Accounting Information Systems

FOURTH EDITION

Accounting Information Systems

FOURTH EDITION

Vernon J. Richardson
University of Arkansas
Baruch College

C. Janie Chang
University of California, Davis

Rodney Smith
California State University, Long Beach

Mc Graw Hill

ACCOUNTING INFORMATION SYSTEMS

Published by McGraw Hill LLC, 1325 Avenue of the Americas, New York, NY 10019.

Some ancillaries, including electronic and print components, may not be available to customers outside the United States.

This book is printed on acid-free paper.

1 2 3 4 5 6 7 8 9 LWI 28 27 26 25 24 23

ISBN 978-1-266-18835-0
MHID 1-266-18835-5

Cover Image: *Andreas Schindl/123RF; stockcreations/Shutterstock*

All credits appearing on page or at the end of the book are considered to be an extension of the copyright page.

mheducation.com/highered

About the Authors

Vernon J. Richardson *University of Arkansas; Baruch College*

Vernon J. Richardson is a Distinguished Professor of Accounting and the G. William Glezen Chair in the Sam M. Walton College of Business at the University of Arkansas and a visiting professor at Baruch College. He received his BS, Master's of Accountancy, and MBA from Brigham Young University and a PhD in accounting from the University of Illinois at Urbana–Champaign. He has taught students at the University of Arkansas, University of Illinois, Brigham Young University, and University of Kansas and internationally at Chinese University of Hong Kong Shenzhen, Aarhus University, the China Europe International Business School (Shanghai), Xi'an Jiaotong Liverpool University, and the University of Technology Sydney.

Dr. Richardson is a member of the American Accounting Association. He has served as president of the American Accounting Association Information Systems section. He previously served as an editor of *The Accounting Review* and is currently an editor at *Accounting Horizons.* He has published articles in *The Accounting Review, Journal of Information Systems, Journal of Accounting and Economics, Contemporary Accounting Research, MIS Quarterly, International Journal of Accounting Information Systems, Journal of Management Information Systems, Journal of Operations Management,* and *Journal of Marketing.* Dr. Richardson is also a co-author of McGraw-Hill's *Introduction to Data Analytics for Accounting, Data Analytics for Accounting* and *Introduction to Business Analytics* textbooks.

C. Janie Chang *University of California, Davis*

C. Janie Chang is the Academic Executive Director of the Master of Professional Accountancy program at University of California, Davis. She received her PhD from the University of California–Irvine. Before joining UC Davis in 2023, Dr. Chang was the Vern Odmark Professor at San Diego State University (SDSU). At SDSU, she established the graduate Accounting Information Systems (AIS) program. She also taught students at University of California-Irvine, San Jose State University, and California State University-San Marcos. Dr. Chang's teaching interests in AIS include information systems audit, data modeling, issues in e-business, and business networks and controls.

Dr. Chang is a member of the American Accounting Association and Information Systems Audit and Control Association (ISACA). Dr. Chang has studied issues in auditing, accounting, and information systems to investigate information processing of experts in addition to cross-cultural issues related to professional judgments and decisions. Her studies have been published in *Abacus, Auditing: A Journal of Practice and Theory, Behavioral Research in Accounting, Data Base, International Journal of Accounting, International Journal of Accounting Information Systems, Journal of Accounting Literature, Journal of Accounting and Public Policy,* and *Journal of Emerging Technologies in Accounting,* among others.

Rod Smith *California State University–Long Beach*

Rod Smith is Professor of Accountancy at California State University–Long Beach and Director of the MS in Accountancy program. He received his BS in mathematics from the University of Oregon; MS in financial management from the Naval Postgraduate School, Monterey, California; and PhD in management (accounting) from University of California–Irvine. He previously taught at the University of Arkansas, University of California–Irvine, and University of Alaska.

Dr. Smith has published research in the *Accounting Review, Journal of Information Systems, Journal of Management Accounting Research, Journal of Accounting and Public Policy,* and *International Journal of Accounting Information Systems.* He is a certified public accountant (retired), certified management accountant, chartered global management accountant, and retired captain in the U.S. Coast Guard.

His research interests include use of financial and nonfinancial measures to assess organizational performance; accounting information systems, enterprise systems, business processes, and business value; design science; and systems dynamics and business process simulation.

Dedications

To my wonderful daughter, Bethany. You are a treasure and joy to mom and me.

—Vern Richardson

To my students and my family who have inspired and supported me.

—Janie Chang

To my wife, Gayla.

—Rod Smith

Preface

Whether working in public accounting or in industry, accountants use a variety of technology tools. The International Federation of Accountants (IFAC) describes four roles for accountants with respect to information technology: (1) *users* of technology and information systems, (2) *managers* of users of technology and related information systems, (3) *designers* of information systems, and (4) *evaluators* of information systems. As users, managers, designers, and evaluators of technology and technology-driven business processes, accountants must understand the organization and how organizational processes generate information important to management. Accountants must be business analysts to ensure that process and systems are well documented and continuously improved.

This text aims to provide students with a variety of technology and business analysis concepts and skills most relevant to business operations and decision making. It is intended for use in the first Accounting Information Systems course at both the undergraduate and graduate levels. Ongoing changes in business technology—such as the move to Internet-based systems, data analytics, software as a service, mobile access to enterprise information, as well as increased security and control requirements—make technological skills more important than ever for accounting graduates. This text also aims to show how changes in accounting affect each of these roles. For example, Extensible Business Reporting Language (XBRL) changes system requirements and affects how companies develop and report financial information. We also consider the role of data analytics and how it is used in financial accounting, managerial accounting, and auditing. Additionally, we consider both the COBIT and COSO frameworks to describe how organizations deal with risk management. In their roles as managers, designers, and evaluators, accountants must know how those frameworks affect their accounting and related information systems.

The core competencies of the American Institute of Certified Public Accountants (AICPA) emphasize accounting skills over content. This text emphasizes examples, problems, and projects through which students can develop the technological skills they need for their accounting careers. It uses real-world companies such as **Starbucks**, **Walmart**, **Google**, and **Amazon** that students can relate to. It takes a broad view of accounting information systems that emphasizes the accountants' roles in the use, management, design, and evaluation of the systems and the management information that they produce. To assist accounting students in experiencing the benefit of learning information technology/information services (IT/IS) concepts and using IT/IS skills in accounting, we focus on business processes, business requirements, how information technology supports those requirements, and how accountants contribute. In particular, this text helps students

- **Apply Data Analytics and understand the basic concepts of blockchain and artificial intelligence.** This includes using three different data analytics tools: Excel, Tableau, and Power BI. The use of technology is rapidly changing the accounting profession. The CPA exam now includes material on Data Analytics. Interest in, and use of, blockchain is exploding. Increased computing power and availability of data is driving advances in artificial intelligence. Today's accountant must be familiar with all these topics and able to use prominent tools.
- **Design business processes and represent them with standard documentation tools.** The role of the accounting function has evolved from stewardship and reporting to full partnership, supporting management decisions throughout the

organization. As business analysts, accountants must be able to document business processes, identify potential improvements, and design and implement new business processes. Thus, this text helps develop business process modeling skills.

- **Design and implement well-structured databases to enable business processes.** Accountants must also understand how business processes generate data and how such data are structured, interrelated, and stored in a database system. To ensure that business processes and the database systems are documented and to help make improvements to processes and systems, accountants must understand and be able to model such systems. Thus, this text helps develop data modeling and database implementation skills.
- **Query databases to provide insights about the performance of business operations.** Most organizational information resides in databases. To support management decisions throughout the organization, accountants must understand how those data are structured and how to retrieve information to support business management decisions. Thus, this text develops skills on the use of Microsoft Access and databases in general. This text also develops Data Analytics tools through the use of Microsoft Excel and Tableau.
- **Evaluate internal control systems and apply business rules to implement controls and mitigate information systems risks.** Federal legislation—for example, the Sarbanes–Oxley Act of 2002 and COSO and COBIT guidance—emphasizes the importance of risk mitigation in modern organizations. Internal control systems must constantly evolve to meet a changing risk environment. Accountants are often the internal control experts and must, therefore, understand how internal controls should be implemented in business processes as part of the organization's overall risk mitigation and governance framework. Thus, this text presents specific material on internal control and accounting information systems, as well as general information about computer fraud and security. It also describes how to monitor and audit accounting information systems.

Main Features

Accounting Information Systems, 4th Edition, focuses on the accountant's role as business analyst in solving business problems by database modeling, database design, and business process modeling.

Chapter Maps

Chapter Maps provide a handy guide at the start of every chapter. These remind students what they have learned in previous chapters, what they can expect to learn in the current chapter, and how the topics will build on each other in chapters to come. This allows them to stay more focused and organized along the way.

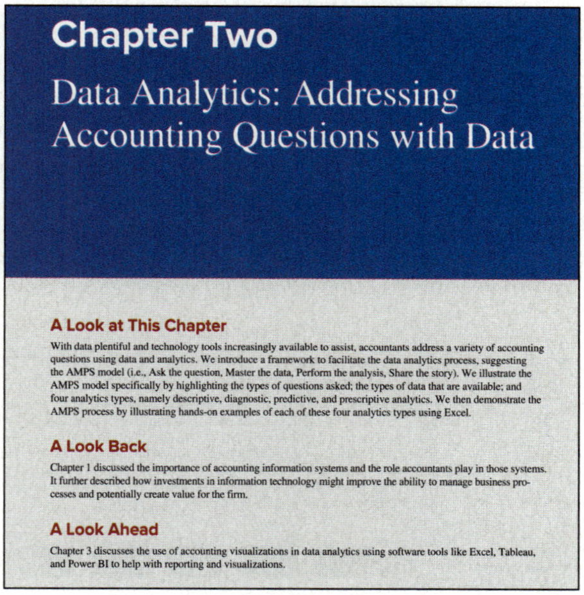
Chapter Two

Data Analytics: Addressing Accounting Questions with Data

A Look at This Chapter

With data plentiful and technology tools increasingly available to assist, accountants address a variety of accounting questions using data and analytics. We introduce a framework to facilitate the data analytics process, suggesting the AMPS model (i.e., Ask the question, Master the data, Perform the analysis, Share the story). We illustrate the AMPS model specifically by highlighting the types of questions asked; the types of data that are available; and four analytics types, namely descriptive, diagnostic, predictive, and prescriptive analytics. We then demonstrate the AMPS process by illustrating hands-on examples of each of these four analytics types using Excel.

A Look Back

Chapter 1 discussed the importance of accounting information systems and the role accountants play in those systems. It further described how investments in information technology might improve the ability to manage business processes and potentially create value for the firm.

A Look Ahead

Chapter 3 discusses the use of accounting visualizations in data analytics using software tools like Excel, Tableau, and Power BI to help with reporting and visualizations.

Chapter-Opening Vignettes

Do your students sometimes wonder how the course connects with their future? Each chapter opens with a vignette, which sets the stage for the rest of the chapter and encourages students to think of concepts in a business context.

"I like how it relates many of the concepts to real companies, like Starbucks."

—Linda Wallace, Virginia Tech

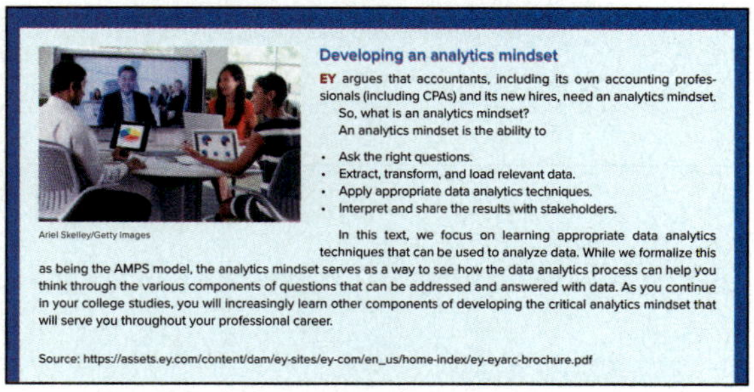
Ariel Skelley/Getty Images

Developing an analytics mindset

EY argues that accountants, including its own accounting professionals (including CPAs) and its new hires, need an analytics mindset.

So, what is an analytics mindset?

An analytics mindset is the ability to

- Ask the right questions.
- Extract, transform, and load relevant data.
- Apply appropriate data analytics techniques.
- Interpret and share the results with stakeholders.

In this text, we focus on learning appropriate data analytics techniques that can be used to analyze data. While we formalize this as being the AMPS model, the analytics mindset serves as a way to see how the data analytics process can help you think through the various components of questions that can be addressed and answered with data. As you continue in your college studies, you will increasingly learn other components of developing the critical analytics mindset that will serve you throughout your professional career.

Source: https://assets.ey.com/content/dam/ey-sites/ey-com/en_us/home-index/ey-eyarc-brochure.pdf

Chapter Outline

Each chapter opens with an Outline that provides direction to the students about the topics they can expect to learn throughout the chapter.

Learning Objectives

Learning Objectives are featured at the beginning of each chapter. The objectives provide students with an overview of the concepts they should understand after reading the chapter. These Learning Objectives are repeated in the margin of the text where they apply.

CHAPTER OUTLINE

Introduction
The Impact of Data Analytics on Business and Accounting (2-1)
Impact of Data Analytics on Business
Impact of Data Analytics on Accounting
The Diversity of Accounting Data Enhances Accounting Analytics (2-2)
The Data Analytics Process: The AMPS Model (2-3)
The Cyclical, Recursive Nature of the AMPS Model
Illustration of the AMPS Analytics Model: Predicting Inventory Needs
The AMPS Model: Ask the Question (2-4)
The AMPS Model: Master the Data (2-5)
The AMPS Model: Perform the Analysis (2-6)
The AMPS Model: Share the Story
Demonstration Labs (Illustrating the AMPS Model) (2-7)
Demonstration Lab 1: Descriptive Data Analytics: Accounts Receivable Aging
Demonstration Lab 2: Diagnostic Data Analytics: Segregation of Duties
Demonstration Lab 3: Predictive Data Analysis: Predicting Bankruptcy
Demonstration Lab 4: Prescriptive Data Analytics: Estimating the Breakeven Point

LEARNING OBJECTIVES

After reading this chapter, you should be able to:

2-1 Understand the impact of data analytics on business and accounting.
2-2 Characterize the diversity of accounting data available to address accounting questions.
2-3 Explain how the AMPS model describes the data analytics process.
2-4 Describe the first stage of the AMPS model—asking appropriate questions.
2-5 Describe the second stage of the AMPS model—mastering the data.
2-6 Define and demonstrate the third stage of the AMPS model—performing the analysis—using different analytics types.
2-7 Demonstrate each of the four analytics types using the AMPS model.

43

"Well-written with great examples. Students should like reading this book."

—Marcia Watson, Mississippi State University

Integrated Project

Projects can generate classroom discussion, foster good teamwork, and prepare students for their accounting careers. Chapter 10 provides guidance to students on how to approach a systems project; related material provides information and data for the projects. There are now three different projects, so instructors can select the project level of difficulty to match the time available or the sophistication of their students. The two main integrated projects require students to apply the different techniques they have learned in Chapters 7, 8, and 9 to a realistic situation. One project focuses on inventory management in a small business with multiple retail stores and a central warehouse. The second project also involves a small wholesale distribution business with multiple stores but without inventory management complications. Students use Microsoft Access to implement their data models and prepare financial reports in both projects. Students also apply data analytics concepts from Chapters 1, 2, and 3.

LO 10-3

Develop an integrated UML class diagram for a business.

Prepare Structure Diagram

Exhibit 10.6 outlines the tasks to prepare structure diagrams. Using the information gained from discovering the business requirements, the project team then prepares an integrated UML class diagram that shows the data requirements for the organization. The class diagram should articulate with the BPMN activity diagrams. In other words, the class diagram must include resources, events, and agents that capture information reflected by each data object in the activity diagrams. Material in Chapters 5, 6, and 7 of this text provides standard patterns that can be the basis for the integrated diagram.

EXHIBIT 10.6
Prepare Structure Diagram Subprocess

This example starts with a UML class diagram based on the generic REA framework for the sales process as shown in Exhibit 10.7. Remember this involves six classes, two resources (*Inventory* and *Cash*), two events (*Sales* and *Cash Receipts*), and two agents (*Customers* and *Employees*). The second step is to determine the associations, starting with the basic associations from the generic sales model and then refining to address specific business requirements. Third, process requirements define appropriate multiplicities. This diagram implements the data structures to support the interactions between Customers and Your Company shown in Exhibit 10.3.

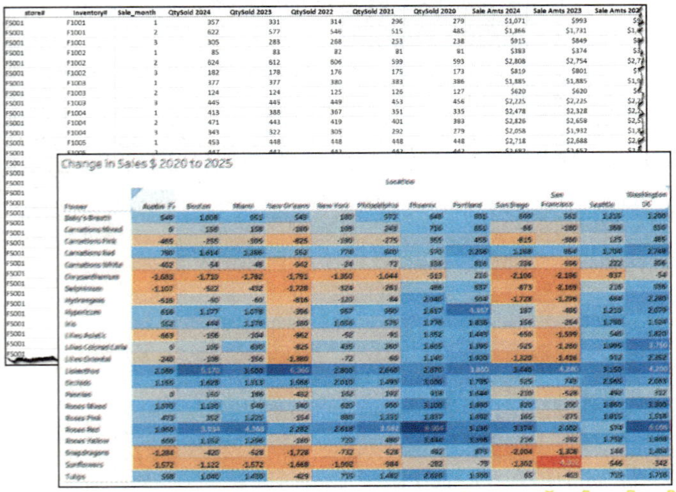

Data Analytics

Due to its importance and popularity, we expanded coverage on Data Analytics and moved it forward in the text. Chapter 2 introduces the importance and impact of Data Analytics in the business world, specifically in the accounting profession. It introduces a framework to facilitate the Data Analytics process, suggesting the AMPS model (i.e., ask the question, master the data, perform the analysis, share the story). We illustrate the AMPS model specifically by highlighting the types of questions asked; the types of data that are available; and four types of analyses, including descriptive, diagnostic, predictive, and prescriptive analysis. Chapter 3 continues the discussion and introduces students to using tools such as Excel, Tableau, and Power BI to help with reporting and visualizations.

Step-by-step instructions and videos associated with the data analytics labs are provided in Connect.

The Cyclical, Recursive Nature of the AMPS Model

After completing all stages of the AMPS model, oftentimes the decision maker is now more knowledgeable and better able to ask another deeper, more refined question, which suggests the AMPS model should best be viewed as recursive in nature. Data analytics might be viewed as successively peeling the layer of an onion. By peeling the first layer of the onion, you now are able to see the next layer and evaluate it and remove it to get to the third layer, and so on. Oftentimes, the AMPS model must be performed multiple times, refining the question (ask the question), possibly considering different types of data (master the data), performing additional analysis (perform the analysis), and retelling the story in each iteration (sharing the story) before the issue/problem/challenge can be finally addressed with some confidence as shown in Exhibit 2.4.

EXHIBIT 2.4
The Recursive Nature of the Data Analytics Process Using the AMPS Model

136 Chapter 3 *Data Analytics: Data Visualizations*

LABS ASSOCIATED WITH CHAPTER 3 connect

- **LAB 3-1 EXCEL** Creating Column Charts, Line Charts and Pie Charts for Tesla Sales and Earnings
- **LAB 3-2 POWER BI** Creating a Word Cloud
- **LAB 3-3 EXCEL** Using Scatterplots and Regression to Understand the Relationship between Advertising Expenditures
- **LAB 3-4 EXCEL** Time Series Analysis of IBM Sales and Earnings
- **LAB 3-5 TABLEAU** Time Series Analysis of IBM Sales and Earnings
- **LAB 3-6 POWER BI** Time Series Analysis of IBM Sales and Earnings
- **LAB 3-5 EXCEL** Create a Dashboard Using PivotTables and Slicers

The multiple choice assessment questions for each lab are assignable via Connect. Materials are also available for courses not utilizing Connect via the Solutions Manual.

Progress Checks

These self-test questions and problems in the body of the chapter enable the student to determine whether he or she has understood the preceding material and to reinforce that understanding before reading further. Detailed solutions to these questions are found at the end of each chapter.

"I really like the Progress Check box. It is a great tool for students' self-assessment."

—Chih-Chen Lee, Northern Illinois University

PROGRESS CHECK

1. A database is an organized collection of data for various uses. Name three uses for a sales database at **Walmart**.
2. Relational data models allow changes to the data model as information needs change. How does the use of a data model help database designers and database users to understand the business processes?

LO 6-2
Explain basic relational database principles.

FUNDAMENTALS OF RELATIONAL DATABASES

Entities and Attributes

First, it is important to describe entities and attributes of a relational database. As introduced in Chapter 5, a class (also called an entity) in the relational database model could be a person, place, thing, transaction, or event about which information is stored. Customers, sales, products, and employees are all examples of classes. Classes could be grouped into resources (R), events (E), and agents (A) in data modeling.[1] *Resources* are those things that have economic value to a firm, such as cash and products. *Events* are the various business activities conducted in a firm's daily operations, such as sales and purchases. *Agents* are the people who participate in business events, such as customers and salespeople.

Data Modeling and Microsoft Access

Chapter 5 describes how data modeling supports the design, implementation, and operation of database systems. Basic modeling tools are used throughout the rest of the text.

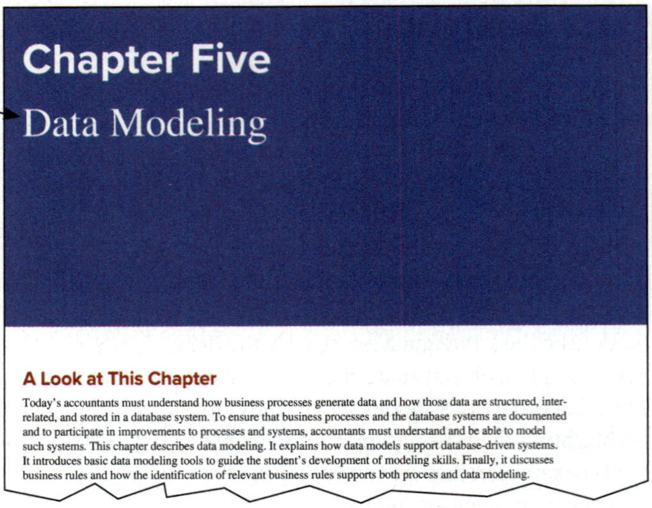

Chapter Five

Data Modeling

A Look at This Chapter

Today's accountants must understand how business processes generate data and how those data are structured, interrelated, and stored in a database system. To ensure that business processes and the database systems are documented and to participate in improvements to processes and systems, accountants must understand and be able to model such systems. This chapter describes data modeling. It explains how data models support database-driven systems. It introduces basic data modeling tools to guide the student's development of modeling skills. Finally, it discusses business rules and how the identification of relevant business rules supports both process and data modeling.

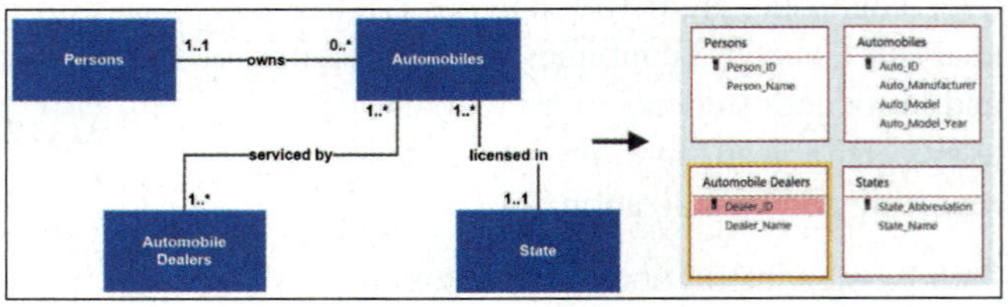

"This textbook would be good when using the database approach. It provides the information needed to develop and use a database without getting into the details of transaction processing (activities, documents, and internal control)."

—Janice Benson, University of Wyoming

Connect Accounting for *Accounting Information Systems*

The 4th Edition of Accounting Information Systems has a full Connect package, with the following features available for instructors and students.

- **SmartBook 2.0®** A personalized and adaptive learning tool used to maximize the learning experience by helping students study more efficiently and effectively. Smartbook 2.0 highlights where in the chapter to focus, asks review questions on the materials covered and tracks the most challenging content for later review recharge.
- **Multiple Choice Questions.** The multiple choice questions from the end-of-chapter materials are assignable in Connect, providing students with instant feedback on their answers.
- **Problems.** Select problems from the text are available for assignment in Connect to ensure students are building an analytical skill set.

- **Comprehensive Review Exercises and Integrated Project.** The setup information for the Comprehensive Review Exercises for Chapters 7, 8, and 9 and the Integrated Project in Chapter 10 have been added to Connect, along with the ability for students to upload their submission files for their instructors to grade.
- **Lecture Videos:** Video-based walk-throughs are available for each chapter to reinforce select concepts.
- **Test Bank:** The Test Bank for each chapter has been updated and expanded to stay current with new and revised chapter material, with all questions available for assignment through Connect. Instructors can also create tests and quizzes from the Test Bank through our Test Builder software.

  Available within McGraw Hill Connect®, Test Builder is a cloud-based tool that enables instructors to format tests that can be printed, administered within a Learning Management System, or exported as a Word document. Test Builder offers a modern, streamlined interface for easy content configuration that matches course needs, without requiring a download.

  Test Builder allows you to:
  - access all test bank content from a particular title.
  - easily pinpoint the most relevant content through robust filtering options.
  - manipulate the order of questions or scramble questions and/or answers.
  - pin questions to a specific location within a test.
  - determine your preferred treatment of algorithmic questions.
  - choose the layout and spacing.
  - add instructions and configure default settings.
- The Instructor and Student Resources have been updated for the 4th edition and are available in the Connect Instructor Resources page. Available resources include Solutions Manuals, Comprehensive Exercise and Integrated Project setup and solutions files, PowerPoint presentations, and other ancillary materials. All applicable Student Resources including databases and data files, will be available in a convenient file that can be distributed to students for classes either directly, through Connect, or via courseware.

AIS 4e Content Updates

General Updates for the 4th Edition

- Now in full color!
- Expanded and relocated coverage of data analytics to chapter 1-3 to demonstrate how data analytics is performed and creates value.
- Added more Tableau and Power BI Labs for data analysis.
- Added Alteryx and UiPath labs for process automation.
- Added end-of-chapter multiple-choice questions and problems throughout the text.
- Significantly revised many end-of-chapter problems for availability and auto-grading within Connect.
- Revised and added many new discussion questions in most chapters.
- Updated integrated projects to apply data analytics concepts.
- Added a new integrated project that emulates accounting software to complete the accounting process for a store.
- Updated Lecture Videos in Connect.

Chapter-by-Chapter Updates

Chapter 1

- Added explanation of a cost accounting system in relation to the various enterprise system components.
- Added two data analytics labs to demonstrate what value can be derived from an accounting information system.

Chapter 2

- Updated discussion on the impact of data analytics on various areas of accounting.
- Added four new demonstration data analytics labs focusing on the different analytics types.

Chapter 3

- Rewrote chapter to emphasize importance of data visualizations.
- Added four new data analytics labs focusing on the different data visualization techniques.

Chapter 4

- Updated introduction to Business Process Modeling and Notation (BPMN).
- Added information about how to develop BPMN models.

Chapter 5

- Updated introduction to Uniform Modeling Language (UML) class diagrams.
- Added information about using business models and business rules to implement internal controls over business processes.
- Added a review exercise for more guided hands-on experience.

Chapter 6

- Updated discussion of relational databases, structured query language (SQL), and Microsoft Access.
- Added hands-on activities.

Chapter 7

- Updated description of sales and collection processes.
- Added new information about planning and implementing internal controls over sales and collections.
- Updated the review exercise to provide more guided hands-on experience.

Chapter 8

- Updated description of the purchases and payments process.
- Added new information about planning and implementing internal controls over purchases and payments.
- Updated the review exercise to provide more guided hands-on experience.

Chapter 9

- Updated description of the conversion (manufacturing) process.
- Added new information about planning and implementing internal controls over the conversion process.
- Added a new review exercise to provide more guided hands-on experience.

Chapter 10

- Substantially updated the two integrated projects to include both process modeling and data analytics components.
- Created a new step-by-step version of the Y Not Flowers project that can be used as students progress through the chapters.
- Created a new project that emulates a small business accounting system such as Quickbooks, and review summary information to complete the accounting process for this store.

Chapter 11

- Added new information about internal controls over financial reporting consistent with new changes to the CPA exam.

Chapter 12

- Updated information about cybersecurity and System and Organization Controls (SOC) examinations to address new changes to the CPA exam and increasing importance of cybersecurity.

Chapter 13

- Updated information on information technology and systems auditing to address new changes to the CPA exam.

Chapter 14

- Updated information about eXtensible Business Reporting Language (XBRL) and inline XBRL.

Chapter 15

- Updated descriptions of Blockchain technology.
- Updated description of AI, machine learning, and robotic process automation.
- Added hands-on labs using Alteryx and UiPath.

Chapter 16

- Updated discussion of the business value of information technology.

Chapter 17

- Updated discussion of planning and implementing IT initiatives.
- Introduced the waterfall and the agile methodologies for systems development.

McGraw Hill connect®

Instructors
The Power of Connections

A complete course platform

Connect enables you to build deeper connections with your students through cohesive digital content and tools, creating engaging learning experiences. We are committed to providing you with the right resources and tools to support all your students along their personal learning journeys.

65%
Less Time Grading

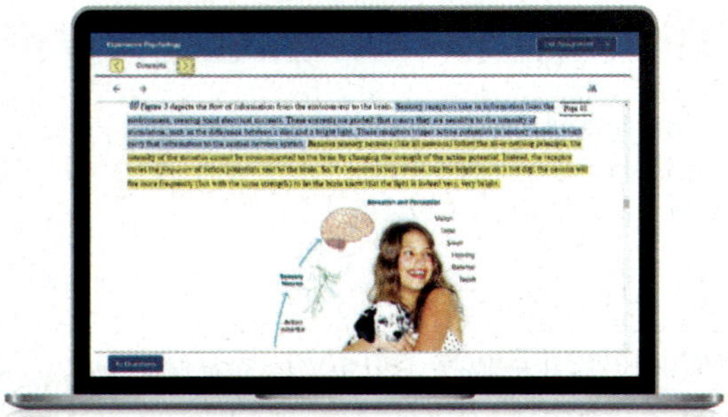

Laptop: Getty Images; Woman/dog: George Doyle/Getty Images

Every learner is unique

In Connect, instructors can assign an adaptive reading experience with SmartBook® 2.0. Rooted in advanced learning science principles, SmartBook 2.0 delivers each student a personalized experience, focusing students on their learning gaps, ensuring that the time they spend studying is time well-spent.
mheducation.com/highered/connect/smartbook

Affordable solutions, added value

Make technology work for you with LMS integration for single sign-on access, mobile access to the digital textbook, and reports to quickly show you how each of your students is doing. And with our Inclusive Access program, you can provide all these tools at the lowest available market price to your students. Ask your McGraw Hill representative for more information.

Solutions for your challenges

A product isn't a solution. Real solutions are affordable, reliable, and come with training and ongoing support when you need it and how you want it. Visit **supportateverystep.com** for videos and resources both you and your students can use throughout the term.

SUPPORT AT every step

Students

Get Learning that Fits You

Effective tools for efficient studying

Connect is designed to help you be more productive with simple, flexible, intuitive tools that maximize your study time and meet your individual learning needs. Get learning that works for you with Connect.

Study anytime, anywhere

Download the free ReadAnywhere® app and access your online eBook, SmartBook® 2.0, or Adaptive Learning Assignments when it's convenient, even if you're offline. And since the app automatically syncs with your Connect account, all of your work is available every time you open it. Find out more at **mheducation.com/readanywhere**

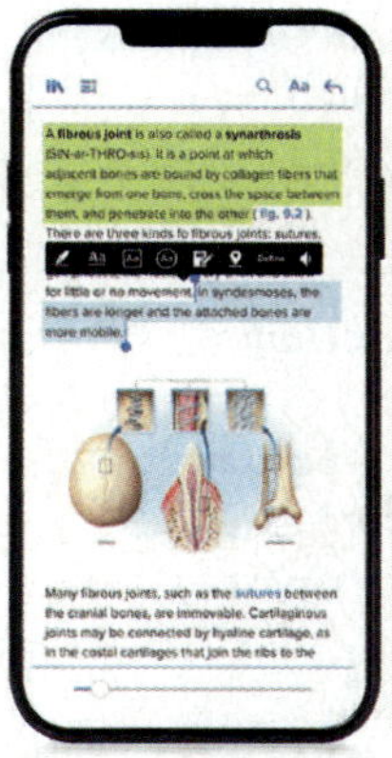

"I really liked this app—it made it easy to study when you don't have your text-book in front of you."

- Jordan Cunningham, Eastern Washington University

iPhone: Getty Images

Everything you need in one place

Your Connect course has everything you need—whether reading your digital eBook or completing assignments for class—Connect makes it easy to get your work done.

Learning for everyone

McGraw Hill works directly with Accessibility Services Departments and faculty to meet the learning needs of all students. Please contact your Accessibility Services Office and ask them to email accessibility@mheducation.com, or visit **mheducation.com/about/accessibility** for more information.

Acknowledgments

Special thanks go to Deniz Appelbaum, Montclair State University; Katherine Boswell, University of Louisiana - Monroe; and Kevin Brennan, University of Akron who were a tremendous help offering suggestions during their accuracy reviews of the text and Connect.

Throughout the development of this book, we were privileged to have the candid and valuable advice of our contributors, reviewers, and survey and focus group participants. These instructors provided us with priceless suggestions, feedback, and constructive criticism. The depth and sincerity of their reviews indicate that they are a devoted group of teacher–scholars. The content of the book over various versions and editions was greatly enhanced because of their efforts.

T. S. Amer
Northern Arizona University
Deniz Appelbaum
Montclair State University
Victoria Badura
Chadron State College
Jon A. Baumunk
San Diego State University
James Bay
University of Utah
Ryan Baxter
Boise State University
Tanya Benford
Florida Gulf Coast University
Janice Benson
University of Wyoming
Jennifer Blaskovich
University of Nebraska, Omaha
Faye Borthick
Georgia State University
Daniel Boylan
University of North Georgia
Kristine Brands
Regis University
Linda Bressler
University of Houston
Kimberly Brickler-Ulrich
Lindenwood University
Sandra Cereola
James Madison University
Siew Chan
Nova Southeastern University
Shifei Chung
Rowan University
Kim Church
Oklahoma State University
Ronald Clark
Auburn University
Curtis Clements
Abilene Christian University
Donna Free
Oakland University
Graham Gal
University of Massachusetts, Amherst
Andy Garcia
Bowling Green State University
David Gelb
Seton Hall University
Jeremy Germann
Centralia College
Jan Gillespie
University of Texas
Terry Glandon
University of Texas, El Paso
Severin Grabski
Michigan State University
Marina Grau
Houston Community College
Gerry Grant
California State University, Fullerton
Jennifer Grennan
Queens University
Michael Griffin
UMASS Dartmouth
Deborah L. Habel
Wayne State University
Rebekah Heath
St. Ambrose University
William Heninger
Brigham Young University
Kenneth Henry
Florida International University
Sarah Hill
Northcentral Technical College
Rani Hoitash
Bentley University
Diane Janvrin
Iowa State University
Jason Jio
Bradley University
Steven Johnson
Minnesota State University, Mankato
Nancy Jones
San Diego State University
Grover Kearns
University of South Florida, St. Petersburg
Andrea Seaton Kelton
Middle Tennessee State University
Kevin Kobelsky
University of Michigan, Dearborn

Joseph Komar
University of St. Thomas
Don Kovacic
California State University, San Marcos
Sabrina Landa
California State University, Long Beach
Brenda Lauer
Davenport University
Mark Lawrence
University of North Alabama
Yvette Lazdowski
Plymouth State University
Maria Leach
Auburn University
Chih-Chen Lee
Northern Illinois University
Picheng Lee
Pace University
Adena LeJeune
Louisiana College
Chan Li
University of Pittsburg
Robert Lin
California State University, East Bay
Qi Liu
University of Rhode Island
Tina Loraas
Auburn University
Sakthi Mahenthiran
Butler University
Lois Mahoney
Eastern Michigan University
Kevin J. McFarlane
Regis University
Britton McKay
Georgia Southern University
James Mensching
California State University, Chico
Mike Metzcar
Indiana Wesleyan University
Pam Meyer
University of Louisiana at Lafayette
Bonnie Morris
West Virginia University
Johnna Murray
University of Missouri, St. Louis
Bruce Neumann
University of Colorado, Denver
Colin Onita
San Jose State University
Oluwakemi Onwuchekwa
University of Central Florida
Debra Petrizzo
Franklin University
Theresa Phinney
Texas A&M University
Ronald Premuroso
University of Montana
Helen Pruitt
University of Maryland
Jeffrey Pullen
University of Maryland
Austin Reitenga
University of Alabama
Jennifer Riley
University of Nebraska Omaha
Juan Roman
American Public University System
Silvia Romero
Montclair State University
Mohd Rujob
Eastern Connecticut State University
Juan Manuel Sanchez
Texas Tech University
Paul San Miguel
Western Michigan University
Arline Savage
Cal Poly, San Luis Obispo
Lloyd Seaton
University of Northern Colorado
George Schmelzle
Missouri State University
Dmitriy Shaltayev
Christopher Newport University
Lewis Shaw
Suffolk University
Robert Slater
University of North Florida
Gary Smith
Georgia State University
Kathleen Sobieralski
University of Maryland
Eileen Taylor
North Carolina State University
Ryan Teeter
University of Pittsburgh
Katie Terrell
University of Arkansas
Barbara Uliss
Metropolitan State University of Denver
Linda Wallace
Virginia Tech
Ting Wang
Governors State University
Marcia Watson
Mississippi State University
Andy Welchel
Furman University
Mitchell Wenger
The University of Mississippi
Veronda Willis
The University of Texas at Tyler
Darryl Woolley
University of Idaho
Al Chen Yuang-Sung
North Carolina State University
David Zhu
California State University, Stanislaus

Brief Contents

Contents

Chapter One

Accounting Information Systems and Firm Value

A Look at This Chapter

Information plays a crucial role in today's information age. In this chapter, we discuss the importance of data and information in accounting information systems and the role accountants play in those systems to create value for the company. In this chapter, we also describe investments in information systems to manage internal and external business processes and how they create value for the firm.

A Look Ahead

Chapter 2 examines the role of accountants as business analysts. The chapter defines business process modeling and describes how it supports the business analyst role of accountants. It explains the potential value of business process modeling and introduces basic modeling tools to guide the accountant's development of modeling skills.

Sorbis/Shutterstock

Walking in to **Starbucks** to order a latte, you notice the atmosphere and the quality and variety of its coffees and related offerings. What you may not immediately notice is the accounting information system that supports the recordkeeping, replenishment, financing, and so on. To be sure, Starbucks has invested immense resources into planning, designing, and developing a number of accounting information systems to track information needed to run an effective business and to report to its shareholders and regulators (e.g., Internal Revenue Service and Securities and Exchange Commission) on its performance. This accounting information system tracks information as diverse as the number of hours worked each day by each of its 383,000 employees throughout the world to the amount of sales taxes to be paid and remitted to local, state, and national tax authorities at its 33,833 stores in 80 countries.

And customers are increasingly using mobile apps to order and pay for their Starbucks transactions. The Starbucks app is the second most used mobile payment app for point-of-sale transactions in the U.S., right after Apple Pay, and is used by over 30 million Americans!

Even Starbucks' Clover coffee machines use technology! By tracking customer preferences and tracking the expiration dates of milk, Starbucks is always collecting information and making it accessible from headquarters as well as each individual store for decision making. Many increasingly view Starbucks as a technology company. Do you? This chapter focuses on the role accounting information systems play in creating value for a firm such as Starbucks.

Source: *CNN Business Profile, https://money.cnn.com/quote/profile/profile.xhtml?symb=SBUX, Insider Intelligence, https://www.insiderintelligence.com/content/how-starbucks-app-energizing-mobile-payment-use* (Accessed August 2022).

CHAPTER OUTLINE

LEARNING OBJECTIVES

After reading this chapter, you should be able to:

1-1 Define an accounting information system, and explain characteristics of useful information.

1-2 Distinguish among data, information, and an information system.

1-3 Distinguish the roles of accountants in providing information, and explain certifications related to accounting information systems.

1-4 Describe how business processes affect the firm's value chain.

1-5 Explain how AIS affects firm value.

1-6 Describe how AIS assists the firm in its internal business processes.

1-7 Assess how AIS facilitates the firm's external business processes.

1-8 Explain how an AIS is used to create a cost accounting system.

1-9 Assess the impact of AIS on firm profitability and stock prices.

Lab 1-1 Excel: Descriptive Analytics: Determining the Most Profitable Products (SKU) and Customers

Lab 1-2 Excel: Descriptive Analytics: Calculating Descriptive Statistics

INTRODUCTION

Data on business facts, numbers, customer preferences, and other useful indicators for business purposes are all around us. When a company combines this data with the appropriate context and uses data analytics to analyze it, it becomes a strategic asset for developing a competitive advantage to run the business better than its competitors.

Starbucks, for example, uses information about its customers, suppliers, and competitors to predict how much coffee it will sell and how much coffee it will need to purchase. If the company predicts more sales to customers than it actually has, it will have excess coffee and likely incur extra carrying costs of its inventory. If Starbucks underestimates the demand for its products, the store could potentially run out of coffee and miss out on profitable sales that will go to competitors. Information is a strategic asset if the firm (1) knows what information it needs; (2) develops systems to collect, store, and process that information; and (3) uses that information (often via data analytics) to make critical decisions that will ultimately affect performance and profitability.

ACCOUNTANTS AS BUSINESS ANALYSTS

LO 1-1

Define an accounting information system, and explain characteristics of useful information.

There are data all around us of every type. In fact, 1.7 megabytes of new information will be soon be created every second for every human being on the planet. With an incredible 2.5 quintillion bytes of data being created every day, 90 percent of the world's data has been created in the last two years alone.[1]

Firms have access to a tremendous amount of data—for instance, transactional data produced from point-of-sale terminals or bank deposits, consumer behavior data on customer preferences and purchases, product availability and costs, and operational statistics generated throughout a supply chain—that can contain valuable insights to enable decision making. With such data, firms can more easily compare and contrast results with relevant benchmarks. In that way, firms can determine the most effective way to allocate resources such as human resource (HR) talent, capital (e.g., equipment and buildings), and budgets (e.g., marketing, advertising, and research and development).[2]

At the same time, however, surveys suggest that 28 percent of senior financial executives say they have little or no information to predict the performance of their firms. Another 54 percent said they had only half the information needed to provide visibility into performance.[3]

Therefore, even with information all around us, it often lacks the needed relevance, clarity, and accuracy. To be sure, as you've learned in your classes to date, accountants keep financial records, prepare financial reports, and perform audits of those financial reports. Because the role of the accountant is to access and attest to the quality of information, accountants may increasingly be considered to be in the best position to serve as a business analyst in looking at the organization as a whole and helping determine how best to optimize overall company performance.

Specifically, as the business analyst, the accountant might be able to use their knowledge of available data from *Accounting Information Systems (AIS)* to provide management with data-driven insights to:

- Address business opportunities like *whether to outsource a portion of the manufacturing function* to Sri Lanka.
- Promote one streaming product over another *based on expected profit margins.*

[1]B. Marr, "How Much Data Is Produced Every Day 2021?," https://www.the-next-tech.com/, Accessed November 2022.

[2]B. McCarthy, "A Manual for the Data-Driven Finance Chief," *CFO.com,* November 6, 2015.

[3]J. Hagel, "Why Accountants Should Own Big Data," *Journal of Accountancy,* November 2013.

- Structure its research and development projects to take advantage of research and development *(R&D) tax credits* in such a way as to minimize current or future taxes.
- Evaluate characteristics of the *journal entries* based on risk scoring (who recorded them, at what amount, who authorized them, rare account combinations, etc.) to find *errors or fraud* in the journal entries.
- Consider how the *product reviews* on **Best Buy**'s website can help predict which inventory items will be sold and which ones won't be sold to determine if the inventory will become obsolete and if the inventory is appropriately valued.
- Predict the *right level of the Allowance for Doubtful Accounts* by classifying which customers will be able to pay their debts based on all the things the company knows about them.
- Give auditors the needed information *to evaluate and verify* account balances to identify potential material misstatements.
- Predict when goodwill is or soon will be impaired using *social media, macroeconomic conditions, the business press, or recent accounting performance.*
- Estimate a product's fixed and variable cost behavior to help *predict the level of sales* required to break even.
- Address the GAAP requirement for the firm *to predict the level of future sales returns* (items returned, refunds, etc.) in order to match it with the current period sales amounts[4] with information from the AIS.

To address such critical, but diverse, business opportunities, accountants need to decide what information is needed or potentially useful for addressing important business questions, then build an information system to gather and access the necessary information, and finally, analyze and communicate this information for use in critical business decision making.[5]

DEFINITION OF ACCOUNTING INFORMATION SYSTEMS

Of the many information systems that are used in a firm, one type of information system is used in every firm: an **accounting information system (AIS)**. An AIS is a system that records, processes, summarizes, reports, and communicates the results of business transactions to provide financial and nonfinancial information to facilitate decision making. An AIS is also designed to ensure appropriate levels of internal controls (important security measures to protect the integrity and privacy of sensitive data) for those transactions.

This is the focus of this book. Some might call an AIS just a financial reporting system (FRS). Others might include in their AIS a much broader set of data that includes nonfinancial information such as customer sales data, sales transactions, and marketing activities or the results of research and development investment. Viewed broadly, an AIS collects, processes, and reports information deemed useful in decision making.

The study of AIS lies at the nexus of two traditional disciplines: information systems and accounting. In this book, we will highlight knowledge from both of these disciplines to more fully understand an AIS. While an AIS could take the form of a paper-and-pencil manual bookkeeping system, we will view an AIS as having all of the capabilities of a computerized system.

[4] FASB, ASU 2014-09.

[5] F. Borthick, "Helping Accountants Learn to Get the Information Managers Want: The Role of the Accounting Information Systems Course," *Journal of Information Systems* 10, no. 2 (1996), pp. 75–85.

A Simple Information System

An AIS, just like any system, can be explained using a general systems approach (as in Exhibit 1.1) with input, storage, processing, and output activities. We cover these activities in subsequent chapters, but the input may come in the form of sales recorded on a **Starbucks** cash register or point-of-sale terminal. Processing those data may take the form of getting the input into storage (such as a database or a data table). Processing might involve querying that database (e.g., using SQL or other queries) to produce the output in the form of a report for management use. As an example, Starbucks may query its sales database to report how much coffee it sells around Christmas to see if additional sales incentives need to be made to increase sales around Christmas in the future. Whether this report has information that is ultimately useful to management for their decision making is covered in the next section.

EXHIBIT 1.1
A Simple Information System

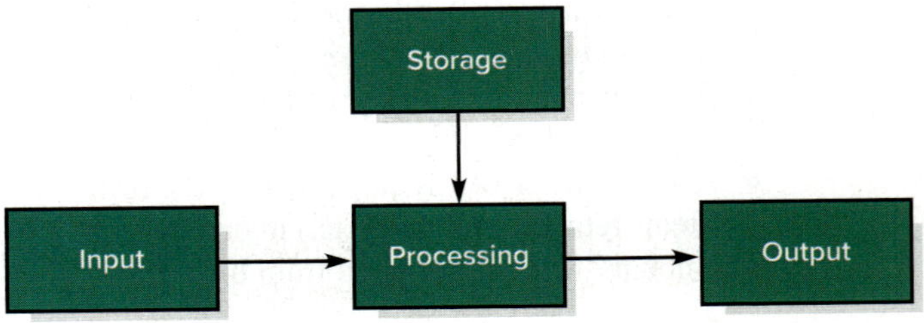

Attributes of Useful Information

To be most useful for decision makers, information from an AIS must both have relevance and give faithful representation of what occurred by having these attributes:

1. **Relevance**
   a. Confirmatory, or feedback, value (corrects or confirms what had been predicted in the past).
   b. Predictive value (helps with forecasting the future).
   c. Materiality (is above a threshold where missing or inaccurate information would impact decisions).
2. **Faithful representation**
   a. Complete (includes all monetary transactions; not missing any).
   b. Neutrality (not biased one way or the other).
   c. Free from error (contains no mistakes or inaccuracies).

Relevance

To be useful, information must be relevant to the decision maker, capable of influencing the decisions of users. In other words, information is relevant when it helps users evaluate how past decisions actually worked out (feedback value) or predict what will happen in the future (predictive value). It is also relevant if the information is material in size, big enough to influence the decisions of its users.

Faithful Representation

Information exhibits faithful representation if the information is complete (i.e., includes all applicable transactions), is neutral (i.e., free from bias), and is free from error. Faithful representation information represents the substance of the underlying economic transaction. If **Amazon** sells Steph Curry athletic shoes for $300, it should be recorded and subsequently reported in its sales revenue account as $300. Accounting information should not be designed to lead users to accept or reject any specific decision alternative, but rather to offer information from transactions that report in essence what happened, free of error or bias.

AISs and accountants exist to provide useful information to decision makers. Considering the attributes of useful information helps AIS designers and users construct a system that delivers useful information to decision makers.

LO 1-2

Distinguish among data, information, and an information system.

Data versus Information

Hal Varian, **Google**'s chief economist, explains that while data are widely available, "what is scarce is the ability to extract wisdom from them." In that short statement, we learn that data and the information actually needed to make decisions may well have different definitions. **Data** are simply raw facts that describe the characteristics of an event that, in isolation, have little meaning.

Walmart has an information system called Retail Link. Retail Link is an Internet-based tool allowing Walmart employees and Walmart suppliers to access the point-of-sale data. Retail Link provides sales and inventory data, by item, store, and day (and time) to its suppliers. That is, it contains a record of every sale of every individual item at every Walmart store for the last 2 years, including time and date of sale, bar code number, price, and quantity purchased. However, to be most useful to Walmart, these data must be processed in a meaningful way to provide information most pertinent for Walmart management. To illustrate, consider the following example:

> At what price should Walmart offer its bananas?
>
> Bananas are the best selling item at Walmart, selling more than 1 billion pounds per year (32 pounds every second of every day). Sometimes Walmart will put bananas at the back of the produce section to get customers to walk through other products before picking up the bananas![6]

To determine price, Walmart management would like the information to potentially address such questions as:

- How many pounds of bananas does Walmart sell on August 1 at its Lawrence, Kansas, store location this year versus last year? How many bananas were available for sale on August 1? How many bananas went bad on August 1 and had to be thrown away (or donated to charity)?
- What is the right price to charge for bananas to maximize Walmart's profits, or that will consistently bring customers in to buy their bananas and other Walmart products?
- What was the trade-off between prices for organic and nonorganic bananas at its locations in Tempe, Arizona; Stamford, Connecticut; and Champaign, Illinois? Does the relative difference in organic and nonorganic bananas depend on location, time of year, size of the price difference, or something else?
- Which other additional items sell best when bananas are bought by our customers? Which items should be set next to the bananas to enhance their chance of being sold?

Information is defined as data organized in a way meaningful to the user. Thus, data are often processed (aggregated, calculated, sorted, manipulated, etc.) and then combined with the appropriate context (year or location, etc.) to turn it into information.

[6]A. Lutz, "Why Bananas Are the Best-Selling Item at Walmart," *Business Insider,* September 27, 2013, https://www.businessinsider.com/bananas-the-best-selling-item-at-walmart-2013-9; A. Swerdloff, "Walmart Is Exploiting Our Love of Bananas to Lure Us through Its Stores," *Munchies,* February 20, 2016, https://munchies.vice.com/en_us/article/bm3adz/walmart-is-exploiting-our-love-of-bananas-to-lure-us-through-its-stores.

Decision makers typically require useful information to make decisions. As an example, while the sales price of a particular toy might be just considered data, subtracting the cost of goods sold from the sales price to compute the net profit would be considered information if the data help a retailer decide whether to carry that particular toy in its inventory, or even where to place it on its shelf to maximize customer exposure. To the extent that computers can assist in processing and organizing data in a way that is helpful to the decision maker, it is possible that there may be so much information available to actually cause **information overload**, which is the difficulty a person faces in understanding a problem and making a decision when faced with too much information. Therefore, an AIS must be carefully designed to provide the most important and useful information without overwhelming the user.

Data are considered to be an input, whereas information is considered to be the output.

The overall transformation from a business need and business event (like each individual transaction including bananas) to the collection of data and information to an ultimate decision is called the **information value chain** and is reflected in Exhibit 1.2. If Walmart needs to know how many bananas it should have at each location (i.e., business need), it will collect transactions involving banana sales (i.e., business event). Then it can take those data and turn them into information that might be used to make decisions on banana supply levels at each store. Certainly, the transformation from data to information is a key part of that value chain. Information that is useful (i.e., exhibiting characteristics of relevance or faithful representation) may get to the point of being knowledge and, ultimately, may be helpful in forming the basis for a decision.

EXHIBIT 1.2
Information Value Chain

Source: Statements on Management Accounting, Institute of Management Accountants, 2008.

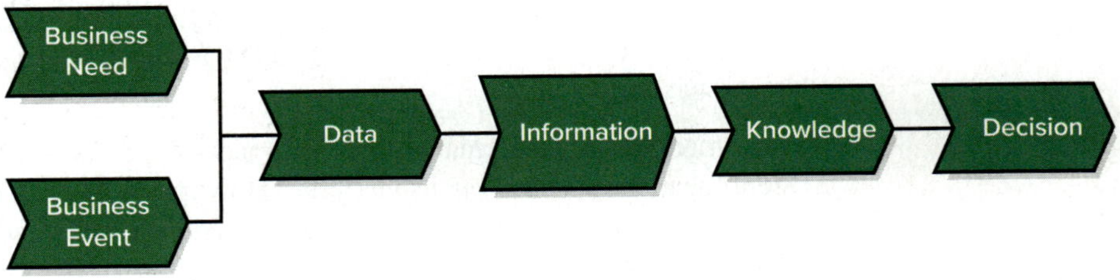

Discretionary versus Mandatory Information

Because you have already taken a few accounting classes, you understand the types of information that are recorded, processed, and subsequently reported for different purposes, including managerial, financial, or tax purposes. Managerial accounting information is generally produced for internal information purposes and would usually be considered to be **discretionary information** because there is no law requiring that it be provided to management. Management simply decides what information it needs to track and builds an information system to track it. For example, management may want an activity-based costing (ABC) system to figure out which cost drivers should be used to allocate overhead costs at **Tesla** to different products (like Tesla's Model 3, Model X, and Model S). The value of information equals the difference between the benefits realized from using that information and the costs of producing it. Because discretionary information is not required, management must determine if the benefits of receiving that information are greater than the costs of producing it.

As early as 1989, **Starbucks** installed a costly computer network and hired a specialist in information technology from **McDonald's** Corporation to design a point-of-sale (cash register) system for store managers to use. Every night, stores passed their sales information to the Seattle headquarters, which allowed managers to highlight regional buying trends almost instantly. Because this information is not required by regulators, this would be considered to be an example of discretionary information.

An AIS is used to support the mandatory information required by tax returns.

Digital Vision/Getty Images

In contrast, much of the financial and tax accounting information is produced by the company for external information purposes such as for investors, banks, financial analysts, bondholders, and the Internal Revenue Service (IRS) in the form of tax returns or audited financial statements. This financial and tax accounting information would generally be considered to be **mandatory information**.

While discretionary information should be produced if the value of the information it provides to management is worth more than the cost to produce it, mandatory information is usually produced at the lowest possible cost of compliance with the laws or regulations from such entities as the Securities and Exchange Commission, IRS, state banking commission, and state tax commission.

PROGRESS CHECK

1. Propose useful information that is relevant to a college football coach. Also, propose useful information that exhibits qualities of faithful representation to a college football coach.
2. Give an example of data versus information at a **T-Mobile** store.
3. Provide two types of discretionary information and two types of mandatory information that might come from an accounting information system for **Samsung**.

LO 1-3

Distinguish the roles of accountants in providing information, and explain certifications related to accounting information systems.

ROLE OF ACCOUNTANTS IN ACCOUNTING INFORMATION SYSTEMS

In today's age, technology is a key tool in creating information systems for businesses. As a result, accounting and information technology are now more closely linked than ever. As information technology (IT) has gained operational and strategic importance in the business world, the role of accountants, understandably, must adjust as well. The International Federation of Accountants (IFAC) notes:

> IT has grown (and will continue to grow) in importance at such a rapid pace and with such far reaching effects that it can no longer be considered a discipline peripheral to accounting. Rather, professional accounting has merged and developed with IT to such an extent that one can hardly conceive of accounting independent from IT.[7]

[7]"Information Technology Competencies in the Accounting Profession: AICPA Implementation Strategies for IFAC International Education Guideline No. 11," American Institute of Certified Public Accountants, 1996.

Indeed, accountants have a role as business analysts and business partners; that is, they gather information to solve business problems or address business opportunities. They determine what information is relevant in solving business problems, work with the AIS (and/or other data provider) to create or extract that information, and then analyze the information to give needed information to the decision maker. Some even characterize the accountant as the "interpreter" between the data provider (or data scientist) and the decision maker.

An AIS provides a systematic means for accountants to get needed information and solve a problem. Another illustration of the role of accountants in AIS comes from the Institute of Management Accounting. In this definition, note the role of the accountant in devising planning and performance information systems:

> Management accounting is a profession that involves partnering in management decision making, devising planning and performance management systems, and providing expertise in financial reporting and control to assist management in the formulation and implementation of a firm's strategy.[8]

Specific Accounting Roles

Understanding the design, use, and management of information technology is of vital importance to not only management accountants, but to all of those within the accounting profession. To recognize the needed competencies for accountants with respect to information technology, it is important to recognize the potential role of accountants in accounting information systems, including the following:

1. The accountant as *user* of accounting information systems—whether it be inputting journal entries into an accounting system, using a financial spreadsheet to calculate the cost of a product, or using antivirus software to protect the system, accountants use an AIS.
    - As an example, accountants serving in an audit role should be able to understand how to access their client's AIS and how to use at least one major computer-assisted auditing package such as IDEA, Robotic Process Automation (RPA) tool such as UIPath or PowerAutomate, an online or local database system, or a professional research tool.
2. The accountant as *manager* of accounting information systems (e.g., financial manager, controller, CFO).
    - Accountants serving as managers of AISs must be able to plan and coordinate accounting information systems and be able to organize and staff, direct and lead, and monitor and control those information systems.
3. The accountant as *designer* of accounting information systems (e.g., business system design team, producer of financial information, **systems analyst**).
    - Accountants serving in a design capacity must have significant practical exposure as they work to develop a system that will meet the needs of users. Specifically, they need to work with key phases of system analysis and design, such as the preparation of a feasibility analysis; information requirements elicitation and documentation techniques; data file design and documentation techniques; and document, screen, and report design techniques. In particular, accountants must understand the underlying business processes and the information requirements of other related systems.
4. The accountant as *evaluator* of accounting information systems (e.g., IT auditor, assessor of internal controls, tax advisor, general auditor, consultant)
    - As will be discussed in Chapter 12, the **Sarbanes–Oxley Act of 2002 (SOX)** requires an evaluation of the internal controls in an AIS. As part of that act, and as part of a standard audit, accountants must be able to tailor standard evaluation approaches to a firm's AIS

[8]Institute of Management Accountants, *Statements on Management Accounting,* 2008.

and offer practical recommendations for improvement where appropriate. In addition, the accountant must be able to apply relevant IT tools and techniques to effectively evaluate the system. They must also understand enough cybersecurity to evaluate whether the data in its system can be adequately protected.

In considering the information technology competencies in the accounting profession, the American Institute of Certified Public Accountants (AICPA) and International Federation of Accountants (IFAC) assume that, at a minimum, all accountants will be proficient in the AIS user role and at least one of the other listed roles (e.g., manager, designer, or evaluator). Accountants will be better users, managers, and evaluators of AISs if they understand how the AIS is designed. Thus, throughout this textbook, we touch on all of the roles that accountants have in the firms, but we particularly emphasize skills most relevant to the designer role.

Certifications in Accounting Information Systems

In addition to the various roles that accountants play, accountants and related professionals may also seek various certifications to show they are proficient in specific areas of AISs. This will show their competence to specific employers or clients that need some specific services. There are three primary certifications that most directly apply to accounting and information systems (see Exhibit 1.3).

Name	Certifying Body	Who They Are and What They Do	How to Qualify
Certified Information Systems Auditor (CISA)	Information Systems Audit and Control Association (ISACA) www.isaca.org	The CISA designation identifies those professionals possessing IT audit, control, and security skills. Generally, CISAs will perform IT audits to evaluate the accounting information system's internal control design and effectiveness.	To qualify as a CISA, a candidate must take an examination and obtain specialized work experience.
Certified Information Technology Professional (CITP)	American Institute of Certified Public Accountants (AICPA) www.aicpa.org	The CITP designation identifies accountants (CPAs) with a broad range of AIS knowledge and experience. The CITP designation demonstrates the accountant's ability to leverage technology to effectively and efficiently manage information while ensuring the data's reliability, security, accessibility, and relevance. CITPs may help devise a more efficient financial reporting system, help the accounting function go paperless, or consult on how an IT function may transform the business.	A CPA can earn a CITP designation with a combination of business experience, lifelong learning, and an optional exam.
Certified Internal Auditor (CIA)	Institute of Internal Auditors (IIA) http://www.theiia.org/	The CIA designation is the only globally accepted certification for internal auditors and is the standard to demonstrate their competency and professionalism in the internal auditing field.	An individual can earn a CIA designation by having the required education, professional experience, and character references. The individual must also pass the CIA examination.

EXHIBIT 1.3
Certifications in Accounting Information Systems

The AICPA recently announced a CPA Evolution initiative transforming the CPA examination and licensure model to recognize the rapidly changing skills and competencies the practice of accounting requires today and will require in the future, especially those that address accounting information systems, data analytics and associated technologies (such as blockchain, cybersecurity, and information technology controls). Such technology concepts will be incorporated into all aspects of the exam, both core and specific disciplines as the impact of advances in technology on the CPA profession continues to grow.[9]

PROGRESS CHECK

4. Would an IT auditor be considered to be a user, manager, evaluator, or designer of a client firm's accounting information system?
5. What would be the appropriate designation for someone who wants to be an IT auditor?
6. Let's suppose that **ExxonMobil** is hiring accountants for an entry-level financial accounting position. Is it reasonable to expect accounting graduates to be proficient in information technology? How do the recent changes made by the AICPA to the CPA exam, suggesting an increasing amount of information technology evaluation of prospective candidates, affect this expectation?

LO 1-4

Describe how business processes affect the firm's value chain.

THE VALUE CHAIN AND ACCOUNTING INFORMATION SYSTEMS

Information technology (IT) is increasingly omnipresent! Worldwide spending on IT was expected to exceed $4.4 trillion in 2022.[10] Clearly, information technology is a huge investment that firms make, and they expect to create value through its use. How IT assists firms to carry out their internal and external business processes and, in turn, creates value is an important topic of this chapter.

A firm makes money by taking the inputs (raw materials, talented workers, buildings, equipment, etc.) and producing a more valuable output (iPhones available for sale, completed audit financial statements, etc.). Let's take universities as an example. Universities admit students to the university (as inputs) and use the institution's resources (curriculum, faculty, buildings, computers, textbooks, labs, etc.) to create a job-ready, educated graduate (the output). Arguably, universities create value. If they were not creating value in one form or the other, they probably would not continue to survive.

Let's continue the discussion by defining **business value** as all those items, events, and interactions that determine the financial health and/or well-being of the firm. This value may come from suppliers, customers, or employees or even from information systems. Business value does not necessarily need to be determined by stock price or net income. A not-for-profit group like the **International Red Cross** may define business value as how many lives are saved, the amount of blood donated, or the number of children that are immunized.

To consider how value is created, we begin by looking at the business processes. A business process is a coordinated, standardized set of activities conducted by both people and equipment to accomplish a specific task, such as invoicing a customer. To evaluate the effectiveness of each of its business processes, a firm can use Michael Porter's value chain analysis. A **value chain** is a chain of business processes for a firm. Products pass through all activities of the chain in order; at each activity, the product is expected to gain some value. It is important not to confuse the concept of the value chain with the actual cost of performing those activities. One way of looking at this is by considering a rough

[9] "New Model for Licensure, New CPA Exam Expected to Launch 2024," https://www.evolutionofcpa.org/, Accessed February 2023.

[10] "Gartner Forecasts Worldwide IT Spending to Reach $4.4 Trillion in 2022," Gartner Press Release, April 6, 2022.

diamond. Although the cutting activity of a diamond may have a very low cost, this cutting activity adds much of the value to the end product because a cut diamond is much more valuable than a rough diamond. And a diamond cut well adds more value than a diamond cut poorly.

The value chain illustrated in Exhibit 1.4 shows both primary activities and support activities. Primary activities directly provide value to the customer and include the following five activities:

1. **Inbound logistics** are the activities associated with receiving and storing raw materials and other partially completed materials and distributing those materials to manufacturing when and where they are needed.
2. **Operations** are the activities that transform inputs into finished goods and services (e.g., turning wood into furniture for a furniture manufacturer; building a house for a home builder).
3. **Outbound logistics** are the activities that warehouse the finished goods and distribute them to the customers.
4. **Marketing and sales activities** identify the needs and wants of customers to help attract them to the firm's products and, thus, buy them.
5. **Service activities** provide the support of customers after the products and services are sold to them (e.g., warranty repairs, parts, instruction manuals).

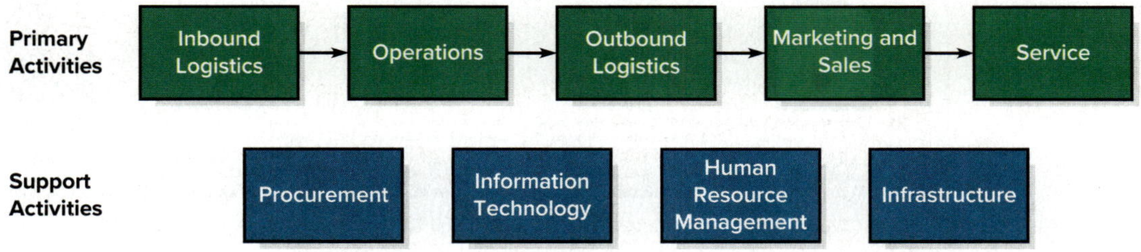

EXHIBIT 1.4
The Value Chain

These five primary activities are sustained by the following four support activities:

1. **Firm infrastructure** activities are all of the activities needed to support the firm, including the chief executive officer (CEO) and the finance, accounting, and legal departments.
2. **Human resource management** activities include recruiting, hiring, training, and compensating employees.
3. **Technology** activities include all of the technologies necessary to support value-creating activities. These technologies also include research and development to develop new products or determine ways to produce products at a cheaper price.
4. **Procurement** activities involve purchasing inputs such as raw materials, supplies, and equipment.

An AIS can add value to the firm by making each primary activity more effective and efficient. For example, AISs can assist with inbound and outbound logistics by finding efficiencies and cost savings (transportation and warehousing costs, etc.). Specifically, use of AISs and geographic information systems help identify the lowest cost of getting items from one location to another. AISs can make marketing, sales, and service activities more valuable by summarizing data about key customers to help manage and nurture a firm's interactions with its clients.

LO 1-5

Explain how AIS affects firm value.

As an example, **Amazon** is one of the best at fostering its interaction with its customers by keeping a record of their past purchases and product searches and using that information to recommend other similar products for its customers to consider. Exhibit 1.5 shows an example of "Recommended for You" at Amazon. In this instance since gloves were ordered previously, winter hats appeared as a future recommendation. The site shows this type of prediction of the items that the customer might be interested. As another example, as the loan officers at a bank learn more about the financial products currently being used by its bank's customers through its AIS, they will be able to help identify additional bank products (insurance, CDs, mutual funds, additional savings accounts, etc.) to sell to their clients. **Netflix** also uses data to help recommend TV shows people should watch—more than 80 percent of the TV shows customers watch are attributed to Netflix's recommendation system.[11]

EXHIBIT 1.5
Amazon.com: "Recommended for You"

Amazon.com

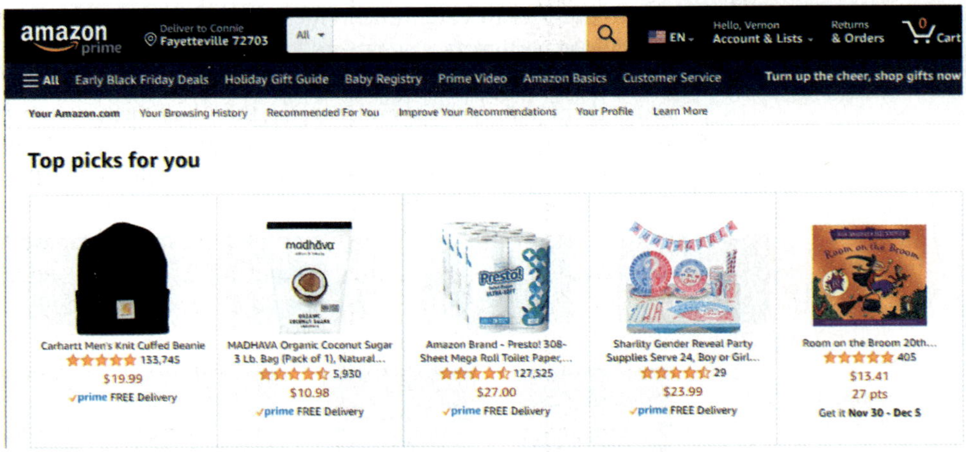

As detailed here, AIS can add value to the firm by making each support activity more effective and efficient. An AIS

- Gives access to management information relevant to the decision makers.
- May also help provide the internal control structure needed to make sure the information is secure, reliable, and free from error (as discussed in Chapter 13).
- Helps produce external and internal financial reports efficiently and helps decision makers get timely access to the processed information. This may give the information to the decision maker in time to influence the decision.
- Supports the human resources function by assisting employees, who are arguably the most valuable asset of the firm. This assistance includes easy access to payroll information, compensation policies, benefits, tax benefits, and so on.
- Assists procurement by improving the effectiveness and efficiency of the supply chain. This helps ensure that the right product is at the right location at the right time, including receipts of raw material from suppliers to delivery of finished goods to the customers.
- Delivers high quality information to employees to perform data analytics on the data to address management questions.

[11] Dave Burstein, Infographic: How Netflix Uses Big Data to Drive Success, DataConomy. https://dataconomy.com/2018/03/infographic-how-netflix-uses-big-data-to-drive-success/, Accessed 2/8/2019.

PROGRESS CHECK

7. Consider the value chain for **Tesla**. In your opinion, which primary activity is the most critical to creating value for the firm?
8. How does an AIS help **Wish.com** (a popular range of products coming directly from China) find the right marketing strategy?
9. An AIS adds value to the supporting activities by making access to financial results available on a more timely basis. Why does this matter?

LO 1-6

Describe how AIS assists the firm in its internal business processes.

AIS AND INTERNAL BUSINESS PROCESSES

Our discussion now turns to how an AIS can assist the firm with its internal business processes. An AIS within a firm is usually the foundation for an **enterprise system (ES)**—also called an enterprise resource planning (ERP) system. An enterprise system is a centralized database that collects data from throughout the firm. This includes data from orders, customers, sales, inventory, and employees. These data are then accumulated in the centralized database and made available to all enterprise system users, including accounting, manufacturing (or operations), marketing, and human resources. As the data are integrated into one single, centralized database to become useful information, authorized employees throughout the firm (from the CEO all the way to the lowest-paid line worker) have access to the information they need to make a decision. For most firms, the informational benefits of these integrated data include enhanced completeness, transparency, and timeliness of information needed to effectively manage a firm's business activities.

As an example, an enterprise system can automate a business process such as order fulfillment. The enterprise system can take an order from a customer, fill that order, ship it, and then create an invoice to bill the customer. When a customer service representative receives a customer order into an enterprise system, they have all the information needed to approve and complete the order (e.g., the customer's credit rating and order history from the finance module of the centralized database, the firm's inventory levels to see if the product is available from the warehouse module of the centralized database, and the shipping dock's trucking schedule from the logistics module of the centralized database). Once the order is complete, the enterprise system routes the order to the warehouse and shipping department for order fulfillment and shipping and then back to the finance department to make sure the customer is invoiced. During the process, all workers in the various departments can see the same information and update it as needed. As problems arise (e.g., backordered products, returned products, trucker strikes), the enterprise system gives all within the firm the most current, real-time information to address these issues.

Specific enterprise accounting information systems that record and manage information on internal business processes include the financial reporting system and the human resource management system

Financial Reporting System

A **financial reporting system (FRS)** measures and records accounting transactions to the general ledger and related journal entries from the general journal and special purpose journals and subledgers. The FRS summarizes and communicates the results of the accounting transactions in financial reports, including financial statements, footnotes and related disclosures. For example, data from a FRS might used as primary inputs into a cost accounting system to determine the cost of producing and delivering goods and services to customers.

Human Resource Management System

A **human resource management system (HRMS)** records and tracks interactions of a company's employees, such as employee records, payroll, benefits, attendance management, career progression, and performance evaluations. Since company employees are generally regarded as the company's most important and most valuable asset, such a system helps a company manage and evaluate its labor force to see if it is ready and prepared to carry out company strategy.

The enterprise system serves as the backbone of the firm's internal business processes and serves as a connection to the external business processes with external partners as discussed in the next section.

LO 1-7

Assess how AIS facilitates the firm in its external business processes.

AIS AND EXTERNAL BUSINESS PROCESSES

Firms do not work in isolation. They are always connected to both their suppliers and customers and their wants and needs. As shown in Exhibit 1.6, the AIS assists in business integration with external parties such as suppliers and customers. The firm's interaction with the suppliers is generally called *supply chain management,* and the interaction with its customers is generally called *customer relationship management.*

EXHIBIT 1.6
AIS and External Business Processes

The Supply Chain

Supply chain refers to the flow of materials, information, payments, and services from raw materials suppliers, through factories and warehouses, all the way to the final customers of the firm's products. A supply chain also includes the firms and processes that create and deliver products, information, and services to the final customers. The supply chain refers to a network of processes that delivers a finished good or service to the final customer. Exhibit 1.7 reflects the sourcing, manufacturing (making), and delivering to the customer for each member of the supply chain (assuming the **Unilever** product is made in China, sold to **Sam's Club** and convenience stores, and ultimately sold to an end customer picking it up at the convenience store).

The supply chain also handles the product returns from the firm's customers back to the firm's suppliers, which represents a significant process that requires substantial planning.

To make the supply chain function efficiently, supply chain tasks include processes such as purchasing, payment flow, materials handling, production planning and control, logistics and warehousing, inventory control, returns, distribution, and delivery, and is usually assisted by supply chain software.

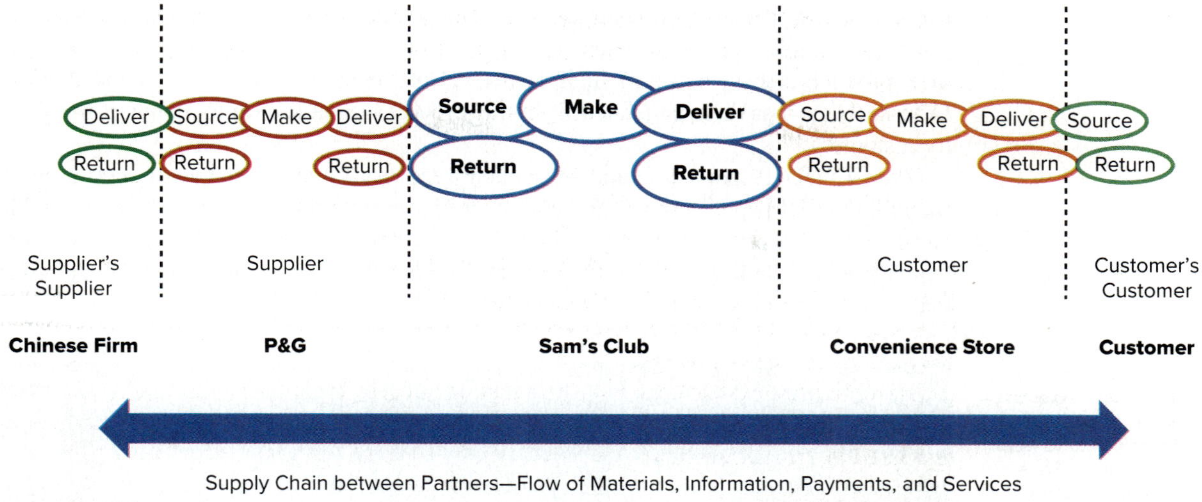

EXHIBIT 1.7
The Supply Chain

As an illustration of how the supply chain system works, Michael Dell of **Dell Technologies Inc.** explained Dell's interaction with its suppliers in this way:

> We tell our suppliers exactly what our daily production requirements are so it is not, "Well, every two weeks deliver 5,000 to this warehouse, and we'll put them on the shelf, and then we'll take them off the shelf." It is, "Tomorrow morning we need 8,562, and deliver them to door number seven by 7 am."[12]

The AIS used to connect the focal firm with its suppliers is generally referred to as **supply chain management system (SCMS)**. This AIS addresses specific segments of the supply chain, especially in manufacturing scheduling, inventory control, and transportation. This SCMS is designed to facilitate decision making and optimize the required levels of inventory to be ordered and held in stock. In the preceding example, Dell might produce expected demand for its products for the next year. As the dates get closer, the estimate is refined so the supplier has a better idea of what exactly will be needed. It is expected that this use of SCMS will optimize inventory and, in turn, will reduce the required amount of raw materials and finished goods inventory the firm will have to hold and thus lower product costs.

An academic study found that firms implementing SCMS are able to reduce the amount of raw materials inventory on hand and reduce selling, general, and administrative expenses. They are also able to increase their gross margins and overall inventory turnover. This suggests that supply chain management systems allow inventory to be optimized to lower the amount of required inventory on hand while not decreasing sales.

Walmart has long been regarded as having one of the best supply chain systems in the world.[13] One aspect of Walmart's supply chain management system is simply communicating the results of its retail sales to its top suppliers. Walmart's Retail Link database

[12]A. A. Thompson, A. J. Strickland, and J. Thompson, *Strategic Management: Concepts and Cases*, 11th ed. (New York: McGraw-Hill, 2006).

[13][[text missing]]

is one of the world's largest databases and allows many of its suppliers to view real-time sales data of its products for each store. This allows suppliers to assess the demand for their products and to optimize their own level of inventory and related logistics costs. In turn, the cost savings generated from this process are passed on to Walmart itself and its customers.

The COVID-19 pandemic and subsequent recovery found shortages of certain goods (including toilet paper, lumber, and computer chips) certainly put an emphasis on SCMS and maintaining efficient supply chains. Such shortages made customers hoard supplies which caused a bullwhip effect, further exacerbating the shortage and supply chain issues that are now taking years to work themselves out.

Walmart uses its supply chain expertise to lower prices and fulfill its motto to help its customers "Save Money, Live Better."
QualityHD/Shutterstock

Connection with Practice

One way of measuring the effectiveness of a supply chain is to calculate the fill rate. The fill rate is a calculation of the service level between two parties—generally, a supplier and a customer. The fill rate is a measure of shipping performance usually expressed as a percentage of the total order. The fill rate is often calculated as the value of order lines shipped on the initial order divided by the total value of the order. If the fill rate increases over time, this means the overall service level is improving. Supply chain management software would be expected to improve the fill rate and, in turn, the overall service levels.

Customer Relationship Management

The more a company can learn about its customers, the more likely it will be able to satisfy their needs. **Customer relationship management system (CRM)** is a term that describes the system used to manage and nurture a firm's interactions with its current and potential clients. A CRM system often includes the use of database marketing tools to learn more about customers and to develop strong firm-to-customer relationships. A CRM system also includes using IT to manage sales and marketing for current sales and customer service and technical support after the sale is done.

As mentioned in the opening vignette of this chapter, a good example of the need for CRM is **Starbucks**. After its quick expansion in the early 2000s, Starbucks felt like it had lost some of the original Starbucks customer coffeehouse experience. This caused a desire within Starbucks to make sure it understood its customers and their coffeehouse needs. Therefore, an initiative at Starbucks was implemented to learn more about its customers. The new chief information officer, Stephen Gillett, argues that his most crucial duty is to enhance Starbucks' ability to mine its customer data to help "reignite our passion with our customers." Starbucks uses loyalty cards (Starbucks' Rewards cards) and surveys to track its customers' purchases and build profiles of its customers.[14]

As another example, **Royal Bank** (formerly Royal Bank of Canada) considers its CRM system to be such an important part of its strategy that the stated objective of the bank is "to capture the full potential of our customer base through the use of customer information to deliver the right solutions in a consistent, professional manner at every point of contact."[15]

Connection with Practice

Salesforce is a popular vendor of CRM software. Note the explanation of CRM on the home page of its website:

> Customer Relationship Management helps companies understand their customers' needs and solve problems by better managing customer information and interactions—all on a single platform that's always accessible from any desktop or device.

Source: https://www.salesforce.com/products/what-is-salesforce/ (accessed August 2022).

PROGRESS CHECK

10. Give an example of how supply chain management software might work for **General Motors**. What type of information does General Motors need to share with its suppliers?
11. Using CRM techniques, what information could universities gather about their current and prospective customers, the students? What information might be most useful to them in recruiting future students?

LO 1-8

Explain how an AIS is used to create a cost accounting system.

USING AIS TO CREATE A COST ACCOUNTING SYSTEM: AN EXAMPLE

As an example of how various AISs are used to capture internal and external business processes, we'll illustrate using a company's cost accounting system. As you recall, a **cost accounting (or costing) system** is designed to aggregate, monitor, and report to

[14]T. Wallgum, "Starbucks' Next-Generation CIO: Young, Fast and in Control," *CIO Magazine,* January 2009, www.cio.com/article/474127/Starbucks_Next_Generation_CIO_Young_Fast_and_In_Control?page=3&taxonomyId=3123.

[15]"CRM Case Study: The Analytics That Power CRM at Royal Bank (of Canada)," www.mindbranch.com.

management information about revenues, costs, and profitability to allocate overhead, formulate job and process costing data, and create budget information. As shown in Exhibit 1.8, a cost accounting system receives data inputs from various enterprise systems that cover internal and external business processes, including the financial reporting system (FRS), the human resource management system (HRMS), the manufacturing system (MS), supply chain system (SCS), and the customer relationship management system (CRM).

- The **financial reporting system (FRS)** contributes information of the amounts paid for direct and indirect costs for each cost object. The FRS includes the general ledger and related journal entries from the general journal and special purpose journals and subledgers.
- The **human resource management system (HRMS)** contributes information on direct labor (as reflected by the arrow from the HRMS to direct labor) and indirect labor to indirect costs (as reflected by the arrow from the HRMS to indirect costs).
- The **manufacturing system (MS)** contributes information on direct materials (as reflected by the arrow from the MS to direct materials) and indirect materials as reflected by the arrow from the MS to indirect costs), by reporting on the various processes and jobs completed. If the company does not manufacture goods, to the extent applicable this input may come from the **supply chain system (SCS).**
- The **customer relationship management system (CRM)** contributes information on revenues to help assess profitability at a detailed customer, product, and company level to help evaluate whether business value was created (as reflected by the arrow from the CRM to sales revenue and on to the cost accounting system).

EXHIBIT 1.8
Inputs from Various AIS into a Company's Cost Accounting System

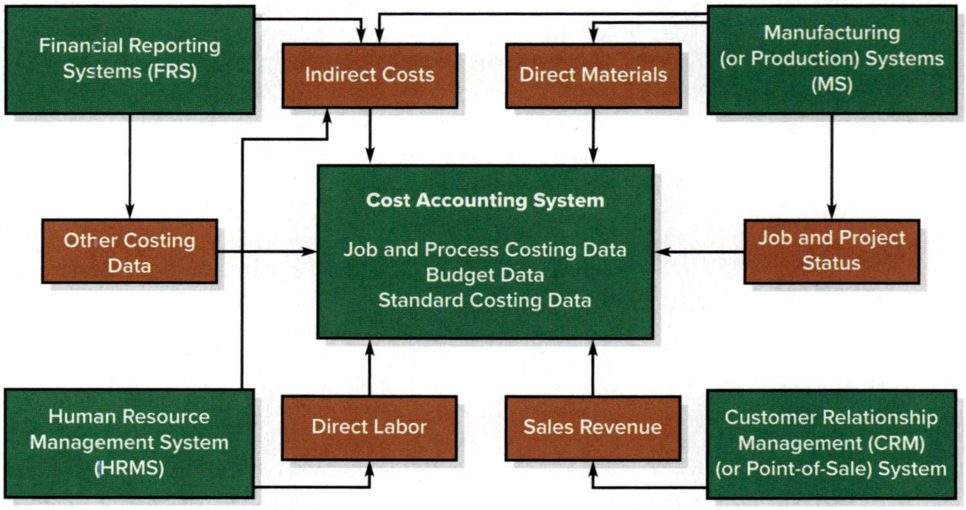

PROGRESS CHECK

12. How does the use of supply chain management software reduce the cost of goods sold for a retailer like **Home Depot**?
13. What does a CRM provide to a cost accounting system?
14. If the company provides services rather than products (like a hospital providing medical services), how will the inputs to this cost accounting system differ from those to a manufacturing company?

LO 1-9

Assess the impact of AIS on firm profitability and stock prices.

AIS AND VALUE CREATION

Throughout this chapter, we have tried to make the case that AIS facilitates value-creating activities. This section explains a path of how investment in AIS, in fact, may be associated with greater profitability and enhanced firm value.

AIS and Firm Profitability

Using Data Analytics to Create Value

If accountants have the needed high-quality data from their AIS, they are in a position to analyze that data to specifically address management's questions. To do so, accountants apply data analytics, analyzing data with the purpose of deriving data-driven insights for decision making. For example, if we could use data analytics (1) to target the firm's most profitable products to customers, (2) determine how product pricing could be optimized to maximize revenue, or (3) use data analytics to better predict demand and not hold excessive product in the warehouse, profitability could be maximized.

LAB CONNECTION

Lab 1-1 Excel uses data analytics techniques to determine the most profitable product and most profitable customer. Determining the most profitable products and customers allow the company to focus its efforts on profitability.

Lab 1-2 Excel uses data analytics techniques (including Excel formulas and the Analysis Toolpak in Excel) to compute descriptive, or summary, statistics on the gross profit margin and gross profit margin percentages of various products. Examining the distribution of gross profit margins and percentages gives the company a fuller knowledge of its product offering.

We'll highlight how accountants use data analytics to address management questions and create value specifically in Chapters 2 and 3 of the textbook.

Which Specific Accounts Show AIS-Created Value?

Another way to consider how AIS creates value is to look at an income statement. Accountants understand that to make more profits, a firm either needs to increase revenues or decrease expenses (or both!). Accountants apply data analytics, analyzing data with the purpose of drawing conclusions for decision making. Exhibit 1.9 illustrates how AIS affects the income statement, making the case for how an AIS may increase profitability.

In an academic study,[16] a positive association was found between the level of the firm's annual AIS investment and its subsequent accounting earnings (as measured by return on assets and return on sales), suggesting that AIS investment does in fact create value. In a completely different study,[17] researchers found both an improvement in profitability as well as stock returns around the implementation of supply chain information systems.

[16] K. Kobelsky, V. J. Richardson, R. Smith, and R. W. Zmud, "Determinants and Consequences of Firm Information Technology Budgets," *The Accounting Review* 83 (July 2008), pp. 957–96.

[17] K. B. Hendricks, V. R. Singhal, and J. K. Stratman, "The Impact of Enterprise Systems on Corporate Performance: A Study of ERP, SCM and CRM System Implementations," *Journal of Operations Management* 25, no. 1 (January 2007), pp. 65–82.

EXHIBIT 1.9
The Potential Effect of AIS on an Income Statement

Income Statement	Effect of AIS on Income Statement
Revenues	Customer relationship management systems (CRM) are used to attract new customers, or analytics are performed to identify the most profitable customers) to generate additional sales revenue.
Less: Cost of Goods Sold	A cost accounting system helps a company track and ultimately reduce their costs. A supply chain management system (SCM) or manufacturing system (MS) allows firms to carry the right inventory and have it in the right place at the right price. This, in turn, will lower obsolescence of their inventory as well as logistics, storage and procurement costs.
Gross Margin	The gross margin will change as the result of changes in revenues or cost of goods sold due to the effects of an AIS.
Less: Selling, General, and Administrative Expenses (SG&A)	An efficient enterprise system can significantly lower the cost of support processes included in sales, general, and administrative expenses. HRMS could also be used to efficiently assign employees to the most important tasks.
Less: Interest Expense	SCM allows the firm to carry less inventory. Less inventory on hand leaves fewer assets to finance, potentially reducing the amount of debt and the related interest to service the debt.
Net Income	All combined, a well-designed and well-functioning AIS with investments in enterprise systems, SCM, and/or CRM may be expected to improve net income.

PROGRESS CHECK

15. How does an AIS make the cost of support lower, and thus reduce SG&A expenses? Provide an example.

Summary

- Accountants play a critical role in recording, processing, and reporting financial information for decision making and control. An accounting information system (AIS) is defined as an information system that records, processes, and reports on transactions to provide financial information for decision making and control.
- The accounting profession (including the IFAC and the AICPA) recommends that accountants develop proficiency in at least two areas of information systems: as a user and as a manager, designer, or evaluator of information systems. Accountants often seek certification in information systems to show their level of proficiency to both prospective employers and clients. The recent proposed changes to the CPA exam that emphasize data, data analytics, cybersecurity, and accounting information systems signal how important AIS training is to all aspects of the accounting profession.
- Firms invest in AIS to create value. The value chain illustrates how, during each primary activity, the product should gain some value. An AIS serves an important role in providing value in each primary and supporting activity.
- An AIS creates value by managing internal and external business processes. Enterprise systems, sometimes called an ERP or back-office systems, generally manage transactions within the firm. Supply chain management software is used to manage

transactions and communications with suppliers. Customer relationship management software is used to manage and nurture the relationship with current and potential customers.

- An AIS generally helps make business processes more efficient and effective. A well-designed and well-functioning AIS can be expected to create value by finding opportunities to increase revenues as well as reduce expenses by using and analyzing important information needed to make decisions.

Key Words

accounting information system (AIS) ***(5)*** A system that records, processes, reports, and communicates the results of business transactions to provide financial and nonfinancial information to make decisions and have appropriate levels of internal controls for those transactions.

business value ***(12)*** Items, events, and interactions that determine the financial health and well-being of the firm.

Certified Information Systems Auditor (CISA) ***(11)*** The CISA designation identifies those professionals possessing IT audit, control, and security skills. Generally, CISAs will perform IT audits to evaluate the accounting information system's internal control design and effectiveness.

Certified Information Technology Professional (CITP) ***(11)*** The CITP designation identifies accountants (CPAs) with a broad range of technology knowledge and experience.

Certified Internal Auditor (CIA) ***(11)*** The CIA designation is the certification for internal auditors and is the standard to demonstrate competency and professionalism in the internal auditing field.

cost accounting (or costing) system ***(19)*** a system designed to aggregate, monitor, and report to management about revenues, costs, and profitability to formulate job and process costing data, budget information, and standard costing data and allocate overhead.

customer relationship management system (CRM) ***(18)*** Information system used to manage and nurture a firm's interactions with its current and potential clients. CRM software often includes the use of database marketing tools to learn more about the customers and to develop strong firm-to-customer relationships.

data ***(7)*** Raw facts or statistics that, absent a context, may have little meaning.

discretionary information ***(8)*** Information that is generated according to one's own judgment.

enterprise system (ES) ***(15)*** A centralized database that collects data from throughout the firm. Commercialized information system that integrates and automates business processes across a firm's value chain located within and across organizations.

financial reporting system (FRS) ***(16)*** a system that measures and records accounting transactions and summarizes and communicates the results of the accounting transactions using financial reports, (e.g., financial statements, footnotes and related disclosures).

firm infrastructure ***(13)*** Activities needed to support the firm, including the CEO and the finance, accounting, and legal departments.

human resource management ***(13)*** Activities include recruiting, hiring, training, and compensating employees.

human resource management system (HRMS) ***(16)*** A system that records and tracks interactions of a company's employees, such as employee records, payroll, attendance management, and performance evaluations.

inbound logistics ***(13)*** Activities associated with receiving and storing raw materials and other partially completed materials and distributing those materials to manufacturing when and where they are needed.

information ***(7)*** Data organized in a way meaningful to the user.

information overload *(8)* The difficulty a person faces in understanding a problem and making a decision as a consequence of too much information.

information value chain *(8)* The overall transformation from a business need and business event to the collection of data and information to an ultimate decision.

mandatory information *(9)* Information that is required to be generated or provided by law or regulation.

manufacturing system *(20)* Software that reports on the status of various jobs in the manufacturing process.

marketing and sales activities *(13)* Activities that identify the needs and wants of their customers to help attract them to the firm's products and buy them.

operations *(13)* Activities that transform inputs into finished goods and services.

outbound logistics *(13)* Activities that warehouse and distribute the finished goods and distribute them to the customers.

procurement *(13)* Activities that involve purchasing inputs such as raw materials, supplies, and equipment.

Sarbanes–Oxley Act of 2002 (SOX) *(10)* A response to business scandals such as Enron, WorldCom, and Tyco International; requires public companies registered with the SEC and their auditors to annually assess and report on the design and effectiveness of internal control over financial reporting.

service activities *(13)* Activities that provide the support of customers after the products and services are sold to them (e.g., warranty repairs, parts, instruction manuals, etc.).

supply chain *(16)* The flow of materials, information, payments, and services from raw materials suppliers, through factories and warehouses, all the way to the final customers of the firm's products.

supply chain management system (SCMS) *(17)* Software that connects the focal firm with its suppliers. It generally addresses segments of the supply chain, including manufacturing, inventory control, and transportation.

systems analyst *(10)* Person responsible for both determining the information needs of the business and designing a system to meet those needs.

technology *(13)* Supports value-creating activities in the value chain. These technologies also include research and development to develop new products or determine ways to produce products at a cheaper price.

value chain *(12)* A chain of critical business processes that creates value at a company.

ANSWERS TO PROGRESS CHECKS

1. Useful relevant information may include how often the opposing team runs or passes, the number of times out of the shotgun, the number of times it runs a jet sweep play, or how often they blitz on defense. Receiving this relevant information in a timely manner may help the team prepare for its upcoming football games or even while the game is being played. An example of useful information that exhibits qualities of faithful representation might include the information collected and verified by an independent official keeping the score and statistics of a football game. This information might include the score of the game, the pass completion percentages, the numbers of sacks or interceptions by each team and player, the total offense statistics, etc. Having an unbiased source of information allows the coach to use the information received without having to worry about whether the information is biased.
2. Data at **T-Mobile** might be any random factoid without context. An example might be that one store in the United States generated $0.3 million in annual telephone coverage yesterday. It is only when put in context that the data become useful. If we know that the store is in Tucson, Arizona, and that on the same date, a year earlier, the store had sales of $0.1 million, the data become information.

3. Two types of discretionary information include the cost of manufacturing each **Samsung** Galaxy Pad or the type of pastry that sells best with a latte at **Starbucks**. Two types of mandatory information might be the amount of sales taxes collected and remitted to the state tax commission or the sales returns a company has that is reported to the Securities and Exchange Commission.
4. Generally, an IT auditor would be considered to be an evaluator of a client firm's accounting information system. In general, IT auditors will assess the accounting information system to ensure the audit risk (the risk of reaching an incorrect conclusion based on the audit findings) associated with a company's information system will be limited to an acceptable level. They will address questions such as whether backups are made, cybersecurity is effective, passwords are changed regularly, etc.
5. The Certified Information Systems Auditor (CISA) designation would be the most appropriate credential for an IT auditor. In some cases, the Certified Information Technology Professional (CITP) designation would also be an appropriate credential.
6. Most, if not all, entry-level financial accounting positions at **ExxonMobil** (or other similar companies) would expect some reasonable level of proficiency as a user of accounting information systems, such as the ability to use a basic accounting/bookkeeping package (QuickBooks, Peachtree, Microsoft Excel, Xero, etc.) However, the International Federation of Accountants suggests accountants have proficiency not only as a user, but also as at least one of these other roles in an accounting information system: evaluator, manager, or designer. (Some of that desirable proficiency will be gained in this textbook, so read carefully!). The AICPA, as noted in its recently announced CPA Evolution initiative, is continuing to emphasize information technology proficiency overall of its CPA licensure candidates.
7. Clearly, all portions of the value chain have to be working well for **Tesla** to be successful and create value for the firm and its shareholders. A case could be made for any and all of the primary activities. We will argue that marketing and sales are the most important because, to be successful, companies need to completely understand and then meet their customers' needs.
8. **Wish.com** is a popular app/e-commerce company that features a variety of very inexpensive products coming directly from China. An AIS may help Wish.com find the right marketing strategy by figuring out where to advertise Wish.com product offerings (banner ads, referral pages, Facebook ads, emails, etc.) to its customers. AIS may also help Wish.com figure out which products sell best and which products have the biggest profit margins to best know which products to emphasize.
9. An AIS can add value to the firm by providing financial results in time to make a difference to the decision maker. As an example, if the firm finds out quickly that one of its products is too expensive to manufacture, the firm may choose to discontinue the product, modify the product by reducing features of it, or find a cheaper way to manufacture it. If that financial information is not received until weeks or months later, the firm will have lost profits.
10. Let's suppose that **General Motors** will decide how many Chevrolet Silverado EV's (electric vehicles) to produce at each plant. Once General Motors knows how many it will likely produce, the supply chain management software can immediately compute the specific parts needed and share this information with its suppliers. The suppliers can then plan and begin production of the parts they provide. For example, if General Motors plans to produce 50,000 Silverado EV at its Indianapolis, Indiana, assembly plant, the tire suppliers can plan on producing and delivering 200,000 tires to meet those needs.
11. Universities are increasingly using CRM techniques to catalog information about their students from overall trends about the new millennials (who prefer more choices, experiential learning, flexibility, etc.) to archiving individual inquiries (email, Snapchat, Instagram, Facebook, Twitter, etc.) by each prospective student. Students generally don't like to be treated as one among the masses, so any information that might target a specific student need (such as information about their desired major) or interest would be particularly useful to recruiters.

12. Supply chain software can help reduce procurement, logistics, and inventory-carrying costs for **Home Depot**. If the whole supply chain has a better idea of the final customer's ultimate demand for the product, it will reduce the need to carry more inventory than is needed or to miss customer sales by not having enough product on hand. This, in turn, will reduce procurement, logistics, and inventory-carrying costs and potentially allow the company to carry less debt to support unnecessary inventory assets on hand.
13. CRM will give the cost accounting system an idea of the sales revenue it might generate from sales of the product. This will help management determine profit margins, contribution margins and gross profit margins.
14. The key inputs for a hospital might include equipment, direct and indirect staff labor, professional fees, software, data center charges, prescription drugs, and so on.
15. If an AIS allows a company to hold less product due to efficiency, this will allow less storage expense, less warehouse personnel, and less work at transportation product. In turn, this will reduce SG&A expenses.

Multiple Choice Questions connect

1. **(LO 1-1)** Accounting information systems
   a. are always computerized.
   b. report only financially related information.
   c. are information systems that record, process, and report on transactions to provide financial and nonfinancial information for decision making and control.
   d. require a CITP designation to understand.
2. **(LO 1-1)** Which of the following is a characteristic of relevance?
   a. Materiality
   b. Timeliness
   c. Verifiable
   d. Cost to generate
3. **(LO 1-2)** Which of the following is considered to be mandatory information required by a regulatory body?
   a. 10-Q submission to the Securities and Exchange Commission
   b. The cost to produce a Samsung Galaxy
   c. The number of organic bananas that are sold at Whole Foods on July 28
   d. The cost to build an all-new Starbucks restaurant in Shenzhen, China
4. **(LO 1-4)** The correct order of events in the value chain is
   a. Inbound logistics → Operations → Service.
   b. Inbound logistics → Outbound logistics → Marketing and sales.
   c. Inbound logistics → Operations → Outbound logistics.
   d. Inbound logistics → Operations → Marketing and Sales.
5. **(LO 1-8)** Which system contributes information on direct labor to a cost accounting system?
   a. Supply chain management system (SCMS)
   b. Financial reporting system (FRS)
   c. Customer Relational Management System (CRM)
   d. Human resource management system (HRMS)

6. **(LO 1-7)** A supply chain
   a. supplies jewelry chains.
   b. refers to the flow of materials, information, payments, and services.
   c. is similar in function and purpose to the value chain.
   d. does not apply to a service firm like an accounting firm.
7. **(LO 1-7)** Customer relationship management software does *not* include information about
   a. current customers.
   b. prospective customers.
   c. former customers.
   d. current employees.
8. **(LO 1-6)** An information system that measures and records accounting transactions and reports them in the financial statements is called a
   a. financial reporting system (FRS).
   b. enterprise system (ES).
   c. manufacturing system (MS).
   d. cost accounting system.
9. **(LO 1-3)** What is the name of the position for a person responsible for determining information needs of a business and designing a system to meet those needs?
   a. Chief information officer
   b. Controller
   c. IT auditor
   d. Systems analyst
10. **(LO 1-9)** The balance sheet account most likely affected by an AIS investment in supply chain management software would be
   a. inventories.
   b. fixed assets.
   c. cash and cash equivalents.
   d. unearned revenue.
11. **(LO 1-7)** The software/system that helps make sure the retail firm doesn't have a stockout is
   a. supply chain management software.
   b. customer relationship management software.
   c. enterprise systems.
   d. human resource systems.
12. **(LO 1-9)** Data analytics performed to identify the most profitable customers would be most likely to affect which income statement account?
   a. Selling, general, and administrative expenses (SG&A)
   b. Interest expense
   c. Revenues
   d. Cost of goods sold
13. **(LO 1-7, LO 1-9)** Customer relationship management systems would generally be considered to be an
   a. internal business process.
   b. external business process.
   c. interior business process.
   d. exterior business process.

14. **(LO 1-3)** An auditor testing internal controls would generally be considered to fill which role with respect to accounting information systems?
    a. User
    b. Manager
    c. Designer
    d. Evaluator
15. **(LO 1-2)** Which of these represents the proper transformation from data to decision according to the information value chain?
    a. Data → Information → Knowledge → Decision
    b. Data → Knowledge → Information → Decision
    c. Data → Business event → Information → Decision
    d. Data → Analysis → Information → Decision

Discussion Questions connect

1. **(LO 1-2)** Brainstorm a list of discretionary information that might be an output of an accounting information system and be needed by **Starbucks**. Prioritize which items might be most important, and provide support.
2. **(LO 1-2)** Explain the information value chain. How do business events turn into data, then into information, and then into knowledge? Give an example starting with the business event of the purchase of a Super Smash Bros. Nintendo Switch game at **GameStop** all the way to giving useful information for the CEO and other decision makers.
3. **(LO 1-2)** Give three examples of types of discretionary information at your college or university, and explain how the benefits of receiving that information outweigh the costs.
4. **(LO 1-2)** After an NCAA women's basketball game, a box score is produced detailing the number of points scored, assists made, and rebounds retrieved (among other statistics). Using the characteristics of useful information discussed at the beginning of the chapter, please explain how this box score meets (or does not meet) the characteristics of useful information.
5. **(LO 1-3)** Some would argue that the role of accounting is simply an information provider. Will a computer ultimately completely take over the job of the accountant? As part of your explanation, explain how the role of accountants in information systems continues to evolve.
6. **(LO 1-3)** How do you become a Certified Internal Auditor (CIA)? What do they do on a daily basis?
7. **(LO 1-3)** How do you become a Certified Information Technology Professional (CITP)? What do they do on a daily basis?
8. **(LO 1-4)** Explain the value chain for an appliance manufacturer, particularly the primary activities. Which activities are most crucial for value creation (in other words, which activities would you want to make sure are the most effective)? Rank the five value chain–enhancing activities in importance for an appliance manufacturer.
9. **(LO 1-4)** Which value chain–supporting activities would be most important to support a healthcare provider's primary activities? How about the most important primary activities for a university?
10. **(LO 1-4)** Where does new-product development fit in the value chain for a pharmaceutical company? Where does new-product development for a car manufacturer fit in the value chain?
11. **(LO 1-5)** List and explain three ways that an AIS can add value to the firm.
12. **(LO 1-6)** An enterprise system is a centralized database that collects and distributes information throughout the firm. What type of financial information would be useful for both the marketing and manufacturing operations?

13. **(LO 1-7)** Customer relationship management software is used to manage and nurture a firm's interactions with its current and potential clients. What information would **Airbus** want to know about its current and potential airplane customers? Why is this so critical?

14. **(LO 1-6, LO 1-8)** What data from internal business processes will serve as inputs into a cost accounting system for your university? From which specific enterprise systems will this data be recorded and managed?

15. **(LO 1-9)** How would an AIS help a company identify the products with the highest profit margins? Why is that important to a company?

Problems connect

1. **(LO 1-1)** Accenture recently published an article titled "Meet the Finance 2020 Workforce,"[18] suggesting that accountants will need to not only embrace traditional financial questions of "What happened?" and "Why did it happen?" but also the question of "What should we do?" How is that consistent with the idea argued in the chapter that the accountant should serve as a business analyst?

2. **(LO 1-1)** Accenture recently published an article titled, "Meet the Finance 2020 Workforce,"[19] suggesting that accountants will need to embrace new financial roles to analyze new business opportunities and ways the organization can profit from them. Explain how an accountant might map internal and external business processes to their relevant AIS systems with the goal of analyzing business opportunities and suggesting strategies to profit from them.

3. **(LO 1-1)** If computers and enterprise systems do much of the traditional work of recording transactions and processing journal entries and other accounting information, what role is left for the accountant to perform?

4. **(LO 1-4)** Match the value chain activity in the left column with the scenario in the right column:

1. Service activities	A. Surveys for prospective customers
2. Inbound logistics	B. Warranty work
3. Marketing and sales activities	C. Assembly line
4. Firm infrastructure	D. Delivery to the firm's customer
5. Human resource management	E. New-product development
6. Technology	F. Receiving dock for raw materials
7. Procurement	G. CEO and CFO
8. Outbound logistics	H. Buying (sourcing) raw materials
9. Operations	I. Worker recruitment

5. **(LO 1-4)** Match the value chain activity in the left column with the scenario in the right column.

1. Customer call center	A. Operations
2. Supply schedules	B. Inbound logistics
3. Order taking	C. Procurement
4. Accounting department	D. Firm infrastructure
5. Staff training	E. Human resource management
6. Research and development	F. Technology
7. Verifying quality of raw materials	G. Service activities
8. Distribution center	H. Outbound logistics
9. Manufacturing	I. Marketing and sales activities

[18] David A. J. Axson and Sharad Mistry, "Meet the Finance 2020 Workforce," 2017, https://www.accenture.com/t20170511T060010Z__w__/us-en/_acnmedia/PDF-50/Accenture-Finance-2020-Workforce.pdf.
[19]ibid

6. **(LO 1-7)** **John Deere**'s $4 billion commercial and consumer equipment division implemented supply chain management software and reduced its inventory by $500 million. As sales continued to grow, the company has been able to keep its inventory growth flat. How did the SCM software implementation allow John Deere to reduce inventory on hand? How did this allow the company to save money? Which income statement accounts (revenue, cost of goods sold, SG&A expenses, interest expense, etc.) would this affect?
7. **(LO 1-7)** **Dell Technologies** used customer relationship management software called IdeaStorm to collect customer feedback. This customer feedback led the company to build select consumer notebooks and desktops pre-installed with the Linux platform. Dell also decided to continue offering Windows 10 as a pre-installed operating system option in response to customer requests. Where does this fit in the value chain? How will this help Dell create value?
8. **(LO 1-9)** **Ingersoll Rand** operates as a manufacturer in four segments: Air Conditioning Systems and Services, Climate Control Technologies, Industrial Technologies, and Security Technologies. It installed an Oracle enterprise system, a supply chain system, and a customer relationship management system. The company boasts the following results.[20]
   - Decreased direct product costs by 11 percent.
   - Increased labor productivity by 16 percent.
   - Increased inventory turns by four times.
   - Decreased order processing time by 90 percent and decreased implementation time by 40 percent.
   - Ensured minimal business disruption.
   - Streamlined three customer centers to one.

   Take each of these results and explain how the three systems (enterprise system, supply chain system, and customer relationship management system) affected these financial results and created value for the firm.
9. **(LO 1-9)** Information systems have impact on financial results. Using Exhibit 1.9 as a guide, which system is most likely to impact the following line items on an income statement? The systems to consider are enterprise systems, supply chain systems manufacturing system, human resource management system, and customer relationship management systems.

Income Statement Item	System
Revenues	
Cost of goods sold	
Sales, general, and administrative expenses	
Interest expense	
Net Income	

10. **(LO 1-3)** Accountants have four potential roles in accounting information systems: user, manager, designer, and evaluator. Match the specific accounting role to the activity performed.
    1. Controller meeting with the systems analyst to ensure accounting information system is able to accurately capture information to meet regulatory requirements
    2. Cost accountant gathering data for factory overhead allocations from the accounting information system
    3. IT auditor testing the system to assess the internal controls of the accounting information system
    4. CFO plans staffing to effectively direct and lead accounting information system

[20] http://www.ediguys.net/pages/SCIS/ingersoll-rand-siebel-casestudy.pdf.

11. **(LO 1-6, LO 1-7)** Which firm information system (customer relationship management, financial reporting system, human resource management system, supply chain management) would address each of the following questions?

Questions	Information System (Customer Relationship Management, Financial Reporting System, Human Resource Management System, Supply Chain Management)
What is the value of fixed assets (property, plant, and equipment) on the balance sheet?	
How much does **Airbus** owe **General Electric** for its turbine engines?	
When will the shampoo products from **Procter & Gamble** arrive at the **Walmart** distribution center?	
Which customers should we no longer sell to due to poor credit?	
When was the depreciation adjusting journal entry made?	
How long does it take **Microsoft** to get electronic parts from Vietnam?	
Who is **Apple**'s most profitable customer?	
What is the salary of the web page designers most recently hired at **Netflix**?	

12. **(LO 1-6, LO 1-7)** Management has questions. Accountants have answers. These answers should come from either internal or external business processes. And come from which firm information system (customer relationship management, enterprise system, supply chain)?

Questions	Internal or External Business Process	Information System (Customer Relationship Management System, Financial Reporting System, Human Resource Management System, Supply Chain Management System)
What is the value of fixed assets (property, plant, and equipment) on the balance sheet?		
Which shoes are least desired by **Zappo**'s customers?		
When will the **United Parcel Service** (UPS) deliver the inventory?		
What is the salary of the accounting staff most recently hired at **Home Depot** headquarters?		
How long does it take to close the books at the end of the period?		
How long does it take to deliver tires from **Nissan** to its car dealers?		

13. **(LO 1-3)** Identify the certification required to address each of the following questions/tasks, including Certified Internal Auditor (CIA), Certified Public Accountant (CPA), Certified Information Technology Professional (CITP), and Certified Information Systems Auditor (CISA).

Questions	Certification [Certified Internal Auditor (CIA), Certified Public Accountant (CPA), Certified Information Technology Professional (CITP), and Certified Information Systems Auditor (CISA)]
Who helps determine if the internal controls are designed properly and working?	
Who helps an individual file taxes with the IRS?	
Who performs IT audits for Deloitte (a Big 4 auditor)?	
Who designs a more efficient financial reporting system?	
Who looks for fraudulent financial transactions and works for the audit committee?	
Who performs an external audit for a company before filing with the Securities and Exchange Commission?	
Who helps design and implement a financial reporting system be done without paper?	
Who evaluates whether there is a threat of a cybersecurity breach to the financial reporting system of a company it is auditing?	

14. **(LO 1-7)** The appropriate amount of an Allowance for Doubtful Accountants (that serves as a contra asset to Accounts Receivable) is generally determined by figuring out how long the underlying receivables have remained unpaid. How might a customer relationship management system be able to help determine whether an outstanding accounting might be paid?

LABS ASSOCIATED WITH CHAPTER 1

Connect

LAB 1-1 EXCEL	Descriptive Analytics: Determining the Most Profitable Products (SKU) and Customers
LAB 1-2 EXCEL	Descriptive Analytics: Calculating Descriptive Statistics

The multiple choice assessment questions for each lab are assignable via Connect. Materials are also available for courses not utilizing Connect via the Solutions Manual.

Lab 1-1 Excel: Descriptive Analytics: Determining the Most Profitable Products (SKU) and Customers

Keywords

SKU, product profitability, inventory management

Lab Insight

Merchandising companies sell product to customers. The company makes money by selling the product for more than the cost of the product. In this lab, we compute the gross margin for each product and then determine the most profitable products to sell. By highlighting the most profitable products, the merchandising company can focus its efforts on selling the products with the highest gross profit, and thus make more overall profits for the company.

Required:

1. Calculate the gross margin for each sale recorded in the sales journal.
2. Sort the products by gross margin achieved during the month.

Ask the Question

Which products (SKUs) have made the highest profit during the month?

Master the Data

SkyDio sells drones to U.S. customers by mail order. The company has a sales journal where it keeps track of each sale by invoice #, customer #, SKU for the month with the following data dictionary:

Data Dictionary

Date: Date of the sale

Invoice #: The invoice number of the sales transaction

Customer #: The customer number of customer buying SkyDio products

SKU: SkyDio SKU (unique code for each inventory item sold) - A SKU stands for stock-keeping unit and serves as an alphanumeric identification to track a particular product for inventory purposes.

Description: Description of each inventory item sold

Sales price: Sales price of product

Cost: Total cost of product

Open Excel File Lab 1-1 Data.xlsx, which has the monthly sales journal for SkyDio (as shown in Lab Exhibit 1-1.1).

Lab Exhibit 1-1.1

	A	B	C	D	E	F	G
1	Date	Invoice #	Customer #	SKU	Description	Sales Price	Cost
2	10/1/2025	6001	3061	SK2-JOY	Joystick Controller	179	107
3	10/2/2025	6002	3095	SKY-CHG	Dual Charger	129	77
4	10/2/2025	6002	3036	SKY-PRK	Skydio 1 Pro Kit	2299	1234
5	10/3/2025	6003	3043	SKY-PRK	Skydio 1 Pro Kit	2299	1234
6	10/3/2025	6004	3081	SKY-PLR	Skydio 1 Propellers	25	14
7	10/3/2025	6005	3009	SKY-BAT	Skydio 1 Battery	115	66
8	10/3/2025	6006	3020	SK2-CHG	Dual Charger	149	86
9	10/3/2025	6007	3083	SK2-USB	Skydio Controller USB-C to Lightning Cable	19	11
10	10/3/2025	6007	3010	SKY-CHG	Dual Charger	129	77
11	10/3/2025	6008	3064	SK2-BEA	Skydio 2 Beacon	219	114
12	10/3/2025	6009	3037	SK2-CIK	Skydio 2 Cinema Kit	1799	1060
13	10/3/2025	6009	3061	SKY-BAT	Skydio 1 Battery	115	66
14	10/3/2025	6010	3054	SKY-BAT	Skydio 1 Battery	115	66

Perform the Analysis

Step 1

We first need to compute the gross margin for each invoice line item.

We'll start by going to cell H1, typing the title, "Gross Margin," and inserting a bottom border. In cell H2, we'll compute the gross margin for each line item of the invoice. To do so, we must subtract the cost in cell G2 from the sales in cell F2 by inserting the formula "=F2-G2". Then hit enter (as shown in Lab Exhibit 1-1.2).

Lab Exhibit 1-1.2

	A	B	C	D	E	F	G	H
1	Date	Invoice #	Customer #	SKU	Description	Sales Price	Cost	Gross Margin
2	10/1/2025	6001	3061	SK2-JOY	Joystick Controller	179	107	72
3	10/2/2025	6002	3095	SKY-CHG	Dual Charger	129	77	52
4	10/2/2025	6002	3036	SKY-PRK	Skydio 1 Pro Kit	2299	1234	1065
5	10/3/2025	6003	3043	SKY-PRK	Skydio 1 Pro Kit	2299	1234	1065
6	10/3/2025	6004	3081	SKY-PLR	Skydio 1 Propellers	25	14	11
7	10/3/2025	6005	3009	SKY-BAT	Skydio 1 Battery	115	66	49
8	10/3/2025	6006	3020	SK2-CHG	Dual Charger	149	86	63
9	10/3/2025	6007	3083	SK2-USB	Skydio Controller USB-C to Lightning Cable	19	11	8
10	10/3/2025	6007	3010	SKY-CHG	Dual Charger	129	77	52
11	10/3/2025	6008	3064	SK2-BEA	Skydio 2 Beacon	219	114	105
12	10/3/2025	6009	3037	SK2-CIK	Skydio 2 Cinema Kit	1799	1060	739
13	10/3/2025	6009	3061	SKY-BAT	Skydio 1 Battery	115	66	49
14	10/3/2025	6010	3054	SKY-BAT	Skydio 1 Battery	115	66	49

Now copy that formula down for every sale below from cell H3:H230.

Step 2

Our objective is to compute the gross margin earned for each product and highlight which products make the highest gross margin during the month.

To do so, we'll use a PivotTable. To do so, click **Insert > PivotTable** and select the data in Table/Range Sheet1!$A$1:$H$230.

Drag [SKU] from **PivotTable Fields** into the **Rows** and [Sales Price], [Cost] and [Gross Margin] from **FIELD NAME** into ΣValues fields in the PivotTable. We'll check the ΣValues area to make sure we are computing the sum of sales price, sum of cost, and sum of gross margin. If they do not, you can adjust them by clicking on the downward chevron, and adjusting the value field settings.

The resulting PivotTable will look like as shown in Lab Exhibit 1-1.3.

Lab Exhibit 1-1.3

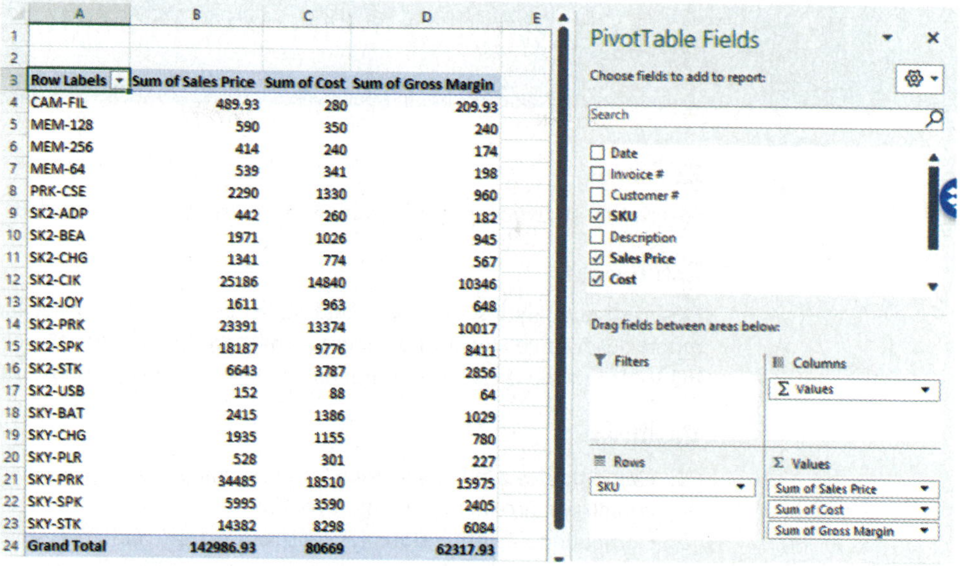

Row Labels	Sum of Sales Price	Sum of Cost	Sum of Gross Margin
CAM-FIL	489.93	280	209.93
MEM-128	590	350	240
MEM-256	414	240	174
MEM-64	539	341	198
PRK-CSE	2290	1330	960
SK2-ADP	442	260	182
SK2-BEA	1971	1026	945
SK2-CHG	1341	774	567
SK2-CIK	25186	14840	10346
SK2-JOY	1611	963	648
SK2-PRK	23391	13374	10017
SK2-SPK	18187	9776	8411
SK2-STK	6643	3787	2856
SK2-USB	152	88	64
SKY-BAT	2415	1386	1029
SKY-CHG	1935	1155	780
SKY-PLR	528	301	227
SKY-PRK	34485	18510	15975
SKY-SPK	5995	3590	2405
SKY-STK	14382	8298	6084
Grand Total	142986.93	80669	62317.93

Right click on the Column Title "Sum of Gross Margin" and select "Sort", and finally select "Sort Largest to Smallest" to identify the SKU that produced the highest gross margin during the month.

Share the Story

We can share the story by reporting our findings to the sales staff, production staff and company management to promote those inventory items that are most profitable. Potentially, we could send additional advertising emails to our customers promoting these specific inventory items.

Assessment:

1. Take a screenshot of the final pivot table sorting gross margins by SKU from high to low, and paste it into a Word document named "Lab 1-1 Excel SS.doc".
2. Answer the questions in Connect and upload your Lab 1-1 Excel SS.doc, if assigned.

Lab 1-1 Alternate

Using the same dataset as Lab 1-1, for Alt Lab 1-1 calculate the gross margin by customer (instead of SKU profitability as calculated in Lab 1-1) using an Excel pivot table.

Required:

1. Calculate total gross margin by customer for the month. (Hint: In your pivot table, put customer # in your rows and sum of gross margin in your ΣValues area).
2. Sort the gross margin by customer from high to low total gross margin.

Assessment:

1. Take a screenshot of the first 30 lines of the final pivot table sorting gross margins by customer from high to low, and paste it into a Word document named "Alt Lab 1-1 Excel SS.doc".
2. Answer the questions in Connect and upload your Alt Lab 1-1 Excel SS.doc, if assigned.

Lab 1-2 Excel: Descriptive Analytics: Calculating Descriptive Statistics

Keywords

descriptive statistics, gross margin, gross margin percentage, data analysis toolpak

Lab Insight

Descriptive analytics uses facts and statistics to explain what happened. In this lab, we report descriptive statistics for a company's product listing. DJI sells drones. They are trying to determine the gross margin and gross margin percentage of their product listing.

Required:

1. Compute descriptive statistics for gross margin and gross margin percentage for a company's product list using formulas.
2. Compute descriptive statistics for gross margin and gross margin percentage for a company's product list using Excel's Data Analysis Toolpak.

Ask the Question

What is the mean, median, maximum, minimum, and range of gross margin and gross margin percentage for a company's product list?

Master the Data

The reported results of financial performance are included in the dataset for DJI's product listing.

Data Dictionary

SKU: SKU (unique code for each inventory item sold at DJI) - A SKU stands for stock-keeping unit and serves as an alphanumeric identification to track a particular product for inventory purposes.

Description: Description of each inventory item sold

Sales Price: Sales price of product

Cost: Total cost of product

Perform the Analysis

Open Excel File Lab 1-2 Data.xlsx (the spreadsheet should appear as shown in Lab Exhibit 1-2.1).

Lab Exhibit 1-2.1

	A	B	C	D
1	SKU	Description	Sales Price	Cost
2	DJI-IFB	DJI FPB Intelligent Flight Bat	159	101
3	DJI-MI2	DJI Mini 2	449	285
4	OSM-A11	Osmo Action	199	125
5	DJI-2FI	DJI Air 2S ND Filters Set	99	62
6	MAV-AI2	Mavic Air 2 Intelligent Flight	115	72
7	MAV-AR2	Mavic Air 2	799	499
8	DJI-GBA	DJI FPV Goggles Battery	29	18
9	DJI-AIF	DJI Air 2S Fly More Combo	1749	1082
10	DJI-FPV	DJI FPV Combo	1299	802
11	DJI-AIR	DJI AIR 2S	999	616
12	DJI-PO2	DJI Pocket 2	439	270
13	DJI-MMC	DJI Motion Controller	199	122
14	MAV-2II	Mavic 2	1599	976
15	DJI-FLP	DJI OM Fill Light Phone Clam	59	36
16	OSM-P11	Osmo Pocket	299	182
17	DJI-DSC	DJI Action 2 Dual-Screen Cor	519	315
18	DJI-FMK	DJI FPV Fly More Kit	299	181
19	DJI-OM4	DJI OM 4 SE	119	72
20	DJI- OM5	DJI OM 5	159	96
21	DJI--SMC	DJI Smart Controller	749	450
22	DJI-AC2	DJI Action 2	519	311
23	DJI-2PC	DJI Action 2 Power Combo	399	239
24	DJI-P2D	DJI Pocket 2 Do-It-All Handle	99	59
25	DJI-MIN	DJI Mini Bag+	39	23

We will now learn how to get the descriptive statistics for the gross margin and gross margin percentage.

Step 1

We first need to compute the gross margin for each invoice line item.

We'll start by typing the title, "Gross Margin," in cell E1 and the title, "Gross Margin Percentage," in cell F1 and inserting a bottom border beneath both. In cell E2, we'll compute the gross margin for each line item of the invoice. To do so, we must subtract the cost in cell D2 from the sales in cell C2 by inserting the formula "=C2-D2". Then hit enter. To calculate the gross margin percentage, divide gross margin by the sales price, by entering the formula "=E2/C2" in cell F2, and hit enter. Copy the results in cells E2 and F2 to cells E3:F25 (as shown in Lab Exhibit 1-2.2).

Lab Exhibit 1-2.2

	A	B	C	D	E	F
1	SKU	Description	Sales Price	Cost	Gross Margin	Gross Margin Percentage
2	DJI-IFB	DJI FPB Intelligent Flight Bat	159	101	58	0.364779874
3	DJI-MI2	DJI Mini 2	449	285	164	0.365256125
4	OSM-A11	Osmo Action	199	125	74	0.371859296
5	DJI-2FI	DJI Air 2S ND Filters Set	99	62	37	0.373737374
6	MAV-AI2	Mavic Air 2 Intelligent Flight	115	72	43	0.373913043
7	MAV-AR2	Mavic Air 2	799	499	300	0.375469337
8	DJI-GBA	DJI FPV Goggles Battery	29	18	11	0.379310345
9	DJI-AIF	DJI Air 2S Fly More Combo	1749	1082	667	0.381360778
10	DJI-FPV	DJI FPV Combo	1299	802	497	0.382602002
11	DJI-AIR	DJI AIR 2S	999	616	383	0.383383383
12	DJI-PO2	DJI Pocket 2	439	270	169	0.384965831
13	DJI-MMC	DJI Motion Controller	199	122	77	0.386934673
14	MAV-2II	Mavic 2	1599	976	623	0.389618512
15	DJI-FLP	DJI OM Fill Light Phone Clam	59	36	23	0.389830508
16	OSM-P11	Osmo Pocket	299	182	117	0.391304348
17	DJI-DSC	DJI Action 2 Dual-Screen Cor	519	315	204	0.393063584
18	DJI-FMK	DJI FPV Fly More Kit	299	181	118	0.394648829
19	DJI-OM4	DJI OM 4 SE	119	72	47	0.394957983
20	DJI- OM5	DJI OM 5	159	96	63	0.396226415
21	DJI--SMC	DJI Smart Controller	749	450	299	0.399198932
22	DJI-AC2	DJI Action 2	519	311	208	0.400770713
23	DJI-2PC	DJI Action 2 Power Combo	399	239	160	0.401002506
24	DJI-P2D	DJI Pocket 2 Do-It-All Handle	99	59	40	0.404040404
25	DJI-MIN	DJI Mini Bag+	39	23	16	0.41025641

Step 2

To compute the mean, median, maximum, minimum, and range of gross margins, we'll first use formulas.

In cell D27, enter the title "Mean" and in E27 insert the formula =Average($E$2:$E$25).

In cell D28, enter the title "Median" and in E28 insert the formula =Median($E$2:$E$25).

In cell D29, enter the title "Maximum" and in E29 insert the formula =Max($E$2:$E$25).

In cell D30, enter the title "Minimum" and in E30 insert the formula =Min($E$2:$E$25).

In cell D31, enter the title "Range" and in E31 insert the formula =E29-E30 to help see the distance between the minimum and maximum observations.

Enter similar formulas in column F for each row to calculate descriptive statistics for gross margin percentage, remembering to include the cell range ($F$2:$F$25) in the calculations. After formatting cells to 3 decimals in column F, the result should be as shown in Lab Exhibit 1-2.3):

Lab Exhibit 1-2.3

	A	B	C	D	E	F
1	SKU	Description	Sales Price	Cost	Gross Margin	Gross Margin Percenta
2	DJI-IFB	DJI FPB Intelligent Flight Bat	159	101	58	0.365
3	DJI-MI2	DJI Mini 2	449	285	164	0.365
4	OSM-A11	Osmo Action	199	125	74	0.372
5	DJI-2FI	DJI Air 2S ND Filters Set	99	62	37	0.374
6	MAV-AI2	Mavic Air 2 Intelligent Flight	115	72	43	0.374
7	MAV-AR2	Mavic Air 2	799	499	300	0.375
8	DJI-GBA	DJI FPV Goggles Battery	29	18	11	0.379
9	DJI-AIF	DJI Air 2S Fly More Combo	1749	1082	667	0.381
10	DJI-FPV	DJI FPV Combo	1299	802	497	0.383
11	DJI-AIR	DJI AIR 2S	999	616	383	0.383
12	DJI-PO2	DJI Pocket 2	439	270	169	0.385
13	DJI-MMC	DJI Motion Controller	199	122	77	0.387
14	MAV-2II	Mavic 2	1599	976	623	0.390
15	DJI-FLP	DJI OM Fill Light Phone Clar	59	36	23	0.390
16	OSM-P11	Osmo Pocket	299	182	117	0.391
17	DJI-DSC	DJI Action 2 Dual-Screen Cor	519	315	204	0.393
18	DJI-FMK	DJI FPV Fly More Kit	299	181	118	0.395
19	DJI-OM4	DJI OM 4 SE	119	72	47	0.395
20	DJI- OM5	DJI OM 5	159	96	63	0.396
21	DJI--SMC	DJI Smart Controller	749	450	299	0.399
22	DJI-AC2	DJI Action 2	519	311	208	0.401
23	DJI-2PC	DJI Action 2 Power Combo	399	239	160	0.401
24	DJI-P2D	DJI Pocket 2 Do-It-All Handle	99	59	40	0.404
25	DJI-MIN	DJI Mini Bag+	39	23	16	0.410
26						
27				Mean	183.25	0.387
28				Median	117.5	0.388
29				Maximum	667	0.410
30				Minimum	11	0.365
31				Range	656	0.045

To run the descriptive statistics, we need to make sure our Analysis Toolpak is loaded, by looking at the Analysis group of the Data tab (**Data > Analysis**) and seeing if the Analysis Toolpak Add-In has been installed (as shown in Lab Exhibit 1-2.4).

Lab Exhibit 1-2.4

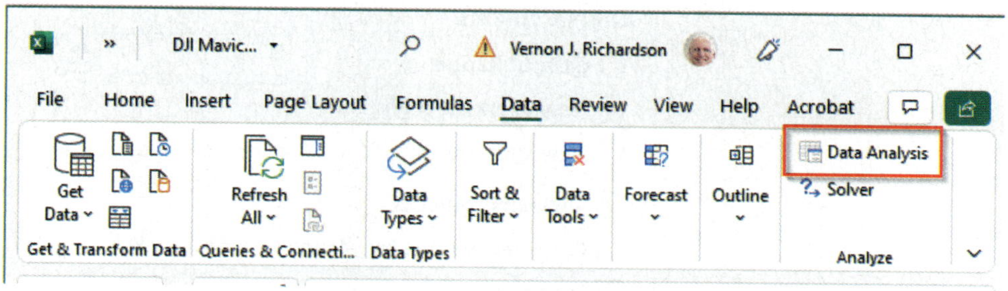

If it has not yet been added, go to **File> Options > Add-Ins>Manage Excel Add-Ins,** select the Analysis Toolpak, and select OK (as shown in Exhibit 1-2.5). (Methods vary depending on the version of Microsoft Excel and on the Mac or the PC.)

Lab Exhibit 1-2.5

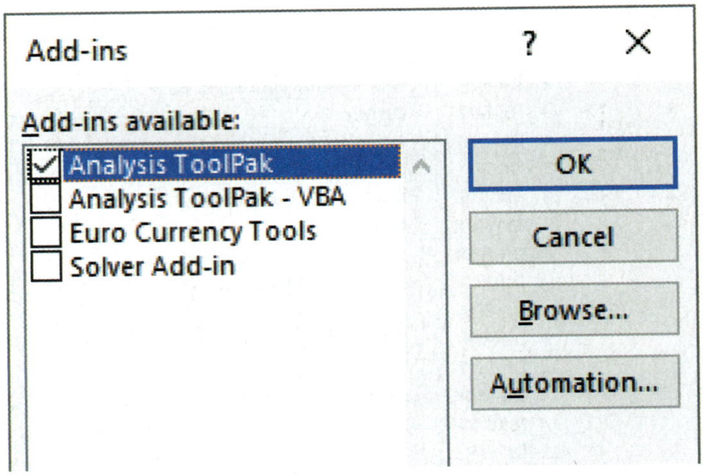

Step 2

To perform the descriptive statistics, select **Data > Analysis > Data Analysis.** A dialog box will open. Select descriptive statistics, and click OK.

We will compute the summary statistics for gross margin and gross margin percentage. For the input range, we select cells $E$1:$F$25 (including the title).

Check "Labels in First Row" to show that we have labels in the first row.

It will default to option, "New Worksheet Ply:".

Check the box next to "Summary statistics," and click OK.

The completed dialog box appears as shown in Lab Exhibit 1-2.6.

Lab Exhibit 1-2.6

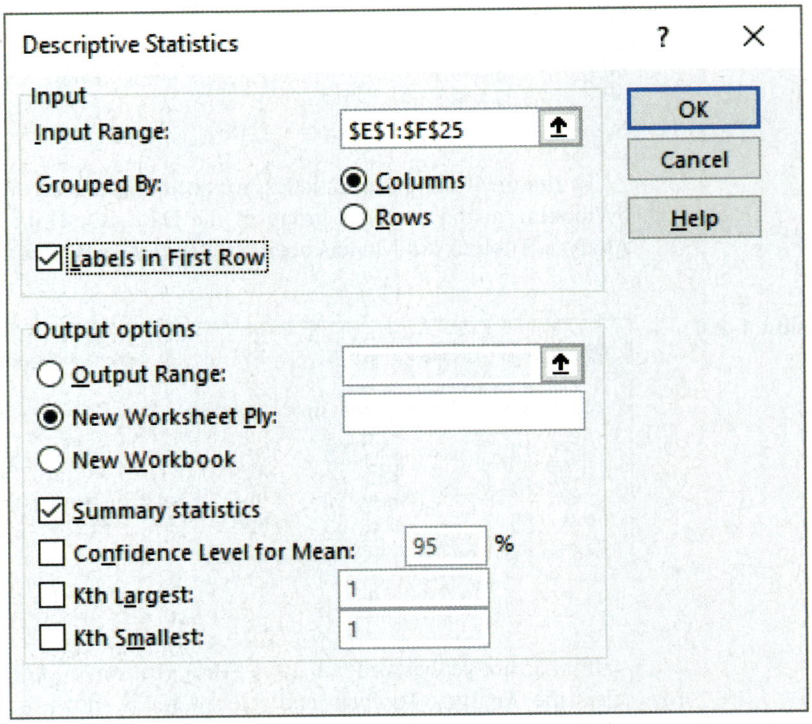

The resulting worksheet tab is shown in Lab Exhibit 1-2.7. We note the mean, median, minimum, maximum, and range for gross margin and gross margin percentages. Note the identical statistics to those computed by formula above.

Lab Exhibit 1-2.7

	A	B	C	D
1	*Gross Margin*		*Gross Margin Percentage*	
2				
3	Mean	183.25	Mean	0.38702
4	Standard Error	38.55178	Standard Error	0.002499
5	Median	117.5	Median	0.388277
6	Mode	#N/A	Mode	#N/A
7	Standard Deviation	188.8644	Standard Deviation	0.012241
8	Sample Variance	35669.76	Sample Variance	0.00015
9	Kurtosis	1.380179	Kurtosis	-0.68572
10	Skewness	1.4659	Skewness	-0.13025
11	Range	656	Range	0.045477
12	Minimum	11	Minimum	0.36478
13	Maximum	667	Maximum	0.410256
14	Sum	4398	Sum	9.288491
15	Count	24	Count	24

Share the Story

Descriptive statistics are used to understand what has happened. We showed two different ways to compute the descriptive statistics.

Assessment:

1. Take a screenshot of your summary statistics for gross margin and gross margin percentage, calculated using formulas, paste it into a Word document named "Lab 1-2 Excel SS.doc", and label the screenshot Submission 1.
2. Take a screenshot of your summary statistics for gross margin and gross margin percentages calculated using Excel's Data Analysis Toolpak, paste it into your Word document named "Lab 1-2 Excel SS.doc", and label the screenshot Submission 2.
3. Answer the questions in Connect and upload your Lab 1-2 Excel SS.doc, if assigned.

Lab 1-2 Alternate

Using skills learned in Lab 1-2, and the same Excel data source (Lab 1-2 Data), compute the mean, median, maximum, minimum, and range for the sales price of DJI's product list.

Required:

1. Compute descriptive statistics for the sales price for a company's product list using either Excel formulas or Excel's Data Analysis Toolpak.

Assessment:

1. Take a screenshot of your summary statistics for sales price for each product, calculated using formulas, paste it into a Word document named "Alt Lab 1-2 Excel SS.doc", and label the screenshot Submission 1.
2. Take a screenshot of your summary statistics for sales price for each product calculated using Excel's Data Analysis Toolpak, paste it into your Word document named "Alt Lab 1-2 Excel SS.doc", and label the screenshot Submission 2.
3. Answer the questions in Connect and upload your Alt Lab 1-2 SS.doc, if assigned.

Unless otherwise credited screenshots: Source: Microsoft Excel

Chapter Two

Data Analytics: Addressing Accounting Questions with Data

A Look at This Chapter

With data plentiful and technology tools increasingly available to assist, accountants address a variety of accounting questions using data and analytics. We introduce a framework to facilitate the data analytics process, suggesting the AMPS model (i.e., Ask the question, Master the data, Perform the analysis, Share the story). We illustrate the AMPS model specifically by highlighting the types of questions asked; the types of data that are available; and four analytics types, namely descriptive, diagnostic, predictive, and prescriptive analytics. We then demonstrate the AMPS process by illustrating hands-on examples of each of these four analytics types using Excel.

A Look Back

Chapter 1 discussed the importance of accounting information systems and the role accountants play in those systems. It further described how investments in information technology might improve the ability to manage business processes and potentially create value for the firm.

A Look Ahead

Chapter 3 discusses the use of accounting visualizations in data analytics using software tools like Excel, Tableau, and Power BI to help with reporting and visualizations.

Ariel Skelley/Getty Images

Developing an analytics mindset

EY argues that accountants, including its own accounting professionals (including CPAs) and its new hires, need an analytics mindset.

So, what is an analytics mindset?

An analytics mindset is the ability to

- Ask the right questions.
- Extract, transform, and load relevant data.
- Apply appropriate data analytics techniques.
- Interpret and share the results with stakeholders.

In this text, we focus on learning appropriate data analytics techniques that can be used to analyze data. While we formalize this as being the AMPS model, the analytics mindset serves as a way to see how the data analytics process can help you think through the various components of questions that can be addressed and answered with data. As you continue in your college studies, you will increasingly learn other components of developing the critical analytics mindset that will serve you throughout your professional career.

Source: https://assets.ey.com/content/dam/ey-sites/ey-com/en_us/home-index/ey-eyarc-brochure.pdf

CHAPTER OUTLINE

LEARNING OBJECTIVES

After reading this chapter, you should be able to:

2-1 Understand the impact of data analytics on business and accounting.

2-2 Characterize the diversity of accounting data available to address accounting questions.

2-3 Explain how the AMPS model describes the data analytics process.

2-4 Describe the first stage of the AMPS model—asking appropriate questions.

2-5 Describe the second stage of the AMPS model—mastering the data.

2-6 Define and demonstrate the third stage of the AMPS model—performing the analysis—using different analytics types.

2-7 Demonstrate each of the four analytics types using the AMPS model.

LO 2-1

Understand the impact of data analytics on business and accounting.

THE IMPACT OF DATA ANALYTICS ON BUSINESS AND ACCOUNTING

Advancing technology and increasing data availability affects almost everything we do and continues to impact accounting. As these trends continue to grow, business leaders gain greater understanding of the power of this technology and recognize the value that data can have in an increasingly competitive global marketplace.

Impact of Data Analytics on Business

With a wealth of data on their hands, companies are empowered by using data analytics to discover various patterns, investigate anomalies, forecast future behavior, and so on. A study from **McKinsey Global Institute** estimates that data and analytics could create value worth between $9.5 trillion and $15.4 trillion.[1] Analyzing available data could very much transform the manner in which companies run their businesses in the near future. According to a study produced by **CapGemini** and **EMC,** it is clear that increasing data availability is a disruptive force and must be addressed.[2] That is, the real value of data comes from data analytics.

For example, with insight provided through data analytics, companies could do more directed marketing campaigns based on patterns observed in their data, giving them a competitive advantage over companies that do not use this information. Patterns discovered from historical data enable businesses to identify future opportunities and risks. In addition to producing more value externally, studies show that data analytics affects internal processes, improving productivity, utilization, and growth.[3]

According to the results of the 18th Annual Global CEO Survey conducted by **PricewaterhouseCoopers (PwC),** many CEOs indicate that they put a high value on data analytics, and 80 percent place data mining and analysis as the second-most important strategic technology for CEOs. In fact, per PwC's 6th Annual Digital IQ survey of more than 1,400 leaders from digital businesses, the area of investment that tops CEOs' list of priorities is business analytics.[4] In its survey of executives, 82 percent believe that "organizations are increasingly using data to drive critical and automated decision-making, at unprecedented scale."[5]

Impact of Data Analytics on Accounting

Financial Reporting

Financial reporting is the internal responsibility of the firm of issuing financial statements and reports; an effort generally led by the chief financial officer (CFO) and controller. Financial reporting includes a number of estimates and valuations that might be better assessed through use of data analytics. Both internal and external data could be used to

[1]McKinsey Global Institute, "Accelerating Data and Analytics Transformations in the Public Sector," https://www.mckinsey.com/industries/public-and-social-sector/our-insights/accelerating-data-and-analytics-transformations-in-the-public-sector, March 2021 (accessed November 2022).

[2]Louis Columbus, "56% of Enterprises Will Increase Their Investment in Big Data over the Next Three Years," *Forbes,* http://www.forbes.com/sites/louiscolumbus/2015/03/22/56-of-enterprises-will-increase-their-investment-in-big-data-over-the-next-three-years/, March 22, 2015 (accessed January 9, 2016).

[3]Joseph Kennedy, "Big Data's Economic Impact," https://www.ced.org/blog/entry/big-datas-economic-impact, December 3, 2014 (accessed January 9, 2016).

[4]"Data Driven: What Students Need to Succeed in a Rapidly Changing Business World," PwC, https://www.pwc.com/us/en/faculty-resource/assets/pwc-data-driven-paper-feb2015.pdf, February 2015 (accessed February 11, 2019).

[5]"Redefine Your Company Based on the Company You Keep," Accenture, https://www.accenture.com/t20180227T215953Z__w__/in-en/_acnmedia/Accenture/next-gen-7/tech-vision-2018/pdf/Accenture-TechVision-2018-Tech-Trends-Report.pdf#zoom=50 (accessed February 11, 2019).

address many of the questions that face financial reporting. Many financial statement numbers are just estimates, so accountants often ask themselves questions like these to evaluate those estimates:

1. How much of the accounts receivable balance will be collected?
2. Is any of our inventory obsolete? Are customers still interested in it? Should our inventory be valued at market or cost (applying the lower-of-cost-or-market rule)?
3. Is our goodwill correctly valued, or has it been impaired? Due to conservatism, do we need to write it down or write it off?
4. Is our property, plant, and equipment overvalued in the current real estate market?

One way to answer these questions may include the possibility of using data analytics to scan the environment—that is, scanning social media to identify potential risks and opportunities to the firm. For example, in a business intelligence sense, it may allow a firm to monitor its competitors and its customers to better understand opportunities and threats around them. The analytics may uncover answers to questions such as are their competitors, customers, or suppliers facing financial difficulties that might affect their interactions with them? Data analytics may also allow an accountant or auditor to assess the probability of a goodwill write-down, warranty claims, or the collectability of bad debts based on what customers, investors, and other stakeholders are saying about the company in blogs or on social media. This information might help the firm determine both its optimal response to the situation and the appropriate adjustment to its financial reporting.

Management Accounting

Management accounting exists to address questions to either (1) create business value and/or (2) to meet company goals. The management accountant's deep knowledge of the costs associated with the production and distribution of the company's product or service, as well as the factors that can affect those costs impacting the company's profitability, make them particularly well-suited to identify the questions to help make strategic decisions utilizing data analysis.

Increasingly the management accountant's role could be increased by using their accounting- and business-specific knowledge to serve as data analysts, analyzing relevant financial and nonfinancial data. This is possible because management accountants understand the accounting and related data, what it provides, how transactions are measured, and how the company evaluates performance. For example, management may want an activity-based costing (ABC) system to figure out the true cost of making a product (like an Apple Watch™) or to help formulate a cash budget to help plan future finance needs to prepare for holiday sales.

Auditing

Data Analytics plays a very critical role in the future of auditing. "As the business landscape for most organizations becomes increasingly complex and fast-paced, there is a movement toward leveraging advanced business analytic techniques to refine the focus on risk and derive deeper insights into an organization."[6] In fact, in **PwC**'s 18th Annual Global CEO Survey, 86 percent of CEOs say they find it important to champion digital technologies and emphasize a clear vision of using technology for a competitive advantage, while 85 percent say they put a high value on data analytics. This sentiment has been reverberating through industry circles for several years now and has triggered many public accounting firms to

[6]"Adding Insight to Audit: Transforming Internal Audit through Data Analytics," Deloitte, https://www2.deloitte.com/content/dam/Deloitte/ca/Documents/audit/ca-en-audit-adding-insight-to-audit.pdf (accessed February 11, 2019).

invest in technology and personnel to capture, organize, and analyze this data to provide expanded services and added value to their clients. As a result, data analytics is expected to be the next innovation in the evolution of the audit and professional accounting industry.

Given the fact that operational data abounds and is easier to collect and manage, combined with CEOs' desires to utilize this data, accounting firms will be approaching their engagements with a different mindset. No longer will they be simply checking for material misstatements, fraud, and risk in financial statements or merely reporting their findings at the end of the engagement. Now, audit professionals will be collecting and analyzing the company's data similarly to how an internal cost accountant or business analyst would in order to help management make better business decisions. This means that external auditors will stay engaged with clients beyond the audit. This is a significant paradigm shift. The audit process will be changed from a traditionally manually driven process toward a more automated one, which will allow audit professionals to focus more on the logic and rationale behind data queries, and less on the gathering of the actual data.[7] As a result, audits will not only yield important findings from a financial perspective, but also information that can help companies refine processes, improve efficiency, and anticipate future problems.

"It's a massive leap to go from traditional audit approaches to one that fully integrates big data and analytics in a seamless manner."[8]

Data analytics also expands auditors' capabilities in services like testing for fraudulent transactions and automating compliance-monitoring activities (like filing financial reports to the SEC or to the IRS). This increase in automation will also result in both a higher quality and consistency of the audit and will help auditors identify issues earlier, thereby reducing surprises.[9] Greater insight into the client's operations would result in a more thorough audit and a better client experience. The ability to accurately identify risks would become more transparent whether the risks consist of security breaches or just simply flawed processes. Additionally, corporate compliance with changing regulations could be more accurately monitored.

The benefits of competent data analytics services are not limited to the audit services. IT advisory/consulting and tax services would also benefit from the greater insight provided by data analytics from the audit team because the analyses could provide a seamless big picture between functional areas. Financial and operational projection models could be developed to allow for quick and accurate "what if clear" business forecasting.

It is clear that data analytics will transform the audit profession in several ways. Both internal and external auditors can benefit significantly through the use of data analytics. By using data analytics, auditors are able to spend less time looking for evidence, which will allow more time for presenting their findings and making judgments. This will help eliminate some of the mundane tasks involved with audits and will lead to a more interesting and challenging experience for auditors. Data analytics will also allow auditors to vastly expand sampling beyond current traditional sample sizes and, in many cases, be able to test the full population of transactions. With data analytics, auditors will also be able to work from anywhere at any time, given that the data will be at the ready, and there will no longer be a need to pull data at the client site.

[7]"Data Driven: What Students Need to Succeed in a Rapidly Changing Business World," PwC, https://www.pwc.com/us/en/faculty-resource/assets/pwc-data-driven-paper-feb2015.pdf, February 2015 (accessed February 11, 2019).

[8]"How Big Data and Analytics Are Transforming the Audit," EY, https://www.ey.com/en_gl/assurance/how-big-data-and-analytics-are-transforming-the-audit (accessed February 11, 2019).

[9]"Simplifying the Audit through Innovation," PwC, http://www.pwc.com/us/en/audit-assurance-services/financial-statement-audit.html (accessed February 11, 2019).

Another aspect of the audit profession that will change as a result of data analytics is the clients' expectations. Clients will begin to expect deeper and broader insights, faster and more efficient delivery, as well as innovative thinking from their auditors.[10] Overall, the use of data analytics brings forth significant and exciting changes to the audit profession. Auditors who adapt early to these changes will have a significant advantage over slow movers because the harnessing of data analytics will provide notable benefits in the upcoming years.

Tax Accounting

With more and more data available, just like in other areas of accounting, there is an increased focus on tax analytics. New regulators are requiring greater detail, and tax regulators are getting more adept at the use of analytics. Additionally, tax filers now have more data to support their tax calculations and perform tax planning.

An example of how data analytics might support tax planning is the capability to predict and minimize the amount of taxes paid for a potential international merger or acquisition, R&D investment, or for an estate.

PROGRESS CHECK

1. How will data analytics change the external audit?
2. How can data analytics allow an accountant or auditor to assess the probability of a goodwill write-down, warranty claims, or the collectability of bad debts?

LO 2-2

Characterize the diversity of accounting data available to address accounting questions.

THE DIVERSITY OF ACCOUNTING DATA ENHANCES ACCOUNTING ANALYTICS

To better understand the available data and the accounting questions it can answer, it is important to consider the diversity of available accounting-related data. Such diverse data is often described with these four V's (as shown in Exhibit 2.1):

- Volume
- Variety
- Velocity
- Veracity

Volume is the sheer amount of data, regardless of its source. It might come from corporate systems, clickstream data from social media (e.g., Facebook, Instagram, blogs), from the government (e.g., census records), from Internet search engines (e.g., Google, Yahoo!), or just from the Internet in general.

Variety is the form of the data. **Structured data** is highly organized. It fits neatly in a table or in a database. The best example of structured accounting data is a balance sheet or income statement, which comes in tabular format and would be considered structured. **Unstructured data** is data without internal organization (or structure or outline). Blogs and social media, and pictures posted in Instagram would be examples of unstructured data. Some estimates suggest that 80 percent of enterprise data (things like emails, blogs, social

[10] Joe Ucuzoglu, "How and Why the Audit Has to Evolve Rapidly?," *Financial Reporting (Financial Executives International)*, http://daily.financialexecutives.org/how-and-why-the-audit-has-to-evolve-rapidly/, March 26, 2015 (accessed February 6, 2019).

EXHIBIT 2.1
The 4Vs of Data: Volume, Variety, Velocity, and Veracity

Source: EY, "Big Data: Changing the Way Businesses Compete and Operate," Insights on Governance, Risk, and Compliance, April 2014, p. 2, https://www.ey.com/Publication/vwLUAssets/EY-_*Bigdata:changing_the_way* businesses_operate/%24FILE/EY-Insights-on-GRC-Bigdata.pdf.

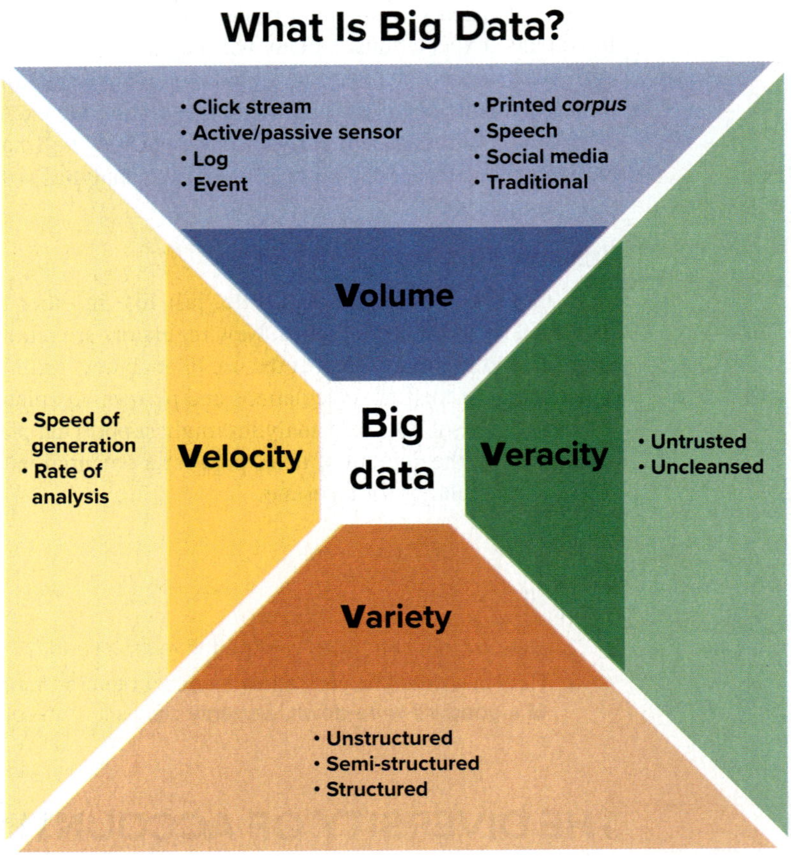

media posts, PDFs, and other documents) is unstructured![11] In between those two extremes would be **semi-structured data** with elements of both structured and unstructured data.

Velocity is the speed that the data is being generated (like stock prices that change on a micro-second basis) or the rate that data is being analyzed (like continuous monitoring of a heart rate to analyze heart health). Stock prices are generated and analyzed much more frequently than a company's financial statements (which are usually generated and analyzed on a quarterly basis).

Veracity is the quality of the data. The quality of the data incorporates much of the attributes of useful information considered in Chapter 1. Some data is cleaner (without errors or data integrity issues), more reliable (closer to fact than fiction), or more representationally faithful than other data. Data with greater veracity is oftentimes more impactful, carrying more weight in data analysis than data with lesser veracity. Even in accounting, data that is generally considered to be factual (the amount of cash a company has in the bank) has more veracity and other data that is considered to be simply an estimate (the value of the allowance for doubtful accounts or the number of years fixed assets such as buildings and equipment will last) has less veracity. Knowing the level of veracity, or cleanliness and quality of the data, is important to the data analyst.

[11] J. Rizkallah, "The Big (Unstructured) Data Problem," *Forbes,* 2017, https://www.forbes.com/sites/forbestechcouncil/2017/06/05/the-big-unstructured-data-problem/#532a74a4493a (accessed November 16, 2018).

PROGRESS CHECK

3. How would considering weather patterns to predict corn production qualify as data analytics?
4. Using their definitions and the textbook discussion, compare and contrast Big Data and data analytics.

LO 2-3

Explain how the AMPS model describes the data analytics process.

THE DATA ANALYTICS PROCESS: THE AMPS MODEL

Recall the analytics mindset proposed by **EY** (from the opening chapter vignette) that all of their accounting professionals will ultimately need. Exhibit 2.2 details the components of the analytics mindset.

EXHIBIT 2.2
The Analytics Mindset

- Ask the right questions.
- Extract, transform, and load relevant data.
- Apply appropriate data analytics techniques.
- Interpret and share the results with stakeholders.

Source: EY, https://assets.ey.com/content/dam/ey-sites/ey-com/en_us/home-index/ey-eyarc-brochure.pdf (accessed May 10, 2022).

Closely related to the analytics mindset, in what we consider to be an effective approach to thinking about the data analytics, is the use of a framework that explains the steps involved in the data analytics process. Specifically, we recommend the AMPS model be used as a framework for the data analytics process. AMPS stands for

1. **A**sk the question.
2. **M**aster the data.
3. **P**erform the analysis.
4. **S**hare the story.

Exhibit 2.3 connects components of the analytics mindset to the AMPS model of data analysis. There is a one-to-one correspondence between them.

EXHIBIT 2.3
Connecting the Analytics Mindset to the AMPS Model

Analytics Mindset	AMPS Model Stage
Ask the right questions	**A**sk the question
Extract, transform, and load relevant data	**M**aster the data
Apply appropriate data analytics techniques	**P**erform the analysis
Interpret and share the results with shareholders	**S**hare the story

The Cyclical, Recursive Nature of the AMPS Model

After completing all stages of the AMPS model, oftentimes the decision maker is now more knowledgeable and better able to ask another deeper, more refined question, which suggests the AMPS model should best be viewed as recursive in nature. Data analytics might be viewed as successively peeling the layer of an onion. By peeling the first layer of the onion, you now are able to see the next layer and evaluate it and remove it to get to the third layer, and so on. Oftentimes, the AMPS model must be performed multiple times, refining the question (ask the question), possibly considering different types of data (master the data), performing additional analysis (perform the analysis), and retelling the story in each iteration (sharing the story) before the issue/problem/challenge can be finally addressed with some confidence as shown in Exhibit 2.4.

EXHIBIT 2.4
The Recursive Nature of the Data Analytics Process Using the AMPS Model

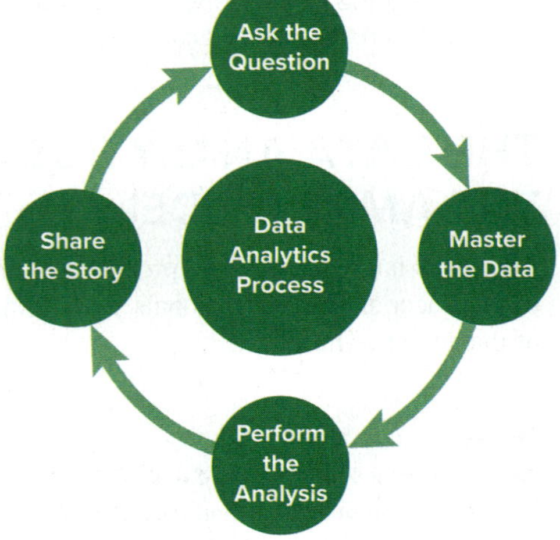

Illustration of the AMPS Analytics Model: Predicting Inventory Needs

Imagine that a **Honda** automobile dealership in Tulsa, Oklahoma, is trying to predict the quantity of Honda Pilot SUVs to have available for sale to customers for the following year.

Ask the question.

How many **Honda** Pilots should we have in inventory for sale to our customers in the Tulsa, Oklahoma, area next year?

Master the data.

Gather relevant data:

- How many **Honda** Pilots were purchased at our dealership last year?
- How many SUVs similar to the **Honda** Pilot were sold nationwide last year?
- In what year did the last model come out?
- In what year will the next model come out?
- How well is the economy performing overall?

Perform the Analysis.

- Use data visualizations (including graphs and trend charts) to summarize past sales and evaluate sales trends.
- Use data-driven forecasting to predict **Honda** Pilot sales at the Tulsa, Oklahoma, dealership.
- Predict how sales of the **Honda** Pilot at the dealership might change under different assumptions, considering best-case, worst-case, and most likely case scenarios.
- Compare sales projections to industry forecasts.

Share the story.

- Determine whether a written report, a visualization (such as a chart or graph), or some combination of text and visuals is the best way to communicate the findings.

- Report the results of the best-case scenario, the worst-case scenario, and the most likely case scenario to the Honda dealer.
- Evaluate your work: Did the analytics address the question posed? Does the **Honda** dealer have what they need to make a decision now? Is additional analysis needed?

In the following sections, we look more closely at each stage in the AMPS model.

PROGRESS CHECK

5. Why is the AMPS model considered recursive?
6. Which stage of the AMPS model would be finding the needed data to assess whether a car dealership needs to change its credit policy of giving loans to customers?

LO 2-4

Describe the first stage of the AMPS model—asking appropriate questions.

The AMPS Model: Ask the Question

The best way to develop critical thinking skills is to ask questions, which is the first step in the analytics mindset.[12] Given that analyzing data strengthens critical thinking (and vice versa),[13] students should ask questions, which they can often solve using data and data analytics. Ask questions that might address a problem the company is facing, such as

1. Which product is most profitable at stores in Missouri?
2. Is it more profitable to produce an item in the United States or in Mexico (or Indonesia)?
3. How much overhead should we apply to each one of our products?
4. Why are our costs increasing in the West but decreasing in the East?
5. What is the probability that our audit client will go bankrupt or need to restate its financial statements?
6. How will the company respond to the various possible scenarios considered in tax legislation?
7. How will increasing petroleum prices (and therefore greater shipping expenses) affect our level in sales to break even?

Generally the more succinct the question, the better. For example, it is hard to think about a question like "How does Walmart grow net income?" but easier to potentially address a question like "How do we sell more bicycles at Walmart in Fayetteville, Arkansas, store 359?" Narrowing the scope of the question helps enhance the focus on a specific question.

In data analysis, the axiom "your data won't speak unless you ask it the right data analysis questions"[14] really speaks to the expertise the accountant can offer by asking questions that are answerable by the data. Given accountants' knowledge of business processes, how information flows through the organization (from customer to order desk to shipping dock to customer), and how and when transactions hit the income statement, accountants can help management create specific questions to address the heart of the problem, opportunity,

[12] J. Sullivan, "How Does Bloom's Taxonomy Relate to Critical Thinking Information?" *CLASSROOM*, 2018, https://classroom.synonym.com/blooms-relate-critical-thinking-information-6233382.html (accessed January 21, 2019).

[13] K. F. Reding and C. Newman, "Improving Critical Thinking through Data Analysis," *Strategic Finance*, June 2, 2017, https://sfmagazine.com/post-entry/june-2017-improving-critical-thinking-through-data-analysis/ (accessed January 21, 2019).

[14] M. Lebied, "Your Data Won't Speak unless You Ask It the Right Data Analysis Questions," *datapine*, June 21, 2017, https://www.datapine.com/blog/data-analysis-questions/ (accessed January 23, 2019).

or challenge at hand. Moreover, accountants should have a thorough knowledge of an organization's data to determine what internal data can potentially answer the question and what additional (external) information should be gathered.

Once we know what specific question we are addressing, we can continue to the next step of accessing appropriate data to address the question.

LO 2-5

Describe the second stage of the AMPS model—mastering the data.

The AMPS Model: Master the Data

Once the accountant understands the question, they start to consider appropriate data that could be used to address the question. Characteristics and qualities of the data quickly arise, including the following:

1. *Data accessibility*
   - What data will be needed to answer the question? Do we have access to it?
   - What is the potential *cost* of acquiring and processing the data as compared to the potential *value* provided by use of the data?
2. *Data reliability*
   - Is it clean, reliable data? Does it have lots of missing values? Does it need to be cleaned or transformed in some way before it can be used?
   - How old is the data? Will it address the question we have now if it is really old data?
3. *Data integrity*
   - Does the data exhibit high levels of **data integrity**, where data is accurate, valid, and consistent over time? Accountants need to understand the trade-offs between relevant data and reliable data (such as data that might exhibit more representational faithfulness).
4. *Data ethics*
   - Was the data gathered and protected in an ethical manner? Was privacy maintained? We define **data ethics** as the moral responsibility associated with gathering and protecting data, and an understanding of how such responsibility affects individuals.
   - Are there privacy concerns associated with our data? Are we allowed to use it? What would happen if there is a data breach and the data is exposed?
5. *Data type*
   - Is the data unstructured, semi-structured, or structured? Does this help determine how we will use it in our analysis?
   - Is the data internal or external to the company?
   - Is the data machine readable? If the data item is stuck in a PDF file, will it be hard to extract and use in our analysis?
   - Does the data come categorical or numerical? Whereas **numerical data** has logical order, **categorical data** has no logical order and can't be easily translated into a numerical value (like sex or hair color).

Sources of Accounting Data

Exhibit 2.5 provides an example of data sources for each of the four branches of accounting, including financial accounting, managerial accounting, and auditing and tax accounting.

The Cost of Acquiring and Storing Data

The data itself might have a cost to acquire (such as the cost to acquire weather pattern data, Twitter data, economic data, etc.). Another cost is that raw data must be scrubbed from extraneous data and noise to become useful. This is generally referred to as the **extract, transform, and load (ETL)** process. Reformatting, cleaning, and consolidating large

Financial Accounting	Managerial Accounting	Auditing	Tax Accounting
• General journal and general ledger • Financial Statements • SEC filings (10-K, 10-Q, etc.) • Conference call transcripts • Press releases	• Budget data • Standard cost data • Point-of-sale transaction data • Supply chain data • Customer relationship management (CRM) data • Human resource (HR) data	• Financial statements • General journal, general ledger and subledgers (accounts), potentially shared through use of audit data standards (See Exhibit 2-X)	• General journal and general ledger (detailed financial transactions) • Prior and current tax returns • Tax-specific information

EXHIBIT 2.5
Accounting Data Sources for the Four Main Branches of Accounting

volumes of data from multiple sources and platforms can be especially time consuming. In fact, data analytics professionals estimate that they spend between 50 percent and 90 percent of their time cleaning data so it can be analyzed.[15] This, too, has an explicit cost that includes the salaries of data scientists and data analysts and the cost of the technology to prepare and analyze the data that needs to be included in the cost of performing data analytics.

Exchange of Data between Auditors and Audit Clients: The Use of Audit Data Standards

We noted above that the extract, transform, and load (ETL) processes to get needed data for analysis can take a great deal of effort—as much as 50 percent to 90 percent of the data analyst's time.

External auditors (like **Grant Thornton**, **PwC**, **Deloitte**, Robert Resutek CPA Firm, etc.) require clients to share their data that supports their financial statements. If both the audit client and its external auditor agreed on the same data standards to share their data, this cost of cleaning and formatting the data could be alleviated. For this reason, the American Institute of Certified Public Accountants (AICPA) worked to develop **Audit Data Standards (ADS)**. ADS is a set of standards for data files and fields typically needed to support an external audit in a given financial business process area. These standards also include questionnaires that may need to be considered to ensure that the data to be accessed is a complete and valid population. While the AICPA's most immediate goal is to support the financial statement audit process, in practice there may be very similar data requirements for external audit, internal audit, and compliance testing.[16]

Because there is wide variability in the file and field names and data types in underlying accounting and enterprise systems, the objective of the ADS is to produce data in a standard structure that can then be used consistently across financial audits of most organizations. The potential benefits include the following:

- Reduces the time and effort involved in accessing data by
  - Providing a precise request of what data is required and the format in which it should be provided.
  - Reducing the risk that incorrect or incomplete data will be provided by IT.
  - Reducing the need for an IT specialist to clean or scrub the data.
  - Potentially having financial reporting systems (such as SAP or Oracle) to output this information directly.

[15]"One-Third of BI Pros Spend Up to 90% of Time Cleaning Data," http://www.eweek.com/database/one-third-of-bi-pros-spend-up-to-90-of-time-cleaning-data.html, June 2015 (accessed March 15, 2016).
[16]Audit Standard Library (as of July 2015), http://www.aicpa.org/interestareas/frc/assuranceadvisoryservices/pages/auditdatastandardworkinggroup.aspx (accessed February 6, 2019).

- Works well with standard audit and risk analytic tests often run against data sets in specific accounts or groups of accounts (such as inventory or accounts receivable or sales revenue transactions).
- Allows software vendors, such as **ACL Inc.,** to produce data extraction programs for given enterprise systems to help facilitate fraud detection and prevention and risk management.
- Facilitates testing of the full population of transactions, rather than just a small sample.
- Connects/interacts well with XBRL GL Standards (as introduced in Chapter 9.)

In Exhibit 2.6, we present the general ledger standards suggested under the Audit Data Standards by the AICPA. You'll note the fields, field names, data types, and lengths, as well as a description of what is included in the general ledger. Note, for example, field 12, which specifies whether this is a debit or credit as well as field 17, which is the User ID of the individual that approved the journal entry.

EXHIBIT 2.6
Standards for the General Ledger under Audit Data Standards

Source: https://www.aicpa.org/InterestAreas/FRC/AssuranceAdvisoryServices/DownloadableDocuments/AuditDataStandards/Audit-DataStandards.GL.July2015.pdf (accessed February 6, 2019).

Field Number	Field Name	Data Type	Length	Description
1	Journal_ID	TEXT	100	Identifier that is unique for each journal entry. May require concatenation of multiple fields.
2	Journal_ID_Line_Number	TEXT	100	Identifier that is unique for each line within a journal entry.
3	JE_Header_Description	TEXT	256	Description of the entire journal entry as described by the journal entry header.
4	JE_Line_Description	TEXT	256	Description of the individual line within the journal entry.
5	Source	TEXT	25	Posting source (code for source form which the journal entry originated, such as sales journal, cash receipts, journal, general journal, payroll journal, accountant manual entry, and spreadsheet).
6	Business_Unit_Code	TEXT	25	Used to identify the business unit, region, branch, and so on, at the level that financial statements are being audited and for which the trial balance is generated.
7	Effective_Data	DATE		The date of the journal entry, no matter what date the entry is received or entered.
8	Fiscal_Year	TEXT	4	Fiscal year in which Effective_Date occurs—YYYY for delimited, CCY-MM-DD fiscal year end (ISO 8601).

EXHIBIT 2.6
(continued)

Field Number	Field Name	Data Type	Length	Description
9	Period	TEXT	10	Fiscal period in which the Effective_Date occurs. Examples include W1–W53 for weekly periods, M1–M12 for monthly periods, and Q1–Q4 for quarterly periods.
10	GL_Account_Number	TEXT	100	Identifier for the GL financial account. The GL_Account_Number in this file must match the GL_Account_Number used in the Trial_Balance and Chart_of_Accounts files.
11	Amount	NUMERIC		Transaction monetary amount recorded in the functional or group currency for the entity under audit.
12	Amount_Credit_Debit_Indicator	TEXT	1	Indicates whether the amount is a credit or debit. C = credit; D = debit.
13	Amount_Currency	TEXT	3	The functional or group currency related to the amount.
14	Entered_By	TEXT	25	User_ID (from User_Listing file) for person who created the record.
15	Entered_Date	DATE		Date the journal entry was entered into the system. This is sometimes referred to as the creation date.
16	Entered_Time	TIME		The time this transaction was entered into the system. ISO 8601 representing time in 24-hour time (hhmm) (e.g., 1:00 p.m. = 1300)
17	Approved_By	TEXT	25	User ID (from User_Listing file) for person who approved the entry.
18	Approved_Date	DATE		The date the entry was approved.
19	Last_Modified_By	TEXT	25	User_ID (from User_Listing file) for the last person modifying this entry.
20	Last_Modified_Date	DATE		The date the entry was last modified before posting.
21	Reporting_Amount	NUMERIC		The amount recorded in the currency in which a reporting entity prepares its financial statements.

(continued)

EXHIBIT 2.6
(continued)

Field Number	Field Name	Data Type	Length	Description
22	Reporting_Amount_Currency	TEXT	3	The currency in which a reporting entity prepares its financial statements (e.g., USD, EUR).
23	Local_Amount	NUMERIC		Amount in the local country currency where the transaction originated.
24	Local_Amount_Currency	TEXT	3	The currency used for local country reporting requirements (e.g., USD, EUR; see ISO 4217 coding).
25	Reversal_Indicator	TEXT	1	Indicates whether this entry is a reversal or to be reversed. 1 = entry is a reversal; 2 = entry is to be reversed; empty ("") = none of the above or system generated indicators.
26	Reversal_Journal_ID	TEXT	100	When the Reversal_ Indicator = 1, this identifies the Journal_ID of the entry being reversed.

While the actual financial reporting system a company uses may vary (**Oracle, Peoplesoft, SAP,** etc.), the idea is that they all have the ability to output a file with these characteristics, which would then be easily imported into an external auditor's software.

PROGRESS CHECK

7. Why are the use of audit data standards (ADS) helpful for the external auditor?
8. Why are the use of audit data standards (ADS) helpful for the company being audited?

LO 2-6

Define and demonstrate the third stage of the AMPS model—performing the analysis—using different analytics types.

The AMPS Model: Perform the Analysis

In this section, we discuss the process of evaluating data, or the "perform the analysis" part of the AMPS model. However, the analysis we do depends on the question we are asking.

Common data analytics questions can be divided into four types of questions:

1. What happened?
2. Why did it happen?
3. Will it happen in the future?
4. What should we do, based on what we expect will happen?

There is a specific type of analytics that corresponds to each of these questions, namely, descriptive, diagnostic, predictive, and prescriptive analytics.[17] Each analytics type addresses a different type of question. Exhibit 2.7 provides an example of accounting questions asked by branch of accounting and analytics type.

[17]Tschakert, N, J. Kokina, S. Kozlowski, and M. Vasarhelyi, "The Next Frontier in Data Analytics." *Journal of Accountancy* 222, no. 2 (2016), p. 58.

Accounting Questions by Branch of Accounting and Data Analytics Type	Financial Accounting	Managerial Accounting	Audit	Tax Accounting
Descriptive: What happened? What is happening?	What is the balance of inventory on hand? What are the descriptive performance statistics (e.g., means, medians, maximums, and minimums) for the retail industry? What were the return on asset, asset turnover, and return on sales ratios last year?	What percentage of United Airlines' flights departed on time this past month? What was the revenue growth for each division? Which product is the most profitable for the company?	How long have the existing accounts receivable (amounts that our customers owe us) been outstanding? Which sales come from a related party (pre-existing business relationship or common interest)?	How much did the company pay in federal taxes last year? What effective tax rate did we pay? How big is the difference between our taxable income and net income?
Diagnostic: Why did it happen? What are the root causes of past results? Why are the actual results different than expected?	Why did SG&A (sales, general, and administrative) expenses decrease as compared to the industry?	Why is revenue up on the West Coast but down in the Midwest? How can the computation of price variance and labor rate variance help determine the root causes of the operational results? Why did the collectability of receivables (amount our customers owe us) fall in the current quarter (as compared to the past)?	Which large transactions had proper management approval, which did not have proper management approval, and why? Why were checks recorded out of sequence?	Why did the average effective tax rate change? Why did overall income tax increase even though net income did not? Why is the difference between taxable income and net income getting bigger?
Predictive: Will it happen in the future? What is the probability something will happen? Can we forecast what will happen?	Can we forecast future revenues/cash flows/earnings with reasonable accuracy? What is the chance the company will go bankrupt?	Will a prospective borrower be able to repay their loan? What forecast of future sales should be used to set the budget?	Can we predict if the financial statements might contain errors (or be misstated)? Should we accept this company as an audit client?	Can the IRS use predictive techniques to find those who are evading taxes? Can we predict whether the IRS will audit us or not?
Prescriptive: What should we do, based on what we expect will happen? How do we optimize our performance based on potential constraints?	Will **Novartis** be more profitable if the FDA approves its new pharmaceutical product?	Should the company lease or buy its headquarters office building? Should the company make its products or outsource to other producers? What level of sales will allow us to break even? How can revenues be maximized (or costs be minimized) if there is a trade war with another country?	How will audit work scheduling change if we acquire a Korean company as a client? If an auditing company has all 12/31 year-end audit clients, how will it organize its audit work in the new year?	Should we move operations from the United States to Ireland to minimize taxes? How will our taxes change if certain tax laws change after the next U.S. Congress legislative section?

EXHIBIT 2.7

Accounting Data Analytics: The Different Types of Accounting Questions in the Four Main Branches of Accounting

For example, these are the types of questions that go with each analytics type:

1. *Descriptive analytics: Addresses questions like "What happened? What is happening?"* **Descriptive analytics** are analytics performed that characterizes, summarizes, and organizes features and properties of the data. Descriptive analytics techniques include using counts, sums, totals, averages, graphs, histograms, and financial statements to address questions like
   a. Did the company make a profit last year?
   b. Did return on assets improve or decline over the past year?
   c. Did the airline company's on-time departures improve this past month?
   d. How much did the company pay in federal taxes last year?
   e. How long have the existing accounts receivable been past due?
   f. Which product is the most profitable one for the company?

LAB CONNECTION

Labs 1-1 and 1-2 are examples of descriptive analytics techniques.

Lab 1-1 Excel uses descriptive analytics techniques to determine the most profitable product and most profitable customer.

Lab 1-2 Excel uses descriptive analytics techniques (including Excel formulas and the Analysis Toolpak in Excel) to compute descriptive, or summary, statistics on the gross profit margin and gross profit margin percentages of various products.

Demonstration Lab 1 detailed below uses descriptive analytics techniques to age receivables to help us determine the appropriate allowance for doubtful accounts.

2. *Diagnostic analytics: Addresses questions like "Why did it happen? What are the root causes of past results? Why are the actual results different than expected?"* We define **diagnostic analytics** as analysis performed to investigate the underlying cause that cannot be answered by simply looking at the descriptive data. Diagnostic analytics techniques include hypothesis testing, variances, differences from expectations, outliers/anomalies, correlations, drill-downs and roll-ups to get needed detail, and pivot tables (cross-tabulations) to address questions like
   a. Why is revenue up on the West Coast but down in the Midwest?
   b. Why did sales, general, and administrative expenses increase relative to the industry?
   c. Why did overall taxes increase even though net income did not?
   d. Why were checks recorded out of sequence?
   e. Why did labor expenses increased over the past year when overall production was down?

LAB CONNECTION

Demonstration Lab 2 detailed below uses diagnostic analytics techniques to evaluate whether transactions violate the segregation of duties.

Lab 2-1 uses diagnostic analytics techniques to see how actual cost differs from standard cost performing variance analysis.

Lab 2-2 details a bank reconciliation performed using conditional formatting, a diagnostic analytics technique.

3. *Predictive analytics: Addresses questions like "Will it happen in the future? What is the probability something will happen? Can we forecast what will happen?"* We define **predictive analytics** as analysis performed to provide foresight by identifying patterns in historical data to judge likelihood or probability. Predictive analytics techniques include time series, classifications, and regression analysis to address questions like:
   a. Can interested shareholders forecast future sales, earnings, and cash flows?
   b. What is the chance the company will go bankrupt?
   c. Will a potential borrower be able to repay their loan?
   d. Can the IRS predict which individuals or corporations are evading taxes?

LAB CONNECTION

Demonstration Lab 3 detailed below uses predictive analytics techniques to evaluate whether a company will go bankrupt.

Lab 2-3 uses predictive analytics techniques to forecast product sales using time series analysis.

4. *Prescriptive analytics: Addresses questions like "What should we do based on what we expect will happen? How do we optimize our performance based on potential constraints?"* We define **prescriptive analytics** as analysis performed that identifies best possible options given constraints or changing conditions. Prescriptive analytics techniques include to address questions like
   a. What is the level of sales that will allow us to break even?
   b. If we have all 12/31 year-end audit clients, how will we organize our audit work in the new year?
   c. Should the company move operations from the United States to Ireland to minimize taxes?
   d. Should the company rent or own their headquarters office building?
   e. Should the company make its products or outsource to other producers?
   f. What is the optimal price for each product we sell, and what is the appropriate product mix the company provides to the market?

LAB CONNECTION

Demonstration Lab 4 detailed below prescriptive analytics techniques uses goal-seek analysis to find the breakeven point in product sales.

Lab 2-4 details how to perform sensitivity analysis using prescriptive analytics techniques and conditional formatting.

So, in summary, each of these four general categories of questions corresponds to each analytics type:

1. *Descriptive analytics:* What happened? What is happening?
2. *Diagnostic analytics:* Why did it happen? What are the causes of past results? Why are the actual results different than expected?

3. *Predictive analytics:* Will it happen in the future? What is the probability something will happen? Can we forecast what will happen?
4. *Prescriptive analytics:* What should we do, based on what we expect will happen? How do we optimize our performance based on potential constraints?

Exhibit 2.8 provides a summary of the four data analytics types, their definitions, and the types of specific analytics techniques employed in each.

The AMPS Model: Share the Story

We will fully explore this step in Chapter 3, but sharing the story is communicating the findings of the data analysis to decision makers using reports, statistics, and visualizations. Chapter 3 emphasizes the use of visualizations as an effective means of sharing the story.

Accounting Data Analytics Type	Questions Accountants Try to Address	Definition	Specific Analytics Techniques Employed
Descriptive	What happened? What is happening?	Analysis performed that characterizes, summarizes, and organizes features and properties of the data to facilitate understanding.	Counts, totals, sums, averages, financial statements, histograms, pivot tables
Diagnostic	Why did it happen? What are the root causes of past results? Can we explain why it happened?	Analysis performed to investigate the underlying cause that cannot be answered by simply looking at the descriptive data but may include hypothesis testing.	Hypothesis testing, variances, differences from expectations, outliers/anomalies, correlations, drill-downs and roll-ups to get needed detail, pivot tables (cross-tabulations)
Predictive	Will it happen in the future? What is the probability something will happen? Is it forecastable?	Analysis performed to provide foresight by identifying patterns in historical data to judge likelihood or probability.	Classifications, regressions, time series
Prescriptive	What should we do based on what we expect will happen? How do we optimize our performance based on potential constraints?	Analysis performed that identifies best possible options given constraints or changing conditions.	Optimization, what-if scenarios, simulation; sensitivity analysis, make-or-buy analysis, goal-seek analysis

EXHIBIT 2.8
Accounting Data Analytics Types, Definitions, and Specific Analytics Techniques Employed

LO 2-7

Demonstrate each of the four analytics types using the AMPS model.

DEMONSTRATION LABS (ILLUSTRATING THE AMPS MODEL)

We next demonstrate the four analytics types using Excel as the analytics software tool. Exhibit 2.9 details the accounting questions, the data required, and the analytics performed. We now provide step-by-step detail of each of these four labs.

Accounting Data Analytics Type	Ask the Question: Specific Question Addressed	Master the Data: Data Required to Answer the Question (Source)	Perform the Analysis: Specific Types of Analysis Employed
Demonstration Lab 1: Descriptive Analytics	How long have the existing accounts receivable been outstanding?	Customer Accounts Receivable balances and days past due (Source: A/R ledger or Customer Relationship Management system)	Pivot table to produce report of aged receivables
Demonstration Lab 2: Diagnostic Analytics	How did entry and approval of various transactions violate the segregation of duties?	Journal entries: Who entered the journal entry and who approved the journal entry (Source: Financial Reporting System)	Pivot tables (cross-tabulations)
Demonstration Lab 3: Predictive Analytics	What is the chance a company will go bankrupt?	Financial ratios from financial statements (Source: Company Balance Sheet and Income Statement)	Employ research performed by Altman (1969)* based on various weightings
Demonstration Lab 4: Prescriptive Analytics	What is the level of sales that will allow us to break even?	Unit Revenue, Unit Variable Costs, Total Fixed Costs, Number of Units in Sales (Source: Cost Accounting System)	Excel what-if analysis

*Edward I. Altman, "Financial Ratios, Discriminant Analysis and the Prediction of Corporate Bankruptcy," *Journal of Finance* 23, no. 4 (1968), pp. 589–609.

EXHIBIT 2.9
Demonstration Labs, Accounting Questions, Data Sources, and Specific Analytics Employed

Demonstration Lab 1: Descriptive Data Analytics: Accounts Receivable Aging

Lab Insight: To evaluate the status and collectability of accounts receivable, companies analyze how long the receivables have been outstanding. Knowing the current status of accounts receivable helps us understand the potential to ultimately collect the receivables. How does that help? The longer the receivables go unpaid, the less likely they will ever be repaid. Aging receivables helps the company accountant and internal and external auditors assess the right amount of the Allowance for Doubtful Accounts account.

In this lab, we show an easy way to age the receivables by putting them in 30-day buckets. We also show the composition of each bucket.

Required:

1. Age the receivables in six 30-day buckets including 1–30 days, 31–60 days, 61–90 days, 91–120 days, 121–150 days, and 151–180 days.
2. Detail the receivables from the 61–90 day bucket.

Ask the Question

What is the distribution of aged receivables owed to the company?

Master the Data

Open Excel File Lab 1 Data.xlsx.

Note that the data lists 200 receivables that are all past their due date.

Data Dictionary

Customer: Name of the customer

Invoice Amount: Amount of invoice amount that remains unpaid; the amount of the receivable owed to the company

Due Date: Date the invoice was due

Perform the Analysis

The use of PivotTables in Excel allows for an easy way to age the receivables and put them into their appropriate aged buckets.

Step 1

Copy the data to a new sheet called "working data." In D1 add the heading: "Days Past Due."

Begin by calculating the days past due by taking today's date (assume today's date is 12/31/2025) and subtracting the invoice due date (as shown in Exhibit 2.10).

EXHIBIT 2.10

	A	B	C	D	E	F	G
1	Customer	InvoiceAmount	Due Date	Days Past Due		Today's Date	12/31/2025
2	Noodles	269.65	7/21/2025	=$G$1-C2			
3	Noodles	456.16	7/22/2025				
4	Tasty Thai	157.11	7/25/2025				
5	Grandma's Greasy Spo	243.05	7/25/2025				
6	7 Brews	127.75	7/26/2025				

When entering the equation for "Days Past Due," select <F4> (or input with dollar signs so it appears as '$G$1') to make the reference to today's date an absolute reference. (Note: Column D must be formatted as a number.)

We then copy this formula all the way to the bottom (Row 201) (as shown in Exhibit 2.11).

EXHIBIT 2.11

	A	B	C	D	E	F	G
1	Customer	InvoiceAmount	Due Date	Days Past Due		Today's Date	12/31/2025
2	Noodles	269.65	7/21/2025	163			
3	Noodles	456.16	7/22/2025	162			
4	Tasty Thai	157.11	7/25/2025	159			
5	Grandma's Greasy Spo	243.05	7/25/2025	159			
6	7 Brews	127.75	7/26/2025	158			
7	Grandma's Greasy Spo	416.56	7/27/2025	157			
8	Tasty Thai	492.93	7/27/2025	157			
9	Pita Pan	98.73	7/28/2025	156			
10	Noodles	370.26	7/30/2025	154			
11	Noodles	235.79	8/1/2025	152			
12	Wok Delight	96.39	8/2/2025	151			

Step 2

Before creating a PivotTable from the data, format the data as a table by selecting one cell within the spreadsheet range and selecting <Ctrl>-T (or <Command>-T for Macs). Be sure to check the box indicating that your table has headers; otherwise, Excel will include the first row in the data. Select "OK."

To get started on a PivotTable, we go to the Table Tools Design menu (You must have the cursor inside the table to see the Table Tools.) Select "Summarize with PivotTables" (as shown in Exhibit 2.12).

EXHIBIT 2.12

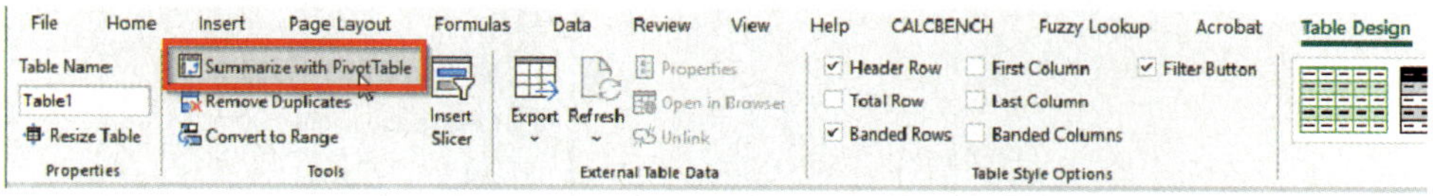

Select "Table1" for the Table/Range and select "OK."

Step 3

We are trying to sort and summarize the accounts receivable by the number of days past due. To do so, Drag [Days Past Due] from **FIELD NAME** into the **Rows** and [Invoice Amount] into ΣValues fields in the PivotTable. The ΣValues may default to either sum or count of Invoice Amount. Use Value Field Settings to change summarization to sum (as shown in Exhibit 2.13).

Inputs into PivotTable

Columns:

Rows: [Days Past Due]

ΣValues: [Invoice Amount]

EXHIBIT 2.13

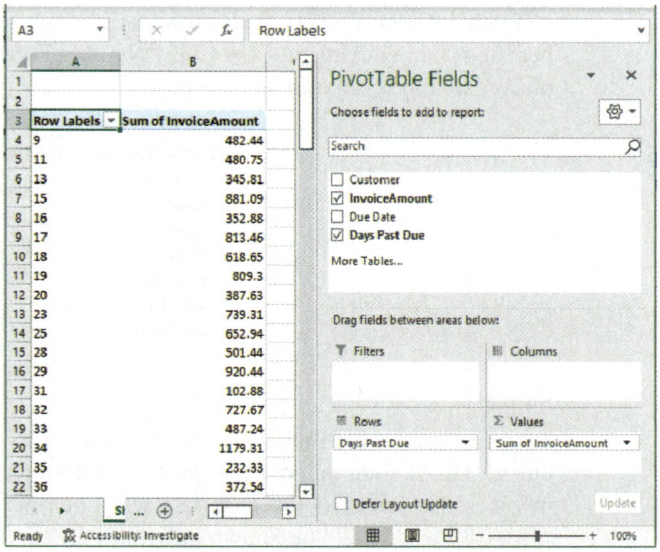

Name the new sheet "Aging of AR."

Step 4

To put the sum of the invoices into Accounts Receivable buckets, including 1–30 days, 31–60 days, 61–90 days, 91–120 days, 121–150 days, and 151–180 days, right click on any row of the row labels inside the PivotTable, select Group, and specify starting at 1, ending at 180, by groups of 30 (as shown in Exhibit 2.14).

EXHIBIT 2.14

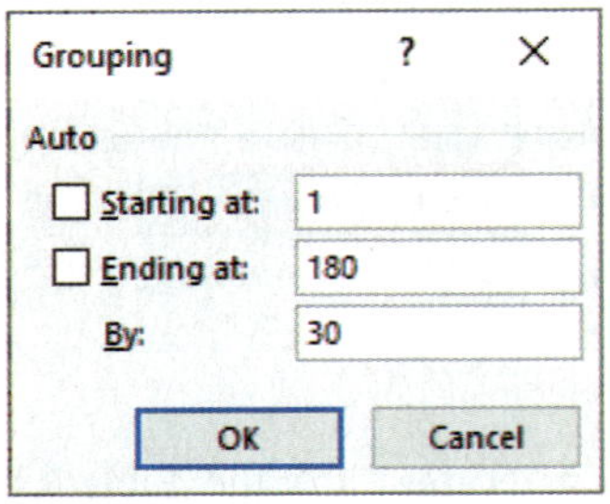

Exhibit 2.15 shows the result of the PivotTable.

EXHIBIT 2.15

Row Labels	Sum of InvoiceAmount
1-30	7986.14
31-60	11880.62
61-90	12574.47
91-120	9104.01
121-150	11499.66
151-180	3336.51
Grand Total	**56381.41**

Step 5

Next, format the PivotTable.

Double click the "Row Labels" title and replace "Row Labels" with "Days Late." Also replace "Sum of Invoice Amount" by double clicking on that Cell and typing "Total Amount Due."

Optional step: You could also format the numbers as Currency by highlighting the numbers and right clicking and selecting "Number Format" and "Currency" with two decimal places, so it looks like Exhibit 2.16.

EXHIBIT 2.16

Days Outstanding	Total Amount Due
⊞ 1-30	$7,986.14
⊞ 31-60	$11,880.62
⊞ 61-90	$12,574.47
⊞ 91-120	$9,104.01
⊞ 121-150	$11,499.66
⊞ 151-180	$3,336.51
Grand Total	**$56,381.41**

Step 6

To see exactly which invoices are due in the 151–180 day time period, double click on the $3,336.51 total amount due in the PivotTable. The detailed listing of the individual invoices that are 151–180 days late will open in a new sheet, which you should name "151–180-day detail" (as shown in Exhibit 2.17).

EXHIBIT 2.17

Customer	InvoiceAmount	Due Date	Days Past Due
Wok Delight	96.39	8/2/2025	151
Pita Pan	98.73	7/28/2025	156
7 Brews	127.75	7/26/2025	158
Tasty Thai	157.11	7/25/2025	159
Noodles	235.79	8/1/2025	152
Grandma's Greasy Spoon	243.05	7/25/2025	159
Noodles	269.65	7/21/2025	163
Noodles	370.26	7/30/2025	154
One in a Million	372.13	8/2/2025	151
Grandma's Greasy Spoon	416.56	7/27/2025	157
Noodles	456.16	7/22/2025	162
Tasty Thai	492.93	7/27/2025	157

Share the Story

Now that you have aged the receivables, the company is better able to estimate its allowance for doubtful accounts (the contra receivable accounts that reduces gross accounts receivable into net accounts receivable). As a rule, as accounts receivable age, they are less likely to be collected.

Check Your Answers to Assure Learning

1. What is the gross amount of receivables outstanding for this dataset?
   ANSWER: $56,381.41; We see this amount as the total of our PivotTable which summarizes the number of days outstanding and the aging schedule that we created (as shown in Exhibit 2.18).

EXHIBIT 2.18

Days Outstanding	Total Amount Due
1-30	$7,986.14
31-60	$11,880.62
61-90	$12,574.47
91-120	$9,104.01
121-150	$11,499.66
151-180	$3,336.51
Grand Total	$56,381.41

2. What is the gross amount of receivables due in the 151–180 day A/R aging bucket?
   Answer: $3,336.51; We see this amount as the total of the 151–180 day A/R aging buck we created using a PivotTable (as shown in Exhibit 2.19).

EXHIBIT 2.19

Days Outstanding	Total Amount Due
1-30	$7,986.14
31-60	$11,880.62
61-90	$12,574.47
91-120	$9,104.01
121-150	$11,499.66
151-180	$3,336.51
Grand Total	$56,381.41

3. If Taste of Thai has an invoice date of 7/25/2025 and today's date is 12/31/2025, what is the number of days past due?
   Answer: 159 Days Past Due; We can find this by either searching for the customer and date for all the invoices, or (1) selecting search and filter in the Home menu, (2) setting the parameters for the filter, (3) 2025 (for year), (4) July (for month), (5) 25 (for day or month), and (6) finding the answer of 159 days past due (as shown in Exhibit 2.20).

EXHIBIT 2.20

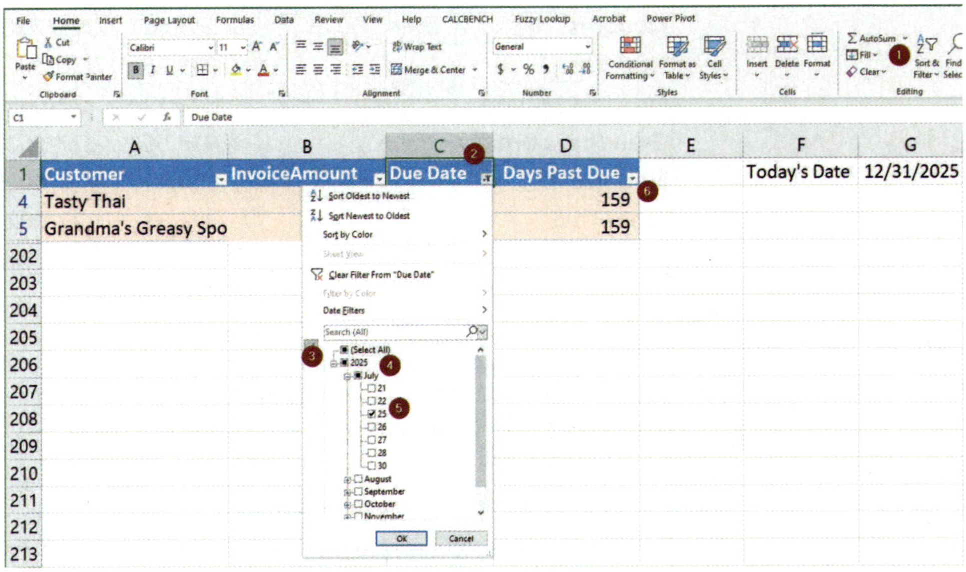

4. In the 121–150 A/R aging bucket, what is the total receivables owed by 7 Brews?
   Answer: $459.80; Found by double-clicking on the Total Amount due for the 121–150 A/R Bucket (or $11,499.81) and finding the two 7 Brews invoices in the 121–150 A/R Bucket (as shown in Exhibit 2.21).

EXHIBIT 2.21

1	Customer	InvoiceAmount	Due Date	Days Past Due
2	Pita Pan	77.93	8/19/2025	134
3	Grandma's Gı	93.14	8/21/2025	132
4	Soup 'r Salad	96.17	8/17/2025	136
5	Thai Tap	97.89	8/29/2025	124
6	Tequila Taste	100.78	8/4/2025	149
7	Tasty Thai	130.84	8/17/2025	136
8	Grandma's Gı	160.61	8/10/2025	143
9	Soup 'r Salad	164.42	8/28/2025	125
10	Wok Delight	168.81	8/11/2025	142
11	Thai Tap	170.13	9/1/2025	121
12	7 Brews	188.93	8/20/2025	133
13	Grandma's Gı	202.62	8/25/2025	128
14	Wok Delight	206.37	8/15/2025	138
15	Thai Tap	207.96	8/28/2025	125
16	Noodles	217.81	8/5/2025	148
17	The Godfathe	220.19	8/14/2025	139
18	Tasty Thai	221.42	8/12/2025	141
19	Planet of the	238.52	8/30/2025	123
20	The Godfathe	240.24	9/1/2025	121
21	Thai Tap	248.76	8/23/2025	130
22	Tequila Taste	250.48	8/16/2025	137
23	One in a Mill	256.1	8/8/2025	145
24	The Godfathe	260.56	8/23/2025	130
25	Wok Delight	261.41	8/11/2025	142
26	Tequila Taste	268.95	8/13/2025	140
27	Planet of the	270.11	8/21/2025	132
28	7 Brews	270.87	8/16/2025	137

5. In the 1–30 A/R aging bucket, what is the total receivables owed by One in a Million? Answer: $228.98; Found by double-clicking on the Total Amount due for the 1–30 A/R Bucket (or $7,986.14) and finding the One in a Million invoices in the 1–30 A/R Bucket (as shown in Exhibit 2.22).

EXHIBIT 2.22

	A	B	C	D
1	Customer	InvoiceAmount	Due Date	Days Past Due
2	Tequila Taste	78.59	12/3/2025	28
3	The Godfather	87.37	12/8/2025	23
4	Tasty Thai	91.18	12/6/2025	25
5	One in a Million	103.84	12/15/2025	16
6	One in a Million	125.14	12/6/2025	25
7	Planet of the Grapes	125.87	12/2/2025	29

Demonstration Lab 2: Diagnostic Data Analytics: Segregation of Duties

Lab Insight: One of the first things we learn about internal controls is that different people should have different roles in the accounting function. For example, in terms of the cash function, some important internal controls include the following:

1. Separate those who handle cash from those who keep the records or write the journal entries.
2. Separate those who authorize payments from those who handle cash.
3. Separate bookkeepers' duties so that each bookkeeper does not perform the other bookkeepers' tasks.
4. Separate those who bill customers for goods delivered or services performed from those who handle cash.
5. Separate those who reconcile cash from those who make bank deposits and control the general ledger.

In this lab, we test to see if those who entered the journal entry and who approved the journal entry maintained the internal control of separation of duties by using pivot tables. This diagnostic analysis will help us to see if there is a problem and if so, how or why it occurred.

Required:

1. Perform a test of the separation of duties by comparing who entered and approved journal entries to see if all transactions maintained adequate separation of duties.

Ask the Question: How did entry and approval of various transactions violate the segregation of duties?

Master the Data: AttackID begins business 1/1/2022 and has 52 journal entries in the first month, which we have now input into an Excel spreadsheet.

Here is the data dictionary for the dataset:

Data Dictionary

Date: Date of Journal Entry MM/DD/YYYY

JE#: Number of Journal Entry from 0 to 51

Account: Account Name

Debit: The debit entry of the journal entry

Credit: The credit entry of the journal entry

Entered: Initials of person inputting journal entry. Authorized personnel to input include "VR" and "MW."

Approved: Initials of person authorizing journal entry. Authorized personnel to approve include "AC" and "DH."

Open Excel File Lab 2 Data.xlsx
Here's a snippet of the spreadsheet (as shown in Exhibit 2.23):

EXHIBIT 2.23

	A	B	C	D	E	F	G
1	Date	JE#	Account Name	Debit	Credit	Entered	Approved
2	1/3/2022	0	Cash	50,000		VR	AC
3	1/3/2022	0	Common Stock		50,000	VR	AC
4	1/3/2022	1	Travel Expense	250		VR	AC
5	1/3/2022	1	Cash		250	VR	AC
6	1/3/2022	2	Building	32,000		VR	AC
7	1/3/2022	2	Cash		32,000	VR	AC
8	1/5/2022	3	Utilities Expense	1,600		VR	AC
9	1/5/2022	3	Cash		1,600	VR	AC
10	1/6/2022	4	Equipment	19,300		VR	AC
11	1/6/2022	4	Notes Payable		19,300	VR	AC
12	1/7/2022	5	Salaries Expense	5,200		VR	AC
13	1/7/2022	5	Cash		5,200	VR	AC
14	1/7/2022	6	Payroll Tax Expense	1,100		VR	AC
15	1/7/2022	6	Cash		1,100	VR	AC
16	1/8/2022	7	Accounts Receivabl	10,000		VR	AC
17	1/8/2022	7	Service Revenue		10,000	VR	AC
18	1/8/2022	8	Cash	12,000		VR	AC
19	1/8/2022	8	Notes Payable		12,000	VR	AC
20	1/9/2022	9	Repairs Expense	7,000		VR	AC
21	1/9/2022	9	Cash		7,000	VR	AC

Let's now use Excel's PivotTable function to create a trial balance.

Step 1:

In the Excel menu, select **Insert> PivotTable.** This dialog box will open (as shown in Exhibit 2.24):

EXHIBIT 2.24

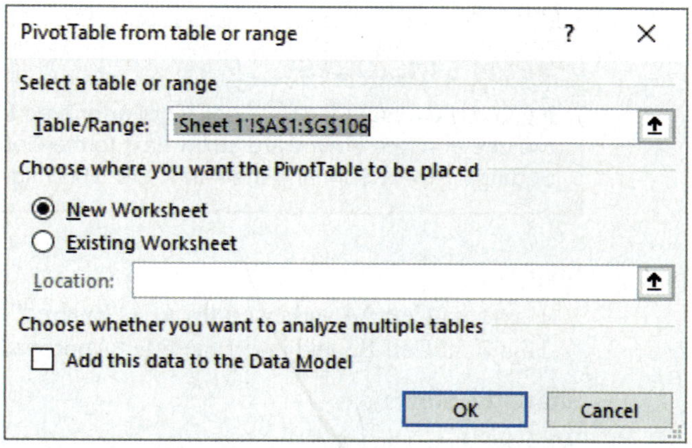

In the dialog box, select the Table/Range that includes the account titles and all of the data (debits and credits), and select "New Worksheet"; then click OK. The empty pivot table will open up in a new worksheet, ready for Step 2.

Step 2:

Co umns: [Approved]
Rows: [Entered]
ΣValues: [Debit]

Inputs into PivotTable

Drag [Approved] from **FIELD NAME** into the **Columns,** [Entered] into **Rows,** and [Debit] into ΣValues fields in the PivotTable. The ΣValues will default to "Count of Debit" in this way (as shown in Exhibit 2.25):

EXHIBIT 2.25

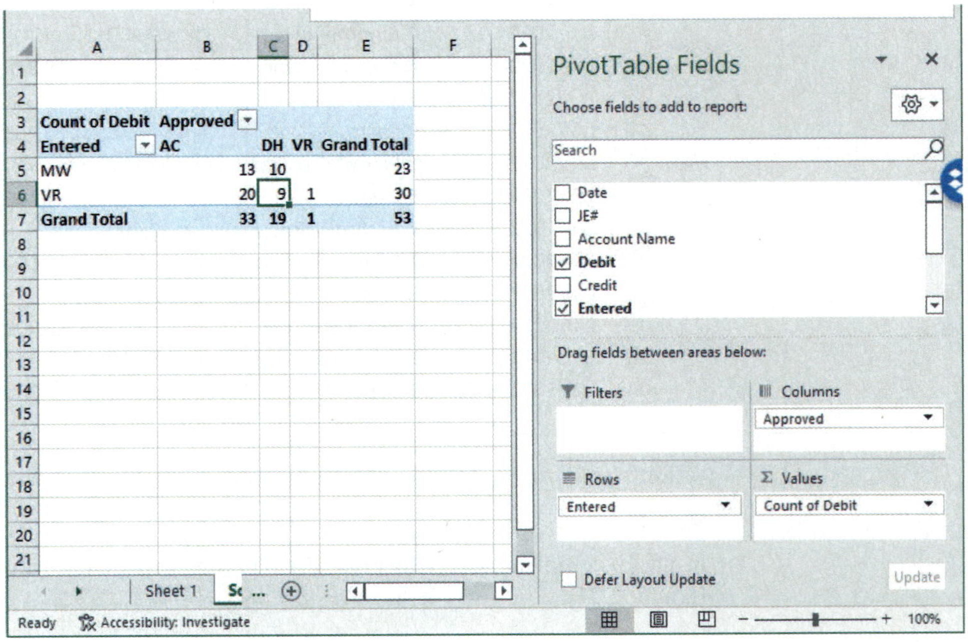

VERN'S INSIGHTS

If you'd like to sum the total dollars of approved transactions, you can **right click** on the chevron (the downward arrow next to the Count of Debit) and **select** Value Field Settings. **Select** Sum and then **click** OK. This might be helpful for the lab questions.

Step 3:

Highlight Cell A4 and insert the title "Entered".
Highlight Cell B3 and insert the title "Approved".

Share the Story:

We can share the story by reporting our findings to the Internal Audit Department or potentially to the CFO (where appropriate) to see what interventions are needed (such as training or reassignment of duties). Separation of duties is a basic internal control and it is important that it be tested and maintained to ensure financial reporting and financial statements free of error.

Check Your Answers to Assure Learning

1. According to the PivotTable results, who violated the separation of duties?
   Answer: VR; We see that VR both approved and entered the transaction (as shown in Exhibit 2.26).

EXHIBIT 2.26

Count of Debit	Approved			
Entered	AC	DH	VR	Grand Total
MW	13	10		23
VR	20	9	1	30
Grand Total	33	19	1	53

2. Using the PivotTable to summarize, VR entered how many debits that were also approved by AC?
   Answer: 20; We see in the PivotTable using count of debit transactions, VR entered 20 transactions that were approved by AC (as shown in Exhibit 2.27).

EXHIBIT 2.27

Count of Debit	Approved			
Entered	AC	DH	VR	Grand Total
MW	13	10		23
VR	20	9	1	30
Grand Total	33	19	1	53

3. Using the PivotTable to summarize, MW entered how many debits that were also approved by DH?
   Answer: 10; We see in the PivotTable using count of debit transactions, MW entered 10 transactions that were approved by DH (as shown in Exhibit 2.28).

EXHIBIT 2.28

Count of Debit	Approved			
Entered	AC	DH	VR	Grand Total
MW	13	10		23
VR	20	9	1	30
Grand Total	33	19	1	53

4. Using the PivotTable to summarize, how many dollars in total debits of journal entries were entered this period?
   Answer: \$297,927 in debit transactions were entered during the period. Change the Σ Values to Sum of Debit by clicking on the downward chevron, selecting value field settings in the drop down menu, and then selecting sum. You can then see the total number of transactions in dollars during the period (as shown in Exhibit 2.29).

EXHIBIT 2.29

Sum of Debit	Approved			
Entered	AC	DH	VR	Grand Total
MW	31777	36625		68402
VR	151050	77975	500	229525
Grand Total	182827	114600	500	297927

5. Using the PivotTable to summarize, who entered the least total dollars (in total debits) of journal entries?
   Answer: MW. Change the Σ Values to Sum of Debit by clicking on the downward chevron, selecting value field settings in the drop down menu, and then selecting sum.

You can then see that MW has lower dollars entered, as compared to VR (as shown in Exhibit 2.30).

EXHIBIT 2.30

Sum of Debit	Approved			
Entered	AC	DH	VR	Grand Total
MW	31777	36625		68402
VR	151050	77975	500	229525
Grand Total	**182827**	**114600**	**500**	**297927**

Demonstration Lab 3: Predictive Data Analysis: Predicting Bankruptcy

Background Information for Lab 3 on Predicting Bankruptcy

In 1968, Edward Altman published a paper predicting bankruptcy using an analysis called Altman's Z.[18] The basic calculation he did in 1968 is still used today, more than 50 years later.

Why is it a classification exercise? It's because we are trying to put companies into classes: whether we expect companies to go bankrupt or not.

The base of his analysis predicts whether certain common business ratios could be used to classify bankrupt firms as compared to a matched sample of firms.

Altman considered more than 20 possible ratios of firm performance, but the resulting analysis found that bankruptcy prediction is a linear combination of five common business ratios:

1. X1: Working capital/Total assets
    - Measures how liquid, or cash-like, assets are (or liquidity level in relation to the size of the company).
2. X2: Retained earnings/Total assets
    - Measures long-term profitability over the life of the company.
3. X3: Earnings before interest and taxes/Total assets
    - Measures recent, or short-term, profitability of the company.
4. X4: Market value of stockholders' equity/Book value of total debt owed (total liabilities)
    - Measures long-term solvency of the company, or whether the company will have sufficient funds to pay its debt as it comes due.
5. X5: Sales/Total assets
    - A measure of efficiency, or how well assets are utilized.

In essence, the higher each of these five common business ratios (X1 to X5) is, the less likely the company would be to go bankrupt.

Altman performed his analysis based on 33 bankrupt manufacturing firms and 33 non-bankrupt manufacturing firms, and small firms with assets of less than $1 million were not included. His analysis showed this linear combination, weighted by coefficients, determined by statistical analysis.

The original Z-score formula was as follows:

$$Z = 1.2X_1 + 1.4X_2 + 3.3X_3 + 0.6X_4 + 1.0X_5$$

[18]E. I. Altman, "Financial Ratios, Discriminant Analysis and the Prediction of Corporate Bankruptcy." *The Journal of Finance 23,* no. 4 (1968), pp. 589–609.

Altman found that the ratio profile for the bankrupt group was, on average, –0.25 but was an average of 4.48 for the nonbankrupt group. As a way of separating firms into two or more classes, Altman used the following cutoffs to establish expectations for bankruptcy:

Decision Rules:

If Z < 1.80	⇒ Classify as significant risk of bankruptcy, or in the "distress zone"
If Z >= 1.80 and Z < 3.0	⇒ Classify as at risk of bankruptcy, or "gray zone"
If Z >= 3.00	⇒ Classify as not currently at risk of bankruptcy, or "safe zone"

Let's consider the case of Apple Computer in 1997. At that time, Windows had just come out for the IBM PC, and many were questioning the value of Apple Computer, which did not interface well with the IBM PC or necessarily do well in the corporate world. At that point, many believed that Apple was on the verge of bankruptcy. Using Altman's Z-score to see how close Apple came to bankruptcy, we compute each of the five predictive factors of bankruptcy, multiply them by their respective weights as noted in the original Z-score formula above, and calculate the Z-score as follows:

			Altman Z		
Apple Computer	**Year 1997**		**Weights**		**Total**
X1: Working capital (Current assets−Current liabilities)/ Total assets	0.379	×	1.2	=	0.4548
X2: Retained earnings/Total assets	0.139	×	1.4	=	0.1946
X3: Earnings before interest and taxes (EBIT)/Total assets	−0.253	×	3.3	=	−0.8349
X4: Market value of stock/Book value of total liabilities	0.896	×	0.6	=	0.5376
X5: Sales/Total assets	1.673	×	1.0	=	1.6730
Z-score (sum of the individual scores)					**2.0251**

We get an Altman Z-score of 2.0251 by adding each of the components together. With a score of 2.0251, the analysis shows that Apple was close to the 1.80 cutoff for bankruptcy by being in the "gray zone" (where Z >= 1.80 and Z < 3.0). And in truth, they were very close to bankruptcy in 1997, but Steve Jobs rejoined Apple in July 1997, and the company started developing iPods, iPhones, and iPads and has since become one of the world's most valuable companies.

This is a classic example of a prediction analysis activity performed by current and potential investors and, potentially, by auditors in planning the audit.

How about today?

Lab 3 takes a look at the retail (base dataset) and the manufacturing (alt dataset) industries. The retail industry has been undergoing transformation primarily as the emergence of Amazon and their e-commerce initiatives that has placed pressure on many of the traditional brick and mortar retail companies to change their business model or potentially go bankrupt. The manufacturing industry has also undergone transformation with the emergence of Chinese manufacturing and other locations where labor is cheaper.

LAB 3: Predicting Bankruptcy Using Altman's Z

Keywords

predicting bankruptcy, distress, classification

Lab Insight

In 1968, Edward Altman published a paper predicting bankruptcy using an analysis called Altman's Z. The basic terminology is still used today more than 50 years later. The base of his analysis predicts whether certain common business ratios could be used to classify bankrupt firms as compared to a matched sample of firms.

Why is predicting bankruptcy considered a classification exercise? It's because we are trying to put companies into classes, for example, whether companies will likely become bankrupt or not. Altman's analysis predicts whether certain common business ratios could be used to classify bankrupt firms as compared to a matched sample of firms.

Altman considered more than 20 possible ratios of firm performance, but the resulting analysis found that bankruptcy prediction is a linear combination of five common business ratios including the following:

1. X1: Working capital/Total assets
   - Measures how liquid the cash-like assets are (or liquidity level in relation to the size of the company).
2. X2: Retained earnings/Total assets
   - Measures long-term profitability over the life of the company.
3. X3: Earnings before interest and taxes/Total assets
   - Measures recent or short-term profitability of the company.
4. X4: Market value of stockholders' equity/Book value of total debt owed
   - Long-term solvency of the company, or whether the company will have sufficient funds to pay its debt as it comes due.
5. X5: Sales/Total assets
   - A measure of efficiency, or how well assets are utilized.

Required:

1. Compute the five Altman factors/ratios used to predict bankruptcy.
2. Weight each of those factors/ratios using Altman's bankruptcy prediction weights to arrive at Altman's Z-score.
3. Classify each company as either in the distress zone, gray zone, or safe zone for bankruptcy using Altman's classifications through use of a histogram.

Ask the Question

Which companies do we predict will go bankrupt?

Master the Data

Financial data was gathered for each publicly traded firm in the retail sector.

Open Excel File Lab 3 Data.xlsx and view the variables (as shown in Exhibit 2.31).

	A	B	C	D	E	F	G	H	I	J	K	L
1	gvkey	conm	fyear	act	at	ebit	lct	lt	ni	re	sale	ME
2	034066	111 INC -A	2021	441.051	495.219	-101.403	335.302	361.615	-105.442	-464.439	1956.092	289.3695
3	122519	1-800-FLO	2021	400.059	1076.679	154.49	265.938	567.609	118.652	285.857	2122.245	2071.677
4	036399	1847 GOEI	2021	121.318	375.984	10.622	105.341	170.381	7.67	-19.056	362.314	255.3288
5	038824	1STDIBS.C	2021	175.887	192.254	-22.017	32.211	34.816	-20.963	-268.711	102.731	475.2799
6	039500	A.K.A. BRA	2021	184.332	687.846	37.678	108.015	236.82	-5.968	-2.91	562.191	1189.994
7	063643	ABERCROI	2021	1507.759	2939.491	311.257	1015.24	2102.167	263.01	2271.45	3712.768	2066.415
8	037054	ACADEMY	2021	1715.747	4584.94	907.947	1127.11	3117.994	671.381	1268.06	6773.128	3387.373
9	145977	ADVANCE	2021	6275.476	12194.21	901.527	5180.307	9065.918	616.108	4583.164	10997.99	14874.72
10	162425	AEGIS BRA	2021	2.993	20.32	-6.582	4.979	12.417	-7.914	-86.909	10.876	16.4933

EXHIBIT 2.31

Here is the data dictionary for the dataset:

Data Dictionary

gvkey: A unique code for each company given by Compustat, the data provider for this financial statement data
conm: Company name
fyear: Fiscal year
act: Current assets ($ millions)
at: Total assets ($ millions)
ebit: Earnings before interest and taxes ($ millions)
lct: Current liabilities ($ millions)
lt: Total liabilities ($ millions)
ni: Net income ($ millions)
re: Retained earnings ($ millions)
sale: Net sales ($ millions)
ME: Market value of equity ($ millions)

The dataset contains details on 256 companies with all necessary data from either 2020 or 2021.

Step 1

1. In cell M1, insert the title "X1".
2. In cell N1, insert the title "X2".
3. In cell O1, insert the title "X3".
4. In cell P1, insert the title "X4".
5. In cell Q1, insert the title "X5".
6. In cell R1, insert the title "Altman's Z".
7. In Excel, calculate the five financial ratios (labeled as X1:X5) useful in predicting bankruptcy as follows:

   X1: Working capital/Total assets; calculate in cell M2 using the variable names in the data dictionary as "=(act-lct)/at"or (=(D2-G2)/E2).

   - Measures how liquid the cash-like assets are (or liquidity level in relation to the size of the company).

   X2: Retained earnings/Total assets; calculate in cell N2 using the variable names in the data dictionary as "=re/at". (=J2/E2).

   - Measures long-term profitability over the life of the company.

   X3: Earnings before interest and taxes/Total assets; calculate in cell O2 using the variable names in the data dictionary as "=ebit/at". (=F2/E2).

   - Measures recent or short-term profitability of the company.

   X4: Market value of stockholders' equity/Book value of total debt owed; calculate in cell P2 using the variable names in the data dictionary as "=ME/lt". (=L2/H2).

   - Long-term solvency of the company, or whether the company will have sufficient funds to pay its debt as it comes due.

X5: Sales/Total assets; calculate in cell Q2 using the variable names in the data dictionary as "=sale/at". (=K2/E2).

- A measure of efficiency, or how well assets are utilized.

The formulas in the Excel spreadsheet should look as shown in Exhibit 2.32.

EXHIBIT 2.32

M	N	O	P	Q
X1	X2	X3	X4	X5
=(D2-G2)/E2	=J2/E2	=F2/E2	=L2/H2	=K2/E2
=(D3-G3)/E3	=J3/E3	=F3/E3	=L3/H3	=K3/E3
=(D4-G4)/E4	=J4/E4	=F4/E4	=L4/H4	=K4/E4
=(D5-G5)/E5	=J5/E5	=F5/E5	=L5/H5	=K5/E5
=(D6-G6)/E6	=J6/E6	=F6/E6	=L6/H6	=K6/E6
=(D7-G7)/E7	=J7/E7	=F7/E7	=L7/H7	=K7/E7

Copy the results from M1:Q1 to M2:Q257 to get the result shown in Exhibit 2.33.

EXHIBIT 2.33

M	N	O	P	Q	R
X1	X2	X3	X4	X5	ALTMAN'S
$0.21	($0.94)	($0.20)	0.800214	3.949953	
$0.12	$0.27	$0.14	3.649832	1.971103	
$0.04	($0.05)	$0.03	1.498576	0.963642	
$0.75	($1.40)	($0.11)	13.65119	0.53435	
$0.11	($0.00)	$0.05	5.024888	0.817321	
$0.17	$0.77	$0.11	0.982993	1.263065	

Perform the Analysis

Step 2

Altman's Z is a bankruptcy prediction using a linear combination of five common business ratios. In essence, the higher each of these common business ratios is, the less likely the company would be to go bankrupt.

The original Z-score formula was as follows:

$$Z = 1.2X_1 + 1.4X_2 + 3.3X_3 + 0.6X_4 + 1.0X_5.$$

8. In cell R2, calculate the Z-score by weighting each of the factors X1–X5, "=(1.2*M2)+(1.4*N2)+(3.3*O2)+(0.6*P2)+(Q2*1)" as shown in Exhibit 2.34.

EXHIBIT 2.34

M	N	O	P	Q	R	S	T	U
X1	X2	X3	X4	X5	ALTMAN'S Z			
$0.21	($0.94)	($0.20)	0.800214	3.949953	=(1.2*M2)+(1.4*N2)+(3.3*O2)+(0.6*P2)+(Q2*1)			

9. Copy the results in cell R2 to cells R3:R257 to get the result showing in Exhibit 2.35.

EXHIBIT 2.35

M	N	O	P	Q	R
X1	X2	X3	X4	X5	ALTMAN'S Z
$0.21	($0.94)	($0.20)	0.800214	3.949953	2.697625
$0.12	$0.27	$0.14	3.649832	1.971103	5.155692
$0.04	($0.05)	$0.03	1.498576	0.963642	1.936053
$0.75	($1.40)	($0.11)	13.65119	0.53435	7.287175
$0.11	($0.00)	$0.05	5.024888	0.817321	4.140235
$0.17	$0.77	$0.11	0.982993	1.263065	3.485184
$0.13	$0.28	$0.20	1.086395	1.477256	3.323846
$0.09	$0.38	$0.07	1.640729	0.901903	2.764271
($0.10)	($4.28)	($0.32)	1.328284	0.535236	-5.84183
$0.01	$0.05	$0.10	0.317986	2.620137	3.214305

Altman found he could accurately classify the firms into three "zones," or classes, using the following cutoffs:

Decision Rules:

If Z < 1.80	⇒ Classify as significant risk of bankruptcy, the "distress zone"
If Z > = 1.80 and Z < 3.0	⇒ Classify as at risk of bankruptcy, the "gray zone"
If Z > = 3.00	⇒ Classify as not currently at risk of bankruptcy, the "safe zone"

To evaluate the Altman Z-scores to see if any fall in these zones, let's do additional analysis that includes a histogram to count how many are in each bin, or zone.

To create the histogram, you'll need to install and access Excel's Data Analysis Toolpak (Exhibit 2.36).

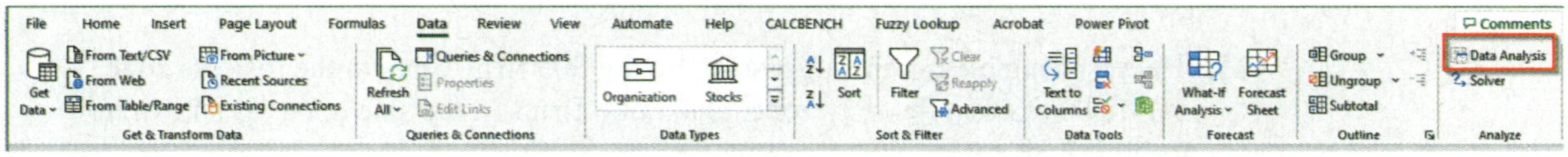

EXHIBIT 2.36

10. In cell T1, insert the title "Bins".
11. In cell T2, insert the number "1.799999". This will be the highest number of the lowest bin to help count the number of firm-years where Altman's Z falls in the distress zone.
12. In cell T3, insert the number "2.999999". This will be the highest number of the middle bin to help count the number of firm-years where Altman's Z falls in the gray zone.
13. We'll now create a histogram. Select Data > Analysis > Data Analysis, select Histogram, and click OK (as shown in Exhibit 2.37).

EXHIBIT 2.37

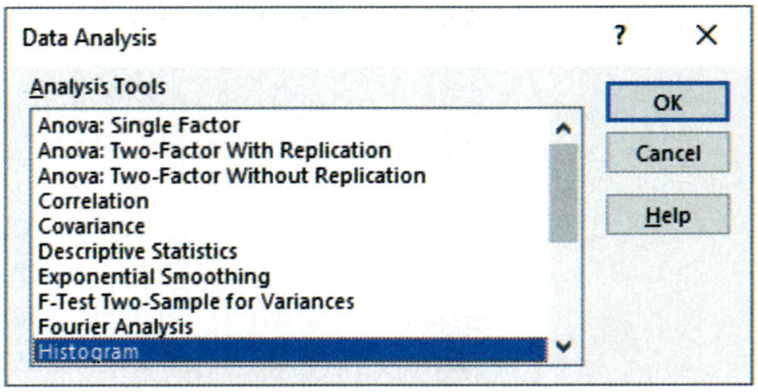

14. Input " $R$1:$R$257" in the input range and "$T$1:$T$3" in the bin range, and select Labels. This tells the histogram where to look for the data and what bins should be used for the various zones included in the data. The Histogram dialog box should appear (as shown in Exhibit 2.38).

EXHIBIT 2.38

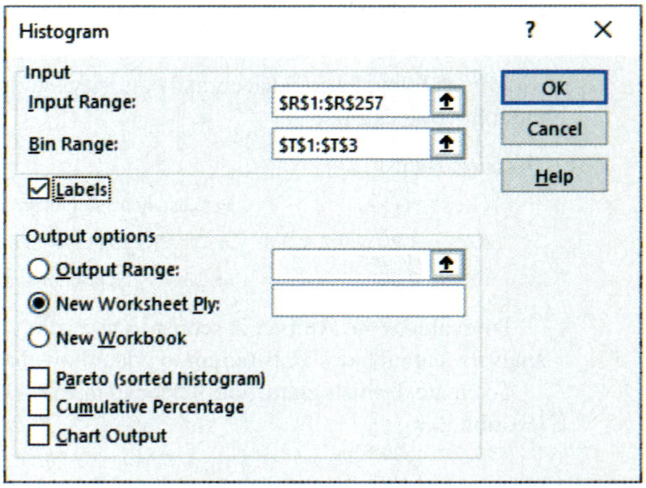

15. The resulting histogram suggests there are 305 firm-years in the distress zone, 516 firm-years in the gray zone, and 1,508 firms in the safe zone (as shown in Exhibit 2.39).

EXHIBIT 2.39

Bins	*Frequency*
1.799999	63
2.999999	61
More	132

Share the Story

We now have a bankruptcy prediction for every retail company with availability date for each firm-year combination. Auditors can use this score to understand the financial risk facing their client. Investors can use this score to understand the financial risk they face if they invest in the firm. Banks and lenders can also use this score to decide if the company will be around to pay the loan back when it is due.

Check Your Answers to Assure Learning

1. According to the analysis and the histogram, how many firms have an Altman's Z-score greater than 3 and fall in the "Safe Zone"?
   Answer: 2090; See histogram for frequency in the safe zone (as shown in Exhibit 2.40).

EXHIBIT 2.40

Bins	*Frequency*
Distress zone	2530
Grey zone	817
Safe zone	2090

2. Based on Altman's Z formula, the higher each of the five factors (or financial ratios), does that increase or decrease the likelihood of bankruptcy?
   Answer: Higher; The greater each factor, the lower the chance of bankruptcy. Note Altman Z's formula equals (1.2*X1 (Factor 1))+(1.4*X2 (Factor 2))+(3.3*X3 (Factor 3))+(0.6*X4 (Factor 4))+(1*X5(Factor 5)). Therefore, the greater each factor is, the greater the Altman Z score and prediction for bankruptcy.
3. According to the analysis and the histogram, how many firms have an Altman's Z-score less than 1.8 and fall in the "Distress Zone"?
   Answer: 2530; See histogram for frequency in the distress zone (as shown in Exhibit 2.41).

EXHIBIT 2.41

Bins	*Frequency*
Distress zone	2530
Grey zone	817
Safe zone	2090

4. If each factor equaled 1 for a company, what would be the total Altman Z score?
   Answer: 7.5; Note Altman Z's formula equals (1.2*X1 (Factor 1)+(1.4*X2 (Factor 2))+(3.3*X3(Factor 3))+(0.6*X4 (Factor 4))+(1*X5(Factor 5)), or (1.2+1.4+3.3+0.6+1= 7.5).
5. Would this be considered descriptive, diagnostic, predictive, or prescriptive analytics? And why?
   Answer: This would be considered predictive analytics, because it predicts the possibility of bankruptcy in the future based on prior history and performance.

PROGRESS CHECK

9. Why do you think Altman's first factor, X1: Working capital (Current Assets-Current liabilities)/Total assets, is associated with bankruptcy? Why would you expect that a greater X1 value is associated with a lower chance of bankruptcy?
10. If a company is classified as being in the distress zone, does that mean it will definitively go bankrupt in the following year?

Demonstration Lab 4: Prescriptive Data Analytics: Estimating the Breakeven Point

Lab Insight:

Managers use historical data to predict costs and prices of products. What-if analysis helps managers estimate the breakeven point. The estimated breakeven point identifies the threshold for the positive net income and the goal for the minimum sales.

In this lab, we use the goal-seek solver in Excel to estimate breakeven point.

Required:

1. Use goal-seek solver in Excel to predict breakeven point.

Ask the Question

What is the breakeven point given costs and sales prices?

Master the Data

Jing LCC is a food company. The costs of ingredients for food production varies by season. In terms of costs and sales prices of 2025, the manager wants to estimate the breakeven points for product A of each month in 2026 to set up minimum sales targets.

Data Dictionary

Price: The unit price of product A

Unit of sales: The expected unit of sales of product A per month

Unit cost: The variable costs per product A

Fixed cost: The fixed costs per month

Variable cost: Total variable costs of product A per month

Total cost: The total costs of product A per month

Sales Revenue: The sales revenue of product A per month

Net income: The net income of product A per month

Perform the Analysis

1. Open Excel File Lab 2-4 Data.xlsx.
2. Browse the spreadsheet to make sure there isn't any obvious error in the Excel file.
3. Calculate the total variable costs of product A in January. Variable costs = Unit of sales × Unit costs as shown in Exhibit 2.42.

EXHIBIT 2.42

	A	B	C	D
1		Jan	Feb	March
2	Price	7.00	7.00	7.00
3	Unit of sales	300.00	300.00	300.00
4	Unit cost	4.50	4.40	4.30
5	Fixed cost	1000.00	1000.00	1000.00
6	Variable cost	=B3*B4		
7	Total cost			
8	Sales revenue			
9	Net income			

4. Calculate the total cost of product A in January. Total cost = Variable cost + Fixed costs, as shown in Exhibit 2.43.

EXHIBIT 2.43

	A	B	C	D	E
1		Jan	Feb	March	April
2	Price	7.00	7.00	7.00	7.00
3	Unit of sales	300.00	300.00	300.00	300.00
4	Unit cost	4.50	4.40	4.30	4.20
5	Fixed cost	1000.00	1000.00	1000.00	1000.00
6	Variable cost	1350.00			
7	Total cost	=B5+B6			
8	Sales revenue				
9	Net income				

5. Calculate sales revenue of product A in January. Sales revenue = Price × Unit of sales, as shown in Exhibit 2.44.

EXHIBIT 2.44

	A	B	C	D
1		Jan	Feb	March
2	Price	7.00	7.00	7.00
3	Unit of sales	300.00	300.00	300.00
4	Unit cost	4.50	4.40	4.30
5	Fixed cost	1000.00	1000.00	1000.00
6	Variable cost	1350.00		
7	Total cost	2350.00		
8	Sales revenue	=B2*B3		
9	Net income			

6. Calculate net income of product A in January. Net income = Sales revenue – Total costs, as shown in Exhibit 2.45.

EXHIBIT 2.45

	A	B	C	D
1		Jan	Feb	March
2	Price	7.00	7.00	7.00
3	Unit of sales	300.00	300.00	300.00
4	Unit cost	4.50	4.40	4.30
5	Fixed cost	1000.00	1000.00	1000.00
6	Variable cost	1350.00		
7	Total cost	2350.00		
8	Sales revenue	2100.00		
9	Net income	=B8-B7		

7. In cell B9, estimate the breakeven for revenue and total costs using the what-if solver. Using the Data tab in the ribbon, in the section of Forecast, click What-If Analysis. In the submenu, click Goal Seek. The screenshots should be like Exhibits 2.46 and 2.47.

EXHIBIT 2.46

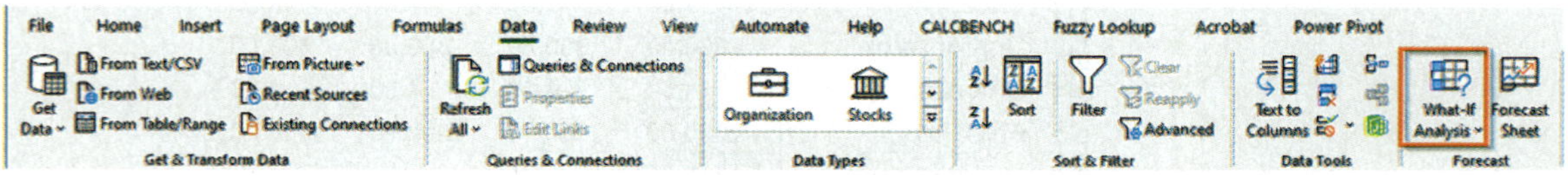

EXHIBIT 2.47

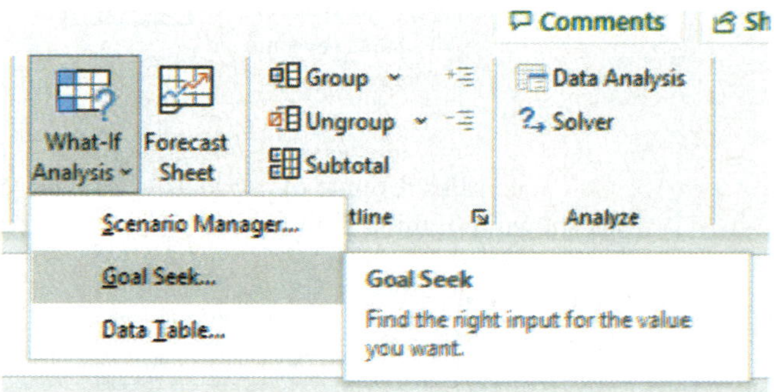

8. Estimate the unit of sales when net income equals zero. In the window of Goal Seek, select net income in January (data under a condition) in the box next to Set cell; type 0 (the condition) in the box next to "To value", select unit of sales in January (click on Cell B3) in the box next to By changing cell. It should look similar to Exhibit 2.48.

EXHIBIT 2.48

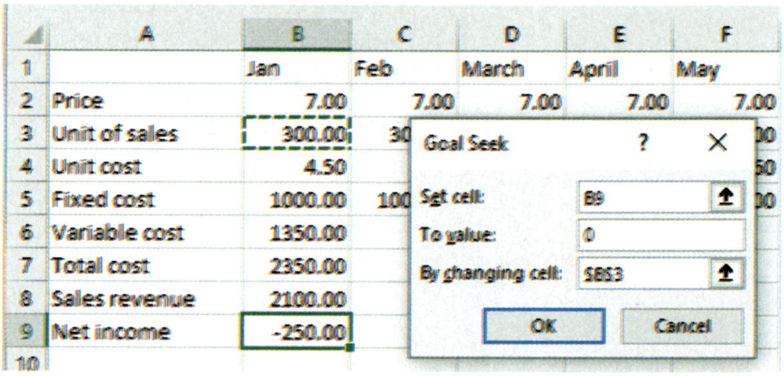

9. Click OK in the Goal Seek window. Once you press OK, notice that the number of units in B3 changes to 400. This indicates 400 is the estimated unit of sales in January, which will result in net income equal to zero, or breakeven (as shown in Exhibit 2.49).

EXHIBIT 2.49

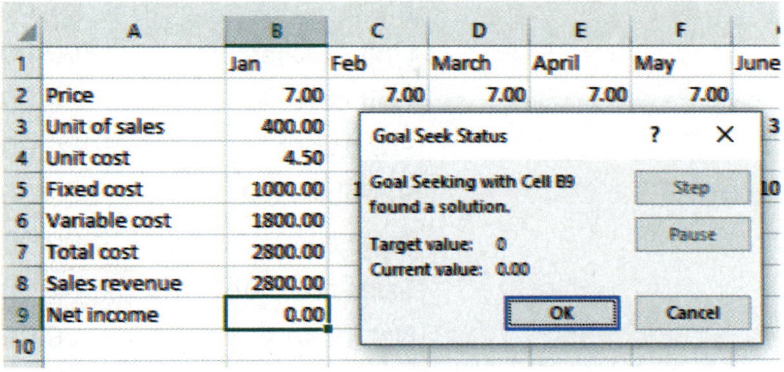

10. Follow steps 3 through 9 for each month to identify the number of units sold in order to result in a net income equal to zero, or breakeven.

Share the Story

Using what-if analysis, managers can estimate the minimum unit of sales for breakeven net income. Managers set the minimum unit of sales as the threshold and adjust sales strategies in terms of the difference between actual sales and the breakeven level.

Check Your Answers to Assure Learning

1. What is the number of sales units at the breakeven point in February?
   Answer: 384.62 (as shown in Exhibit 2.50).

EXHIBIT 2.50

	Jan	Feb
Price	7.00	7.00
Unit of sales	400.00	384.62
Unit cost	4.50	4.40
Fixed cost	1000.00	1000.00
Variable cost	1800.00	1692.31
Total cost	2800.00	2692.31
Sales revenue	2800.00	2692.31
Net income	0.00	0.00

2. What is the total sales revenue at the breakeven point in January?
   Answer: $2800 total sales revenue (as shown in Exhibit 2.51). Or Breakeven unit of sales units 400 @ $7 each = $2800.

EXHIBIT 2.51

	Jan	Feb
Price	7.00	7.00
Unit of sales	400.00	384.62
Unit cost	4.50	4.40
Fixed cost	1000.00	1000.00
Variable cost	1800.00	1692.31
Total cost	2800.00	2692.31
Sales revenue	2800.00	2692.31
Net income	0.00	0.00

3. What are the total costs at the breakeven point in January?
   Answer: $2800 total costs (as shown in Exhibit 2.52). Note Sales Revenue at breakeven is $2800 and total cost is also $2800, giving the company profits of zero.

EXHIBIT 2.52

	Jan	Feb
Price	7.00	7.00
Unit of sales	400.00	384.62
Unit cost	4.50	4.40
Fixed cost	1000.00	1000.00
Variable cost	1800.00	1692.31
Total cost	2800.00	2692.31
Sales revenue	2800.00	2692.31
Net income	0.00	0.00

4. What is the total sales revenue at the breakeven point in December?
   Answer: $3043.48 total sales revenue (as shown in Exhibit 2.53). Or Breakeven unit of sales is 434.78 @ $7 each = $3043.48.

EXHIBIT 2.53

	Nov	Dec
Price	7.00	7.00
Unit of sales	350.88	434.78
Unit cost	4.15	4.70
Fixed cost	1000.00	1000.00
Variable cost	1456.14	2043.48
Total cost	2456.14	3043.48
Sales revenue	2456.14	3043.48
Net income	0.00	0.00

5. What are the total costs at the breakeven point in December?
   Answer: $3043.48 total costs (as shown in Exhibit 2.54). Note Sales Revenue at breakeven is $3043.48 and total cost is also $3043.48, giving the company profits of zero.

EXHIBIT 2.54

	Nov	Dec
Price	7.00	7.00
Unit of sales	350.88	434.78
Unit cost	4.15	4.70
Fixed cost	1000.00	1000.00
Variable cost	1456.14	2043.48
Total cost	2456.14	3043.48
Sales revenue	2456.14	3043.48
Net income	0.00	0.00

PROGRESS CHECK

11. What is the difference between predictive and prescriptive analytics?
12. Why would predicting bankruptcy be considered predictive analytics and determining the breakeven sales be considered prescriptive analytics?

Summary

- Big Data are datasets that are too large and complex for businesses' existing systems to handle utilizing their traditional capabilities to capture, store, manage, and analyze these datasets, whereas data analytics is the science of examining raw data (now often described as Big Data), removing excess noise from the dataset, and organizing the data with the purpose of drawing conclusions for decision making.
- There are often significant costs associated with getting data ready for analysis, including the cost to acquire the data as well as the cost to extract and reformat it to get it ready for analysis.
- Data analytics may help businesses unlock value in their firms by improving marketing strategies; identifying future opportunities and risks; and improving productivity, utilization, and growth.
- Data analytics may impact the financial reporting and internal and external auditing areas. In financial reporting, for example, scanning social media might be helpful in identifying potential risks and opportunities to the firm. In auditing, Data analytics might be useful in helping both internal and external auditors perform audit tests on the population of transactions rather than just a sample.
- The AMPS model was introduced as a way of framing all of the activities associated with data analytics, all the way from carefully specifying the initial question (Ask the

Question), finding appropriate data to address the question (Master the Data), analyzing the data itself (Perform the Analysis), and finally communicating the results to interested stakeholders (Share the Story).

- The American Institute of Certified Public Accountants (AICPA) worked to develop Audit Data Standards (ADS) to set standards on the data files and fields typically needed to support an external audit in a given financial business process area.

Key Words

Audit Data Standards (ADS) (*53*) A standard format for data files and fields typically needed to support an external audit in a given financial business process area that was developed by the AICPA.

categorical data (*52*) Data that has no logical order and can't be translated into a numerical value.

data ethics (*52*) The moral responsibility associated with gathering and protecting data, and an understanding of how such responsibility affects individuals.

data integrity (*52*) Maintaining and assuring the accuracy and consistency of data during transmission and at storage.

descriptive analytics (*58*) Analysis performed that characterizes, summarizes, and organizes features and properties of the data to facilitate understanding.

diagnostic analytics (*58*) Analysis performed to investigate the underlying cause that cannot be answered by simply looking at the descriptive data.

Extract, Transform, and Load (ETL) (*52*) The process of cleaning and scrubbing the data before data analysis can take place.

numerical data (*52*) Data associated with a number and that has logical order.

predictive analytics (*59*) Analysis performed to provide foresight by identifying patterns in historical data by judging likelihood or probability.

prescriptive analytics (*59*) Analysis performed that identifies best possible options given constraints or changing conditions.

semi-structured data (*48*) Data that has elements of both structured (highly organized) and unstructured (not highly organized) data.

structured data (*47*) Highly organized data that fits nicely in a table or in a database. A balance sheet or income statement is a good example.

unstructured data (*47*) Data without internal organization (or structure). Blogs and social media and pictures posted in Instagram are examples of unstructured data.

ANSWERS TO PROGRESS CHECKS

1. Data analytics will allow external auditors to spend less time looking for evidence and allow more time for presenting their findings and making judgments.
2. Data analytics may also allow an accountant or auditor to assess the probability of a goodwill write-down, warranty claims, or the collectability of bad debts based on what customers, investors, and other stakeholders are saying about the company in blogs and in social media. Such information might help the firm determine both its optimal response to the situation and an appropriate adjustment to its financial reporting.
3. Analyzing weather patterns and correlating them with corn production is an example of data analytics. We generally know that rain and exposure to sun are key components of

corn production, so knowing and measuring rain, sun, temperature, and humidity might all be useful data. Data analytics would figure out how to remove excess noise from the dataset and organize the data in such a way as to draw conclusions and highlight the relationship between weather patterns and characteristics with corn production. Understanding weather patterns might help a farmer choose a variety of corn seed engineered to be resistant to drought or flood, or decide how much to plant, and so on.

4. Big Data is defined as datasets that are too large and complex for businesses' existing systems to handle utilizing their traditional capabilities to capture, store, manage, and analyze these datasets, while data analytics is the science of examining raw data, removing excess noise from the dataset, and organizing the data with the purpose of drawing conclusions for decision making. Big Data seems to highlight the size of the data—that it is simply so big and unmanageable—but data analytics uses context to figure out what is needed to draw conclusions to be useful in decision making. Specifically, data analytics provides a way to search through large and unstructured data to identify unknown patterns or relationships.
5. It may take many attempts of asking the question, getting the needed data to perform the analysis, learning from the analysis, and then refocusing and refining the question to begin the AMPS process anew.
6. Mastering the data is the stage of the AMPS process where we find the right data that can potentially answer our questions.
7. Audit Data Standards (ADS) allow the external auditor to receive the data needed to perform the audit testing without having to clean, scrub, reformat, or extract the data. This will save them time, effort, and expense.
8. Audit Data Standards (ADS) allow the company to provide the required data to the external auditor in a fairly effortless and costless way. It will be especially effortless if the financial reporting system/enterprise system has an option that automatically provides this data with little extra effort on the company's part.
9. Altman's first factor, X1, is a measure of liquidity and measures whether the company has the needed cash or liquid assets to pay debts and bills as they come due. The greater the liquidity available to pay these debts and bills, the lower the chance of bankruptcy.
10. The results of the bankruptcy analysis are simply a prediction, but not necessarily deterministic on whether bankruptcy will or will not happen. If a company is classified as being in the distress zone, it would certainly have a higher likelihood of going bankrupt than a company in the safe zone.
11. Predictive analysis focuses on whether or not something is expected to happen, like whether a company would go bankrupt. In contrast, prescriptive analysis is more likely to optimize something based on what we think might happen. For example, if rising (or falling) gas prices affect our cost structure, prescriptive analysis would help us envision the scenarios and how we would respond.
12. Bankruptcy prediction would be predictive analytics because we are predicting whether something will happen or not happen. Determining the breakeven sales depends on changing dollar and unit sales as well as changing fixed and variable costs. As those variables change, the breakeven sales level will also change. Determining the level of breakeven sales would thus be prescriptive analytics.

Multiple Choice Questions connect

1. **(LO 2-2)** Big Data is often described by the 4 Vs, or
   a. Volume, velocity, veracity, and variability.
   b. Volume, velocity, veracity, and variety.
   c. Volume, volatility, veracity, and variability.
   d. Volume, volatility, veracity, and variety.
2. **(LO 2-5)** According to estimates considered in the chapter, up to what percentage of a data analyst's time is spent cleaning (or scrubbing) the data to be ready for analysis?
   a. 40 percent
   b. 0 percent
   c. 20 percent
   d. 90 percent
3. **(LO 2-5)** The acronym ETL, in the process of readying data for use in data analysis, refers to what three words?
   a. Extrapolate, transform, and learn
   b. Extrapolate, transpose, and load
   c. Extract, transform, and load
   d. Extract, transform, and learn
4. **(LO 2-1)** Which term is used to describe the science of examining raw data, removing excess noise from the dataset, and organizing the data with the purpose of drawing conclusions for decision making?
   a. Big Data
   b. Data Analytics
   c. Audit Analytics
   d. Extract, transform, and load
5. **(LO 2-5)** ADS is a standard format for data files and fields typically needed to support an external audit in a given financial business process area that was developed by the AICPA. The acronym ADS stands for what three words?
   a. Accounting Data Specification
   b. Accounting Data Standards
   c. Audit Data Standards
   d. Auditor Data Standards
6. **(LO 2-4)** Which type of question does prescriptive analytics address?
   a. What happened?
   b. What should we do based on what we expect will happen?
   c. Why did it happen?
   d. Will it happen in the future?
7. **(LO 2-4)** Which type of question does predictive analytics address?
   a. What happened?
   b. What should we do based on what we expect will happen?
   c. Why did it happen?
   d. Will it happen in the future?
8. **(LO 2-4)** What type of analytics addresses questions of "Why did it happen"?
   a. Descriptive analytics
   b. Diagnostic analytics

c. Predictive analytics
d. Prescriptive analytics

9. **(LO 2-6)** What type of analytics would address the question of whether a customer will ultimately pay if credit is granted?
   a. Descriptive analytics
   b. Diagnostic analytics
   c. Predictive analytics
   d. Prescriptive analytics
10. **(LO 2-6)** If we wanted to know what score we needed to get on the final in this class based on our expected performance before the final, we would call that ______________ analytics.
   a. Descriptive
   b. Diagnostic
   c. Predictive
   d. Prescriptive

Discussion Questions

1. **(LO 2-1)** How might an airline use data analytics to evaluate different services provided to business and casual travelers to maximize revenue?
2. **(LO 2-2)** What is the difference between Big Data and data analytics? Give an example of the difference.
3. **(LO 2-5)** Why is it important to have software vendors, such as **ACL Inc.,** use the Audit Data Standards?
4. **(LO 2-5)** What efficiencies are there for external auditors to use Audit Data Standards?
5. **(LO 2-5)** In field 17 of **Exhibit 2.6**, Audit Data Standards includes a record of who approved the journal entry. Why do you think the external auditor might be interested in this field? Why do you think they might also be interested in who modified a journal entry (field 19 of Exhibit 2.6) and on what date (field 20 of Exhibit 2.6)?
6. **(LO 2-6)** What is the difference between descriptive and diagnostic analytics?
7. **(LO 2-6)** What type of analytics (descriptive, diagnostics, predictive, or prescriptive analytics) is required to find the needed product sales to break even? Why?

Problems

1. **(LO 2-3)** Data analytics can be disaggregated into four steps as part of the AMPS. Which of these AMPS processes would be considered mastering the data [or ETL (extract, transform, and load)] or performing the analysis?
   a. Removing extraneous data and noise
   b. Looking for trends in the data that might predict new sales opportunities
   c. Finding the necessary data from the financial reporting system to give to the external auditor for analysis
   d. Performing test of internal controls by the external auditor
   e. Considering Champaign, Illinois, weather patterns to predict corn production in the immediate area
   f. Consolidating large volumes of data from multiple sources and platforms

2. **(LO 2-1)** Match these definitions with the four Vs of Big Data that it best describes:

   1. Unstructured and unprocessed data, such as comments in social media, emails, global positioning system measurements, etc.
   2. The massive amount of streaming data involved
   3. Data coming in at fast speeds or in real time, such as streaming videos and news feeds
   4. Opinions or facts
   5. Data with a lot of missing observations
   6. Stock market data that updates every 5 seconds
   7. Financial statement data that appears in tables
   8. All Twitter data from 2021

   A. volume
   B. velocity
   C. variety
   D. veracity

3. **(LO 2-1, LO 2-5, LO 2-6)** Match the definition of the keywords with their terms.

   1. A standard format for data files and fields typically needed to support an external audit
   2. Datasets that are too large and complex for businesses' existing systems to handle using their traditional capabilities to capture, store, manage, and analyze these datasets
   3. The process of cleaning and scrubbing the data before data analytics can take place
   4. Process of determining how separation of duties was violated at the company
   5. Process of summarizing accounts receivable by how long it has been outstanding
   6. Delivering the findings to the decision maker of which firms our company should approve for credit

   A. Audit Data Standards
   B. Big Data
   C. Descriptive analytics
   D. Diagnostic analytics
   E. AMPS: Master the data
   F. AMPS: Share the story

LABS ASSOCIATED WITH CHAPTER 2

LAB 2-1 EXCEL	Diagnostic Analytics: Computing Variances and Using Conditional Formatting
LAB 2-2 EXCEL	Diagnostic Analytics: Bank Reconciliations Using Conditional Formatting
LAB 2-3 EXCEL	Predictive Analytics: Prediction of Product Sales
LAB 2-4 EXCEL	Prescriptive Analytics: Sensitivity Analysis of Profitability under Changing Volume, Sales Price, and Fixed and Variable Cost Assumptions

The multiple choice assessment questions for each lab are assignable via Connect. Materials are also available for courses not utilizing Connect via the Solutions Manual.

Lab 2-1 Excel: Diagnostic Analytics: Computing Variances and Using Conditional Formatting

Keywords

managerial accounting, direct materials variance, direct labor variance

Lab Insight

In managerial accounting, the use of standard costs and the calculation of variances are useful in performance evaluation. Why did the actual materials and labor usage vary from what is expected?

Karina Inc. manufactures leather jackets using Columbian leather in Cucuta, Colombia. These sell at a premium in export markets. Karina is attempting to reduce its costs to become more profitable. Karina establishes standard costing for both direct materials and direct labor in order to evaluate actual spending by evaluating variances. Karina could hire cheaper labor but wonders if cheaper laborers would waste more material than if Karina used more expensive labor. A performance evaluation of materials and labor variances will allow him to do that.

A favorable cost variance is present when the actual cost is less than the standard cost. An unfavorable cost variance occurs when the actual cost is greater than the standard cost.

Required:

1. Using performance standards for the materials used in manufacture of jackets, calculate the direct materials variances, including price and quantity variances.
2. Use conditional formatting to identify favorable and unfavorable variances.

Ask the Question

How can an evaluation of direct materials and direct labor variances contribute to better profitability?

Master the Data

Open the template we'll use for our analysis, namely Excel file Lab 2-1 Data.xlsx.

Note that the direct materials variance calculations are on the upper part of the spreadsheet with the direct labor variance calculations in the lower part.

Note the direct materials variance is composed of a materials price variance and materials quantity variance. Likewise, note that the direct labor variances are composed of a labor rate variance and labor efficiency variance.

Karina will make 4,000 jackets with standard quantity of leather per jacket of 120.03 square inches of material @$0.25/square inch. The actual quantity leather per jacket for those 4,000 jackets produced was leather per jacket 122.53 square inches of material @0.24/square inch. The standard labor to produce each jacket is one hour for each jacket with a cost of $16.50/hour. The actual labor used to produce each jacket was 1.06 hours at $16/hour.

We're now ready to perform the analysis.

Perform the Analysis

Step 1: Input Actual Quantities and Prices

In cell D8, insert the actual quantity of 4,000 jackets *122.53 square inches/jacket, by inputting "=4000*122.53".

In cell D9, insert the actual price per square inch of 0.24, by inputting "0.24".

In cell G8, insert the actual quantity of 4,000 jackets *122.53 square inches/jacket, by inputting "=4000*122.53".

In cell G9, insert the standard price per square inch of 0.25, by inputting "0.25".

In cell J8, insert the standard quantity of 4,000 jackets *120.03 square inches/jacket, by inputting "=4000*120.03".

In cell J9, insert the standard price per square inch of 0.25, by inputting "0.25".

In cell D11, calculate the actual total cost by multiplying actual quantity by actual price, by inputting "=D8*D9".

In cell G11, calculate the actual total cost by multiplying actual quantity by standard price, by inputting "=G8*G9".

In cell J11, calculate the actual total cost by multiplying standard quantity by standard price, by inputting "=J8*J9".

The spreadsheet should now appear as shown in Lab Exhibit 2-1.1:

	A	B	C	D	E	F	G	H	I	J
1	Calculation of Direct Materials and Direct Labor Variance									
2										
3	**Direct Materials Variance**									
4				**Actual Cost**					**Standard Cost**	
5				Actual Quantity		Actual Quantity			Standard Quantity	
6				@ Actual Price		@ Standard Price			@ Standard Price	
7										
8			Actual Quantity (AQ)	490,120		Actual Quantity (AQ	490,120		Standard Quantity (SQ)	480,120
9			Actual Price (AP)	0.24		Standard Price (SP)	0.25		Standard Price (SP)	0.25
10										
11			**Actual Cost (AQ * AP)**	**$117,628.80**		**Actual Quantity @ Standard Price (AQ * SP)**	**$122,530.00**		**Standard Cost (SQ * SP)**	**$120,030.00**

Lab Exhibit 2-1.1

Step 2: Compute Materials Price and Materials Quantity Variances

Next, we will compute the materials price variance; that is, how much of the variance is due to the change in price from $0.25/square inch standard cost to $0.24/square inch actual cost.

In cell E16, subtract actual cost from actual quantity at standard price by inserting the formula, "=G11-D11", as shown in Lab Exhibit 2-1.2, to compute the materials price variance. We compute a favorable variance of 4901.20.

Lab Exhibit 2-1.2

	C	D	E	F	G
1	d Direct Labor Variance				
2					
3					
4		**Actual Cost**			
5		Actual Quantity		Actual Quantity	
6		@ Actual Price		@ Standard Price	
7					
8	Actual Quantity (AQ)	490,120		Actual Quantity (AQ	490,120
9	Actual Price (AP)	0.24		Standard Price (SP)	0.25
10					
11	**Actual Cost (AQ * AP)**	**117628.80**		**Actual Quantity @**	**122530.00**
12				**Standard Price (AQ * SP)**	
13					
14	=		Materials		
15			Price Variance		
16			=G11-D11		

In cell H16, subtract actual quantity at standard price by inserting the formula, "=J11-G11" to compute the materials price variance. We compute an unfavorable variance of -2500, as shown in Lab Exhibit 2-1.3.

Lab Exhibit 2-1.3

	F	G	H	I	J
8	Actual Quantity (AQ	490,120		Standard Quantity (SQ)	480,120
9	Standard Price (SP)	0.25		Standard Price (SP)	0.25
10					
11	**Actual Quantity @**	**122530.00**		**Standard Cost (SQ * SP)**	**120030.00**
12	**Standard Price (AQ * SP)**				
13					
14			Materials		
15			Quantity Variance		
16			**-2500.00**		

Next, we'll compute the total direct materials variance by summing the materials price variance and the materials quantity variance. In cell B16, insert the formula, "=E16+H16" as shown in Lab Exhibit 2-1.4.

	A	B	C	D	E	F	G	H	I	J
1	Calculation of Direct Materials and Direct Labor Variance									
2										
3	**Direct Materials Variance**									
4				**Actual Cost**					**Standard Cost**	
5				Actual Quantity		Actual Quantity			Standard Quantity	
6				@ Actual Price		@ Standard Price			@ Standard Price	
7										
8			Actual Quantity (AQ)	490120		Actual Quantity (AQ	490120		Standard Quantity (SQ)	480120
9			Actual Price (AP)	0.24		Standard Price (SP)	0.25		Standard Price (SP)	0.25
10										
11			**Actual Cost (AQ * AP)**	**117628.8**		**Actual Quantity @**	**122530**		**Standard Cost (SQ * SP)**	**120030**
12						**Standard Price (AQ * SP)**				
13										
14		Total Direct	=		Materials			Materials		
15		Materials Variance			Price Variance			Quantity Variance		
16		=E16+H16			4901.2			-2500		

Lab Exhibit 2-1.4

We calculate an overall favorable direct materials variance of $2041.20. To check that figure, we'll compare actual cost to standard cost. In cell A17, insert the word "Check". In cell B17, insert the formula, "=J11-D11" as shown in Lab Exhibit 2-1.5.

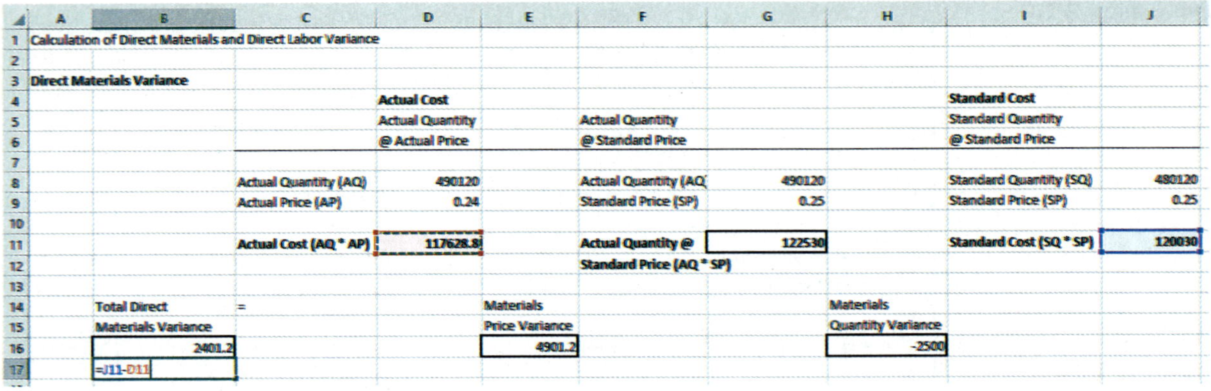

Lab Exhibit 2-1.5

Once again, we compute $2401.20 as a check figure for the total direct materials variance, suggesting that Karina both used more quantity than standard (quantity variance) and paid more than expected (price variance) which resulted in spending more overall than anticipated.

Step 3: Formatting, Conditional Formatting, and Variances

Next, we'll format the cells with "$" signs, commas, and decimal points. For each of the cells with dollar figures, hold the control key and highlight cells D11, G11, J11, B16, E16, and H16 and then right-click and select "Format Cells".

Select Currency and "2" decimal places and Select OK. All of the currency cells should be formatted appropriately.

Next, format cells D8, G8, and J8 as "Number" with zero decimal places.

Next, we will conditionally format each of the cells to highlight favorable and unfavorable variances.

To do so, select the cells we would like to conditionally format, namely cells B16, E16, and H16, and select **Conditional Formatting>Highlight Cells Rules> Less than** in the ribbon as shown in Lab Exhibit 2-1.6.

Lab Exhibit 2-1.6

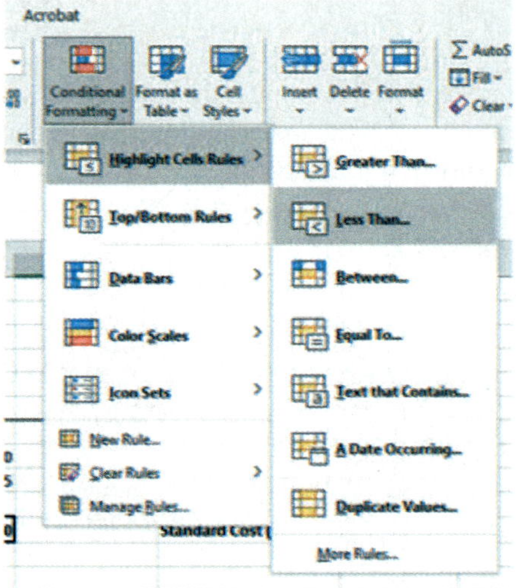

Input "0" to format cells that are less than zero, and then select "Red Text" and Select OK, as shown in Lab Exhibit 2-1.7.

Lab Exhibit 2-1.7

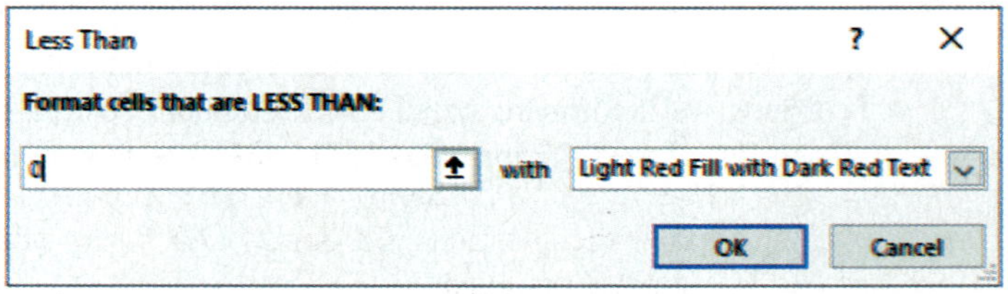

Again, select the cells we would like to conditionally format, namely cells B16, E16, and H16, and select Conditional Formatting>Highlight Cells Rules> Greater than in the ribbon. Input "0" to format cells that are greater than zero, and then select "Green Fill with Dark Green Text" and Select OK.

The final product will be as shown in Lab Exhibit 2-1.8.

Calculation of Direct Materials and Direct Labor Variance									
Direct Materials Variance									
			Actual Cost					**Standard Cost**	
			Actual Quantity		Actual Quantity			Standard Quantity	
			@ Actual Price		@ Standard Price			@ Standard Price	
		Actual Quantity (AQ)	490,120		Actual Quantity (AQ	490,120		Standard Quantity (SQ)	480,120
		Actual Price (AP)	0.24		Standard Price (SP)	0.25		Standard Price (SP)	0.25
		Actual Cost (AQ * AP)	**$117,628.80**		**Actual Quantity @**	**$122,530.00**		**Standard Cost (SQ * SP)**	**$120,030.00**
					Standard Price (AQ * SP)				
	Total Direct	=		Materials			Materials		
	Materials Variance			Price Variance			Quantity Variance		
	$2,401.20			$4,901.20			-$2,500.00		
Check	$2,401.20								

Lab Exhibit 2-1.8

Share the Story

We have computed the quantity variance. Once we compute the labor variance, we will be able to decide if hiring less expensive workers is associated with an unfavorable materials variance and decide what is best both for overall quality as well as its ability to maintain low costs.

Assessment:

1. Take a screenshot of your variance analysis, paste it into a Word document named "Lab 2-1 Excel SS.doc" and label the screenshot Submission 1.
2. Answer the questions in Connect and upload your Lab 2-1 Excel SS.doc via Connect if assigned.

Lab 2-1 Alternate

Apply the same general steps as Lab 2-1 to Alt Lab 2-1, but now calculate the direct labor variance. The template exists in Lab 2-1 Data.xlsx to assist you in your analysis. Open Excel file Lab 2-1 Data.xlsx.

Karina will make 5,000 jackets with standard quantity of leather per jacket of 120.03 square inches of material @$0.25/square inch. The actual quantity of leather per jacket for those 5,000 jackets produced was 122.53 square inches of material @0.24/square inch. The standard labor to produce each jacket is one hour for each jacket with a cost of $16.50/hour. The actual labor used to produce each jacket was 1.06 hours at $16/hour.

Required:

1. Using performance standards for the labor utilized in the manufacture of jackets, calculate the direct labor variances, including rate and efficiency variances.
2. Use conditional formatting to identify favorable and unfavorable variances.

Assessment:

1. Take a screenshot of your variance analysis, paste it into a Word document named "Alt Lab 2-1 Excel SS.doc" and label the screenshot Submission 1.
2. Answer the questions in Connect and upload your Alt Lab 2-1 Excel SS.doc via Connect if assigned.

Lab 2-2 Excel: Diagnostic Analytics: Bank Reconciliations Using Conditional Formatting

Keywords

cash account, bank and GL reconciliation, conditional formatting

Lab Insight

An important internal control for cash is the reconciliation of the cash general ledger account to the bank statement on a regular basis. We call this a bank reconciliation and provide it here as an example of diagnostic analytics. In general, the expectation is that the company and the bank have recorded the same transactions, and any transactions not recorded by both are in need of reconciliation.

To perform a reconciliation, the company needs to reconcile the cash balance recorded in its general ledger (GL) with the cash that the bank collected or charged (disbursed) without the company's knowledge. At the same time, the company needs to reconcile the cash balance on the bank statement with the transactions recorded in the GL but not known at the bank. We also use reconciliations to find recording errors that either the bank or the company have made.

In this lab, we use conditional formatting to find items that need to be reconciled.

Required:

1. Find the items that need to be reconciled between the company's general ledger and the bank statement.

Ask the Question

Can we use conditional formatting to highlight reconciling items for a bank reconciliation?

Master the Data

We Consult You has cash transactions recorded in the general ledger and cash transactions reported on the bank statement, including checks, deposits, bank notes, NSF checks, and bank fees. There are several different ways the company and the bank might report different cash items, including the following:

Outstanding checks are checks written by the company but not yet processed by the bank.

Outstanding deposits are deposits recorded by the company but not yet processed by the bank.

NSF checks are checks reported as received by the company, but the bank does not recognize them because the check writer has insufficient funds.

Notes (loans made to customers collected by the bank) and *interest* (owed on notes from the customers and collected by the bank) collected by banks. The company may not find out about these items until it receives the bank statement.

Bank service fees are fees the bank charges for its banking services and checking accounts. The bank deducts these fees directly from the company's checking account. The company may not find out about the fee until it receives the monthly bank statement.

Errors are sometimes made by the company or the bank in recording a transaction. Accountants do not find these errors until they compare the amounts for each transaction in the general ledger and each transaction in the bank statement.

Perform the Analysis

Open Excel File Lab 2-2 Data.xlsx.

Use Excel's conditional formatting function to find the items that need to be reconciled. Conditional formatting applies a format (or a highlight) to cells differently depending on the content of the individual cells (as shown in Lab Exhibit 2-2.1).

Lab Exhibit 2-2.1

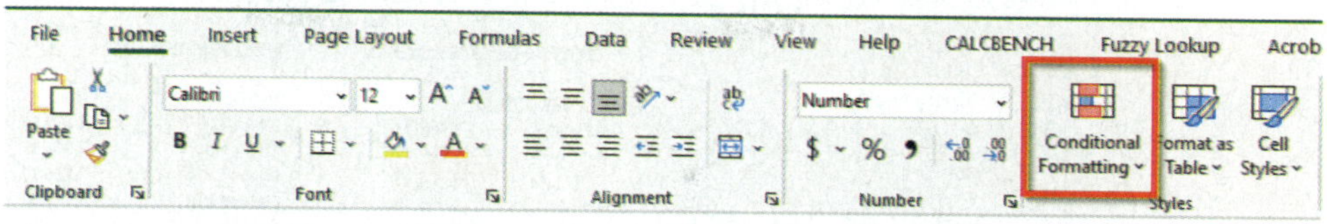

In this lab, you will use conditional formatting to find general ledger (GL) cash transactions that are different from those reported by the bank. In this case, conditional formatting reveals the unique items in the two columns of numbers that will be important to our cash reconciliation.

Step 1

Copy the data to a new worksheet called "working data."

Next, hold the Control Key and highlight both columns of numbers. Then, select Conditional Formatting and click on New Rule.

Select "Format only unique or duplicate values" and select "unique" under Format all. Click on the Format. . . command to set the Fill color to light orange (or peach) to show the unique values.

Select OK, and the screen will format the unique numbers as follows, highlighting the numbers in each column that need to be reconciled (as shown in Lab Exhibit 2-2.2).

Lab Exhibit 2-2.2

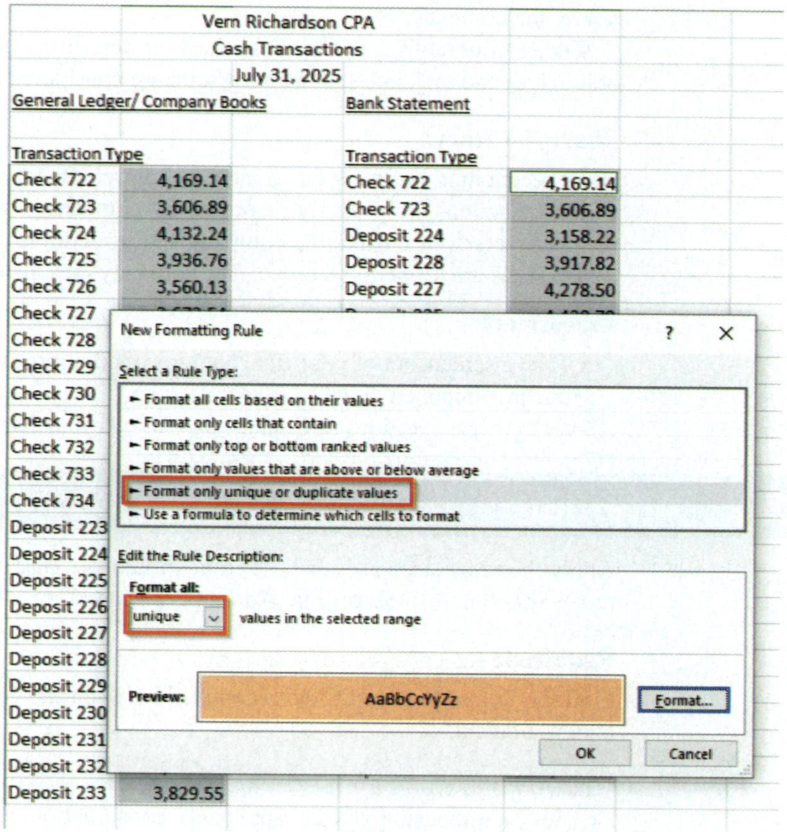

The cells highlighted are those items that need to be reconciled (as shown in Lab Exhibit 2-2.3).

Lab Exhibit 2-2.3

We Consult You Cash Transactions July 31, 2025			
General Ledger/ Company Books		Bank Statement	
Transaction Type		Transaction Type	
Check 722	4,169.14	Check 722	4,169.14
Check 723	3,606.89	Check 723	3,606.89
Check 724	4,132.24	Deposit 224	3,158.22
Check 725	3,936.76	Deposit 228	3,917.82
Check 726	3,560.13	Deposit 227	4,278.50
Check 727	3,673.54	Deposit 225	4,430.78
Check 728	3,742.57	Deposit 226	2,871.63
Check 729	3,351.13	Deposit 223	3,352.37
Check 730	3,025.09	Deposit 229	3,426.75
Check 731	3,408.65	Deposit 230	3,164.18
Check 732	3,174.59	Check 725	3,936.76
Check 733	4,249.97	Check 726	3,560.13
Check 734	2,879.02	Check 727	3,673.54
Deposit 223	3,352.37	Check 728	3,742.57
Deposit 224	3,158.22	Check 729	3,351.13
Deposit 225	4,430.78	Check 730	3,525.09
Deposit 226	2,871.63	Note Collect 1	3,000.00
Deposit 227	4,278.50	Interest Earned	1,511.05
Deposit 228	3,917.82	NSF Check 713	4,145.05
Deposit 229	3,426.75	NSF Check 717	2,424.17
Deposit 230	3,164.18	NSF Fees 1	18.00
Deposit 231	2,979.91	NSF Fees 2	19.00
Deposit 232	3,755.74	Deposit 231	2,979.91
Deposit 233	3,829.55		

The cells in the general ledger column highlighted are items recorded by the company but not by the bank. The checks highlighted would be considered outstanding checks. The deposits highlighted would be considered outstanding deposits.

The cells in the bank statement column highlighted are items recorded by the bank but not by the company.

The cells pertaining to the same check or deposit number highlighted in both the general ledger and the bank statement column are considered to be errors.

Share the Story

Bank reconciliations are a basic internal control used by companies to ensure that their cash transactions are properly recorded. By comparing the cash transactions to the independent records of a bank, the company and its auditors can be more certain that its cash transactions are properly recorded. The company may also use this to identify bank errors.

Assessment:

1. Take a screenshot of your final bank reconciliation, and paste it into a Word document named "Lab 2-2 Excel SS.docx".
2. Answer the questions in Connect and upload your Lab 2-2 Excel SS.docx, if assigned.

Lab 2-2 Alternate

Apply the same steps as Lab 2-2 to the Alt Lab 2-2 Data.xlsx dataset that includes a bank reconciliation. Open Excel File Alt Lab 2-2 Data.xlsx.

Required:

Find the items that need to be reconciled between the company's general ledger and the bank statement.

Assessment:

1. Take a screenshot of your final bank reconciliation, paste it into a Word document named "Alt Lab 2-2 Excel SS.docx", and label the screenshot Submission 1.
2. Answer the questions in Connect and upload your Alt Lab 2-2 Excel SS.docx, if assigned.

Lab 2-3 Excel: Predictive Analytics: Prediction of Product Sales

Keywords

predictive analysis, forecasting, time series, product demand

Decision-Making Context: There are many reasons to forecast future product demand. For example, future product demand is used to ensure that a company has adequate product available for sale.

Hike 'Em Hiking Boots is a fictitious company that sells hiking boots and works hard to have the right products on hand and available for sale.

Required:

Using Excel's forecasting sheet and available product demand from 2021 to 2024, forecast product demand for Hike 'Em Hiking Boots from 2025 to 2026.

Ask the Question

What will be the monthly demand for Hike 'Em Hiking Boots during 2025 and 2026?

Master the Data

Open Excel file Lab 2-3 Data.xlsx.

> **Data Dictionary**
>
> **Month:** Month of the year from 2021 to 2024
>
> **Monthly Product Demand:** Product demand (in thousands of dollars sold)

Perform the Analysis

Step 1: Analyze Past Trends.

1. To start the forecast analysis, highlight one of the numbers in column B (Monthly Product Demand), and then click on Data > Forecast > Forecast Sheet as shown in Lab Exhibit 2-3.1.

Lab Exhibit 2-3.1

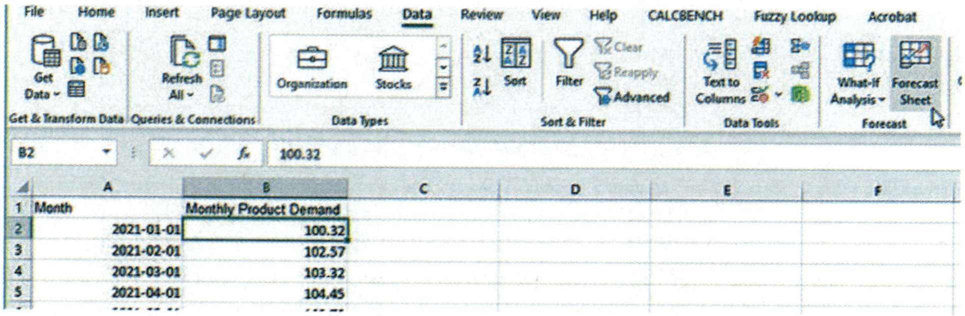

The dialog box in Lab Exhibit 2-3.2 will open, beginning our forecast of Hike 'Em Hiking Boots sales for 2025 and 2026. The forecast sheet capability is available only on Excel for Windows, and not on Excel for Mac. If you work mostly on a Mac, you may need to use a PC in a computer lab or a virtual desktop to access this functionality.

Lab Exhibit 2-3.2

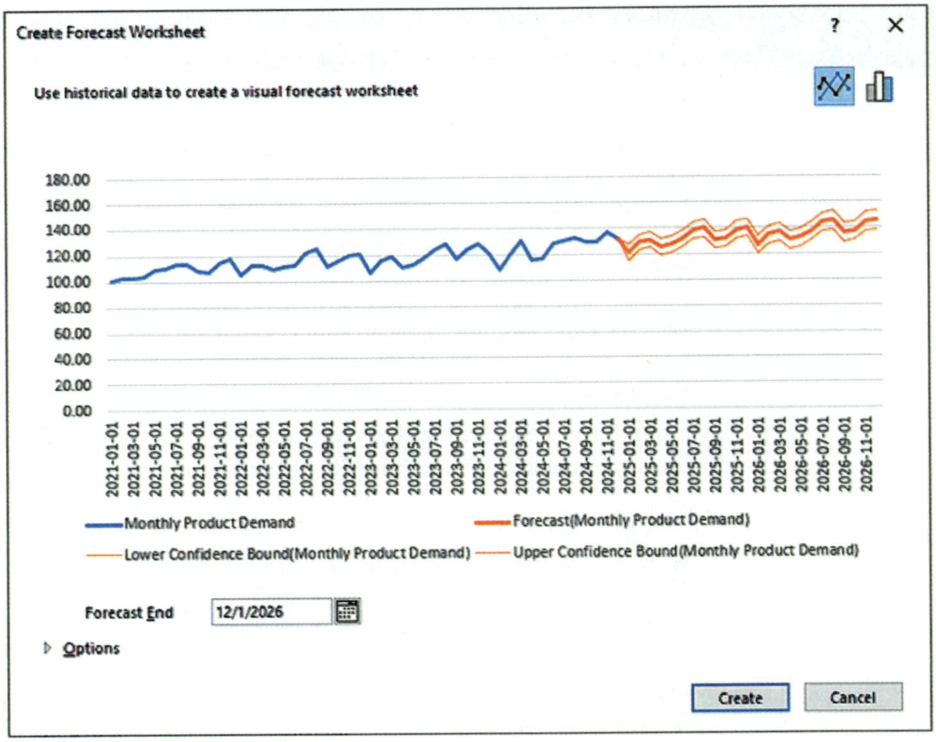

2. Note the seasonality of the data with the reasonably consistent crest and trough over the four quarters each year. Click on the chevron next to Options near the bottom left.
3. Consider the various options, including the dates that the forecast starts and ends, the confidence interval, the timeline range and value range, and how missing points and duplicates are handled.

Step 2: Forecast Future Performance.

1. Select "Include forecast statistics" near the bottom left and then select "Create".
2. Note the new spreadsheet tab with forecast statistics and forecasts for each month in 2025 and 2026. Also note the lower and the upper confidence bound of the forecast. The forecast sheet suggests that there is a 95 percent chance that the actual sales will be in the range between the lower and the upper confidence bound.
3. The forecast graph should look as shown in Lab Exhibit 2-3.3.

Lab Exhibit 2-3.3

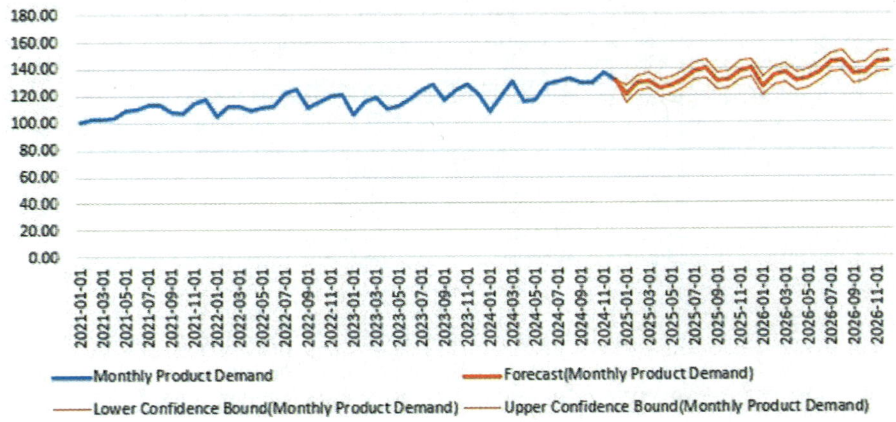

Share the Story

We have now developed a forecast for future product demand that the management of Hike 'Em Hiking Boots can use to plan its future operations and sales. In addition to using time series analysis, we can work to develop other predictors of product demand beyond prior product demand. Perhaps we can determine if there are other relevant predictors of performance, such as competitor performance, industry performance, or macroeconomic performance.

Assessment:

1. Take a screenshot of the forecast spreadsheet of product demand, paste it into a Word document named "Lab 2-3 Excel SS.docx", and label the screenshot Submission 1.
2. Take a screenshot of the forecast graph of product demand, paste it into the same Word document, and label the screenshot Submission 2.
3. Answer the questions in Connect and upload your Lab 2-3 Excel SS.docx via Connect if assigned.

Lab 2-3 Alternate

Using Excel's forecasting sheet and available product demand, forecast product demand for Adventure Shoes from 2025 to 2026. Open Excel file Alt Lab 2-3 Data.xlsx.

Data Dictionary

Month: Month of the year from 2021 to 2024

Monthly Product Demand: Product demand (in thousands of dollars sold)

Required:

Using Excel's forecasting sheet and the available product demand from 2021 to 2024, forecast the product demand for Adventure Shoes from 2025 to 2026.

Assessment:

1. Take a screenshot of the forecast graph of product demand, paste it into a Word document named "Alt Lab 2-3 Excel SS.docx", and label the screenshot Submission 1.
2. Take a screenshot of the forecast spreadsheet of product demand, paste it into the same Word document, and label the screenshot Submission 2.
3. Answer the questions in Connect and upload your Alt Lab 2-3 Excel SS.docx via Connect if assigned.

Lab 2-4 Excel: Prescriptive Analytics: Sensitivity Analysis of Profitability under Changing Volume, Sales Price, and Fixed and Variable Cost Assumptions

Keywords

sensitivity analysis, cost-volume-profit, conditional formatting, changing assumptions

Lab Insight

Profitability is function of number of units sold, price sold, and fixed and variable costs.

What happens if we change the assumptions we make? How sensitive are the results to changes say in the number of units sold or the variable cost per unit? How much will profit change?

By examining how sensitive the profitability is to the changing assumptions, we are able to make a more informed decision on pricing and manufacturing, as well as margins.

This provides an example of prescriptive analytics, evaluating the impact of changing conditions or changing assumptions faced by the company. Specifically, we evaluate how changing volume sold, sales price, and fixed and variable costs will affect firm profitability. We'll also use conditional formatting to visualize the differing levels of profitability.

Required:

1. Determine how sensitive the profits are with changing assumptions of the numbers of units sold and level of variable costs per unit.
2. Apply conditional formatting to the differing levels of profitability in the data table.

Ask the Question

How sensitive are company profitability levels given assumptions of the inputs?

Master the Data:

1. Open a new file in Excel. There is no other data file provided for this lab.
2. In cell A1, type the word "Assumptions:" and then bold it and underline it.
3. In cell A2, type the word "Price" and in cell B2, enter the number "28" (no need to enter quotation marks, just the number or text).
4. In cell A3, type the word "Units Sold" and in cell B3, enter the number "300".
5. In cell A4, type the words "Total Revenues" and in cell B4, enter the formula "=B2*B3" as shown in Lab Exhibit 2-4.1.

Lab Exhibit 2-4.1

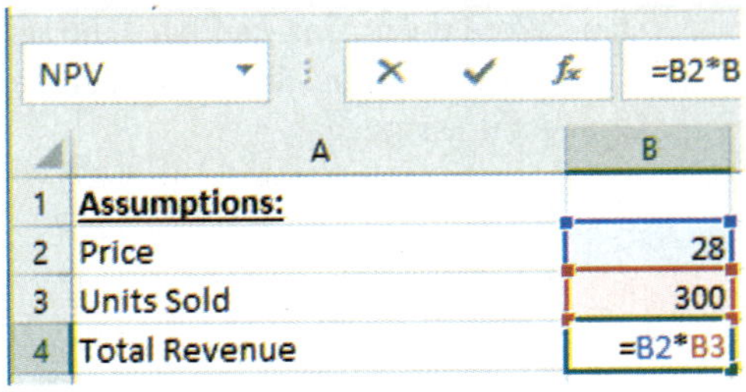

6. In cell A5, type the word "Cost per Unit" and in B5, enter the number "20".
7. In cell A6, type the word "Total Variable Costs" and in B6, enter the formula "=B3*B5".

8. In cell A7, type the word "Total Fixed Costs" and in B7, enter the number "1500".
9. In cell A8, type the word "Total Costs" and in B8, enter the formula "=B6+B7".
10. In cell A9, type the word "Profit" and in B9, enter the formula "=B4-B8", that is Total Revenues less Total Expenses. At this point, the spreadsheet should appear as shown in Lab Exhibit 2-4.2.

Lab Exhibit 2-4.2

	A	B
1	**Assumptions:**	
2	Price	28
3	Units Sold	300
4	Total Revenue	8400
5	Variable Cost per Unit	20
6	Total Variable Cost	6000
7	Total Fixed Costs	1500
8	Total Costs	7500
9	Profit	900

Perform the Analysis

Step 1: Input the range of assumptions.

11. In this lab, we'll assess how profitability changes based on changes in the assumptions regarding the variable cost per unit and the number of units sold.
12. In cell H2, input the words "Variable Cost per Unit".
13. In cell H3, input "$4". In cells I3:Q3, input from $8 to $40, increasing by $4 in each cell in this way as shown in Lab Exhibit 2-4.3.

Lab Exhibit 2-4.3

H	I	J	K	L	M	N	O	P	Q
Variable Cost per unit									
$ 4.00	$ 8.00	$ 12.00	$ 16.00	$ 20.00	$ 24.00	$ 28.00	$ 32.00	$ 36.00	$ 40.00

14. In cell E5, input the words "Units Sold". In cell G4, input "50". In cells G5:G14, input from 100 to 550 in increments of 50 down the column as shown in Lab Exhibit 2-4.4:

Lab Exhibit 2-4.4

	G
4	50
5	100
6	150
7	200
8	250
9	300
10	350
11	400
12	450
13	500
14	550

15. In cell G3, insert the formula "=B9". That link references the total profits and is the result that will change based on different assumptions in the data table. In this table, we will see the impact of changing assumptions on variable cost per unit and number of units sold.
16. Highlight cells G3:Q14 and go to **Data>What-if Analysis> Data Table** as shown in Lab Exhibit 2-4.5.

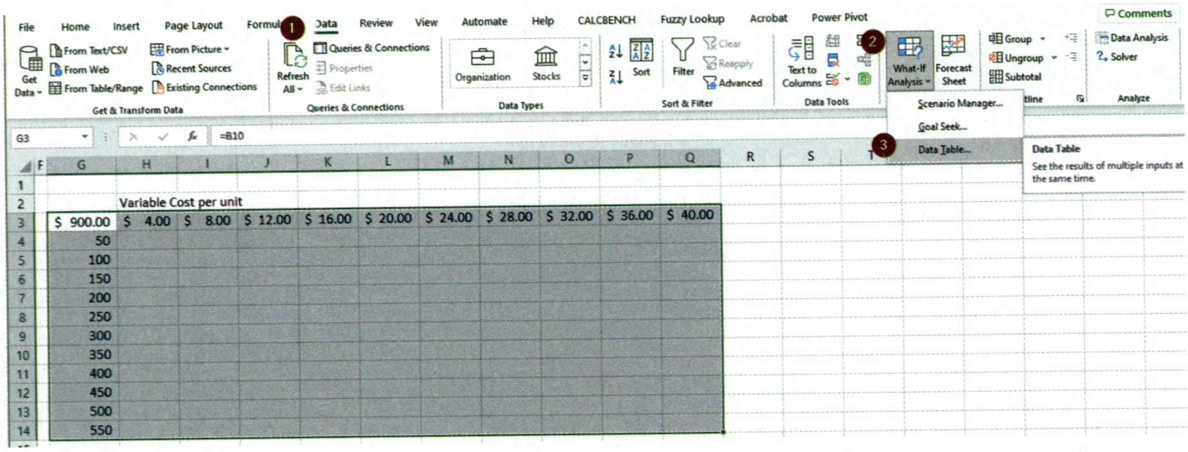

Lab Exhibit 2-4.5

17. In the Data Table Dialog Box, input cell "$B$5" for row input cell suggesting the row input varies by variable cost. Input "$B$3" for column input cell suggesting that column input varies by the number of units sold, as shown in Lab Exhibit 2-4.6. Select "OK."

Lab Exhibit 2-4.6

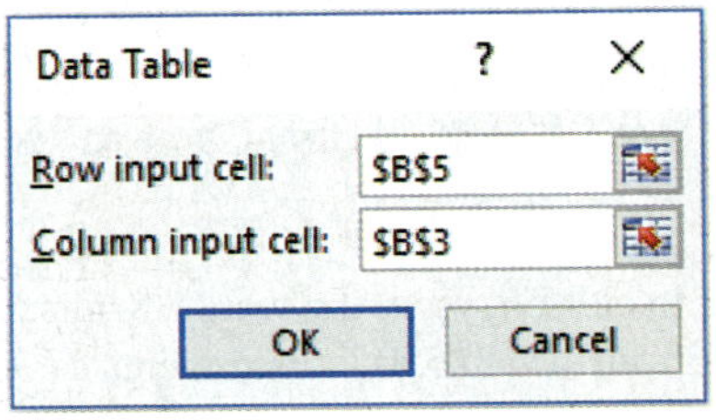

18. The output will appear as follows representing the total profits in each of these scenarios. Note the base case scenario (highlighted below in Lab Exhibit 2-4.7) with a $20 variable cost and 300 units sold, gives a profit of $900.

		Variable Cost per unit									
	$ 900.00	$ 4.00	$ 8.00	$ 12.00	$ 16.00	$ 20.00	$ 24.00	$ 28.00	$ 32.00	$ 36.00	$ 40.00
	50	-300.00	-500.00	-700.00	-900.00	-1100.00	-1300.00	-1500.00	-1700.00	-1900.00	-2100.00
Units Sold	100	900.00	500.00	100.00	-300.00	-700.00	-1100.00	-1500.00	-1900.00	-2300.00	-2700.00
	150	2100.00	1500.00	900.00	300.00	-300.00	-900.00	-1500.00	-2100.00	-2700.00	-3300.00
	200	3300.00	2500.00	1700.00	900.00	100.00	-700.00	-1500.00	-2300.00	-3100.00	-3900.00
	250	4500.00	3500.00	2500.00	1500.00	500.00	-500.00	-1500.00	-2500.00	-3500.00	-4500.00
	300	5700.00	4500.00	3300.00	2100.00	900.00	-300.00	-1500.00	-2700.00	-3900.00	-5100.00
	350	6900.00	5500.00	4100.00	2700.00	1300.00	-100.00	-1500.00	-2900.00	-4300.00	-5700.00
	400	8100.00	6500.00	4900.00	3300.00	1700.00	100.00	-1500.00	-3100.00	-4700.00	-6300.00
	450	9300.00	7500.00	5700.00	3900.00	2100.00	300.00	-1500.00	-3300.00	-5100.00	-6900.00
	500	10500.00	8500.00	6500.00	4500.00	2500.00	500.00	-1500.00	-3500.00	-5500.00	-7500.00
	550	11700.00	9500.00	7300.00	5100.00	2900.00	700.00	-1500.00	-3700.00	-5900.00	-8100.00

Lab Exhibit 2-4.7

19. Next, we will visualize the trends in intrinsic value using conditional formatting. Highlight cells H4:Q14 and then go to the **Home>Conditional Formatting>Color Scales** and click on Green-Yellow-Red Color Scale as shown in the Lab Exhibit 2-4.8.

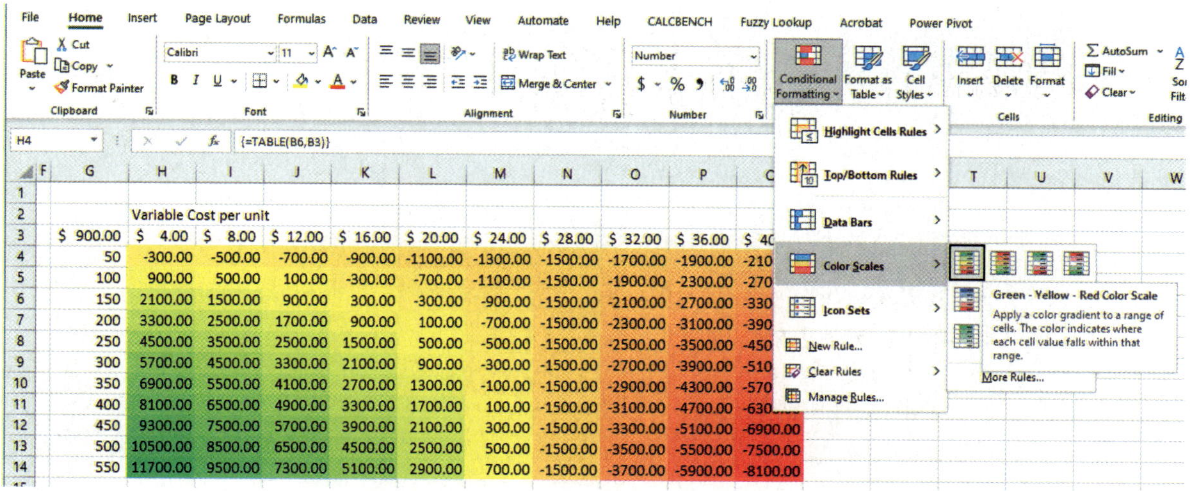

Lab Exhibit 2-4.8

Share the Story

We have now completed the analysis that will help us assess basic profitability levels based on a set of alternate assumptions. We can use these to help with decision making or refine further with additional analysis.

Assessment:

1. Take a screenshot of your completed profitability analysis, and paste it into a Word document named "Lab 2-4 Excel SS.doc".
2. Answer the questions in Connect and upload your Alt Lab 2-4 Excel SS.doc, if assigned.

Lab 2-4 Alternate

Apply the same base scenario as Lab 2-4 to Alt Lab 2-4, but now vary the fixed costs from 500 to 3,000 (in increments of 250) and vary sales price from $5 to $50 (increments of $5) and see how profitability varies on these two dimensions.

Required:

1. Determine how sensitive the profits are with changing assumptions of the level of total fixed costs and sales price.
2. Apply conditional formatting to the differing levels of profitability in the data table.

Assessment:

1. Take a screenshot of your completed profitability analysis, and paste it into a Word document named "Alt Lab 2-4 Excel SS.doc".
2. Answer the questions in Connect and upload your Alt Lab 2-4 Excel SS.doc, if assigned.

Chapter Three

Data Analytics: Data Visualizations

A Look at This Chapter

Data analytics emphasizes the use of visualizations both to perform the analysis and to share the story. We'll compare and contrast exploratory data visualizations and explanatory data visualizations. Visualizations depend on the data type as well as the needs of the analyst and decision maker.

A Look Back

In Chapter 2, we discussed the analytics mindset and presented the AMPS model as a framework for the data analytics process.

A Look Ahead

Chapter 4 describes the roles of accountants as users, managers, designers, and evaluators of technology and technology-driven business processes. To perform in those roles, accountants need to ensure that processes and systems are documented—and to participate in improvements to processes and systems. Thus, accountants must be business analysts. The chapter continues to introduce types of business process models as well as the potential value of business process modeling.

Nata Fuangkaew/Shutterstock

Using Big Data, **Starbucks** knows its customers better every day. Customers make more than 90 million purchases from the 25,000 Starbucks stores worldwide each day. The Starbucks mobile app has more than 17 million users, and its rewards program has 13 million active users. There is an overwhelming amount of data that can be segmented to improve customers' experiences, grow sales, and increase profit.

The mobile app and rewards program allows Starbucks to track purchase patterns even when customers visit different stores. Starbucks knows what those customers buy and what time of day they buy it. Then, it can personalize each customer's Starbucks experience. The app can suggest new products that are likely of interest to a customer based on what they usually buy. Starbucks' *Digital Flywheel Program,* a cloud-based artificial intelligence system, is smart enough to change its recommendations based on local weather, holidays, or locations. The same intelligence system supports custom emails going out to customers offering discounts and special offers based on each customer's purchase history.

Another business intelligence system helps Starbucks plan where to locate new stores. It evaluates volumes of data considering proximity to existing stores, traffic patterns, demographics, and more to recommend new store locations. It can even estimate the impact on existing stores from opening a new store. Data also drives Starbucks' menu selections. There are more than 87,000 drink combinations available, and Starbucks monitors sales for each one to determine menu changes.

Such analysis of Starbucks' business intelligence system requires unique and clever ways to share the story to with the decision makers. What visualizations allow the user to efficiently and effectively understand what is going on? In this chapter, we'll highlight some visualizations that are used to both understand the data and communicate the results.

Source: Bernard Marr, "Starbucks: Using Big Data, Analytics and Artificial Intelligence to Boost Performance," *Forbes,* May 28, 2018; Anshu Sharaf "How Starbucks uses Big Data AI in its business," February 25, 2022, https://www.linkedin.com/pulse/how-starbuck-uses-big-data-ai-its-business-anshu-sharaf-/?trk=articles_directory.

CHAPTER OUTLINE

LEARNING OBJECTIVES

After reading this chapter, you should be able to:

3-1 Define data visualizations.

3-2 Compare and contrast exploratory data visualizations and explanatory data visualizations.

3-3 Outline the basic activities associated with data visualizations.

3-4 Determine the best visualizations for categorical data.

3-5 Determine the best visualizations for numerical (quantitative) data.

3-6 Explain the importance of storytelling using visualizations and written reports to share the story.

LO 3-1

Define data visualizations.

DATA VISUALIZATIONS

Data visualizations are important tools for helping accountants to see data relationships and for using graphical representations to present information to decision makers. We define **data visualization** as a graphic representation of data, often in the form of a graph, chart, or other image.

In Chapter 1, we discussed how the information value chain (Exhibit 1.2) collects data based on business needs and business events. Those data are turned into information to create knowledge that is communicated to decision makers and used to support their decisions. That is why preparing relevant, effective data visualizations is an important component of the analytics mindset and the AMPS model, as discussed in Chapter 2.

Data visualizations are often preferred to be written content to both help perform the data analysis and communicate results to others for the following reasons:

- 91 percent of people prefer visual content over written content.[1] For example, on Facebook, photos have an interaction rate of 87 percent, compared to 4 percent or less for other types of posts, such as links or text.
- The brain processes images 60,000 times faster than it processes text.[2]
- 90 percent of information transmitted to the brain is visual.[3]

In this chapter, we'll explain how data visualizations assist in both exploratory and explanatory data visualizations and provide examples of data visualizations.

PROGRESS CHECK

1. After reading the summary of various academic studies, why are data visualizations preferred to text?
2. Why do you think the interaction rate of visual content is so much higher than written content?

LO 3-2

Compare and contrast exploratory data visualizations and explanatory data visualizations.

EXPLORATORY AND EXPLANATORY DATA VISUALIZATIONS

One key analytics tool in the PERFORM THE ANALYSIS and SHARE THE STORY steps of the AMPS analytics model is the use of data visualizations. Data visualizations are an important part of how analytics are performed, interpreted, and communicated.

There are two types of visualizations: *Exploratory data visualizations* can reveal patterns in the data, which can lead to greater insight in exploratory data analysis as part of PERFORM THE ANALYSIS of the AMPS analytics model. *Explanatory data visualizations* are very useful for communicating the findings of the data analysis to stakeholders as part of SHARE THE STORY of the AMPS analytics model.[4]

[1]Zohar Dayan, "Visual Content: The Future of Storytelling," *Forbes,* April 2, 2018, https://www.forbes.com/sites/forbestechcouncil/2018/04/02/visual-content-the-future-of-storytelling/?sh=2613829a3a46 (accessed August 2022).

[2]Hannah Whiteoak, "Six Reasons to Embrace Visual Commerce in 2018," Pixlee https://www.pixlee.com/blog/six-reasons-to-embrace-visual-commerce-in-2018 (accessed August 2022).

[3]Harry Eisenberg, "Humans Process Visual Data Better," *Thermopylae Sciences + Technology,* September 15, 2014, https://www.t-sciences.com/news/humans-process-visual-data-better (accessed August 2022).

[4]"Explanatory Data Visualizations," Ann Dzuranin, Strategic Finance, January 1, 2022, https://sfmagazine.com/post-entry/january-2022-explanatory-data-visualizations/ (accessed January 7, 2022).

Exploratory Data Visualizations

An **exploratory data visualization** is a graphical representation that is useful for uncovering patterns and useful insights in to the data. These visualizations are typically used during the Analysis step of the AMPS model to explore and understand the data. For example, when performing descriptive or diagnostic analytics to determine what or why something happened, an accountant may decide to graph the data to gain a better understanding of what is occurring. Exploratory data visualization combines with statistical tools to complete **exploratory data analysis**, which is the initial investigation used to discover patterns, spot anomalies or outliers, check assumptions, or test hypotheses and to check assumptions with the help of summary statistics and graphical representations. Exploratory data analysis is generally performed when performing descriptive or diagnostic analytics.

Exploratory data visualizations might help the accountant address the following questions. When paired with statistical tests and tools, an accountant can perform more complete exploratory data analysis. Exhibit 3.1 provides details of accounting questions that are addressed using both exploratory data visualization and statistics tools.

Accounting Questions Addressed through Exploratory Data Analysis	Exploratory Data Visualization Tool	Exploratory Data Statistics Tool
At our company, are increased advertising expenses associated with more sales?	Scatterplot with advertising expense on the x-axis and related sales on the y-axis over multiple time periods. (See Lab 3-3 Excel)	Correlation
What is the distribution of profit margins across different company products?	Histogram (Histogram groups product profit margins into bins and ranges of values and usually shows frequencies)	Descriptive Statistics (Mean, median, maximum, minimum, etc.)
What is the composition of costs of production to help determine the level of fixed and variable costs?	Scatterplot with production on the x-axis and total cost on the y-axis.	Regression analysis with total cost as the dependent variable and total production as the independent variable.
Which variances between actual and budget (or actual and standard) cost need additional analysis?	Conditional formatting to highlight, readily see, and attend to the biggest differences from expectation.	Percentage change calculations highlighting difference from expectation.

EXHIBIT 3.1
Accounting Questions Addressed through Exploratory Data Analysis

Anscombe's Quartet: Using Both Visualizations and Statistical Tools in Exploratory Data Analysis

In 1973, a statistician named Francis Anscombe illustrated the importance of visualizations using four datasets that had nearly identical descriptive summary statistics, yet appeared very different when the distributions were graphed and visualized. It came to be known as "Anscombe's Quartet" and emphasized the importance of visualizations used in tandem with the underlying statistical properties.[5]

As an example of exploratory data visualizations, suppose that an accountant wants to understand how profitability is distributed over time across all the firms trading on a U.S. public exchange. The analyst might choose to plot the return on equity (ROE, which equals

[5]F. J. Anscombe, "Graphs in Statistical Analysis." *The American Statistician* 27, no. 1 (1973), https://www.sjsu.edu/faculty/gerstman/StatPrimer/anscombe1973.pdf (accessed December 23, 2021).

net income divided by stockholders' equity) at each earnings interval across all of those firms. Accounting researchers David Burgstahler and Ilia Dichev[6] did exactly that, creating the visualization shown in Exhibit 3.2 for the period from 1976 to 1994. This exploratory visualization shows what earnings were reported over the time period in each earnings (or profitability) interval, so it is a type of descriptive analytics.

EXHIBIT 3.2
Distribution of Return on the Market Value of Stockholders' Equity, 1976–1994

Source: David Burgstahler and Ilia Dichev, "Earnings Management to Avoid Earnings Decreases and Losses," *Journal of Accounting and Economics* 24, no. 1 (1997).

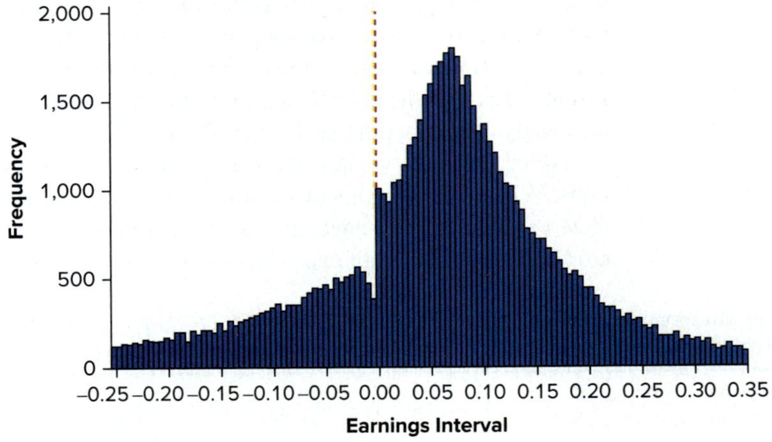

For the most part, the visualization displays the expected bell-shaped distribution of earnings that often shows up in stock market returns. However, the visualization shows an anomaly—in this case, a discontinuity, right around zero. Just below zero, there seem to be missing observations or a lower-than-expected frequency, suggesting some type of an anomaly. And just above zero, there seem to be extra observations (or a higher-than-expected frequency), again suggesting an anomaly.

This exploratory data visualization will likely lead to additional questions:

- What explains the differences in profitability level from company to company?
- Are managers responsible for the higher-earning companies' high profit levels?
- Do managers use the flexibility within accounting standards to make earnings higher (or lower) than expected? If they do manage earnings, how do they do that? What incentives do managers have to manage earnings up or down?
- Do managers manage earnings to maximize their own bonuses?

LAB CONNECTION

Lab 3-3 Excel provides an example of the use of a scatterplot to better understand the relationship between advertising expenditures and revenues. As such, it provides an example of exploratory data visualizations.

Labs 3-3 Excel, 3-4 Tableau, and 3-5 Power BI provide an example of exploratory analytics by seeing the past trend of sales and earnings and using time series analysis to help forecast the future.

[6]David Burgstahler and Ilia Dichev, "Earnings Management to Avoid Earnings Decreases and Losses," *Journal of Accounting and Economics* 24, no. 1 (1997), pp. 99–126.

Explanatory Data Visualizations

The accountant often serves as an interpreter, or liaison, between the data scientist and decision-makers. Indeed, an accountant should be particularly good at reporting the results to decision-makers and all other interested parties. Very often the report includes **explanatory data visualizations** that are useful in communicating the findings of the analysis to stakeholders. Data visualizations are one way we *share* the story.

The visualizations might be reported just once in a **static report** that is not constantly updated. Or the report may undergo continuous, real-time updates (a **dynamic report**) delivered through a **dashboard**, which is a graphical summary of various measures continuously tracked by a company.

LAB CONNECTION

Lab 3-7 Excel provides an example of a dashboard in Excel using a PivotTable, PivotCharts, and slicers, as an example of a dynamic, interactive report.

PROGRESS CHECK

3. In which step of the AMPS model are exploratory visualizations typically created? Which step uses explanatory visualizations?
4. If a company would like to track actual daily sales as compared to its sales targets, should it use a dynamic report or a static report? Explain.

LO 3-3

Outline the basic activities associated with data visualizations.

DATA VISUALIZATION CONCEPTS

There are three basic activities underlying data visualizations.

1. *Understanding the data.* This involves finding relevant sources, selecting data, preparing it for use, and questioning how the data supports the overall goal of the visualizations. It also includes selection of appropriate metrics. This is closely related to the extract, transform, and load (ETL) processes described in Chapter 2.
2. Select appropriate data visualization software tool(s). There are several widely used tools for data visualization included Excel, Tableau, and Power BI described later in this chapter. Each data analytics software product includes its own data visualization tool. Well-known tools include the following (with Exhibit 3.3 providing a description of various tools and their specialties in different parts of the AMPS model):
   a. Excel supports data processing and presentation.
   b. Tableau desktop is data visualization software designed to integrate with an extensive list of data sources, such as Excel, Oracle, IBM DB2, MySQL, Redshift, and Hadoop.
   c. Power BI desktop from **Microsoft** is data visualization software also designed to integrate with various data sources, such as Excel, Microsoft Access, and various Azure data (Azure is Microsoft's cloud computing platform). It is part of the Microsoft Office Suite.
   d. Python is a programming language with extensive data manipulation capabilities and the ability to create basic charts.

EXHIBIT 3.3
Data Analysis and Visualization Software Tools by AMPS Model Component and Data Analysis Specialty

AMPS Model Component	Data Acquisition and Preparation Tools	Data Analysis Tools	Data Visualization Tools
Master the Data [Extract, Transform and Load (ETL)]	Excel (basic) Alteryx SQL (Structured Query Language) Tableau Prep (Tableau) Power Query (Power BI)		
Perform the Analysis		Excel (basic analysis) SAS, SPSS, Stata (advanced analysis) R and Python (advanced analysis)	**Exploratory Data Visualizations** Excel (basic) Tableau Desktop (advanced) Power BI (advanced) SAS, Stata, SPSS, Python, R(basic)
Share the Story			**Explanatory Data Visualizations** Excel (basic) Tableau Desktop (advanced) Power BI (advanced) SAS, Stata, SPSS, Python, R(basic)

e. R statistical software is an open-source statistical programming language with a variety of libraries for creating visuals.
f. SAS, Stata, and SPSS are examples of statistical software with data processing and visualization capabilities.

LAB CONNECTION

Labs 3-4 Excel, 3-5 Tableau, and 3-6 Power BI all provide examples of analytics and related visualization associated with forecasting products and sales. The labs show how this is performed on the same time series data in Excel (Lab 3-4 Excel), Tableau (Lab 3-5 Tableau), and Power BI (Lab 3-6 Power BI).

3. *Developing and presenting the visualization.* This is the design function that is critical to the effective presentation of information. The visualization must focus the decision maker's attention and avoid information overload. Information overload occurs when the level of information is greater than the decision maker's information processing capability. Important considerations:

   a. **Keep the user/decision maker in mind:** The visualization must create or reinforce knowledge.
   b. **Match the right chart to the appropriate data type:** Some examples of selection criteria and visualization types are presented in Exhibit 3.4.
   c. **Direct the user to the most important information:** Use color, size, and other visual cues to draw attention to important data.

d. **Curate the visualization with explanatory titles:** Focus on the question at hand and provide key insights using meaningful titles.
e. **Define axis labels and numbers clearly** so the reader easily understands the relationships.

Type of Data	Type of Chart	Purpose	Examples	Potential Problems/ Suggested Limits
Categorical	Vertical bar, horizontal bar, treemaps, bubble charts	Comparisons of performance metrics	Revenue or profit comparisons among divisions or stores	Too many categories; limit number of bars (fewer for vertical than horizontal)
Univariate	Histograms	Frequencies, range of values, most likely values	Stock returns, stock betas for an industry	Bins too large to show detail
Multivariate relationships	Scatter plots	Relationships, correlations	Comparing return on equity and stock returns	Too many trees to see forest (too much detail and lack of clear relationship)
Geospatial	Maps, symbol maps	Comparisons among locations	Relative sales by state	Too few symbols to spread out; too many symbols on the map
Time trends	Line charts	Comparison over time	Sales by year and quarter	Too many lines; limit to five or less
Proportional	Pie charts, doughnut charts, treemaps	Comparison of parts to a whole	Division net profit slices in total; company net profit pie	All slices similar size; too many slices; limit to five slices or less

EXHIBIT 3.4
Surveying the Set of Visualization Types

PROGRESS CHECK

5. What kind of visualization would be used to understand if there is a relationship between two variables?
6. What kind of visualization is used to show a single variable over time?

LO 3-4

Determine the best visualizations for categorical data.

APPROPRIATE VISUALIZATIONS FOR CATEGORICAL DATA

As noted in the previous section, it is critical to match the visualization to the appropriate data type. We'll next discuss categorical and numerical data types and appropriate visualizations.

- **Categorical data** are a form of qualitative data that are represented either by words or by nonmeaningful numerical data. For example, categorical data might group people by age (e.g., adult or child), gender (male, female, nonbinary), label transaction types (e.g., sales versus returns), or specify a depreciation method (e.g., straight line, sum-of-the-years digits, or double-declining balance).
  - **Nominal data** are a type of categorical data that cannot be ranked, such as eye color and transaction type (purchase, return).

- **Ordinal data** are a type of categorical data with natural, ranked categories, such as letter grades (A, B, C, D, F) and Olympic medals (gold, silver, and bronze).
- **Numerical data** are meaningful numbers that represent quantities, such as transaction amount, net income, age, or score on an exam.

Charts Appropriate for Categorical Data

Because categorical data and numerical (quantitative) data have different characteristics, they require different types of visualizations. The charts most frequently used to visualize categorical data include:

- **Pie charts,** which are data visualizations in the form of a circle divided into sections representing the category's proportion of the whole.
- **Bar (column or vertical) charts,** which are data visualizations using vertical/horizontal bars that represent the total amount of observations in that category.
- **Stacked bar (column) charts,** a type of bar chart data visualization that represents the proportional contribution of individual data points as compared to the total.

The pie chart is probably the most common data visualization for categorical data. It shows the parts of the whole; in other words, it represents the proportion of each category as it corresponds to the whole dataset. A **proportion** is the number of observations in one category divided by the total number of all observations.

Another way to show the proportions of each category is through the use of a bar chart. In most cases, a bar chart is easier to interpret than a pie chart because our brains are more skilled at comparing the height of columns (or the lengths of horizontal bars) than they are at comparing the sizes of pie slices, especially when the proportions are relatively similar.

EXHIBIT 3.5
Pie Chart and Bar (Column) Chart Illustrate Proportions in Different Ways

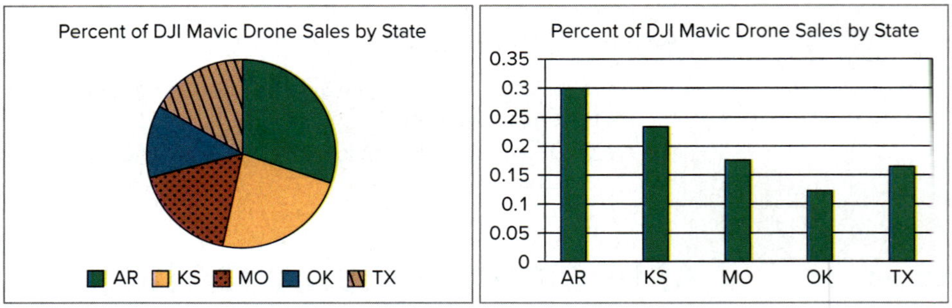

Consider the two different charts in Exhibit 3.5. Both charts represent the sales of DJI Mavic Drone in various states. The size of the difference between the two largest pieces of pie in Arkansas and Kansas is almost impossible to see in the pie chart. This difference is easier to see in the bar chart. We could improve the pie chart by adding the percentages associated with each proportion in the chart, as shown in Exhibit 3.6, but it is much easier to see the difference in proportions by glancing at the order and length of the bars in the bar chart in Exhibit 3.5.

A good rule of thumb to follow with pie charts is to avoid using them when there are more than six categories. As the number of categories (slices of pie) increases, it becomes increasingly difficult to distinguish between the size of the slices. It is particularly difficult to read a pie chart with many skinny slices of pie (e.g., see Exhibit 3.7).

EXHIBIT 3.6
Pie Chart Showing Proportion Detail

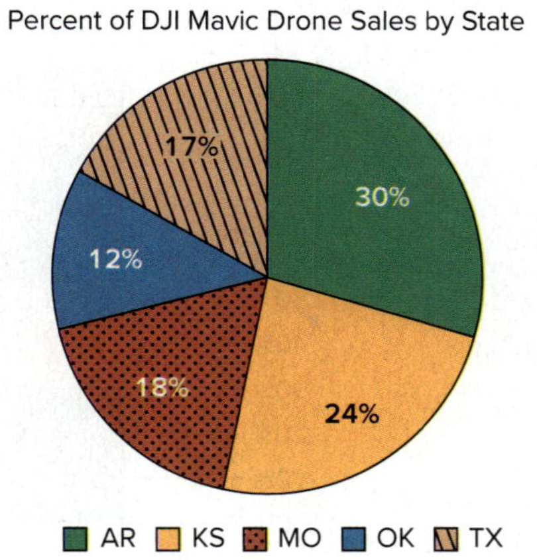

EXHIBIT 3.7
Pie Chart Showing Proportion Detail with Arguably Too Many Slices

Source: AICPA 2021 Trends Report, page 36. (https://www.aicpa.org/professional-insights/download/2021-trends-report, accessed August 2022)

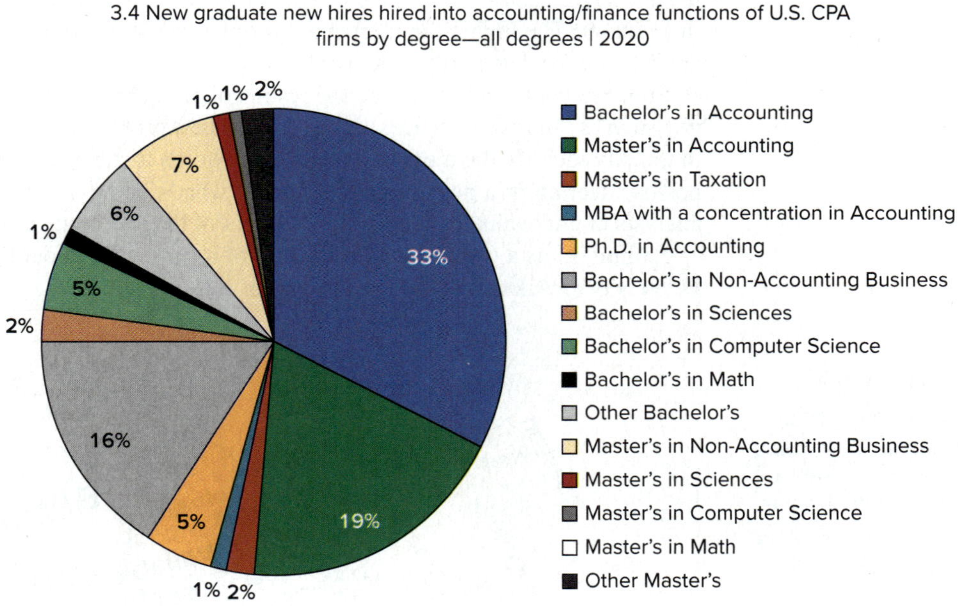

We can also represent the same set of data in a stacked bar chart or a 100 percent stacked bar chart, as shown in Exhibit 3.8. A stacked bar chart can take less space on a page or a PowerPoint slide than a traditional bar chart. The left axis label of Exhibit 6.7 is a stacked bar (column) chart that shows the proportion of drones sold in each state. The 100 percent stacked bar chart on the right side shows the proportion expressed in terms of percentage of the whole. Note that the Y-axes begin at zero and increase as the count (number) or percentage increases.

While it is sometimes difficult to compare two values in stacked bar charts, they work well when you are trying to break down and compare parts of the whole. For example, you could prepare a stacked bar chart with two columns, one for 2025 sales and one for 2026 sales, with each chart showing the breakdown by state.

Several other types of charts also work well for showing proportions:

If you are working with text data, you can use a word cloud to identify the most commonly used words. A **word cloud** is a collection of words depicted in different sizes, with

EXHIBIT 3.8
Stacked Bar (Column) Charts

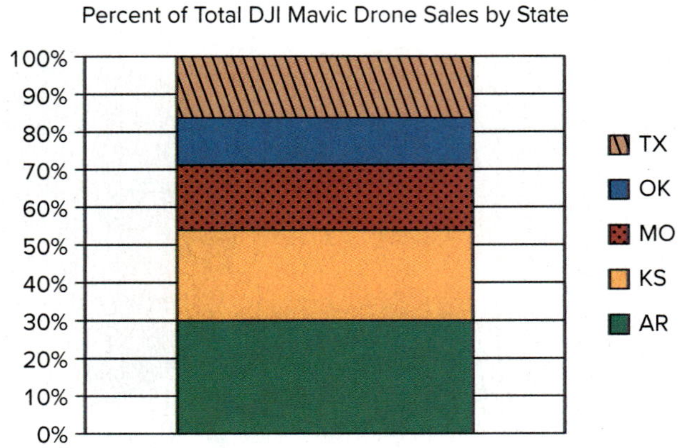

larger font size (and often the bolder the font) reflecting greater frequency of the word in the underlying dataset. The basis of a word cloud is the frequency of each word mentioned in a dataset. The higher the frequency (proportion) of a given word, the larger and bolder are the font for that word in the word cloud.

Suppose you want to analyze the results of an open-ended response question on a survey such as "In four sentences, describe your best professor". A word cloud is a great way to quickly identify the most frequently used words to determine if the respondents have a positive feeling or a negative feeling about what's being surveyed. Additional sentiment analysis might evaluate the overall sentiment of the text being examined.

Exhibit 3.9 is a word cloud for the text of a survey filled out by college students at the University of Arkansas (and used as part of Lab 3-2).

EXHIBIT 3.9
Word Cloud from Students Describing Their Best Professor at the University of Arkansas (Based on Lab 3-2 Power BI)

A **filled geographic map** is useful for expressing categorical data proportions across geographic areas such as states or countries. Exhibit 3.10 shows the number of sales by U.S. state. Notice that the heat map used in combination with the filled map shows relative proportions across different geographic regions, it is not the best choice for visualizing your data if a greater degree of precision is necessary.

EXHIBIT 3.10
Filled Geographic Map (Sales by State)

Tableau Software

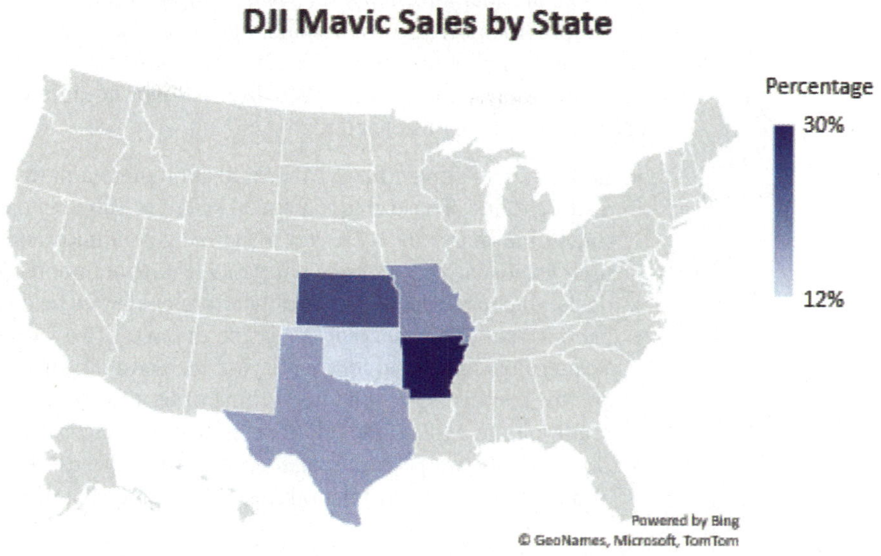

LAB CONNECTION

Lab 3-2 Power BI provides an example of how to build a word cloud to answer the question "How do you describe your best professor?".

PROGRESS CHECK

7. What type of chart would you use to summarize the results of a text analysis of **Home Depot**'s annual financial report?
8. What is wrong with the pie chart in Exhibit 3.7?

LO 3-5

Determine the best visualizations for numerical (quantitative) data.

DETERMINING APPROPRIATE VISUALIZATIONS FOR NUMERICAL DATA

Charts Appropriate for Numerical (Quantitative) Data

An important characteristic of numerical data is whether the data is continuous or discrete. We define those terms further here:

- **Continuous data** are numerical data that can take on any numerical value, not just whole numbers, meaning there is an infinite set of values between any two observations in a continuous data scale. Examples of continuous data are height, sales, income, cash flows, and currency.
- **Discrete data** are numerical data that only take on whole-number (integer) values and have a finite set of values between any two observations. An example of discrete data is the number of products in inventory (you can have 0 items or 150 SKUs in inventory, but in most cases you cannot have 143.27 items in inventory).

There are many methods for visualizing quantitative data. All the methods mentioned in the previous section for visualizing categorical data, except for the word cloud, can work for depicting numerical data, but the following chart types are particularly useful for depicting more complex data. We discuss them in more detail, and provide examples of each, a bit later in this chapter.

- *Line charts.* A **line chart** is a visualization of data in the form of points that connect in a straight line. These charts are well suited to showing data changes or trend lines over time. Line charts are useful for visualizing continuous data, while bar charts are often used for visualizing discrete data. Line charts are not recommended for qualitative data, which are categorical and therefore can never be continuous.
- *Scatterplots.* A **scatterplot** is a graph that plots two variables each on its own axis. Scatterplots are useful for identifying the possible correlation between two variables and for identifying a trend line or line of best fit. (Lab 3-3 Excel, for example, uses a scatterplot to explain the relationship between sales and advertising expenditures.)
- *Box-and-whisker plots and histograms.* These are useful for visualizing the distribution of a dataset and identifying outliers that might exist in the data.

Bar Charts and Line Charts to Visualize Numerical Data

Bar charts, line charts, and pie charts can all be useful in exploratory business analytics. Let's begin with a simple example. Exhibit 3.11 is a simple table showing **Amazon**'s net income and sales from 2012 through 2021. Presented in tabular form, it is difficult to see how net income and sales change over time.

EXHIBIT 3.11
Table of Financial Performance for Amazon, 2012–2021 ($ in millions)

Source: Amazon Income Statements 2012–2021

Year	Net Income	Sales
2012	(39)	61,093
2013	274	74,452
2014	(241)	88,988
2015	596	107,066
2016	2,371	135,987
2017	3,033	177,866
2018	10,073	232,887
2019	11,588	280,522
2020	21,331	386,064
2021	33,364	469,822

When the same data are visualized using a bar chart, as in Exhibit 3.12, you can quickly see that Amazon's sales have grown steadily each year. Note the chart components and how they align with the basic elements of a chart that you learned in earlier in this chapter:

- The vertical axis has a scale from 0 to 500,000, with tick marks indicating each incremental 50,000 increase.
- The labels on the horizontal axis indicate the years from 2012 through 2021.
- The bars indicate the data series with the total sales data point for each year.

Bar charts should be sorted logically. When visualizing **time series data** (values taken on by a variable at different points in time: days, months, or years), it typically makes sense to sort the data chronologically. However, bar charts also lend themselves

EXHIBIT 3.12
Bar Chart Amazon Sales, 2012–2021 ($ in millions)

Source: Amazon Income Statements 2012–2021

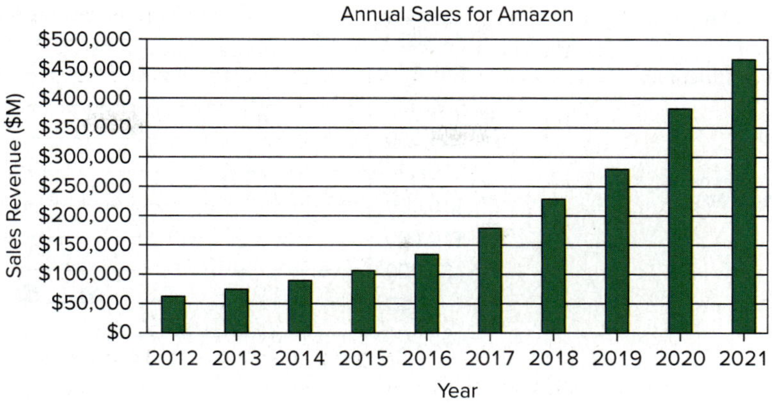

to sorting based on the numerical value of the variable. In this case, Amazon's sales increased each year, so the bar graph would not change if we sorted it in ascending order based on sales.

Because Amazon's sales data are time series data, we can also use a line chart to visualize the data effectively. Line charts should always be sorted chronologically. Recall the bar chart in Exhibit 6.4, which compared sales from five different companies. Using the same set of data to create a line chart would not make sense because there is nothing that inherently connects the different companies' sales totals. However, if you had yearly sales data for each of those five companies, you could place those data in a line chart to see how total sales compare across the companies over time.

The data for **Amazon**'s net income in Exhibit 3.11 can be depicted as a line chart (Exhibit 3.13) because the net income is provided over a 10-year period. In addition to being useful for visualizing time series data, line charts work well in visualizing numerical data that extend below 0. In this example, Amazon had negative income in 2012 and 2014.

EXHIBIT 3.13
Line Chart of Amazon's Net Income, 2012–2021 ($ in millions)

Source: Amazon Income Statements 2012–2021

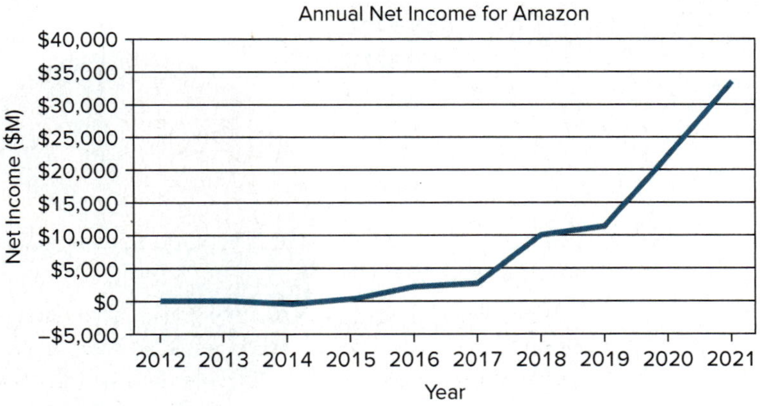

These net income data could also be depicted with a bar chart, as shown in Exhibit 3.14. However, this bar chart is clunkier than the line chart. The data point for 2012 is barely visible on the bar chart because it is very close to 0, and the negative value for 2014 is also difficult to see. Line charts are preferable when you want to communicate the overall trend rather than specific data points. In addition, line charts provide more flexibility with scales.

EXHIBIT 3.14
Bar Chart of Amazon's Net Income, 2012–2021 ($ in millions)

Source: Amazon Income Statements 2012–2021

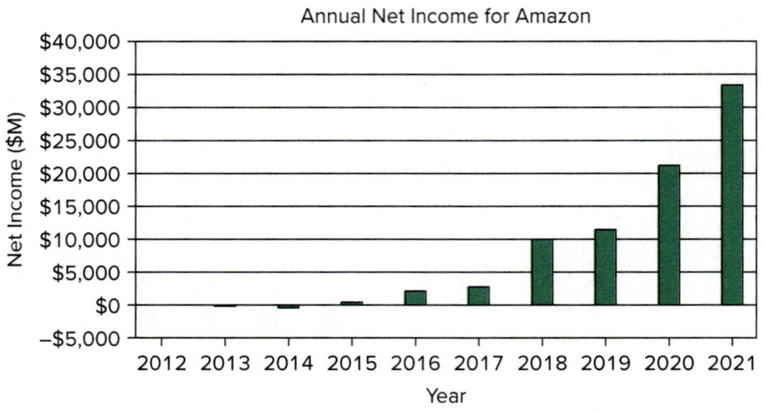

Pie charts are also useful for showing proportion and visualizing categorical data as a part of exploratory business analytics. Recall that categorical data tend to be represented by words, such as transaction types (e.g., sales and returns). Pie charts show proportion, which is calculated as the number of observations in one category divided by the grand total of observations. However, note that Exhibit 3.15 is a poor use of a pie chart. The proportion of each year's sales over a 10-year period is not particularly useful; dollar values are included, but percentages are not. Also, it is difficult to determine the year that each slice represents, even though a legend is included at the bottom. As noted earlier, pie charts are rarely preferred when there are six or more categories (or "slices" of pie).

EXHIBIT 3.15
Pie Chart of Amazon's Sales, 2012–2021 ($ in millions)

Source: Amazon Income Statements 2012–2021

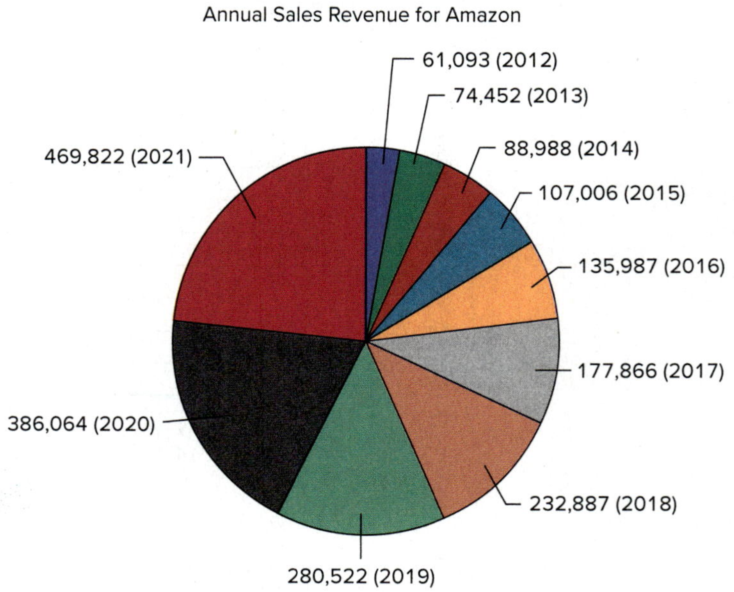

LAB CONNECTION

Lab 3-1 Excel provides multiple examples of creating column charts, line charts, and pie charts for Tesla sales and net income.

PROGRESS CHECK

9. When is a line chart preferred over a bar chart?
10. When visualizing data over time, which charts are the best options?

Visualizations Often Depend on User Preference

Visualizations Exhibit 3.16 show three ways of showing a time series and forecast visually (as performed in Labs 3-4 Excel, 3-5 Tableau, and 3-6 Power BI. They each represent the sales forecast for sales revenue at **IBM.**

Exhibit 3.16 provides an example of a sales forecast using time-series analysis for IBM made using Excel's Forecast Sheet. We note some seasonality, or variation by quarter; some quarters consistently have higher or lower sales than other quarters. Also, note the forecast of future sales beginning in 2022 and ending in 2024, as shown by the boldfaced orange line (in panel A) and other ways in the other panels. There is also a lower and an upper confidence bound, equal to ± two standard deviations, around the predicted level of sales, representing the worst- and best-case scenarios. All other things equal, there is a 95 percent chance that the future actual sales will be in the range between the lower and the upper confidence bound.

Which do you prefer? Why is that so?

EXHIBIT 3.16
IBM Sales Forecast Using Time Series Analysis

(B, C): Tableau Software

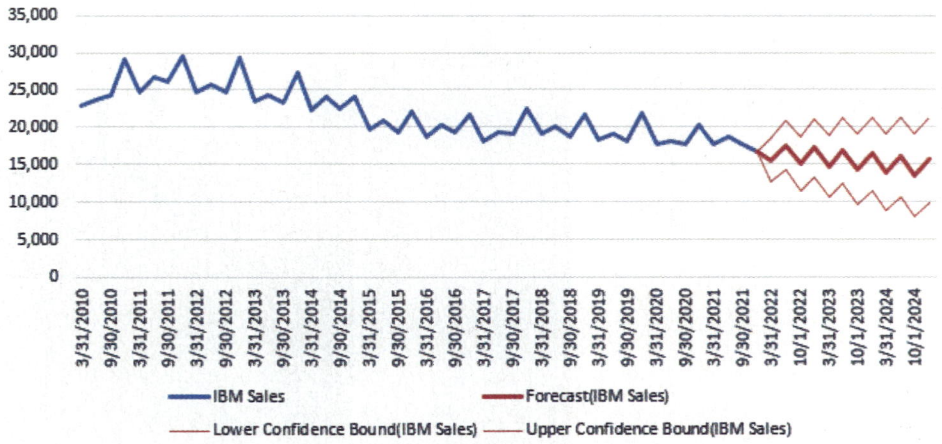

Panel A: Prediction of Earnings Using Line Graphs (Output from Excel–From Lab 3-4 Excel)

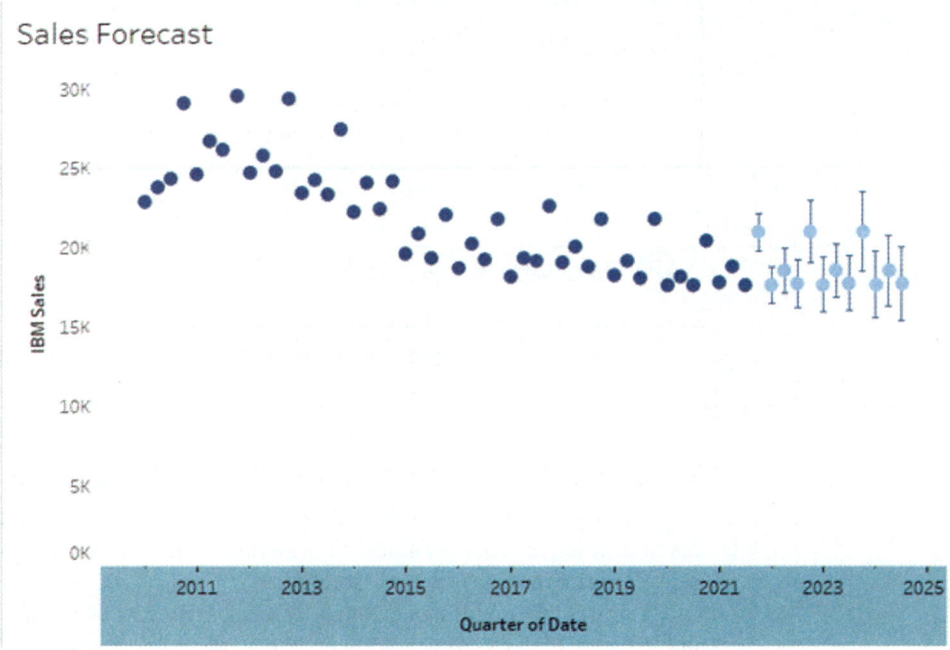

Panel B: Prediction of Earnings Using Circles (Output from Tableau–from Lab 3-5 Tableau)

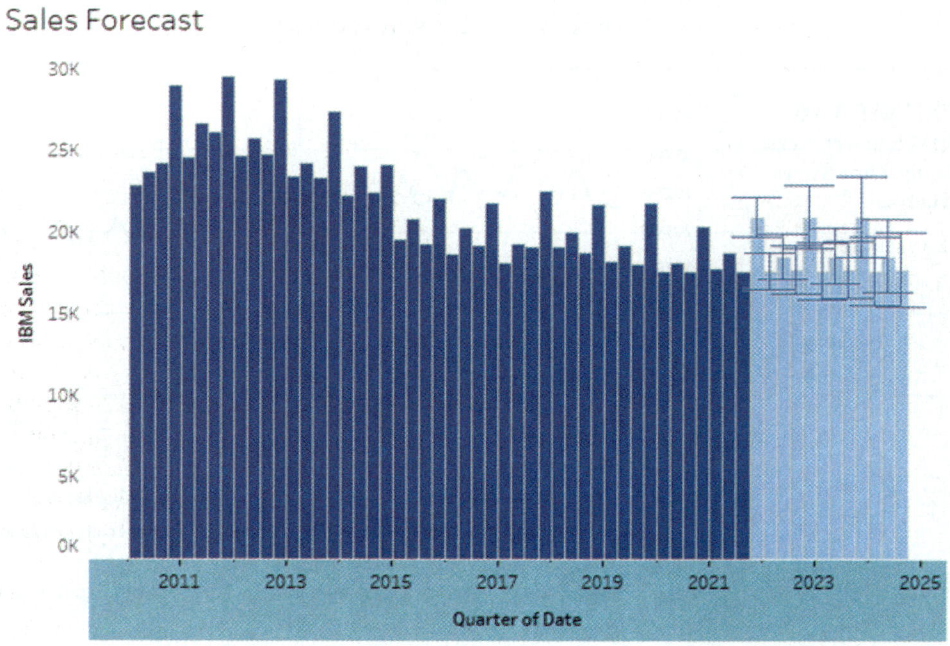

Panel C: Prediction of Earnings Using Line Graphs (Alternate Output from Tableau) Left Column Content

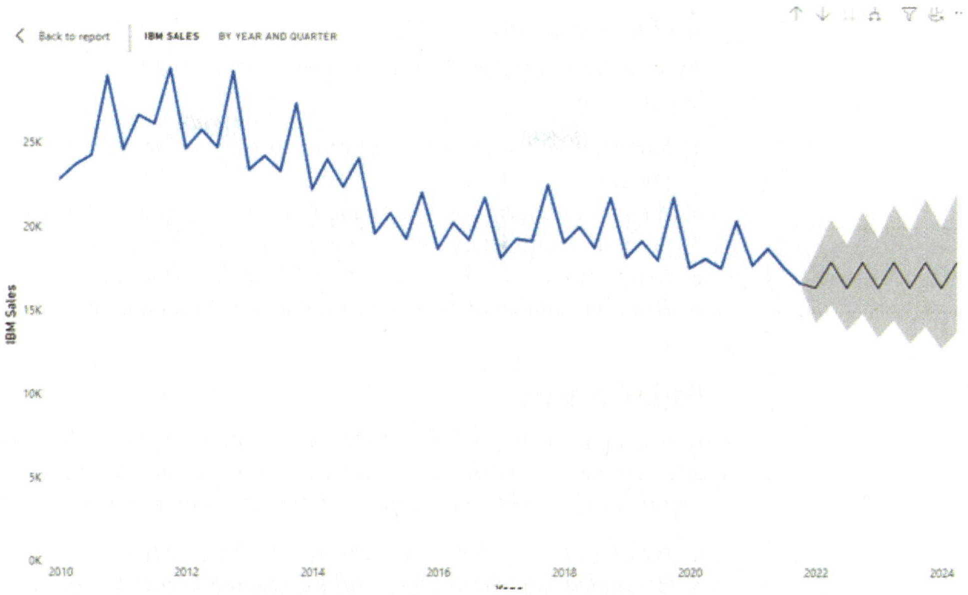

Panel D: Prediction of Earnings Using Line Graphs (Alternate Output from Power BI–from Lab 3-6 Power BI)

PROGRESS CHECK

11. Is it possible for actual (realized sales) to be greater than the upper confidence bound?
12. The panels of Exhibit 3.16 all show forecasts of future performance including the expected future value and the upper and lower confidence bound? Which panel do you prefer?

LO 3-6

Explain the importance of storytelling using visualizations and written reports to share the story.

SHARE THE STORY: STORYTELLING WITH VISUALIZATIONS AND WRITTEN REPORTS

The last step in the AMPS model is to Share the Story. Some data analysts refer to this part of sharing the story as storytelling. **Storytelling** works to ensure that the message conveyed by the analyst (in this case, the accountant) is meaningful and relevant.

Having the most effective storytelling requires understanding your target audience. Some target audiences prefer explanatory visualizations and others prefer written summaries such as executive summaries or full(er) reports. And some, of course, want all of the detail of the written report, along with all the visualizations (even if they are all just included in an appendix at the end of the report). For example, a production line manager making the Ford Maverick truck will more likely want to see a full explanation with a detailed report and statistical charts whereas the Ford CEO may prefer to capture the gist (highlights) of the analysis through an executive summary.

Depending on the amount of information you want to convey and how much your audience is interested in the detail, you may choose to prepare an *executive summary* or a *full report* (which usually includes the executive summary).

Executive Summary

An executive summary, which is typically not longer than a page, includes the following key sections:

- *Statement of the problem, question, or opportunity* that initiated the business analytics project.
- *A concise description of why the project is relevant to the audience.* It is important to tailor all communications (written and otherwise) to your intended audience.
- *Brief summary of the results,* possibly including visualizations.
- *Brief recommendation(s)* for a course of action based on the results.

Full Report

If you are providing a full report, the executive summary may serve as an introduction to and summary of what your audience will learn throughout the rest of the more detailed report. In addition to an executive summary, a full report should include:

- *A description of the method* chosen for the analytics project.
- *Expanded summary of the results discussed in the executive summary.* The report should go beyond the brief results provided in the executive summary to include:
- Assumptions made and estimates used. All analysis requires assumptions and estimates. Explaining these might help the audience better understand the output, and whether it might vary if different assumptions are made.
- *Pertinent data outputs,* such as correlations, results from the tests of various hypotheses (that might include the results of correlations, statistical tests, or regression tests. When providing these data outputs in a report, it is necessary to interpret the results. This fuller interpretation helps the reader better understand the details that support the results.
- *Data visualizations that help to communicate the findings and help with the storytelling.* Provide a written summary of the information that the visualization provides. For example, if you provide a line chart that is skewed positively or negatively, explain what the skew signifies.
- *Expanded recommendation(s)* beyond brief recommendations in the executive summary that reiterate the significance of the project and how it will affect your audience.

Regardless of the exact manner in which the story is shared, it is important to meet the needs of the one receiving the report to ensure that the message conveyed by the analyst (in this case, the accountant) is meaningful and relevant.

PROGRESS CHECK

13. What is the difference between an executive summary and a full report?
14. Why would some users prefer a fuller report with all the details as compared to an executive summary?

Summary

- Data visualizations are graphical representations that present information to decision makers. They are a communications tool that allows accountants to turn data into information to create knowledge for decision makers.

- Selecting the right visualization (and visualization tool) requires an understanding of the decision maker's goals and issues involved in the decision. The selection of the right chart depends on the type of data. Users must get data, set relationships, select or create attributes, and select and modify the visualization.
- There are common steps in preparing data and developing visualizations regardless of the visualization tool.
- Microsoft Excel provides several tools to support data analytics and visualization. First, tables allow direct analysis using totals and filters. Pivot tables provide a robust reporting and charting tool.
- Applications such as Tableau desktop and Power BI desktop are specifically designed for Data Analytics and visualizations. They provide easy-to-use analysis tools with extensive charting options.

Key Words

bar (or column) chart (*116*) A data visualization using vertical/horizontal bars that represent the total amount of observations in that category.

categorical data (*115*) A form of qualitative data that are represented either by words or by non-meaningful numerical data.

continuous data (*119*) Numerical data that can take on any numerical value.

dashboard (*113*) A graphical summary of various measures tracked by a company.

data visualization (*110*) The graphic representation of data, often in the form of a graph, chart, or other image.

discrete data (*119*) Numerical data that take on whole number (integer) values.

dynamic report (*113*) A report characterized by constant update, change, or activity.

explanatory data visualization (*113*) A graphical representation useful in communicating the findings of the analysis to stakeholders.

exploratory data analysis (*111*) An initial investigation of the data generally using summary statistics and graphical representations.

exploratory data visualization (*111*) A graphical representation that is useful for uncovering patterns and useful insights in to the data, generally as part of descriptive or diagnostic analytics.

filled geographic map (118) A graphical representation that uses shading, tinting, or patterns to display how a value differs across geographic regions, such as states or countries.

line chart (*120*) A visualization of data in the form of points that connect in a straight line.

nominal data (*115*) Categorical data that cannot be ranked (such as transaction type (purchase or return).

numerical data (*116*) Data represented by meaningful numbers, such as a transaction amount, net sales, or the score on an exam.

ordinal data (*116*) Categorical data with natural, ranked categories [such as letter grades (e.g., A, B, C, D, and F) and Olympic medals (e.g., gold, silver, and bronze)].

pie chart (*116*) A data visualization in the form of a circle divided into sections representing the category's proportion of the whole.

proportion (*116*) The number of observations in one category; that number is then divided by the grand total number of all available observations.

scatterplot (*120*) A graphical representation that plots two variables each on its own axis.

stacked bar chart (*116*) A type of bar chart data visualization that represents the proportional contribution of individual data points as compared to the total.

static report (*113*) A one-time report that remains unchanged.

storytelling (*125*) As part of communicating the results to the stakeholder, ensuring that the message conveyed by the analyst (accountant) is meaningful and relevant.

time series data (*120*) Values for a single variable at different points over time such as days, months, or years.

word cloud (*117*) A collection of words depicted in different sizes, with the larger font size reflecting the greater frequency of the word in the underlying dataset.

Appendix A

A Review of Sample Charts and Their Uses

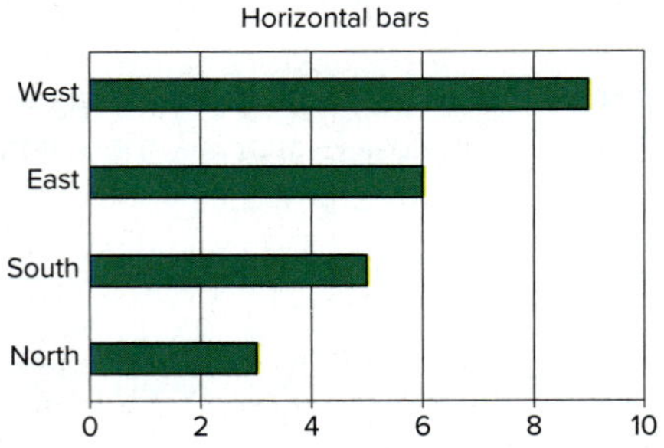

Use horizontal bar charts to show categorical information at a single point in time; the categories are typically nominal variables—that is, names of things. Horizontal bar charts can be used to show more categories/things than column charts. The purpose is to compare information among categories.

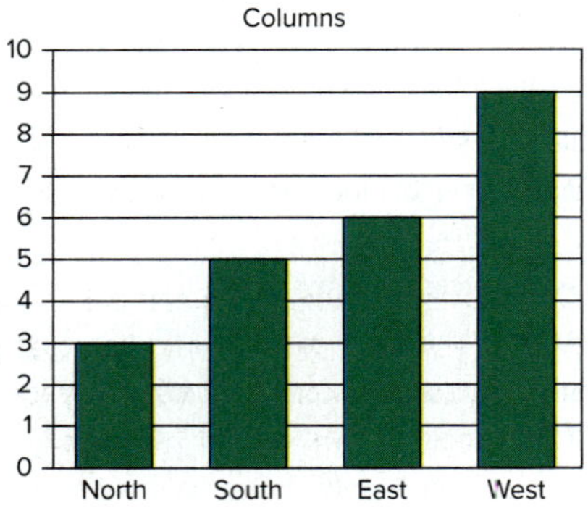

Use vertical column charts to show categorical information; the categories are typically ordinal variables—that is, ordered within a series. Column charts are generally used to show fewer categories than bar charts. The purpose is to compare information among categories.

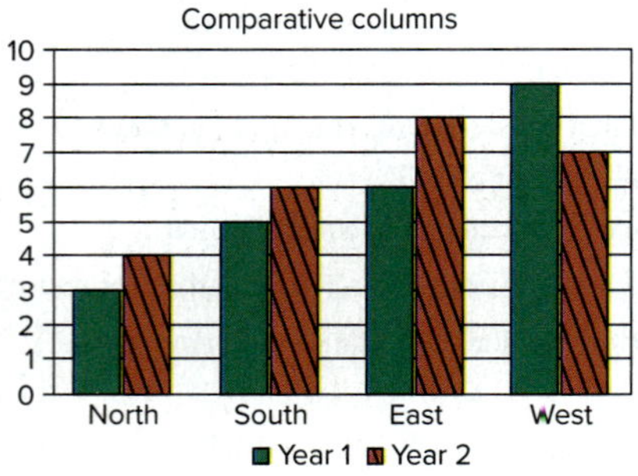

Use comparative column charts to compare among a few different comparative categories, such as sales this year versus sales last year. Comparative column charts are often also displayed as stacked columns where both categories are shown in each column, differentiated by color. The purpose is to compare information among categories.

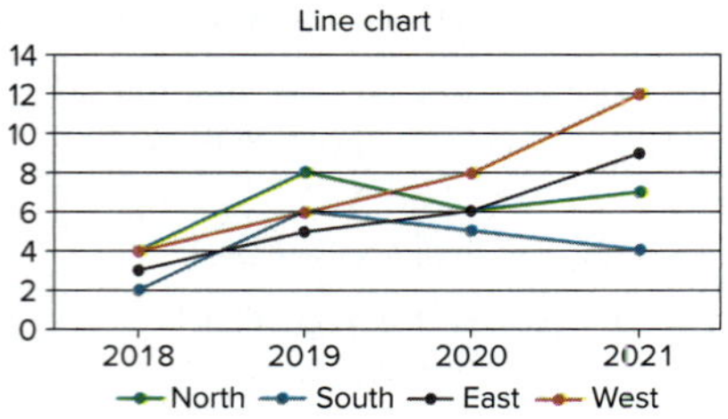

Line charts are used to show values over time, often to see trends. They can be used to show many categories over a few periods (column charts can also be used) or a few categories over many periods. The purpose is to compare information among categories.

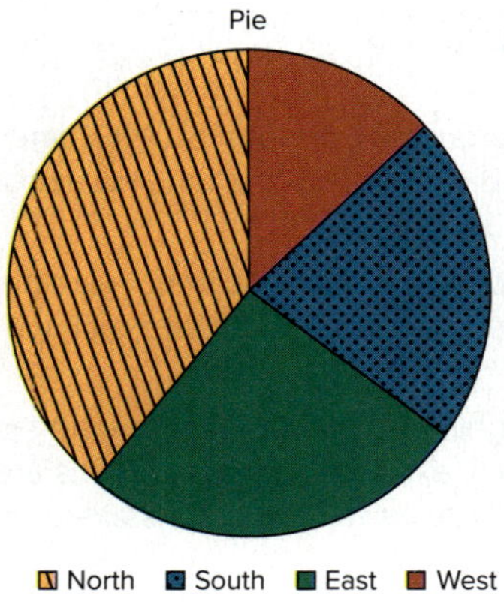

Pie charts show shares of a total for nominal variables at a single point in time. Pie charts should be limited to six or fewer slices with clear differences in size. Pie charts only show positive numbers. The purpose of a pie chart is to show the composition of a whole.

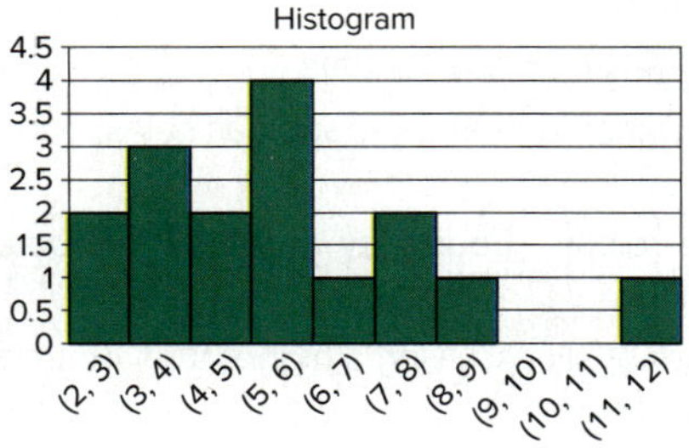

Histograms show the distribution of a single variable across a range of values. Histograms are grouped into bins and ranges of values and usually show frequencies (number of occurrences in that bin).

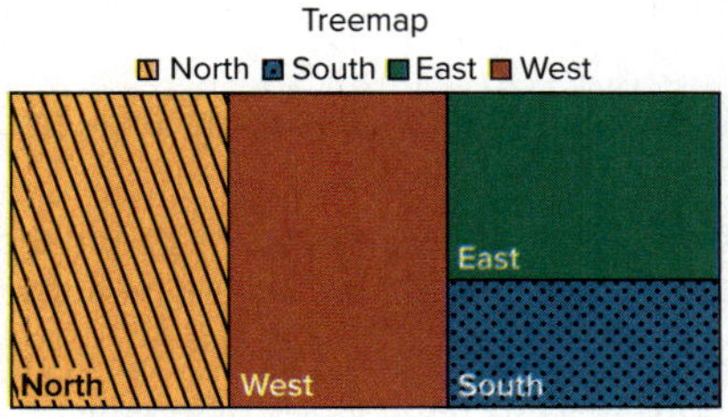

Treemaps show composition and relationships among nested categories at a single point in time. Each (positive) value is shown as a rectangle; the color and size of each rectangle depict the relative proportion of the overall tree based on a single dimension of the data.

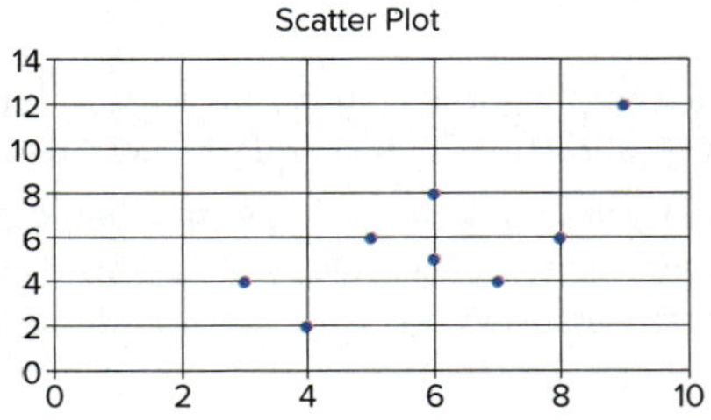

Scatter plots show correlations between two continuous variables, such as height and weight or GPA and SAT scores. Scatter plots present detailed data for the two variables; each dot represents a single data point. The data is usually accompanied by a regression line summarizing the relationship and showing outliers.

ANSWERS TO PROGRESS CHECKS

1. Visual content is more desirable because the brain processes images 60,000 times faster than it processes text (according to academic studies). For this and other reasons, 90 percent of information transmitted to the brain is visual.
2. Because of the challenges processing text, your brain will sometimes skip or not give the same attention to the written content as to visual content. The interaction rate on Facebook is higher for visual content.
3. While exploratory visualizations works to discover insights and patterns in the data (as part of the Perform the Analysis step in the AMPS model), explanatory visualizations are used to communicate the insights and findings of the analytics to interested stakeholders (as part of Share the Story in the AMPS model).
4. Tracking daily sales would require frequent updating, which would require dynamic reports, rather than static reports (which do not change much).
5. A scatterplot is used to evaluate the relationship between two variables.
6. A line chart is typically used to visualize a single variable over time, such as sales, earnings, or cash flows.
7. A word cloud could be used to summarize the relative frequency of words in Home Depot's annual report.
8. The primary deficiency in Exhibit 3.7 is the number of slices. Using a higher than optimal number of slices makes it difficult to understand the relative proportion of each of the many parts.
9. Line charts are better than bar (or column) charts at showing trends, or visualizing data over time.
10. Line graphs are generally preferred for showing trends of the past and the expected trend in the future.
11. While 95 percent of the sales observations are expected to be within the upper and the lower confidence bound, 5 percent of the time the true sales observations will be above or below these bounds.
12. The different software tools display the prior and predicted time series differently. In general, since line graphs (as illustrated in panels A and D) generally are better at showing trends, they are preferred.
13. While executive summaries briefly summarize the analysis (generally in one page, a full report provides much more detail including a combination of both text and visualizations.
14. Some report users want fuller detail to understand what was done. To gain data-derived insights into a business problem or business opportunity, some will want to know all the details, including assumptions, estimates, full data outputs, and a host of data visualizations.

Multiple Choice Questions connect

1. **(LO 3-1)** Which of the following best describes a data visualization?
   a. Part of the information value chain
   b. A tool for preparing the data
   c. A tool for recording data transactions
   d. A graphical representation that presents information to decision makers
   e. None of the above

2. **(LO 3-5)** Which of the following charts is used to show trend over time?
   a. Symbol maps
   b. Scatter plots
   c. Line charts
   d. Pie charts
   e. Treemaps
3. **(LO 3-4)** Which of the following charts is generally considered the best way to show proportions?
   a. Bar charts
   b. Scatter plots
   c. Line charts
   d. Pie charts
   e. Treemaps
4. **(LO 3-3)** Which of the following software is best at data analysis, as compared to visualizations?
   a. Power BI
   b. Excel
   c. Tableau
   d. Powerpoint
5. **(LO 3-3)** The use of visualizations to help perform the analysis is called
   a. explanatory visualizations.
   b. diagnostic visualizations.
   c. exploratory visualizations.
   d. interpretive visualizations.
6. **(LO 3-3)** The use of visualizations to communicate the results to decision makers is called
   a. explanatory visualizations.
   b. prescriptive visualizations.
   c. exploratory visualizations.
   d. diagnostic visualizations.
7. **(LO 3-4)** Which of the following statements is true?
   a. Scatterplots show values of two variables each plotted on its own axis to exhibit potential trends.
   b. Scatterplots show values of two variables each plotted on its own axis to exhibit potential correlation.
   c. Graphs show values of two variables each plotted on its own axis to exhibit potential trends.
   d. Graphs show values of two variables each plotted on its own axis to exhibit potential correlation.
   e. None of the above
8. **(LO 3-4)** Assume that **Netflix** wants to show the relative frequency of its sales by state. Which of the following would be most appropriate?
   a. Word cloud
   b. Filled geographic map
   c. Bar chart
   d. Pie chart
   e. None of the above

9. **(LO 3-4)** Which of the following software tools is more associated with getting the data ready for analysis?
   a. Tableau Desktop
   b. Tableau Prep
   c. Python
   d. SAS
   e. None of the above
10. **(LO 3-6)** If the CEO prefers less detail in their written report, the analyst might suggest
    a. an executive summary.
    b. a complete set of visualizations.
    c. a full report.
    d. a sampling of the most important visualizations
    e. None of the above

Discussion Questions connect

1. **(LO 3-2)** If Excel offers data analytics capabilities, why would anyone choose Tableau or Power BI?
2. **(LO 3-2, LO 3-6)** How are the data visualization concepts applicable to writing a report for one of your classes?
3. **(LO 3-2)** There are literally dozens of data analytics software products. If you were buying one of them, how would you compare them? Prepare a list of criteria.
4. **(LO 3-2)** Use your criteria from Discussion Question 3, compare the desktop products from Qlik Sense (www.qlik.com) and Rapid Miner (www.rapidminer.com). How do they differ from Tableau and Power BI?
5. **(LO 3-1, LO 3-4, LO 3-5)** Based on your personal experience, what kinds of charts do you use most often? What kinds of charts would accountants use most often? Why?
6. **(LO 3-1, LO 3-5)** Some argue that a picture is worth a thousand clicks. Argue for and against the use of data visualizations when reporting the results using explanatory visualizations.
7. **(LO 3-2)** Explain the difference between exploratory and explanatory visualizations. Why are their aims different from each other?

Problems connect

1. **(LO 3-2, LO 3-4, LO 3-5)** Match the data visualization listed with type of data analytics (descriptive, diagnostic, predictive, or prescriptive) it is most associated with.
   - Scatterplot
   - Time series data with forecast
   - Sensitivity analysis table evaluating assumptions made
   - Pie charts
   - Break-even graph
   - Line and bar charts
   - Box plots highlighting extreme observations
   - Histograms

2. **(LO 3-2, LO 3-4, LO 3-5)** Match each term with its definition.

Term	Definition
1. Categorical Data	a. The values of two variables, each plotted on its own axis to exhibit possible correlation
2. Trend	b. The number of observations in a particular category divided by the grand total of observations
3. Proportion	c. General direction in which something is moving
4. Numerical data	d. Data represented by meaningful numbers, such as a transaction amount, net sales, or the score on an exam
5. Scatterplot	e. Values taken on by a variable at different points in time
6. Time series data	f. A form of qualitative data that are represented either by words or by non-meaningful numerical data

3. **(LO 3-2, LO 3-4, LO 3-5)** Determine whether each of the following terms is more likely to be associated with exploratory data visualizations or explanatory data visualizations.
   - Visualizations in executive summary
   - Scatterplot
   - Visualizations in written report
   - Past time series of data to forecast performance
   - Plotting data to see if it departs from expectations as part of diagnostic analytics
   - Dashboard with dynamic updates to track performance

4. **(LO 3-1, LO 3-5)** What does the following data visualization tell us about the relationship between labor cost per lawn mowed and monthly (profit) margin (the extent to which revenues exceed expenses) as shown on the vertical axis?

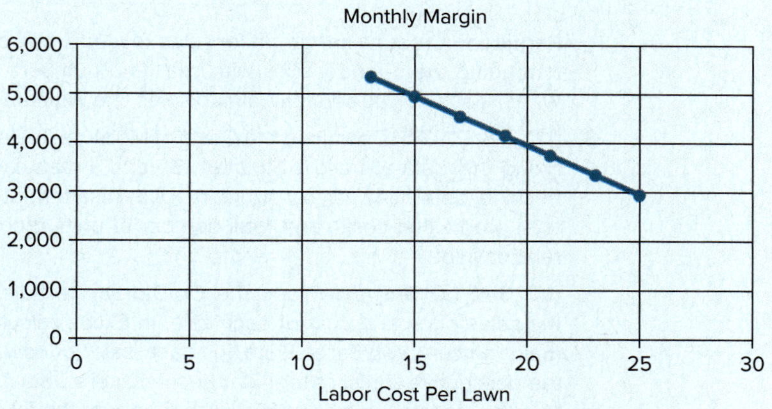

5. **(LO 3-1, LO 3-5)** Is the data visualization in Exercise 4 immediately above better or worse than the same data in the following tabular format?

Labor Cost per Lawn	Monthly Margin
13	5,350
15	4,950
17	4,550
19	4,150
21	3,750
23	3,350
25	2,950

6. **(LO 3-4, LO 3-5)** Download the dataset, Sales Growth Dataset.xlsx, which has sales data for years 20X1 and 20X2 for a set of publicly traded companies over a recent year. Calculate the sales growth using (New–Old)/Old or $(Sales_{20X2}–Sales_{20X1})/Sales_{20X2}$ for each company.

Required

1. Use Excel, Tableau, or Power BI to plot the results using a column chart, histogram, or a box plot. Which of these data visualization types will be most useful in diagnostic analytics to find outliers or anomalies?
2. Do the results skew to the left or to the right? What would you conclude from the results?

7. **(LO 3-5)** Use the following data to graph the sales revenue and net income for Walmart from 2012 to 2020 in Excel.

The data file, Walmart Trend Analysis.xlsx, is available in Connect or via the Additional Student Resources page. (Note the data is in $ millions.)

Year	Sales Revenue	Net Income
2012	$ 468,651	$ 17,756
2013	$ 476,294	$ 16,695
2014	$ 485,651	$ 17,099
2015	$ 482,130	$ 15,080
2016	$ 485,873	$ 14,293
2017	$ 500,343	$ 10,523
2018	$ 514,343	$ 6,670
2019	$ 523,964	$ 14,881
2020	$ 559,151	$ 13,510

Required: Create a bar graph for sales revenue, and create a line graph for net income, formatting the x- and y-axes with year and numbers inserting appropriate chart titles. What trends do you see for Walmart sales and Walmart net income over this time period?

8. **(LO 3-4, LO 3-5)** Download the Costs of Moistureshield Production dataset in Excel. Analyzing this data will allow **Moisture Shield,** a manufacturer of wood-plastic composite decking, determine its cost structure. Use a scatterplot to show the relationship between total production costs, and total number of units produced. Add a trendline to see the relationship.

9. **(LO 3-4, LO 3-5)** Download the SkyDio Drone Sales Journal dataset in Excel. Note the sales price and cost of each sale. In Excel, calculate the gross margin percentage (Sales Price–Cost)/Sales Price for each sale (or row in the sales journal). Use either the descriptive statistics tool featured in Excel's Data Analysis ToolPak or Excel functions to compute the summary statistics and answer the following questions.

Required:

a. Create a histogram of the gross margin percentages. (Hint: **Insert > Charts > Statistic Chart > Histogram** after selecting data range.) Submit this screenshot to your instructor if assigned.

b. How many transactions were for 47 percent or higher?

c. How many transactions were for 40 percent or lower?

10. **(LO 3-4, LO 3-5)** Download the sp-500-historical-annual-returns dataset in Excel from Connect or Additional Student Resources.[7] Note the annual stock market returns to investment in the S&P 500. Create a visualization in Excel using a bar chart. Note the volatility of returns over the years, which is an indicator that the stock market is a risky investment.

[7]Source: https://www.macrotrends.net/2526/sp-500-historical-annual-returns.

Required:

1. Create a bar chart of the annual returns (*Hint:* **Insert > Charts > Bar Chart**) or column chart of the annual returns (*Hint:* **Insert > Charts > Column Chart**).
2. Label the vertical axis as "Annual Percentage Return", the horizontal axis as "Year", and the chart title as "Annual Returns to the S&P 500 Index".

11. **(LO 3-4, LO 3-5)** Download the nasdaq-by-year-historical-annual-returns dataset in Excel from Connect or Additional Student Resources.[8] Note the annual stock market returns to investment in the NASDAQ stock market index. Use any type of visualization (such as histograms, bar charts, or column charts) that will allow you to complete the following requirements.

Required:

1. Create a chart of the annual returns (*Hint:* **Insert > Charts**). Submit this screenshot to your instructor if assigned.
2. What is the average return on the NASDAQ market? The median return? *Hint:* Use AVERAGE() and MEDIAN() functions in Excel.
3. Based on the visualization, how many annual returns were 20 percent or higher? *Hint:* Perform a count.
4. Based on the visualization, how many annual returns were negative? *Hint:* Perform a count.

[8]Source: https://www.macrotrends.net/2623/nasdaq-by-year-historical-annual-returns.

LABS ASSOCIATED WITH CHAPTER 3

The multiple choice assessment questions for each lab are assignable via Connect. Materials are also available for courses not utilizing Connect via the Solutions Manual.

Lab 3-1 Excel: Creating Column Charts, Line Charts and Pie Charts for Tesla Sales and Earnings

Keywords

Data visualizations, line charts, bar charts, pie charts

Lab Insight

Data visualizations are powerful ways to communicate results. What is the most effective way to communicate a company's performance?

The goal of this lab is to communicate **Tesla's** performance using various types of visualizations.

Required:

Create Column Charts, line graphs, and pie charts for Tesla's net sales and net income from 2008 to 2021.

Ask the Question

What data visualizations best display Tesla financial performance from 2008 to 2021?

Master the Data

Open Excel file Lab 3-1 Data.xlsx. Here is the data dictionary:

Data Dictionary

Year: Year of financial performance reported
Net Income: Net Income for Tesla during the named year
Net Sales: Net sales for Tesla during the named year

Perform the Analysis

Analysis Task 1: Create Column Chart, Line Chart, and Pie Chart for Tesla Sales Revenue

1. Highlight cells C2:C15.
2. Select **Insert>Chart>2D Column (or Bar) Chart.**
3. Select Chart Design>Data>Select Data and the popup box as shown in Lab Exhibit 3-1.1.

Lab Exhibit 3-1.1

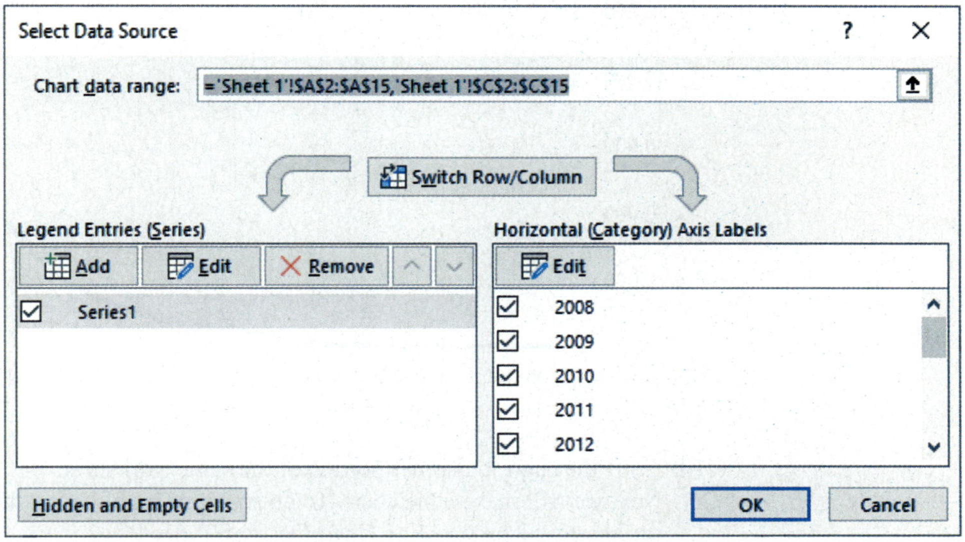

4. Under Horizontal (Category) Axis Labels, click Edit. Highlight cells A2:A15 (as shown in Lab Exhibit 3-1.1) to put the years in as the x-axis labels.
5. Change the "Chart Title" to "Annual Tesla Sales Revenue".
6. The resulting Column Chart will be as shown in Lab Exhibit 3-1.2.

Lab Exhibit 3-1.2

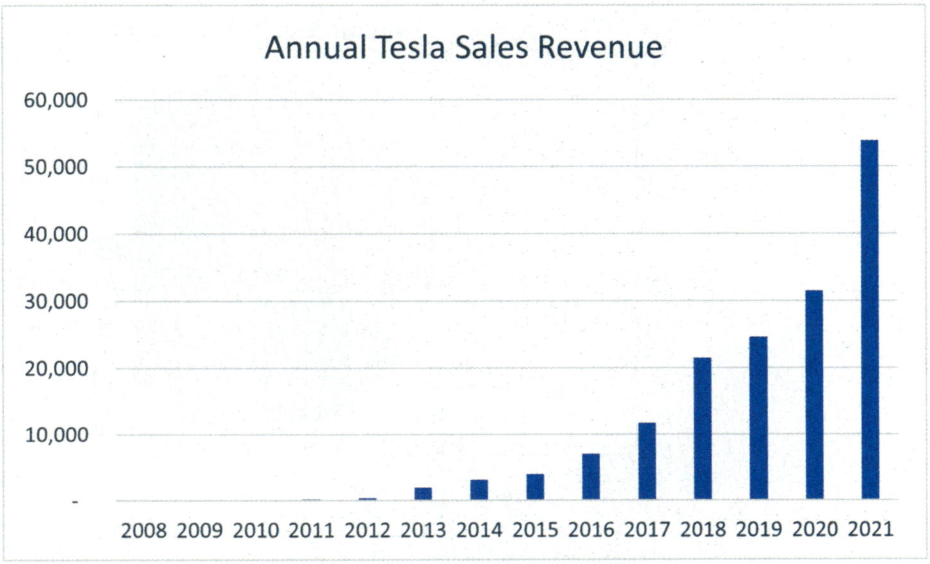

7. Copy the chart to another portion of the same worksheet.
8. Next we will make a line chart. To do so, while highlighting the copied chart, change the chart type by selecting **Chart Design>Type>Line.**

9. The resulting line graph is as shown in Lab Exhibit 3-1.3.

Lab Exhibit 3-1.3

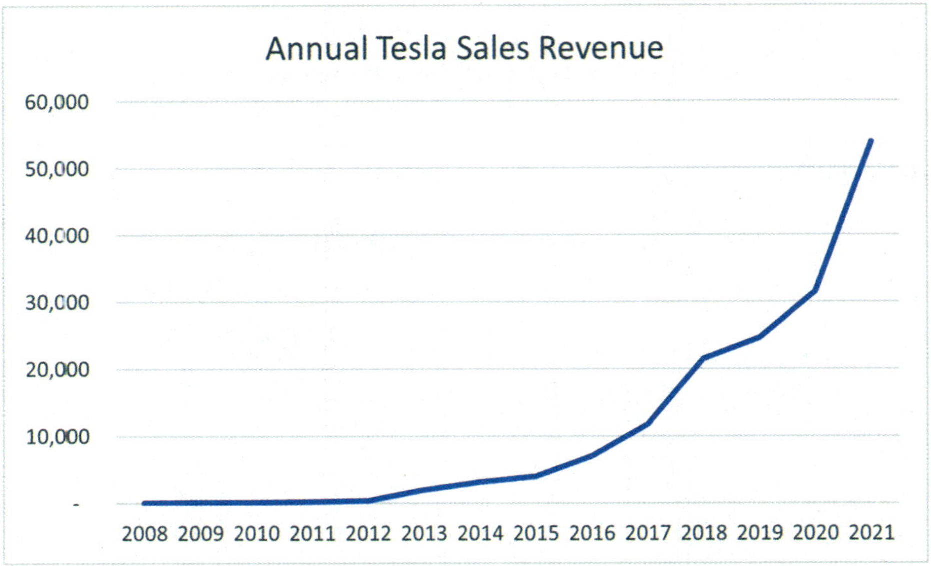

10. Copy the chart to another portion of the same worksheet.
11. Next we will make a pie chart. To do so, while highlighting the copied chart, change the chart type by selecting Chart Design>Type>Pie.
12. To show the years, add a legend by selecting **Chart Design> Add Chart Element > Legend > Bottom.**
13. Right-click on the pie chart itself, and select "Add Data Labels" to add the specific numbers to each slice of the pie (as shown in Lab Exhibit 3-1.4).

Lab Exhibit 3-1.4

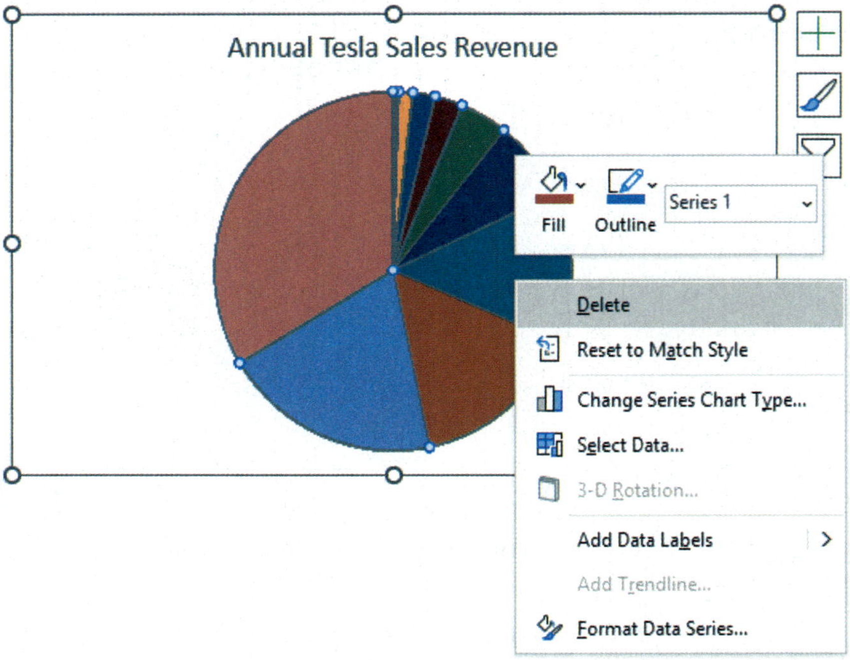

14. The final visualization is as shown in Lab Exhibit 3-1.5.

Lab Exhibit 3-1.5

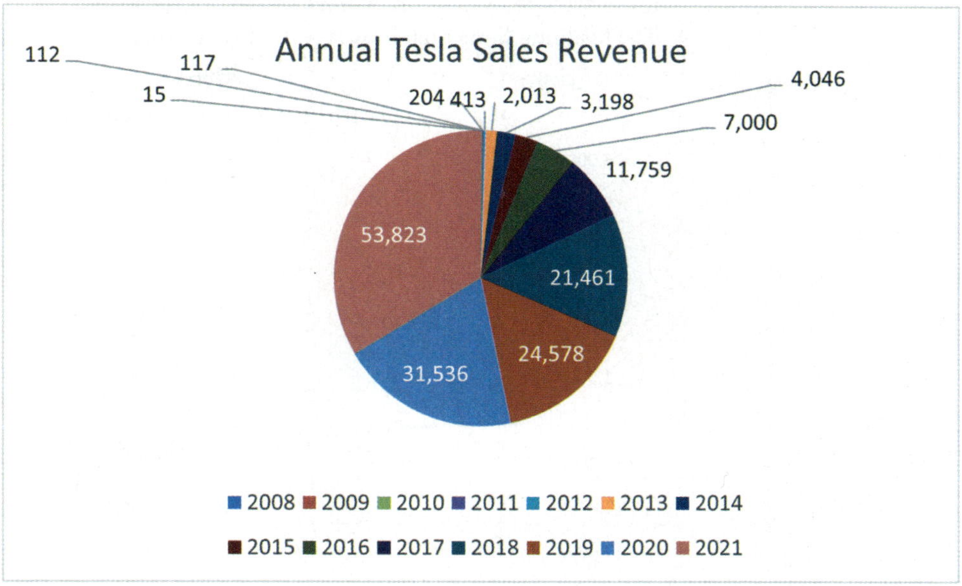

Analysis Task 2: Create Column Chart, Line Chart and Pie Chart for Tesla Net Income

1. Highlight cells B2:B15.
2. Select **Insert>Chart>2D Column (or Bar) Chart.**
3. Select Chart Design>Data>Select Data.
4. Under Horizontal (Category) Axis Labels, click Edit. Highlight cells A2:A15 to put the years in as the x-axis labels.
5. Change the "Chart Title" to "Annual Tesla Net Income".
6. The resulting Column Chart will be as shown in Lab Exhibit 3-1.6.

Lab Exhibit 3-1.6

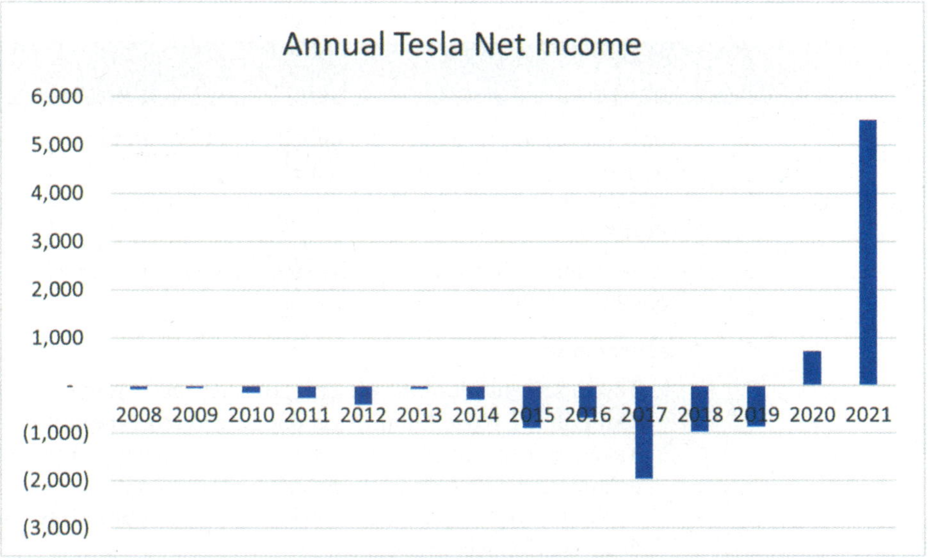

7. Copy the chart to another portion of the same worksheet.
8. Next we will make a line chart. To do so, while highlighting the copied chart, change the chart type by selecting **Chart Design>Type>Line.**
9. The resulting line graph is as shown in Lab Exhibit 3-1.7.

Lab Exhibit 3-1.7

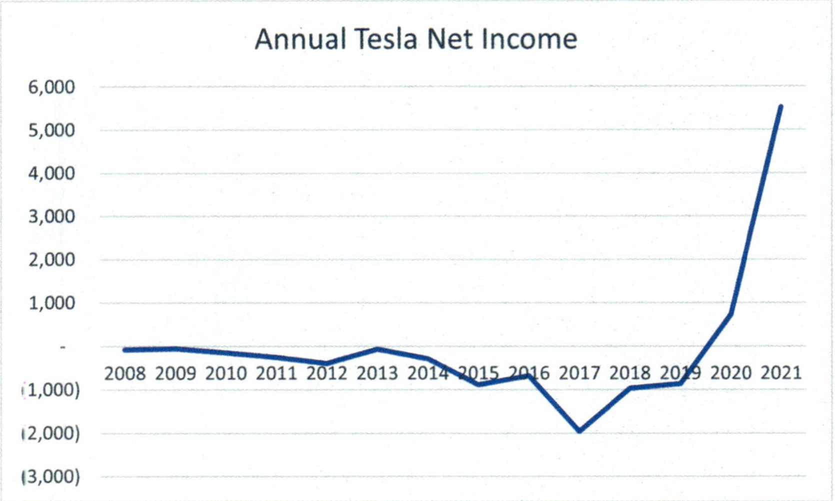

Share the Story

As part of the analysis performed in this lab, we have made many visualizations. Which ones are best? Which ones would be given to management, or should we give them all of the visualizations to better see the story?

Assessment:

1. Take a screenshot of the pie chart of sales, paste it into a Word document named "Lab 3-1 Excel Submission.docx", and label the screenshot Submission 1.
2. Take a screenshot of the line chart of net income, paste it into the same Word document, and label the screenshot Submission 2.
3. Answer the questions in Connect and upload your Lab 3-1 Excel Submission.docx via Connect if assigned.

Lab 3-1 Alternate

Apply the same procedures as applied in Lab 3-1 to the time series of Amazon sales and net income. Open Alt Lab 3-1 Data.xlsx.

Required:

Create column charts, line graphs, and pie charts for Amazon's net sales and net income from 2008 to 2021.

Assessment:

1. Take a screenshot of the pie chart of sales, paste it into a Word document named "Alt Lab 3-1 Excel Submission.docx", and label the screenshot Submission 1.
2. Take a screenshot of the line chart of net income, paste it into the same Word document, and label the screenshot Submission 2.
3. Answer the questions in Connect and upload your Lab Alt 3-1 Excel Submission.docx via Connect if assigned.

Lab 3-2 Power BI: Creating a Word Cloud

Keywords

Data visualization, frequency data visualization, categorical data

Lab Insight

Data visualizations are powerful ways to communicate results. What is the effective way to summarize a survey with lots of words? We'll consider word clouds to answer the question, "What attributes did your best professor to date have?".

We will perform the analysis in Power BI, since it has an easy add-in.

Required:

Create a word chart summarizing the survey.

Ask the Question

What attributes did your best professor to date have?

Master the Data

Open Excel file Lab 3-2 Data.xlsx in Excel. Browse the data and see how it is all stacked in one column.

Perform the Analysis

Analysis Task 1: Load the Data in Power BI.

1. Open Power BI.
2. Select **File>Get data>Excel Workbook** and then select Lab 3-2 Data.xlsx.
3. Put a checkmark in Survey Response and select Load (as shown in Lab Exhibit 3-2.1.

Lab Exhibit 3-2.1

Microsoft Power BI

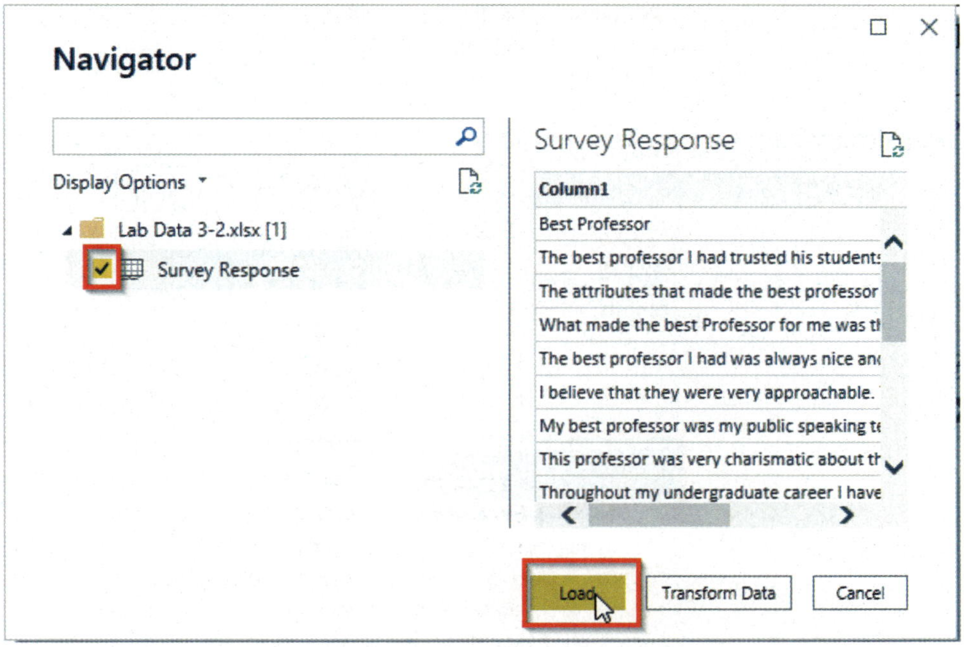

Analysis Task 2: Load the Word Cloud Visualization in Power BI.

1. Once the data is loaded, in the visualizations area, click on the three dots to "Get more visuals" as shown in Lab Exhibit 3-2.2.

Lab Exhibit 3-2.2

Microsoft Power BI

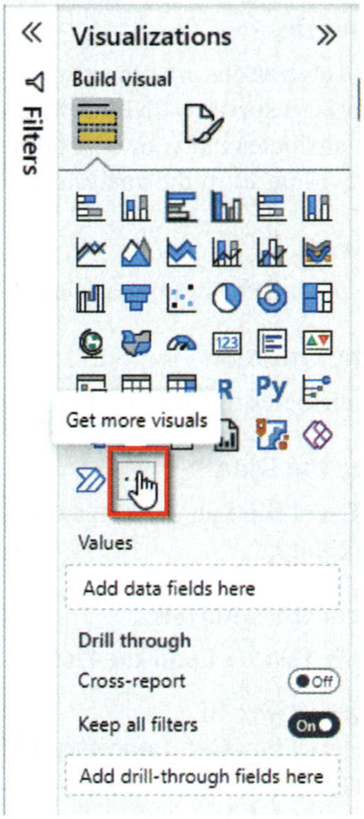

2. A dialog box will open up. Search "Word Cloud". Add the word cloud visual, as shown in Lab Exhibit 3-2.3.

Lab Exhibit 3-2.3

Microsoft Power BI

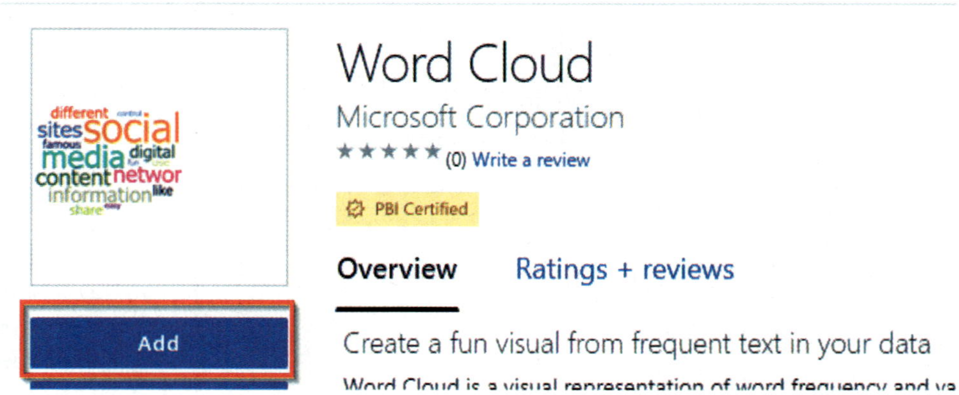

Analysis Task 3: Create the Word Cloud

1. In the visualizations area, click on the Word Cloud visual (as shown in Lab Exhibit 3-2.4).

Lab Exhibit 3-2.4

Microsoft Power BI

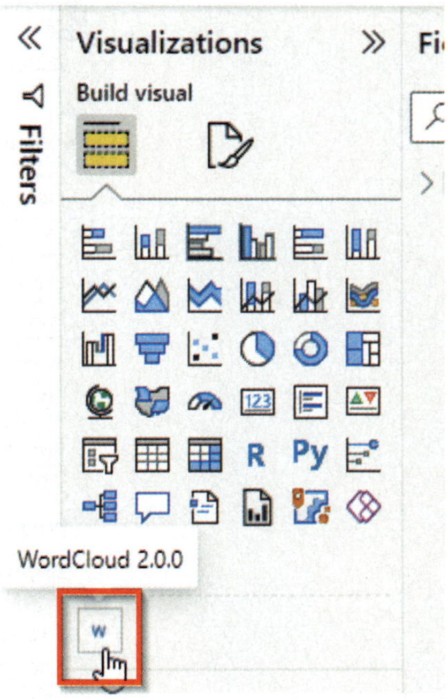

2. Under Fields, Select "Survey Response" and then put a check mark next to column 1. The word cloud will appear. We'll next work to refine it.
3. Under Visualizations, Formatting, Visual, General, make these three modifications (as shown in Lab Exhibit 3-2.5)
   A. Change the Max Number of Words to 50, to allow us to highlight fewer words.
   B. Make sure Stop Words are toggled to "On" and click toggle to "On" for the Default Stop Words. This takes out commonly occurring words like "and" and "the".
   C. Add three words to the Stop Words, to take out words that are part of the question.

Lab Exhibit 3-2.5

Microsoft Power BI

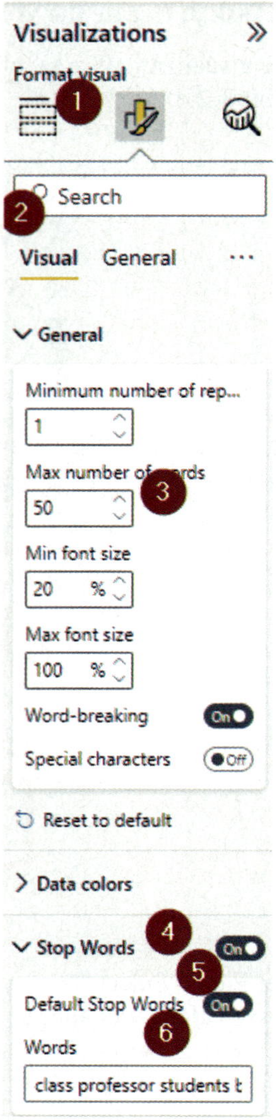

4. The resulting word cloud visualization is as shown in Lab Exhibit 3-2.6.

Lab Exhibit 3-2.6

Microsoft Power BI

Share the Story

The word cloud visualization serves as an effective means of summarizing the most important words when describing the best professor. This will cause the analyst to reflect on the attributes that characterize the best professor.

Assessment:

1. Take a screenshot of the final word cloud, paste it into a Word document named "Lab 3-2 Submission.docx".
2. Answer the questions in Connect and upload your Lab 3-2 Submission.docx via Connect if assigned.

Lab 3-2 Alternate

Apply the same procedures in Power BI as applied in Lab 3-2 to the new dataset in Alt Lab 3-2 Data.xlsx. Change the max number of words in the word cloud to 100, and make sure the default stop words are on, and remove the words "class", "university", and "best". This dataset summarizes student responses to determine the attributes of student's best university class.

Required:

Create a word chart summarizing the survey.

Assessment:

1. Take a screenshot of the final word cloud, paste it into a Word document named "Alt Lab 3-2 Submission.docx".
2. Answer the questions in Connect and upload your Alt Lab 3-2 Submission.docx via Connect if assigned.

Lab 3-3 Excel: Using Scatterplots and Regression to Understand the Relationship between Advertising Expenditures and Sales

Keywords

advertising, sales revenue

Lab Insight

Are revenues dependent on advertising expenses? The more consumers know or are reminded about a product and its qualities via advertising, the more of that product they supposedly will buy. However, it isn't always clear how big that impact is. Each company will be interested in knowing what the returns are to the advertising expenses for their *specific firm.* For this reason, companies will evaluate the relationship both by 1) using a visualization (scatter plot) and 2) running a regression to further understand that relationship. The outcome variable is sales revenue that arguably comes as a result of the input variable, advertising expenses.

- Dependent variable: Sales revenue
- Independent variable: Advertising expenses

Required:

1. Create a scatter plot evaluating the relationship between advertising expenditures and sales revenue.
2. Using regression analysis, determine the relationship between advertising expenditures and sales revenue.

Ask the Question

What is the relationship between advertising expense and sales for our company?

Master the Data

Open Excel File Lab 3-3 Data.xlsx, and browse the data.

Data Dictionary

Month: The month number from the beginning of the analysis until the end of the analysis

Date: Month when revenues and advertising expenses are realized

Revenues: The monthly revenue for this company

Advertising Expenses: The monthly advertising expenses for this company

Step 1:

Let's start off by plotting the data. Highlight C1:D37. Select **Insert > Charts > Scatter** from the menu bar (as shown in Lab Exhibit 3-3.1).

Lab Exhibit 3-3.1

	A	B	C	D
1	Month	Date	Advertising Expenses	Revenues
2	1	1/1/2025	51,891	1,000,052
3	2	2/1/2025	52,750	1,001,166
4	3	3/1/2025	50,668	1,001,966
5	4	4/1/2025	51,106	1,003,704
6	5	5/1/2025	51,316	1,004,956
7	6	6/1/2025	52,841	1,005,937

Choose layout 3 from the Quick Layout on the ribbon (as shown in Lab Exhibit 3-3.2).

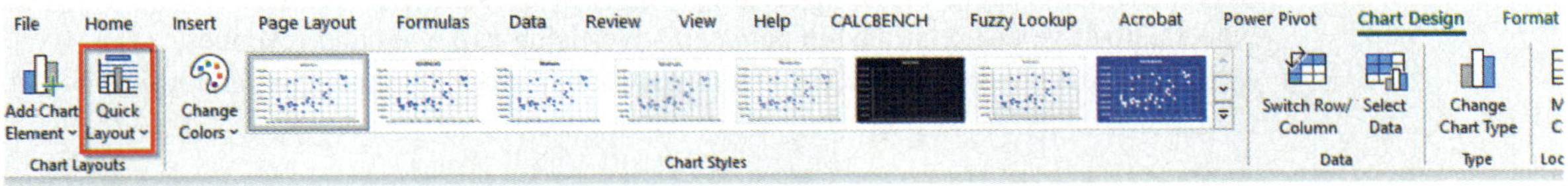

Lab Exhibit 3-3.2

The result is a graph plotting revenues and expenses (as shown in Lab Exhibit 3-3.3).

Lab Exhibit 3-3.3

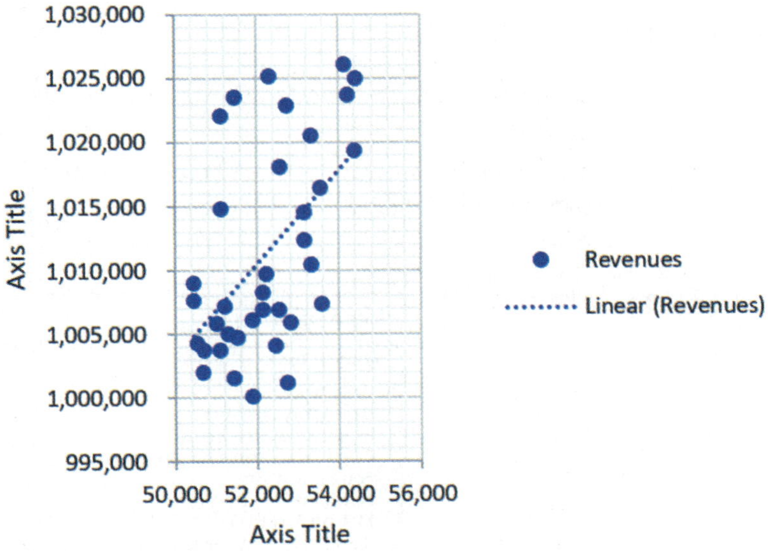

Format the X-axis as Advertising Expense and the Y-axis as Revenues. Given this graph

- Does it appear that there is a relationship between advertising expenses and revenues? Does the relationship appear to be positive? Why did we put the advertising expenses on the X-axis? Is it because we believe that advertising expenses might be a predictor of revenues? Or that revenue is a function of expenses [Revenues = f(Advertising expense)]?

Step 2: Regression Analysis

To see if there is a statistical relationship between advertising expenses and sales revenue, run a regression specifying the following:

- Dependent variable: Sales revenue
- Independent variable: Advertising expenses

We're now ready to perform the analysis.

Regression analysis is a way of using mathematics and statistics to determine if a variable has an impact on an outcome and how big that impact is on the outcome. Regression analysis helps to answer the following questions: Which factors matter most in predicting the outcome? Which factors can we ignore?

Sometimes it is good to think through the variables; for example, it would seem that the greater the advertising expense, the more likely sales will increase. Therefore, we would expect a positive (+) relationship between advertising expenses and revenues.

To run the regression, select the Data Analytics Toolpak (as shown in Lab Exhibit 3-3.4).

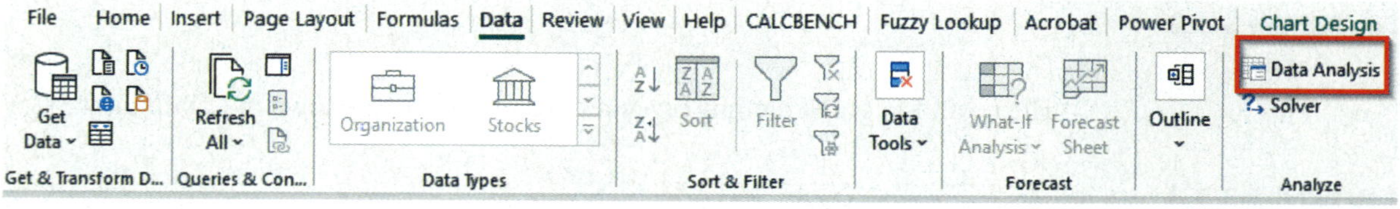

Lab Exhibit 3-3.4

Step 3

To perform the regression, select **Data > Analysis > Data Analysis.** A dialog box (as shown in Lab Exhibit 3-3.5) will open. Select Regression and click OK.

Lab Exhibit 3-3.5

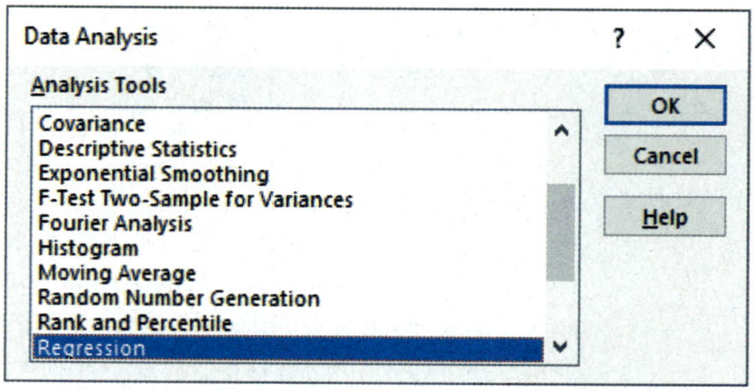

Select the dependent variable (or Y Range). Our dependent variable is Revenues, so enter $D$1:$D$37 in the Input Y Range.

Next select the independent variable (or X Range). The variable Advertising Expenses are independent variables, so enter $C$1:$C$37 in the Input X Range.

Because we highlighted the labels in the data range, click on "Labels". Select "New Worksheet Ply" to get the results in a new worksheet. Click OK. The result should appear as shown in Lab Exhibit 3-3.6.

Lab Exhibit 3-3.6

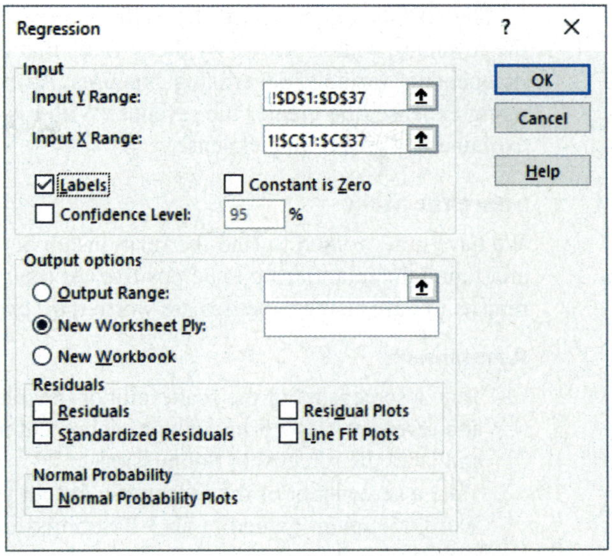

Select "OK" to get the regression results shown in Lab Exhibit 3-3.7.

Exhibit 3-3.7

SUMMARY OUTPUT					
Regression Statistics					
Multiple R	0.5359				
R Square	0.2872				
Adjusted R Square	0.2663				
Standard Error	6938.7347				
Observations	36				
ANOVA					
	df	*SS*	*MS*	*F*	*Significance F*
Regression	1	659621859.2	6.6E+08	13.70044	0.000755105
Residual	34	1636965319	48146039		
Total	35	2296587178			
	Coefficients	*Standard Error*	*t Stat*	*P-value*	*Lower 95%*
Intercept	819247.455	51893.259	15.787	0.000	713787.665
Advertising Expenses	3.678	0.994	3.701	0.001	1.658

There are many things to note about this regression. The first is that the regression did better than chance at predicting revenues. We note that the "Significance F" result is very small, even zero, suggesting there is virtually zero probability that the revenues can be explained by no independent variables rather than by a model that has independent variables. This is exactly the situation we want, which suggests that we will be able to identify those factors that explain revenues.

There is another statistic used to measure how well the model did at predicting the dependent variable of interest rates. The adjusted R-squared is a value between 0 and 1. An adjusted R-squared value of 0 represents no ability to explain the dependent variable, and an adjusted R-squared value of 1 represents perfect ability to explain the dependent variable. In this case, the adjusted R-squared value is 0.266, which represents a low ability to explain the level of revenues given advertising expenses.

The statistics also report that taking advertising expenses into account helps predict the revenues. This is shown by the "t-Stat" that is greater than 2 (or less than −2) for the independent variable, advertising expenses. As expected, the greater the amount of advertising expense, the greater the revenue. With a *p*-value of less than 0.05, revenues can be explained by advertising expense.

Share the Story

We have now worked to find the relationship between advertising expenses and revenues and found the relationship to be positive. At this point, management needs to decide if the returns to advertising expenses are worth their expected payoff.

Assessment:

1. Take a screenshot of the scatterplot of the relationship between advertising expenses and revenues, paste it into a word document named "Lab 3-3 Submission.docx", and label the screenshot Submission 1.
2. Take a screenshot of the regression output predicting revenues, paste it into a Word document named "Lab 3-3 Submission.docx", and label the screenshot Submission 2.
3. Answer the questions in Connect and upload your Lab 3-3 Submission.docx, if assigned.

Lab 3-3 Alternate

Apply the same steps as Lab 3-3 to the Alt Lab 3-3 Data.xlsx dataset.

Required:

1. Using regression analysis, determine the relationship between advertising expenses and sales revenue.

Open Excel File Alt Lab 3-3 Data.xlsx. Here is the data dictionary for the dataset:

Data Dictionary

Month: The month number from beginning of the analysis until the end of the analysis

Date: Month when revenues and advertising expenses are realized

Advertising Expenses: The monthly advertising expenses for this company

Revenues: The monthly revenue for this company

Assessment:

1. Take a screenshot of the scatterplot of the relationship between advertising expenses and revenues, paste it into a Word document named "Alt Lab 3-3 Excel SS.docx", and label the screenshot Submission 1.
2. Take a screenshot of the regression output predicting revenues, paste it into your Word document named "Alt Lab 3-3 Excel SS.docx", and label the screenshot Submission 2.
3. Answer the questions in Connect and upload your Alt Lab 3-3 SS.docx, if assigned.

Unless otherwise credited screenshots: Source: Microsoft Excel

Magnifying glass: PureSolution/Shutterstock

Lab 3-4 Excel: Time Series Analysis of IBM Sales and Earnings

Keywords

Predictive Analysis, Forecasting, Time Series

Lab Insight

There are many reasons to forecast a company's future performance. For example, it may need to predict sales to determine needed manufacturing capacity, or it may be predicting cash flows to determine if it will need a loan or have sufficient cash on hand without taking a loan. In addition, an investor might be forecasting a company's earnings to determine whether the company's stock will be a good investment.

The goal of this lab is to forecast sales and earnings for **IBM** using Excel's Forecast Sheet. (*Note:* Excel's Forecast Sheet is not available on Excel for Mac computers.)

Required:

1. Using Excel's Forecast Sheet, forecast future sales for IBM.
2. Using Excel's Forecast Sheet, forecast future income before extraordinary items for IBM.

Ask the Question

What will IBM's 2022, 2023, and 2024 quarterly sales and earnings be given times series (past quarterly sales and earnings from 2010 to 2021)?

Master the Data

Looking at IBM's financial statements, we accumulate the values of quarterly sales and earnings from 2010 to 2021.

Open Excel file Lab 3-4 Data.xlsx. Here is the data dictionary:

Data Dictionary

Date: Quarter end date

Net Sales: Net sales for IBM during the respective quarter

Income: Income (before extraordinary items) for IBM during the respective quarter

Perform the Analysis

Analysis Task 1: Forecast Sales.

1. To start the forecast analysis, highlight one of the numbers in column B (for sales), and then click on **Data > Forecast > Forecast Sheet.** The dialog box in Lab Exhibit 3-4.1 will open up, beginning our forecast of IBM net sales in 2022, 2023, and 2024. The Forecast Sheet is available only for Windows, and not for Macs. If you use a Mac, you may need to use a computer lab or a virtual desktop to get access to this functionality.

Lab Exhibit 3-4.1

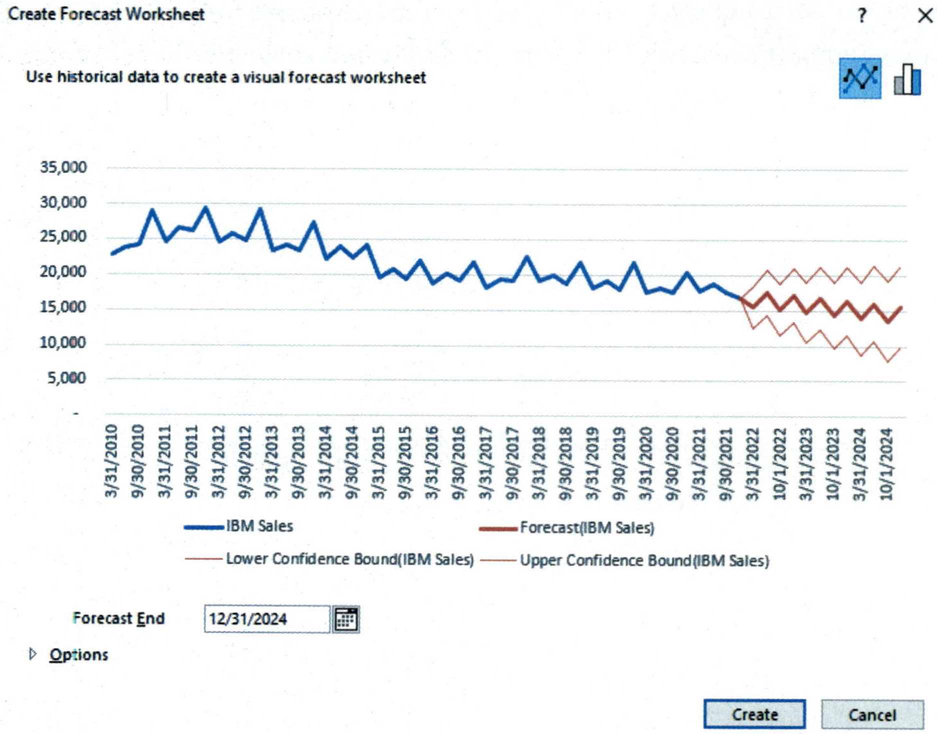

2. Note the seasonality of the data with reasonably consistent crests and troughs over the four quarters. Click on the chevron next to Options near the bottom left.
3. Consider the various options, including the dates forecast start and end, the confidence interval, the timeline range and value range, and how missing points and duplicates are handled.
4. Select "Include forecast statistics" near the bottom left and select the Create button at the bottom.
5. Note the new tab with forecast statistics with forecasts for each quarter in 2022, 2023, and 2024. Also note the lower and the upper confidence bound of the forecast. The forecast sheet suggests that there is a 95 percent chance that the actual sales will be in the range between the lower and the upper confidence bound.
6. The forecast graph should look as shown in Lab Exhibit 3-4.2.

Lab Exhibit 3-4.2

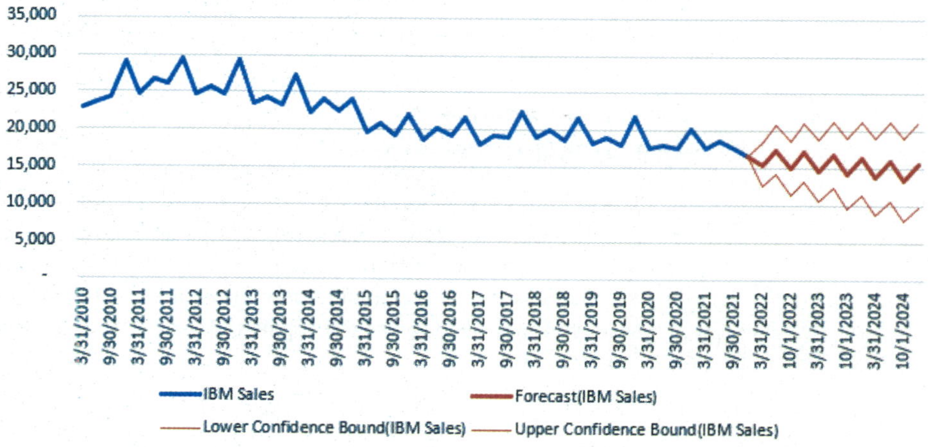

7. Note the widening between the confidence bounds on the graph. Calculate the difference between the lower and the upper bound, noting that, over time, the difference between the lower and upper confidence bounds get larger because the further we get out in time, the less certainty we have of the outcome.
   - At 3/31/2022, the difference between upper and lower confidence bound is 18,441.04–12,569.56 = 5,871.48.
   - At 12/31/24, the difference between upper and lower confidence bound is 21,317.63–9,822.83 = 11,494.80.

Analysis Task 2: Forecast Earnings (Income Before Extraordinary Items).

1. Do the same analysis for Income Before Extraordinary Items with the data in Sheet1 in column E, repeating steps 1–6 in Analysis Task 1 with the new data. We choose income before any possible extraordinary items because predicting extraordinary items is very difficult to do.
   A. The graph for the forecast of future income from extraordinary items is as shown in Lab Exhibit 3-4.3.

Lab Exhibit 3-4.3

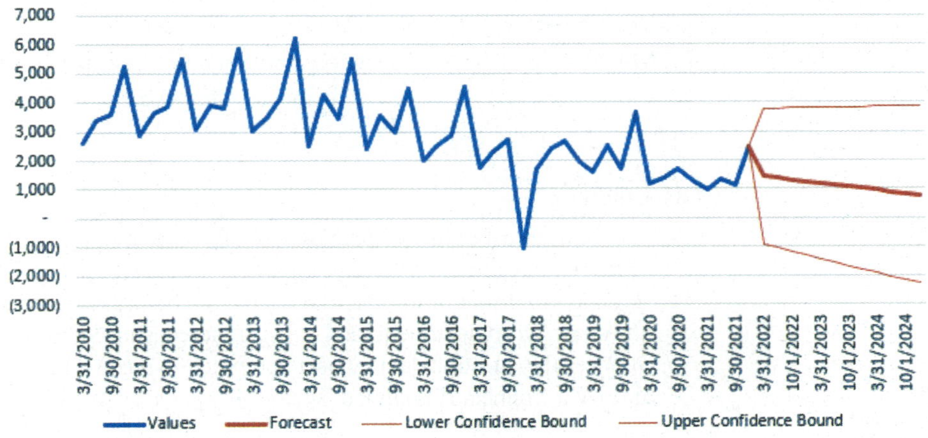

Share the Story

We have now developed a forecast for future sales and income before extraordinary items. This forecast will be helpful for management, investors, lenders, and other stakeholders.

Assessment:

1. Take a screenshot of the forecast of sales, paste it into a Word document named "Lab 3-4 Excel Submission.docx", and label the screenshot Submission 1.
2. Take a screenshot of the forecast of income before extraordinary items, paste it into the same Word document, and label the screenshot Submission 2.
3. Answer the questions in Connect and upload your Lab 3-4 Excel Submission.docx via Connect if assigned.

Lab 3-4 Alternate

Apply the same procedures as applied in Lab 3-4 to the new dataset in Alt Lab 3-4 Data.xlsx. While Lab 3-4 procedures were for the time series analysis for IBM, this alternate dataset will be for Netflix.

Required:

1. Using Excel's Forecast Sheet, forecast future sales for Netflix.
2. Using Excel's Forecast Sheet, forecast future income before extraordinary items for Netflix.

Open Excel file Alt Lab 3-4 Data.xlsx. Here is the data dictionary:

Data Dictionary

Date: Quarter begin date

NFLX Sales: Net sales for Netflix during the respective quarter

NFLX Income from Extraordinary Items: Income before extraordinary items for Netflix

Assessment:

1. Take a screenshot of the forecast of sales, paste it into a Word document named "Alt Lab 3-4 Excel Submission.docx", and label the screenshot Submission 1.
2. Take a screenshot of the forecast of income before extraordinary items, paste it into the same Word document, and label the screenshot Submission 2.
3. Answer the questions in Connect and upload your Alt Lab 3-4 Excel Submission.docx via Connect if assigned.

Lab 3-5 Tableau: Times Series Analysis of IBM Sales and Earnings

Keywords

Predictive Analysis, Forecasting, Time Series

Lab Insight

There are many reasons to forecast a company's future performance. For example, it may need to predict sales to determine needed manufacturing capacity, or it may be predicting cash flows to determine if it will need a loan or have sufficient cash on hand without taking a loan. In addition, an investor might be forecasting a company's earnings to determine whether the company's stock will be a good investment.

The goal of this lab is to forecast sales and earnings for **IBM** using Tableau.

Required:

1. Using Tableau's forecasting options, forecast future sales for IBM.
2. Using Tableau's forecasting options, forecast future income before extraordinary items for IBM.

Ask the Question

What will IBM's quarterly sales and earnings be for 2022, 2023, and 2024, given time series (past quarterly sales and earnings from 2010 to 2021)?

Master the Data

Looking at IBM's financial statements, we accumulate the values of quarterly sales and earnings from 2010 to 2021.

Open Tableau and connect to Excel file Lab 3-5 Data.xlsx.

Data Dictionary

Date: Quarter end date

Net Sales: Net sales for IBN during the respective quarter

Income: Income (before extraordinary items) for IBM during the respective quarter

Perform the Analysis

Analysis Task 1: Forecast Sales.

Make sure the data loaded correctly. Click on Sheet 1. To start the forecast analysis, double-click **IBM Sales** from Tables. Then double-click **Date** also from Tables (as shown in Lab Exhibit 3-5.1).

Lab Exhibit 3-5.1

Tableau Software

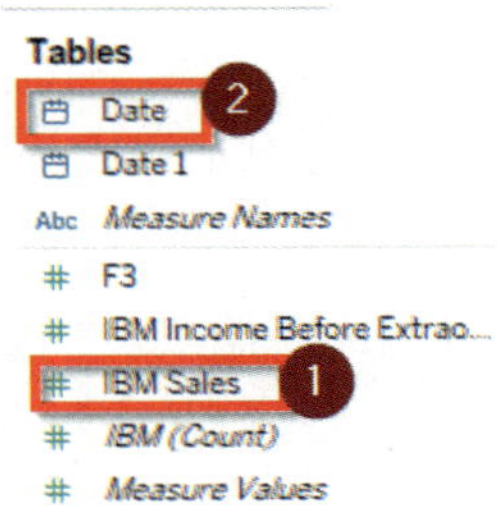

1. Tableau should have defaulted the visualization type to a continuous line chart, but if it did not, you can change it from the Show Me tab (Lab Exhibit 3-5.2).

Lab Exhibit 3-5.2

Tableau Software

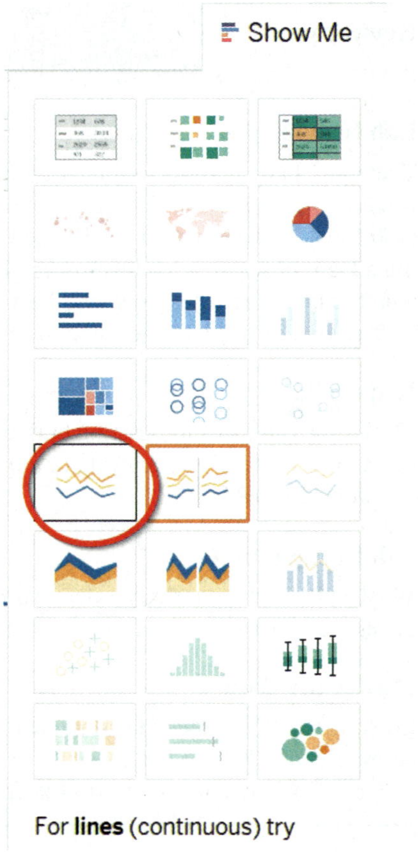

Tableau interacts with dates in two ways, as either "Continuous" or "Discrete." Regardless of the way Tableau chose to display your dates when you added them to your visualization, you can change the field to the right display quite easily.

2. From the **Columns** shelf, right-click the **YEAR(Quarter)** pill and select **Quarter Q2 2015** (Lab Exhibit 3-5.3).

Lab Exhibit 3-5.3

Tableau Software

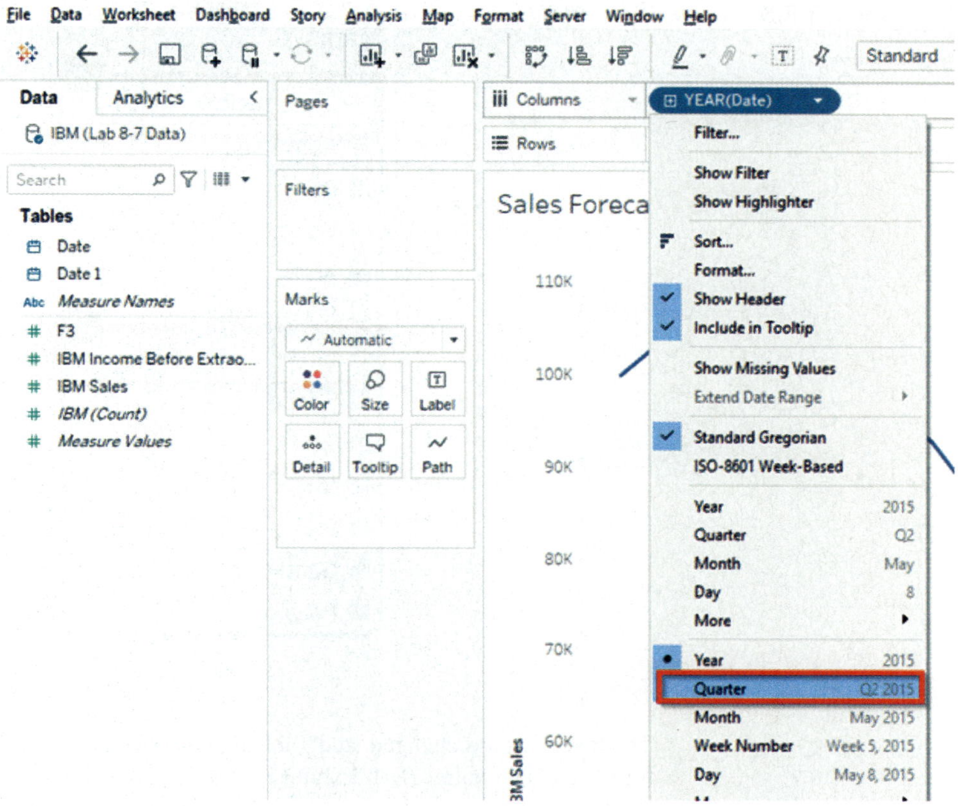

3. To expand this line chart to show a Forecast, select the **Analysis Tab > Forecast > Show Forecast** (Lab Exhibit 3-5.4).

Lab Exhibit 3-5.4

Tableau Software

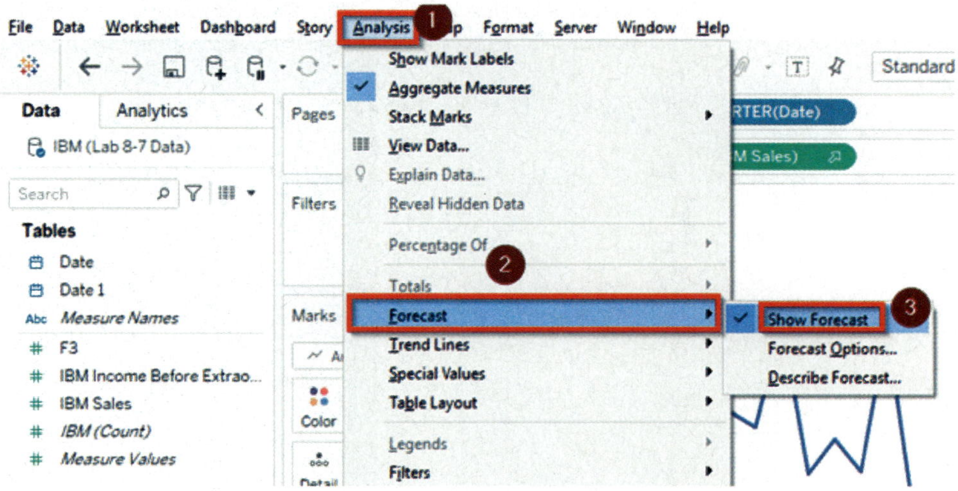

You can now select a variety of options to refine this forecast.

4. From the Marks shelf, change the default mark to Circle (Lab Exhibit 3-5.5).

Lab Exhibit 3-5.5

Tableau Software

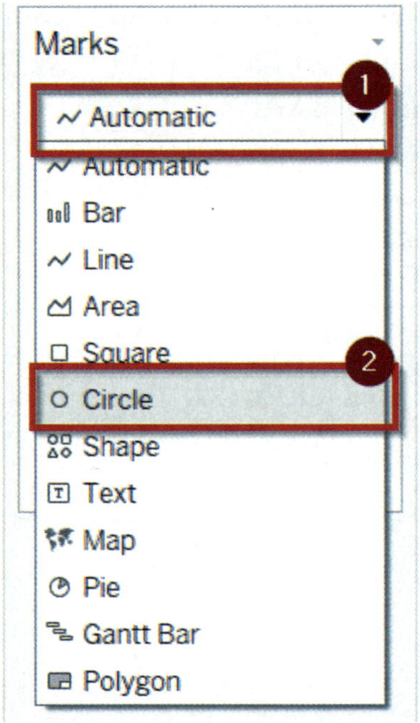

The line chart has changed, and Tableau has provided whiskers around each of the forecasted data points (Lab Exhibit 3-5.6).

Lab Exhibit 3-5.6

Tableau Software

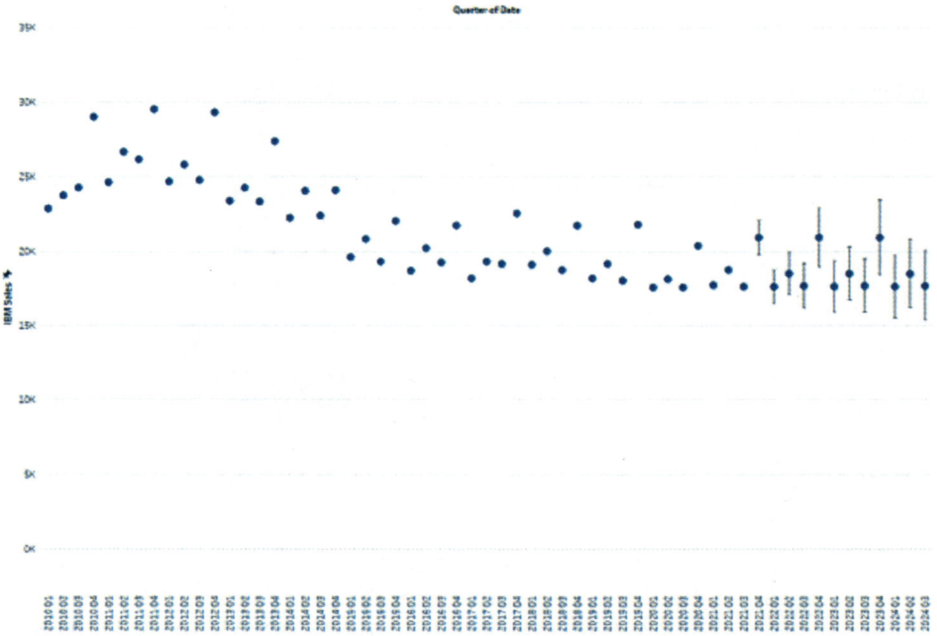

5. You can also adjust the amount of time you are forecasting. From the Analysis Tab, select **Forecast > Forecast Options** (Lab Exhibit 3-5.7).

Lab Exhibit 3-5.7

Tableau Software

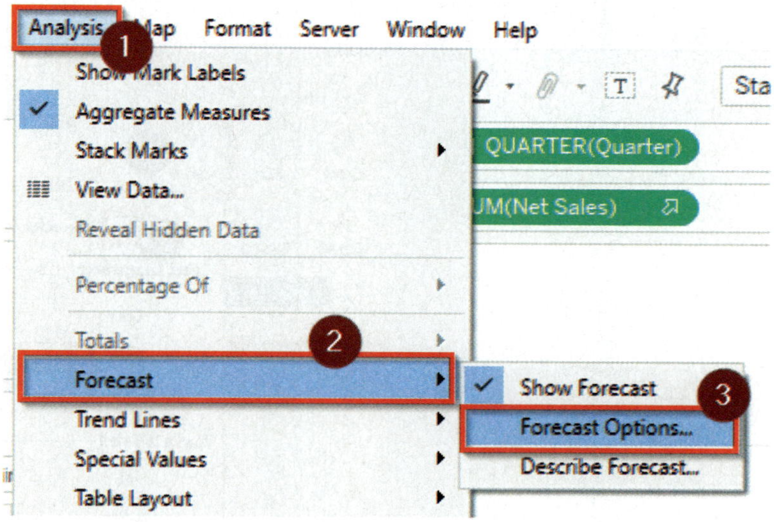

6. Adjust the **Forecast Length** to Exactly 3 Years, then click OK (Lab Exhibit 3-5.8).

Lab Exhibit 3-5.8

Tableau Software

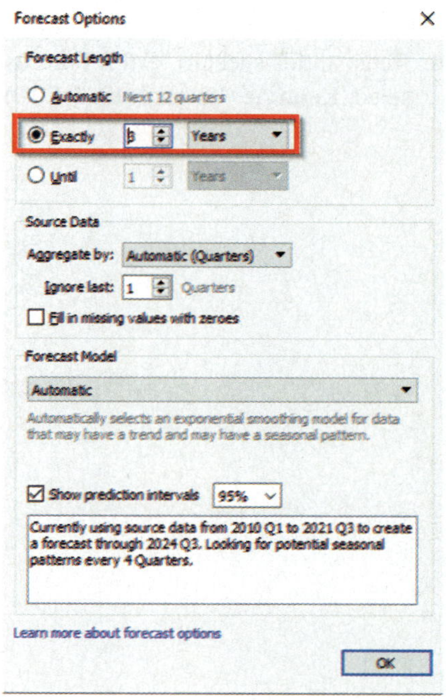

As you make the change, you can see how the chart adjusted to provide more data. You can also see that the whiskers around the dates extend as you reach further into the future, due to increasing uncertainty about the outcome.

7. Notice that the labels indicating the month and product demand (either actual or estimated) do not appear by default. To add the labels, click **Label** in the Marks shelf and add a check mark next to **Show mark labels** (Lab Exhibit 3-5.9).

Lab Exhibit 3-5.9

Tableau Software

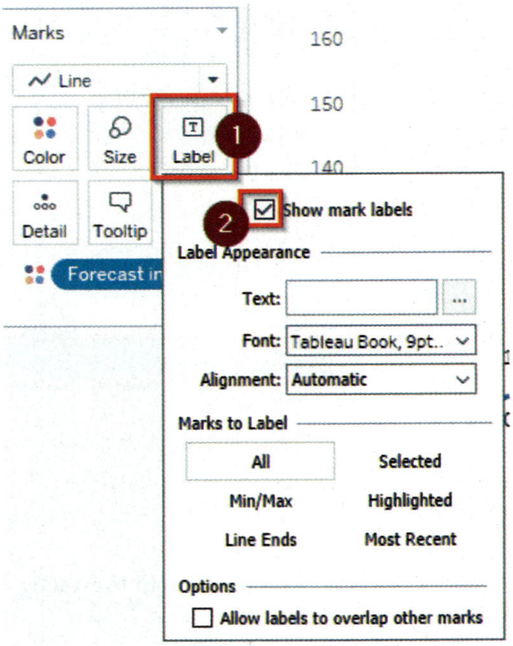

8. Rename this sheet to "Sales Forecast with Box Plots". Right-click on Sheet 1 and select **Rename** (Lab Exhibit 3-5.10).

Lab Exhibit 3-5.10

Tableau Software

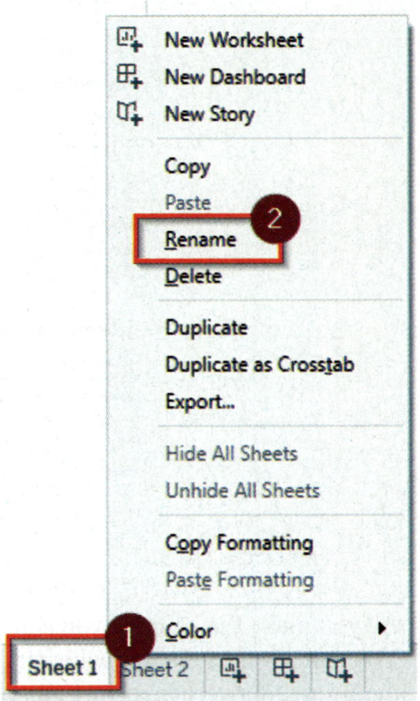

9. Tableau does not default to providing the values for the upper and lower prediction levels the way Excel does. Remember, Tableau is based primarily on visualizing data. However, when forecasting, it can be useful to see not only the marks for the predicted values but also the upper and lower prediction levels.
   To see these levels, we need to duplicate our current sheet as a cross-tab. Right-click **Sales Forecast with Box Plots** and select **Duplicate as Crosstab** (Lab Exhibit 3-5.11).

Lab Exhibit 3-5.11

Tableau Software

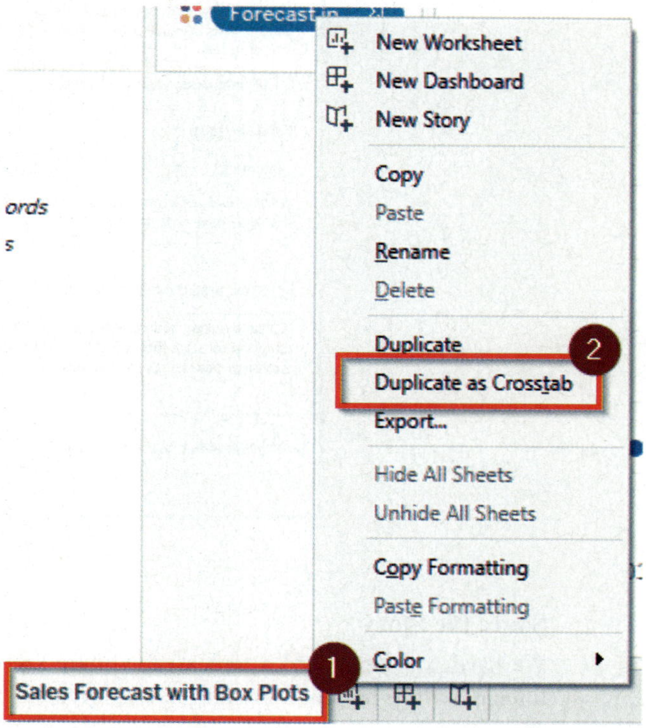

10. You will see a new sheet titled Sales Forecast with Box Plots (2). Rename this sheet to "Sales Forecast Crosstab Data."
11. Click into your new **Sales Forecast with Crosstab Data** sheet to view the cross-tab data. If you scroll to the right, you will see data for the upper and lower bounds.

Analysis Task 2: Forecast Earnings (Income Before Extraordinary Items).

1. Create a new sheet and perform the same analysis for Income before extraordinary items, repeating steps 1–12 from Analysis Task 1 with the new data (the only change is using the Income measure instead of Net Sales). We choose income before any possible extraordinary items because predicting extraordinary items is very difficult to do.
   If you completed Lab 3-3 before this lab, you will notice that the forecast is vastly different. This is because Tableau has defaulted to leaving out the last quarter from its analysis.
2. Select **Analysis Tab > Forecast > Forecast Options** and adjust the default from 1 to 0 in **Ignore Last Quarters.** Then click OK (Lab Exhibit 3-5.12).

Lab Exhibit 3-5.12

Tableau Software

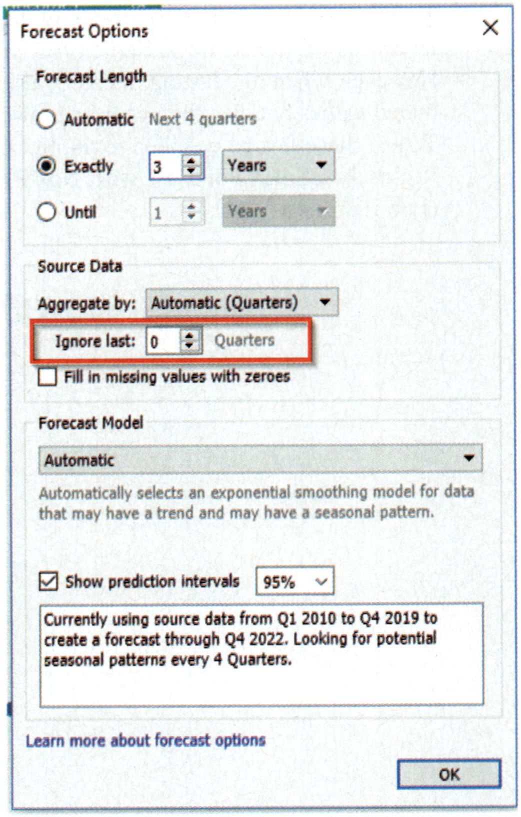

Share the Story

We have now developed a forecast for future sales and income before extra items. This forecast will be helpful for management, investors, lenders, and other stakeholders.

Assessment:

1. Take a screenshot of the forecast of sales, paste it into a Word document named "Lab 3-5 Tableau Submission.docx", and label the screenshot Submission 1.
2. Take a screenshot of the forecast of income, paste it into the same Word document, and label the screenshot Submission 2.
3. Answer the questions in Connect and upload your Lab 3-5 Tableau Submission.docx via Connect if assigned.

Lab 3-5 Alternate

Predictive Analytics: Forecasting Future Performance of Netflix

Using Lab 3-5 Tableau as a guide, forecast future sales and income before extraordinary items for **Netflix**.

Required:

1. Using Tableau's forecasting options, forecast future sales for Netflix.
2. Add a duplicate of the sheet to show the cross-tab data.

3. Using Tableau's Forecasting options, forecast future income before extraordinary items for Netflix. (Don't forget to adjust the amount of quarters ignored to 0.)
4. Add a duplicate of the sheet to show the cross-tab data.

Open Tableau and connect to Excel file Alt Lab 3-5 Data.xlsx.

Data Dictionary

Date: Quarter end date

Net Sales: Net sales for Netflix during the respective quarter

Income: Income before extraordinary items for Netflix during the respective quarter

Assessment:

1. Take a screenshot of the forecast of sales, paste it into a Word document named "Alt Lab 3-5 Tableau Submission.docx", and label the screenshot Submission 1.
2. Take a screenshot of the forecast of income, paste it into the same Word document, and label the screenshot Submission 2.
3. Answer the questions in Connect and upload your Alt Lab 3-5 Tableau Submission.docx via Connect if assigned.

Lab 3-6 Power BI: Time Series Analysis of IBM Sales and Earnings

Keywords

predictive analysis, forecasting, time series

Lab Insight

There are many reasons to forecast a company's future performance. For example, it may need to predict sales to determine needed manufacturing capacity, or it may be predicting cash flows to determine if it will need a loan or have sufficient cash on hand without taking a loan. In addition, an investor might be forecasting a company's earnings to determine whether the company's stock will be a good investment.

The goal of this lab is to forecast sales and earnings for **IBM** using Power BI.

Required:

1. Using Power BI's forecasting options, forecast future sales for IBM.
2. Using Power BI's forecasting options, forecast future income before extraordinary items for IBM.

Ask the Question

What will IBM's quarterly sales and earnings be for 2022, 2023, and 2024, given time series (past quarterly sales and earnings from 2010 to 2021)?

Master the Data

Looking at IBM's financial statements, we accumulate the values of quarterly sales and earnings from 2010 to 2021.

Open Power BI and connect to Excel file Lab 3-6 Data.xlsx. Click the IBM sheet and click Load.

> **Data Dictionary**
>
> **Date:** Quarter end data
>
> **Net Sales:** Net sales for IBM during the respective quarter
>
> **Income:** Income (before extraordinary items) for IBM during the respective quarter.

Perform the Analysis

Analysis Task 1: Forecast Sales.

1. To start the forecast analysis, click the Line chart button in the Visualizations pane. Check the boxes next to **IBM Sales** and **Date** in the Fields pane to add them to your visual as Y-axis and X-axis, respectively.
2. To show the dates by Year and Quarter, remove the Month and Day designation in the Date of the X-axis, as shown in Lab Exhibit 3-6.1.

Lab Exhibit 3-6.1

Microsoft Power BI

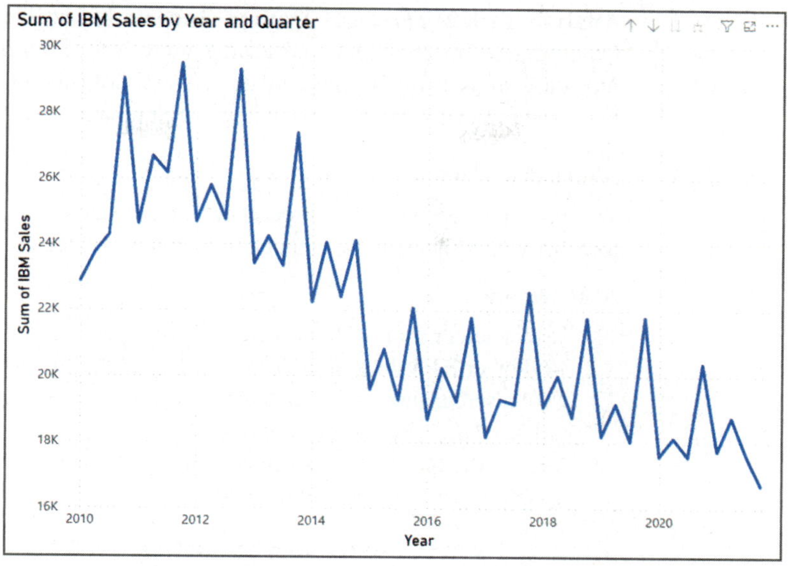

3. To expand this line chart to show a Forecast, click the **Analytics** magnifying glass button in the Visualizations pane. Expand the **Forecast** header and click Add (as shown in Lab Exhibit 3-6.2).

Lab Exhibit 3-6.2

Microsoft Power BI

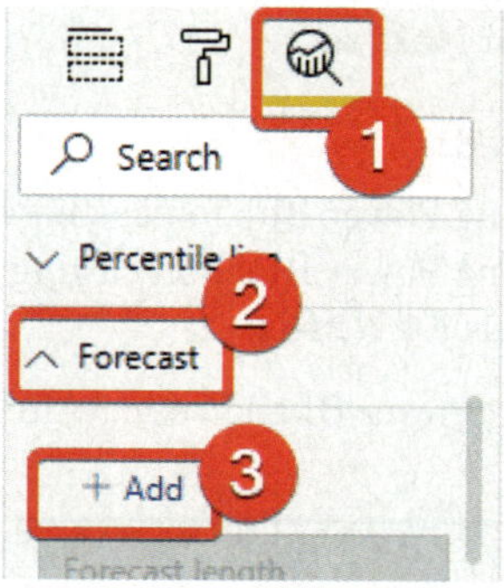

4. Adjust the **Forecast length** to Exactly 3 Years (Lab Exhibit 3-6.3). Click Apply.

Lab Exhibit 3-6.3

Microsoft Power BI

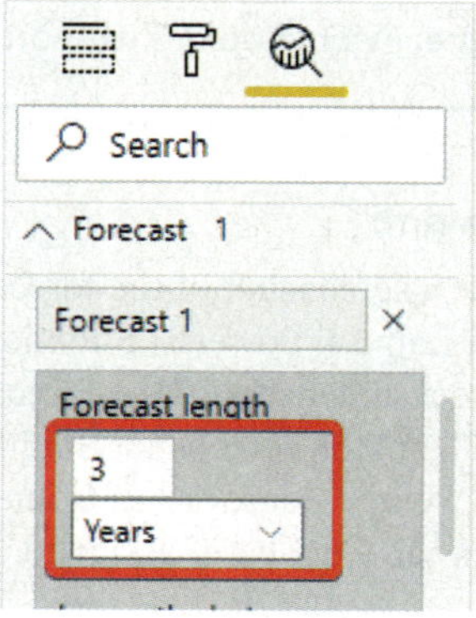

Analysis Task 2: Forecast Earnings (Income Before Extraordinary Items).
Create a new line chart and do the same analysis for **Income before Extraordinary Items,** repeating steps 1–6 with the new data. We choose income before any possible extraordinary items because extraordinary items are rare and hard to predict.

Share the Story

We have now developed a forecast for future sales and income before extra items. This forecast will be helpful for management, investors, lenders, and other stakeholders.

Assessment:

1. Take a screenshot of the forecast of sales, paste it into a Word document named "Lab 3-6 Power BI Submission.docx", and label the screenshot Submission 1.
2. Take a screenshot of the forecast of income, paste it into the same Word document, and label the screenshot Submission 2.
3. Answer the questions in Connect and upload your Lab 3-6 Power BI Excel Submission.docx via Connect if assigned.

Lab 3-6 Alternate

Predictive Analytics: Forecasting Future Performance of Netflix
Using Lab 3-6 Power BI as a guide, forecast future sales and income before extraordinary items for **Netflix**.

Required:

1. Using Power BI's forecasting options, forecast future sales for Netflix.
2. Using Power BI's Forecasting options, forecast future income before extraordinary items for Netflix.

Open Power BI and connect to Excel file Alt Lab 3-6 Data.xlsx.

Data Dictionary

Date: Quarter end date

Net Sales: Net sales for Netflix during the respective quarter

Income: Income before extraordinary items for Netflix during the respective quarter

Assessment:

1. Take a screenshot of the forecast of sales, paste it into a Word document named "Alt Lab 3-6 PowerBI Submission.docx", and label the screenshot Submission 1.
2. Take a screenshot of the forecast of income, paste it into the same Word document, and label the screenshot Submission 2.
3. Answer the questions in Connect and upload your Alt Lab 3-6 Power BI Submission.docx via Connect if assigned.

Lab 3-7 Excel: Create a Dashboard Using PivotTables and Slicers

Keywords

pivot
table, pivot chart, dashboard, slicer

Lab Insight

This lab will demonstrate how placing multiple pivot tables and pivot charts in the same spreadsheet can present opportunities for interesting analysis.

We will create a dashboard that consists of three pivot tables, three associated pivot charts, and two separate slicers to filter the dashboard components.

**Note: the dataset will not work on Excel for Mac.

PivotTables and Related Charts

1. Sum of Quantity Sold for each product (and a related bar (column) chart).
2. Count of Sales Orders that have each product on them (and a related bar (column) chart).
3. Both measures (sum of quantity sold and count of sales orders) for each product over time (and a related line chart).

Slicers

1. A dashboard-level slicer to filter each pivot table and pivot chart at once based on Customer state.
2. A report-level slicer to filter only the sales of product over time pivot table and pivot chart by product.

The slicer will be for state, so that we can see the changes in products sold for each separate region interactively.

Ask the Question

What are the different reports and charts that would be useful to place together for regular analysis?

Master the Data

Step 1

Open the dataset Lab 3-7 Data.xlsx.

Insert a PivotTable from any of the tables in the Excel workbook. When doing so, place a check mark in the box next to Add this data to the Data Model as shown in Lab Exhibit 3-7.1. This connects the individual tables in each tab to each other using common fields that we'll learn more about in Chapter 6.

Lab Exhibit 3-7.1

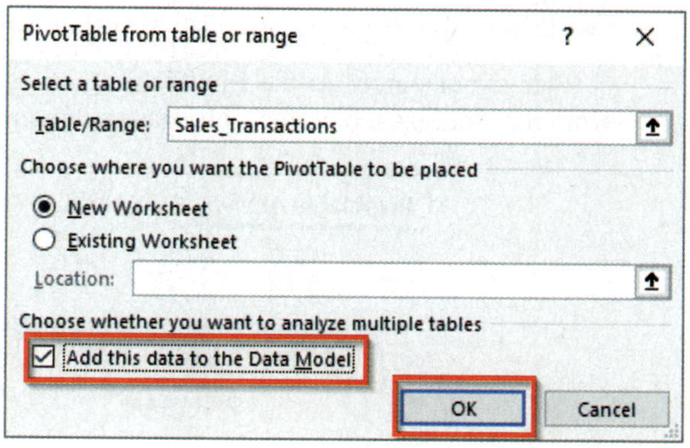

In the PivotTable field list, click "All" as shown in Lab Exhibit 3-7.2 to show the fields from each of the three tables in the workbook and click on the arrows to see the fields. The relationships between the tables have already been created in this dataset.

Lab Exhibit 3-7.2

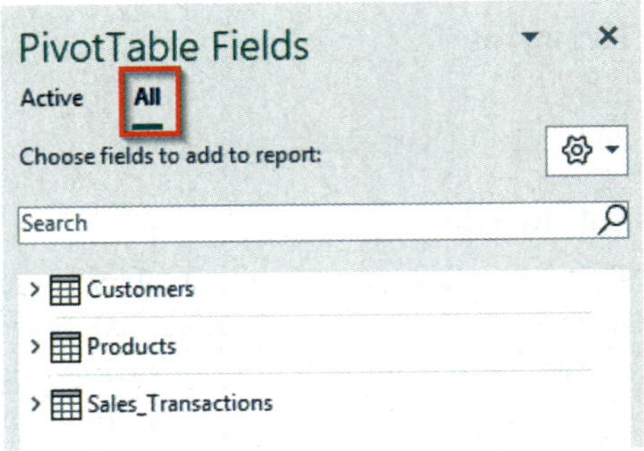

Step 2

Place the following fields in your PivotTable (as shown in Lab Exhibit 3-7.3):

Lab Exhibit 3-7.3

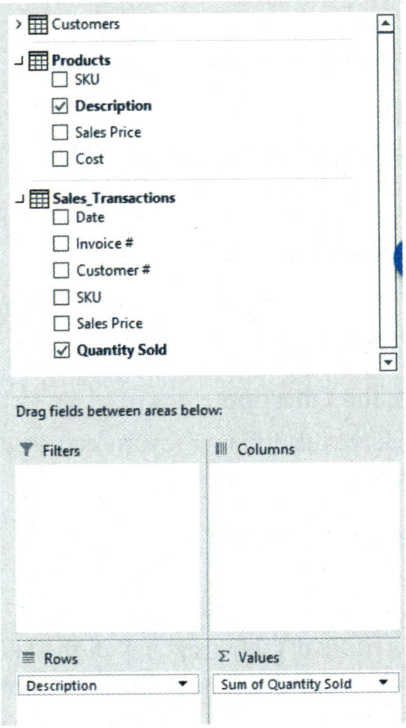

- Quantity Sold (from the Sales_Transactions sheet) in Values
- Description (from the Products sheet) in Rows

Place your cursor in the PivotTable then create a pivot chart by clicking PivotChart from the Analyze tab on the ribbon as shown in Lab Exhibit 3-7.4.

Lab Exhibit 3-7.4

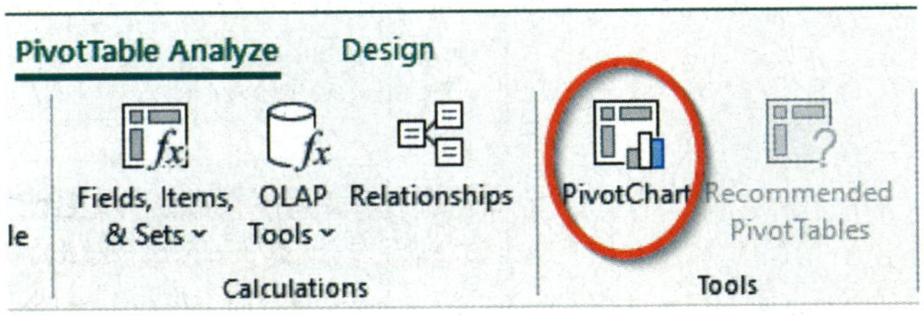

Insert the Column Chart (the default) by clicking OK.

To create a second PivotTable, copy the table you just created. Make sure you select all the fields, then click Ctrl + C on your keyboard (or right click the selection with your mouse and select copy). Paste the copy of the existing PivotTable a few rows beneath the existing one.

In this new PivotTable, edit the field in the Values section to reflect a Count of Invoice # (as shown in Lab Exhibit 3-7.5). This field may default to a sum, so change its count if necessary.

Lab Exhibit 3-7.5

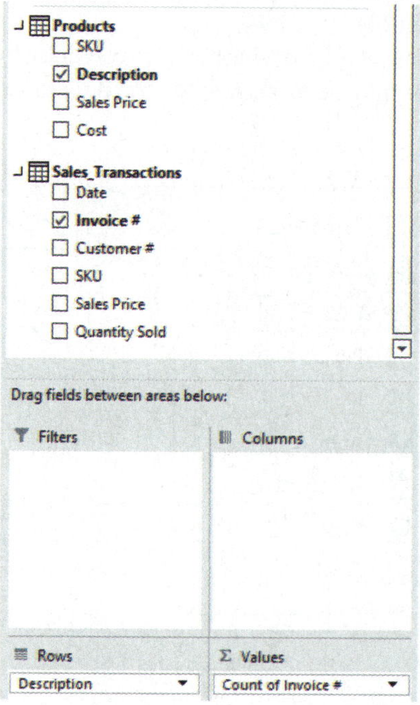

Add a pivot chart for this PivotTable and click OK to create the default Column Chart.

Finally, create your third PivotTable. To do so, once again copy one of your existing PivotTables, and then paste the new PivotTable a few records below the existing PivotTables.

For your third PivotTable, use the following fields (as shown in Lab Exhibit 3-7.6):

Lab Exhibit 3-7.6

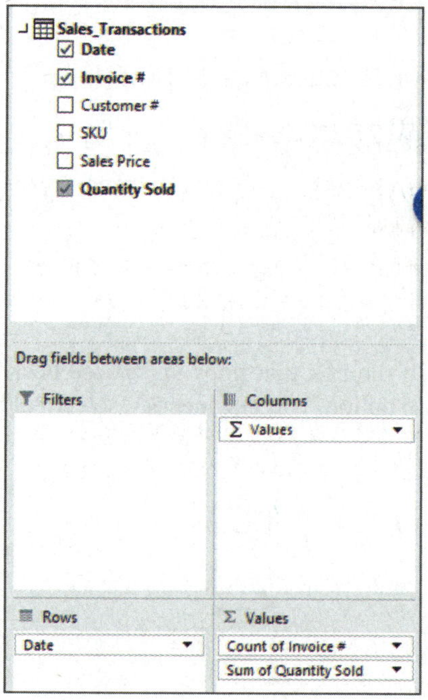

- Date in Rows
- Invoice # in Values (Count)
- Quantity Sold in Values (Sum)

Depending on your version of Excel, it may have automatically created a date hierarchy in the rows. If that's the case, remove all fields except for Sales_Order_Date (that is, remove Sales_Order_Date (year), Sales_Order_Date (Quarter), and Sales_Order_Date (Month)).

Insert a Line chart as a PivotChart for this PivotTable as shown in Lab Exhibit 3-7.7. (You may need to override the default in the PivotChart window.) Click OK.

Lab Exhibit 3-7.7

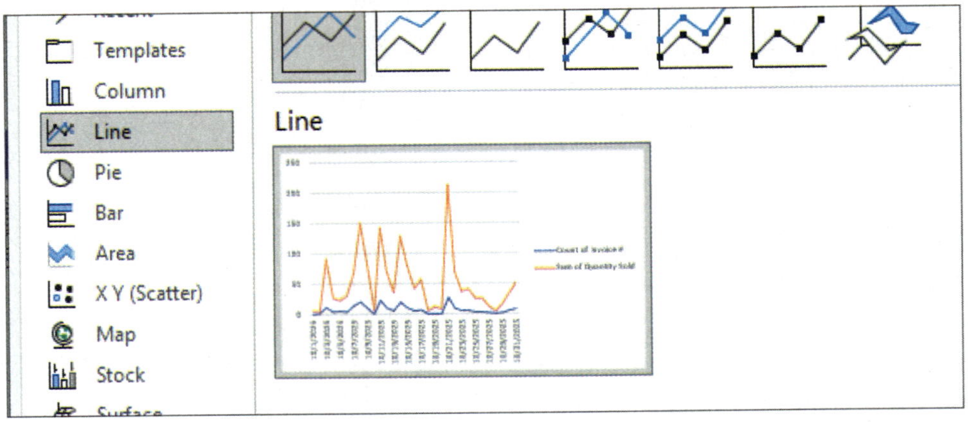

Step 3

Add in your slicers.

Click into any of the PivotTables and select Insert Slicer from the Analyze (or PivotTable Analyze) tab on the ribbon as shown in Lab Exhibit 3-7.8.

Lab Exhibit 3-7.8

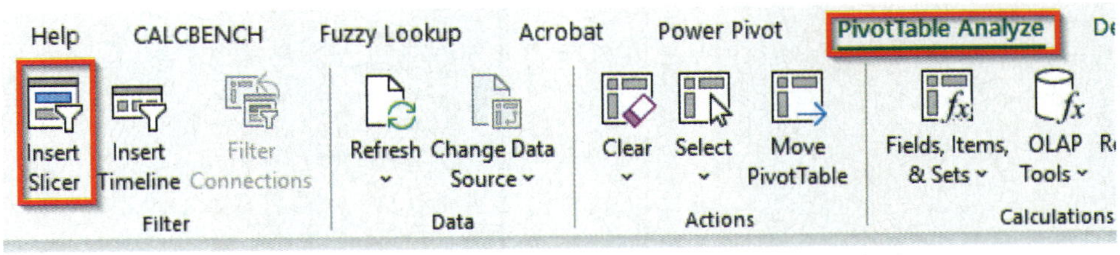

In the box that pops up, place check marks next to State and Description. To see the State option, you may need to select All as shown in Lab Exhibit 3-7.9.

Lab Exhibit 3-7.9

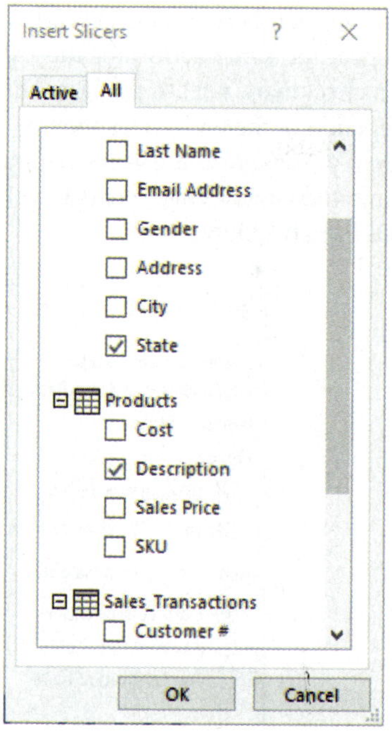

Arrange the Slicers so they are visible (and rearrange the PivotCharts if necessary).

On the State Slicer, right click anywhere. From the options provided, click Report Connections. . . as shown in Lab Exhibit 3-7.10.

Lab Exhibit 3-7.10

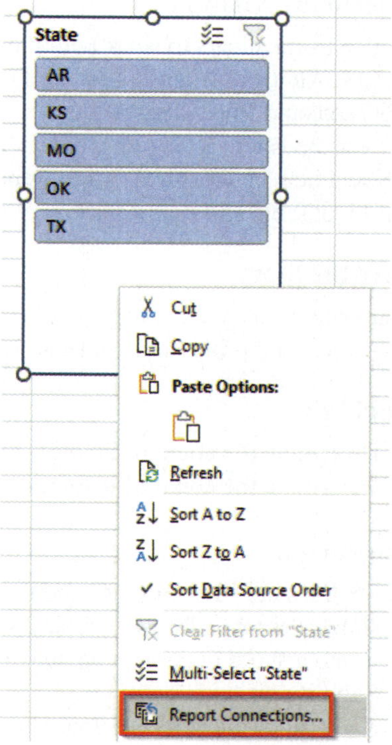

Ensure that there is a checkmark next to each of the three PivotTables.

Repeat the same action for the Description slicer, but for this one, ensure that there is only a checkmark next to the last. This will ensure that the slicer only filters the last PivotTable, and not the entire Dashboard.

Finally, rename the Slicers. Right click the State filter and select Slicer Settings. . . Rename the slicer "Dashboard-Level Filter: State" in the Caption field; then click OK as shown in Lab Exhibit 3-7.11.

Lab Exhibit 3-7.11

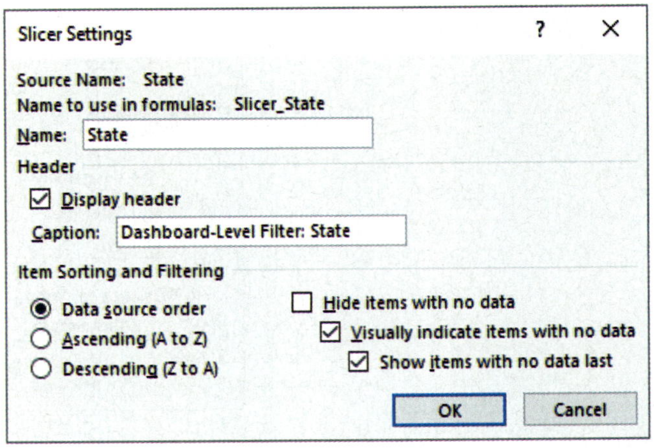

Repeat the same process for the Description slicer, but for this one, name it "Report-Level Filter: Product".

Perform the Analysis

Practice using slicers to work with the dashboard.

Click AR (for Arkansas) in the Dashboard-Level Filter: State slicer to see how each PivotTable and PivotChart reacts.

Clear the filter.

Now click Mavic Air 2 in the Report-Level Filter: Product slicer to see how only the final PivotTable and PivotChart react.

Share the Story

Dashboards serve the purpose of sharing a story—providing the information in an easy-to-use and professional format for decision making.

Required:

1. Determine the count of invoices and quantity sold of Mavic Air 2 in AR (Arkansas).
2. Determine the count of invoices and quantity sold of all products in all locations.

Assessment:

1. Set the state filter to "AR" and the product filter to "Mavic Air 2", so that your report shows the totals for Mavic Air 2 sales to Arkansas customers, take a screenshot, paste it into a Word document named "Lab 3-7 Excel SS.docx", and label the screenshot Submission 1.
2. Clear all of the filters in your slicers, take a screenshot of the entire dashboard, paste it into your Word document named "Lab 3-7 Excel SS.docx", and label the screenshot Submission 2.
3. Answer the questions in Connect and upload your Lab 3-7 Excel SS.docx, if assigned.

Lab 3-7 Alternate

Use the same dataset created in Lab 3-7 to answer additional questions in Alt Lab 3-7.

Required:

1. Determine the count of invoices and quantity sold of Osmo Pocket in KS (Kansas).
2. Determine the count of invoices and quantity sold of Osmo Action in OK (Oklahoma).

Assessment:

1. Set the state filter to "KS" and the product filter to "Osmo Pocket", so that your report shows the totals for Osmo Pocket sales to Kansas customers, **take** a screenshot, **paste** it into a Word document named "Alt Lab 3-7 Excel SS.docx", and **label** the screenshot Submission 1.
2. Set the state filter to "OK" and the product filter to "Osmo Action", so that your report shows the totals for Osmo Action sales to Oklahoma customers, **take** a screenshot, **paste** it into a Word document named "Alt Lab 3-7 Excel SS.docx", and **label** the screenshot Submission 2.
3. **Answer** the questions in Connect and **upload** your Lab 3-7 Excel SS.docx, if assigned.

Chapter Four

Accountants as Business Analysts

A Look at This Chapter

As users, managers, designers, and evaluators of technology and technology-driven business processes, accountants must understand the organization and how organizational processes generate information important to management. To ensure that processes and systems are documented—and to participate in improvements to processes and systems—accountants must also be business analysts. This chapter introduces business process modeling and describes how it supports the roles of accountants. It explains the potential value of business process modeling. Finally, it describes the types of business process models and introduces basic modeling tools to guide the student's development of modeling skills.

A Look Back

Chapter 3 reviewed data analytics tools and practices for accountants. It described how to compare and contrast exploratory data visualizations and explanatory data visualizations. It is important to remember that data visualizations address business problems, and identifying business problems depends on the accountant's understanding of business processes.

A Look Ahead

Chapter 5 introduces data modeling. It describes how data modeling supports the design, implementation, and operation of database systems. It introduces basic modeling tools that will be used throughout the rest of the text.

Sorbis/Shutterstock

One recent morning, I stopped at a very busy **Starbucks.** I looked at the line coming out of the door and immediately thought that it would take at least 20 minutes to get my morning coffee. Instead, I was pleasantly surprised at the efficiency of the employees who got me through that line in less than 2 minutes.

I watched closely as the Starbucks partners behind the counter executed the workflow of the process. One partner took my order and relayed my pastry order to another partner behind the pastry case. He also relayed my coffee order to the barista at the other end of the counter. As I moved through the line to the register, my order arrived just as I did, and a fourth partner checked the order and took my payment. Within those 2 minutes, they had served at least a dozen other customers, too.

I thought about the number of options they had to deal with, the variety of hot and cold drinks, the pastries and other breakfast items, while also keeping a supply of freshly brewed coffee ready. I was sure that Starbucks had analyzed the process in detail to eliminate waste and enhance their partners' productivity. Then, they had to train all their partners in that process so they could work as one highly synchronized team. Finally, they delivered a hot cup of coffee to a grateful customer on a cool San Francisco morning.

CHAPTER OUTLINE

Changing Roles of Accountants in Business
- *IMA Competency Framework*
- *CGMA Competency Framework*
- *IFAC Accountant Roles*

Business Process Documentation
- *Definitions*
- *Purposes of Documentation*
- *Value of Business Models*

Types of Business Models

Activity Models
- *Business Process Modeling Notation*
- *Building Blocks for BPMN Diagrams*
- *Example of a Business Process Diagram*
- *Identifying Participants in Business Process Diagrams*
- *Messages in BPMN*
- *Extended Building Blocks for BPMN Diagrams and Modeling Concepts*
- *Subprocesses and Repeating Activities*
- *Data Objects, Datastores, and Associations*
- *Rules for Connecting Symbols with Sequence Flows and Message Flows*
- *Steps to Prepare Business Process Models*

Appendix A: Flowcharting

Appendix B: Data Flow Diagrams

LEARNING OBJECTIVES

After reading this chapter, you should be able to:

4-1 Describe the roles of the accounting/finance function in business and why those roles require knowledge of technology and business processes.

4-2 Understand the importance of business process documentation.

4-3 Recognize the value of business models.

4-4 Articulate the characteristics of activity models.

4-5 Understand and apply the building blocks for BPMN (activity) diagrams.

4-6 Use pools and lanes to identify process participants.

4-7 Apply message flows to show interactions between pools.

4-8 Understand and apply flow object types.

4-9 Recognize and model repeating activities.

4-10 Understand and apply data objects and datastores to model data created, updated, transferred, and deleted in a process.

4-11 Understand and apply a structured process of business process model development.

LO 4-1

Describe the roles of the accounting/finance function in business and why those roles require knowledge of technology and business processes.

CHANGING ROLES OF ACCOUNTANTS IN BUSINESS

The role of the accountant in business has changed. In the past, accountants typically focused on stewardship and reporting functions; they kept financial records, prepared financial reports, and performed audits. Now, they face the challenge of helping the enterprise to optimize its processes (financial, administrative, and operational) to achieve competitive performance levels and maximize shareholder value.

At its heart, the accounting and financial management function assembles financial and nonfinancial information, analyzes that information, advises decision-makers, and applies subsequent decisions to achieve desired results. In a broad sense, accounting roles involve reporting, questioning, developing solutions, and deploying those solutions. Accountants remain a trusted source of high integrity financial and related reports, but they now have a broader responsibility to deliver value to the organization. Exhibit 4.1 summarizes the traditional stewardship and reporting and accounting management roles, as well as the increasingly important business management support roles. Exhibit 4.2 describes the new accounting value matrix.

It is clear that accountants need to develop new skills to be competitive. They not only need to know traditional accounting functions, they also need to understand business processes and how technology affects those processes.

EXHIBIT 4.1
Roles of the Accounting/Finance Function in Business

Source: Based on *Improving Decision Making in Organisations: The Opportunity to Transform Finance* (London: CIMA, 2007), Exhibit 3.

Stewardship and Reporting	Accounting/Finance Operations	Business Management Support
Regulatory compliance	Finance and accounting processes (procure to pay, order to cash, record to report, and payroll and treasury)	Assembling and analyzing management information
Tax returns	Financial close—completing period-end accounts	Planning, budgeting, and forecasting
Stakeholder assurance	Financial consolidation, reporting, and analysis	Performance measurement, reporting, and analysis
Investor relations	Providing comprehensive management information	Performance management
Raising capital and loans	People management	Risk management—from strategic to operational, including fraud risk
Board reports	Using IT to make finance and accounting processes more efficient and effective	Investment appraisal and professional expertise (e.g., merger and acquisition or tax)
Statutory reporting		Cost, supply chain, value-based, project, and change management
		Capital structure and dividend policy
		Strategic planning

IMA Competency Framework

Recently, prominent accounting organizations articulated the skills and competencies that accountants need to be successful in the 21st century. The Institute of Management Accountants developed the *IMA Management Accounting Competency Framework.* It defines six areas of skills that accounting professionals need to remain relevant in the digital age and adapt to rapidly changing technologies:

EXHIBIT 4.2
Accounting Function Value Matrix

Source: *The Changing Role and Mandate of Finance: Creating a Vision for the Future* (New York: CGMA and AICPA 2018).

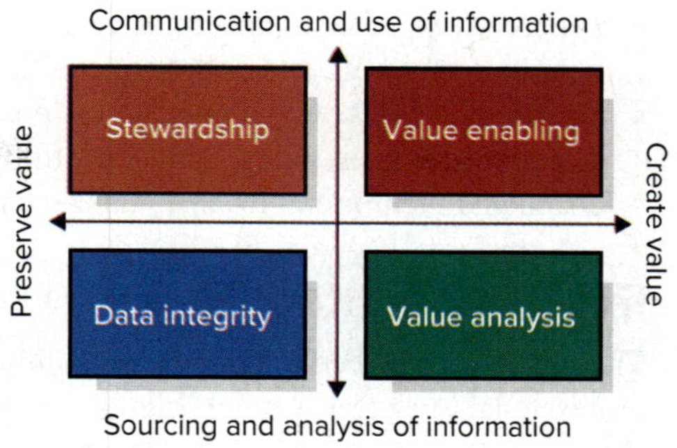

- ***Strategic management.*** Accountants must possess the skills necessary to lead the strategic planning process, guide decision making, manage organizational risks, and monitor performance. They include the ability to develop financial plans consistent with an organization's strategic goals and implement corresponding performance management systems.
- ***Reporting and control.*** Accountants must possess the skills necessary to measure and report organizational performance in compliance with appropriate standards.
- ***Technology and analytics.*** Accountants must possess skills necessary to manage technology and analyze data to enhance organizational success.
- ***Business acumen and operations.*** Accountants must be able to contribute as a cross-functional business partner and contribute to all areas of organizational operations.
- ***Leadership.*** Accountants must possess leadership skills required to facilitate collaboration and inspire others to achieve organizational goals.
- ***Professional ethics and values.*** Accountants must demonstrate commitment to professional values, ethical behavior, and legal compliance critical to a sustainable business model.

CGMA Competency Framework

Similarly, the American Institute of CPAs, in conjunction with the Chartered Institute of Management Accountants, created the Chartered Global Management Accountant (CGMA) designation. Together, they created the CGMA Competency Framework to articulate the broad set of skills and technological expertise needed for important accounting roles. The framework describes four important sets of skills anchored by a commitment to ethics, integrity, and professionalism:

- ***Technical skills.*** Accountants must possess these skills to help develop an organization's strategic goals and ensure that their performance contributes to strategic success. These skills include those necessary to manage implementation of new or updated accounting standards; conduct accounting operations efficiently and effectively; develop and apply appropriate costing techniques; translate business strategy into financial targets and apply related financial modeling, planning, and forecasting processes; identify and mitigate enterprise risk; and develop and manage appropriate accounting and enterprise technology.
- ***Business skills.*** Accountants must understand the organization's environment and its overall strategic direction. These skills include possessing the analytical skills necessary to advise on strategic options, planning and managing business processes to achieve desired levels of performance, working with stakeholders to meet organizational objectives, and developing and implementing complex projects to create value to the organization.

- ***People skills.*** Accountants must possess the skills necessary to manage effectively, communicate well, and collaborate with a diverse set of stakeholders.
- ***Leadership skills.*** Accountants must possess the skills required to drive performance from subordinates, peers, and teams throughout the organization. They must be able to coach and mentor employees, manage change, and motivate and inspire others.

IFAC Accountant Roles

The International Federation of Accountants also articulated the need for accounting professionals to offer a much higher contribution to their organizations. Due to rapidly changing competitive environments and technology, accountants must look beyond financial reporting to develop the skills necessary to provide useful, forward-looking insights. Enterprise performance management is evolving. Accountants must evolve to be able to deliver insights based on financial and nonfinancial, internal and external, and structured and unstructured data and information. Accountants need to harness data and models, technology, talent, and organization culture to support dynamic planning and forecasting as well as integrated performance analysis. They must be able to analyze costs, profitability, productivity, and operational performance to allow the organization to respond proactively to current performance and deliver long-term value. Every accountant should be able to articulate ideas and communicate the business case for new technologies.

AICPA and NASBA CPA Evolution

The Association of International Certified Professional Accountants in conjunction with the National Association of State Boards of Accountancy conducted a public accounting practice analysis. This analysis resulted in the CPA Evolution initiative establishing new foundational knowledge for newly licensed CPAs. This new licensure model recognizes the important role of technology on the accounting, auditing, and taxation practices of public accountants. Furthermore, it creates a new discipline for the CPA examination involving information systems and controls. The new CPA exam structure, scheduled for introduction in 2024, highlights the importance of business knowledge and technical skills for accountants.

LO 4-2

Understand the importance of business process documentation.

BUSINESS PROCESS DOCUMENTATION

Definitions

Before we describe how business analysis and business process modeling can support accountants' roles, we first present some definitions:

- **Business process**: A defined sequence of business activities that use resources to transform specific inputs into specific outputs to achieve a business goal. A business process is constrained by business rules.
- **Business analysis**: The process of defining business process requirements and evaluating potential improvements. Business analysis involves ascertaining, documenting, and communicating information about current and future business processes using business process modeling and related tools.
- **Business model**: A simple, abstract representation of one or more business processes.[1] A business model is typically a graphical depiction of the essential business process information.

[1]In other contexts, the term "business model" is often used to describe the plan by which a company generates revenue.

- **Documentation**: Explains how business processes and business systems work. Documentation is "a tool for information transmission and communication. The type and extent of documentation will depend on the nature of the organization's products and processes."[2]

Purposes of Documentation

Documentation includes business process models, business rules, user manuals, training manuals, product specifications, software manuals, schedules, organization charts, strategic plans, and similar materials that describe the operation, constraints on, and objectives of business processes and systems. Although documentation has always been important for accounting information systems, the Sarbanes–Oxley Act of 2002 made documentation essential for businesses. This act requires managers to assess and attest to the business's internal control structure and procedures. The U.S. Securities and Exchange Commission (SEC) rules require "management to annually evaluate whether ICFR (internal control of financial reporting) is effective at providing reasonable assurance and to disclose its assessment to investors. Management is responsible for maintaining evidential matter, including documentation, to provide reasonable support for its assessment. This evidence will also allow a third party, such as the company's external auditor, to consider the work performed by management."[3] The act also requires external auditors to audit management's assessment of the effectiveness of internal controls and express an opinion on the company's internal control over financial reporting.[4] Thus, documentation is necessary for internal audit to support management's assertions as well as for external auditors to evaluate management's assertions on internal control over financial reporting.

Documentation supports audits of business processes.

RapidEye/Getty Images

In addition to Sarbanes–Oxley compliance requirements, documentation is important for the following reasons:

- *Training.* User guides, employee manuals, and operating instructions help employees learn how business processes and systems operate.
- *Describing current processes and systems.* Documentation provides an official description of how business processes and systems, including AIS, work. Thus, documentation supports internal and external audit requirements; establishes accountability; and standardizes communications within the business and between the business and its customers, suppliers, and other stakeholders.
- *Auditing.* Documentation provides audit trails, which can assist auditors in determining the effectiveness of internal controls.
- *Accountability.* Documentation includes checklists, delegations of authority, and similar assignments of responsibility. Thus, documentation would specify who is authorized to approve orders or sign checks, for example.

[2]ISO 9001:2008, International Standards Organization.

[3]SEC Interpretive Guidance 33-8810, issued June 27, 2007.

[4]See Public Company Accounting Oversight Board (PCAOB) Auditing Standard No. 5, *An Audit of Internal Control Over Financial Reporting That Is Integrated with an Audit of Financial Statements.*

- *Standardized interactions.* Documentation clearly describes the inputs and outputs of business processes and systems and thus provides a common language for all parties that interact with the process or system.
- *Facilitating process improvement.* Because it describes the way processes currently work, documentation is also the basis for determining what should be changed. Well-managed businesses regularly review all processes with a view to continuous improvement in four major areas:

  1. Effectiveness: Are the outputs of the process obtained as expected?
  2. Efficiency: Can the same outputs be produced with fewer inputs and resources?
  3. Internal control: Are the internal controls working?
  4. Compliance with various statutes and policies: Does the process comply with constantly changing local, state, federal, and international laws and regulations?

LO 4-3

Recognize the value of business models.

Value of Business Models

Imagine a map of a city like Los Angeles, California, or even a small city like Fayetteville, Arkansas. How many words would it take to provide the same information as the map? Undoubtedly, the graphical representation (map) presents the information more concisely and perhaps more clearly than a written description. Business processes and systems can also be difficult to describe concisely using words alone. Thus, business models allow us to depict the important features of business processes and systems clearly and concisely.

Organizational change—including mergers, acquisitions, outsourcing, offshoring, product innovation, and continuous process improvement—and other business transformations are common. Change, however, can be expensive and risky. Careful planning is necessary to implement change in a way that minimizes those costs and risks. This is where business models create value. Business models provide communication, training, analysis, and persuasion tools that are particularly suited for planning business transformations. Business models allow managers to assess what needs to be changed and plan how to make the change. In particular, business models create value in the following ways:

- *Managing complexity.* Models are simpler than the processes and systems they depict, but they incorporate the essential elements.
- *Eliciting requirements.* Models offer a communications tool that can be used to interview involved parties and discuss the impact of possible changes.
- *Reconciling viewpoints.* Models can combine various local views into one integrated view. Some models can be used to simulate potential outcomes from a change to better assess the impact of the change.
- *Specifying requirements.* Models can be the basis for documentation of the changed process or system. Additionally, some models can be used to generate working software directly.
- *Managing compliance.* Models can be used to identify legal and regulatory requirements and how those requirements affect business processes. When new laws are passed, the models quickly show where changes must be made to comply.
- *Supporting training.* Models can support training of employees on how to implement new business processes.
- *Managing and reusing knowledge.* Models support knowledge management, the practice of systematically capturing individuals' knowledge and making it available where needed throughout the organization. Business models can convert tacit knowledge, found only in people's heads, to explicit knowledge that can be taught to others.

PROGRESS CHECK

1. How would documentation help accountants perform some of the roles listed in Exhibit 4.1?
2. From your own experience, describe how models (or pictures or maps) have helped you understand a complex issue.

LO 4-4

Articulate the characteristics of activity models.

TYPES OF BUSINESS MODELS

This textbook will focus on three different elements of business process models. To be complete, concise, and useful, business process models need to describe process activity, data structures, and the business rules that constrain and guide process operations (see Exhibit 4.3). This chapter focuses on activity models, and Chapter 5 introduces structure models.

EXHIBIT 4.3
Business Process Models and Business Rules

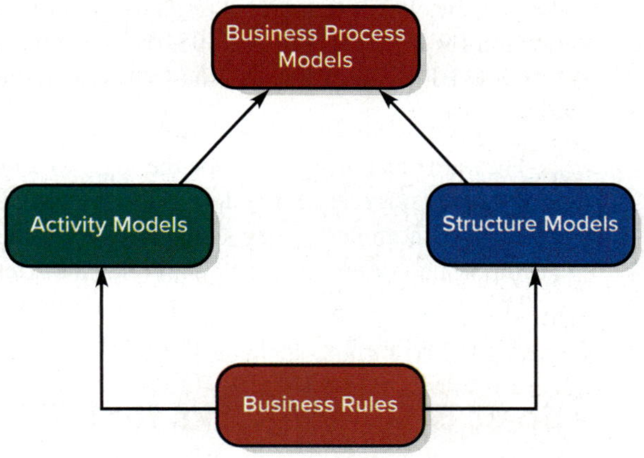

ACTIVITY MODELS

Activity models describe the sequence of workflow in a business process or processes. While the purpose of structure models is to create a blueprint for the development of a relational database to support the collection, aggregation, and communication of process information, the purpose of activity models is to represent the sequential flow and control logic of a set of related activities. They are tools for planning, documenting, discussing, and implementing systems; however, they also facilitate the use of those systems once implemented. Furthermore, they are important tools for analyzing and improving business processes.

Activity models, such as flowcharts, have been used to analyze business processes and design changes since well before 1920.[5] As technology changed, designers developed a variety of activity models, such as data flow diagrams, business process maps, and the IDEF0 functional modeling method,[6] to document and analyze business process workflow.

[5]D. J. Couger, "Evolution of Business System Analysis Techniques," *Computing Surveys* 5, no. 3 (1973), pp. 167–98. The article describes the use of flowcharts for industrial engineering by Frederick W. Taylor and others prior to 1920.

[6]See Federal Information Processing Standards Publication 183, www.idef.com.

Regardless of the specific modeling notation, workflow models must be able to describe

1. Events that start, change, or stop flow in the process.
2. Activities and tasks within the process.
3. The sequence of flow between tasks.
4. Decision points that affect the flow.
5. Division of activity depending on organizational roles.

Business Process Modeling Notation

LO 4-5

Understand and apply the building blocks for BPMN (activity) diagrams.

For this textbook, we employ **business process modeling notation (BPMN)** for activity models, although the concepts discussed also apply to other modeling notation, such as UML activity diagrams and data flow diagrams.[7] The Object Management Group (OMG) also maintains the specifications for BPMN. The original specification for BPMN was issued in 2004. Since then, BPMN has been widely adopted because it was specifically designed for process modeling in a way that can be understood by businesspeople rather than software engineers (in contrast with UML activity diagrams). Additionally, there are free or inexpensive software products that support modeling and subsequent simulation of the process. The International Organization for Standardization (ISO) has adopted a specification for BPMN (ISO/IEC 19510:2013) that is identical to OMG BPMN 2.0.1.

Good BPMN models have the following important characteristics:

1. They are valid. They do not violate BPMN standards.
2. They are clear. They describe the logic of a business process unambiguously, although they may not present the details of how individual tasks are performed.
3. They are complete. They show how the process starts, all the significant ends, and all important communications with relevant external parties.
4. They are accurate. Given the same facts about the process logic, all modelers should create similar models of the process consistent with the facts.

Basic Building Blocks for BPMN Diagrams

Events include start, intermediate, and end events. Basic events are modeled as small circles, as shown in Exhibit 4.4. Start events have a single thin line circle. End events have a single thick line circle. Intermediate events have a double thin line circle. Intermediate events affect the flow of a process, but do not start or end the process. Icons placed in events are used to further define event categories, such as message, timer, or error events.

Activities represent specific steps in the business process. Basic activities are modeled as rounded rectangles. Each activity is described with a short verb phrase placed within the rectangle (e.g., process credit card payment or bill customer). An activity can depict a single action or some logical combination of actions depending on the required level of detail to achieve the objectives of the business process analysis.

Sequence flows are represented by arrows to indicate the progression of activity within the process. The diagram should show the sequence of activity from left to right and top to bottom.

Gateways show process branching and merging as the result of decisions. Basic gateways are depicted as diamonds. Usually, gateways appear as pairs on the diagram. The first gateway shows the branching, and the second gateway shows merging of the process branches.

[7]Data flow diagrams encompass elements of both activity and structure models, but they are primarily used to depict the sequence of data flows related to activities in a business process.

Element	Description	Symbol
Events	Events are things that happen; they affect the flow of the business process when they occur. For example, a start event begins a process, an intermediate event may change the flow, and an end event signals the end of the process.	start; intermediate; end
Activities	Activities are where the work takes place; they can represent processes, subprocesses, or tasks depending on the diagram's level of detail.	Activity
Sequence Flows	An arrow shows the normal sequence flow—i.e., the order of activities—in a business process diagram.	Sequence Flow
Gateways	Gateways control the branching and merging of flow paths in the business process.	Gateway
Annotations	Text annotations allow the analyst to add descriptive information to the diagram.	text annotation

EXHIBIT 4.4
Basic Elements of Business Process Diagrams

Annotations allow the modeler to add additional descriptive information to the model. Annotations are modeled with text inside a bracket connected to other model symbols with a dashed line.

Example of a Business Process Diagram

Exhibit 4.5 illustrates a simple business process activity diagram showing the checkout process at a retail store. In this process, the customer presents items for checkout. The clerk scans items and identifies payment method. Then, the process branches depending on the nature of payment. The payment is accepted, and the process branches merge. The clerk bags the items for the customer, and the process ends. Note that the start event can be labeled to explain the start event, and the gateway branches can be labeled to show the purpose of the branches (handling cash or credit payment in this case).

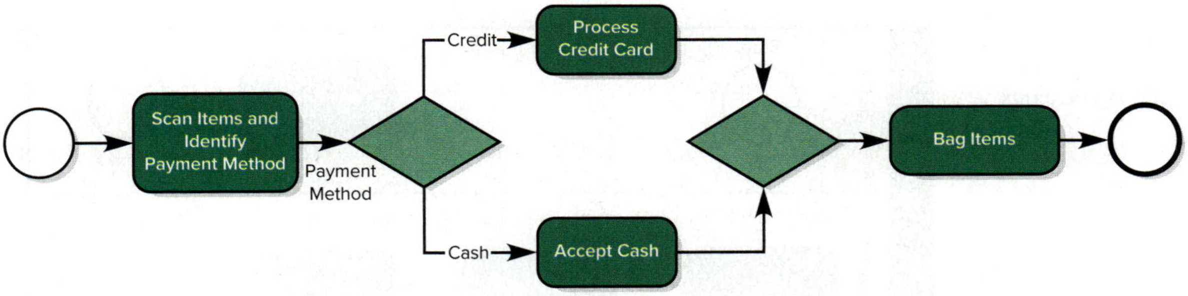

EXHIBIT 4.5
Sample Business Process Diagram

Exhibit 4.5 also demonstrates some other features of BPMN models. First, the models are usually presented left to right or top to bottom. All processes start with a start event and end with an end event, although there may be more than one end event. The flow of the process is shown by the sequence flow arrows. The sequence flows following the branching gateway are labeled to describe the circumstances under which the process would follow that specific flow. Each step in the process, each task, is named to describe the nature of the task. Tasks are named with a verb and an object, such as *bag items* and *accept cash,* that imply the outcome of the task. The branching gateway represents an important question that affects the subsequent flow; in this case, the gateway questions the payment method. However, the gateway is not a decision. The information to answer the question is determined in the task labeled "Scan Items and Identify Payment Method." The second gateway shows that the two paths merge and the flow then continues. In this model, the second, merging, gateway is optional. Later, you will see models where the merging gateway is not optional.

PROGRESS CHECK

3. Draw a business process model (using BPMN) of a drive-through window at a fast-food restaurant. What starts the process? What ends the process? What are the important steps? Are there any decision points that would require gateways?

LO 4-6

Use pools and lanes to identify process participants.

Identifying Participants in Business Process Diagrams

It is often important to identify who performs which activity in a business process. A participant is an actor or person that performs activities and interacts with other participants in a process. Participants include people, systems, organizations, and machines. Participants can also be identified by the role of the actor in the process. BPMN provides notation to identify both the organizations and the departments or individual actors participating in a process. The organization is identified by a **pool** and the department is identified by **lanes** within the pool, as shown in Exhibit 4.6. Every diagram contains at least one pool, but if there is only one pool, the pool may be presented without a boundary. Activities can be assigned to only one participant, and thus may appear in only one pool or lane.

Let's examine Exhibit 4.6 more closely. You should note that regardless of the number of lanes in the pool, there is still one start event per pool and at least one end event. Each task is located in only one lane. Tasks may not span lanes. In other words, one task cannot be performed by two departments. The sequence must flow continuously from the start event to each end event, but the sequence flows can cross lane boundaries. Sequence flows, however, do not extend beyond one pool.

EXHIBIT 4.6
Pools and Lanes to Identify Participants

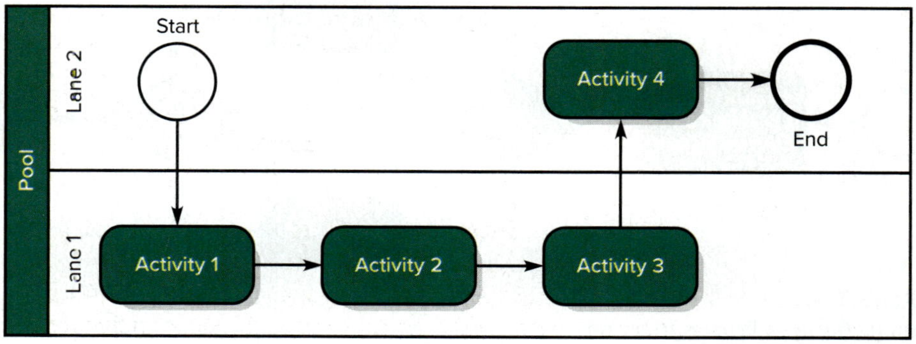

LO 4-7

Apply message flows to show interactions between pools.

Messages in BPMN

BPMN represents exchanges between two participants (pools) in the same process as message flows. For example, in a sales process with a customer pool and a store pool, the customer order would be represented as a message flow. The activities within a pool are organized by sequence flow, but the interactions between pools are represented as **message flows**. A message flow is shown as a dashed arrow with a small circle at the starting end, as shown in Exhibit 4.7.

EXHIBIT 4.7
Message Flow Symbol

Exhibit 4.8 provides a simple example of message flows between two pools. One pool represents a patient and the other pool represents the doctor's office. The patient becomes ill and calls the doctor's office for an appointment. The doctor's office receives the request and assigns the appointment. Each pool has a start event and in the case one end event. The sequence flows are continuous from the start events to the end events and do not cross pool boundaries. The message flows are between pools and not within pools. While the nature of each message flow is pretty clear in this model, it is good practice to label the message flows. As models become more refined, it is sometimes necessary to define the specific content of each message flow to aid the implementation of the process.

EXHIBIT 4.8
Message Flow Example

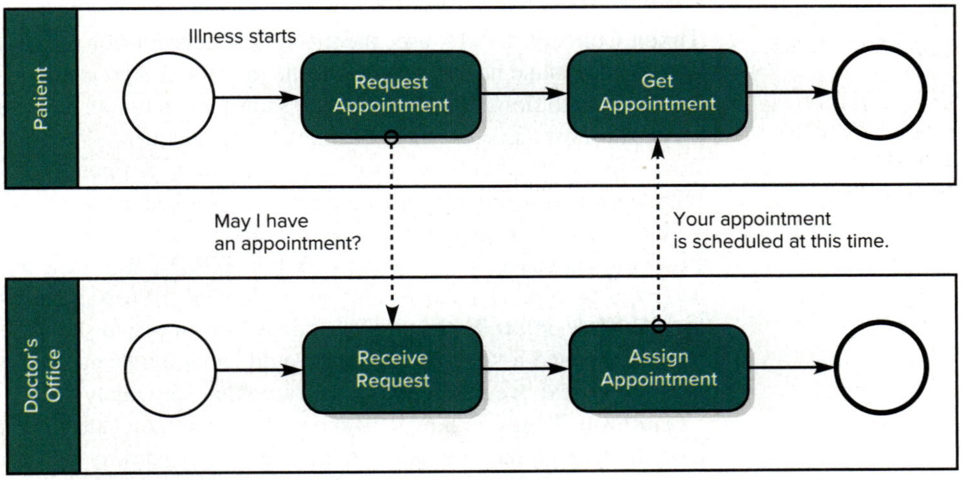

PROGRESS CHECK

4. Using Exhibit 4.8 as a guide, draw a simple model of a customer interacting with **Amazon's** website (www.Amazon.com) to purchase an item. Assume the customer is an Amazon Prime™ member and can buy an item with 1-click (i.e., Amazon already has the credit card information). Use two pools and the associated message flows.

Usually, modelers are not very interested in activities in the external pool. So, if we are modeling the doctor's office process in Exhibit 4.8, we might not care about the activities in the patient's pool. Yet, we remain concerned about the message flows between the pools. So, we can make the patient's pool opaque, hiding the activities but still showing the

EXHIBIT 4.9
Message Flow to Edge of Pool

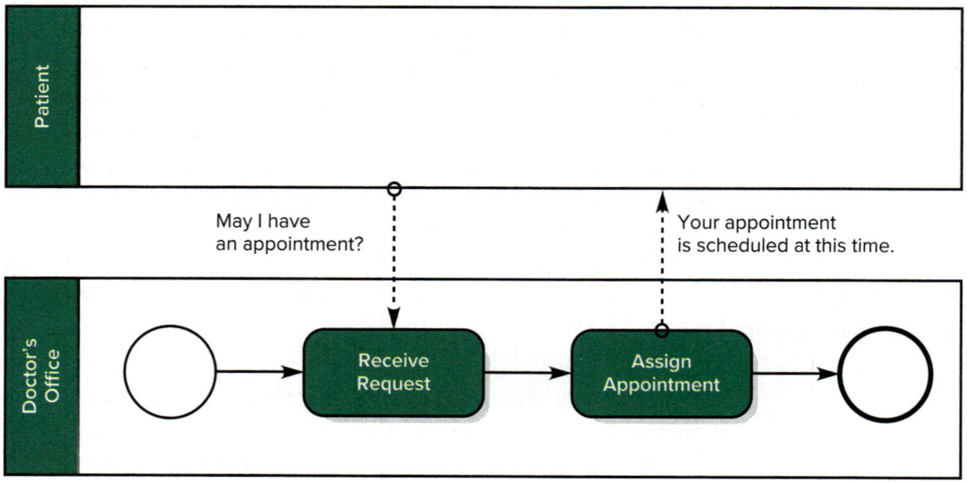

message flows. Exhibit 4.9 shows the opaque patient's pool. Note that the message flows now attach to the edge of the patient's pool.

LO 4-8

Understand and apply flow object types.

Extended Building Blocks for BPMN Diagrams and Modeling Concepts

Token Concept. BPMN uses the theoretical concept of a token flowing through the process to understand how various elements interact. A start event generates a token that must then be able to flow through the process until it reaches an end event, which consumes the token. In most cases, tokens only travel along sequence flows and pass through process flow objects. Process flow object behavior can be defined by how that element interacts with a token as it flows through the process. A token does not traverse message flows.

Flow Object Types. Flow objects include events, activities, and gateways. Sequence flows only connect to flow objects. Within BPMN, each flow object can be further characterized by type. To show the type of element, BPMN includes a type icon within the specific flow object. For example, a "timer" event would show the event with a clock face icon inside, and a "message" event would show the event with an envelope icon inside. Within this text, we will focus on the types that are widely used.

Gateway Types. Exhibit 4.10 shows three common gateway types. Exclusive gateways pass the token along the path established by the gateway conditions. Inclusive gateways

EXHIBIT 4.10
Gateway Types

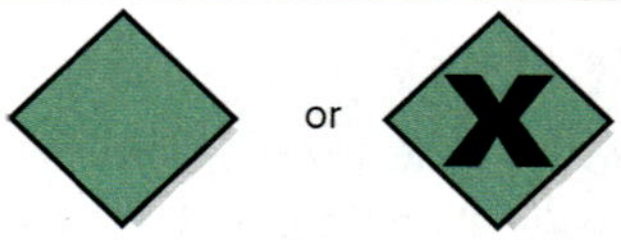	**Exclusive gateway.** For branching, only one path can be taken out of the gateway for each instance of a process.
	**Inclusive gateway.** For branching, one or more paths can be taken out of the gateway for each instance of a process. Merging inclusive gateways synchronize the flow.
	**Parallel gateway.** For branching, all paths are taken out of the gateway for each instance of a process. Merging parallel gateways synchronize the flow.

can create additional tokens depending on the number of paths taken after the branching gateway. Parallel gateways also create additional tokens for each path leaving the gateway. The merging gateways synchronize the process. For inclusive and parallel gateways, the merging gateways delay the flow until all tokens for that instance arrive, then one token proceeds along the exiting sequence flow.

Consider the process of planning a trip. Exhibit 4.11 shows an example of an exclusive gateway where the trip will involve either traveling by air or traveling by car. In Exhibit 4.12, an inclusive gateway indicates that the planned trip could involve either traveling by air or traveling by car or both. In Exhibit 4.13, a parallel gateway indicates that the trip will involve air travel, car travel, and hotel stays.

EXHIBIT 4.11
Exclusive Gateway Example Where the Trip Involves Air Travel or Car Travel but Not Both

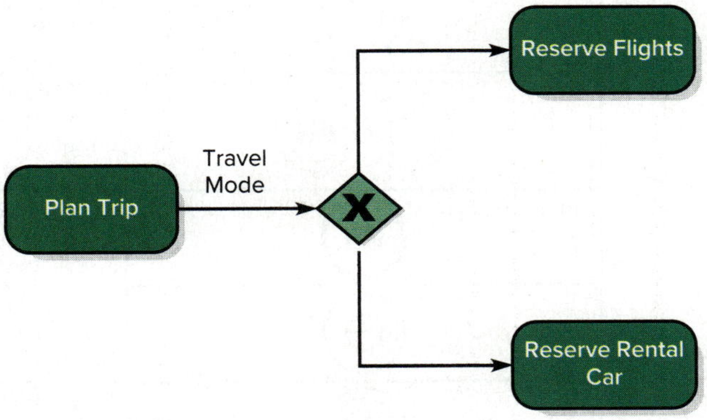

EXHIBIT 4.12
Inclusive Gateway Example Where the Trip May Involve Either Air Travel, Car Travel, or Both

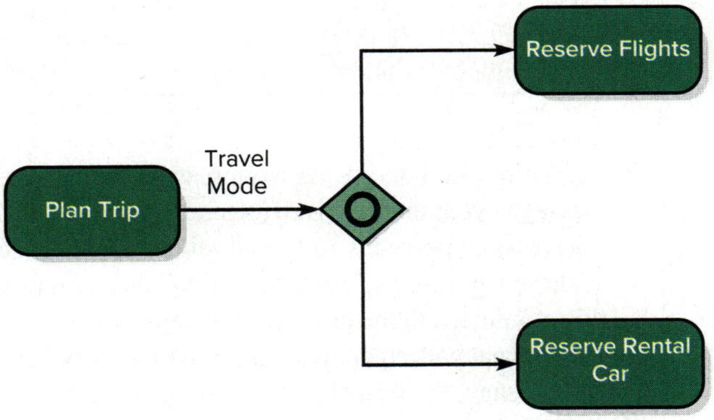

EXHIBIT 4.13
Parallel Gateway Example Where the Trip Involves Air Travel, Car Travel, and Hotel Stays

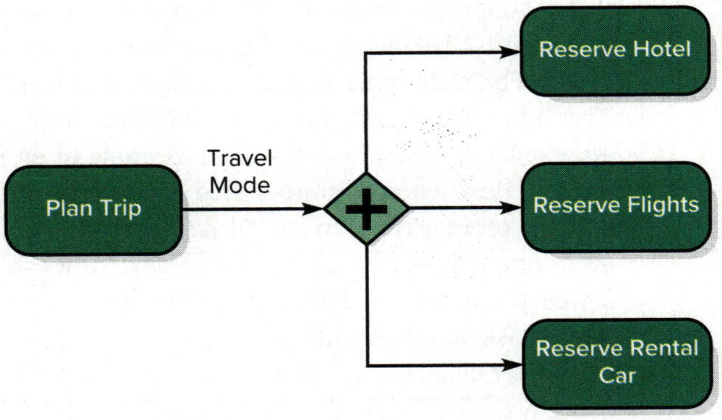

Event Types. The basic flow objects include start events, intermediate events, and end events. Like Gateway types where the icon indicates the unique characteristics of that Gateway, BPMN also identifies types of start, intermediate, and end events. Exhibit 4.14 shows some of the most common event types. First, message events either create (throw) or receive (catch) messages. Messages are communications between participants (pools) in a process, which are modeled as message flows. Second, timer events indicate a delay until a specific time and/or date or a specific cycle (such as 8 hours, 2 weeks). Third, error events indicate an interruption to the process. Intermediate error events are "boundary" events; they are attached to an activity and indicate an alternate process flow when an error occurs.

EXHIBIT 4.14
Event Types

	**Start message (catching) event.** Used to begin a process based on an incoming message, such as a sales order. Start events only receive (catch) messages and not send (throw) them.
	**Intermediate message events.** The event with the white envelope catches messages and the event with the black envelope throws (sends) messages to external participants.
	**End message (throwing) event.** Used to send a message when the process ends. End events cannot receive (catch) messages.
	**Start timer event.** Used to indicate that the process starts at a particular time or date, such as preparing budgets at the end of each month.
	**Intermediate timer event.** Used to indicate a delay in the process flow until a specified time or date or for a specified period of time.
	**Intermediate error event.** A boundary event, discussed in more detail below, that indicates the start of an alternate process flow when an error occurs in an activity.

Exhibit 4.15 shows an example using message events. The process starts with a start message event that receives (catches) the "Request" message from the external participant. The process proceeds to the "Evaluate Request" task, and then the intermediate message event sends (throws) the "Evaluation" message flow to the external participant. The process flow continues to the next intermediate message event, where it waits (the token stops) until the external participant responds with the "Confirm" message flow. When the event catches the message, the sequence flow continues to the "Do Something" task and then the process ends. The end message event throws a message to the external participant that the process is done. Note that in this simple interaction between an external pool and the process, the pool that contains the process is implied and does not need to be included on the diagram.

Exhibit 4.16 shows an example using timer events and a boundary intermediate error event. The start timer begins the process 2 weeks before the birthday to be celebrated. The "Plan Party" task has an intermediate error event attached to its boundary (a boundary event). Specifically, this is an example of an interrupting boundary event that affects process flow when an unspecified error occurs in the Plan Party task. If an error occurs, then the process flows to the "Cancel Party" task and then ends. However, if the Plan Party task completes successfully, the process flows to the intermediate timer event and waits 2 weeks (the token waits to proceed). After 2 weeks, the process continues to the "Hold Party" task and then ends.

In later chapters, we will discuss other types of boundary events, both interrupting and noninterrupting. Note that you could also model the process shown in Exhibit 4.16 using

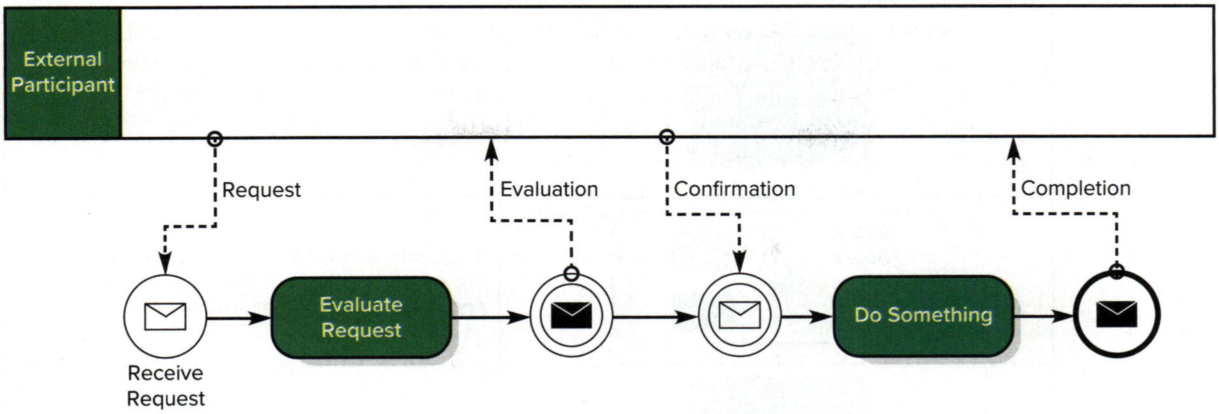

EXHIBIT 4.15
Message Events Example

EXHIBIT 4.16
Timer and Error Events Example

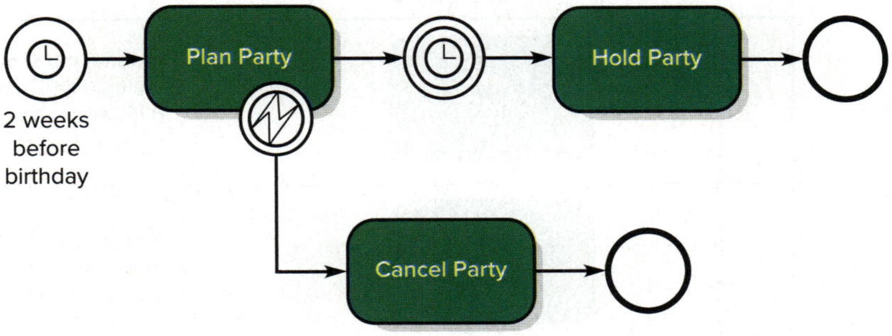

a task to test whether the plans are good and then using a gateway to branch to the Cancel Party task if the plans fail. The use of the error boundary event provides a clear and more concise way to show the error handling option.

Task Types. Finally, BPMN offers different task types, but task types are used less often than gateway and error types. There are tasks to send and receive messages. These would be modeled with envelope icons (white for receiving, black for sending) in the upper left corner of the task rectangle. These tasks correspond to catching and throwing message events, and in most cases, the message events are preferred. Normally, you would use the send and receive tasks when you need to attach boundary events to the task as you can't do that with events. Modelers are often tempted to use the send and receive tasks to forward work to the next task in the process. This is unnecessary because the sequence flow implies that the work is forwarded. So, send and receive tasks are only related to message flows. Next, there are business rules tasks. In a business rules task, one or more business rules are applied in order to produce a result or make a decision. There are several other task types, such as user, script, manual, and service, and users can define their own tasks. In most cases, there is little need to use other than the general abstract task type (without any type icon). In this textbook, we will generally not use task types.

Subprocesses and Repeating Activities

LO 4-9

Recognize and model repeating activities.

Activities are the places where work occurs in BPMN diagrams. An activity can represent a process, subprocess, or task. So far, we've focused on tasks, but sometimes it is helpful to show a higher level of abstraction. In other words, we might want to lump several related tasks together into a subprocess. Exhibit 4.17 shows how subprocesses

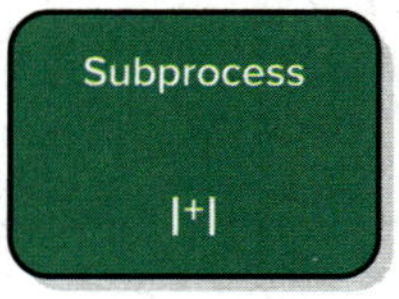	**Collapsed subprocess.** Contains another process that is hidden from view. The details of the other process are normally shown in another diagram.
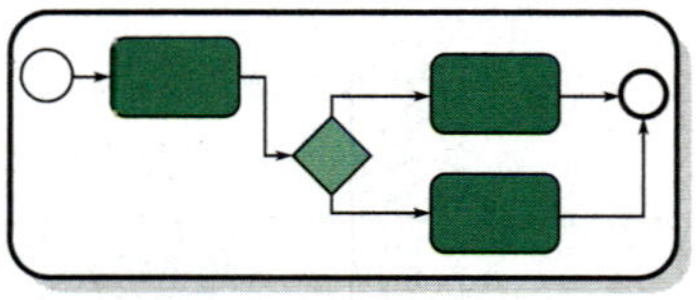	**Expanded subprocess.** Used when embedding the subprocess in the current process and showing the details of the subprocess.
	**Looping activity/task.** Indicates that the activity or task loops until a condition is satisfied, such as "all email in the inbox has been read."
	**Parallel multi-instance task.** Task is performed multiple times in parallel, such as when several different people are doing the same task at the same time.
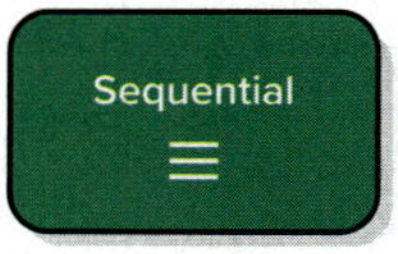	**Sequential multi-instance task.** Task is performed multiple times in sequence, such as when instructor grades tests for students in a class.

EXHIBIT 4.17
Subprocesses and Repeating Activities

and repeating activities are modeled. Subprocesses can be used to show processes that are reused in several other processes. They are a useful modeling tool when the modeler doesn't want to add unnecessary detail to a diagram, especially when that detail will be presented in another model.

Sometimes, we want to show that the same task is performed multiple times. In this case, we can show the task as looping. Looping tasks repeat until a condition is satisfied. This has the same effect as using a gateway that directs process flow to repeat the task if the condition is not satisfied. When the number of times that a task will repeat is known in advance, we can use a multi-instance task. A parallel multi-instance task is performed several times by different actors at the same time. A sequential multi-instance task is performed several times by the same actor in sequence. Think about taking a test. Each student takes the test at the same time, so this would be an example of a parallel multi-instance task. Then, the instructor grades the tests sequentially, so this would be an example of a sequential multi-instance task.

LO 4-10

Understand and apply data objects and datastores to model data created, updated, transferred, and deleted in a process.

Data Objects, Datastores, and Associations

Processes create, update, transfer, and delete data in various forms. Sometimes the data management is implicit. At other times, it is important to explicitly model where data are created or used. The two main BPMN elements used to model data are the data object and the datastore, as shown in Exhibit 4.18. Data objects are modeled with document icons. Datastores are modeled with the computer disk icon. Associations are dotted lines that show the movement of data between the data objects and datastores and activities. Associations may use arrowheads to show the direction of data flow.

EXHIBIT 4.18
Data Objects, Datastores, and Associations

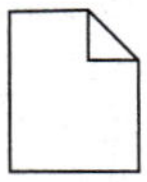	**Data object.** Represents data (e.g., an invoice) that is only available for the duration of the process.
	**Datastore.** Represents data that is available across processes, such as information in a database.
	**Association.** Connects data objects or datastores to activities. The arrowhead shows the direction of the data flow when necessary.

Exhibit 4.19 shows alternative examples of one simple process with a data object. The process starts when the actor buys concert tickets. Time passes until the date of the concert and then the actor attends the concert using the tickets. The same data object, tickets, can be repeated in the process as necessary to avoid confusing associations. In our simple example, the first alternative seems to make more sense because it is clear that one ticket data object is created and then used. When the tickets information is shared across processes rather than only within one process, then tickets should be modeled as a datastore.

EXHIBIT 4.19
Examples of Process Using Data Objects

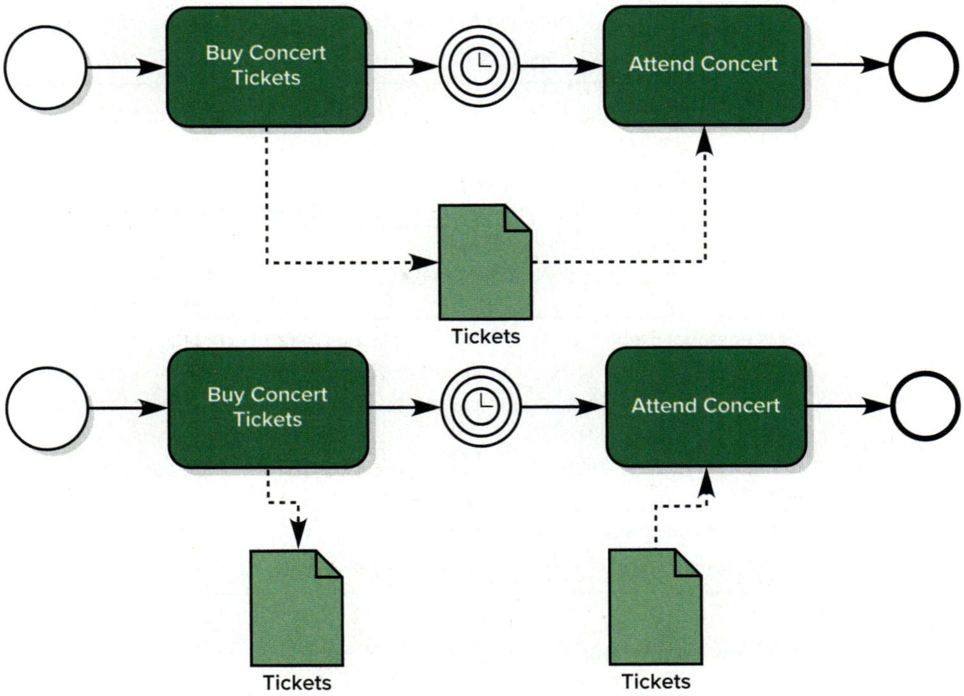

Rules for Connecting Symbols with Sequence Flows and Message Flows

Pools represent participants in a process. If the process has only one participant, it is not necessary to use a pool symbol. Sequence flows are used within pools. Message flows are used between pools. Exhibit 4.20 describes the general rules for connecting sequence flows. For example, a sequence flow can connect an activity to another activity, collapsed subprocess, gateway, intermediate event, or end event, but a sequence flow cannot connect to a start event. Exhibit 4.21 describes the general rules for connecting message flows. For example, a message flow can connect an external pool to a start message event, but a start message event cannot initiate a message flow to another pool. Activities can initiate or receive (throw or catch) message flows. Again, a message flow must connect a pool or a symbol within a pool to the edge of another pool or symbol in that other pool.

To avoid errors in your BPMN diagrams, there is one basic good practice to follow. Although not required by the BPMN specification, activities should have one incoming and one outgoing sequence flow. If you need more than one incoming or outgoing flow, use a gateway to branch or merge flows.

EXHIBIT 4.20
Allowable Sequence Flow Connections

		Connecting to Symbol					
		Start Event	**Activity**	**Collapsed Subprocess**	**Gateway**	**Intermediate Event**	**End Event**
Connecting from Symbol	Start Event	NO	YES	YES	YES	YES	YES
	Activity	NO	YES	YES	YES	YES	YES
	Collapsed Subprocess	NO	YES	YES	YES	YES	YES
	Gateway	NO	YES	YES	YES	YES	YES
	Intermediate Event	NO	YES	YES	YES	YES	YES
	End Event	NO	NO	NO	NO	NO	NO

		Connecting to Symbol (in Current Pool)						
		Start (Message) Event	**Pool**	**Activity**	**Collapsed Subprocess**	**Gateway**	**Intermediate (Message) Event**	**End (Message) Event**
Connecting from Symbol	Start (Message) Event	NO	NO	NO	NO	NO	NO	NO
	Pool	YES	YES	YES	YES	YES	YES	NO
	Activity	YES	YES	YES	YES	YES	YES	NO
	Collapsed Subprocess	YES	YES	YES	YES	YES	YES	NO
	Gateway	YES	YES	YES	YES	YES	YES	NO
	Intermediate (Message) Event	YES	YES	YES	YES	YES	YES	NO
	End (Message) Event	YES	YES	YES	YES	YES	YES	NO

EXHIBIT 4.21
Allowable Message Flow Connections

LO 4-11

Understand and apply a structured process of business process model development.

Steps to Prepare Business Process Models

BPMN provides useful tools to create activity diagrams. These diagrams aid in planning, documenting, discussing, implementing, and using systems. To prepare useful business process models, it is helpful to follow a structured and iterative process:

1. Identify the purpose of the business process model. In this step, the modeler defines who the model is for, why it is needed, and how it is going to be used.
2. Define the model context. In this step, the modeler identifies external actors, exchanges between processes and those actors, and any boundaries for the model.
3. Outline basic business process flows. In this step, the modeler builds on information gathered in step two to define inputs to each process and expected outcomes from that process. Then, the modeler lays out the expected activity sequence to deliver the expected outcome.
4. Define the activities in the process. In this step, the modeler determines what takes place in each activity, who performs that activity, and what outcomes are reasonable, including expected error situations.
5. Refine diagrams and decompose activities into any needed lower-level processes. In this step, the modeler adds detail as necessary to achieve the purpose of the model.
6. Validate the model with stakeholders. In this step, the modeler reviews the diagrams with stakeholders that perform the process, stakeholders that are customers of the process, and stakeholders that are responsible for the process.

Review Exercise: Preparing a Basic BPMN Diagram

This review exercise focus on business process modeling with BPMN.

1. The purpose of this review exercise is to describe the passenger check-in process at the airport using automated kiosks. We are assuming that this will be used to provide a passenger guide in the future.
2. The context of the model will include steps beginning with the passenger's arrival at the airport terminal and end when the passenger has been checked in, checked any luggage, and received a boarding pass. Thus, the diagram will not include elements of transportation to the airport, transiting security, and boarding the plane. The context of the model is established by interviews with stakeholders or review of any documentation. In this case, the context includes two participants, the automated kiosk and the passenger, and the communications between them.
3. The process takes place as follows:
    - The passenger approaches the kiosk. The kiosk screen requests the customer to identify themselves.
    - The passenger scans the required identification.
    - The kiosk uses the passenger identification to find and display the passenger's flight information.
    - The passenger confirms the flight information.
    - The kiosk asks how many bags to be checked.
    - The passenger responds with the count of bags to be checked.
    - The kiosk prints the requested number of tags.
    - The passenger affixes the tags to the bags.
    - The kiosk prints the boarding pass(es).

4. Using this information, complete the following:
   - Create a context diagram using two pools (Kiosk and Passenger) and showing the message flows between the two pools.
   - Outline basic business process flows. Identify the sequence of activities that the passenger performs in the process and prepare an initial BPMN model.
   - Define the activities. For this exercise, the activities are pretty clear. In more complicated situations, you would examine closely the content of each activity.
   - Refine the diagram. Next, add the external pool (kiosk) and the message flows between the passenger and kiosk. Modify the process flow with gateways that branch and merge so that the passenger doesn't receive and affix tags when they are not checking any bags.
   - Validate with stakeholders. Review our diagram with process users (fellow students in this case).

Summary

- Accountants' roles in business are evolving rapidly.
- Accountants are increasingly involved in business management support.
- Business process documentation is essential for training, describing current processes and systems to support internal and external audits, establishing accountability, and communicating among employees and various stakeholders.
- Business process documentation provides a starting point for business process improvement.
- Business models manage complexity, elicit requirements, reconcile viewpoints, and specify operating requirements for business processes.
- There are two major types of business process models: activity models and structure models.
- Activity models show the flow of work in a business process.
- BPMN provides a notation for specifying workflow.
- BPMN notation includes flow objects: events, activities, sequence flows, and gateways that allow process branching.
- BPMN allows the identification of participants in a process through the use of pools and swimlanes.
- BPMN message flows document exchanges between pools.
- External pools may be opaque with message flows attached to the edge of the pool.
- The token concept is a method to understand sequence flow within a process.
- BPMN establishes types for flow objects—that is, events, gateways, and tasks—to help describe specific uses.
- Intermediate error events are an example of boundary events that interrupt the normal flow of a process when an error condition occurs.
- Timer events are used to indicate events that occur at a specific time or date or cause the process to wait for a specific period of time.
- Subprocesses represent collections of tasks.
- Data objects and datastores allow modeling of process information processing requirements.

Key Words

activities (*182*) In business process modeling, activities represent specific steps in a business process.

activity models (*181*) Models that describe the sequence of workflow in a business process or processes.

annotations (*183*) Model elements that allow the modeler to add additional descriptive information to the model. Annotations are modeled with text inside a bracket connected to other model symbols with a dashed line.

business analysis (*178*) The process of defining business process requirements and evaluating potential improvements. Business analysis involves ascertaining, documenting, and communicating information about current and future business processes using business process modeling and related tools.

business model (*178*) A simple, abstract representation of one or more business processes. A business model is typically a graphical depiction of the essential business process information.

business process (*178*) A defined sequence of business activities that use resources to transform specific inputs into specific outputs to achieve a business goal.

business process modeling notation (BPMN) (*182*) A standard for the description of activity models.

Any separately identifiable collection of things (objects) about which the organization wants to collect and store information. Classes can represent organization resources (e.g., trucks, machines, buildings, cash, investments), persons (e.g., customers, employees), events (e.g., sales, purchases, cash disbursements, cash receipts), and conceptual structures (e.g., accounts, product categories, budgets). Classes are typically implemented as tables in a relational database, where individual instances of the class are represented as rows in the table.

Another type of activity model that graphically shows the flow of data through a system and also incorporates elements of structure models.

documentation (*179*) An information transmission and communication tool that explains how business processes and business systems work.

events (*182*) Events: (UML) Classes that model the organization's transactions, usually affecting the organization's resources, such as sales and cash receipts; (BPMN) important occurrences that affect the flow of activities in a business process, including start, intermediate, and end events.

flowcharts (*196*) Visualizations of a process activity; they are activity models much like models using BPMN.

gateways (*182*) Show process branching and merging as the result of decisions. Basic gateways are depicted as diamonds. Usually, gateways appear as pairs on the diagram. The first gateway shows the branching, and the second gateway shows merging of the process branches.

lanes (or swimlanes) (*184*) BPMN symbols that provide subdivisions of pools to show, for example, functional responsibilities within an organization.

message flows (*185*) BPMN represents exchanges between two participants (pools) in the same process as message flows, which are modeled as dashed arrows.

pools (*184*) BPMN symbols used to identify participants, actors, or persons that perform activities and interact with other participants in a process.

process maps (*196*) Simplified flowcharts that use a basic set of symbols to represent a business process activity.

sequence flows (*182*) BPMN symbols that show the normal sequence of activities in a business process. Sequence flows are modeled as solid arrows, with the arrowhead showing the direction of process flow.

Appendix A

Flowcharting

WHAT IS A FLOWCHART?

Like business process models, **flowcharts** are visualizations of a process activity. Flowcharts have been widely used since they were first introduced in the 1920s. Modern techniques such as UML activity diagrams and BPMN are extensions of flowcharts. Flowcharts are useful tools for systems development, process documentation, and understanding internal controls. Three types of flowcharts are often used by accountants. These three types typically differ in the level of detail modeled.

1. *Systems flowcharts* provide an overall view of a system, including the inputs, activities, and outputs of the process.
2. *Process maps* use the basic set of flowchart symbols to provide a representation of the steps within a business process. **Process maps** are conceptually similar to business process diagrams created with BPMN.
3. *Document flowcharts* present the flow of documents through an entity, often describing the areas within the entity with responsibility for particular tasks.

BASIC BUILDING BLOCKS FOR FLOWCHARTS

The basic flowchart symbols shown in Exhibit 4.A1 are similar to, and serve the same basic functions as, the BPMN symbols for activity models.

- *Start/End.* Each flowchart should show the flow of process activities from one start to one or more logical ends. The start and end steps are drawn as ovals.
- *Tasks/Activities.* Tasks or activities represent specific steps in the business process. Basic activities are modeled as rectangles. Each activity is described with a short verb

Element	**Description**	**Symbol**
Start/End	The Start/End steps indicate the beginning and ending of the process flow.	Start
Tasks/Activities	Tasks/Activities are the steps that describe the work; they can represent individual tasks or collections of tasks depending on the diagram's level of detail.	Task/Activity
Sequence Flows	An arrow shows the normal direction of flow—i.e., the order of activities—in a diagram.	—— Sequence Flow ——>
Decisions	Decision ciamonds portray the nature of the decision and the exit options.	Decision

EXHIBIT 4.A1
Basic Elements of Flowcharts

phrase placed within the rectangle (e.g., process credit card payment or bill customer). An activity can depict a single action or some logical combination of actions depending on the required level of detail to achieve the objectives of the business process analysis.

- *Sequence Flows.* Sequence flows are represented by arrows to indicate the progression of activity within the process. The diagram should show the sequence of activity from left to right and top to bottom.
- *Decisions.* Decisions are modeled as diamonds with multiple exits (sequence flows) based on the result of decisions.

EXAMPLE OF BUSINESS PROCESS FLOWCHART

Exhibit 4.A2 shows a simple business process activity diagram depicting the checkout process at a retail store. In this process, the customer presents items for checkout. The clerk scans items and identifies payment method. Then the process branches depending on the nature of payment. The payment is accepted, and the process branches merge. The clerk bags the items for the customer, and the process ends. Note that the start event can be labeled to explain the start event, and the gateway branches can be labeled to show the purpose of the branches (handling cash or credit payment in this case).

EXHIBIT 4.A2
Sample Business Process Flowchart

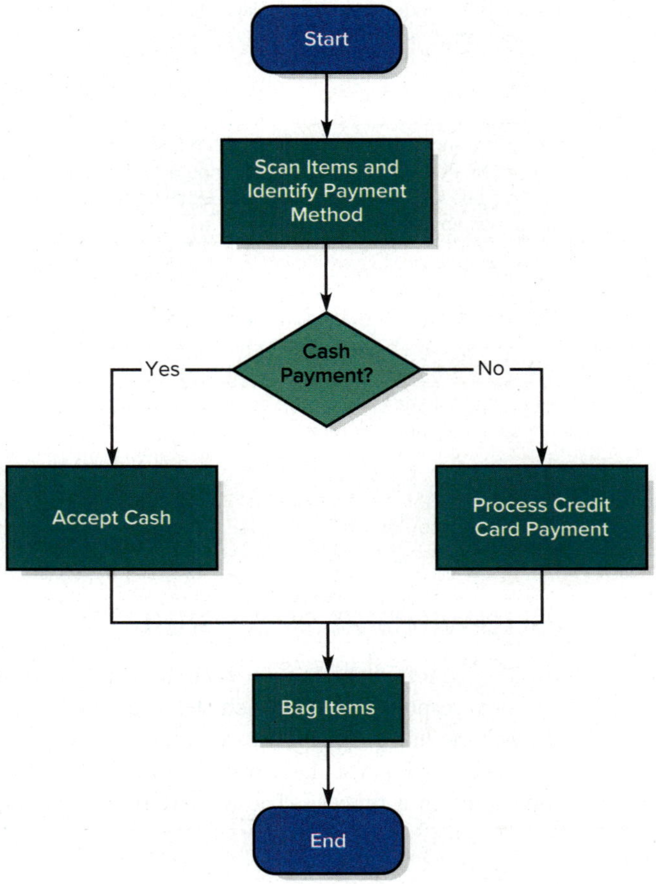

ADDITIONAL FLOWCHART SYMBOLS

The additional symbols shown in Exhibit 4.A3 are also widely used to depict specific operations within flowcharts. While none of these symbols are necessary for system flowcharts, they are often used in document flowcharts to differentiate manual and system operations and the media used in the process.

Element	Description	Symbol
Input/Output; Journal/ Ledger	The parallelogram is a generalized symbol for input or output when the medium is not specified.	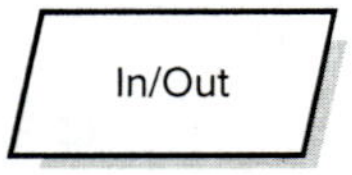
Input/Output of Document(s) or Report(s)	The document symbol indicates hard-copy documents or reports coming into or going out of the process.	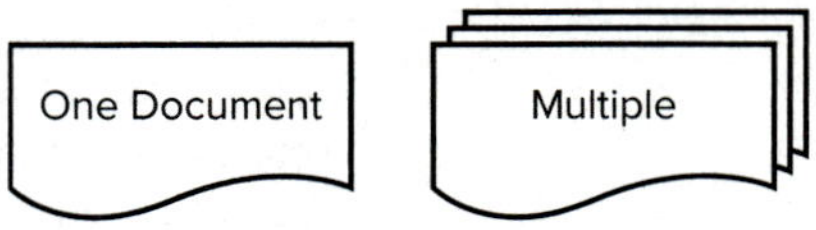
Online Keying	This symbol indicates data entry using online devices such as a computer or a handheld device.	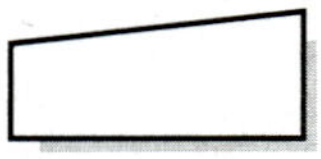
Storage Offline	This symbol indicates storage, typically of documents, not accessible by computer. File-ordering sequence is indicated as follows: N = numerically, A = alphabetically, and D = by date.	
Magnetic Disc Storage	This symbol includes database (online) storage accessible by computer.	
Manual Task/Activity	This symbol indicates a manual task. If the flowchart differentiates between manual and computer operations, the basic task/activity symbol shown in Exhibit 4.A1 then shows a computer operation.	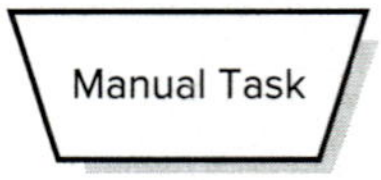
On/Off Page Connectors	These symbols facilitate modeling by allowing a connection between two points on the same page or on different pages.	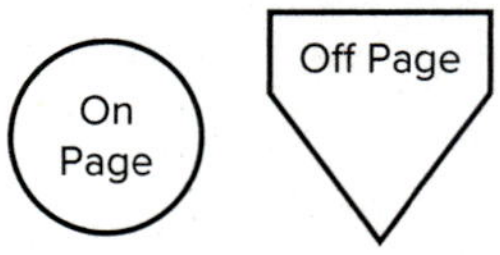
Annotation	This symbol s to add descriptive comments or explanatory notes to clarify the process.	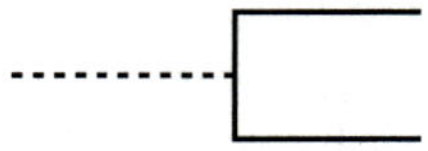

EXHIBIT 4.A3
Additional Flowchart Symbols

SHOWING RESPONSIBILITY

Deployment flowcharts show both the sequence of steps in a process as well as the organizational responsibility for each step. Like business process models (BPMN), deployment flowcharts use swimlanes to represent different organizational units or functions. These flowcharts are particularly useful in identifying the multiple handoffs between organization units in a process. These handoffs can be sources of problems, and making these

EXHIBIT 4.A4
Flowchart with Swimlanes Showing Responsibility

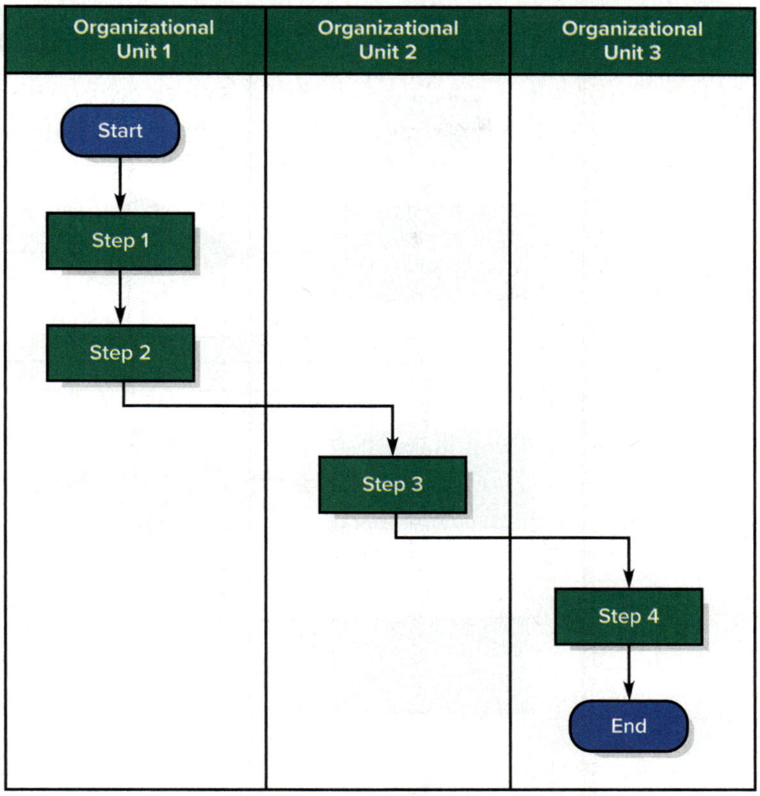

steps clear can help identify those problems. Additionally, deployment flowcharts are useful in documenting processes for activities such as employee training. The flowchart in Exhibit 4.A4 illustrates swimlanes and responsibilities.

SHOWING OPPORTUNITY

Opportunity flowcharts highlight opportunities for improvement by, for example, separating value-added from cost-added activities within a process. Opportunity flowcharts use swimlanes to separate the activities that add value from those that add to the costs of the process, such as the costs of redoing work, waiting for information, waiting for parts, or correcting problems in general. Value-added activities are those that are essential to producing the process's product or service given the current state of technology, even if the process runs perfectly every time. Cost-added-only activities are those related to checking for defects, reworking, or supplying missing information.

For example, Exhibit 4.A5 shows the simple process of printing out and turning in an assignment document. If the process went as expected, we would select the printer, print the document, and turn in the assignment. The example assumes that, in some cases, the printer can be out of paper, which requires adding more paper before proceeding, or that the print cartridges could be out of ink, which requires replacing the cartridges and reprinting the document.

EXHIBIT 4.A5
Opportunity Flowchart Example of a Document Printing Process

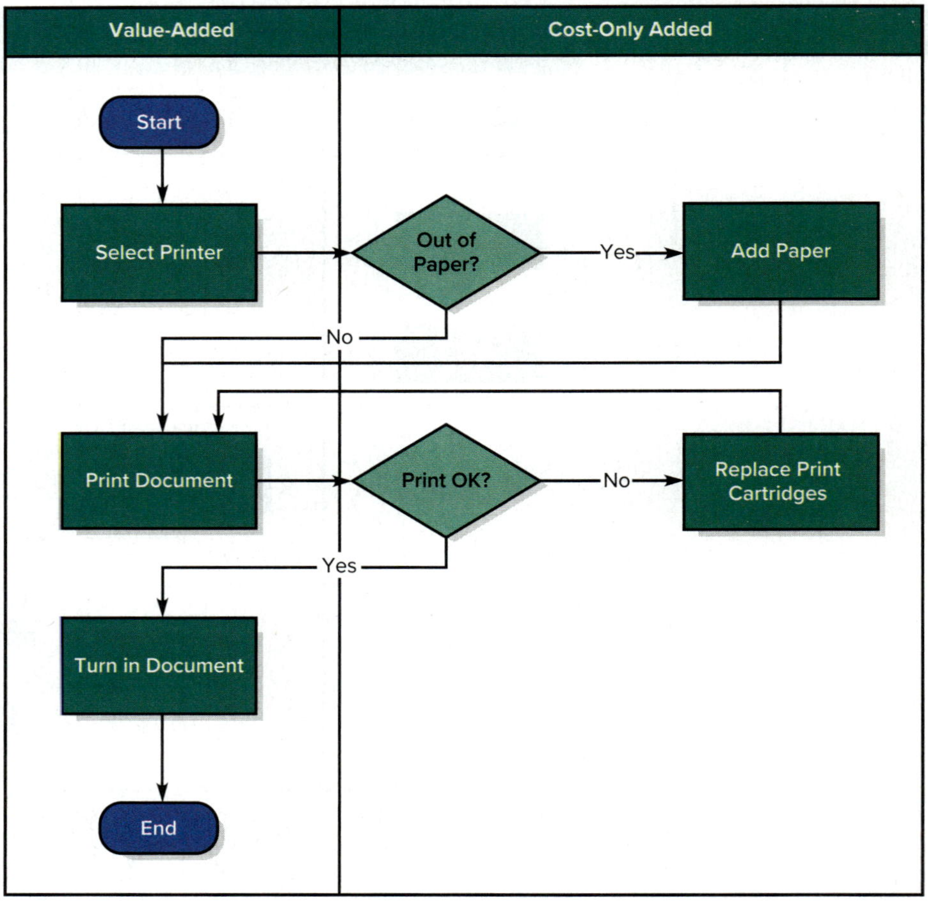

Appendix B

Data Flow Diagrams

WHAT IS A DATA FLOW DIAGRAM (DFD)?

A **data flow diagram (DFD)** represents graphically the flow of data through a system, such as one or more business processes. Data flow diagrams are often used to perform structured systems analysis and design, whereby a system is described at increasing levels of detail to facilitate new systems design. DFDs use a limited set of symbols (see Exhibit 4.B1) and are easily read and understood. Unlike most flowcharts, DFDs specifically represent the datastores—that is, the system files affected by or supporting the process—as well as the data that flow to and from the datastores. DFDs have no start and end symbols, which is also unlike flowcharts and BPMN business process diagrams. Instead, data flow diagrams present the external sources of—or destinations for—the data.

BASIC BUILDING BLOCKS FOR DATA FLOW DIAGRAMS

The following describes basic building blocks for data flow diagrams. The structure of these diagrams is substantially different from the structure of BPMN activity models.

EXHIBIT 4.B1
Basic Elements of Data Flow Diagrams

Element	Description	Symbol
Process	The activities within a system that use or generate data (e.g., receive customer order).	Process
Data Source or Destination	The entities that interact with the system (e.g., customers, employees, or bank).	Source/ Destination
Datastores	This symbol describes the physical or electronic data storage.	Datastore
Data Flows	This symbol shows the flow of data (e.g., an order coming from a customer); data flows are named to indicate the data content.	data flow 1

- *Processes* are activities that use or generate data. Depending on the software tools used to draw DFDs, processes may be represented with circles or rectangles with rounded corners. As with BPMN diagrams and flowcharts, processes are given names using short verb phrases (e.g., receive customer order). A process must have at least one or more data flows coming in and going out.
- *Terminators* are external entities that are either sources or destinations for data. Terminators are typically represented with rectangles. Examples of terminators are customers, suppliers, or other entities external to the particular system being represented.
- *Datastores* represent the physical or electronic repositories of data within the system. Datastores are typically represented as rectangles with one or both ends open.
- *Data flows* represent the flow of physical or electronic data through the system. These are represented by arrows that show the direction of data flow.

EXAMPLE OF A DFD

Exhibit 4.B2 shows a simple example of a DFD showing the checkout process at a retail store. In this process, the customer (external source) presents items for checkout. The system includes scanning and bagging the items and accepting payment while updating sales and inventory records.

NESTING OR EXPLODING DFDs

DFDs describe a system at increasing levels of detail to facilitate new systems design. The context diagram shows the entire system as one process and identifies all relevant external sources and destinations for data, as well as the type of data coming from or going to those external entities. Then, subsequent models showing increasing detail would be identified as level 0, level 1, and level 2. Each process in a DFD is designated by the level and the number of the process. In Exhibit 4.B2, for example, assuming that is the level 0 diagram, then *Scan Items* could be designated process 1.0. If any subprocesses of *Scan Items* are subsequently modeled, those would be designated 1.1, 1.2, and so on.

BEST PRACTICES FOR DFDs

There are several best practices to ensure that DFDs provide useful descriptions of systems. Similar to flowcharts and BPMN diagrams, DFDs are a communications tool. Thus, the names given to processes, datastores, data flows, and external entities are important.

EXHIBIT 4.B2
Sample Level 1 DFD of Customer Checkout System

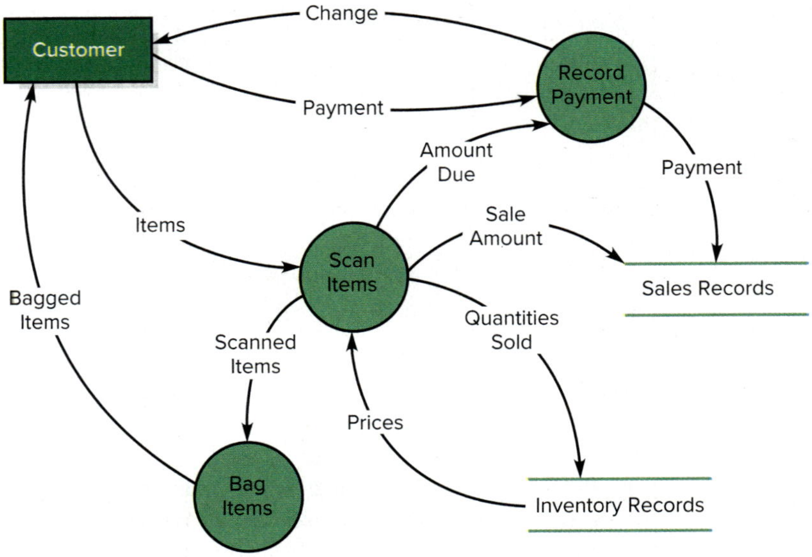

The names should be clear to the system users. With regard to modeling specific elements of the diagram, modelers should remember that processes do not spontaneously generate or absorb data. Processes only modify data; therefore, all processes should have at least one data flow coming in and going out, and the data flow out of a process should be different than the data flow in. Datastores support the system's processing requirements, so every datastore should be connected to at least one process in the system. Finally, systems are developed to respond to inputs from external entities or to deliver information to external entities, so every external entity must be connected to at least one data flow.

USING DFDs FOR SYSTEM DOCUMENTATION

To form complete documentation for a system, the business analyst would augment the DFDs with additional information. For example, the analyst would define each datastore completely, specifying the fields, data types, data limits, and formats. The analyst would also define each element of a data flow in terms of the specific fields that it contains. Plus, the analyst would describe the business rules or logic for each process and confirm those with the process owners.

ANSWERS TO PROGRESS CHECKS

1. Documentation is important to almost all accounting/finance functions listed.
2. The answer depends on the student, but all of us have used maps. Many of us have assembled a product from **IKEA.** Most of us have installed software on our computers.
3. Here's a simple business process model (without pools and swimlanes) for a fast-food drive-through:

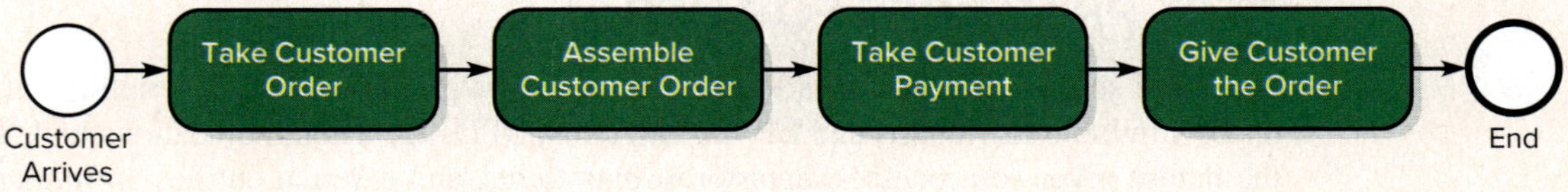

4. Here is one possible example of a process model using pools and message flows to show a customer interacting with Amazon.com's website to purchase an item.

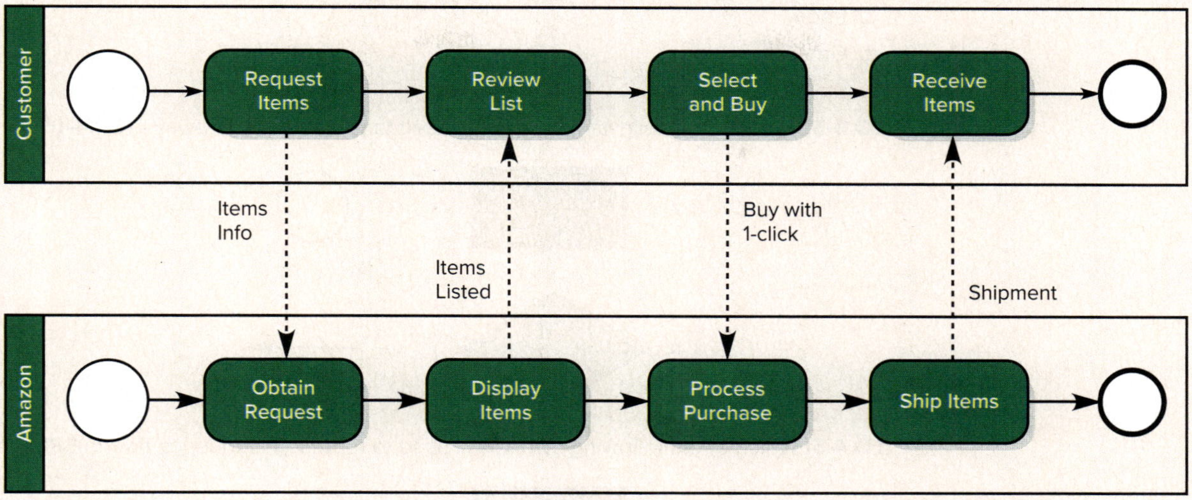

Multiple Choice Questions connect

1. **(LO 4-1)** Which of the following is not a role of the accounting function in business?
   a. Financial close
   b. Regulatory compliance
   c. Project management
   d. Using IT to make finance and accounting processes more efficient
   e. All of these are roles of the accounting function
2. **(LO 4-2)** Which of the following is not an example of business process documentation?
   a. Business process models
   b. Training manuals
   c. Organization charts
   d. Internal audit
   e. All of these are examples of business process documentation
3. **(LO 4-2)** Which of the following is not a purpose of business process documentation?
   a. Facilitating process improvement
   b. Specifying accountability
   c. Training
   d. Supporting internal audit
   e. All of these are purposes of business process documentation
4. **(LO 4-3)** Which of the following best describes the value of business models?
   a. A communication tool
   b. A planning tool
   c. A process improvement tool
   d. A tool for managing complexity
   e. All of these describe values of business models.

5. **(LO 4-6)** Which of the following describes how participants in a process are identified in BPMN?
   a. Message flows
   b. Sequence flows
   c. Pools
   d. Gateways
   e. Start events
6. **(LO 4-5)** Which of the following symbols is used to represent a gateway in BPMN?

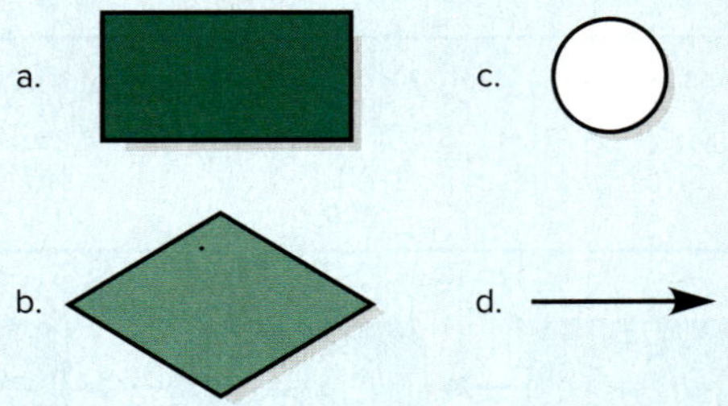

7. **(LO 4-5)** Which of the following symbols is used to represent sequence flow in BPMN?

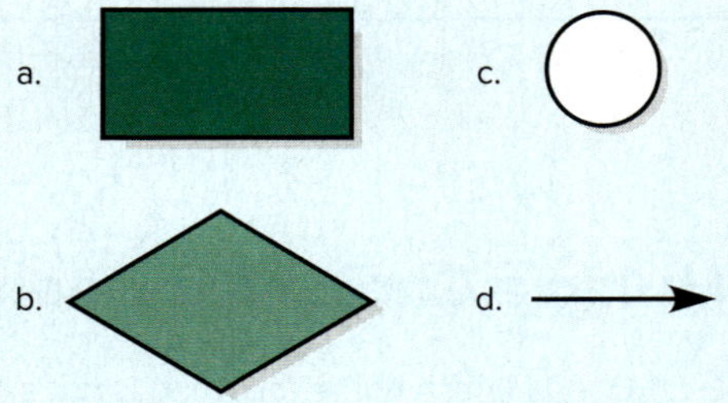

8. **(LO 4-5)** Which of the following statements about BPMN is not true?
   a. Arrows represent sequence flows.
   b. The BPMN specification is maintained by the Object Management Group (OMG).
   c. Events are modeled with a rectangle symbol.
   d. Annotations allow the modeler to add descriptive text.
   e. All of these statements are true.
9. **(LO 4-5)** Which of the following describe characteristics of good BPMN models?
   a. They are clear.
   b. They are complete.
   c. They are consistent.
   d. They are valid.
   e. All of these options.
10. **(LO 4-5)** Which of the following statements about sequence flows is not true?
    a. Sequence flows are continuous from the start event through activities and gateways, if any, to an end event in a pool.
    b. Sequence flows may not cross pool boundaries.
    c. Sequence flows may not cross lane boundaries.
    d. Tokens move along sequence flows.
    e. Sequence flows are modeled with solid arrows.
11. **(LO 4-7)** Which of the following best describes message flows?
    a. Message flows are continuous within each pool.
    b. Message flows are modeled with solid arrows.

c. Message flows represent exchanges between pools.
d. Message flows may not cross pool boundaries.
e. Message flows may not cross lane boundaries.

12. **(LO 4-8)** Which of the following is the best description of the token concept?
    a. The token concept is a theoretical concept that describes process flow.
    b. The start event generates a token.
    c. The end event consumes the token.
    d. Tokens do not traverse message flows.
    e. All of these options describe the token concept.
13. **(LO 4-8)** Which of the following is not a flow object?
    a. Gateways
    b. Message events
    c. Activities
    d. Message flows
    e. Timer events
14. **(LO 4-8)** Which of the following best describes an exclusive gateway?
    a. The only gateway in a BPMN diagram.
    b. A gateway that does not connect to message flows.
    c. A gateway with only one exit path per instance of a process.
    d. A gateway where all exit paths are taken for each instance of a process.
    e. None of these options describe an exclusive gateway.
15. **(LO 4-8)** Which of the following best describes an inclusive gateway?
    a. The gateway that is shared among two pools.
    b. A gateway with one or more exit paths per instance of a process.
    c. A gateway with only one exit path per instance of a process.
    d. A gateway where all exit paths are taken for each instance of a process.
    e. None of these options describe an inclusive gateway.
16. **(LO 4-8)** Which of the following is true about start events?
    a. A start event can catch a message.
    b. A start event cannot be a timer event.
    c. A start event can throw a message.
    d. A start event cannot be a message event.
    e. None of these statements are true.
17. **(LO 4-8)** Which of the following is true about end events?
    a. An end event can catch a message.
    b. An end event can throw a message.
    c. An end event can be a timer event.
    d. An end event can be shared among pools.
    e. None of these statements are true.
18. **(LO 4-8)** Which of the following is true about intermediate timer events?
    a. The process delays until a specific date or time.
    b. The process delays until a message is thrown.
    c. The process delays for an unspecified amount of time.
    d. The process delays until a message is received.
    e. The process is timed up to that point.

19. **(LO 4-8)** Which of the following best describes an intermediate error event?
    a. It is a boundary event attached to the boundary of an activity.
    b. It indicates alternate sequence flow begins when an error occurs.
    c. It is modeled with a leaning Z or flash sign.
    d. All of the above describe intermediate error events.
    e. None of the above describes intermediate error events.
20. **(LO 4-9)** Which of the following best describes a looping task?
    a. The task repeats until a condition is satisfied.
    b. A looping task only repeats twice.
    c. A looping task is modeled as a subprocess.
    d. A looping task happens multiple times in parallel.
    e. None of these options describe a looping task.
21. **(LO 4-10)** Which of the following is not true about data objects?
    a. They are modeled with a document icon.
    b. They represents data that are only available for the duration of the process.
    c. They are linked to activities with data associations.
    d. They are similar to but different from datastores.
    e. They can be linked to other pools with message flows.
22. **(LO 4-10)** Which of the following are not true about data associations?
    a. They are modeled as a dotted arrow.
    b. The association arrowhead shows the direction of data flow.
    c. They connect data objects to activities.
    d. They connect data objects to intermediate events.
    e. They connect datastores to activities.
23. **(LO 4-11)** Which of the following is not a step in preparing process models?
    a. Outline basic process flows
    b. Define model context
    c. Refine diagram
    d. Review BPMN standard
    e. Validate with stakeholders

Discussion Questions

1. **(LO 4-1)** Do you think that your accounting education has prepared you for all roles of an accountant in business (see Exhibit 4.1)? Which roles do you feel best prepared for? Which roles do you feel least prepared for? Why?
2. **(LO 4-1)** Consider the Stewardship and Reporting role of accountants shown in Exhibit 4.1. What information would you need to collect and use to manage the regulatory compliance function?
3. **(LO 4-1)** Download the CGMA Competency Framework (currently at https://www.cgma.org/resources/tools/cgma-competency-framework.html). Create a checklist that evaluates the skills you currently have and those you need to work on. Revisit the list at the end of the class to monitor improvements.
4. **(LO 4-1)** Download the IMA Competency Framework (currently at https://www.imanet.org/career-resources/management-accounting-competencies?ssopc=1). Create a checklist that evaluates the skills you currently have and those you need to work on. Revisit the list at the end of the class to monitor improvements.
5. **(LO 4-1)** Compare the CGMA and IMA competency frameworks. Which emphasizes technology more? How can improving your technology and analytics skills improve your overall accounting skills?

6. **(LO 4-1)** Review the IMA Competency Framework for mention of "processes." How does process documentation in the form of business process models (either BPMN, flowcharts, or data flow diagrams) affect process-related skills?
7. **(LO 4-1)** Review the CGMA Competency Framework Technical Skills. How do business process models facilitate an understanding of accounting applications?
8. **(LO 4-1)** Choose one of the Accounting/Finance Operations roles in Exhibit 4.1. How could a BPMN activity model help an accountant better understand that role?
9. **(LO 4-1, LO 4-4)** Compare BPMN activity diagrams with flowcharts and DFDs. What is different? What is the same? When would one notation be better or worse than another?
10. **(LO 4-3, LO 4-4)** Consider the Stewardship and Reporting role of accountants shown in Exhibit 4.1. What information would you need to collect and use to manage the regulatory compliance function?
11. **(LO 4-5)** Assume that your company has BPMN diagrams of all their main processes. How could they use this information?
12. **(LO 4-6)** Describe some situations that might lead you to conclude that a BPMN diagram is not complete.
13. **(LO 4-5, LO 4-8)** Each activity/task can only be assigned to one pool or lane. Why is that an important rule?
14. **(LO 4-8)** Describe situations where you would use exclusive, inclusive, and parallel gateways?
15. **(LO 4-8)** Your process waits until you receive a response from your customer. What kind of flow object would you use to show this?
16. **(LO 4-4)** Give some examples based on your experience of processes that would start with a timer event.
17. **(LO 4-11)** Outline and explain the basic steps in preparing business process models.

Problems

1. Using the following description, prepare a business process model using BPMN to describe the interactions between a Starbucks barista and a customer at a **Starbucks** branch:

   A Starbucks customer entered the drive-through lane and stopped to review the menu. He then ordered a Venti coffee of the day and a blueberry muffin from the barista. The barista recorded the order in the cash register. While the customer drove to the window, the barista filled a Venti cup with coffee, put a lid on it, and retrieved the muffin from the pastry case and placed it in a bag. The barista handed the bag with the muffin and the hot coffee to the customer. The customer has an option to pay with cash, credit card, or Starbucks gift card. The customer paid with a gift card. The barista recorded the payment and returned the card along with the receipt to the customer.

   a. **(LO 4-5)** Briefly describe the purpose of the model.
   b. **(LO 4-5, LO 4-9)** Use pools and message flows to describe the context of the business process model.
   c. **(LO 4-5, LO 4-8)** Outline the basic business process flows from the viewpoint of the Starbucks barista. What initiates the process? What are the basic steps to complete the process? What is the final outcome?
   d. Refine the diagram by adding the external customer pool and the message flows exchanged between the barista and the customer. Then, include the two following refinements.
      1. The barista prepares each item in the order before delivering the order to the customer. Model the process to include a looping task.
      2. **(LO 4-5, LO 4-6, LO 4-7)** The coffee needs time to brew and isn't immediately available. The barista asks the customer if he wants to wait. If the customer waits, 5 minutes will pass, and then the coffee can be prepared. Model the process to include an intermediate error event and an intermediate timer event.

2. Prepare a business process model using BPMN to describe how Larry gets to school. Consider the following narrative describing the process of going to class:

   Larry awoke to his alarm clock buzz. He got up and dressed for the day. Then, he ate a hearty breakfast of oatmeal, toast, orange juice, and coffee. He grabbed his books and prepared to leave for school. Before he left home, he checked the weather. If it looked like rain, he put on a jacket and took his umbrella, and he drove to school. If it looked sunny, he left his jacket and umbrella at home and walked to school. If he drove to school, he parked his car and walked to class. If he walked to school, he went straight to class.

   a. **(LO 4-5)** Briefly describe the purpose of the model.
   b. **(LO 4-5, LO 4-9)** The next step would be to use pools and message flows to describe the context of the business process model; however, there is not external pool in this lab.
   c. **(LO 4-5, LO 4-8)** Outline the basic business process flows from Larry's viewpoint. What initiates the process? What are the basic steps to complete the process? What is the final outcome?
   d. Refine the model to include the following:
      1. **(LO 4-5, LO 4-8)** Larry arrives at school early. Use an intermediate timer event to show the delay between arriving at school and going to class.
      2. **(LO 4-5)** Larry doesn't own a car. If it is raining, he texts his friend Jazmin for a ride. She texts back whether she's available or not, and Larry either rides with her or walks to school in the rain.

3. Prepare a business process model using BPMN to describe the process of planning a vacation:

   Yannis is planning a trip to Hawaii with a friend. They first decide when they want to go and how much they can afford to spend. Then, they make their flight and hotel reservations using a prominent travel website. After reserving flight and hotel, they wait until the scheduled departure. They travel to Hawaii and check into the hotel. While in Hawaii, they enjoy a number of tourist activities. When their time in Hawaii is done, they check out of their hotel, return to the airport, and fly home.

   a. **(LO 4-5)** Briefly describe the purpose of the model.
   b. **(LO 4-5, LO 4-9)** Use pools and message flows to describe the context of the business process model.
   c. **(LO 4-5, LO 4-8)** Outline the basic business process flows from Yannis's viewpoint. What initiates the process? What are the basic steps to complete the process? What is the final outcome?
   d. Refine the diagram by adding the following:
      1. **(LO 4-5, LO 4-9)** When in Hawaii, they enjoy a number of tourist activities. Include a looping task to show this.
      2. **(LO 4-5, LO 4-8)** There is a possibility that the hotel room and/or flights aren't within their budget. If reservations are too expensive, they will try different dates. If reservations are still too expensive, they will cancel their trip. Use a collapsed subprocess and an intermediate error event to model these assumptions.

4. Prepare a business process model using BPMN to describe the process of preparing and filing an income tax return:

   Each year before April 15, you prepare to file your income taxes. You collect multiple W-2 and 1099 documents. You download multiple required forms from the IRS website. You fill out the forms, double-check your work, and then print them out. If you owe money, you write a check. You mail your tax return along with the check if you owe money. If you are getting a refund, you mail your tax return and wait to receive your refund by check. When you receive the refund, you deposit it in your bank account.

   a. **(LO 4-5)** Briefly describe the purpose of the model.
   b. **(LO 4-5, LO 4-9)** Use pools and message flows to describe the context of the business process model.

c. **(LO 4-5, LO 4-8)** Outline the basic business process flows from your viewpoint. What initiates the process? What are the basic steps to complete the process? What is the final outcome?

d. Refine the diagram per the following:

1. When you prepare your tax return, you use cloud-based tax software. You answer the questions and the tax software prepares the tax return for you. Once you've double-checked your work, you enter your checking account details and file your return electronically.
2. **(LO 4-8)** If you owe money, the IRS will automatically deduct the amount from your checking account in 7 days. If you are getting a refund, the IRS will deposit the refund directly into your checking account.

5. Prepare a business process model using BPMN to describe the process of registering a car with the Department of Motor Vehicles (DMV):

Heide lives in California and it is time to renew her automobile registration. The California DMV sends her a renewal form and indicates that she needs a smog check for her automobile. She takes her car to the smog check station. She completes the smog check. If the smog check is successful, she can then go to the DMV website and renew her registration, paying with a credit card. Two weeks later she receives a new registration form and tags for her license plates. She puts the registration in the glove box of her car and places the tags on her license plates. If the smog check is not successful, she takes her car to her mechanic to make the necessary repairs. When those are complete, she repeats the smog check.

a. **(LO 4-5)** Briefly describe the purpose of the model.

b. **(LO 4-5, LO 4-9)** Use pools and message flows to describe the context of the business process model.

c. **(LO 4-5, LO 4-8)** Outline the basic business process flows from Heide's viewpoint. What initiates the process? What are the basic steps to complete the process? What is the final outcome?

d. Refine the diagram per the following:

1. **(LO 4-8)** Use a messaging start event to begin the process.
2. **(LO 4-8, LO 4-10)** Heide uses the renewal form information at the smog check station. The smog check station provides a smog check certificate that Heide submits along with the renewal form to update her registration via the DMV website. She then downloads her new registration document and places it in her car. Use data objects to represent these documents.

Design Element: Duncan Smith/Getty Images

Chapter Five
Data Modeling

A Look at This Chapter

Today's accountants must understand how business processes generate data and how those data are structured, interrelated, and stored in a database system. To ensure that business processes and the database systems are documented and to participate in improvements to processes and systems, accountants must understand and be able to model such systems. This chapter describes data modeling. It explains how data models support database-driven systems. It introduces basic data modeling tools to guide the student's development of modeling skills. Finally, it discusses business rules and how the identification of relevant business rules supports both process and data modeling.

A Look Back

Chapter 4 described the roles of accountants as users, managers, designers, and evaluators of technology and technology-driven business processes. To perform in those roles, accountants need to ensure that processes and systems are documented—and to participate in improvements to processes and systems. Thus, accountants must be business analysts. The chapter continued to introduce types of business process models as well as the potential value of business process modeling.

A Look Ahead

In the next several chapters, we use business process and data models to examine sales, acquisition, conversion, and related management processes.

Monkey Business Images/Shutterstock

Recently, **Starbucks** replaced a variety of systems with **Oracle**'s application suite. According to Karen Metro, vice president of global business system solutions for Starbucks, "Many of our systems had grown up in silos and were loosely connected, and we were having a hard time keeping them upgraded or getting the functionality we needed out of those systems. **Accenture** came in to help us review the state of the environment and put together a global program to deploy standardized business processes and systems around the world." About 200 people from both Accenture and Starbucks worked full time for 3 years on the project. The software was first implemented in Europe, then North America, and finally China. Starbucks expects a variety of performance benefits, including improved margins. In particular, the software will help Starbucks understand where its money is spent and "leverage that with our suppliers around the world."

Source: Information provided by Accenture case study posted on its website, www.accenture.com, 2009.

CHAPTER OUTLINE

LEARNING OBJECTIVES

After reading this chapter, you should be able to:

5-1 Understand the purpose of structure models.

5-2 Understand and apply the building blocks for UML class (structure) diagrams.

5-3 Describe multiplicities for a UML class diagram.

5-4 Understand how to implement a relational database from a UML class diagram.

5-5 Understand process decision requirements and how business rules support process decisions.

5-6 Describe decision tables and business rules and the various forms of rules.

5-7 Use business process models and rules to implement internal controls.

LO 5-1

Understand the purpose of structure models.

STRUCTURE MODELS

Structure models describe the data and information structures inherent in a business process or processes. The primary purpose of these models is to create a blueprint for the development of a relational database to support the collection, aggregation, and communication of process information. They are tools for planning, documenting, discussing, and implementing databases; however, they also facilitate the use of databases after they are implemented.

For more than 50 years, **data models** have been used to represent the conceptual contents of databases to communicate with the users of those databases. For example, Charles Bachman developed data structure diagrams, also known as Bachman diagrams, in the 1960s. Using similar notation, Peter Chen developed entity-relationship modeling in 1976 to describe the entities (e.g., people, things, and events) and the relationships among entities in databases. Since then, a number of others have offered a variety of notations to describe the elements of databases, but the concepts in all variations are similar.

A model of logical database structures must be able to describe

1. The entities or things in the domain of interest.
2. The relationships among those things.
3. The cardinalities that describe how many instances of one entity can be related to another.
4. The attributes or characteristics of the entities and relationships.

Unified Modeling Language Class Diagrams

This textbook employs the Unified Modeling Language (UML) class diagram notation for structure models, although the concepts also apply to other notation standards, such as entity-relationship modeling. The Object Management Group is a not-for-profit consortium of computer industry members that maintains and publishes the specification for the UML. **Class diagrams** are one type of diagram within UML and are similar in many ways to entity-relationship diagrams. They describe the logical structure of a database system.

LO 5-2

Understand and apply the building blocks for UML class (structure) diagrams.

Building Blocks for UML Class Diagrams

Classes

A **class** is any separately identifiable collection of things (objects) about which the organization wants to collect and store information. Classes can represent organization resources (e.g., trucks, machines, buildings, cash, investments), persons (e.g., customers, employees), events (e.g., sales, purchases, cash disbursements, cash receipts), and conceptual structures (e.g., accounts, product categories, budgets). Classes are typically implemented as tables in a relational database, where individual instances of objects are represented as rows in the table.

Cash disbursements represent events in a class. The class symbol would include the name only.

Panuwat Phimpha/Shutterstock

Each class is represented by a rectangle with three compartments, as shown in Exhibit 5.1. The top compartment shows the name of the class. The middle compartment shows the attributes (data elements) shared by all instances in the class. The bottom compartment describes operations that each instance in the class can perform. The attribute and operation compartments are optional. In this text, we will typically omit the attribute and operations compartments and use the class symbol with only the name of class when depicting classes.

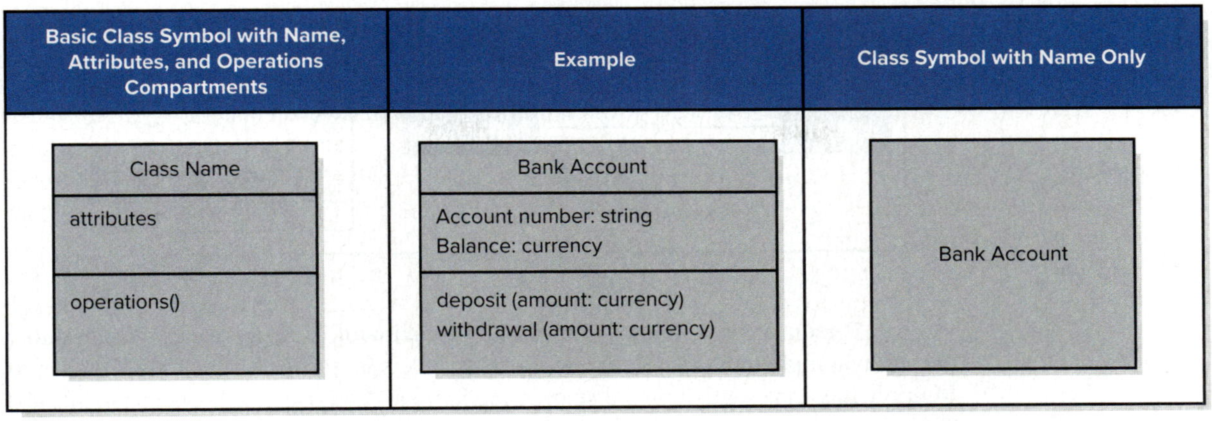

EXHIBIT 5.1
Class Notation

Associations

An **association** depicts the relationship between two classes. For example, customers (class) *participate* in sales (class); professors (class) *teach* courses (class); employees (class) *work for* organizations (class). It allows navigation between instances in one class and instances of another class, such as linking customer information to a particular sale. A generic association is drawn as a line connecting two classes. When the business purpose of the association is not clear, the association can be named by placing the text name on the line, as shown in Exhibit 5.2. Association names are verbs or verb phrases that indicate why instances of one class relate to instances of another class.

EXHIBIT 5.2
Classes with Associations

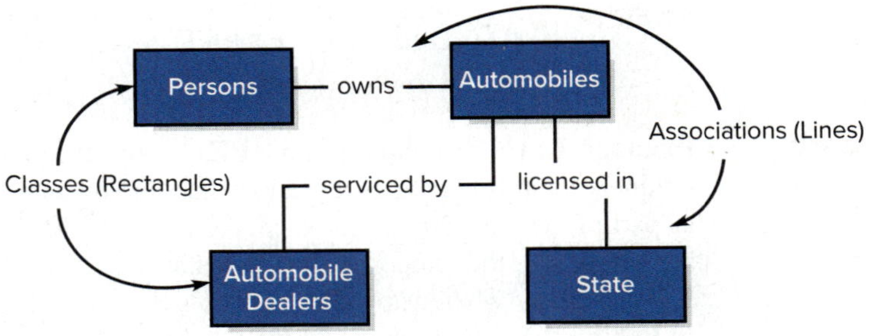

> **LO 5-3**
>
> Describe multiplicities for a UML class diagram.

Multiplicities

Multiplicities describe the minimum and maximum number of times instances in one class can be associated with instances in another class. Multiplicities for a class are represented by a pair of numbers placed on the opposite side of the association. In a binary association, there would then be two sets of multiplicities. Minimum values can be 0 or 1. The minimum values of multiplicities indicate whether participation in the relationship is optional (0) or mandatory (1). The maximum values can be 1 or many (*). In Exhibit 5.3, for example, it is optional for a person to own an automobile, but it is mandatory that each auto be owned by a person (assuming the auto class represents registered automobiles). The maximum values for a pair of multiplicities for a single association describe the nature of the relationship between classes: one-to-one, one-to-many, or many-to-many. In Exhibit 5.3, for example, a person could own many autos, so this is a one-to-many relationship.

EXHIBIT 5.3
Multiplicities

Example of Association with Multiplicities

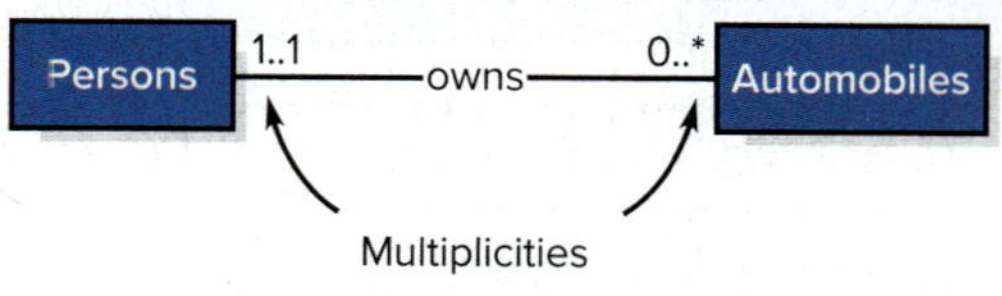

Options for Multiplicities

Indicator	Meaning
0..1	Zero or one
1..1	One only
0..*	Zero or many
1..*	One or many

Each Person owns a minimum of 0 and a maximum of many Autos. Each Auto is owned by a minimum of 1 and a maximum of 1 Person. Please focus on the Options for Multiplicities table in Exhibit 5.3 since it applies to all exercises and problems in this text. There are only four choices for each multiplicity.

Attributes

Attributes are data elements that describe the instances in a class. Exhibit 5.4 lists the attribute names for the classes in a domain of interest (related to taking orders from customers) and identifies primary and foreign keys. The full specification of attributes would also include data type, default value (if any), **constraints** on the value (such as minimum and maximum possible values), and other descriptive information.

EXHIBIT 5.4
List of Tables with Attribute Names

Customers	[Customer_Number (PK), Customer_Name, Customer_City, Customer_State, Customer_Zip, Customer_Phone]
Orders	[Order_Number (PK), Order_Date, Delivery_Date, Order_Amount, Shipping_Cost, Customer_Number (FK)]
Order_Items	[Order_Number + Product_Number (PK), Quantity_Ordered, Price]
Inventory	[Product_Number (PK), Product_Description, Quantity_on_Hand (QOH), Unit_of_Issue, Current_List_Price, Standard_Cost]

Primary Keys. A **primary key (PK)** is an attribute or combination of attributes that uniquely identifies each instance in a class or row in a table. Primary keys can be modeled as part of the attribute list for each class on the UML class diagram; often, however, they are defined in the supporting documentation, such as the table listing shown in Exhibit 5.4, especially when using class symbols that only show the class name, as shown earlier in Exhibit 5.2. The primary key is a unique identifier for each instance in the class. For example, the "State" class in Exhibit 5.2 collectively defines all the states. Each state is an instance in that class, and each state would be identified by a unique primary key, such as the abbreviations AR, CA, WA, and so on.

There are often several candidates for the primary key of a class or database table. There are several important criteria that guide the selection of appropriate primary keys:

- The primary key must uniquely identify each instance of the class (or row of the table). Consequently, the designer should avoid anything that could be duplicated, such as names.
- The primary key cannot be null (blank) under any circumstances. For this reason, the designer should avoid using attributes for the primary key that are potentially unavailable for any instance of the class; for example, not everyone has a Social Security number.
- The primary key cannot change over time.
- The primary key should be controlled by the organization that assigns it. When the assigning organization does not control the primary key values, it becomes difficult to ensure uniqueness. For example, names are not good primary keys.

- A primary key with sequential values makes it easier to recognize gaps in the data.
- All else equal, shorter primary key values are better than longer ones because shorter keys ease data entry, indexing, and retrieval.

Foreign Keys. A **foreign key (FK)** is an attribute or combination of attributes that allows tables to be linked together. A foreign key is linked *to the primary key of another table* to support a defined association. In Exhibit 5.3, for example, the Auto class would include a foreign key to match the primary key for the Person class to support the Owns association. In the table attribute listing shown in Exhibit 5.4, the primary key of the Customers Table is Customer Number. The foreign key Customer Number in the Orders Table allows rows in the Orders Table to be linked to corresponding rows in the Customers Table.

PROGRESS CHECK

1. Consider students enrolled in courses taught by professors. Draw a simple class diagram with associations that describes the registration process. (*Hint:* Include courses, students, and professors.)
2. Add multiplicities to your diagram. Can a student be enrolled in many courses? Can a course have many students enrolled?
3. Create a listing of the tables with attributes. What are the primary keys? What attributes do you think go with each table definition?

Other Relationships

The generic relationship between two classes is modeled as an *association,* as described earlier. However, UML includes modeling notation for other types of relationships: **generalization** (or inheritance), **aggregation**, and **composition**, as shown in Exhibit 5.5. These special-purpose relationship notations should be used when they clarify relationships in a particular model, but they can also be modeled using associations.

<table>
<tr><th>Relationship Notation</th><th>Explanation</th></tr>
<tr><td>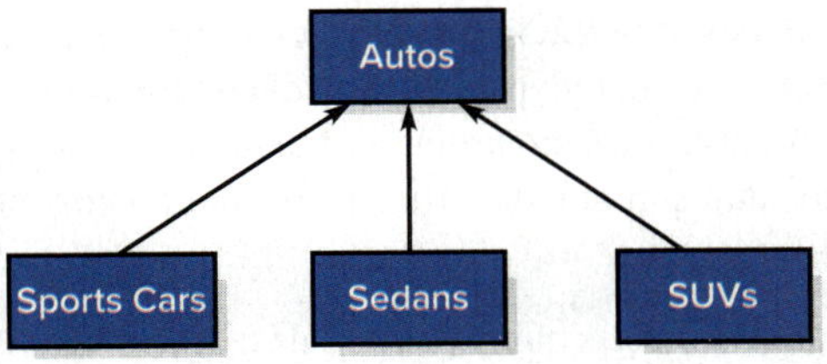
</td><td>Generalization relationships allow grouping of things that share common characteristics. These relationships reduce redundancy since common characteristics only need to be modeled once. For example, sports cars, sedans, and SUVs are all autos and have common elements such as horsepower, gas mileage, etc. The subtypes (sports cars, sedans, and SUVs) also have unique characteristics that separately identify them.</td></tr>
<tr><td>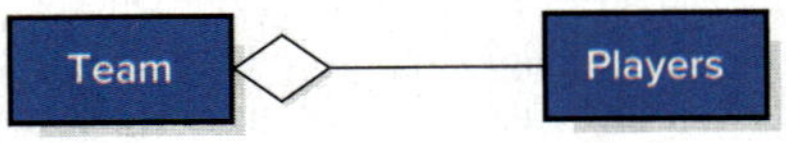
</td><td>Aggregation relationships describe classes that are often considered together. Although players could exist separately from a team, they are part of a team. Aggregation relationships could be nested, for example, when the team is part of a league.</td></tr>
<tr><td>
</td><td>Composition relationships are a form of aggregation. In this case, however, chapters normally do not exist separately from the books.</td></tr>
</table>

EXHIBIT 5.5
UML Notation for Other Relationships

Other Useful UML Class Model Notation

UML is semantically rich; it provides notation that accommodates a wide variety of modeling situations. We have outlined the basic notation that should allow you to build most business process structural models. However, there are three other UML class model notations that can be particularly useful for modeling business processes from an accounting viewpoint. These three notations are described in Exhibit 5.6.

Other Notation	Explanation
	Notes allow the modeler to add explanations. Notes can also be used to describe constraints. A note could be attached to a class with a dashed line.
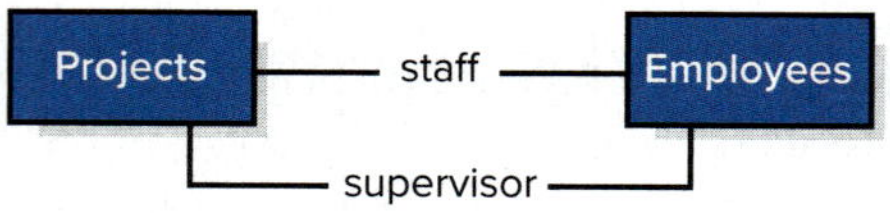	Role designation is helpful when the association between two classes depends on the specific role that objects in one class take on. In this example, employees work on a project, but one employee supervises the project. Different roles often result in different multiplicities.
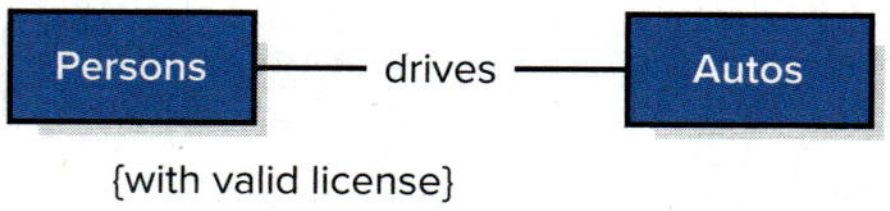	Constraints can be modeled with notes or placed near the constrained end of an association. In this example, only persons with valid drivers' licenses should participate in the association.

EXHIBIT 5.6
Other Useful Class Diagram Notations

Best Practices in Preparing Class Diagrams

The primary objective of a class diagram is to describe the important elements of a domain of interest clearly, concisely, and accurately. As noted previously, class diagrams are tools to aid in planning, documenting, discussing, implementing, and using database systems. Here are some modeling best practices that can enhance the use of models for these purposes:

1. Use common terminology in the organization for class names (e.g., sales, orders, clients), and avoid confusing abbreviations.
2. Link classes on the diagram only when there is a clear business purpose for the relationship.
3. Avoid crossing lines where possible because that increases the potential for misreading the diagram.
4. Use consistently sized class rectangles to avoid an unwanted emphasis on a larger symbol.
5. Avoid running association lines close together because they may be hard to follow.
6. Opt for simplicity; show only what you need to show.
7. Focus first on the accuracy of the content, then address appearance.
8. Use notes to explain more complex situations.

LO 5-4

Understand how to implement a relational database from a UML class diagram.

UML CLASS MODELS FOR RELATIONAL DATABASE DESIGN

As we noted at the beginning of this chapter, the primary purpose of structure models is to create a blueprint for the development of a relational database to support the collection, aggregation, and communication of process information. They are tools for planning, documenting, discussing, and implementing databases. This section describes basic processes for mapping a UML class diagram to a relational database schema, which defines the tables, fields, relationships, keys, etc., in the database.[1]

1. *Map classes to tables.* The first step is to map the classes to tables. In Exhibit 5.7, for example, the UML class diagram (shown earlier in Exhibit 5.2 without multiplicities) would map to four tables in the relational database. Each instance of the class maps to a row in the corresponding table.

EXHIBIT 5.7
Mapping Classes to Tables

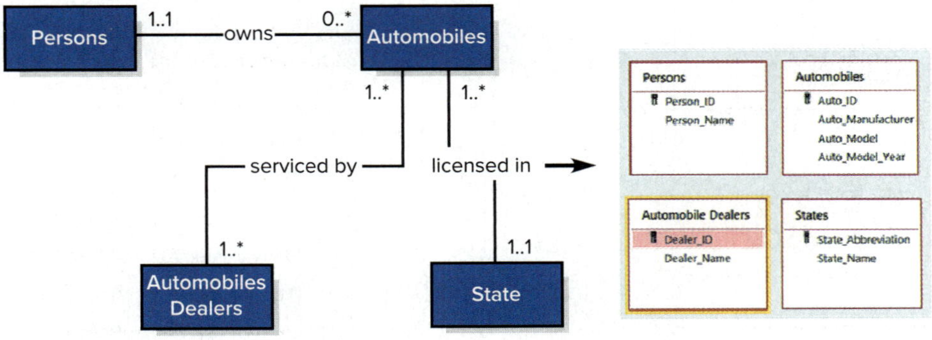

2. *Map class attributes to table fields and assign primary keys.* Map the attributes for each class to fields in the corresponding relational table. If the primary keys have not been designated, determine an appropriate primary key for each relational table. In the example shown in Exhibit 5.7, the primary keys for the tables are indicated by **Microsoft** Access's primary key symbol, a gold key icon.
3. *Map associations to foreign keys.* Each association in Exhibit 5.7, except the "serviced by" association between Dealers and Auto, will be implemented by adding foreign keys. The maximum multiplicities on each side of an association determine the foreign key placement. The exhibit indicates that one person owns a maximum of many autos. This is an example of a one-to-many relationship that will be implemented with a foreign key. A one-to-one relationship occurs when the maximum multiplicity on each side of the association is 1, and, in general, one-to-one relationships will also be implemented with a foreign key.
   a. There is a rule of thumb that can help identify where the foreign key is placed. Remember that each association is implemented in your database with a foreign key or a linking table, as described later. Assume a one-to-many relationship—that is, a relationship where the maximum multiplicity on one side of the association is 1 and the maximum multiplicity on the other side of the association is many. The foreign key is posted toward the "many" side of the association. In other words, the

[1] Schemas can also define other database requirements, such as levels of access, but this section focuses on designing the basic elements.

primary key for the class on the 1 side of the association is posted as a foreign key for the class on the "*" side of the association. Thus, in Exhibit 5.7, the primary key for Person is posted in Auto as a foreign key, and the primary key of State is also posted in Auto as a foreign key. Exhibit 5.8 provides general rules for posting foreign keys based on the type of association between two classes.

EXHIBIT 5.8
Posting Foreign Keys[1]

Multiplicity for A	Multiplicity for B	Relationship Type	General Rules for Posting Foreign Keys
0..1	0..1	One-to-one[2]	Post foreign key in either A or B but not both
0..1	1..1	One-to-one	Post foreign key in A
0..1	0..*	One-to-many	Post foreign key in B
0..1	1..*	One-to-many	Post foreign key in B
1..1	0..1	One-to-one	Post foreign key in B
1..1	1..1	One-to-one	Post foreign key in either A or B but not both
1..1	0..*	One-to-many	Post foreign key in B
1..1	1..*	One-to-many	Post foreign key in B
0..*	0..1	One-to-many	Post foreign key in A
0..*	1..1	One-to-many	Post foreign key in A
0..*	0..*	Many-to-many	Create linking table
0..*	1..*	Many-to-many	Create linking table
1..*	0..1	One-to-many	Post foreign key in A
1..*	1..1	One-to-many	Post foreign key in A
1..*	0..*	Many-to-many	Create linking table
1..*	1..*	Many-to-many	Create linking table

[1]The foreign key is the primary key of the related table; however, foreign keys may be assigned different names if it improves understanding.
[2]Foreign keys can be posted in either table, but the minimum multiplicity of 0 indicates an optional association for that table and a general rule provides the most efficient option for posting the foreign key.

b. The minimum multiplicities are often determined by the timing of entries to both tables involved in one association. If an entry in one table must match an entry in the other table, then the minimum is 1. If an entry in one table can occur without an entry in the other table, then the minimum is 0. In Exhibit 5.7, we've assumed that each auto is owned by one person, and you can't have any auto listed in the Auto table without a corresponding owner in the Person table. Thus, the minimum multiplicity next to Person is 1. Conversely, an individual in the Person table may or may not own an auto. If the individual did not own an auto, there would be no matching auto in the Auto table. In this case, the matching entry is optional and the minimum multiplicity next to Auto is 0. Note that the minimum is 0 even if some individuals own autos. As long as our requirements indicate that some individual may not own an auto, the minimum is 0.

4. *Create new tables to implement many-to-many relationships.* A many-to-many relationship is when the maximum multiplicity is * on both ends of the association, regardless of the minimum multiplicities. In this situation, the database designer creates a new table to implement the association. The default primary key for the new

table is the combination of the two primary keys for the associated tables. In Exhibit 5.7, for example, each Auto can be serviced by many Dealers, and each Dealer can service many Autos. Thus, the "serviced by" association is implemented by creating a new table with a primary key that includes both Auto_ID and the Dealer_ID (called a concatenated or composite key), as shown in Exhibit 5.9.

EXHIBIT 5.9
Implementing a Many-to-Many Relationship
In theory, every relationship type can be implemented with a linking table as shown in this exhibit.

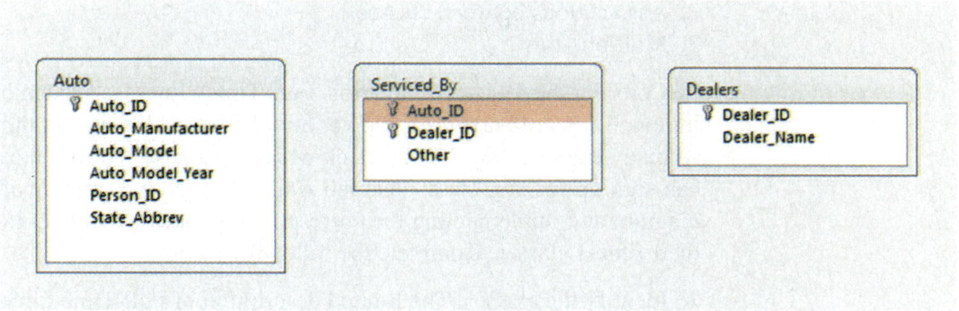

5. *Implement relationships among tables.* Create relationships among the relational tables to match the associations shown on the class diagram. After the foreign keys are posted and the linking tables created for the many-to-many relationships, the database designer can implement the relationships, as shown in Exhibit 5.9. Note that each half of the composite primary key for the Serviced_By table acts as a foreign key: Auto_ID in the Serviced_By table links to Auto_ID in the Auto table and Dealer_ID in Serviced_By table links to Dealer_ID in the Dealers table.

The set of relational tables shown in Exhibit 5.10 then implements the class diagram shown in Exhibit 5.4. In other words, the class diagram is the blueprint from which the database is built. Just as inadequate plans result in substandard buildings, an incomplete or erroneous class diagram will result in an ineffective database. It is easier to change the blueprint than change the building, and it is easier to change the class diagram (and ensure that it is correct) than to change the database.

EXHIBIT 5.10
Mapping Class Diagram Associations to Relationships

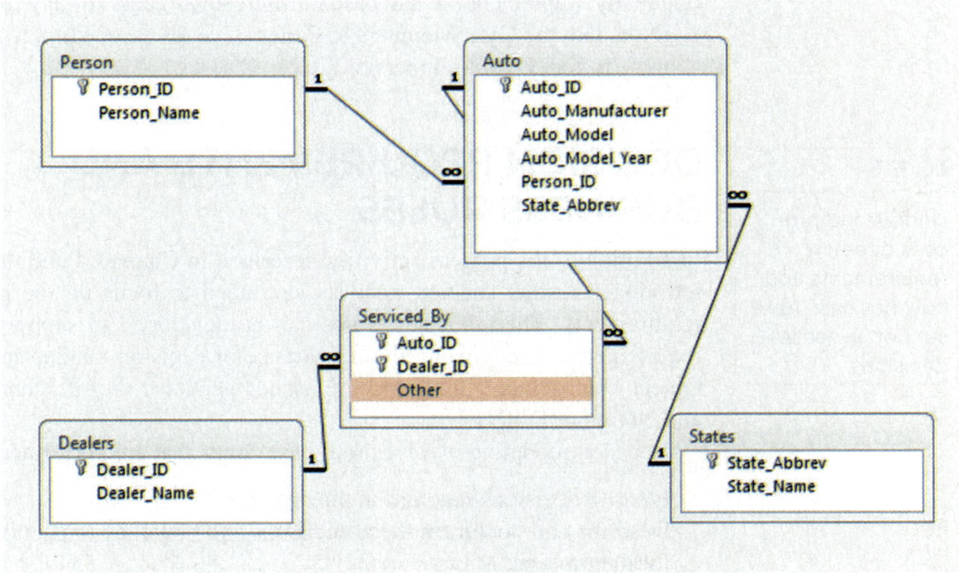

Review Exercise: Preparing and Implementing a UML Class Diagram

Remember that UML class diagrams involve

1. Classes (the objects about which the organization wants to collect and store information).
2. Associations between classes.
3. Multiplicities.

Consider the following situation. Full-Time Fitness is a chain of gyms in Seattle, Washington. They are known for the variety of fitness classes that they offer. Since they offer so many classes, they need to track which instructor will teach each class. Gym members can sign up for any class. This lab walks through the process of preparing a UML class diagram and implementing the corresponding database to help Full-Time Fitness manage their fitness classes. Complete the following steps:

1. Identify the classes. The limited description of Full-Time Fitness suggests that there are three objects of interest: fitness classes, fitness class instructors, and gym members. Draw the corresponding classes.
2. Identify the associations between classes. There are two main associations: gym members sign up for classes, and instructors teach classes. On your diagram, create the associations between classes.
3. Define multiplicities. Before we can define multiplicities, we need some additional information. For Full-Time Fitness, classes include at least one and up to 40 members. Gym members can sign up for no classes or up to 10 classes per week. Class instructors may teach from one to five classes per week. However, new instructors may not have taught any classes. Each class has only one instructor. Add the multiplicities to complete your UML Class Model.
4. To implement the model, map classes to tables and define some basic attributes/fields for the classes/tables. Make up some likely attributes for the tables and designate the primary key(s).
5. Next, assign foreign keys. Use Exhibit 5.8 to guide the assignment of foreign keys or the rule of thumb.
6. Finally, implement the database in Microsoft Access (or any relational database). (Note that the Gym Members to Fitness Classes association is implemented as a new table to link Gym Members to Fitness Classes.)

LO 5-5

Understand process decision requirements and how business rules support process decisions.

DECISION REQUIREMENTS AND BUSINESS RULES

In addition to the process activities described in Chapter 4 and the information structures introduced in this chapter, analysts also need to focus on the process decision-making requirements. Then, business rules can be developed to support those decision-making requirements. Recognizing the importance of decision making in business processes, the Object Management Group recently issued version 1.0 of its standard for Decision Model and Notation (DMN).

Decision modeling involves four basic steps that are performed iteratively:

1. Identify decisions required in the process.
2. Describe and document these decisions and how they impact the business objectives for the process.

3. Specify decision requirements in terms of the information and knowledge required to make the decision.
4. Decompose and refine the requirements, determining where existing business rules apply and where new business rules need to be developed.

Once decisions are identified, the analyst can focus on identifying the decision logic—that is, the business rules—required to make the decision as well as the contextual input data that would be available to decision makers. Operational decisions depend on the business process but can be categorized into several general types as follows:

- Eligibility or approval—is this individual or organization eligible for this product or service?
- Validation—is this claim valid for processing?
- Calculation—what is the correct discount for this product/service for this customer?
- Risk—what is the risk of relying on this supplier's promised delivery date?
- Fraud—how likely is this claim to be fraudulent?
- Opportunity—which of these options is the best opportunity?
- Assignment—to whom should this issue be assigned?
- Targeting—how should we respond to this person?

Consider the simple example shown in Exhibit 5.7. Persons own automobiles that are licensed in states and serviced by dealers. What decisions might be involved in processing this information? Is this person eligible to own this auto? Is this license request valid? Is this auto under warranty? Once each decision is identified, the corresponding business rules must be developed and documented.

LO 5-6

Describe decision tables and business rules and the various forms of rules.

Business Rules and Decision Tables

Business rules support decision making in business processes. They standardize and constrain process action. A **business rule** is a succinct statement of a constraint on a business process. It is the logic that guides the behavior of the business in specific situations. Business rules are typically written in text, not modeled; however, they influence the structure and flow of models. Business rules establish multiplicities in class models, and they set criteria for branching in activity models.

There are several forms of business rules. To put these in context, let's consider a simple example of customer payments at a restaurant. Suppose the restaurant accepts cash or credit card payments as long as the credit card is American Express. Additionally, the restaurant only accepts payments in U.S. dollars, not foreign currency, and it does not accept checks. These payment constraints involve the following rule forms:

- *Obligatory.* This rule form states what should occur: Payment should be made in U.S. dollars.
- *Prohibited.* This rule form states what should not occur: No payments by check.
- *Allowed.* This rule form states what is allowed under what conditions: Credit card payments are allowed if the card is American Express.

Rule: Credit card payments are allowed if the card is American Express.

Kikinunchi/Shutterstock

Rules are stated in short sentences, as described earlier. In an attempt to formalize the statement of rules, the Object Management Group published a standard, titled "Semantics of Business Vocabulary and Business Rules"

(SBVR), in 2008.[2] SBVR sets standards for stating business rules using natural language. The standard describes operative business rules, such as the three forms just described: obligatory, prohibited, and allowed. It also describes similar structural rules that describe fundamental characteristics—such as, "It is necessary that each sale be made to a customer"—rather than operating policy rules that are stated in terms of preferred outcomes.

Rules must be enforceable. So, there must be related enforcement-level information that describes how to deal with potential violations. Enforcement levels include strict enforcement, pre-override, and post-override. If a rule is strictly enforced, violations are not authorized. If a rule is subject to pre-override, violations are allowed if authorized in advance. If a rule is subject to post-override, violations are allowed if authorized after the violation. When rules are subject to override, there should also be a statement of who can authorize a violation. Additionally, certain rules can be considered guidelines, which are generally followed but not enforced. The enforcement level can vary for different parts of the organization.

Rules are valuable because they make modeling business processes easier. They limit the number of options to those allowed by business policy. The rules for a business process establish systems requirements when acquiring new technology. However, rules can also inhibit process improvements because they can be tied to outdated technology. Thus, a close examination of business rules—and the business reasons for them—can reveal unnecessary constraints. In most situations, however, business rules are not stated formally; they are implicit. The process analysis should, therefore, elicit important business rules.

Decision tables combine multiple business rules to support likely circumstances requiring a decision. A decision table consists of a name, a set of inputs, a set of outputs, and a set of rules. The rules associate the inputs to the decision outputs at that point in the process. Exhibit 5.11 presents a sample decision table where three rules are shown as rows in the table. The table name is *Discounts*. The columns *Customer Type* and *Size of Order* are the inputs to the decision. The *Discount to Offer* is the output of the decision. The number column could be indexed to identify the process, decision, and rule, but in this case it simply numbers the three rule options.

EXHIBIT 5.11
Sample Decision Table

Discounts			
Number	**Customer Type**	**Size of Order**	**Discount to Offer**
1	Business	<10	10%
2	Business	>=10	15
3	Individual	All	5

LO 5-7

Use business process models and rules to implement internal controls.

USING BUSINESS PROCESS MODELS AND BUSINESS RULES TO IMPLEMENT INTERNAL CONTROLS

Organizations are designed to accomplish objectives. Organizational governance involves business planning, execution, monitoring, and adapting. During the planning phase, organizational leaders establish those objectives, identify risks that affect achieving those objectives, create processes and systems, and establish internal controls to mitigate those risks. Business process models allow managers to specify business processes and address

[2] For further information on SBVR, see www.omg.org/spec/SBVR/1.0/.

threats to process performance. Business rules articulate constraints on those processes. Thus, models and rules are important tools to help organizations plan and implement an effective system of internal controls.

Business process models and business rules are context specific, but the following provides examples of how they can be used to plan and implement internal controls. Chapter 11 describes internal control and related governance frameworks in more detail, but three main functions of internal control are prevention, detection, and correction of errors and related loss. Preventive controls deter problems. Detective controls find problems that arise. Corrective controls fix those problems. Exhibit 5.12 lists common controls in those three functions with examples of how BPMN activity diagrams, UML Class Models, and Business Rules can be used to implement those controls.

Examples of Business Process Models and Rules to Plan and Implement Controls

BPMN	**UML Class Diagrams**		**Business Rules**
Preventive Controls			
Proper authorization	Include authorization event so process does not proceed until authorization received	Use an association to include the authorization role as shown in Exhibit 5.6	Cash disbursement is prohibited if not authorized by designated person
Segregation of duties	Use lanes as shown in Exhibit 4.6 to define separate responsibilities	Use associations to specify different roles as shown in Exhibit 5.6	One person should not process, approve, and reconcile expenditures
Physical access controls such as locks, keycards, badges, guards	Include tests of physical controls in the process flows; add gateway to branch if control violated	Define data structure to capture status of physical controls	All inventory locations must be locked between 6 PM and 8 AM
Detective Controls			
Transaction reconciliations	Define reconciliation process to start at the end of each month, obtain bank data, compare to book data, report differences, and end	Define Reconciliation class with associations to Cash class to capture reconciliation information	Bank reconciliations must be performed monthly
Physical inventories	Define physical inventory process to start at the end of the quarter, conduct physical counts, update inventory records, report adjustments, and end	Define Physical Inventory Count class with association to Inventory class to capture physical inventory results	Physical inventories must be performed quarterly
Performance reviews	Define performance review processes to start at designated time each year, gather performance information, provide performance review, set plans for upcoming period, and end	Define Performance Review class with associations (supervisor and reviewed employee roles) to Employees to record annual performance review	Performance reviews must be performed annually
Corrective Controls			
Rescind access	Define subprocess to rescind access triggered when employee terminated to update access records and end	Define employee termination class and associate with employees to record terminations; add attributes to employee class to record rescinded access status	Employees should not have access to their computers after termination
Retraining	Define process for staff retraining to start every six months, schedule training, conduct training, evaluate training results and end	Define a training class and associate with employees class for employees trained; add attribute(s) to employees class to record training status	Staff should be retrained every six months

(continued)

Insurance	Define process for making insurance claims to start when loss recognized, contact insurance company, file claim with loss information, collect insurance settlement, and end	Define an insurance class and associations to covered assets; create class to track insurance claims	All assets with value greater than $10,000 must be insured
Disaster recovery	Define disaster recovery process to begin when loss of computing resources, replace equipment, reload software, reload backup data, test, and end	Define a disaster recovery class that would capture the transactions necessary to restore systems	Data systems should be backed up daily

EXHIBIT 5.12
Using BPMN, UML, and Rules to Implement Controls

Exhibit 5.13 shows a BPMN diagram implementing the preventive control, proper authorization, in a business process. The goal of the process is to make payments. Organizations often control the payment process by matching purchase orders, receiving documents, and invoices. The Prepare Documents activity implements the matching, then the process flows to the intermediate event to await authorization. When authorized, the process flows to the Make Payment activity, and then ends.

EXHIBIT 5.13
BPMN Diagram with Authorization Intermediate Event

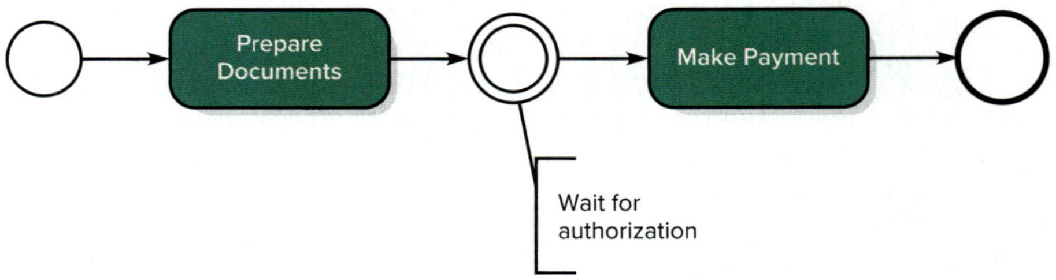

Exhibit 5.14 shows a BPMN diagram implementing the preventive control, segregation of duties, in a business process. The goal of this process is to reconcile an organization bank account. Segregation of duty principles requires bank reconciliation to be done by someone who does not make payments or process receipts. In this example, the process starts and flows to a recurring activity, Make Payments, which would continue throughout the month. The process then flows to the Reconcile Bank Account activity and shows the two activities in different lanes to indicate segregation of duties.

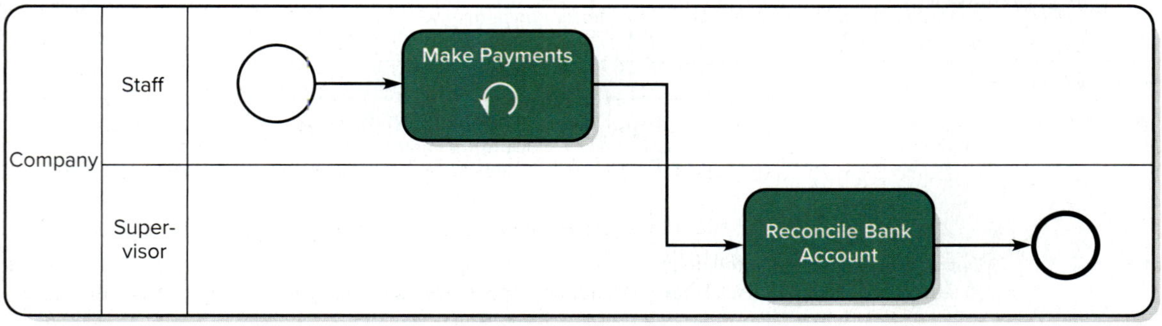

EXHIBIT 5.14
BPMN Diagram with Lanes to Show Segregation of Duties

Exhibit 5.15 shows a different way of describing segregation of duties. In this UML class diagram, the Employees class is related to the Payments class, but the diagram shows two associations to indicate the two roles that employees play in that relationship. One role is the Authorizer of the payment(s), and the other role is the Preparer of the Payments.

EXHIBIT 5.15
UML Class Diagram to Show Different Roles to Support Segregation of Duties

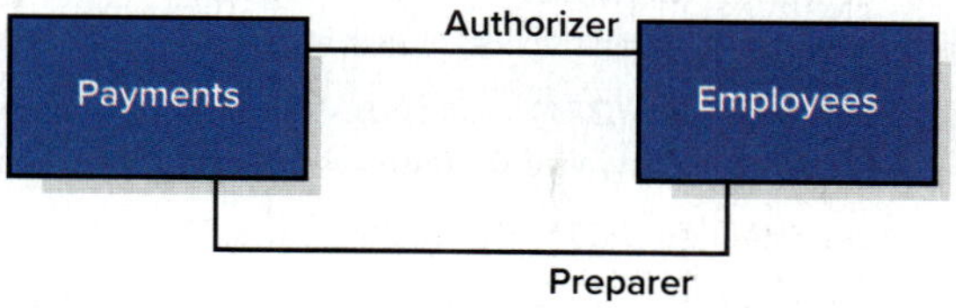

PROGRESS CHECK

4. How would you use a BPMN diagram to implement the detective control, Physical Inventories, listed in Exhibit 5.12?
5. Can you develop a UML class diagram to implement the corrective control, Insurance, listed in Exhibit 5.12?

Summary

- Structure models, such as UML class models, describe the information structures of one or more business processes.
- Structure models allow communication about database design.
- Structure models support the design, implementation, and use of databases.
- The building blocks for UML class diagrams include classes, associations, multiplicities, and attributes.
- Attributes for each class include the primary key, foreign keys, and other attributes describing characteristics of the class.
- Primary keys uniquely define each instance of a class (and each row in a relational database table).
- Foreign keys allow tables to be linked together.
- Foreign keys are primary keys of other tables posted in the current table to allow linking.
- Other class diagram relationships include generalizations, aggregations, and compositions.
- Associations model the business purpose of a relationship between two classes, such as the role that members of one class have with respect to the other class.
- UML class models can be used to create tables by mapping classes to tables, mapping class attributes to table fields, mapping associations to foreign keys depending on the multiplicities of the association, and creating new tables to implement many-to-many relationships.
- Analysts must understand process decision requirements to truly understand how the process should perform.
- Business rules and decision tables establish business policies and constrain business processes.
- Business models and business rules are important tools to improve corporate governance and implement internal controls.

Key Words

aggregation relationship (*215*) A special-purpose UML notation representing the relationship between two classes that are often considered together, such as when a sports league is made up of a collection of teams.

association (*213*) UML symbol that depicts the relationship between two classes; it is modeled as a solid line that connects two classes in a model.

attributes (*214, 227*) Data elements that describe instances in a class, very much like fields in a database table; characteristics, properties, or adjectives that describe each class.

business rule (*221*) Succinct statement of constraints on a business process; it provides the logic that guides the behavior of the business in specific situations.

cardinalities (*227*) *See* multiplicities.

class (*212*) Any separately identifiable collection of things (objects) about which the organization wants to collect and store information. Classes can represent organization resources (e.g., trucks, machines, buildings, cash, investments), persons (e.g., customers, employees), events (e.g., sales, purchases, cash disbursements, cash receipts), and conceptual structures (e.g., accounts, product categories, budgets). Classes are typically implemented as tables in a relational database, where individual instances of the class are represented as rows in the table.

class diagrams (*212*) Structure models prepared using UML notation.

composition relationship (*215*) A special-purpose UML notation representing the relationship between two classes that are often considered together, similar to aggregation relationships, except in composition relationships, one class cannot exist without the other, such as a book and the chapters that compose the book.

constraints (*214*) Optional or mandatory guidance about how a process should perform in certain situations.

data models (*212*) A graphic representation of the conceptual contents of databases; data models support communication about database contents between users and designers of the database.

entities (*227*) The people, things, and events in the domain of interest; in UML notation, entities are modeled as classes.

foreign key (FK) (*215*) Attribute that allows database tables to be linked together; foreign keys are the primary keys of other tables placed in the current table to support the link between the two tables.

generalization relationship (*215*) A special-purpose UML symbol that supports grouping of things that share common characteristics; it reduces redundancy because the shared characteristics need only be modeled once.

multiplicities (*213*) UML symbols that describe the minimum and maximum number of times an instance of one class can be associated with instances of another class for a specific association between those two classes; they indicate whether the two classes are part of one-to-one, one-to-many, or many-to-many relationships.

primary key (PK) (*214*) An attribute or a combination of attributes that uniquely identifies an instance of a class in a data model or a specific row in a table.

relationship (*227*) The business purpose for the association between two classes or two database tables; see association.

structure model (*212*) A conceptual depiction of a database, such as a UML class model or an entity-relationship model.

Entity-Relationship Diagrams

WHAT IS AN ENTITY-RELATIONSHIP DIAGRAM?

An entity-relationship diagram (ERD) represents graphically the logical data structure of a system, such as a database supporting one or more business processes. ERDs were originally proposed in a 1976 paper[3] by Peter Chen as a tool to capture the conceptual design (schema) of a relational database system, and ERD modeling techniques have evolved over time. Fundamentally, ERDs and UML class models are equivalent tools for modeling data structures.

BASIC BUILDING BLOCKS OF ERDS

Not surprisingly, the basic building blocks of ERDs include entities and relationships. Each entity has attributes that describe its characteristics. Entities correspond to tables in a relational database where the attributes are the fields in the table. Each relationship indicates a business purpose for connecting two or more entities. Relationships correspond to the links between tables. Cardinalities (i.e., multiplicities) define how one entity links to another (see Exhibit 5.A1).

Element	Description	Symbol
Entity	Separately and uniquely identifiable things of interest in a system.	
Relationship with Cardinalities	Associations between two entities reflecting a business purpose (information engineering style), where the ends indicate the cardinalities.	

EXHIBIT 5.A1
Basic Elements of Entity-Relationship Diagrams

Entities represent separately and uniquely identifiable things of interest in a system, for example, customers, employees, sales, inventory, and cash receipts. Entities are modeled as rectangles. Entities correspond to classes in UML class models.

Relationships represent associations between entities, for example, customers (entity) *participate in* (relationship) sales (entity). Relationships correspond to associations in UML class models.

Attributes are characteristics of entities; for example, customer attributes could include name, address, city, state, zip code, and credit limit. Attributes correspond to fields in a relational table, so the selection of attributes for an entity should reflect efficient table design, as discussed within Chapter 6.

Cardinalities describe the nature of the relationship between two entities; they describe how many instances of an entity relate to one instance of another entity—for example, each *customer* may *participate in* many *sales*. Cardinalities correspond to multiplicities in UML class diagrams.

[3] P. P. Chen, "The Entity-Relationship Model: Toward a Unified View of Data," *ACM Transactions on Database Systems* 1 (1976), pp. 9–36.

ERD EXAMPLE USING INFORMATION ENGINEERING NOTATION

Exhibit 5.A2 shows an example using information engineering notation. Again, the two entities are Singers and Songs. In this case, however, the purpose of the relationship between the two entities is not as clearly identified. The "crow's feet" markings on the relationship line indicate the cardinalities. The cardinality notation next to the Singers entity indicates there is one singer for each song. Note that a double line symbol (–||–) is sometimes used to indicate one and only one (mandatory). The cardinality notation next to the Songs entity indicates a singer can record many songs (optional). Thus, there may be singers in the database who did not record any songs, but each song must be recorded by one singer.

EXHIBIT 5.A2
ERD Example Using Information Engineering Notation

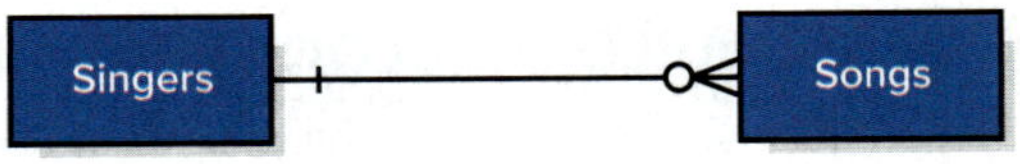

CARDINALITY OPTIONS

In general, there are four options for each cardinality. The minimum can be zero (the relationship is optional) and the maximum can be either one or many, or the minimum can be one (the relationship is mandatory) and the maximum can again be either one or many. Considering the cardinalities at each end of the relationship between two entities (entity A and entity B), there are three basic types of relationships (see Exhibit 5.A3):

- *One-to-one (1:1).* One instance of entity A is related only to one instance of entity B. For example, each sale earns one cash receipt.
- *One-to-many (1:N).* One instance of entity A is related to many instances of entity B (or vice versa). For example, a customer participates in many sales.
- *Many-to-many (M:N).* Many instances of entity A are related to each instance of entity B and many instances of entity B are related to entity A. For example, a sale can include many inventory items, and each inventory item could be sold on many sales.

EXHIBIT 5.A3
Examples of Cardinality Options Using Information Engineering Notation

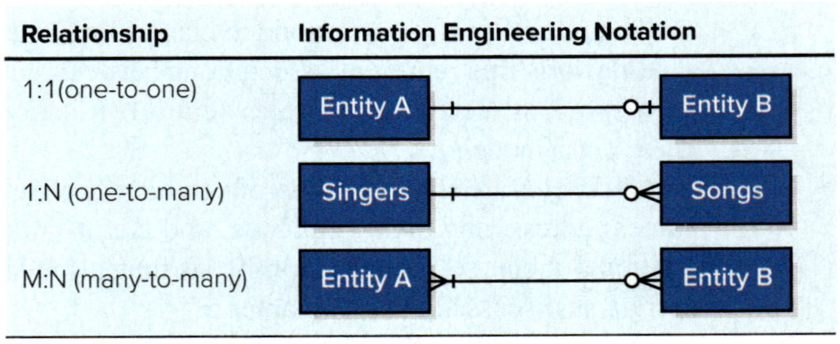

ANSWERS TO PROGRESS CHECKS

1. The class diagram would look something like this:

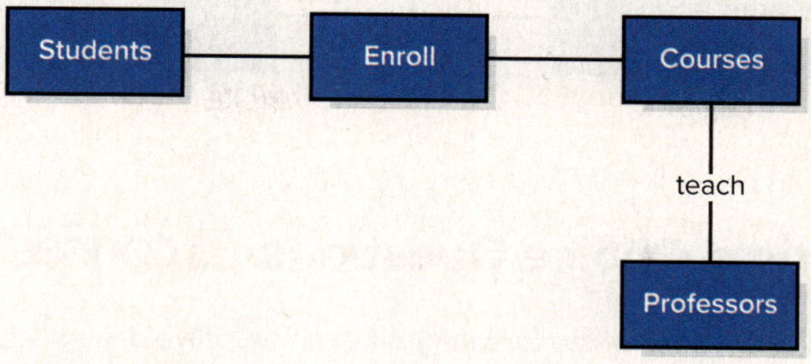

2. With multiplicities:

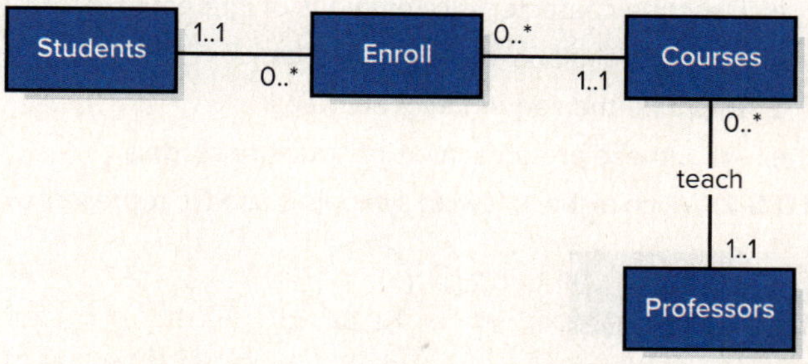

   Note that this assumes that each course only has one professor teaching it and students have not yet enrolled in some courses.

3. The table structure would look something like this:

Students	[Student ID (PK), Student Name, Student Address, Student email,. . .]
Enroll	[Enrollment transaction number (PK), Enrollment date, Student ID (FK),. . .]
Courses	[Course number (PK), Course Name, Course Description, Professor ID (FK),. . .]
Professors	[Professor ID (PK), Professor Name, Professor Department,. . .]

4. The BPMN diagram to implement the detective control physical inventories would look like this:

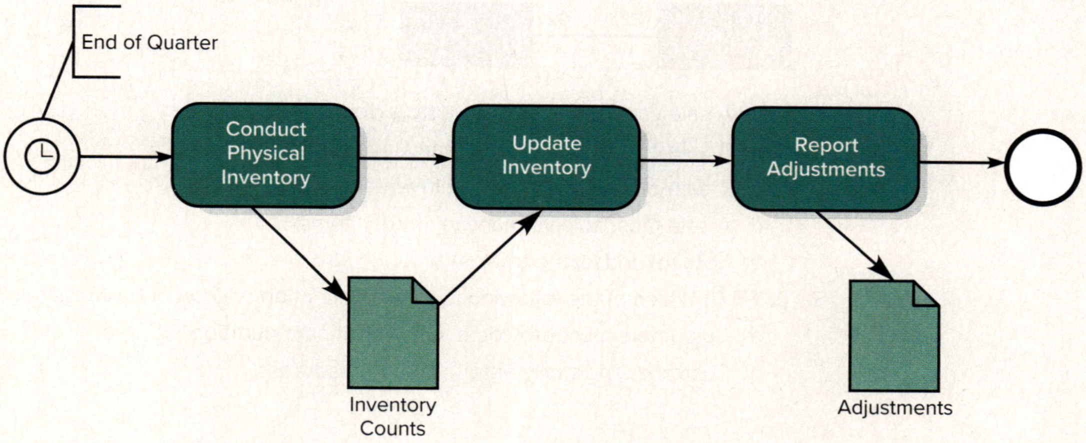

5. The UML class diagram to model insurance would look like this where insurance instances are related to insured assets:

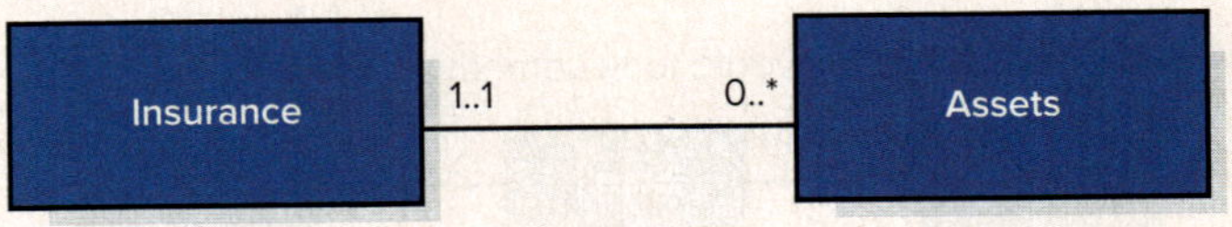

Multiple Choice Questions connect

1. **(LO 5-1)** Which of the following is not an objective of a structure model?
   a. Designate things of interest in the business domain.
   b. Describe characteristics of things of interest in the business domain.
   c. Support relational database design.
   d. Describe the sequence of activities.
   e. All of these are objectives of structure models.
2. **(LO 5-2)** Which of the following symbols is used to represent a class in a UML class diagram?

   a. 

   c. 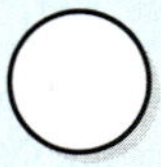

   b. 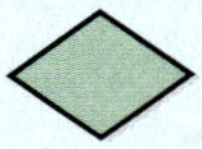

   d.

3. **(LO 5-2, LO 5-3)** Which of the following statements concerning this class diagram with multiplicities is not true?

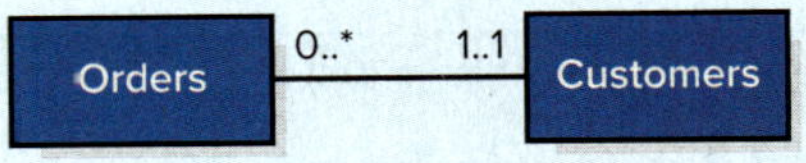

   a. An order can involve only one customer.
   b. A customer can place only one order.
   c. A customer can place many orders.
   d. A customer may not have ordered yet.
   e. All of these statements are true.
4. **(LO 5-2, LO 5-3)** Which of the following statements is true about the following class diagram?

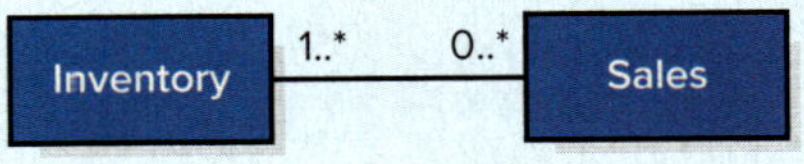

   a. A sale can involve zero inventory items.
   b. A sale can involve one or many inventory items.
   c. A sale can only involve one inventory item.
   d. A sale must involve many inventory items.
   e. Both (b) and (c) are true.
5. **(LO 5-6)** Which of the following is an example of an *obligatory* business rule?
   a. Customers must provide a valid credit card number.
   b. Customers normally enter a shipping address.

c. Customers should not enter a post office box as a shipping address.

d. Customers may use Visa or MasterCard.

e. Both (a) and (b) are obligatory business rules.

6. **(LO 5-6)** Which of the following is not an enforcement level for a business rule?

a. Strict enforcement

b. Optional enforcement

c. Pre-override enforcement

d. Post-override enforcement

e. Guideline

7. **(LO 5-1, LO 5-2, LO 5-3)** Contrast the UML class diagrams with the entity-relationship diagrams shown in Appendix A. Which of the following pairs are not equivalent?

a. Class and Entity

b. Class and Relationship

c. Association and Relationship

d. Multiplicity and Cardinality

e. All of these are equivalent.

8. **(LO 5-2, LO 5-3)** Which of the following best describes the meaning of this diagram?

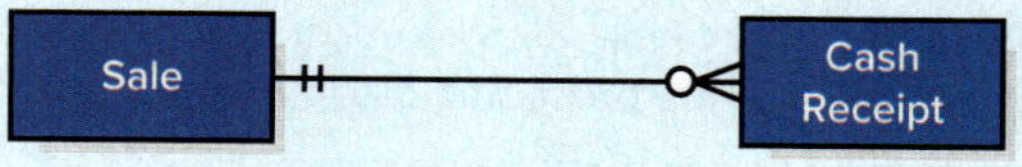

a. Each sale can result in many subsequent cash receipts.

b. Each cash receipt can apply to many sales.

c. All sales must have cash receipts.

d. Each sale can result in only one cash receipt.

e. None of these describe the meaning of the diagram.

9. **(LO 5-2, LO 5-3)** Which of the following best describes the meaning of this UML class diagram?

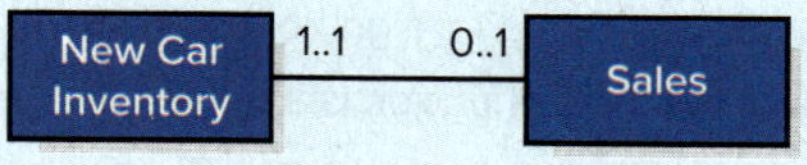

a. Each new car can be sold once.

b. A sale can involve multiple new cars.

c. Each new car can be sold multiple times.

d. No new cars are in inventory.

e. None of these options describe the meaning of the diagram.

10. **(LO 5-2, LO 5-3)** Which of the following best describes the meaning of this UML class diagram?

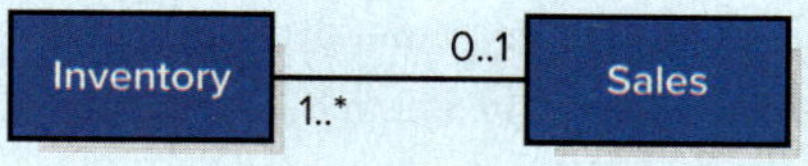

a. Each inventory item can be sold a minimum of 1 and maximum of many times.

b. Each sale includes a minimum of 0 and maximum of 1 inventory items.

c. Each inventory item can be sold a minimum of 0 and maximum of 1 time.

d. Each sales includes a minimum of 1 and maximum of 1 inventory items.

e. None of the options describe the meaning of the diagram.

Refer to this diagram to answer Questions 11 through 20.

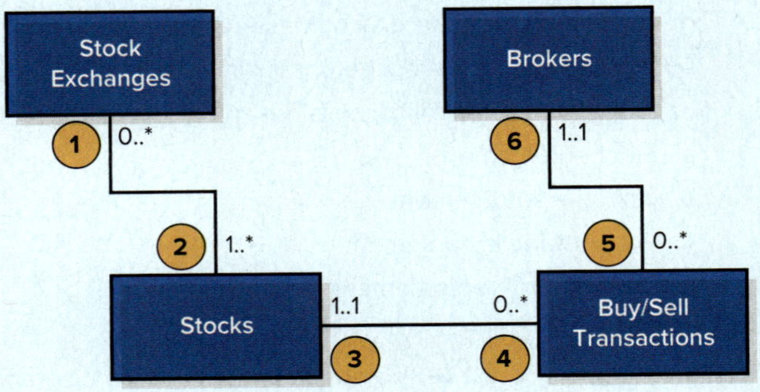

11. **(LO 5-2, LO 5-3)** Which of the following best describes the meaning of the multiplicities next to the number 1 in the preceding diagram?
    a. Stocks are traded in only one exchange.
    b. Stocks are traded in at least one exchange.
    c. Stocks are traded in a minimum of zero exchanges.
    d. Stocks are traded in a maximum of one exchange.
    e. Both (c) and (d) are correct.
12. **(LO 5-2, LO 5-3)** Which of the following best describes the meaning of the multiplicities next to the number 2 in the preceding diagram?
    a. Each exchange trades at least one stock.
    b. Each exchange trades only one stock.
    c. Each exchange trades a minimum of zero stocks.
    d. Each exchange trades a maximum of one stock.
    e. Both (a) and (d) are correct.
13. **(LO 5-2, LO 5-3, LO 5-4)** Which of the following is true about implementing the Stock Exchanges and Stocks classes and the association between them in the preceding UML class diagram in a database?
    a. The primary key of Stocks is a foreign key in Stock Exchanges.
    b. The primary key of Stock Exchanges is a foreign key in Stocks.
    c. The association between Stocks and Stock Exchanges is implemented as a linking table.
    d. Both (a) and (b) are true.
    e. None of these is true.
14. **(LO 5-2, LO 5-3)** Which of the following best describes the meaning of the multiplicities next to the number 3 in the preceding diagram?
    a. Each transaction involves at least one stock.
    b. Each transaction involves only one stock.
    c. Each transaction involves a minimum of zero stocks.
    d. Each transaction involves a maximum of one stocks.
    e. Both (a) and (b) are correct.
15. **(LO 5-2, LO 5-3)** Which of the following best describes the meaning of the multiplicities next to the number 4 in the preceding diagram?
    a. Each stock is bought/sold at least once.
    b. Each stock is bought/sold only once.
    c. Each stock is bought/sold a maximum of many times.
    d. Each stock is bought/sold a minimum of many times.
    e. Both (a) and (c) are correct.

16. **(LO 5-2, LO 5-3, LO 5-4)** Which of the following is the best way to implement the Buy/Sell Transactions and Stocks classes and the association between them in the preceding UML class diagram in a database?
    a. The primary key of Stocks is a foreign key in Buy/Sell Transactions.
    b. The primary key of Buy/Sell Transactions is a foreign key in Stocks.
    c. The association between Stocks and Buy/Sell Transactions is implemented as a linking table.
    d. Both (a) and (b) are true.
    e. None of these is true.
17. **(LO 5-2, LO 5-3)** Which of the following best describes the meaning of the multiplicities next to the number 5 in the preceding diagram?
    a. Each Broker is involved in one Buy/Sell Transaction.
    b. Each Broker is involved in a maximum of many Buy/Sell Transactions.
    c. Each Broker is involved in a minimum of one Buy/Sell Transaction.
    d. Each Broker is involved in a minimum of zero Buy/Sell Transactions.
    e. Both (b) and (d) are correct.
18. **(LO 5-2, LO 5-3)** Which of the following best describes the meaning of the multiplicities next to the number 6 in the preceding diagram?
    a. Each Buy/Sell Transaction involves one Broker.
    b. Each Buy/Sell Transaction involves many Brokers.
    c. Each Buy/Sell Transaction involves a minimum of zero Brokers.
    d. Each Buy/Sell Transaction involves a maximum of many Brokers.
    e. Both (a) and (d) are correct.
19. **(LO 5-2, LO 5-3, LO 5-4)** Which of the following is the best way to implement the Buy/Sell Transactions and Brokers classes and the association between them in the preceding UML class diagram in a database?
    a. The primary key of Brokers is a foreign key in Buy/Sell Transactions.
    b. The primary key of Buy/Sell Transactions is a foreign key in Brokers.
    c. The association between Brokers and Buy/Sell Transactions is implemented as a linking table.
    d. Both (a) and (b) are true.
    e. None of these is true.
20. **(LO 5-2, LO 5-3, LO 5-4)** Which of the following is the best way to implement the Stock Exchanges and Brokers classes in the preceding UML class diagram in a database?
    a. The primary key of Brokers is a foreign key in Stock Exchanges.
    b. The primary key of Stock Exchanges is a foreign key in Brokers.
    c. The association between Brokers and Stock Exchanges is implemented as a linking table.
    d. Both (a) and (b) are true.
    e. None of these is true.
21. **(LO 5-5)** Which of the following is not a general category of operational decision?
    a. Eligibility
    b. Accumulation
    c. Validation
    d. Risk
    e. Opportunity

22. **(LO 5-5)** Which of the following is not a basic step in modeling process decision requirements?
    a. Identify process steps.
    b. Document decisions and how they impact business objectives.
    c. Decompose and refine requirements.
    d. Specify decision information and knowledge requirements.
    e. Identify required decisions.
23. **(LO 5-7)** Which of these is not one of the three main internal control functions?
    a. Preventive controls
    b. Respective controls
    c. Corrective controls
    d. Detective controls
    e. All of these are main internal control functions

Discussion Questions

1. **(LO 5-1, LO 5-2, LO 5-3, LO 5-4)** Consider the following one-to-one association between classes. You are mapping the diagram to a set of relational tables. Where would you post the foreign key? Why would you post it there?

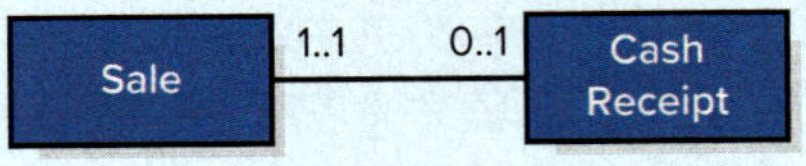

2. **(LO 5-1, LO 5-3)** Consider the sale and cash receipt classes shown in Discussion Question 1. What kind of business is this (in terms of its payment requirements from customers)? How would the multiplicities change if the business (e.g., a used car dealer) accepted multiple payments over time?
3. **(LO 5-1, LO 5-2, LO 5-3, LO 5-4)** Consider the following model and corresponding relational tables. Describe the meaning of the diagram in words. Assume that Students are identified by Student ID Number and Courses are identified by Course Number. List the relational tables that would implement the diagram (you may make assumptions about the nonidentifying fields in the tables).

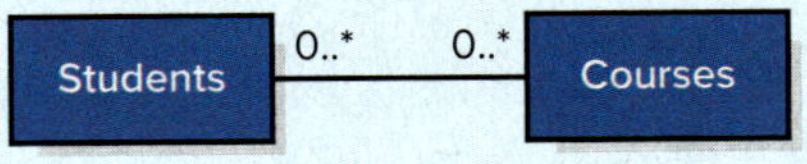

4. **(LO 5-1, LO 5-2)** How would the following model look if you used a composition relationship? Which is more descriptive? (*Hint:* Consider a composition relationship.)

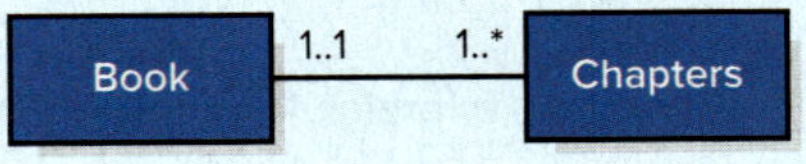

5. **(LO 5-1, LO 5-2)** Consider the diagram in Discussion Question 4. Identify some examples of classes that would be modeled with a composition model. Identify some examples of classes that would be modeled with an aggregation relationship model.
6. **(LO 5-5, LO 5-6)** Think about the process you went through to enroll in this class. What business rules do you think applied to the enrollment process? Are all of these rules written? Why or why not?
7. **(LO 5-5, LO 5-6)** Think about the last time that you purchased something over the Internet. What did the checkout page look like? What categories of operational decisions do you think were made by the website operator. What business rules applied?
8. **(LO 5-1, LO 5-2)** Compare the UML class diagram shown in Exhibit 5.2 with the entity-relationship diagram shown in Exhibit 5.A2. Describe the differences and the similarities.
9. **(LO 5-1, LO 5-2, LO 5-3)** In your college career, you may have attended several universities. Draw a simple UML class diagram or an entity-relationship diagram showing your

relationship with those universities. Now add the multiplicities or cardinalities. Would the multiplicities/cardinalities be different if the diagram was drawn from the university's perspective rather than your perspective? Why or why not?

10. **(LO 5-3, LO 5-4)** Describe some real-world examples of (a) one-to-one relationships, (b) one-to-many relationships, and (c) many-to-many relationships. Which do you think is most common? Which does a relational database handle most easily?

Problems connect

1. **(LO 5-2, LO 5-3)** Identify the classes and associations in the following narrative, and draw a class diagram with multiplicities:

   Dr. Franklin runs a small medical clinic specializing in family practice. She has many patients. When the patients visit the clinic, she may perform several tests to diagnose their conditions. She bills the patient one amount for the visit plus additional amounts for each test.

2. **(LO 5-2, LO 5-3)** Identify the classes and associations in the following narrative, and draw a class diagram with multiplicities:

   Paige runs a small frozen yogurt shop. She buys several flavors of frozen yogurt mix from her yogurt supplier. She buys plastic cups in several sizes from another supplier. She buys cones from a third supplier. She counts yogurt and cones as inventory, but she treats the cups as an operating expense and doesn't track any cup inventory.

3. **(LO 5-4)** Write out a set of relational tables that correspond to the class diagram that you prepared for Problem 1. Identify primary and foreign keys.

4. **(LO 5-4)** Write out a set of relational tables that correspond to the class diagram that you prepared for Problem 2. Identify primary and foreign keys.

5. **(LO 5-2, LO 5-3, LO 5-4)** Consider the following narrative describing the operation of the Multnomah County Library.

   The Multnomah County Library provides a variety of services to citizens of the county. First, the library offers a number of traditional books and movies that may be checked out by patrons. Each patron may check out up to five books and two movies at one time. The library also offers several computers for patron use. The library tracks computer use sessions. Each patron may use the computer for up to 30 minutes per session. The library also maintains a number of small meeting rooms that patrons may reserve for classes or events during normal operating hours. Although library services are offered to all county citizens, each patron must obtain a library card to check out books, use the computers, or reserve a room.

   - Identify the classes described in the narrative.
   - Identify the associations between classes.
   - Define multiplicities for each association.
   - Prepare the UML class diagram.
   - Define tables and create at least three fields for each table, including the primary key.
   - Assign foreign keys.
   - Create an Access database using the UML class diagram and the corresponding tables and attributes. Create relationships among tables to implement the UML class diagram.

Chapter Six

Relational Databases and Enterprise Systems

A Look at This Chapter

Databases serve as a means of organizing information. We focus on relational databases that store information in tables. We explore relational database principles, including primary and foreign keys, basic requirements of database design, and data retrieval using Structured Query Language (SQL). We also explain enterprise systems (or ERP systems) using a relational database system and their relevance to the organization.

A Look Back

Chapter 5 described data modeling, explaining how data models support database-driven systems. It introduced basic data modeling tools to guide the student's development of modeling skills. The chapter also provided a discussion of business rules and how identifying relevant business rules supports both process and data modeling.

A Look Ahead

Chapters 7 through 9 use data models to describe business processes such as sales to cash collection, procurement to pay, and product conversion.

Pere Rubi/Shutterstock

As **Starbucks**' main competitor in the northeast United States, **Dunkin' Donuts** looks to use relational database technology to help determine who ends up on the corner of your block first!

To help it win this race, Dunkin' Donuts is using a new system that helps it more quickly close deals with its new franchisees. Franchisees apply to run a Dunkin' Donuts franchise, pay the franchise fee after the approval process, and then pay royalties on each dollar of sales thereafter. Dunkin' Donuts' management uses the system to manage information about these potential franchisees, including the status of each potential deal and the status of the franchisee financing. This is particularly important in the competition against Starbucks, which doesn't franchise its stores, so its growth isn't delayed by issues with finding suitable franchise operators and getting them signed up to sell coffee in a timely fashion.

Dunkin' Donuts' managers use this dashboard-type system to get a geographic view of regions where deals are stalling; it then has the ability to drill down to see which specific item is slowing down the process. It can identify potential deals in locations that are too close in proximity. Key metrics the company is tracking and monitoring include the average cycle time to complete a franchise deal and the expected size of those deals.

Sources: Informationweek, 2007, www.informationweek.com/news/global-cio/showArticle.jhtml?articleID=199001001; www.betheboss.ca/franchise_news_april_2007%5Cdunkin-donuts-crm161.cfm.

CHAPTER OUTLINE

LEARNING OBJECTIVES

After reading this chapter, you should be able to:

6-1 Describe the advantages of relational databases.

6-2 Explain basic relational database principles.

6-3 Describe how to query using Structured Query Language (SQL).

6-4 Understand the purpose and basic framework for an enterprise system.

6-5 Assess how cloud computing facilitates enterprise systems.

INTRODUCTION

A **database** is a collection of related data for various uses. Databases used in a business setting often maintain information about various types of objects (e.g., raw materials inventory), events (e.g., sales transactions), people (e.g., customers), and places (e.g., retail store). In databases today, three types of data models are used: the hierarchical model, the network model, and the relational model.

Hierarchical data models were widely used in mainframe database management systems. Hierarchical data models organize data into a tree-like structure that allows repeating information using defined parent/child relationships. One example of a tree-like structure is financial statements, where a financial statement element (parent) can be decomposed into finer elements (child). More specifically, assets (parent) can be decomposed into current assets (child 1) and noncurrent assets (child 2). Current assets (parent) could be further decomposed into cash and cash equivalents (child 3), accounts receivable (child 4), and inventory (child 5). You can see how the hierarchical relationships define the relationships among the data elements associated with a balance sheet in a tree-like structure. In a hierarchical data model, data elements are related to each other using a notation known as 1:N mapping (one parent: more than one child), also known as one-to-many relationships.

A **network data model** is a flexible model representing objects and their relationships. The network model allows each record to have multiple parent and child records or M:N mapping, also known as many-to-many relationships. These form a lattice structure (often looking like a big net) connecting parent and child records together.

LO 6-1

Describe the advantages of relational databases.

The **relational data model** is a data model that stores information in the form of related two-dimensional tables. It allows designers and users to identify relationships at the time the database is created or much later whenever new informational requirements from the data model are desired. While hierarchical and network data models require relationships to be formed at the database creation, relational data models can be made up as needed.

Relational data models are the dominant data model form in use today, likely because they offer many advantages over other data models, including

1. ***Flexibility and scalability.*** As business and informational requirements change, relational data models are able to handle these changes quickly and easily. For this flexibility, the relational data model for databases is the most popular data model today.
2. ***Simplicity.*** A relational data model is a relatively simple model that is easy to communicate to both database users and database developers.
3. ***Reduced information redundancy.*** A relational data model requires each piece of data to be recorded only in one place, eliminating the need for information to be stored in multiple places in the organization. This also helps keep the information updated because the information only has to be updated once in one database, which can help avoid data inconsistency.

For the remainder of the chapter, we focus on the use of relational databases.

Definitions for Databases

Before we get into the details of how relational databases are created and used in an organization, it is useful to define a few terms related to databases:

- **Database management system (DBMS)**—The DBMS is a computer program that creates, modifies, and queries the database. Specifically, the DBMS is designed to manage a database's storage and retrieval of information.
- **Data dictionary**—The data dictionary describes the data fields in each database record such as field description, field length, field type (e.g., alphanumeric, numeric), and so on.
- **Database administrator**—The database administrator is responsible for the design, implementation, repair, and security of a firm's database.

PROGRESS CHECK

1. A database is an organized collection of data for various uses. Name three uses for a sales database at **Walmart.**
2. Relational data models allow changes to the data model as information needs change. How does the use of a data model help database designers and database users to understand the business processes?

LO 6-2

Explain basic relational database principles.

FUNDAMENTALS OF RELATIONAL DATABASES

Entities and Attributes

First, it is important to describe entities and attributes of a relational database. As introduced in Chapter 5, a class (also called an entity) in the relational database model could be a person, place, thing, transaction, or event about which information is stored. Customers, sales, products, and employees are all examples of classes. Classes could be grouped into resources (R), events (E), and agents (A) in data modeling.[1] *Resources* are those things that have economic value to a firm, such as cash and products. *Events* are the various business activities conducted in a firm's daily operations, such as sales and purchases. *Agents* are the people who participate in business events, such as customers and salespeople.

Attributes are characteristics, properties, or adjectives that describe each class. Attributes for customers may include the Customer ID, Customer Last Name, Customer First Name, and Customer Address. Attributes for sales could be Invoice Number, Customer ID, Date, and Product Number. Attributes for products may include Product Number, Product Name, and Product Price.

There are three main constructs in a relational database: tables, attributes, and records. The primary construct is called a table or relation for data storage, with rows and columns much like a spreadsheet. Each table in a database represents either a class or a relationship among classes. Tables need to be properly linked to make a relational database. The columns in a table are called fields and represent the attributes or characteristics of the class or relationship. The rows in a table are called records or tuples. A record represents all the specific data values that are associated with one instance.

Products of Gizmos and Gadgets.

Kardasov Films/Shutterstock

Keys and Relationships

Logical relationships within a relational database model are created by using primary keys and foreign keys. A simplistic illustration of a relational database for Gizmos and Gadgets (a reseller of smartphones) appears in Exhibit 6.1. As defined in Chapter 5, a **primary key (PK)** is an attribute or a combination of attributes that uniquely identifies a specific row in a table. Notice the Customer ID in the Customer table is the primary key that uniquely identifies the customer. In this case, the telephone number of the customer serves as the Customer ID. In Exhibit 6.1, the primary key that uniquely identifies a sale in the Sales table is the invoice number, and the primary key that uniquely identifies each product in the product table is the product number.

[1]The REA model was first conceptualized by William E. McCarthy in 1982. See W. E. McCarthy, "The REA Accounting Model: A Generalized Framework for Accounting Systems in a Shared Data Environment," *The Accounting Review*, July 1982, pp. 554–78.

A **foreign key (FK)** in the relational database model serves as an attribute in one table that is a primary key in another table. A foreign key provides a logical relationship, or a link, between two tables. For example, notice the link between the Customer table and the Sales table by use of the foreign key, Customer ID, in Exhibit 6.1. Also, notice the link between the Sales table and the Product table by use of the foreign key Product No. in the Sales table.

EXHIBIT 6.1
Illustration of a Relational Database Using Primary Keys and Foreign Keys for Gizmos and Gadgets, a Phone Reseller

Gizmos and Gadgets
To: Mark Wagstaff
168 Apple Rd., Rockville, MD 20852
602-966-1238

June 12, 2023 Invoice #13131

Product No.	Description	Price	Amount
1233	Apple iPhone 5g	399.00	399.00
		Order Total	399.00

Customer Table			
Customer ID	**Customer Last Name**	**Customer First Name**	**Customer Address**
602-966-1238	Wagstaff	Mark	168 Apple Rd., Rockville, MD 20852
602-251-7513	Waite	Seth	2500 Campanile Dr., NY, NY 10001

Primary Key

Foreign Key

Sales Table			
Invoice No.	**Customer ID**	**Date**	**Product No.**
13131	602-966-1238	6/12/2023	1233
13945	602-966-1238	8/28/2023	1334
14995	602-251-7513	11/21/2023	1233
15123	602-251-7513	12/11/2023	5151
15127	602-251-7513	12/12/2023	3135

Primary Key

Foreign Key

Primary Key

Product Table		
Product No.	**Product Name**	**Product Price**
1233	Apple iPhone 5g	399.00
1334	Motorola Droid	299.00
1233	Apple iPhone 5g	399.00
5151	iPhone cover	32.00
3135	Apple Charger	23.00

Basic Requirements of Tables

The approach of relational database imposes requirements on the structure of tables. If these basic requirements are not fulfilled or if data redundancy exists in a database, anomalies may occur. The requirements include the following:

- The **entity integrity rule**—the primary key of a table must have data values (cannot be null).
- The **referential integrity rule**—the data value for a foreign key must either be null or match one of the data values that already exist in the corresponding table.
- Each attribute in a table must have a unique name.
- Values of a specific attribute must be of the same type (example: alpha or numeric).
- Each attribute (column) of a record (row) must be single-valued. This requirement forces us to create a relationship table for each many-to-many relationship.
- All other nonkey attributes in a table must describe a characteristic of the class (table) identified by the primary key.

PROGRESS CHECK

3. Describe how primary keys and foreign keys link tables in a relational database. (*Hint:* See Exhibit 6.1 to help describe how they work.)

USING MICROSOFT ACCESS TO IMPLEMENT A RELATIONAL DATABASE

Introduction to Microsoft Access

Microsoft Access is a program in the Microsoft Office Suite. Access is a simple database management system that can be used to run databases for individuals and small firms. In practice, many larger firms choose more complicated database systems like MySQL server or Microsoft SQL Server. The Access system is composed of seven objects that are used to implement relational databases.

The basic building block of a database is the *table.* A table is used to store data, which consist of a series of rows (records) and columns (attributes) connected by relationships (links between tables). All data stored in the database will be stored in tables. Tables are linked by the use of foreign keys, forming an interconnected network of records that taken together are the relational database. In Access, Tables are essential objects for data storage.

When users want to find answers to questions in the database, such as "How many customers do I have?" they use **queries**. Queries are a tool used to retrieve and display data derived from records stored within the database. This can range from listing all customers who live in Oregon, which is a subset (dynaset) of records in the customer table, to the balance in Accounts Payable, which must draw data from multiple tables. Calculations and data sorting are often performed with queries.

Forms are database objects to be designed as a user interface. They are utilized by users to enter data into tables and view existing records. In viewing existing records, forms are powered by queries that allow data from multiple tables to be displayed on each form. Often, a firm that uses a fully electronic accounting information system will allow end users to directly update the database through the use of forms.

Reports are used to summarize or integrate data from one or more queries and tables to provide useful information to decision makers. Unlike a form, the report does not allow users to edit database information. In an accounting database, reports might consist of a sales invoice to be mailed to customers or the year-end balance sheet to show stakeholders the financial position of the firm. The applications of reports are limited only by data that have been stored in the database.

Steve's Stylin' Sunglasses

Steve's Stylin' Sunglasses (SSS) is a retail store that designs and manufactures custom sunglasses. Every pair of sunglasses Steve, the owner, creates is unique and is therefore fairly expensive to buy. The excellent reputation for quality products and the stellar customer service provided by SSS have attracted new and returning customers.

To promote sales, Steve allows payments to be made periodically over time based on a zero-interest installment plan. However, a down payment is required. Though most customers pay for their sunglasses in full with either cash or credit card, some choose to take advantage of the payment plan option. Steve has noticed that the installment plan is utilized most frequently by customers buying multiple pairs of sunglasses at one time. Steve's policy on installment sales is that each payment from a customer must be clearly marked for one specific sale.

Because Steve is directly supervising two salespeople, who are paid on commission, he prefers to keep all sales separate to facilitate oversight of the revenue cycle. Steve does not collect any data on his customers until they make their first purchase at the store. However, he insists on storing data on every customer because each customer is entitled to free cleanings and adjustments.

Steve handles the bulk of the behind-the-scenes work at the store, including designing the sunglasses. As a result, he employs two salespeople—Frank and Sandra—who deal with the customers. When a customer walks through the door, the first available salesperson greets and assists that customer from the beginning to the end of the transaction, including helping select the best pair of sunglasses and ringing up the sale on the cash register. To that point, Frank and Sandra also act as the company's cashiers, and in that capacity, they take turns making weekly trips to **Bank of America** to deposit the cash receipts. The company has a few bank accounts with Bank of America.

A Data Model and Attributes for Steve's Stylin' Sunglasses' Sales Process

In Exhibit 6.2, we use a UML class diagram to draft a data model for the sales process of SSS. Notice that an REA data model presents classes in the UML diagram in three general categories: resources, events, and agents.

The central column in Exhibit 6.2 includes two events (i.e., business activities)—Sales and Cash Receipt. The Sales event conducted by SSS involves one resource (Inventory)

EXHIBIT 6.2
The Data Model for Sales Process of Steve's Stylin' Sunglasses

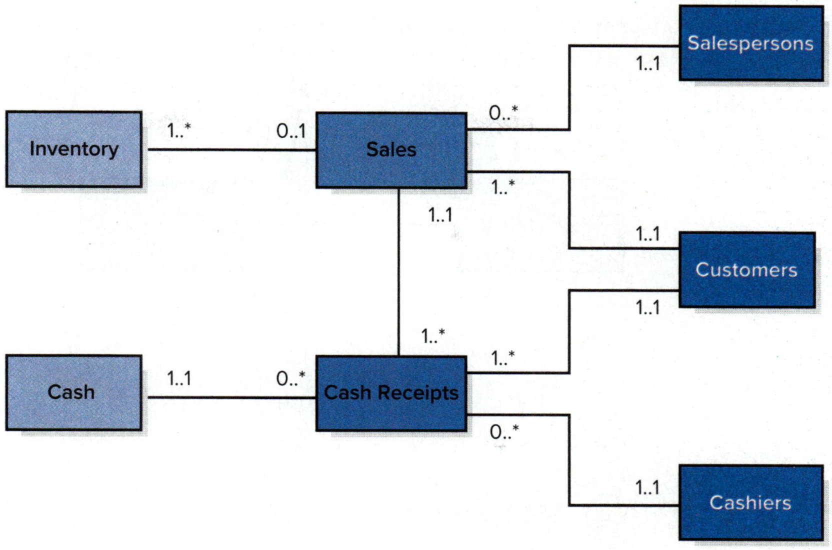

and two agents (Salesperson and Customer). The Cash Receipt event involves one resource (Cash) and two agents (Cashier and Customer). The two events are related. One would decrease the resource of SSS (selling inventories), which leads to the other that would increase the recourse of SSS (collecting cash). They are economic events involving exchanging resources with external agents (i.e., customers).

Please notice that the class Cash contains information of the bank accounts that SSS has. You can consider Cash as Bank Accounts in the diagram. To simplify, you may also consider each record in the Cash Receipt event as a check from a customer.

Multiplicities in Steve's Stylin' Sunglasses' Data Model

Exhibits 6.3, 6.4, and 6.5 explain the multiplicities regarding the sales event of Steve's Stylin' Sunglasses.

A SSS may sell more than one pair of sunglasses to a customer at one time.

B Every pair of sunglasses SSS creates is unique and could be sold once only. Zero means a pair of sunglasses could be designed but not yet sold.

C The shop employs two employees who can act as salespersons. At a minimum, a salesperson (new) may not handle any sale transaction yet, and at most, each salesperson could handle many sale transactions.

D One and only one salesperson greets and assists a customer from the beginning to the end of a sale transaction.

EXHIBIT 6.3
Explanations on Multiplicities Related to the Sales Event

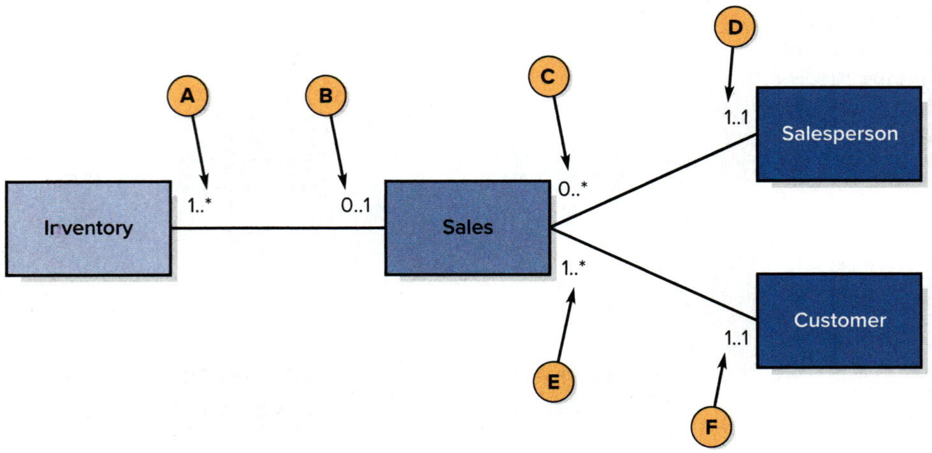

- **E** SSS has repeat customers. Customer data are recorded after the first purchase.
- **F** Each sale involves one and only one customer.

EXHIBIT 6.4
Explanations on Multiplicities Related to the Cash Receipt Event

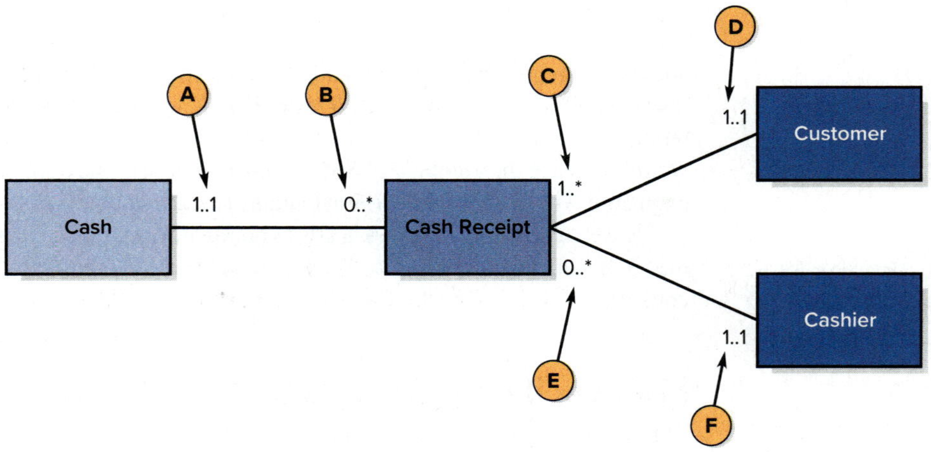

- **A** Each cash receipt is deposited in one and only one bank account.
- **B** Each bank account could have no deposit or many deposits from the cash receipt event.
- **C** Each customer has the option for an installment plan (i.e., SSS will have many cash receipts from one customer). The "1" means a down payment is required.
- **D** Each cash receipt is from one and only one customer.
- **E** The shop employs two employees who can act as cashier. A cashier (new) may not handle any cash receipt yet, or a cashier could take charge of many cash receipts.
- **F** Each cash receipt (e.g., a check from a customer) is handled by one and only one cashier.

EXHIBIT 6.5
Explanations on Multiplicities between the Sales and Cash Receipt Events

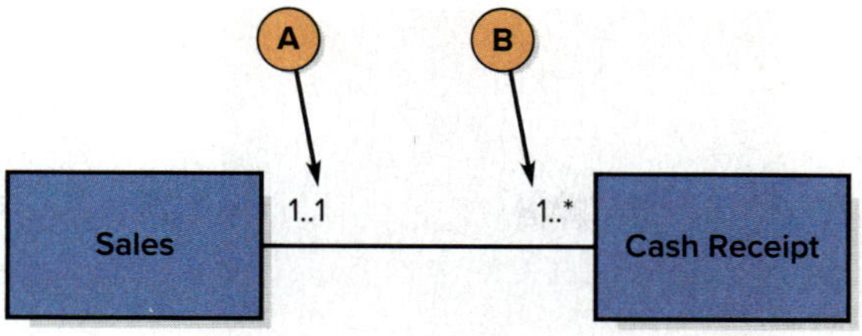

(A) Each cash receipt is for one and only one sale transaction.

(B) Each sale transaction may have at least one cash receipt (i.e., a down payment is required), and at most many cash receipts from customers (i.e., installment sales).

Given the data model in Exhibit 6.2, we assume the following attributes for each table:

Customer	[Customer_Number (PK), Customer_First_Name, Customer_Last_Name, Customer_Address, Customer_City, Customer_State, Customer_Zip, Customer_Email]
Salesperson	[Salesperson_Number (PK), Salesperson_First_Name, Salesperson_Last_Name, Salesperson_SSN]
Cashier	[Cashier_Number (PK), Cashier_First_Name, Cashier_Last_Name, Cashier_SSN]
Sales	[Sale_Number (PK), Sale_Date, Sale_Amount, Payment_Type, Customer_Number (FK), Salesperson_Number (FK)]
Cash_Receipt	[Receipt_Number (PK), Receipt_Date, Receipt_Amount, Customer_Number (FK), Cashier_Number (FK), Sale_Number (FK), Account_Number (FK)]
Cash	[Account_Number (PK), Bank_Name, Bank_Address, Bank_Contact_Person, Balance]
Inventory	[InventoryID_Number (PK), Description, Completion_Date, Cost, Price, Sale_Number (FK)]

Demonstration Lab 1: Using Access to Implement a Simple Database for Steve's Stylin' Sunglasses

Getting Started in Access

Step 1. To start open Access on your computer.

Step 2. On the ribbon bar select **File → New**. The New database menu should appear (see Exhibit 6.6). Select **Blank Database**. The **Blank Database** create menu will appear (see Exhibit 6.7).

EXHIBIT 6.6
Starting Access

Source: Microsoft Access

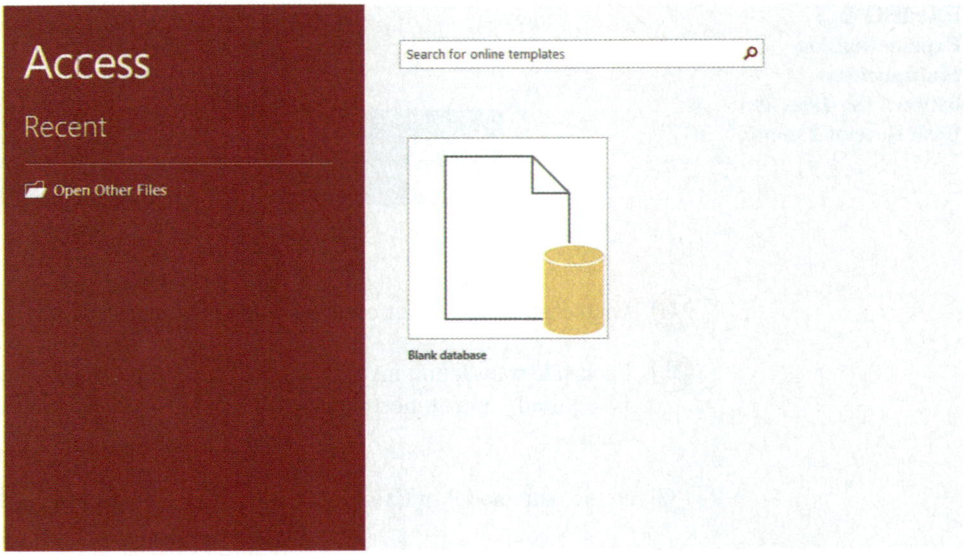

EXHIBIT 6.7
Create and Name a New Database in Access

Source: Microsoft Access

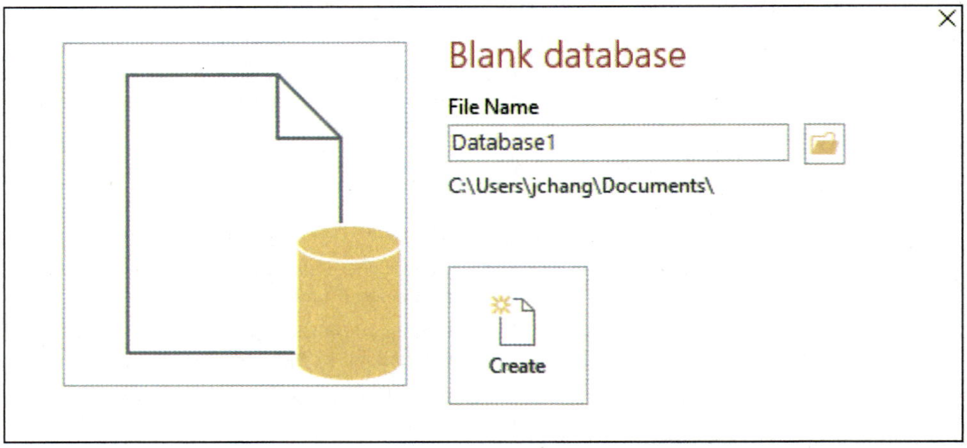

Step 3. Name the database as 'SSS' for Steve's Stylin' Sunglasses. Click on the small folder icon next to the file name and select an appropriate location on your computer to save the file. Click **Create**. See Exhibit 6.8. Exhibit 6.9 shows the home screen for your Database.

EXHIBIT 6.8
Save a Database in Access

Source: Microsoft Access

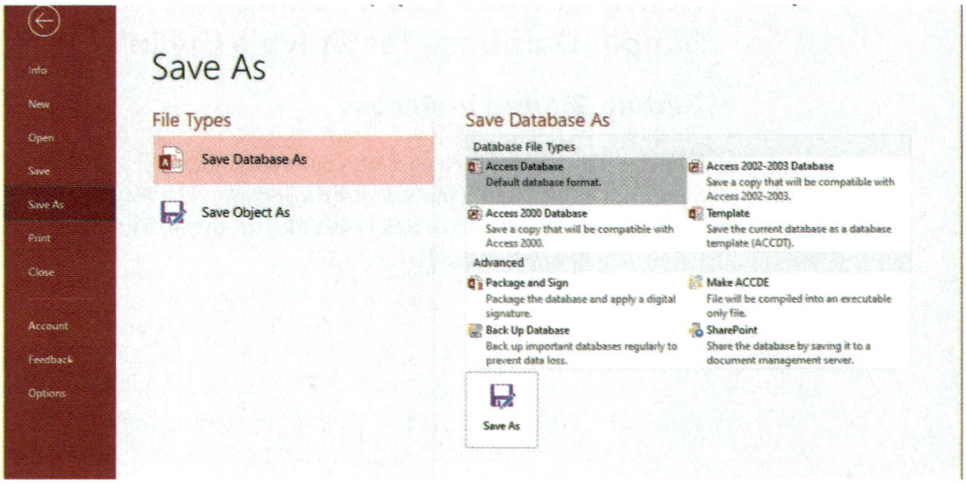

EXHIBIT 6.9
Home Screen of a New Table View in Access

Source: Microsoft Access

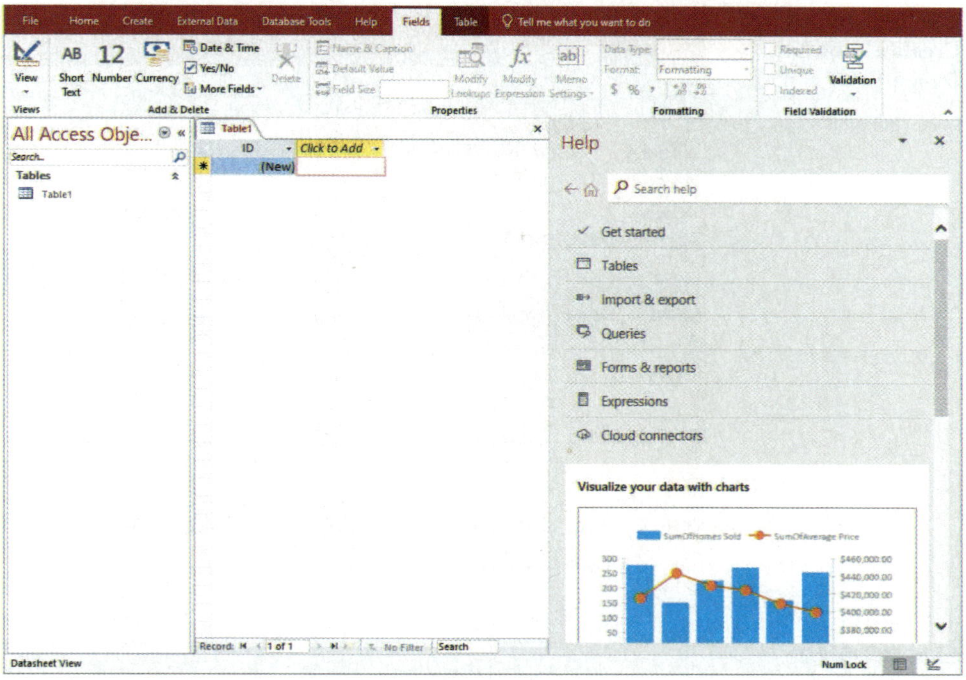

Creating New Tables in Access

Refer to the tables and attributes designed based on the data model of Steve's Stylin' Sunglasses (Exhibit 6.2). That is the database we will be constructing. The first table is the **Customer table**.

Step 1. Click the tab **Create** → **Table**. (Note: The Table Design button will create a table and open it in **Design View**. See Exhibit 6.10.)

EXHIBIT 6.10
Create a Table in Access

Source: Microsoft Access

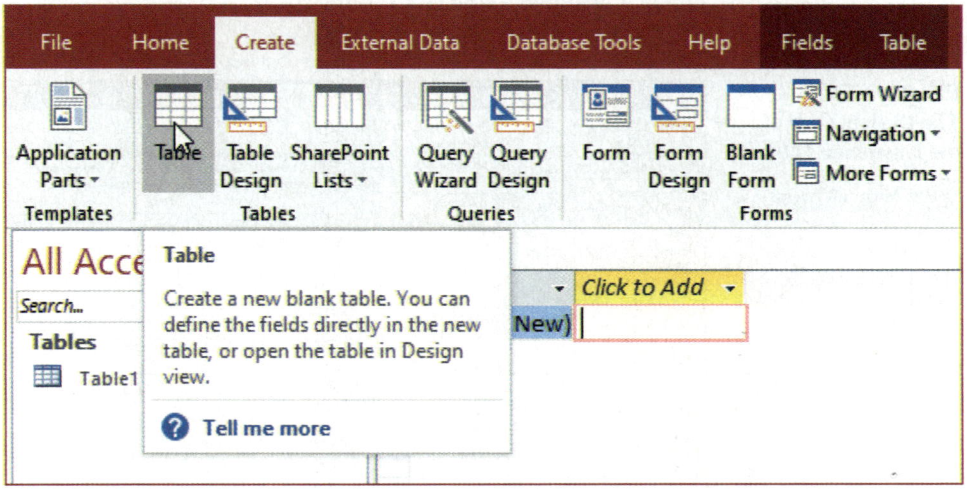

Step 2. Click the tab **Home** → **View** (dropdown menu) → **Design View** (to view the table in **Design View**). See Exhibit 6.11.

EXHIBIT 6.11
Create a Table in Design View

Source: Microsoft Access

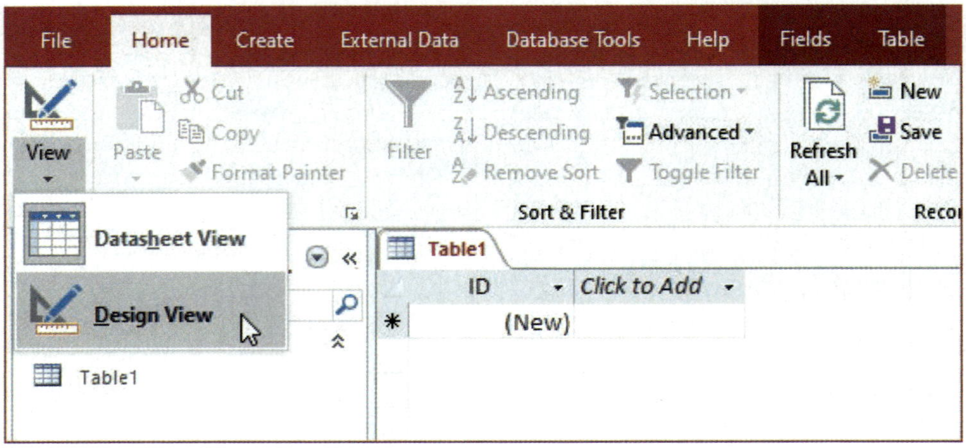

Step 3. You will be prompted to **Save As**, so save the table as "**Customer**" (see Exhibit 6.12).

EXHIBIT 6.12
Name the Customer Table

Source: Microsoft Access

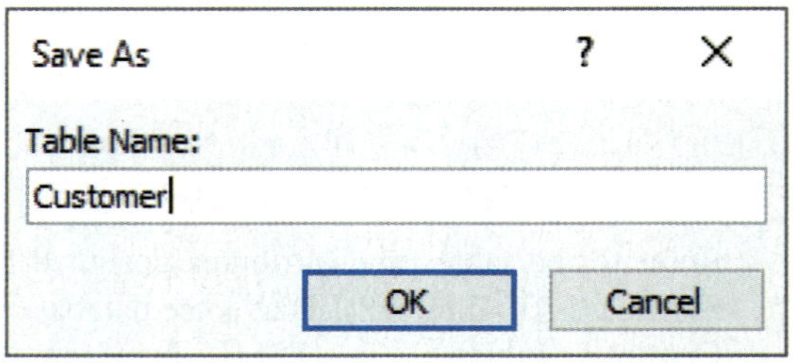

The **Customer Table** will contain the records of Steve's Stylin' Sunglasses' customers. Note the **Field Name, Data Type** and **Description** columns. You will use these to configure the **Customer table** (see Exhibit 6.13).

EXHIBIT 6.13
The Design View of the Customer Table

Source: Microsoft Access

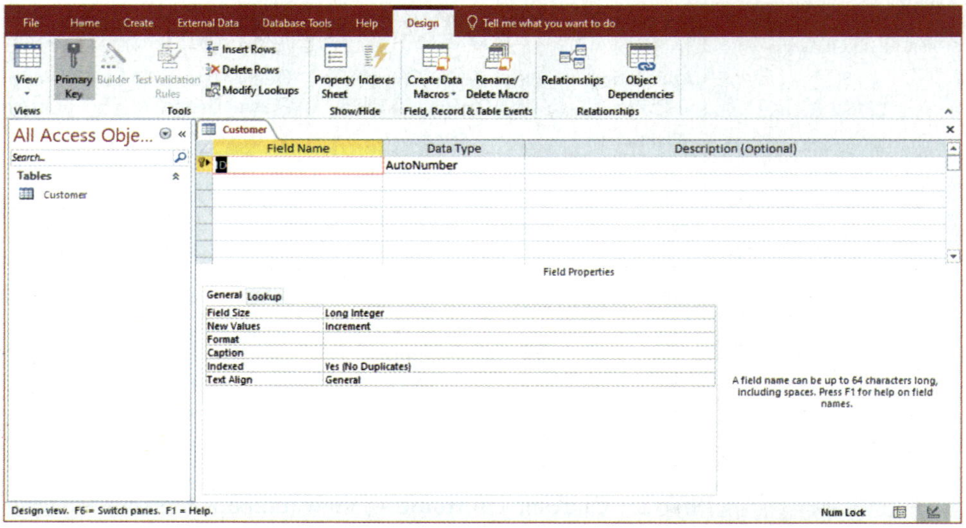

Step 4. The first attribute of the **Customer Table** will be its primary key. Currently, the primary key is named ID. Highlight ID in the **Field Name column** and change it to "**Customer Number**." A field name determines what an attribute is called in a table. It may contain up to 64 characters and may not contain periods, exclamation points, or brackets because they are used in Visual Basic scripts. You should see a key icon next to the **Customer Number** (see Exhibit 6.14). If it is not there, right click on the **gray box** next to the **Customer Number** field and select "**Primary Key**" or look for the primary key button on the design tab of the ribbon.

EXHIBIT 6.14
Create the Primary Key of the Customer Table

Source: Microsoft Access

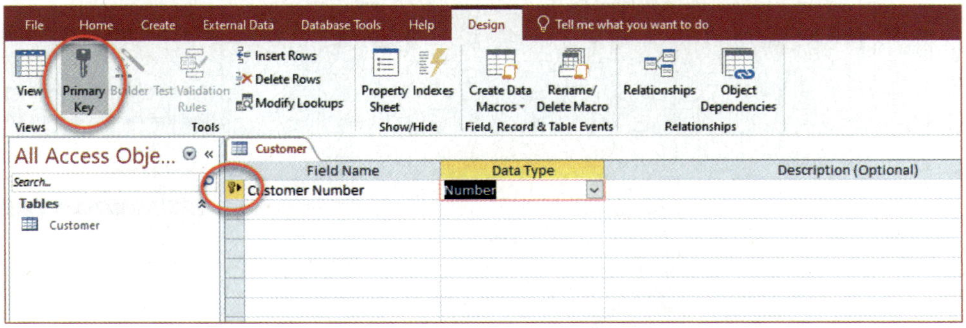

Step 5. Click on the dropdown button for the **Data Type** and select **Number**. Take some time to familiarize yourself with the options on this menu. This will force any data entered into this field to be in the form of a number. The **Description field,** when used, allows useful information about the attribute to be provided to users.

Step 6. It is a good practice to set **Field Properties** for each attribute. For example, for **Customer Number** we would set the **Field Size** to **Long Integer**, the **Validation Rule** to '**Like "######"**.' By doing so, we will ensure that all Customer Numbers are 6 numbers long (i.e., six pound signs). The **Validation Text** of "**Customer Number should be 6 numbers**" provides an error message to tell users what they did wrong. Since this is a primary key, choose the **Required** field as "**Yes**" and the **Indexed** field as "**Yes (No Duplicates)**" (see Exhibit 6.15).

EXHIBIT 6.15
Field Properties for the Primary Key of the Customer Table

Source: Microsoft Access

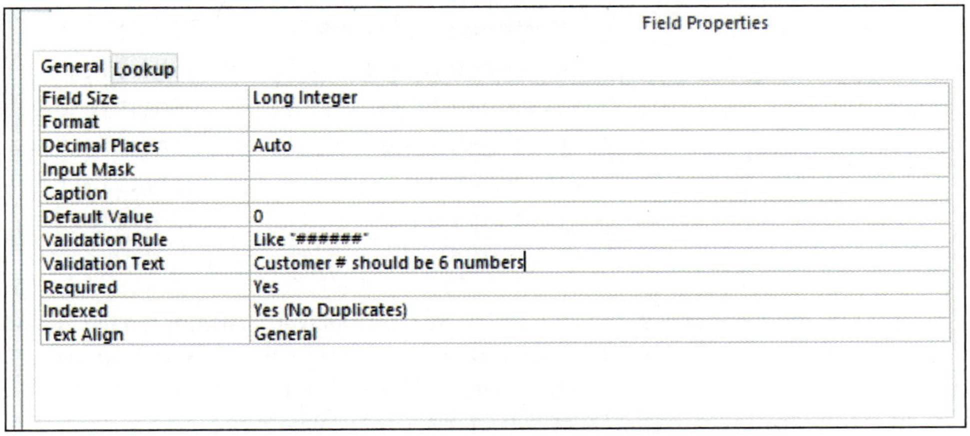
Field Properties

General | Lookup

Field Size	Long Integer
Format	
Decimal Places	Auto
Input Mask	
Caption	
Default Value	0
Validation Rule	Like "######"
Validation Text	Customer # should be 6 numbers
Required	Yes
Indexed	Yes (No Duplicates)
Text Align	General

Step 7. For some fields, it is appropriate to use an **Input Mask**. For example, **Customer Zip** should have an Input Mask. To do this, select the attribute **Customer Zip** and click in the Input Mask area in the Field Properties box. You will see to the right a button with ". . ." on it. Click this button to bring up the **Input Mask Wizard** window as shown in Exhibit 6.16. Select **Zip Code** from the menu and click **Next** and **Finish**.

EXHIBIT 6.16
Input Mask for Customer Zip Field

Source: Microsoft Access

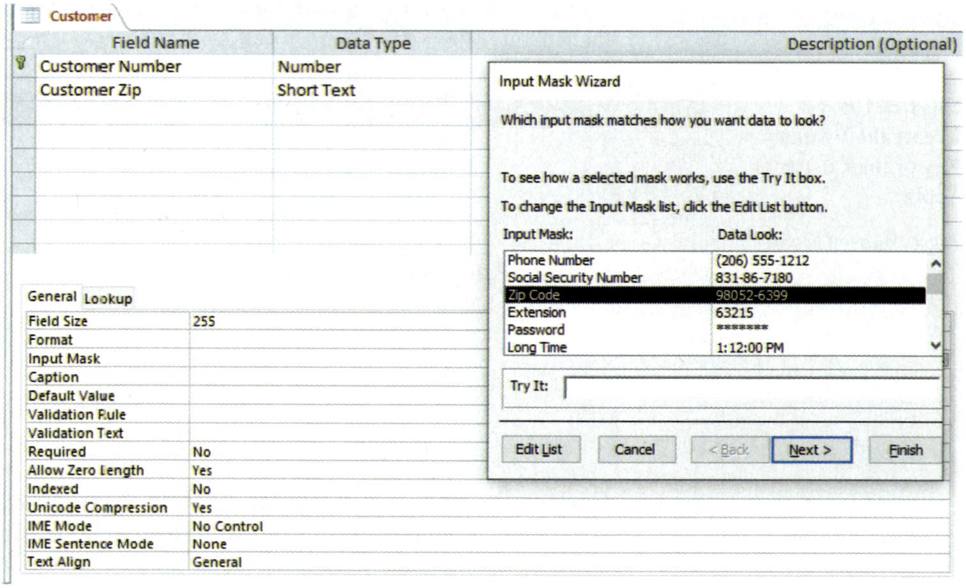

Step 8. Input the remaining fields for the **Customer Table** as shown in Exhibit 6.17. You may **insert rows** between the **Customer Number** field and the **Customer Zip** field. To insert a row left click on a row where you would like to insert a new row. Right click to bring up a drop-down menu. Left click on Insert Row.

EXHIBIT 6.17
Remaining Fields for the Customer Table

Source: Microsoft Access

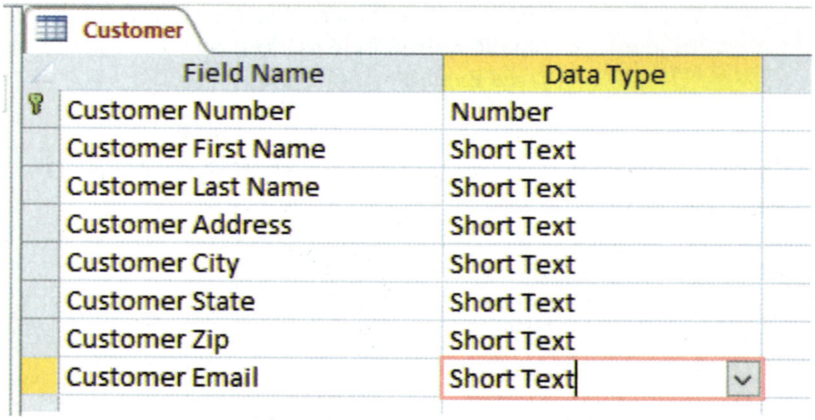

Step 9. Steve's Stylin' Sunglasses creates **custom** sunglasses. When you create the **Inventory Table**, you want to include **Sale Number** as a foreign key as explained above. This will be important later when you create the relationships between the tables. See Exhibit 6.18.

EXHIBIT 6.18
Require Sale Number to Link Tables

Source: Microsoft Access

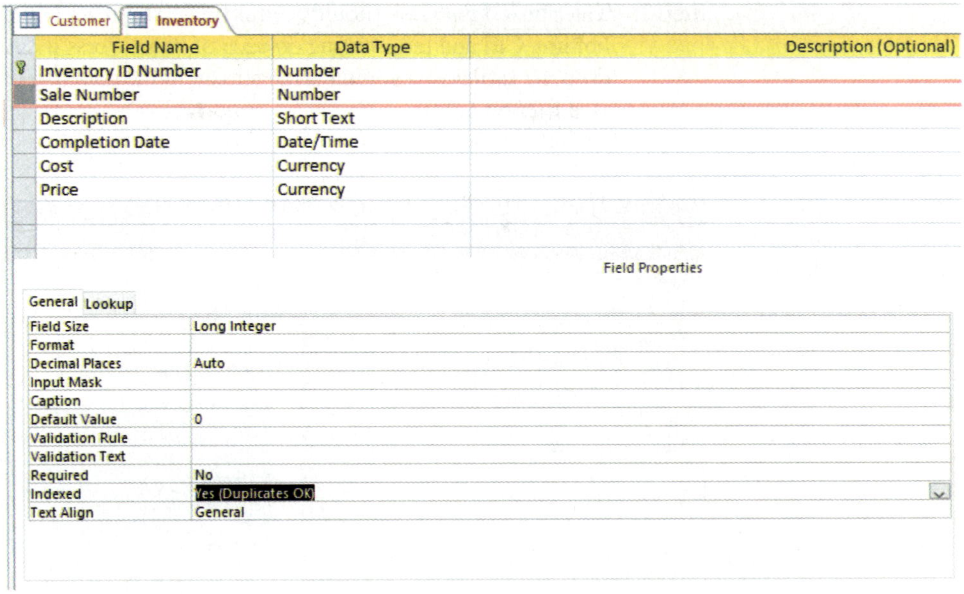

Step 10. Create the rest of the **tables** and **attributes** given before, using appropriate data types and properties. Generally, **validation rules** are used for **primary keys**. The attributes of the **Sales table** are as follows (see Exhibit 6.19). For other fields such as **Sales Date** in the **Sales table** you will also use **Input Masks**.

EXHIBIT 6.19
Attributes of the Sales Table

Source: Microsoft Access

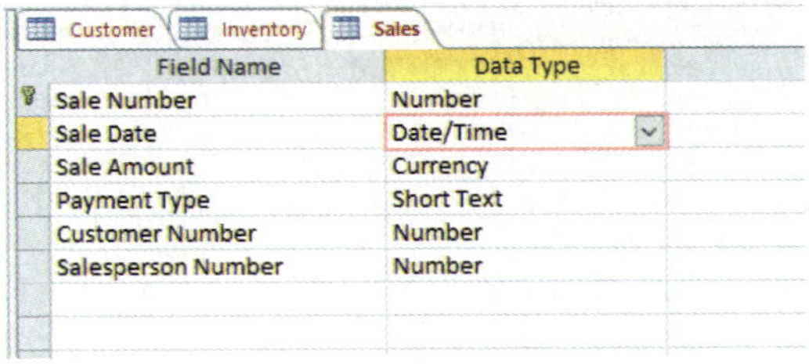

Creating Relationships in Access.

In order to implement a **relationship** in Access, you must use a foreign key. Note that the names of the two fields (the **primary key** in one table and the **foreign key** in the other table) do not have to be the same. You will create links between these similar fields in Access' Relationship window.

Step 1. To pull up the Relationship window, click Database Tools → Relationships (see Exhibit 6.20).

EXHIBIT 6.20
Open the Relationship Window in Access

Source: Microsoft Access

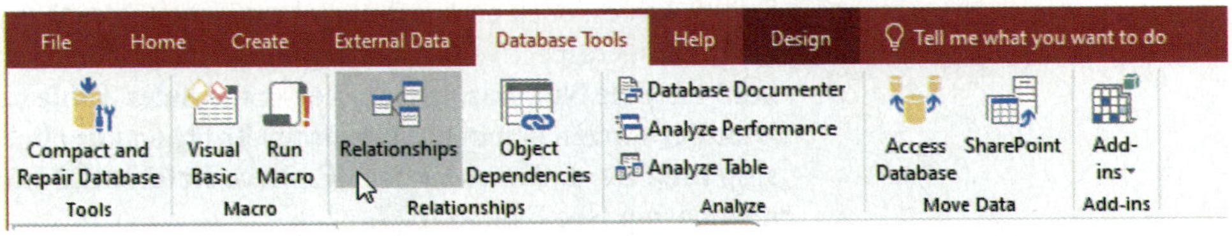

Step 2. The **Show Table** box should appear (see Exhibit 6.21). Select all your tables by holding Ctrl and left clicking on each of them. Press the **Add** button. Drag and drop the **tables** in a similar arrangement to the data model presented in Exhibit 6.2 (see Exhibit 6.22).

EXHIBIT 6.21
Select Tables to Create the Relationships in Access

Source: Microsoft Access

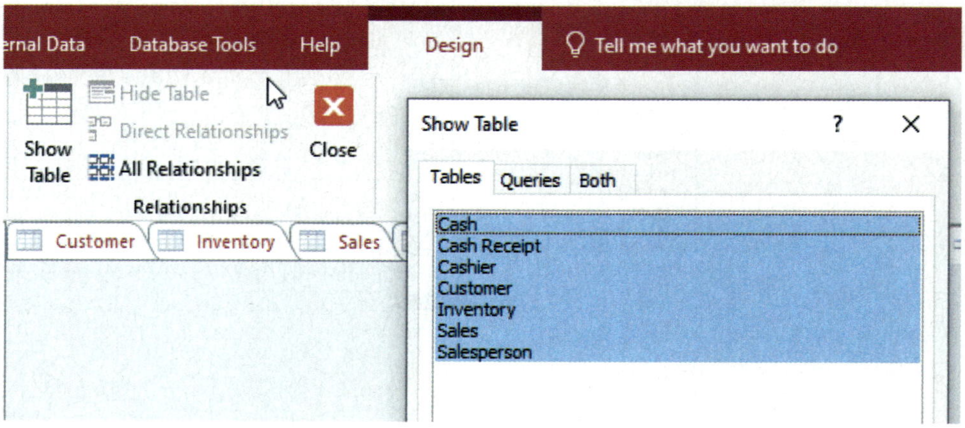

EXHIBIT 6.22
Arrange the Selected Tables before Linking

Source: Microsoft Access

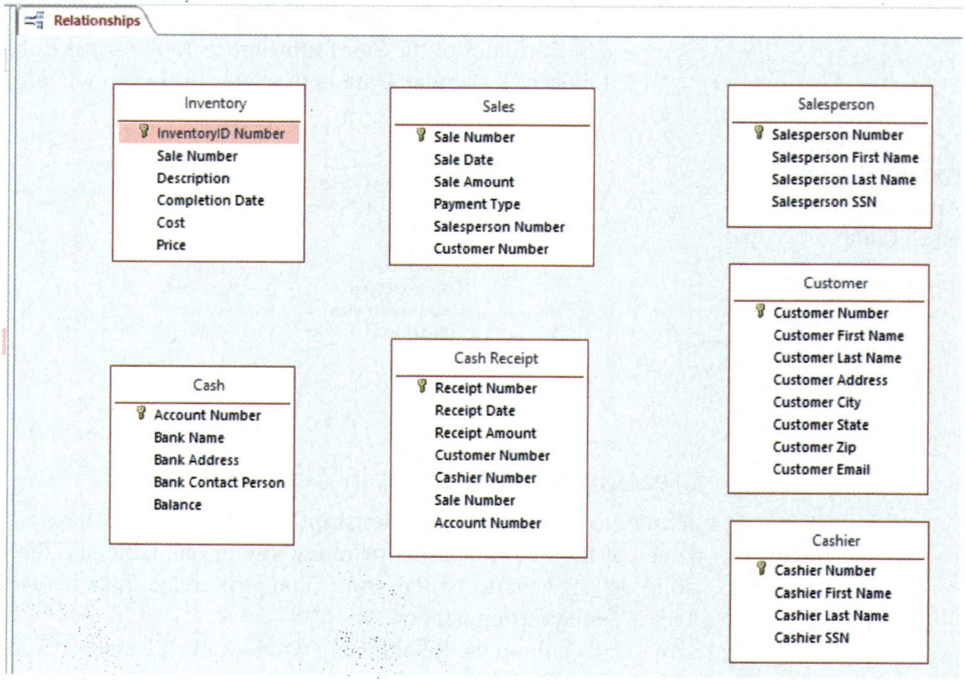

Step 3. To link tables, click each **primary key** of the tables that you want to link and drag it to its respective **foreign key** in another table. Example: **left click** and **hold** the **Sale Number** primary key in the **Sales Table** and drag it to the **Sale Number** foreign key in the **Inventory Table** and **unclick** to create the **relationship link**. Be sure to check the "**Enforce Referential Integrity**" box for each relationship (see Exhibit 6.23).

EXHIBIT 6.23
Enforce Referential Integrity in Linking Tables

Source: Microsoft Access

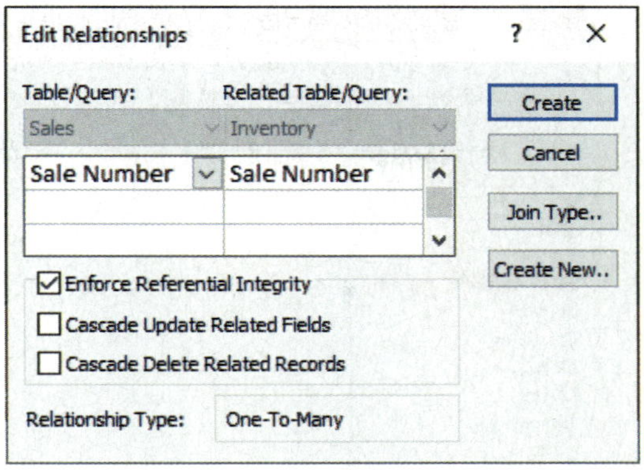

Step 4. When you have completed this process for all relationships among your tables, your Relationship window should look like Exhibit 6.24. You have created a relational database in Access for Steve's Stylin' Sunglasses.

EXHIBIT 6.24
A Database for Steve's Stylin' Sunglasses

Source: Microsoft Access

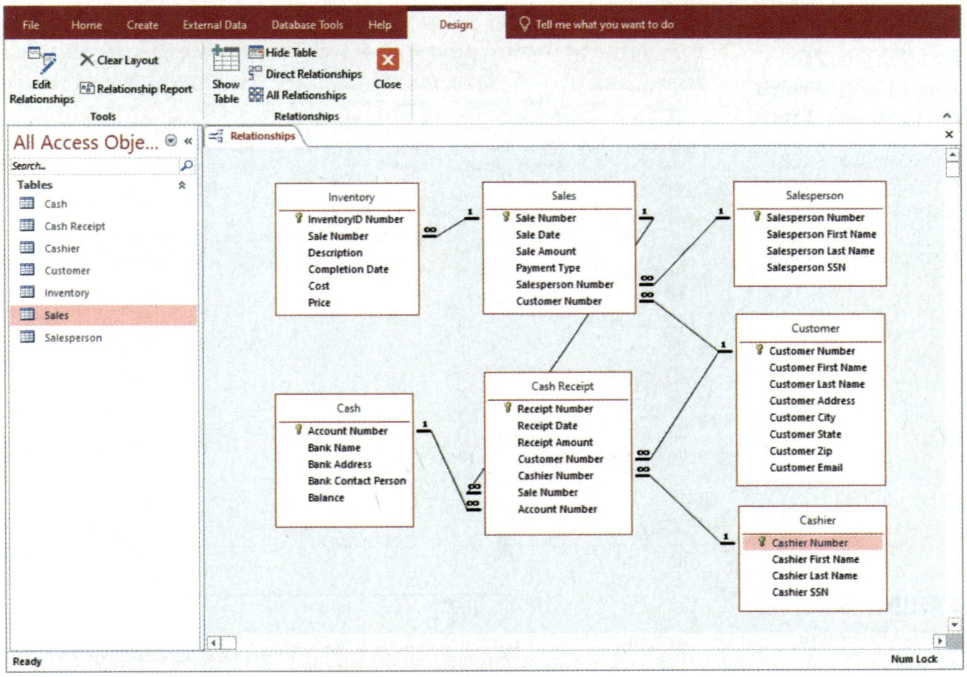

Demonstration Lab 2: Creating a Form for Data Entry and Display

Forms are utilized to enter data into tables and view existing records. This demonstration lab provides a tutorial to create a simple form for Steve's Stylin' Sunglasses (SSS) to enter customer information into the customer table and display the customer records one by one. Please use the relational database which you created for Steve's Stylin' Sunglasses in Microsoft Access to create a Customer Form.

Step 1. Open the database which you created for SSS in Microsoft Access. The database should by default open to the Home tab, see Exhibit 6.25. Click the Enable Content button if necessary (not shown).

EXHIBIT 6.25
Home Tab of SSS in Access

Source: Microsoft Access

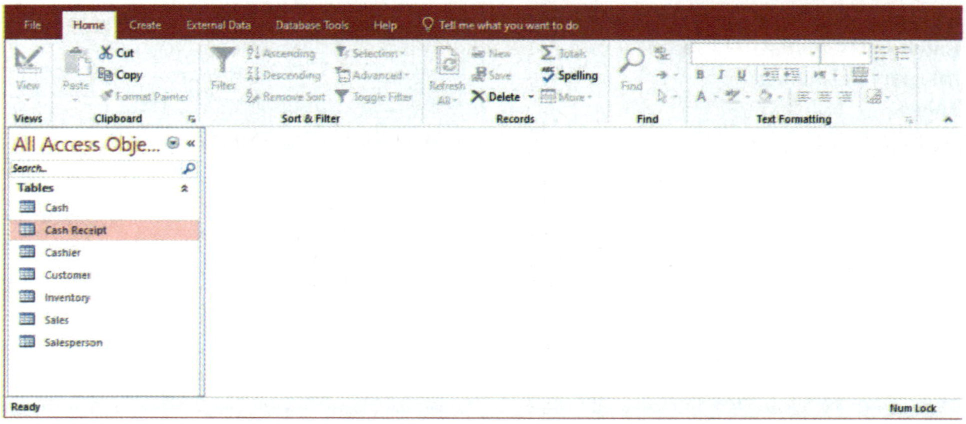

Step 2. In the following order, click on the **Create** tab in the ribbon, click on the **Customer Table** on the left-hand side of the screen and click on the **Form Wizard** button located in the ribbon, see Exhibits 6.26 and 6.27.

EXHIBIT 6.26
Select Form Wizard for Customer Table

Source: Microsoft Access

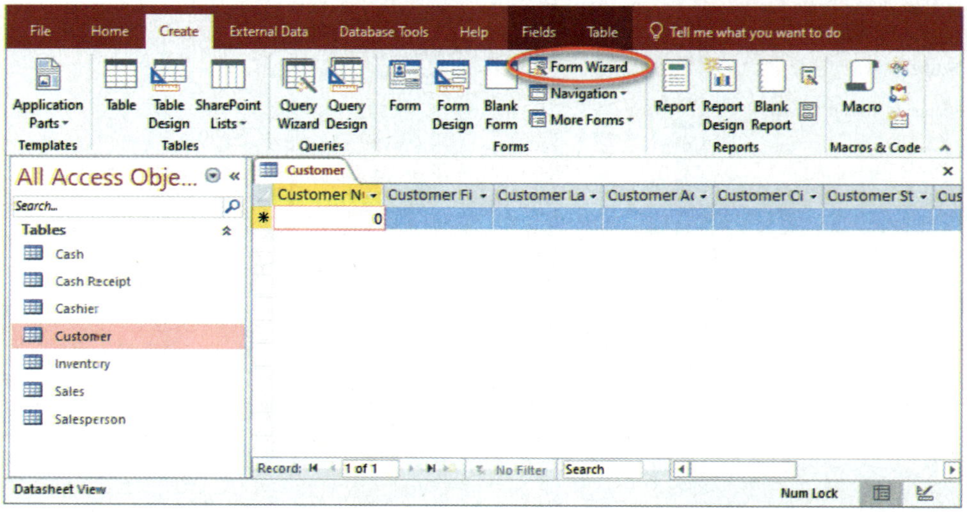

EXHIBIT 6.27
Form Wizard in Access

Source: Microsoft Access

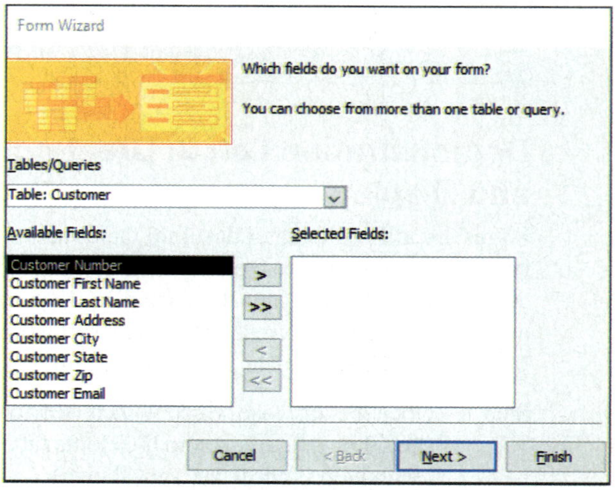

Step 3. In the pop-up Form Wizard window (see Exhibit 6.28), select **Table: Customer** from the **Tables/Queries** drop down menu.

EXHIBIT 6.28
Select Customer Table

Source: Microsoft Access

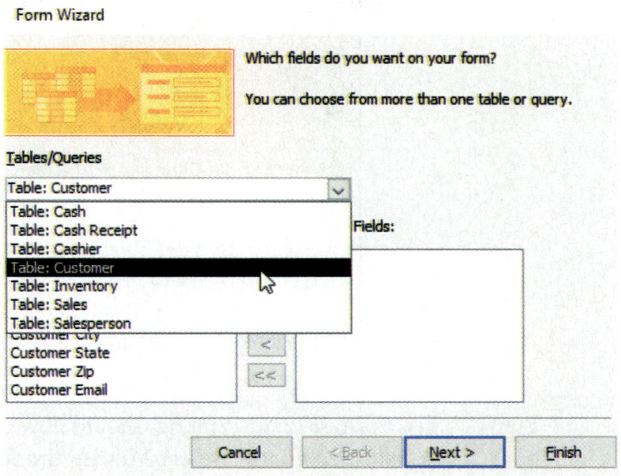

Step 4. In the Form Wizard window, there are two lists of Fields. The Available Fields: and the Selected Fields. Located between these two lists are several buttons. Click on the double arrows pointing to the right, >>. By doing so, you will move all the fields to the **Selected Fields** list, see Exhibit 6.29.

EXHIBIT 6.29
Select Fields of Customer Table

Source: Microsoft Access

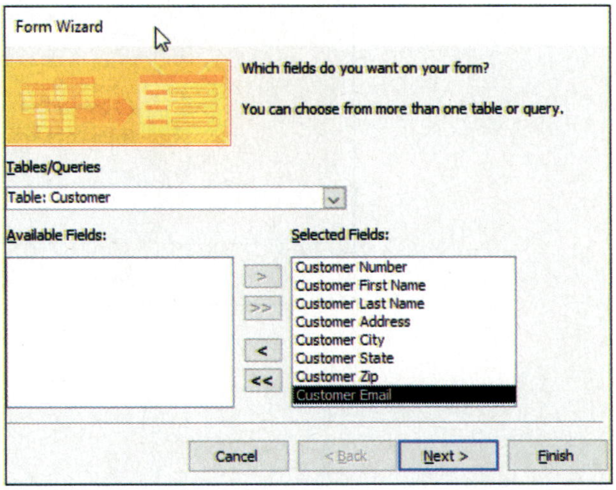

Step 5. Click the **Next** button on the Form Wizard window (see Exhibit 6.30). The Form Wizard window now displays a menu regarding **Layouts**. Select **Columnar** and click **Next**, see Exhibit 6.30.

EXHIBIT 6.30
Select Form Layout of Customer Table

Source: Microsoft Access

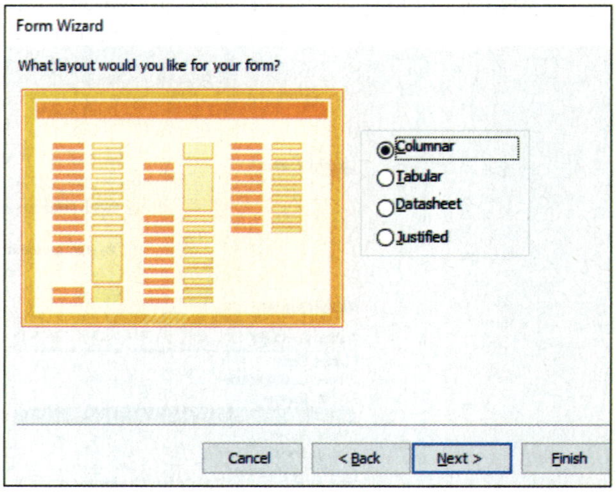

Step 6. The Form Wizard Window should now display a title menu. Name the form "**Customer Form**", select **Modify the form's design**., and click **Finish**, see Exhibit 6.31. The **Design** view of the **Customer Form** should now display, see Exhibit 6.32.

EXHIBIT 6.31
Name the Form as Customer Form

Source: Microsoft Access

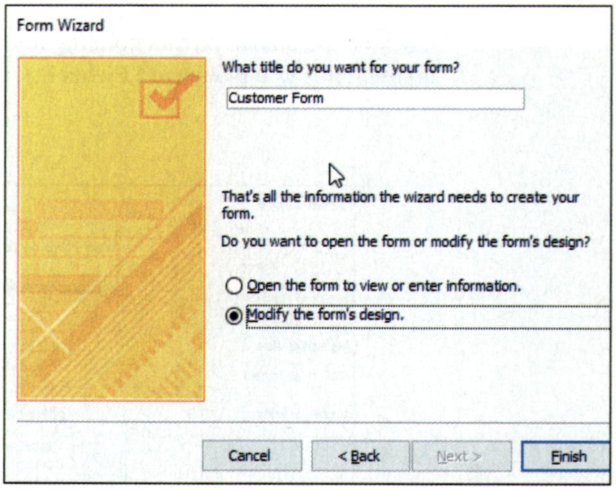

EXHIBIT 6.32
Design View of the Customer Table

Source: Microsoft Access

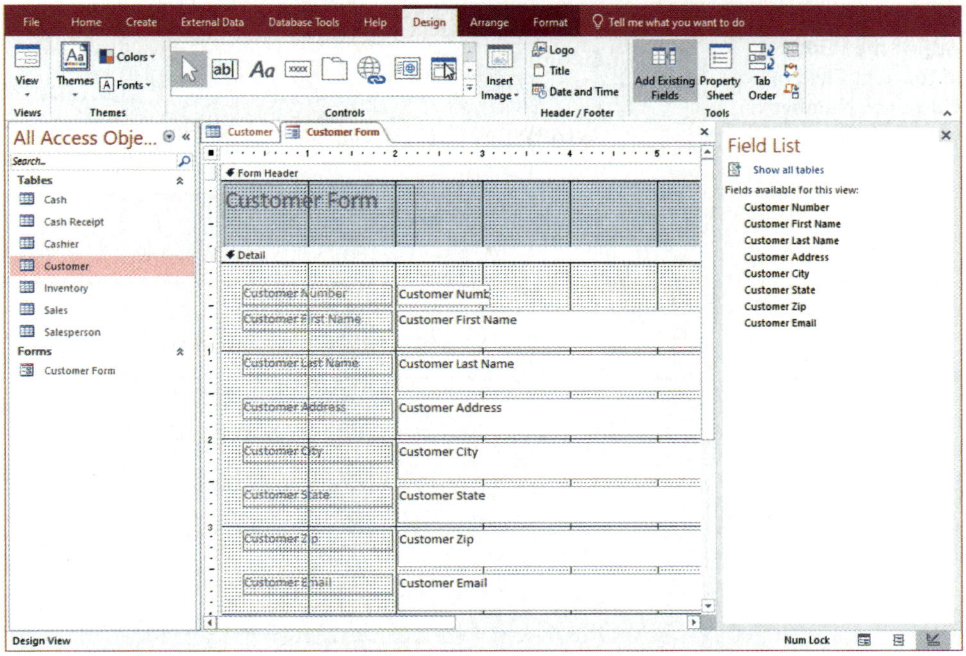

Step 7. Click the **X** button in the top right corner of the **Field List** menu to close the menu, see Exhibit 6.33. The **Customer Form** now lists all the Fields, Customer Number, Customer First Name, etc. Each Field has a **Label Field** and a **Text Field**. The Label Fields are located on the left side and are slightly transparent. The Text Fields are located on the right side and have a plain white background.

EXHIBIT 6.33
Close the Field List Menu

Source: Microsoft Access

Step 8. The sizes of the Text Fields can be changed by clicking on the borders and changing their sizes. Enlarge the **Customer Number Text Field** so its entire text is visible, see Exhibit 6.34. Resize the remaining **Text Fields** so they match Exhibit 6.35.

EXHIBIT 6.34
Adjust the Width of the Text Field of Customer Number

Source: Microsoft Access

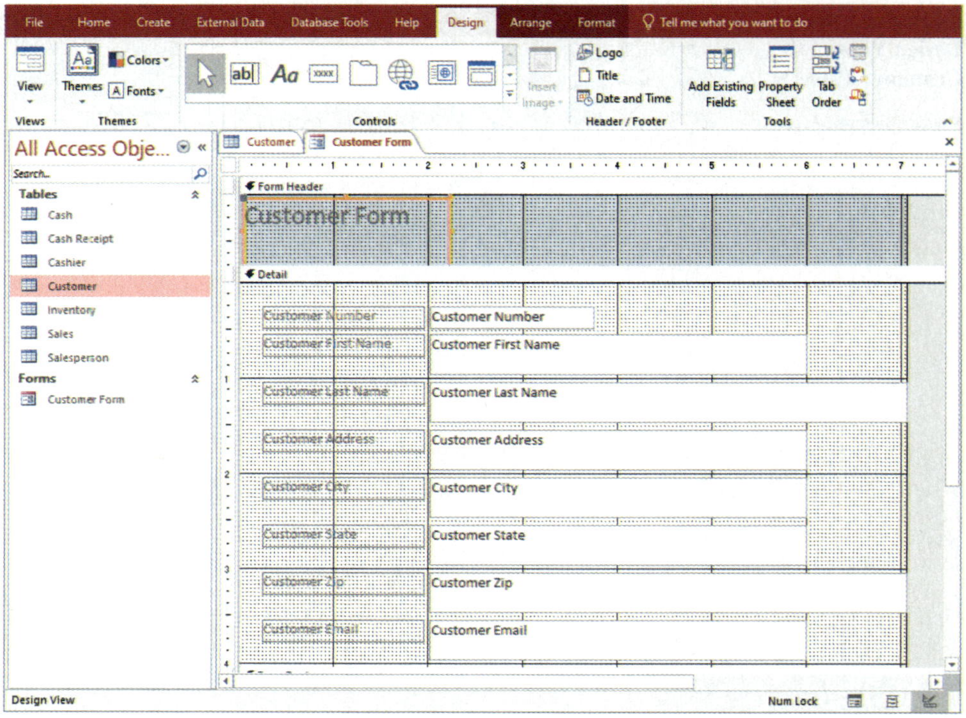

EXHIBIT 6.35
Adjust the Width of All Text Fields of the Customer Form

Source: Microsoft Access

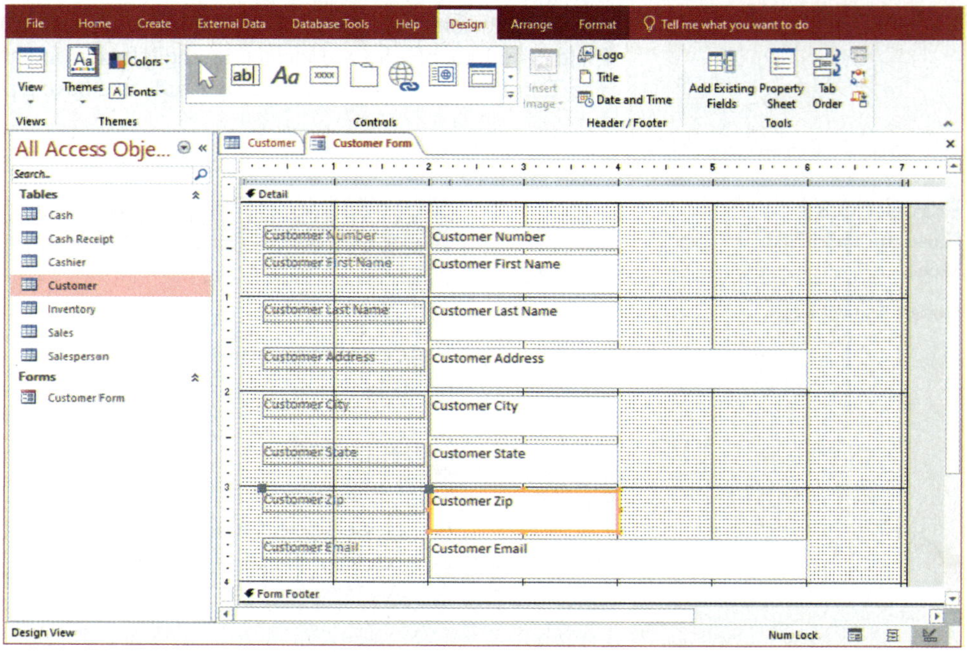

Step 9. Click on the Form View button located in the Views section of the ribbon, see Exhibit 6.36. The Customer Form should now be in Form View, see Exhibit 6.37.

EXHIBIT 6.36
Select the Form View in Access

Source: Microsoft Access

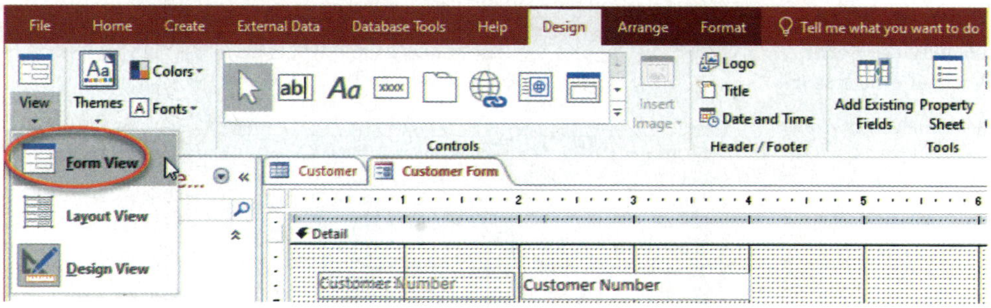

EXHIBIT 6.37
Display the Form View in Access

Source: Microsoft Access

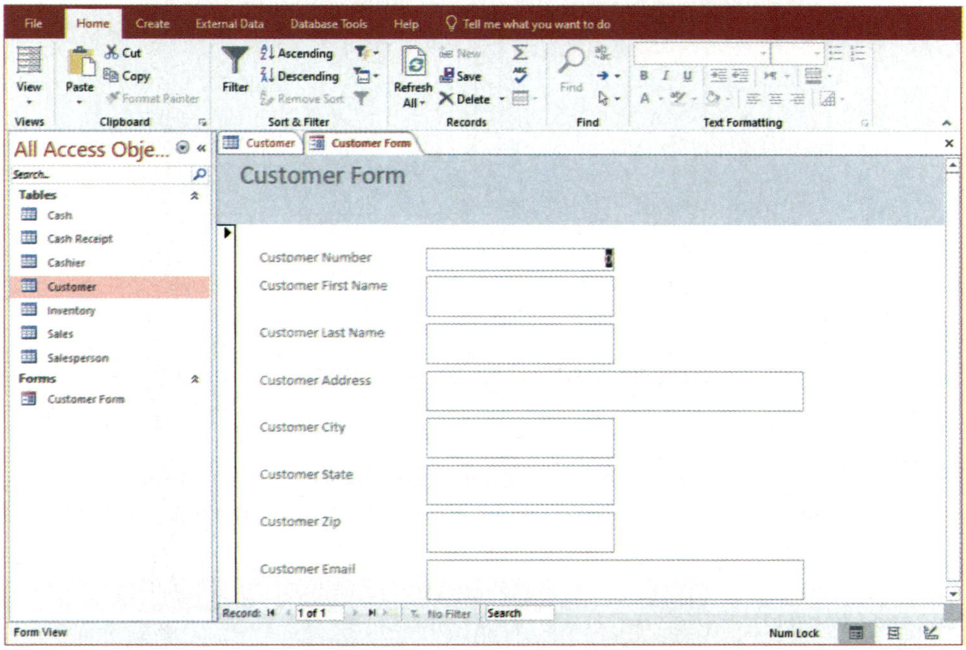

Step 10. In the **Form View**, enter a new customer record with the data values as follows:
Customer Number: 100001
Customer First Name: John
Customer Last Name: Smith
Customer Address: 2105 East Main Street
Customer City: Denver
Customer State: CO
Customer Zip: 80202-4781
Customer Email: JohnS@gmail.com

The Customer Form should look like the following once all the customer information is entered, see Exhibit 6.38. If you would like to add the second record using this form, click on the triangle symbol icon on the record line at the bottom of the Customer Form (see Exhibit 6.39). It will display another blank page for data entry.

EXHIBIT 6.38
Display the Form View of One Record

Source: Microsoft Access

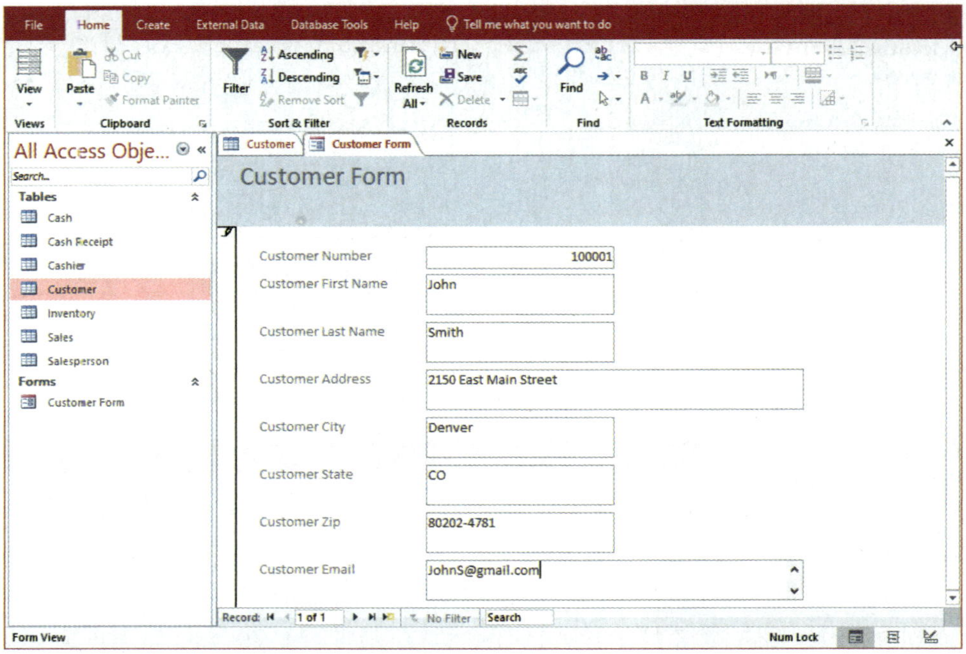

EXHIBIT 6.39
Add a Second Record to SSS Database

Source: Microsoft Access

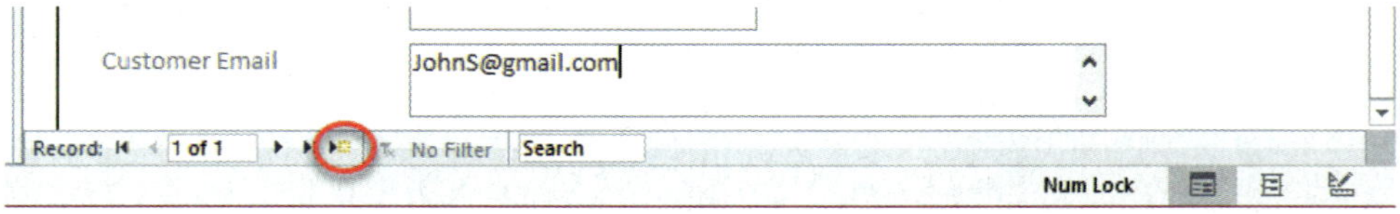

Step 11. Save the database and then close the Customer Form by clicking on the small X button in the upper right-hand corner of the Customer Form, see Exhibit 6.40.

EXHIBIT 6.40
Save and Close the Customer Form

Source: Microsoft Access

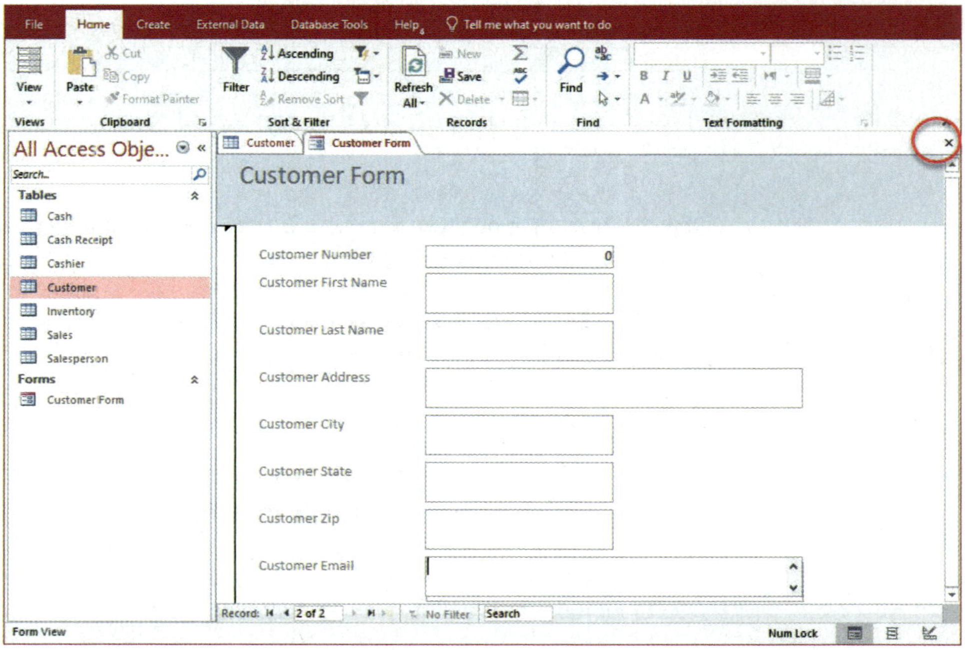

Step 12. Double Click on the Customer Table located on the left side of the database window to open the Customer Table. Notice the Customer Table now displays the data for the customer you just entered using the Customer Form you just created, see Exhibit 6.41.

EXHIBIT 6.41
View the Record in Customer Table

Source: Microsoft Access

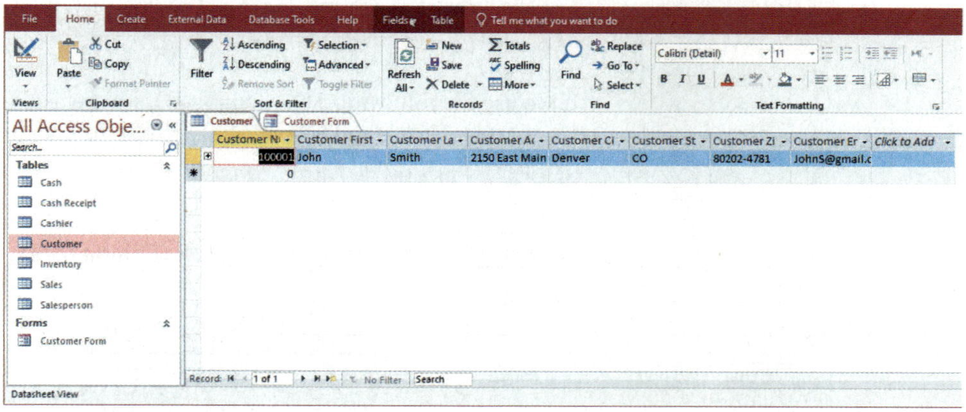

In this demonstration lab, you learned how to create a form to enter customer information into the Customer Table and how to review customer information one by one using the form.

LO 6-3

Describe how to query using Structured Query Language (SQL).

STRUCTURED QUERY LANGUAGE (SQL)

SQL (usually pronounced "Sequel") stands for **Structured Query Language** and is a computer language designed to query data in a relational database. SQL is based on relational algebra and allows a user to query and update the database. In a database, while queries allow the user to access, read, and report on desired data, the responsibility of actually making physical changes to the relational database belongs to the database management system (DBMS). The four most basic operations—Create, Read, Update, and Delete (CRUD)—must be supported in a DBMS. SQL provides the "INSERT" operator (i.e., a command) to create new records, the "SELECT" operator to read or retrieve data, the "UPDATE" operator to update records, and the "DELETE" operator to delete existing records from the database.

The SELECT operator is used to begin a query. The SELECT operator tells the query which columns (or attributes) of a table should be included in the query result. A query includes a list of columns in the final result immediately following the SELECT operator. An asterisk (*) can also be used to specify that the query should return all columns of the queried tables. SELECT is the most useful operator in SQL, with optional keywords and clauses that include the following:

1. The FROM clause to the SELECT operator indicates the name of table(s) from which to retrieve data.

SQL Example 1: Given the attributes in the Customer table in Exhibit 6.42, how is a query used to find the salesperson for each customer?

EXHIBIT 6.42
Customer

Customer#	Name	A/R Amt	SP#
C-1	Bill	345	E-12
C-2	Mick	225	E-10
C-3	Keith	718	E-10
C-4	Charlie	828	E-99
C-5	Ron	3,200	E-10

If we use the following SQL commands, we are asking SQL to select the Customer#, Name, and SP# attributes from the Customer Table:

SELECT Customer#, Name, SP#

FROM Customer;

We will get the following query result (Exhibit 6.43):

EXHIBIT 6.43

Customer#	Name	SP#
C-1	Bill	E-12
C-2	Mick	E-10
C-3	Keith	E-10
C-4	Charlie	E-99
C-5	Ron	E-10

2. The WHERE clause states the criteria that must be met to be shown in the query result. There are many search criteria that you can specify for the final result. Search criteria using relational operators, the BETWEEN operator, and the LIKE operator are very common in SQL commands (Exhibit 6.44).

EXHIBIT 6.44
Cash Receipt

Remittance Advice#	Amount	Bank Account#	Date	Customer Number	Cashier Number
RA-1	1,666	BA-6	25-JUL-2020	C-2	E-39
RA-2	10,000	BA-7	26-JUL-2020	C-2	E-39
RA-3	72,000	BA-7	15-AUG-2020	C-1	E-39
RA-4	32,600	BA-7	15-AUG-2020	C-5	E-39
RA-5	1,669	BA-6	25-AUG-2020	C-2	E-39

SQL Example 2:

If we use the following SQL command, we are asking SQL to retrieve all cash receipt information for customer C-2 from the table called "Cash Receipt."

SELECT *

FROM [Cash Receipt]

WHERE [Customer Number] = 'C-2';

Please note that the asterisk (*) following the SELECT SQL statement is a wild card indicating all columns should be selected. The brackets are needed following the FROM and WHERE clauses because there are spaces in the table and attribute names. In addition, if any table name or attribute name contains one or more spaces, we have to use brackets such as [Cash Receipt] to make sure it is considered as one table or one attribute in SQL.

We will get the following query result (Exhibit 6.45):

EXHIBIT 6.45

Remittance Advice#	Amount	Bank Account#	Date	Customer Number	Cashier Number
RA-1	1,666	BA-6	25-JUL-2020	C-2	E-39
RA-2	10,000	BA-7	26-JUL-2020	C-2	E-39
RA-5	1,669	BA-6	25-AUG-2020	C-2	E-39

Notice the WHERE command eliminated those rows that did not have Customer Number equal to C-2.

SQL Example 3: Assume you would like to use a query to find the salesperson for each customer, and you would like to show the name of each salesperson as part of the result. Data are presented in Exhibits 6.46 and 6.47.

EXHIBIT 6.46
Customer

Customer#	Name	A/R Amt	SP#
C-1	Bill	345	E-12
C-2	Mick	225	E-10
C-3	Keith	718	E-10
C-4	Charlie	828	E-99
C-5	Ron	3,200	E-10

EXHIBIT 6.47
Salesperson

SP#	SP_Name
E-10	Howard
E-12	Pattie
E-34	Stephanie
E-99	David

If we use the following SQL commands, we are asking SQL to select the Customer#, Name, SP#, and SP_Name attributes from the Customer table and Salesperson table:

```
SELECT Customer#, Name, SP#, SP_Name
FROM Customer, Salesperson
WHERE Customer. SP# = Salesperson. SP#;
```

It is critical that we include WHERE here to link two tables. SP# is a foreign key in the Customer table. We use it to link the Salesperson table with the Customer table. We will get the following query result (Exhibit 6.48):

EXHIBIT 6.48

Customer#	Name	SP#	SP_Name
C-1	Bill	E-12	Pattie
C-2	Mick	E-10	Howard
C-3	Keith	E-10	Howard
C-4	Charlie	E-99	David
C-5	Ron	E-10	Howard

The above example shows a "one-to-many" relationship. That is, each customer is served by a salesperson and each salesperson can serve many customers.

3. The GROUP BY operator is used with aggregate functions on the query results based on one or more columns.

SQL Example 4: Refer to the Cash Receipt table in SQL Example 2 (Exhibit 6.44). Assume you would like to know the total cash receipt amount from each customer. If you use the following SQL commands, you can get the result:

```
SELECT [Customer Number], SUM(Amount)
FROM [Cash Receipt]
GROUP BY [Customer Number];
```

The query results will be (Exhibit 6.49):

EXHIBIT 6.49

Customer Number	Amount
C-2	13,335
C-1	72,000
C-5	32,600

4. The ORDER BY clause identifies which columns are used to sort the resulting data. If there is no ORDER BY clause, the order of rows returned by a SQL query will not be defined.

SQL Example 5: Refer to the Cash Receipt table in SQL Example 2 (Exhibit 6.44). If we use the following SQL commands instead, the amount of cash receipt would be ordered in ascending amount (ASC) or descending amount (DESC). The result (Exhibit 6.50) is different from that of Example 2.

```
SELECT *
FROM [Cash Receipt]
WHERE [Customer Number] = 'C-2'
ORDER BY Amount ASC;
```

EXHIBIT 6.50

Remittance Advice#	Amount	Bank Account#	Date	Customer Number	Cashier Number
RA-1	1,666	BA-6	25-JUL-2020	C-2	E-39
RA-5	1,669	BA-6	25-AUG-2020	C-2	E-39
RA-2	10,000	BA-7	26-JUL-2020	C-2	E-39

5. The INSERT INTO operator inserts data into a SQL table. For example, you can insert a row into the Cash Receipt table with the following SQL commands:

```
INSERT INTO [Cash Receipt]
VALUES ('RA-6', 5000, 'BA-7', '28-AUG-2020', 'C-2', 'E-39');
```

After insertion, the Cash Receipt table will have one more row and the result of the execution is as follows (Exhibit 6.51):

EXHIBIT 6.51
Cash Receipt

Remittance Advice#	Amount	Bank Account#	Date	Customer Number	Cashier Number
RA-1	1,666	BA-6	25-JUL-2020	C-2	E-39
RA-2	10,000	BA-7	26-JUL-2020	C-2	E-39
RA-3	72,000	BA-7	15-AUG-2020	C-1	E-39
RA-4	32,600	BA-7	15-AUG-2020	C-5	E-39
RA-5	1,669	BA-6	25-AUG-2020	C-2	E-39
RA-6	5,000	BA-7	28-AUG-2020	C-2	E-39

6. The UPDATE operator is for updating data in a SQL table. For example, you can use the following SQL UPDATE command to change the Amount value from 5000 to 6000 for the inserted entry of RA-6. You often need to use the command SET for the updated data value.

   UPDATE [Cash Receipt]

   SET Amount = 6000

   WHERE [Remittance Advice#] = 'RA-6';
7. The DELETE FROM operator deletes data from a SQL table. For example, to delete the entry previously inserted, you can use the following SQL commands:

   DELETE FROM [Cash Receipt]

   WHERE [Remittance Advice#] = 'RA-6';

   After executing the DELETE command, the record of Remittance Advice# 'RA-6' will be deleted from the Cash Receipt table, and the table will look the same as the original one.
8. The SELECT DISTINCT clause selects a column without showing repetitive values.

   SQL Example 6: Refer to the Cash Receipt table in SQL Example 2 (Exhibit 6.52). You can retrieve each customer number once from the Cash Receipt table with the following command:

   SELECT DISTINCT [Customer Number]

   FROM [Cash Receipt];

   You will get the following query result (Exhibit 6.52):

EXHIBIT 6.52

Customer Number
C-2
C-1
C-5

9. The BETWEEN operator can be used to specify the end points of a range. Possible criteria can be "WHERE Amount BETWEEN 1000 AND 2000" or "WHERE Date BETWEEN '01-JAN-2020' AND '31-DEC-2020'." Assuming that you are interested in finding out cash receipt entries made in July, then you can issue the following SQL command to retrieve those entries:

   SELECT *

   FROM [Cash Receipt]

   WHERE Date BETWEEN '01-JUL-2020' AND '31-JUL-2020'

   The query result will be (Exhibit 6.53):

EXHIBIT 6.53

Remittance Advice#	Amount	Bank Account#	Date	Customer Number	Cashier Number
RA-1	1,666	BA-6	25-JUL-2020	C-2	E-39
RA-2	10,000	BA-7	26-JUL-2020	C-2	E-39

10. Membership Operator (IN) allows you to test whether a data value matches the specified target values.

SQL Example 7: Refer to the Cash Receipt table in SQL Example 2 (Exhibit 6.44). Assume you would like to know the total cash receipt amount from customers C-1 and C-2. If you use the following SQL commands, you can get the result shown in Exhibit 6.54, which is different from that of Example 4:

```
SELECT [Customer Number], SUM(Amount)
FROM [Cash Receipt]
WHERE [Customer Number] IN ('C-1', 'C-2')
GROUP BY [Customer Number];
```

The query results will be

EXHIBIT 6.54

Customer Number	Amount
C-1	72,000
C-2	13,335

In addition, there are six relational operators in SQL. Their definitions are listed here:

Relational Operators	Meaning
=	equal
! = or < >	not equal
<	less than
< =	less than or equal to
>	greater than
> =	greater than or equal to

Given the data in Exhibit 6.44, if you are interested in those entries with an amount $\geq$ 10000, you can use the following SQL commands:

```
SELECT *
FROM [Cash Receipt]
WHERE Amount > = 10000;
```

You will get the following query result back (Exhibit 6.55):

EXHIBIT 6.55

Remittance Advice#	Amount	Bank Account#	Date	Customer Number	Cashier Number
RA-2	10,000	BA-7	26-JUL-2020	C-2	E-39
RA-3	72,000	BA-7	15-AUG-2020	C-1	E-39
RA-4	32,600	BA-7	25-AUG-2020	C-5	E-39

SQL language provides several convenient aggregate functions to be used in SQL commands. These aggregate functions include AVG, SUM, MAX, MIN, and COUNT. Their definitions are as follows:

- AVG(X): gives the average of column X.
- SUM(X): gives the summation of all rows that satisfy the selection criteria for column X.
- MAX(X): gives the maximum value of column X.
- MIN(X): gives the minimum value of column X.
- COUNT(X): gives the number of rows that satisfy the given condition.

To query the total amount and average amount from the Cash Receipt table, use

```
SELECT SUM(Amount), AVG(Amount)
FROM [Cash Receipt];
```

To query the largest amount entry from the Cash Receipt table, use

```
SELECT MAX(Amount)
FROM [Cash Receipt];
```

To query the total amount that occurred in July from the Cash Receipt table, use

```
SELECT SUM(Amount)
FROM [Cash Receipt]
WHERE Date BETWEEN '01-JUL-2020' AND '31-JUL-2020';
```

SQL create commands, update commands, and many other SQL query commands as well as SQL functions are beyond the scope of this textbook. See, for example, www.w3schools.com/sql/ for a list of popular SQL query commands.

PROGRESS CHECK

4. What does the SQL command SELECT * do?
5. What SQL command would you use to order an amount in descending order?
6. What SQL commands would you use if you wanted to query transactions made in July from the Cash Receipt table?

LO 6-4

Understand the purpose and basic framework for an enterprise system.

ENTERPRISE SYSTEMS

Before enterprise systems were developed, each function within the organization (finance, accounting, human resources, procurement, manufacturing, etc.) had its own information system that met its own needs. However, imagine the challenge for a company like **General Motors** to predict, budget, and manage its costs for producing a new Corvette! The company would have to get production information from the manufacturing database, costs from the accounting database, and labor information and costs from the human resources database and attempt to integrate them. Because of these types of problems and the power of integrated information, enterprise systems were developed, including major, commercial enterprise systems such as SAP/ERP, Oracle ERP, and Microsoft Dynamics.

In fact, for a popular ERP product (SAP/ERP) installation, there are more than 10,000 tables that are all linked to each other!

Enterprise systems (ESs), also known as enterprise resource planning (ERP) systems, are commercialized information systems that integrate and automate business processes across a firm's value chain located within and across organizations. Typically, an enterprise system uses a relational data model as a basis for the information system. The use of primary and foreign keys links the hundreds of tables that form the basis for the enterprise system.

As mentioned in Chapter 1, ESs accommodate the integration and support of the various business processes and information needs of a company by integrating multiple modules to help a manufacturer or other business manage the important parts of its business, including product planning, parts purchasing, inventory maintenance, supplier interaction, customer service, and order tracking. ESs can also include application modules for the accounting, finance, and human resources aspects of a business. ESs are applicable to all types of businesses. In fact, most universities now use enterprise systems to manage course registration and student accounts (including the payment of library fines and parking tickets!).

Exhibit 6.56 offers a list of potential modules available from SAP S/4HANA (most current version of SAP's ERP product. See: https://www.tutorialspoint.com/sap/sap_modules.htm). You can quickly see the breadth of the offering that would come from a typical enterprise systems vendor.

EXHIBIT 6.56
List of Modules Available from SAP S/4HANA

List of SAP Modules Available for Implementation	
Financial Applications	
FI	Financial Accounting
CO	Controlling
EPM	Enterprise Performance Management
IM	Investment Management
PS	Project System
Human Resources	
HCM	Human Capital Management
PT	Personnel Time Management
PY	Payroll
Logistics Applications	
SD	Sales and Distribution
MM	Materials Management
PP	Production Planning and Control
SCM	Supply Chain Management
QM	Quality Management
CS	Customer Service

Managers (and auditors) can trace the creation of information throughout business processes and also identify the participants in each process. Therefore, ES has a higher level of internal transparency compared to the typically isolated legacy systems. For example, once one user from the sales department enters a customer order, users from the inventory department can see this information immediately and begin to process the customer order. At the same time, users from the accounting department can use this information to prepare the customer invoice and recognize revenue once it has been earned. Database transactions in ES are often designed to track specific details of any given business transaction, including who entered the data into the system, who modified it, and who actually used it.

The purported informational benefits of an enterprise system include enhanced completeness, transparency, and timeliness of information needed to manage effectively an organization's business activities.[2]

[2]H. Klaus, M. Rosemann, and G. G. Gable, "What Is ERP?" *Information Systems Frontiers 2*, no. 2 (2000), p. 141.

Hershey was not able to deliver Hershey Kisses for Halloween in 1999 right after the first attempt to implement its enterprise system.

Jill Jarsulic/KRT/Newscom

The enterprise system serves as the backbone of the company's internal business processes and serves as a connection with the external business processes for supply chain and customer relationship management systems.

Challenges of Enterprise System Implementation

Although the standard enterprise system software is packaged and technically sound, all types of challenges emerge from both a technical and organizational perspective when it comes time to custom-fit the software to a particular organization's needs. More specifically, organizations face many challenges in implementing enterprise systems, including the following:

1. Integrating various modules within the enterprise system.
2. Integrating with external systems such as the information system of a supplier and/or customer.
3. Integrating with the firm's own existing legacy systems.
4. Converting data from existing legacy systems to the enterprise system.
5. Getting any big project implemented at a firm. This might include scope creep (i.e., increasing the number of changes to the software initially planned), cost overruns, time delays, and so on. In addition, this means getting adequate training for employees and getting them to actually adopt the new software when they might feel their old system seemed to meet their needs just fine.

These challenges can be overwhelming and some are specifically addressed in Chapter 17. Here, we provide an illustration of a few of the high-profile examples of firms that had failed or challenged enterprise system implementations, as well as the resulting damage inflicted on the firm:

1. **Hershey** spent $115 million on a failed enterprise system implementation attempt of SAP R/3, Siebel CRM, and Manugistics supply chain applications during the Halloween season, which caused huge candy disruptions in 1999. This failed attempt prevented Hershey from delivering $100 million worth of Hershey Kisses for Halloween that year, causing a third-quarter sales drop of 12.4 percent. Earnings that year were off by 18.6 percent (compared with the previous year) and that caused the stock price to fall by 8 percent.
2. In 2000, a $400 million i2 upgrade to **Nike**'s supply chain and enterprise systems gave the shoe and athletic company $100 million in lost sales, a 20 percent stock dip, and a collection of class-action lawsuits.
3. In 2004, **HP**'s enterprise system implementation went awry. Gilles Bouchard, then-CIO of HP's global operations, said, "We had a series of small problems, none of which individually would have been too much to handle. But together they created the perfect storm."* The project eventually cost HP $160 million in order backlogs and lost revenue—more than five times the project's estimated cost.

* IDG Communications, Inc.

4. During fall semester of 2004, more than 27,000 students at the University of Massachusetts, Stanford University, and Indiana University were unable to find their classes and unable to collect their financial aid checks due to a flawed ERP system. However, after a couple frustrating days and weeks, everyone eventually got their checks and class schedules![3]
5. **Worth & Co**. is a Pennsylvania-based manufacturing company. In 2014, Worth hired a consulting firm to implement Oracle's E-Business Suite. The original go-live date was in late 2015. In 2019, the project was abandoned after another consulting firm also failed to customize Oracle's suite for Worth & Co.'s purposes.
6. In 2016, cosmetics giant **Revlon** acquired Elizabeth Arden, Inc. Revlon used Microsoft Dynamics AX and Elizabeth Arden used Oracle Fusion Applications. The merged company decided to use SAP HANA. The system rollout was disastrous in 2019 and affected Revlon's own manufacturing operations. Revlon was unable to fulfill product shipments of approximately $64 million of net sales. Revlon's stock prices dropped significantly due to the service-level disruptions. This implementation failure resulted in a rare investor lawsuit.

LO 6-5

Assess how cloud computing facilitates enterprise systems.

Enterprise Systems Computing in the Cloud

Providing sufficient computing power in an organization to run an enterprise system can be challenging. In recent years, **cloud computing** has emerged as a potential alternative to host enterprise systems and other firm computing needs. Cloud computing is Internet-based computing, where shared resources, software, and information are provided to firms on demand. Just like an electrical grid can handle electricity needs on the fly, cloud computing can handle computing needs on the fly. Cloud computing is simply a set of pooled computing resources that are delivered over the Internet.

Cloud computing can easily host enterprise system applications. Enterprise system applications can quickly scale to the requirements of the computing task by making hundreds of servers and related resources available when they are required. When using cloud computing, firms do not need to worry about buying more computers to meet increasing computing traffic demands or about huge computing traffic spikes. They will simply pay for the computing power they use, much like you pay for the amount of electricity you use in your home or work.

Cloud computing, of course, has disadvantages as well. Ensuring that any sensitive data are secure and backed up frequently by the host is often a concern of cloud computing clients. Making sure the host has minimal down time and adequate processing speed at all times are also concerns. But perhaps the biggest concern is that cloud computing requires the client to have a constant Internet connection. If, for some reason, the Internet connection goes down, the system will not function. This represents an obvious downside on a firm's business that uses cloud computing for its interfaces with their enterprise system.

PROGRESS CHECK

7. Why are enterprise systems so much better than legacy systems that firms are willing to invest the time, money, and effort to risk implementing such systems?
8. From Exhibit 6.56, which SAP modules would an accounting firm implement to track its billable hours for the audit staff?

[3] www.cio.com/article/486284/10_Famous_ERP_Disasters_Dustups_and_Disappointments.

Summary

- Relational databases offer efficient, effective databases for a firm. Their flexibility and scalability along with their simplicity offer powerful advantages for a firm and its information systems.
- Relational databases rely on primary and foreign keys to link tables.
- Structured Query Language (SQL) is used with relational databases to query the database.
- Enterprise systems are based on relational databases and link many different modules and functions of the firm to give integrated information to the firm's management and workers throughout the firm.
- Cloud computing is a recent innovation that could host a firm's enterprise systems such as SAP's cloud-based ERP software SAP S/4HANA Cloud. SAP Analytics Cloud provides insight (i.e., business intelligence) based on the data extracted from the ERP system, as well as predictive analytics.

Key Words

attributes (*239*) Data elements that describe instances in a class, very much like fields in a database table; characteristics, properties, or adjectives that describe each class.

cloud computing (*270*) Using redundant servers in multiple locations to host virtual machines.

data dictionary (*238*) Describes the data fields in each database record such as field description, field length, field type (e.g., alphanumeric, numeric), etc.

database (*238*) A shared collection of logically related data for various uses.

database administrator (*238*) The person responsible for the design, implementation, repair, and security of a firm's database.

database management system (DBMS) (*238*) A computer program that creates, modifies, and queries the database. Specifically, the DBMS is designed to manage a database's storage and retrieval of information.

enterprise system (ES) (*267*) A centralized database that collects data from throughout the firm. Commercialized information system that integrates and automates business processes across a firm's value chain located within and across organizations.

entity integrity rule (*240*) The primary key of a table must have data values (cannot be null).

foreign key (FK) (*240*) Attribute that allows database tables to be linked together; foreign keys are the primary keys of other tables placed in the current table to support the link between the two tables.

form (*241*) Forms are utilized by users to enter data into tables and view existing records.

hierarchical data model (*238*) Organizes data into a tree-like structure that allows repeating information using defined parent/child relationships.

network data model (*238*) A flexible model representing objects and their relationships; allows each record to have multiple parent and child records or M:N mapping, also known as many-to-many relationships.

primary key (PK) (*239*) An attribute or a combination of attributes that uniquely identifies an instance of a class in a data model or a specific row in a table.

query (*241*) Query in Access is a tool used to retrieve and display data derived from records stored within the database.

referential integrity rule (*241*) The data value for a foreign key must either be null or match one of the data values that already exist in the corresponding table.

relational data model (*238*) Stores information in the form of related two-dimensional tables.

report (*242*) Reports in Access are used to integrate data from one or more queries and tables to provide useful information to decision makers.

Structured Query Language (SQL) (*261*) A computer language designed to retrieve data from a relational database.

ANSWERS TO PROGRESS CHECKS

1. There could be different answers for this question. Three possible answers are as follows:
   a. Which **Walmart** products are selling the best.
   b. Which products **Walmart** needs to advertise or which need a price reduction.
   c. How many of which product to order for tomorrow, next week, and next month from its suppliers.
2. During the process of creating data models, database designers need to understand the need of database users. When they work together, the designers could learn from the users to understand the business/operation processes. The designers will work with the users to predict information needed for decision making.
3. The primary key of one table serves as a foreign key in another table. When they are matched together, they are able to link two distinct tables in preparation for querying, updating, or modifying.
4. The SQL statement "SELECT *" requests that all columns in a table be selected for use in the query.
5. The SQL clause "ORDER BY Amount DESC" would be used.
6. The following SQL commands should be used.

```
SELECT *
FROM [Cash Receipt]
WHERE Date BETWEEN '01-JUL-2020' AND '31-JUL-2020';
```

7. The power of integration of the various modules and functions (e.g., accounting, marketing, procurement, manufacturing, etc.) across the organization makes an enterprise system particularly valuable to not only management but also to workers throughout the enterprise.
8. The SAP module PT Personnel Time Management appears to be the most applicable module for tracking billable hours for the audit staff.

Multiple Choice Questions connect

1. **(LO 6-2)** In the hierarchical data model, the mapping from parent to child is
   a. 1:1 (one-to-one).
   b. 1:N (one-to-many).
   c. N:N (many-to-many).
   d. N:1 (many-to-one).
2. **(LO 6-1)** Advantages of relational data models generally include
   a. reduced information redundancy.
   b. low cost.
   c. ease of implementation.
   d. efficiency.
3. **(LO 6-2)** A class in a relational database model is defined as
   a. the sum of a whole.
   b. characteristics or properties of a table.
   c. person, place, thing, transaction, or event about which information is stored.
   d. being or existence, especially when considered as distinct, independent, or self-contained.

4. **(LO 6-4)** Which statement about enterprise systems is correct?
   a. Most enterprise systems are designed mainly for accounting and finance functions.
   b. **SAP, Oracle**, and **Microsoft** all offer products for enterprise systems.
   c. Most enterprise systems are designed for the service industry.
   d. Small companies do not use enterprise systems at all.
5. **(LO 6-2)** Refer to Exhibit 6.2; if Steve's Stylin' Sunglasses accepts installments without requiring a down payment, the multiplicities between Sales and Cash Receipts should be changed to
   a. Sales (0..1) - (1..*) Cash Receipts.
   b. Sales (1..1) - (0..*) Cash Receipts.
   c. Sales (1..1) - (1..1) Cash Receipts.
   d. Sales (0..*) - (1..1) Cash Receipts.
   e. None of these is correct.
6. **(LO 6-3)** The FROM clause to the SELECT statement used in SQL indicates
   a. the name of the table(s) from which to retrieve data.
   b. the name of the column(s) from which to retrieve data.
   c. the name of the database(s) from which to retrieve data.
   d. the name of the query from which to retrieve data.
7. **(LO 6-3)** The WHERE clause to the SELECT statement used in SQL states the criteria that must be met
   a. to include a table in the query.
   b. to be included as an attribute in the table.
   c. to be included in the database.
   d. to be shown in the query result.
8. **(LO 6-3)** The "ORDER BY Amount ASC" clause to the SELECT statement used in SQL suggests that
   a. the amount of the query result will be listed in ascending order.
   b. the amount of the query result will be listed in descending order.
   c. the data attribute ASC be shown in order.
   d. None of the above
9. **(LO 6-4)** SAP modules available for implementation include
   a. Payroll, Personnel Time Management, and Enterprise Management.
   b. Payroll, Financial Accounting, and Enterprise Management.
   c. Financial Accounting, Payroll, and Sales and Distribution.
   d. Sales and Distribution, Financial Accounting, and Procurement.
10. **(LO 6-5)** Cloud computing
    a. takes energy from the sun and clouds.
    b. is Internet-based computing, where shared resources, software, and information are provided to firms on demand.
    c. requires a firm to make an extensive investment in hardware and software to meet firm needs.
    d. can meet computing needs today but is not expected to meet tomorrow's computing needs.
11. **(LO 6-1)** What kind of relationship does a network data model represent?
    a. One-to-one relationship
    b. One-to-many relationship
    c. Many-to-one relationship
    d. Many-to-many relationship

12. **(LO 6-2)** Which of the following is a valid primary key for a cash receipt table?
    a. Purchase order number
    b. Check number
    c. Cash receipt number
    d. Receipt amount
13. **(LO 6-3)** Which of the following is used in SQL to begin a query?
    a. BEGIN
    b. SELECT
    c. INPUT
    d. INSERT
14. **(LO 6-3)** The GROUP BY operator in SQL is used to
    a. aggregate functions on the query results based on one or more columns.
    b. identify which columns are used to sort the resulting data.
    c. state the criteria that must be met to be shown in the query result.
    d. indicate the name of the table from which to retrieve data.
15. **(LO 6-2)** When using Microsoft Access, the main function of "Table" is to
    a. store data.
    b. report data.
    c. retrieve data.
    d. analyze data.
16. **(LO 6-2)** Which of the following is a correct statement about primary keys?
    a. The data values of a primary key must be different (i.e., unique).
    b. A primary is always another table's foreign key.
    c. A primary cannot be used in another table as a foreign key.
    d. Most tables in a database may not require primary keys.
17. **(LO 6-2)** Which of the following is a correct statement about foreign keys?
    a. All foreign keys cannot be blank (null).
    b. Most foreign keys should not have any data values.
    c. A foreign key must be another table's primary key.
    d. An attribute cannot be a foreign key used in different tables.
18. **(LO 6-2)** What is referential integrity rule?
    a. Primary keys cannot be null.
    b. Foreign keys cannot be null.
    c. The data values of a forging key always exist in the corresponding table.
    d. Foreign keys could be null.
19. **(LO 6-2)** Which of the following is a correct statement about entity integrity rule?
    a. The rule is regarding how to use foreign keys.
    b. The rule is used to verify the type of data values in each table.
    c. The rule requires each record's primary key cannot be blank (null).
    d. The rule allows each primary key to be used to link tables.
20. **(LO 6-2)** When using Microsoft ACCESS, the main function of "Form" is to
    a. store data.
    b. enter data.

c. retrieve data.

d. analyze data.

21. **(LO 6-2)** When using Microsoft ACCESS, the main function of "Query" is to

    a. store data.

    b. enter data.

    c. retrieve data.

    d. analyze data.

22. **(LO 6-2)** Which of the following is the best primary key for cash disbursement table?

    a. Purchase order number

    b. Check number

    c. Inventory receipt number

    d. Disbursement voucher number

23. **(LO 6-2)** Which of the following could be an "event" in REA data models?

    a. Cash

    b. Sales

    c. Customer

    d. Inventory

24. **(LO 6-2)** Which of the following could be a relationship table (i.e., to link two tables with a many-to-many relationship)?

    a. Purchase order table

    b. Purchase line-item table

    c. Inventory receipt table

    d. Disbursement table

25. **(LO 6-2)** Which of the following is not a valid link between tables?

    a. Linking Sales Table and Inventory Table

    b. Linking Purchases Table with Cash Disbursement Table

    c. Linking Salespeople Table with Customer Table

    d. Linking Vendor Table with Customer Table

Discussion Questions connect

1. **(LO 6-1)** Explain the differences among hierarchical, network, and relational data models. What makes the relational data model the most popular data model in use today?
2. **(LO 6-2)** What are the basic requirements of a relational database?
3. **(LO 6-3)** Structured Query Language (SQL) is used to retrieve data from a database. Why would an accountant need to learn SQL?
4. **(LO 6-4)** Exhibit 6.39 lists the modules available from SAP. List and explain which modules would be most appropriate for either **Maytag** or a manufacturing company you are familiar with.
5. **(LO 6-4)** Given the description of **Hershey**'s failed enterprise system implementation from the chapter, which of the four challenges of the enterprise system described in the chapter seem to best explain what happened? Use **Google** or **Yahoo!** to get more details on this case to help answer this question.

Problems connect

Cash

Account#	Type	Bank	Balance
BA-6	Checking	Boston5	253
BA-7	Checking	Shawmut	48,000
BA-8	Draft	Shawmut	75,000
BA-9	Checking	Boston5	950

1. **(LO 6-3)** Use the Cash table above to show the output for the following SQL query:

   SELECT Account#, Balance
   FROM Cash
   WHERE Balance < 50000;

2. **(LO 6-3)** Use the Cash table above to show the output for the following SQL query:

   SELECT Account#, Balance
   FROM Cash
   WHERE Bank = 'Boston5'
   ORDER BY Amount DESC;

3. **(LO 6-3)** Use the Cash table above to write a SQL query to show a list of checking accounts. (*Hint:* Filter the results on the Type field.)
4. **(LO 6-3)** Use the Cash table above to write a SQL query to show the total of all of the balances. (*Hint:* Use the SUM function.)
5. **(LO 6-2)** Consider the UML diagram used to model Steve's Stylin' Sunglasses' (SSS) sales data. Draw a new UML diagram assuming that SSS sells mass-produced brand-name sunglasses instead of custom sunglasses.
6. **(LO 6-1, LO 6-2)** Think about data collected and used by **Netflix**.
   a. Identify three tables that would contain customer or subscription data.
   b. For each table identified in (a), list five attributes (you may include primary and foreign keys as well as nonkey attributes).
   c. Describe each attribute using elements from a data dictionary (e.g., description, field length, field type, etc.).
   d. Why would Netflix be interested in storing and tracking these attributes (e.g., to enhance customer service or future customer sales, to sell more affiliated products to customers, etc.)?
7. **(LO 6-5)** Cloud computing has plenty of appeal for many firms, especially those that have immense computing needs. Why do you think some might be reluctant to have their data and computing power originating from the cloud?
8. **(LO 6-2)** Use the Access_Practice.accdb database to complete the following tasks in Access.
   a. The database contains three tables containing information about this company's sales process: Inventory, Sales, and SalesItems. Use the Relationships window to link the tables together.
   b. The SalesItems table records the quantity and price of each item sold on each sale (sales may include more than one item). Calculate the extended amount of sale (call it Amt) for each item (Quantity * UnitPrice). Include InvoiceID, InventoryID, Quantity, and UnitPrice in the query. Name the query Item_Extension_Calculation.
   c. Calculate the total dollar amount of *each sale*. Include InvoiceID, InvoiceDate, CustomerID, and EmployeeID from the Sales table and the Amt from the Item_Extension_Calculation query. Name the query Sale_Amount_Calculation.
   d. Calculate total sales for *each inventory item*.

e. Calculate *total sales*.

f. Calculate the month in which each sale occurred. Include InvoiceID and InvoiceDate from the Sales table. Name the query Sales_Months. (*Hint:* Look for the Month function in the expression builder.)

g. Calculate the sum of sales for each month.

9. **(LO 6-2)** This problem continues Problem 8. Use the Access_Practice.accdb database that you have been working on to complete the following tasks.

   a. Go to the Relationships screen and connect the five tables, enforcing referential integrity.

   b. Calculate the total sales for each customer. Include CustomerID and CompanyName from the Customer table and the calculated sale amount from the Sale_Amount_Calculation query. Name the query Total_Customer_Sales.

   c. Generate an email user name for each employee using the first letter of the employee's first name and the first five letters of the employee's last name, for example, Rod Smith = > rsmith. Include EmployeeID, EmployeeFirstName, and EmployeeLastName in the query. Name the query Employee_Email_Generator.

   d. Calculate the total sales for each month.

   e. Determine which customer had the highest average sales amount. (*Hint:* Sort in descending order.)

   f. Assume the employees earn a 5 percent commission on sales. Calculate the total commission due to each employee. Use two queries to do these calculations.

Background for Problems 10 through 14

Ellen Novotny started an online bookstore in 2023. You are Ellen's best friend and promised to help her. Ellen asked you to create a small database to track the information on books and authors. You created the following tables: Author, Book, and Author_Book. The table Author_Book is a relationship table to link the Author table and Book table because of the many-to-many relationship between the two tables. That is, each author may write many books and each book may have multiple authors. In general, each customer can purchase many books in a single transaction. Also, copies of the same book can be sold to different customers. Once an order is processed, the books are shipped right away. Based on these tables you have (see below), help Ellen to extract the information she needs from the database.

Author

Author ID	Last Name	First Name	Email	Phone number
AU-1	Adams	Eric	Eric168@yahoo.com	(714) 833-2419
AU-2	Brown	Jennifer	jenifferb@gmail.com	(619) 596-0012
AU-3	Davis	Keith	keithd@gmail.com	(212) 342-5680
AU-4	Newport	Kevin	kevinn@hotmail.com	(301) 947-7741
AU-5	Pham	John	johnpham@gmail.com	(617) 645-3647
AU-6	Sviokla	Julia	jsviokla@yahoo.com	(805) 498-1688

Book

Book ID	Title	Area	Year	Edition	Publisher
B-1	Accounting Principles	Financial Accounting	2021	8	Wiley
B-2	Cost Management	Management Accounting	2022	3	McGraw-Hill
B-3	Accounting Information Systems	Information Systems	2022	2	McGraw-Hill
B-4	Individual Taxation 2017	Taxation	2023	6	Pearson
B-5	Intermediate Accounting	Financial Accounting	2021	1	Wiley
B-6	Advanced Accounting	Financial Accounting	2022	1	McGraw-Hill

Author_Book

Author ID	Book ID
AU-1	B-2
AU-1	B-5
AU-2	B-6
AU-3	B-2
AU-3	B-3
AU-4	B-2
AU-5	B-4
AU-6	B-1
AU-6	B-6

Customer

Customer ID	Last Name	First Name	Email
C-1	Black	Emily	Ewb2003@yahoo.com
C-2	Brown	Jack	jackjack@gmail.com
C-3	Easton	Anderson	anderson.easton@gmail.com
C-4	Jennix	May	jennixm@hotmail.com
C-5	Venable	Judy	Judy.Venable@gmail.com
C-6	White	Ashley	Ashley2015@yahoo.com
C-7	Williams	Eric	Williams_e@yahoo.com

Sales_Line_Item

Sales Date	Customer ID	Book ID	Quantity	Unit price
9/1/2023	C-7	B-3	1	$205
9/1/2023	C-7	B-1	1	$221
9/1/2023	C-1	B-6	30	$195
9/2/2023	C-5	B-2	60	$199
9/2/2023	C-5	B-5	25	$210
9/2/2023	C-3	B-2	1	$245
9/2/2023	C-3	B-6	1	$215
9/2/2023	C-3	B-4	1	$160
9/3/2023	C-2	B-1	1	$221

10. **(LO 6-2, LO 6-3)** Ellen asks you to give her a list of the books that each author wrote. Write a complete SQL statement to provide the information to Ellen, including author names, book titles, publishers, and the years of publication.
11. **(LO 6-2, LO 6-3)** Ellen wants to know how many books each author wrote. Write a SQL statement to provide such information to Ellen.
12. **(LO 6-2, LO 6-3)** You are going to send emails to inform the customers that the books ordered have been shipped. Write a SQL statement to obtain the complete information on the book title(s), unit price(s), and the number of each book purchased to be sent to the customers.
13. **(LO 6-2, LO 6-3)** Ellen wants to know how many copies of each book were sold. Write a SQL statement to obtain the necessary information you think Ellen wants.

14. **(LO 6-2, LO 6-3)** Ellen wants to know the dollar amount of total sales made on September 1, 2023. Write a SQL statement to obtain the necessary information you think Ellen wants.

15. **(LO 6-2)** The Cash Receipt table below contains seven attributes. Which of those could possibly be foreign keys?

Cash Receipt

Remittance Advice #	Date	Amount	Customer #	Check #	Invoice #	Cashier #
RA-220	12/02/2023	2,549.90	C-12	201	S-101	E-13345
RA-278	12/23/2023	699.90	C-5	1457	S-108	E-13347
RA-276	1/3/2024	1,209.70	C-9	392	S-107	E-13345
RA-289	1/7/2024	949.95	C-28	2558	S-105	E-13346

16. **(LO 6-2)** A sales invoice typically includes the date of sale, salesperson, customer data, items included in the sale, and amount. Which foreign keys should be added to the following table to link all of these data elements?

Sales

Invoice #	Date	Amount
S-101	10/05/2023	2,549.90
S-105	11/01/2023	949.95
S-107	11/02/2023	1,209.70
S-108	11/06/2023	699.90

17. **(LO 6-2, LO 6-3)** Based on the two tables and the attributes below, write SQL commands for each question to retrieve the data from the database.

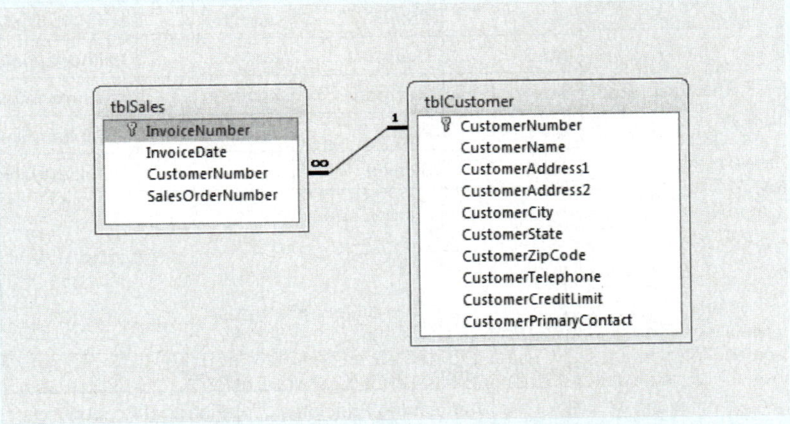

a. How many customer records are stored in the database?
b. List customers who live in New York.
c. List customers with credit limits greater than $50,000.
d. List sales transactions made in July 2024.
e. What's the number of total sales transactions made to each customer?

18. **(LO 6-2, LO 6-3)** Based on the three tables and the attributes below, write SQL commands for each question to retrieve the data from the database.

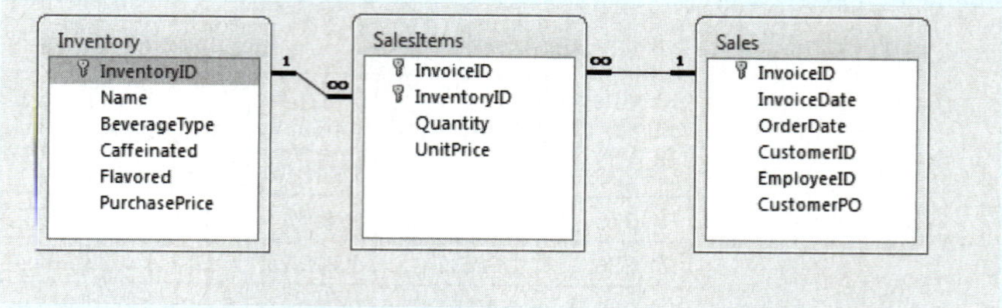

a. What are the foreign keys in the Sales table?
b. How many sales transactions were made in March 2024?
c. Which sales transactions were made by the employee whose ID is "S2038" in the system?
d. List the inventory items with purchase price larger than $6,500.
e. Write a query to find out the dollar amount of each sales transaction.

19. **(LO 6-2)** Identify the primary key of each table in the following partial database.

Author Table

Author ID	Last Name	First Name	Email	Phone number
AU-1	Adams	Eric	Eric168@yahoo.com	(714) 833-2419
AU-2	Brown	Jennifer	jenifferb@gmail.com	(619) 596-0012
AU-3	Davis	Keith	keithd@gmail.com	(212) 342-5680
AU-4	Newport	Kevin	kevinn@hotmail.com	(301) 947-7741
AU-5	Pham	John	johnpham@gmail.com	(617) 645-3647
AU-6	Sviokla	Julia	jsviokla@yahoo.com	(805) 498-1688

Book Table

Book ID	Title	Area	Year	Edition	Publisher
B-1	Accounting Principles	Financial Accounting	2021	8	Wiley
B-2	Cost Management	Management Accounting	2022	3	McGraw-Hill
B-3	Accounting Information Systems	Information Systems	2022	2	McGraw-Hill
B-4	Individual Taxation	Taxation	2023	6	Pearson
B-5	Intermediate Accounting	Financial Accounting	2021	1	Wiley
B-6	Advanced Accounting	Financial Accounting	2022	1	McGraw-Hill

Author_Book Table

Author ID	Book ID
AU-1	B-2
AU-1	B-5
AU-2	B-6
AU-3	B-2
AU-3	B-3
AU-4	B-2
AU-5	B-4
AU-6	B-1
AU-6	B-6

Customer Table

Customer ID	Last Name	First Name	Email
C-1	Black	Emily	Ewb2003@yahoo.com
C-2	Brown	Jack	jackjack@gmail.com
C-3	Easton	Anderson	anderson.easton@gmail.com
C-4	Jennix	May	jennixm@hotmail.com
C-5	Venable	Judy	Judy.Venable@gmail.com
C-6	White	Ashley	Ashley2015@yahoo.com
C-7	Williams	Eric	Williams_e@yahoo.com

Sales_Line_Item

Sales Date	Customer ID	Book ID	Quantity	Unit price
9/1/2023	C-7	B-3	1	$205
9/1/2023	C-7	B-1	1	$221
9/1/2023	C-1	B-6	30	$195
9/2/2023	C-5	B-2	60	$199
9/2/2023	C-5	B-5	25	$210
9/2/2023	C-3	B-2	1	$245
9/2/2023	C-3	B-6	1	$215
9/2/2023	C-3	B-4	1	$160
9/3/2023	C-2	B-1	1	$221

20. **(LO 6-2)** Show how each table in the partial database provided with Problem 19 is linked with to the other table(s).

Chapter Seven

Sales and Collections Business Process

A Look at This Chapter

This chapter examines the sales and cash collection process. We use a comprehensive example to develop activity and structure models of the process. We show how the activity model in conjunction with business rules can be used to develop, implement, and monitor control activities. We show how the structure model can be used to develop a relational database to support information processing requirements. The chapter includes a comprehensive exercise in which students prepare UML class models and then develop the corresponding Microsoft Access database to prepare specific financial information.

A Look Back

Chapters 4 and 5 described types of business process models and introduced basic modeling tools to guide the student's development of modeling skills. Chapter 6 introduced relational databases and Microsoft Access. We use those skills to examine activity and structure models for the sales and collection process.

A Look Ahead

In Chapter 8, we examine the purchasing and cash disbursement process. We again use the basic modeling tools from Chapters 4, 5, and 6 to examine activity and structure models and corresponding database structures for the process.

James Leynse/Getty Images

In April 2008, **Starbucks** started offering additional benefits to registered Starbucks Card holders when they use their cards at Starbucks stores in the United States and Canada:

1. Complimentary customization on select syrups and milk alternatives (e.g., soy milk).
2. Complimentary Tall beverage of choice with the purchase of one pound of whole bean coffee.
3. Free refills on brewed coffee during the same visit.
4. Two hours daily of free, in-store Wi-Fi.
5. The opportunity to join Starbucks in supporting charitable causes.

Speaking about this sales initiative, Starbucks CEO Howard Schultz said, "Already, one in seven customers uses the Starbucks Card, and now we are taking the first steps toward recognizing these customers by providing them value beyond any other coffeehouse. It is the personal relationship our customers have with our brand, our stores, and our baristas that is the foundation of our success. Through this initiative, we are making it even easier to make the Starbucks Experience your own." Now, most cardholders use the Starbucks app to order drinks and food, monitor their spending, and interact with Starbucks.

At the same time, Starbucks introduced its Pike Place Roast, aimed at providing its customers a "unique, consistent, and fresh brewed coffee experience." It also began making coffee in smaller batches to ensure that its coffee is always fresh.

Starbucks' senior management clearly recognizes the importance of its sales process, and the continuing improvement of its customers' experiences, to its success and long-term growth. What kinds of information do you think Starbucks needs to manage and improve its sales process?

Starbucks Corporation

CHAPTER OUTLINE

LEARNING OBJECTIVES

After reading this chapter, you should be able to:

7-1 Describe the business activities that constitute the sales and collection process.

7-2 Develop an activity model of the sales and collection process using BPMN.

7-3 Understand and apply different activity modeling options.

7-4 Develop business rules to implement controls for the sales and collection process.

7-5 Develop a structure model for the sales and collection process using UML class diagrams.

7-6 Use multiplicities to implement foreign keys in relational tables.

7-7 Implement a relational database from the UML class diagram of the sales and collection process.

LO 7-1

Describe the business activities that constitute the sales and collection process.

SALES AND COLLECTION PROCESS

The sales and collection process includes business activities related to selling products and services, maintaining customer records, billing customers, and recording payments from customers. It also includes activities necessary to manage accounts receivable, such as aging accounts and authorizing credit. Certainly, the sales and collection processes generate accounting transactions to record revenue, accounts receivable, and cash receipts. They also affect cost of goods sold and inventory for companies that sell merchandise.

Exhibit 7.1 describes typical accounting transactions resulting from the sales and collection process. **Sales** are typically made in exchange for **cash** or credit. The transaction may also require collection of sales tax. A cash sale increases cash. A credit sale results in an account receivable. **Accounts receivable** are monies owed to the firm from the sale of **products** or services. A sale of goods also results in a corresponding recognition of cost of goods sold expense and reduction of inventory. When the customer subsequently pays for the goods or services sold on credit, cash is increased and accounts receivable are reduced.

EXHIBIT 7.1
Accounting Transactions for the Sales and Collection Process

Oct 1	**Accounts Receivable**	**1,350.54**	
	Sales Tax Payable		**100.04**
	Sales		**1,250.50**
	Sold products on credit to Smith, Inc. Invoice No. 459		
Oct 1	**Cash**	**1,452.87**	
	Sales Tax Payable		**107.62**
	Sales Tax Payable		**1,345.25**
	Sold products for cash		
Oct 1	**Cost of good sold**	**750.30**	
	Inventory		**750.30**
Oct 31	**Cash**	**1,350.54**	
	Accounts Receivable		**1,350.54**
	Received payment from Smith, Inc. for Invoice No. 459		

We apply the tools introduced in Chapters 4, 5, and 6 to a comprehensive example of the sales and collection process. For this example, we take on the role of business analysts helping a small business, Sunset Graphics Inc., document its business processes. In this chapter, we first describe the sales and collection activities using BPMN, and then we define typical information structures using UML class diagrams. Finally, we use the UML class diagrams to build a database to collect and report sales and collection information. Throughout, we describe business rules that establish potential process controls.

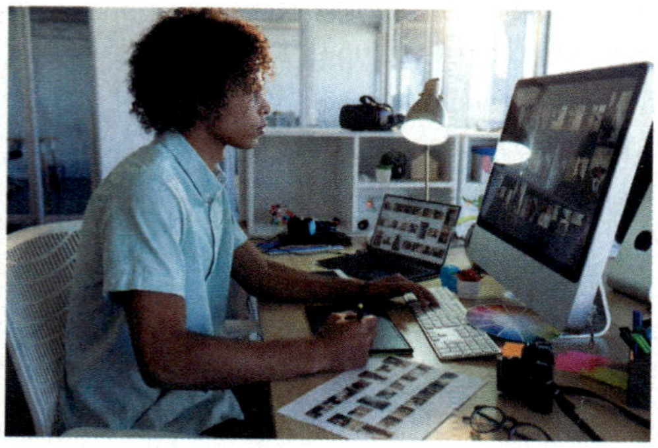

Designing for customer specifications.
wavebreakmediamicro/123RF

SUNSET GRAPHICS EXAMPLE

Company Overview

Virgil B (his family name is Bartolomucci, but everyone calls him Mr. B) started the company over 25 years ago and has grown it into a successful graphic design and printing business. The company designs and sells signs and banners, lettering and vinyl graphics for vehicles and boats, corporate promotional items, and silk-screened t-shirts and embroidered gear, among other products.

Recently, Virgil decided to expand his business onto the Internet. Before he did that, he decided that it was time to review their business processes to develop better documentation, improve processes, and establish consistency in customer service. He also wanted to be sure that effective internal controls were in place since some activity will now be automated.

Sunset Graphics' Sales and Collection Process Description

In the past, most of Sunset's products were designed to customer specifications. Virgil or another Sunset employee prepared a **quote** for the **customer** that carefully described the products and services that Sunset would provide. If the customer liked the quote, they placed the **sales order** for all or part of the quoted products and services. At that point, Sunset often ordered any products not in inventory from their suppliers. When they received the delivery from their supplier, Sunset customized the products by screen printing, applying graphics, embroidering, assembling, and so on. Sunset then delivered the products to the customer. In some cases, Sunset applied the graphics or installed the custom products, such as signs or banners, at the customer's site. After completing the job, Sunset billed the customer. Depending on the customer, Sunset either collected payment immediately or allowed the customer to pay within 30 days.

In the future, Sunset will offer some products for sale over its website. Although this requires more advanced preparation, Virgil thought it would simplify parts of the process. Customers would place orders via the Sunset website, selecting products and then paying by credit card. Sunset employees would prepare the products, apply any graphics (minimal for the online orders), and then ship the products to the customer.

SUNSET GRAPHICS' ACTIVITY MODELS

Basic Sales Activity Model

LO 7-2

Develop an activity model of the sales and collection process using BPMN.

While talking with Virgil about their sales and collection process, we explained the value of business process models and a structured process to develop those models (see Chapter 4). First, we identify the purpose of the model. In this case, that is to document Sunset Graphics current processes in anticipation of expansion. Second, we define the model context. This involves identifying external actors and the exchanges between Sunset Graphics and those actors. Exhibit 7.2 illustrates that context based on Virgil's description.

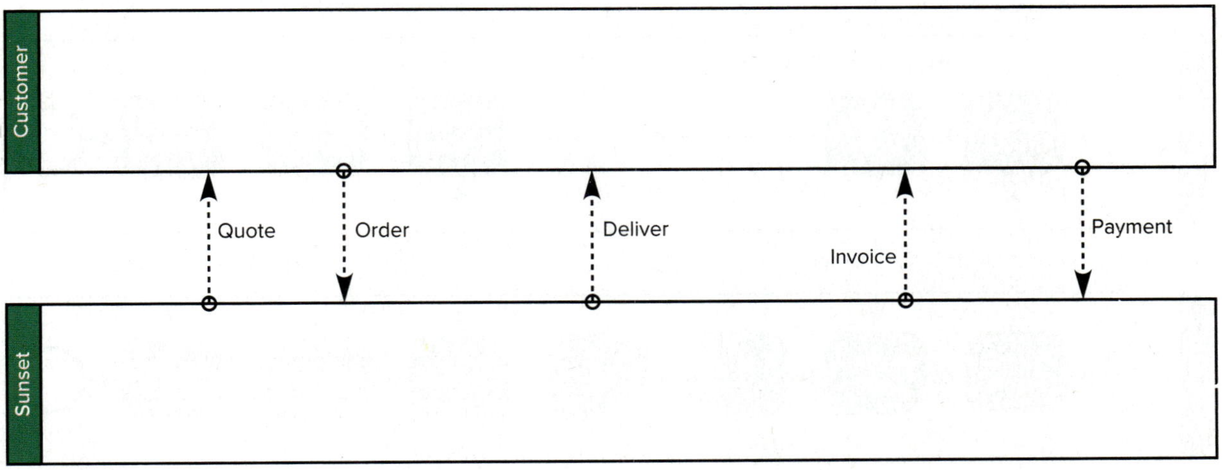

EXHIBIT 7.2
Sunset Graphics Sales Context

Currently, most of his products are custom orders. He provides quotes, accepts orders, delivers the products, invoices his customer, and then accepts payments.

Third, we use the information to outline basic process flows. Using the information from Exhibit 7.2, we draw a simple activity model shown in Exhibit 7.3 using BPMN. Sunset starts the process when the customer requests a quote. Then, a series of tasks takes place in sequence until the customer pays for the products and services and the process ends. Sunset records sales revenue when the products and services are delivered to the customer. Most customers place orders after getting a quote, but some elect to visit other companies to get competing quotes.

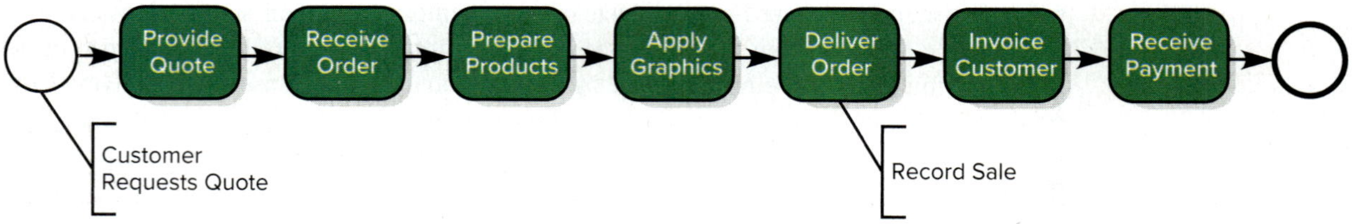

EXHIBIT 7.3
Basic Sales Activity Model

LO 7-3

Understand and apply different activity modeling options.

Refining the Model to Show Collaboration

After thinking about the context diagram and basic model, Virgil asked if we could combine both diagrams to highlight the steps in the process and the interaction with customers. We said that BPMN also allows *pools* that show different participants in a process. *Message flows* (shown by dashed arrows) between pools describe the interaction between participants. *Message flows* are labeled to show the content of the information exchanged between pools. We then prepared Exhibit 7.4 that shows the customer's activities in one pool and Sunset's activities in the other pool. We explained that each pool needs a start and end event, and the *sequence flow* (shown by the solid arrows) within a pool continues from the start event to the end event without a break. This type of activity model is called a **collaboration** model in BPMN, and the interaction between participants is called **choreography**.

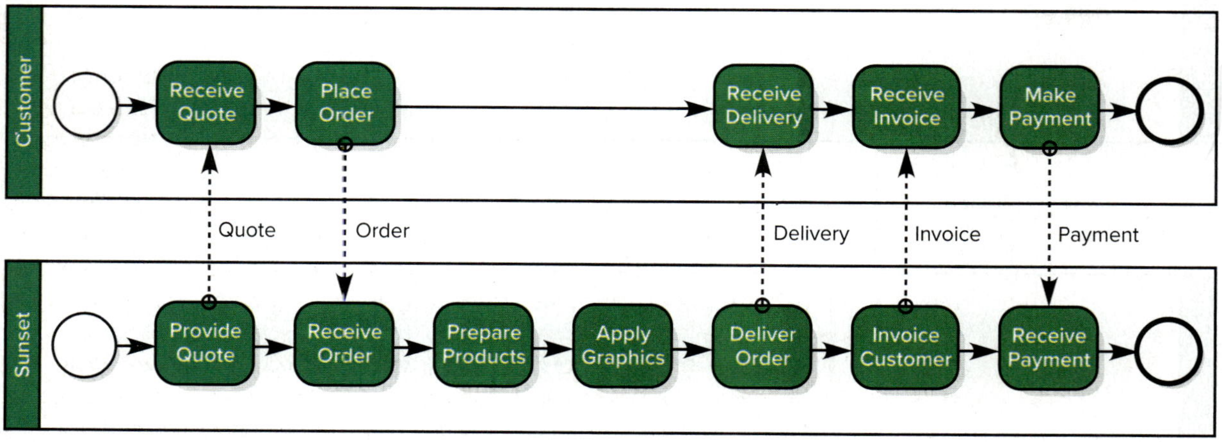

EXHIBIT 7.4
Collaboration Sales Activity Model

Virgil agreed that this model shows the interactions more clearly, but he really did not care about the customers' activities. He was just concerned about the *choreography* of interactions between the pools and the *orchestration* of Sunset's activities (the sequence of activities within one pool is called an **orchestration**). We understood and changed the model. Exhibit 7.5 now hides the customer's activities, but it shows the important message flows between participants. We could also hide Sunset's activities and just show the choreography between participants, but Virgil liked this model.

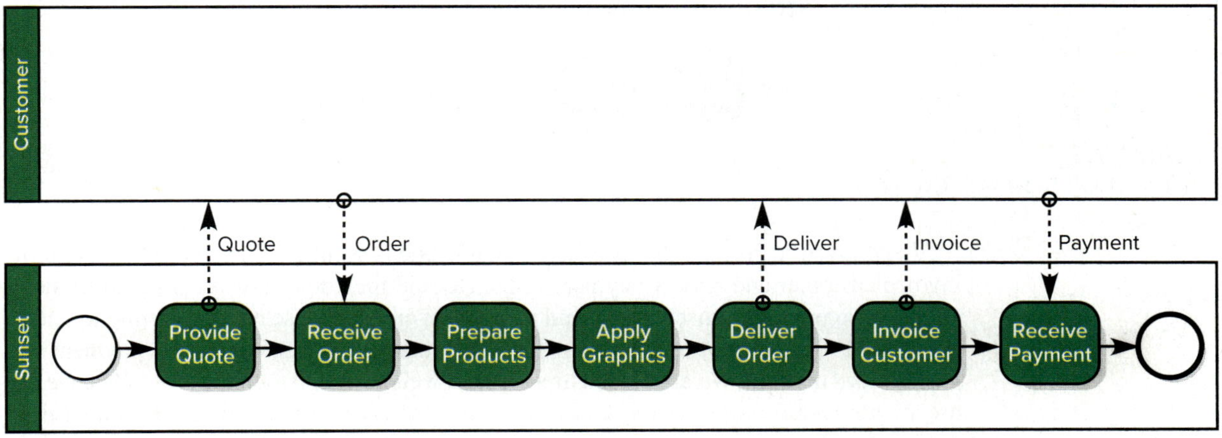

EXHIBIT 7.5
Collaboration Sales Activity Model

PROGRESS CHECK

1. What information does the collaboration model in Exhibit 7.4 tell you that is different from the basic model shown in Exhibit 7.3?
2. From your own experience, describe how you would change Exhibit 7.5 to reflect another sales and collection process.

Refining the Model to Consider Exceptions

Continuing with our structured process of developing our business process model, the next step would be to define the activities in the process, who performs that process, what outcomes are expected, and how to deal with errors. Then, we would continue to refine the model. So, we asked Virgil about potential exceptions to the typical process flow. Virgil said that sometimes Sunset's suppliers don't have the products that Sunset needs to complete the job. Sunset then notifies the customer and cancels the job. We weren't ready to model details of the purchasing process, yet, so we can use a *collapsed* **subprocess** while also allowing for the exception. A collapsed subprocess contains a series of steps that are hidden from view. Later, we will define the purchasing process in detail. Because this was getting more complicated, we temporarily dropped the pools and revised the basic sales model.

Exhibit 7.6 includes the purchasing exception when products are not available. We show the exception that occurs when the product is not available as an *intermediate* **error event** attached to the boundary of the subprocess. When the exception occurs, the customer is notified and the process ends. Under normal conditions, the process continues as before.

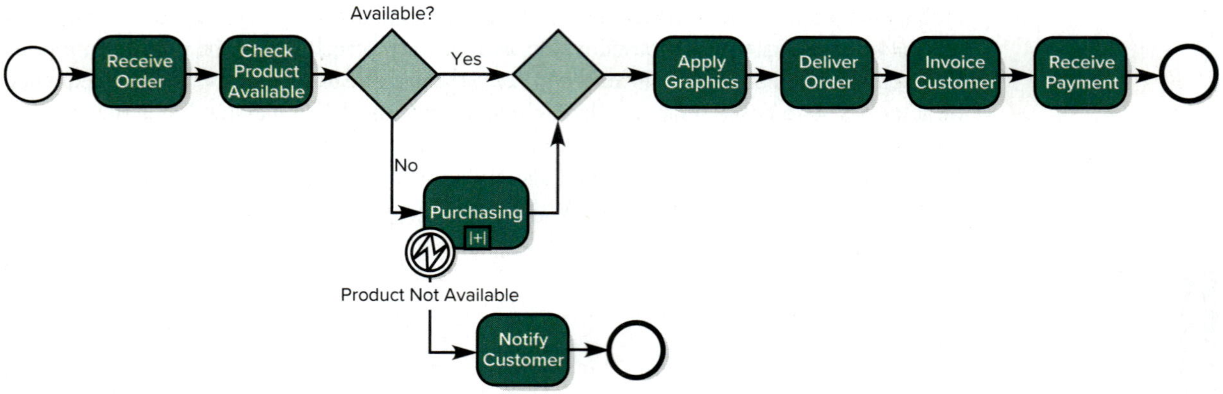

EXHIBIT 7.6
Sales Activity Model with Exception

Virgil loved it. He said that is exactly what happens at times. Then, he asked about the invoice customer and review payment tasks. He said they don't always get paid immediately and sometimes Sunset has to send another invoice. Because he was starting to understand BPMN, he asked if we could also use a boundary event to show that the payment was not received on time. We applauded him for how well he understood the tools. Yes, we can use an *intermediate timer boundary event* to show the exception. Virgil says that he waits 2 weeks after the payment due date to send a new invoice. Exhibit 7.7 adds the intermediate timer boundary event to the process. The timer event would be triggered when the payment is not received within 2 weeks.

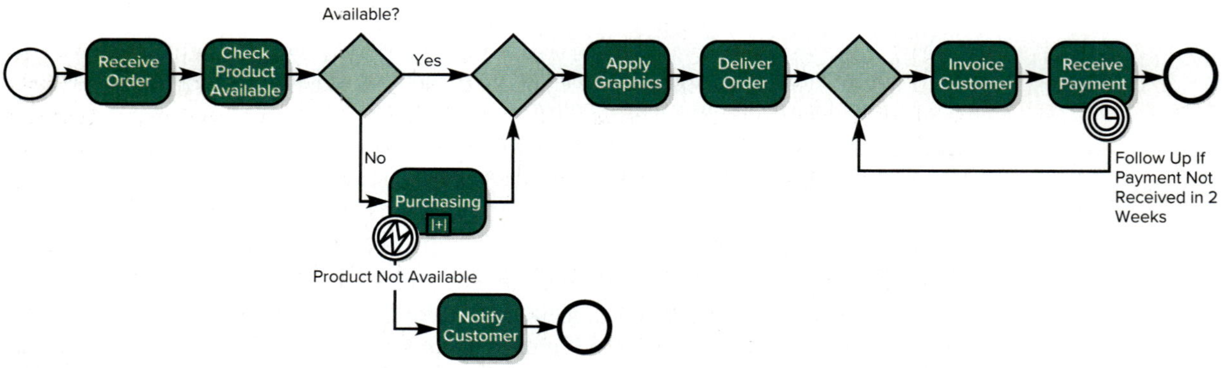

EXHIBIT 7.7
Sales Activity Model with Intermediate Boundary Events

Basic Internet Sales Activity Model

Virgil was satisfied that this represents his sales process when he has face-to-face contact with his customers. We said we could update our collaboration model with this expanded process flow. He didn't think that was necessary yet. Instead, he wondered what the Internet sales process would look like. After discussing his plans, we thought the process would look like a standard web sales process. Customers select items and they are moved to the customer's cart. The customer elects to check out and enters the order and shipping information as well as the credit card payment information. When the credit card payment is confirmed by the credit card processor, Sunset employees prepare the products, apply some limited graphics if ordered, and ship the products to the customer. We presented a draft model of the process as shown in Exhibit 7.8. We used an intermediate error boundary event to show the option that the customer's credit card is not confirmed. At this point, we did not include interactions with the credit card processor, but those could be shown as message flows to another pool.

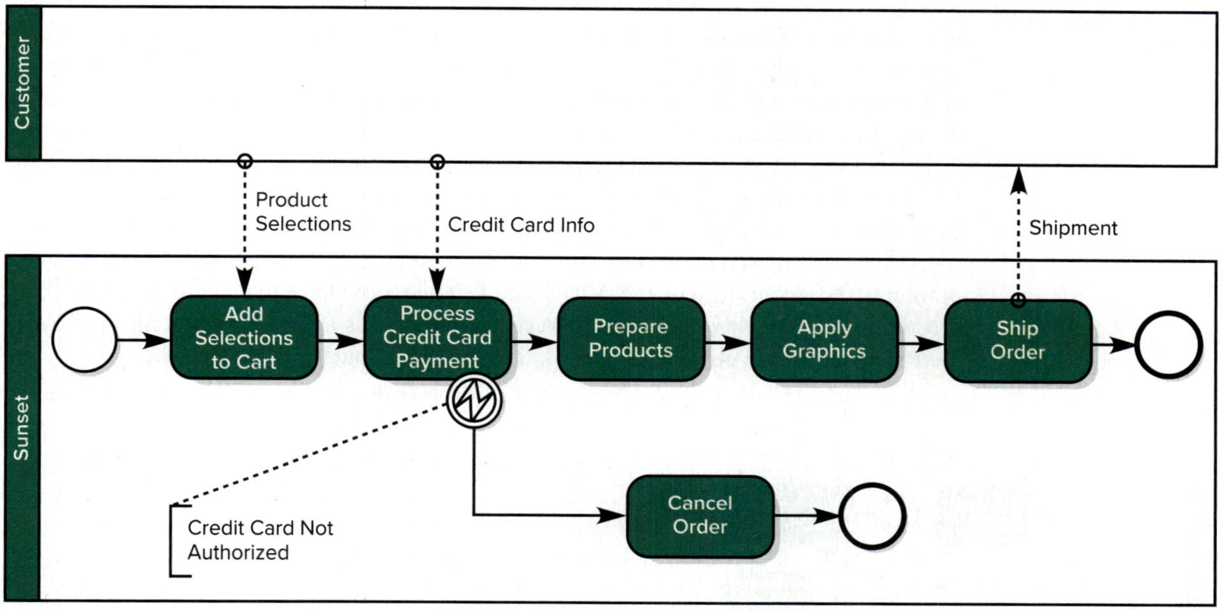

EXHIBIT 7.8
Basic Online Sales Activity Model

Virgil said that this did seem simpler. Plus, the Internet sales would allow him to reach more customers. He was curious, though, about the "Process Credit Card Payment" task. Does this model mean that the customer only gets one attempt to enter acceptable credit card information? We admitted that the model wasn't clear. We explained that we can use a *looping task,* so the customer enters credit card information until confirmed or until the customer exceeds a reasonable number of tries. Exhibit 7.9 shows a looping task for the credit card processing. The number 1 in Exhibit 7.9 represents the incoming sequence flow. The task then loops until the looping criteria are met, and normally the credit card information would be confirmed. The number 2 in Exhibit 7.9 represents the normal outgoing sequence flow. However, when the credit card information is not confirmed after a reasonable number of attempts, the *intermediate error event* is triggered and the process is canceled. The number 3 in Exhibit 7.9 shows that flow. Note that an *intermediate error boundary event* must have one outgoing sequence flow. We planned to update Exhibit 7.8 as modified by Exhibit 7.9 as he got closer to implementing his website.

EXHIBIT 7.9
Modifying the Online Sales Activity Model

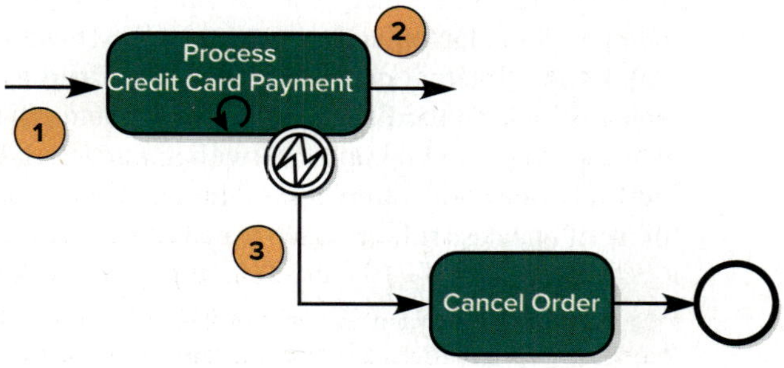

LO 7-4

Develop business rules to implement controls for the sales and collection process.

PLANNING AND IMPLEMENTING SALES AND COLLECTION PROCESS CONTROLS

Next, we wanted to talk about controls over the sales and collection process. We explained to Virgil that we can plan and implement controls with business process models and business rules for the process (see Chapter 5). First, we described three main types of internal controls: preventive, detective, and corrective controls. Preventive controls include proper authorization of transactions and segregation of duties. Exhibit 7.10 provides an example of a process model that includes an intermediate event to authorize the quote and four lanes to describe the possible segregation of duties within the sales and collection process. Virgil saw how the illustrated controls would prevent errors and losses, but he then asked us to give some examples of detective and corrective controls. We explained that detective controls are designed to find any problems that arise and corrective controls fix those problems and repair the damage. Virgil said that he would have to develop some ancillary processes to reconcile orders with invoices and payments and be sure that his employees were retrained when needed. He would have to think about those for a while.

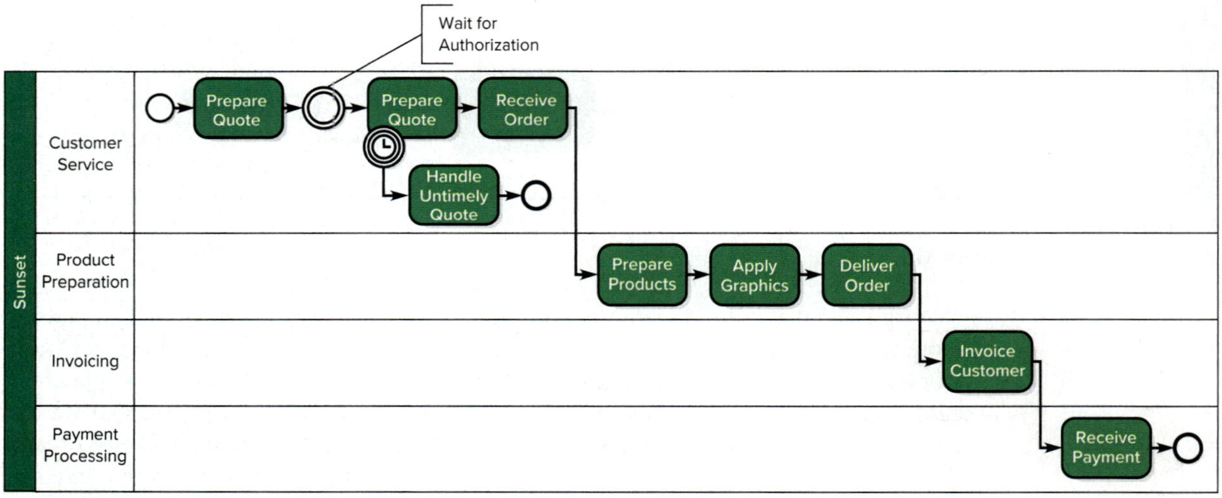

EXHIBIT 7.10
Sunset Graphics Sales Process Controls Example

We also described how he could use business rules to implement internal controls. We explained to Virgil that a *business rule* is a compact statement that constrains some aspect of business activity. Business rules help ensure that processes and the information systems supporting those processes operate in a consistent and effective manner to achieve organizational objectives.

Virgil remarked that business rules do seem similar to internal controls. He quickly pulled out his laptop and went to the COSO website, www.coso.org.[1] He paraphrased its definition, "Internal control is broadly defined as a process designed to provide reasonable assurance regarding the effectiveness and efficiency of operations, reliability of financial reporting, and compliance with applicable laws and regulations." We explained that business rules are not processes; they are constraints on the process. However, you could think of business rules as control activities. COSO describes control activities as including

[1]See Chapter 11 for more complete explanation of COSO (Committee of Sponsoring Organizations of the Treadway Commission) and internal control elements.

approvals, authorizations, verifications, reconciliations, reviews of operating performance, security of assets, segregation of duties, and other activities designed to address risks to achievement of the entity's objectives. After thinking about it, Virgil agreed. He understood that business rules implement specific control activities for a business process. He just wasn't sure how to do it.

We explained that business rules are developed by identifying three elements: event, condition, and action. The first step is to identify important business events. Then, we need to know the conditions that could threaten your intention or objective for each event. Finally, we determine the appropriate actions to take based on the conditions. For example, we've already listed important business events in the activity models, so let's examine Sunset's sales and collection process in Exhibit 7.11 and develop some possible business rules.

Process Steps	Intention	Employee Authority/Action	Access Controls	Application Controls
Provide Quote	Provide quotes promptly and accurately.	Employee must provide quote within 1 business day of request; manager must approve quotes >$5,000.	Employee preparing quotes cannot modify established product and service prices.	System must provide quote number control, default values, range and limit checks, and create audit trail.
Receive Order	Record order promptly and accurately; ensure customer credit is authorized.	Employee must record order within 1 hour of receipt; manager must approve orders >$5,000; credit manager must approve credit order >$1,000.	Employee accepting orders cannot modify established product and service prices; employee accepting orders cannot approve request for customer credit >$1,000.	System must provide order number control, default values, range and limit checks, and create audit trail; system links quote to order.
Prepare Products and Apply Graphics	Prepare products promptly; ensure products match order; ensure quality products.	Employee must check all products for defects and show defective products/graphics to manager; employee must prepare products and apply graphics to meet required delivery schedule.	Employee preparing products cannot modify order.	System must allow the employee to modify only the status information; system must assign current date by default.
Deliver Order	Deliver order on date requested; ensure customer accepts delivery.	Employee delivering order must verify that delivery matches order.	Employee delivering products cannot modify order.	System must supply delivery information and not allow modification.
Invoice Customer	Invoice customer promptly; monitor until paid.	Employee must invoice customer no later than 3 business days after delivery.	Employee preparing invoice cannot modify order; before preparing the invoice, make sure the product has been delivered.	System must supply invoice number; invoice information must be filled in automatically from order.
Receive Payment	Record and deposit receipt promptly.	Employee receiving payment must record receipt immediately and deposit intact on same day.	Employee receiving payment cannot modify order or invoice.	System must supply receipt number, default to current date, default payment value to order amount.

EXHIBIT 7.11
Using Business Rules to Implement Internal Controls

Virgil was now involved, so we started with the first step in the process: provide quote. We asked what his intention was for this step. He replied that his goal was to provide quotes accurately and promptly because the quote was extremely important in winning the customer's business. We then asked about the constraints that should be applied to the activity because a Sunset employee would prepare the quotes in the future. Virgil responded that the employee should provide the quote to the customer within 1 day of the customer's request. He added that they wanted to control approvals so a manager approved large value quotes. That way, he could be sure that Sunset would not be overextended by taking on a large job that it could not accomplish on time.

Since Virgil planned to expand Sunset Graphics, he knew that he would need better information systems. So, we asked him to think about the accounting information system controls over the process. We explained that **access controls** limit who can use and change records in the system. This helps implement appropriate segregation of duties. Virgil said that the employees who provide quotes should not also manage the inventory and set prices, so they should not have access that would allow them to modify product and price information. Finally, we said we need **application controls** to ensure data integrity and an audit trail. For example, we need to control the assignment of quote numbers to make sure all of them are accounted for. Plus, we need to establish appropriate ranges or limits for each value that Sunset's partners can add or change in the system.

With Virgil's input, we were able to develop an initial set of business rules for the sales and collection process. He articulated Sunset's intentions for every step in the process, and then we set business rules to segregate duties and limit employee authority appropriately. Exhibit 7.11 shows the initial set of business rules for Sunset's sales and collection process.

Application Controls

There is an old adage: "garbage-in, garbage-out." Application controls are designed primarily to avoid "garbage-in" from data entry errors. Application controls serve to ensure that data match the original source and correct values as closely as possible. Application controls often limit the new information that any single user can add to the system, requiring the use of validated master data. For example, when scheduling a payment to a vendor, the user should not generally be able to add a new vendor number. Instead, the user should be required to select from a list of validated vendors. Similarly, most users should not be able to enter new employee numbers. Such controls would not limit all potential errors, but they would control entry of valid vendors or employees.

Application controls include a variety of input validation checks:

1. Field checks. These ensure that the entry is the correct data type, for example, numeric. Note that Access automatically checks the data type for entry into a field.
2. Validity checks. These ensure that the entry contains acceptable values. Validity checks are often implemented with dropdown lists of valid options. Access Validation Rules set the requirements for entries for a field; for example, you can set validation rules to require a specific date as shown in Exhibit 7.12. Validation Text provides a notice to the user that the entry failed the Validation Rule as shown in Exhibit 7.13. Access also uses controls such as the DatePicker shown in Exhibit 7.14 to ensure valid

date entries. Access lookup options allow you to limit entries in a field by looking up values from another field, for example, looking up customer numbers for a particular order as shown in Exhibits 7.15 and 7.16.

EXHIBIT 7.12
Default Dates and Validation Rules
Microsoft Access

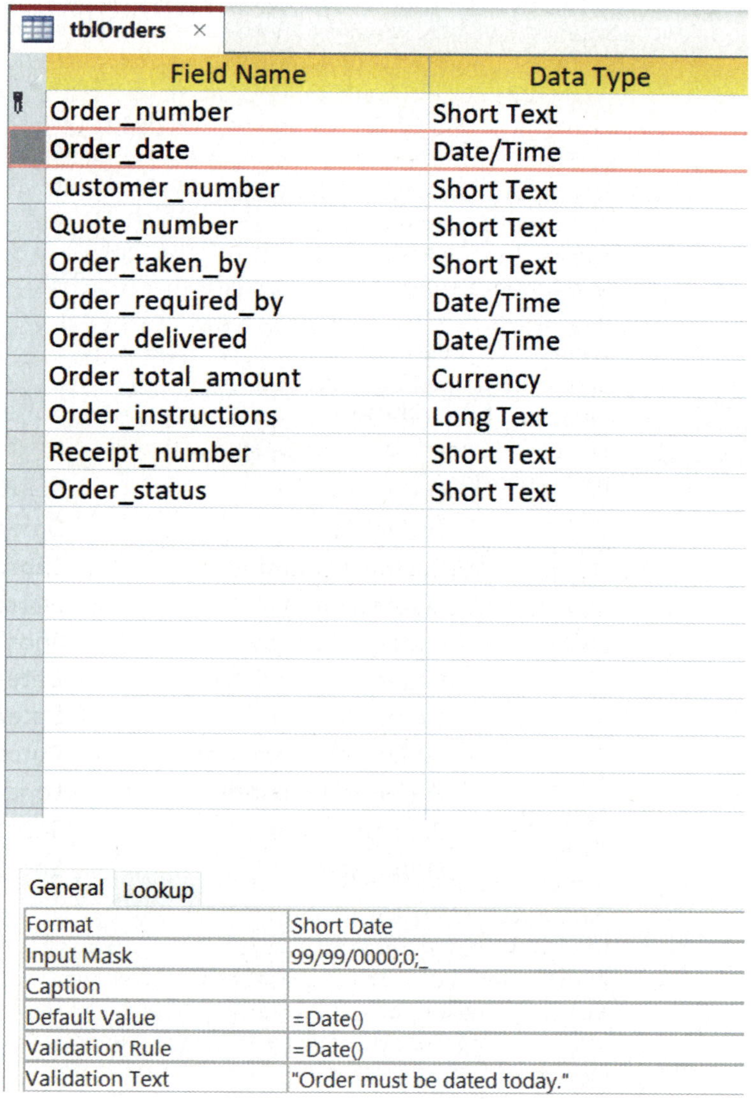

EXHIBIT 7.13
Example of Validation Text
Microsoft Access

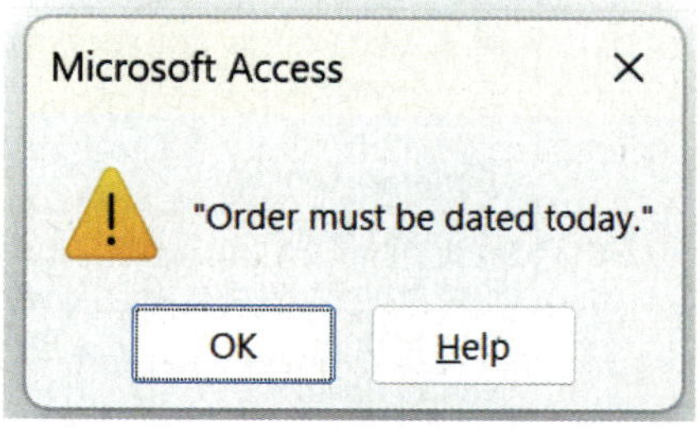

EXHIBIT 7.14
Use of Access Controls for Picking Dates
Microsoft Access

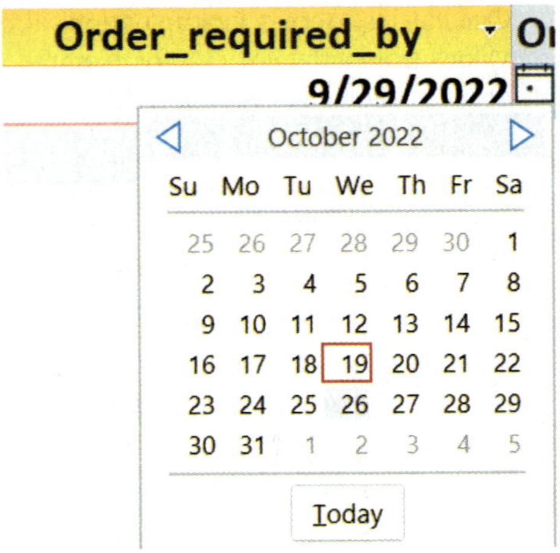

EXHIBIT 7.15
Using Combo Boxes in Access to Ensure Validity
Microsoft Access

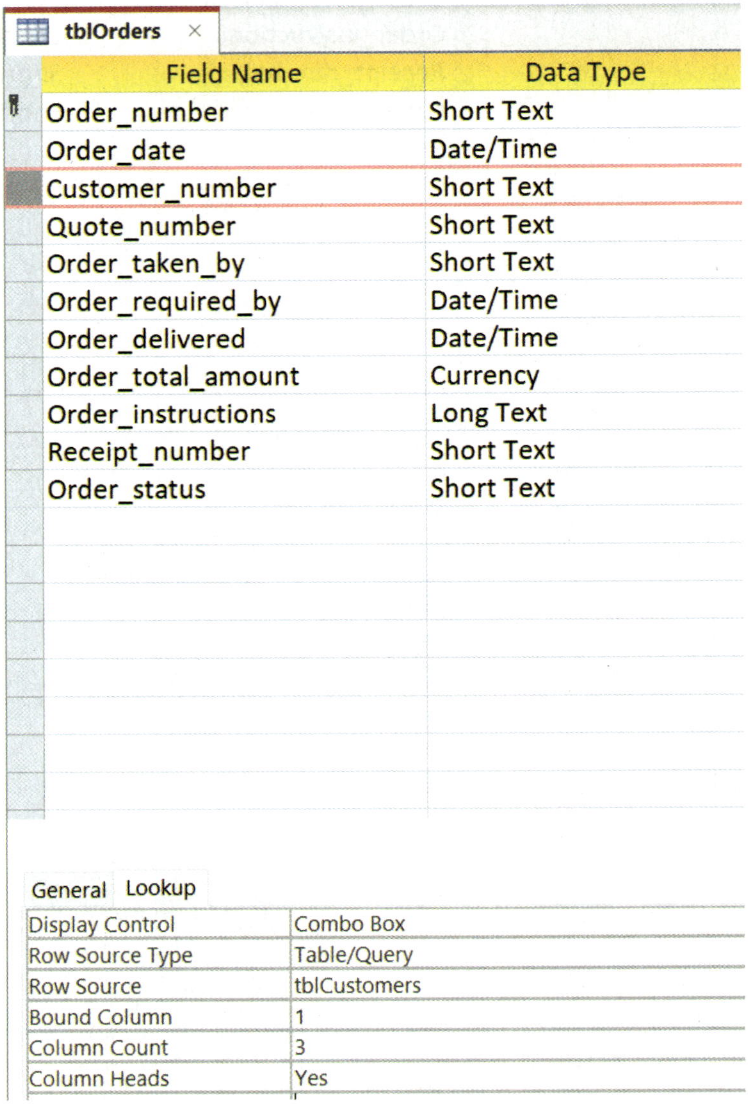

EXHIBIT 7.16
Example of Combo Box to Ensure Selection of Valid Customer Number
Microsoft Access

Customer_number

C1003

Cust#	FName	Addr
C1003	Colt	1115 Emerald Bay
C1004	Bruce	2210 Channel Rd
C1005	Jon	12666 Owens Dr
C1006	Joseph	2974 Los Amigos St
C1007	Greg	1825 W Orange Ave
C1008	Chris	9 Beachcrest

3. Limit and range checks. Limit checks ensure that entries are less than an upper bound, and range checks ensure that entries are between established lower and upper bounds. More sophisticated systems often include dynamic range checks where the bounds change depending on context. For example, they might allow payments up to $10,000 for building rentals but payments only up to $2,500 for utility bills. In Access, limit and range checks are just another type of validation rule as shown in Exhibit 7.17.

EXHIBIT 7.17
Setting Limit Checks in Access
Microsoft Access

tblOrders

Field Name	Data Type
Order_number	Short Text
Order_date	Date/Time
Customer_number	Short Text
Quote_number	Short Text
Order_taken_by	Short Text
Order_required_by	Date/Time
Order_delivered	Date/Time
Order_total_amount	Currency
Order_instructions	Long Text
Receipt_number	Short Text
Order_status	Short Text

General Lookup

Format	Currency
Decimal Places	Auto
Input Mask	
Caption	
Default Value	
Validation Rule	<1000000
Validation Text	"Amount exceeds limit."

4. Reasonableness checks. These compare entries in one field against entries in related fields to ensure that the value is reasonable based on those other fields. For example, pay amount may be compared against job codes. This is similar to a dynamic range check.
5. Completeness checks. These ensure that all required fields are entered before the record can be updated. For example, you have to complete the shipping address when you purchase something online.

Application controls also include the use of scanned or electronically determined data. For example, the user could scan the UPC code of products received, or use RFID or bar code data to confirm inventory transfers.

SUNSET GRAPHICS' STRUCTURE MODELS

LO 7-5

Develop a structure model for the sales and collection process using UML class diagrams.

We proceeded to examine Sunset Graphics' information requirements by preparing UML class diagrams that describe their sales and collection process. As described in Chapter 3, the primary purpose of a UML model of the sales and collection process is to create a blueprint for the development of a relational database to support the collection, aggregation, and communication of process information. To develop UML class diagrams, we follow the **REA** framework (resources, events, and agents) as a proven approach to describing business processes in a way that meets both accounting and broad management information requirements. Appendix A to this chapter provides more information on the REA framework and a generic sales process UML class model using that framework.

UML Class Model for Quotes

Virgil outlined Sunset's process for preparing quotes for customers. A Sunset employee works with the customer to document how Sunset will meet the customer's requirements. The Sunset employee prepares the quote, and the customer can accept the quote. The quote specifies the prices and quantities of Sunset's products and services to be delivered. So, our preliminary model shows Sunset's **resources** (Products), the Quote **event**, and the two **agents** (Sunset Employee and Customer) that participate in the event.

In Exhibit 7.18, we've numbered the three relevant associations: (1) the Sunset Employee to Quote event association, (2) the Customer to Quote event association, and (3) the Quote events to Products resource association. The multiplicities for association number 1 indicates that each Sunset Employee may participate in a minimum of zero Quotes and a maximum of many Quotes, but each Quote involves only one Sunset Employee.[2] Similarly, for association number 2, each Customer may participate in zero to many Quotes and each Quote is prepared for only one Customer. For association number 3 each Quote specifies prices and quantities for at least one product (minimum of one and maximum of many).

EXHIBIT 7.18
UML Class Diagram for Quotes

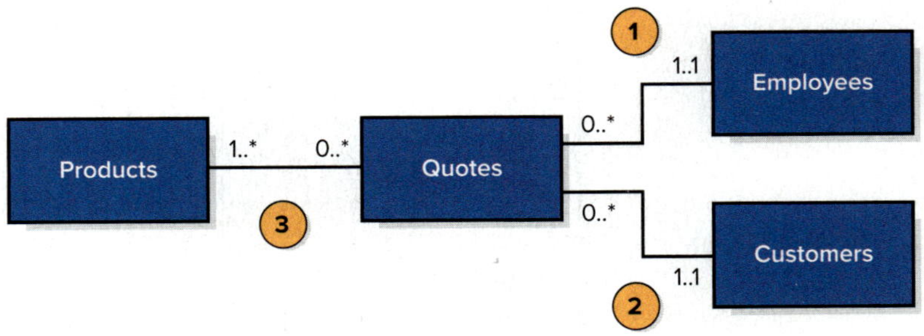

[2]When describing multiplicities, we refer to the instances of the class—for example, Quotes refers to the individual quotes that are instances of the Quote class (or rows in the Quote table).

Each product may be listed on many quotes (but some products may not yet be listed on quotes). Associations 1 and 2 represent **one-to-many relationships** between classes. Association number 3 represents a **many-to-many relationship**. As we discuss later, the nature of these relationships determines how the associations are implemented in the relational database.

UML Class Model for Adding Orders

Next, Virgil described how Sunset's quotes typically result in one or more orders from the customer. Of course, the same customer is involved in both the quote and the order, but a different Sunset employee could take the order. Sunset does not always prepare quotes prior to taking an order because some of its products do not need to be customized. When the customer places the order, Sunset has a formal commitment from the customer that will result in a sale when Sunset completes the delivery. Sunset does not deliver products and services until the order is complete, so there is a one-to-one relationship between orders and subsequent sales.

Exhibit 7.19 adds the Order event. We highlight association 4 because it links the Customer's order to the previous quote. Other associations with Order are similar to associations with Quote. The multiplicities for association 4 indicate that each Quote is related to a minimum of zero Orders, which may happen if the Customer does not place an order but also indicates that orders follow quotes in time (i.e., there can be delay between the quote and the customer order). Each Quote may be related to more than one Order if the Customer places partial orders, such as when the customer needs certain products and services immediately but others can wait. Orders are related to a minimum of zero Quotes and a maximum of one Quote.

EXHIBIT 7.19
UML Class Diagram for Orders and Quotes

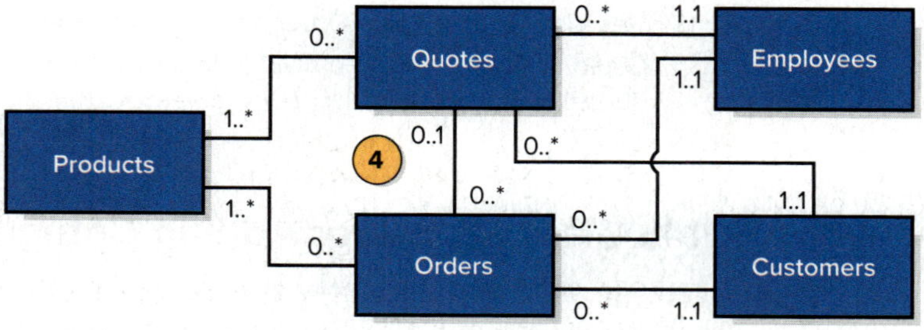

UML Class Model for Adding Cash Receipts

Some customers pay Sunset as soon as it delivers the products and services. However, Virgil said that Sunset's business and government customers are usually offered credit terms. Occasionally, the customers may send one check for several orders. A Sunset partner records the **cash receipt** from the customer. All cash receipts are deposited in Sunset's primary bank account daily.

Exhibit 7.20 adds the Cash Receipt *event* and the Cash *resource* (e.g., bank accounts) to the UML class diagram. As with Orders and Quotes, a Sunset employee and customer both participate in the Cash Receipt *event* and the multiplicities for these associations are like the earlier associations between agents and events. We highlighted the association between Orders and Cash Receipts *events* (number 5) and the association between the Cash Receipts *event* and the Cash *resource* (number 6). For association number 5, the multiplicities indicate that each Cash Receipt is linked with a minimum of one Order and a maximum of many Orders (one customer payment for multiple orders), and each Order is linked to a minimum of zero (not paid yet) and a maximum of one (paid in full) Cash Receipt.

Thus, the delivered Orders for which there are no Cash Receipts define Sunset's accounts receivable. For association number 6, the multiplicities indicate that each Cash Receipt is deposited into one account (Cash *resource*) and each account could have many Cash Receipts. The minimum of 0 next to Cash Receipts indicates that a Cash account does not have to be associated with any cash receipts. The minimum of 1 next to Cash indicates that every cash receipt must be associated with at least one cash account.

EXHIBIT 7.20
UML Class Diagram for Orders and Cash Receipts

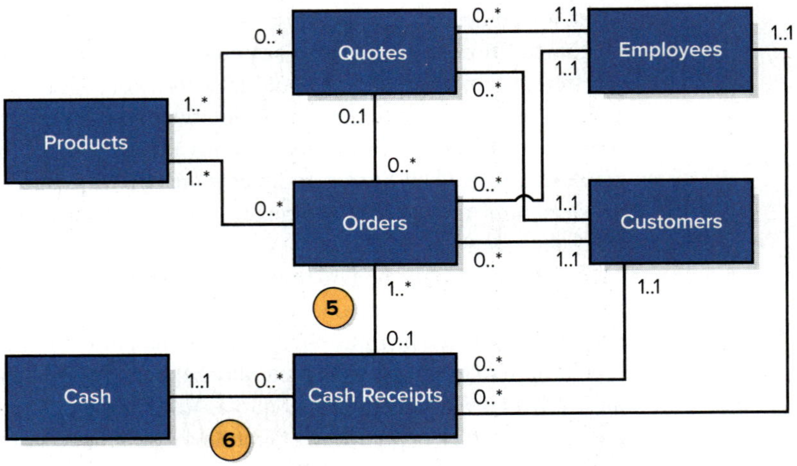

✓ **PROGRESS CHECK**

3. Describe when a Sales/Order might be preceded by the Quote activity.
4. Could the order event be divided into two events: Orders and Sales? If so, when does this make sense?

UML Class Model for Adding Categorical Information

Virgil now agreed that the model generally represents their sales and collection process, but he wondered how to include product categories and order status information that Sunset uses for management. For example, they categorize their products into t-shirts and gear for silk screening and embroidery, lettering material for vehicles and boats, sign and banner material, customer artwork, and printing materials (card stock and stationery items). Additionally, they have a number of different categories for their promotional products. They also track the status of their orders (e.g., waiting for supply, pending graphic application, ready for delivery, and delivered).

Companies often apply guidelines, constraints, and descriptive information to their resources, events, and agents to help manage the business process. Additionally, companies need to summarize the economic activity to support management's information requirements. Generically, these other classes can be called **type images**.[3] Type images are an important extension of the REA framework that allows for the addition of categorial and control information. For Sunset, we can model product category and order status information by adding two classes to the basic model, as shown in Exhibit 7.21.

[3]See, e.g., G. Geerts and W. McCarthy, "Policy Level Specifications in REA Enterprise Information Systems," *Journal of Information Systems* 20, no. 2 (2006), pp. 37–63.

EXHIBIT 7.21
UML Class Diagram for Orders and Cash Receipts with Type Images

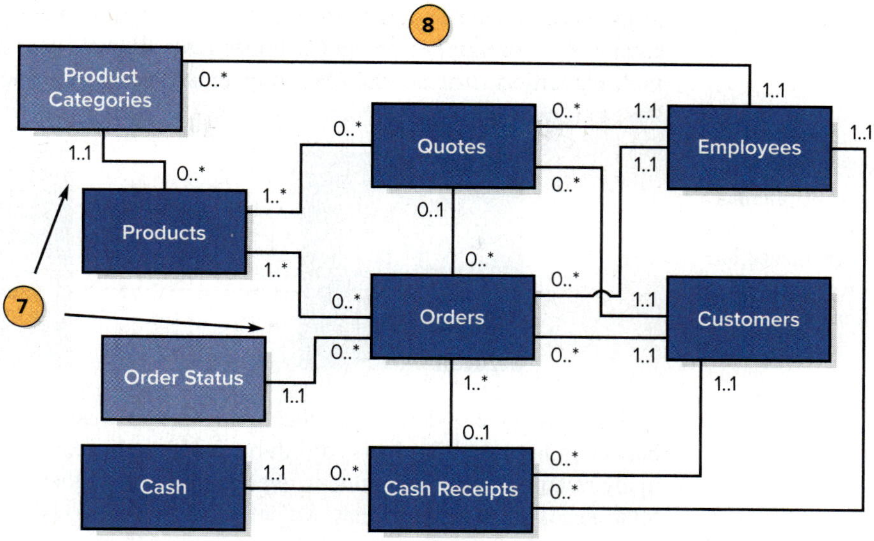

In Exhibit 7.21, the Product Category and Order Status classes allow Sunset to establish appropriate categories for the related classes (i.e., Products for Product Categories and Orders for Order Status). Association number 7 highlights the two association between the underlying class and its type image. The multiplicities for both associations reflect that each category/status can apply to many instances of the underlying class. For example, each Product Category comprises many Products. Once implemented in a relational database, these *type images* allow process information to be summarized by category.

Type images could also support control activities by designating responsibilities. For example, a Sunset Employee could be assigned inventory management responsibility for one or more Product Categories, as shown by association number 8. The multiplicities for association number 8 indicate that one Sunset Partner is assigned to each Product Category, but some Sunset Partners could be assigned to manage multiple Product Categories.

LO 7-6

Use multiplicities to implement foreign keys in relational tables.

UML Class Model for Supporting Relational Database Planning

Virgil B had no more questions about the UML class diagrams of Sunset's sales and collection process, but he did wonder how the model would be implemented in the relational database. He knew that relational databases implement links between tables through foreign keys.[4] "How do you know where to put the foreign keys?" he asked.

We said that once you understand the multiplicities, it is pretty easy to determine where to put the foreign keys. Let's use some of the associations that we've already discussed as examples. Exhibit 7.22 shows the one-to-many relationship between Customers and Orders. We've included some sample attributes for the classes. The <<pk>> notation indicates the primary keys; the <<fk>> notation indicates the foreign keys. Thus, *Cust_num* (customer number) is the primary key for the Customer table, and *Order_num* (order number) is the primary key for the Order table. The multiplicities indicate that each Customer can be linked with multiple Orders, but each Order only involves one Customer. Foreign keys are primary keys of linked tables, so either the *Cust_num* is a foreign key in the Orders table or the *Order_num* is the foreign key in the Customer table. Remember that

[4]See Chapter 4 for a complete discussion of foreign keys and referential integrity.

properly designed relational tables cannot have multivalued fields. Thus, the *Order_num* cannot be a foreign key in the Customer table because each Customer can participate in multiple Orders. Instead, the *Cust_num* must be placed in the Orders table as the foreign key, as shown in Exhibit 5.19.

EXHIBIT 7.22
Using Multiplicities to Determine Foreign Key Implementation for One-to-Many Relationships

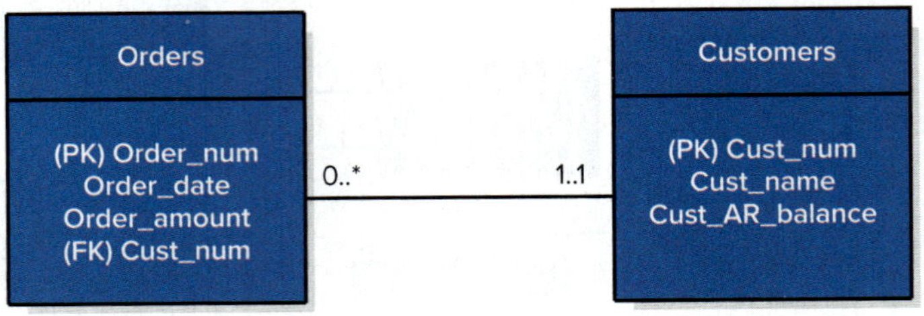

Next, we have to determine what to do with the many-to-many relationships, as shown between Order and Products in Exhibit 7.23. In this case, we need to turn the many-to-many relationship into two one-to-many relationships that can be easily implemented in a relational database. To do that, we define the Order Items class and model a *composition* association between Orders and Order Items as shown in Chapters 5 and 6. Note that the primary key of Order Items is the combination of *Order_num* and *Prod_num* (called concatenated key or composite key): *Order_num* in Order Items links to *Order_num* in Orders and *Prod_num* in Order Items links to *Prod_num* in Products. The Order Items table will include *quantity ordered* and *price* attributes because those attributes depend on both the

EXHIBIT 7.23
Implementing Many-to-Many Relationships

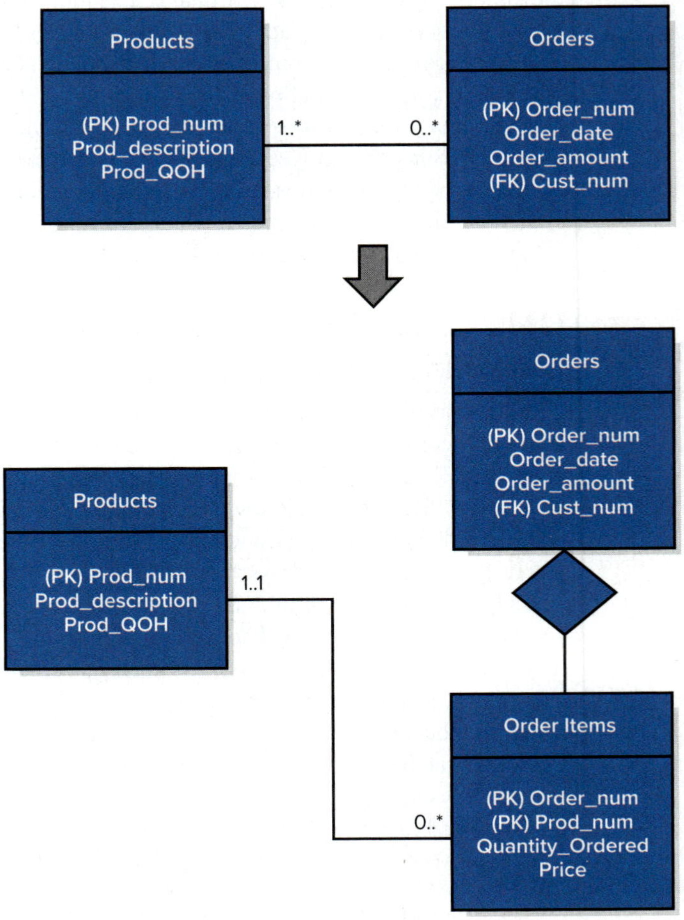

Order and the Product ordered.[5] Although we could have modeled Order Items on the original UML class diagram, identifying the many-to-many relationship serves the same purpose because, in either case, the Order Items table would have to be defined when the model is implemented.[6]

PROGRESS CHECK

5. Refer to Exhibit 7.21. Where does the foreign key go for the Customer to Cash Receipt association?
6. Where would the foreign keys go in the Orders to Cash Receipt association in that figure?

LO 7-7

Implement a relational database from the UML class diagram of the sales and collection process.

SUNSET GRAPHICS' RELATIONAL DATABASE

Virgil was now interested in seeing how the structure model would be implemented in a relational database for Sunset. For this example, we use Microsoft Access, but the process would be similar for any database-driven system. We encourage students to use the following description to implement a relational database to support information requirements for the sales and collection process.

Relational Database Planning for Attributes

During the model development process, we reviewed Sunset's existing documents to determine specific data requirements for each class/table. We then followed the guidance in the previous section to determine allocation of foreign keys. This resulted in a list of tables, attributes, data types, field sizes and primary and foreign keys, as shown in Exhibit 7.24.

EXHIBIT 7.24
Sunset Database Table and Attribute Definitions

PK/FK	Attribute Name	Type	Size
	Table: tblBankAccounts		
PK	Account_number	Text	10
	Bank_routing_number	Text	10
	Bank_balance	Currency	8
	Bank_name	Text	15
	Bank_branch	Text	15
	Bank_phone_number	Text	15
	Table: tblCashReceipts		
PK	Receipt_number	Text	10
	Receipt_date	Date/Time	8
	Receipt_amount	Currency	8
FK	Customer_number	Text	10
	Customer_check_number	Text	10

(continued)

[5]Think about your cash register receipt at the grocery store—one sale includes many items.

[6]Additionally, the Order Items class cannot exist without the Order class, and because it can be derived from other classes, some argue that it should not be modeled.

EXHIBIT 7.24
(continued)

PK/FK	Attribute Name	Type	Size
FK	Received_by	Text	10
FK	Bank_account_number	Text	10
	Receipt_deposit_date	Date/Time	8
	Table: tblCustomers		
PK	Customer_number	Text	15
	Customer_name	Text	30
	Customer_address	Text	30
	Customer_address_2	Text	30
	Customer_city	Text	20
	Customer_state	Text	2
	Customer_zip	Text	5
	Customer_contact	Text	30
	Customer_phone	Text	15
	Customer_established_date	Date/Time	8
	Customer_last_activity	Date/Time	8
	Customer_balance	Currency	8
	Table: tblOrderItems		
PK	Order_number	Text	10
PK	Product_number	Text	10
	Order_quantity	Integer	2
	Order_price	Currency	8
	Table: tblOrders		
PK	Order_number	Text	10
	Order_date	Date/Time	8
FK	Customer_number	Text	10
FK	Quote_number	Text	10
FK	Order_taken_by	Text	10
	Order_required_by	Date/Time	8
	Order_delivered	Date/Time	8
	Order_total_amount	Currency	8
	Order_instructions	Memo	—
FK	Receipt_number	Text	10
FK	Order_status	Text	10
	Table: tblOrderStatus		
PK	Order_status_code	Text	10
	Order_status_description	Text	255
	Table: tblEmployees		
PK	Employee_number	Text	10
	Employee_first_name	Text	15
	Employee_last_name	Text	15

(continued)

EXHIBIT 7.24
(continued)

PK/FK	Attribute Name	Type	Size
	Employee_hire_date	Date/Time	8
	Employee_SocSecNo	Text	11
	Employee_Address	Text	50
	Employee_Address2	Text	50
	Employee_City	Text	20
	Employee_State	Text	2
	Employee_Zip	Text	10
	Employee_phone	Text	14
	Employee_cellphone	Text	14
	Table: tblProductCategory		
PK	Product_category_number	Text	10
	Product_category_description	Text	255
	Product_category_manager	Text	10
	Product_category_notes	Memo	—
	Table: tblProducts		
PK	Product_number	Text	10
	Product_description	Text	255
	Product_price	Currency	8
	Product_unit_of_sale	Text	10
	Product_category	Text	10
	Product_quantity_on_hand	Integer	2
	Product_notes	Memo	—
	Table: tblQuoteItems		
PK	Quote_number	Text	10
FK	Product_number	Text	10
	Quote_quantity	Integer	2
	Quote_price	Currency	8
	Quote_notes	Text	255
	Table: tblQuotes		
PK	Quote_number	Text	10
	Quote_date	Date/Time	8
FK	Customer_number	Text	10
FK	Quote_by	Text	10
	Quote_amount	Currency	8

Create the Database and Define Tables

The next step is to create a new, blank Microsoft Access database and create the tables described in Exhibit 7.24 with the following steps:

1. Create the Table Design as shown in Exhibit 7.25 by selecting the CREATE tab; then select the Table Design icon on the ribbon bar.

EXHIBIT 7.25
Create the Table Design
Microsoft Access

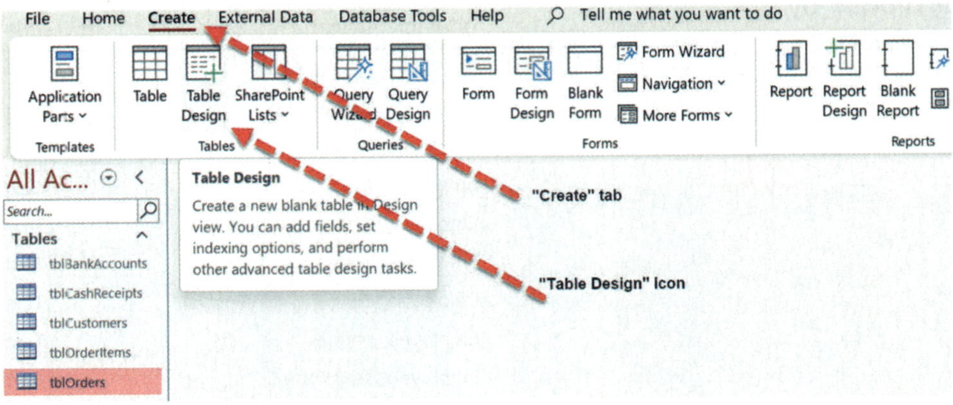

2. Define each attribute listed for the table in Exhibit 7.24 by typing the field name, selecting the data type, and setting the field size, as shown in Exhibit 7.26.

EXHIBIT 7.26
Define the Fields in the Table
Microsoft Access

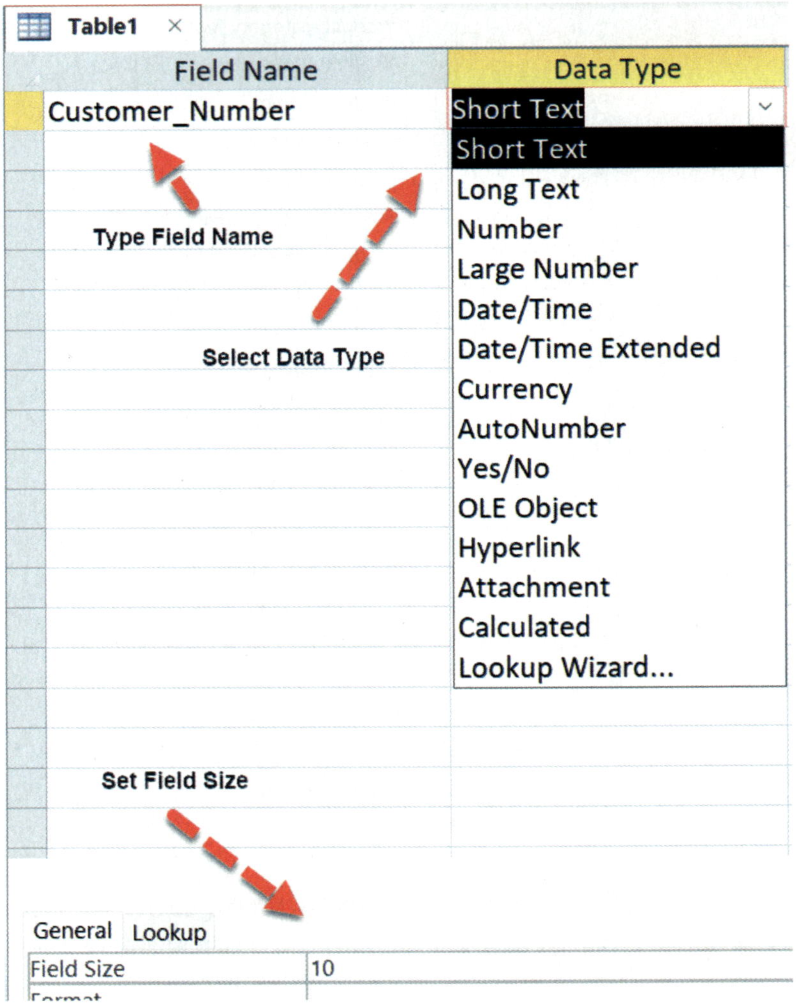

3. Set the primary key by selecting the appropriate field and clicking the Primary Key icon on the ribbon bar, as shown in Exhibit 7.27.

EXHIBIT 7.27
Set the Primary Key for the Table

Microsoft Access

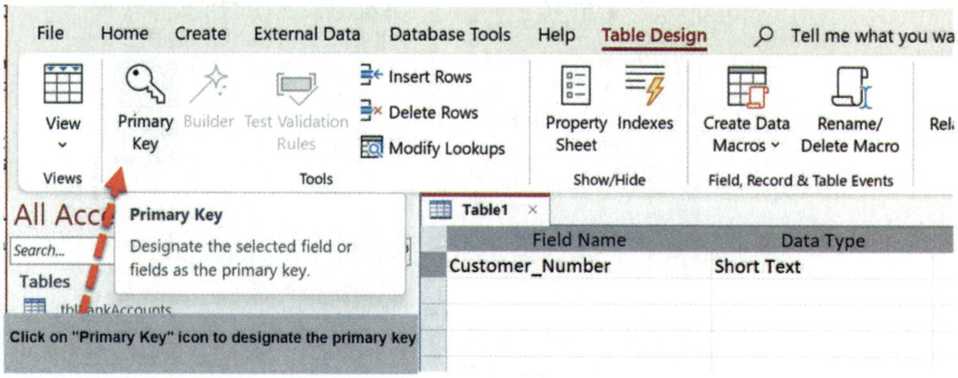

4. Save the table.
5. Repeat until all the tables are defined.

Set Relationships

After the tables are defined, the next step is to establish the links between tables. Click on the DATABASE TOOLS tab and select the Relationships icon on the ribbon bar. Then, as shown in Exhibit 7.28, add all the tables to the relationships screen and connect foreign keys to primary keys as shown in Exhibit 7.29 so that the relationships mimic the UML class diagram shown in Exhibit 7.21.

EXHIBIT 7.28
Set Relationships

Microsoft Access

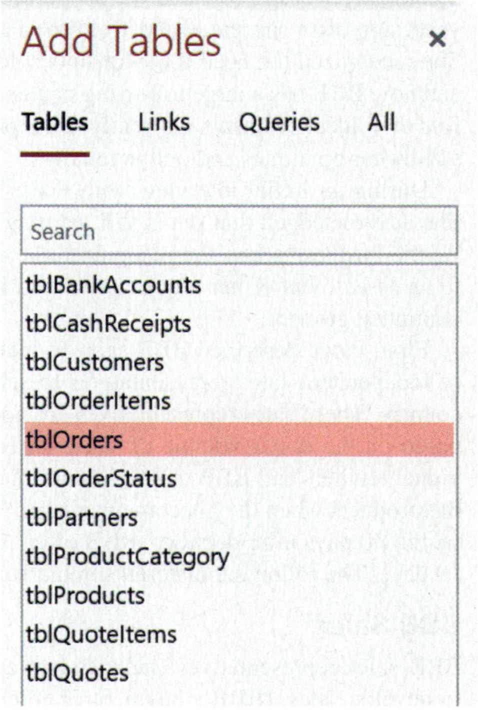

EXHIBIT 7.29
Linked Tables with Referential Integrity Enforced

Microsoft Access

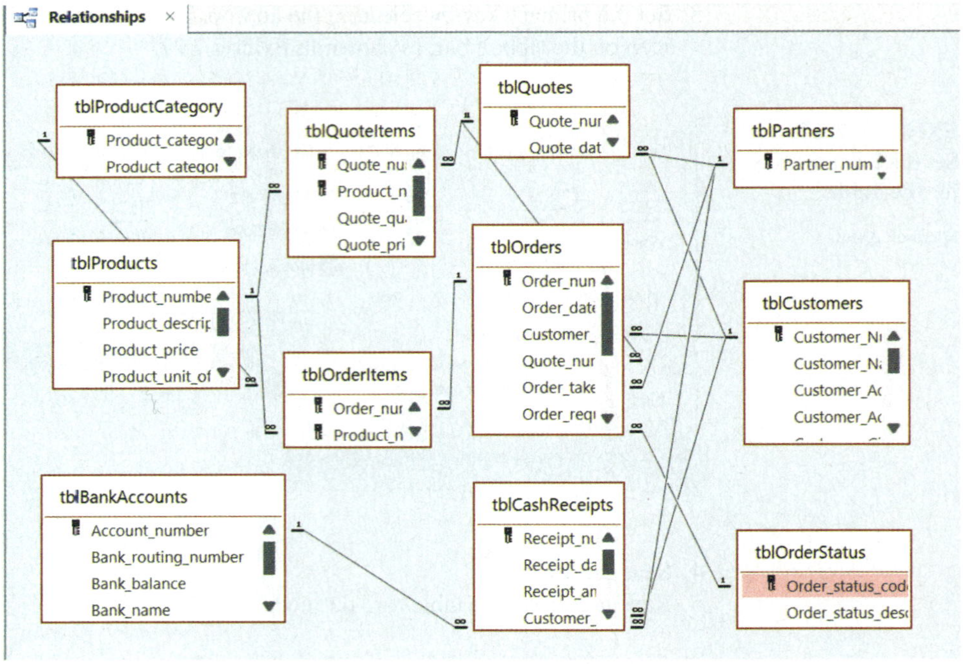

Review Exercise: Baer Belly Bikinis' Sales to Retailers

This review exercise examines the sales process for Baer Belly Bikinis Inc. (BBB), a small business located in Santa Monica, California. It sells swimwear and related products to specialty stores throughout the United States. It also sells its products to individuals over a company website (outside the scope of this lab). Paige Baer founded BBB almost 10 years ago after she graduated from the Fashion Institute of Design and Merchandising. She recognized the need for swimsuits sold as separates. Her business has grown rapidly, and now BBB has a large following of customers who want to be able to mix and match to find their ideal swimsuit. Currently, BBB products are carried in more than 1,000 specialty swimwear boutiques and online retailers.

During an initial interview with Paige Baer, she outlined BBB's business processes. She acknowledged that she is still learning about accounting and information technology. As the business grew, she recognized the importance of both. So, she is looking forward to an assessment of her requirements and recommendations that would position BBB for continued growth.

First, Paige described BBB sales to independent boutique retailers. BBB uses a group of independent sales representatives to sell its products to boutique retailers around the country. These sales representatives are not BBB employees. They are paid commissions based on the dollar volume of sales. After working with the sales representatives, individual retailers call BBB to place their order for the upcoming season. BBB will then ship the products when they become available. The retailers are expected to pay for shipments within 30 days after delivery. BBB offers a prompt payment discount for payment within 10 days. The following material summarizes BBB's activities for their sales process.

BBB Sales

BBB sales representatives (independent agents working on commissions) visit retailers to develop sales. (BBB's payment of commissions to sales representatives is outside the scope of this case, although you should include the Sales Reps in your model and database.) BBB's retailer customers work with the sales representatives to place orders that usually request delivery within 30 days. A BBB customer service employee records sales orders and requested delivery dates. BBB confirms retailers' financial viability before they place any orders.

BBB uses automated equipment to produce its swimwear and related products. The production staff prepares each order separately to meet requested delivery dates. When production is complete and the products are packaged, production staff transfers the products to shipping. The shipping department then schedules and ships products to retailers. Retailers' payments are due 30 days after delivery and include shipping costs. Some retailers pay late. Some take advantage of the prompt payment discounts.

A BBB accounting employee records revenue when the products are shipped. All shipments are made under BBB's contract with a shipping company. BBB charges customers for the cost of the shipment, so the amount due from the retailers depends on the wholesale price of each item, the quantity shipped, and the shipping cost for the shipment. Payments to the shipping company are outside the scope of this case.

BBB Cash Receipts

Retailer customers send payment by check according to the payment terms (BBB standard payment terms are 2% 10 days net 30, meaning they receive a 2% discount on any amount they pay within 10 days with the net balance due within 30 days). The payment from the retailer customer always applies to only one order, but sometimes the retailers send multiple checks for that order. A BBB accounting department employee logs cash receipts from retailers. At the end of the day, the cash receipts are deposited intact into one bank account (BBB's main account). Each cash receipt is tracked by unique sequential cash receipt number.

BBB Finished Goods Inventory

BBB tracks its inventory by catalog number (catalog#). Each product is identified by color code, its use (e.g., tops or bottoms), and its type (e.g., the specific design of the piece). The color codes reflect the color and fabric design options, and they can change each year. Since BBB produces to order, the beginning quantity on hand of each item is zero. The quantity on hand increases when BBB produces the finished products and then decreases as it ships the products to the retailers to fill orders. Those two events happen so close together, BBB does not track the quantity on hand for its finished goods inventory.

Exercise Requirements

1. Based on the preceding information, follow the steps outlined in Chapter 4 to create a business model using BPMN that describes BBB's Sales to Retailers process.
   a. The purpose of the model is to describe BBB's current sales process in preparation for business expansion.
   b. Prepare a context diagram that shows three participants: BBB, retailer customers, and sales representatives and the message flows between them.
   c. Outline the basic process flows and allocate the activities to lanes within the BBB pool. Add the Retailer Customers pool and show the message flows between BBB activities/events and the Retailer Customers.
   d. The next steps in the process are to define the activities, refine the model adding detail, and validate the model with stakeholders (your fellow students and instructor). Students are encouraged to complete those steps on their own.
2. Based on the BBB process description and the attributes list at the end of the lab, prepare a UML class model for BBB's sales to retailers.

3. Use the UML class diagram to create an Access database. Your instructor will provide an Excel spreadsheet with the BBB information. Create a new Access database and import each worksheet in the spreadsheet into the database. Set appropriate primary keys and establish relationships among tables.
4. Use your Access database for BBB to prepare queries to determine BBB's sales revenue in the second quarter (between 4/1/2024 and 6/30/2024), BBB's cash receipts for the same period, and BBB's accounts receivable as of the end of the second calendar quarter.

Attribute Listing for BBB

Bank Name
Cash Account Balance April 1
Cash Account Description
Cash Account#
Cash Receipt#
Customer Address
Customer City State Zip
Customer Name
Customer Phone
Customer#
Delivery Date
Employee Address
Employee City
Employee Department
Employee First Name
Employee Hire Date
Employee Last Name
Employee Pay Amount
Employee Phone
Employee Salary/Wage
Employee Zip
Employee#
Fabric Color Code
Fabric Color Name
Fabric Cost per Yard
Finished Inventory Catalog#
Finished Inventory Description
Finished Inventory Quantity on Hand
Flat Rate Ship Charge
Inventory Type Use
Order Date
Order Employee#
Order#
Quantity Ordered
Receipt Amount
Receipt Date
Requested Date
Retail Price
Sales Rep Area
Sales Rep Email Address
Sales Rep Name
Sales Rep Phone
Sales Rep#
Ship Date
Shipping Employee#
Shipping Cost
Size of Inventory Item
Standard Cost of Inventory Item
Supervisory Employee#
Type Code
Wholesale Price
Yards Fabric Required for This Inventory Type

Summary

- From an accounting standpoint, we must account for sales, accounts receivable, and cash collection in the sales and collection process.
- Sunset Graphics Inc. provides an ongoing example of how to model the sales and collection process.
- Activity models can show the basic steps in the process and the collaborations between the company and its customers, as well as exceptions to the process.
- Business models and business rules help plan and implement internal control activities.
- There is a standard structure model pattern for the sales and collection process that shows the economic reality of the process.
- The standard pattern is tailored to a specific organization by adding type images to collect management information.
- The structure model provides a blueprint for a relational database that will collect, store, and report sales and collection information.
- The demonstration lab reinforces the concepts presented in the chapter.

Key Words

access controls (*292*) Controls that limit who can use and change records in the system; for example, passwords control who can use an application.

accounts receivable (*284*) Monies owed by customers for prior sales of goods or services. In a data modeling context, accounts receivable are calculated as each customer's sales less corresponding cash receipts.

agents (*296*) The people or organizations, such as customers or salespeople, who participate in business events.

application controls (*292*) Controls specific to a subsystem or an application to ensure the validity, completeness, and accuracy of the transaction.

cash (*284*) The organization's monies in bank or related accounts. The instances of the class are individual accounts. This is considered a resource.

cash receipts (*297*) Record receipts of cash from external agents (e.g., customers) and the corresponding deposit of those receipts into cash accounts. This is considered an event.

choreography (*286*) The science of examining raw data (now often Big Data), removing excess noise from the dataset, and organizing the data with the purpose of drawing conclusions for decision making.

collaboration (*286*) A BPMN model showing two participant pools and the interactions between them within a process.

customer (*285*) The external agent in the sales and collection process.

error event (*287*) An intermediate event in a BPMN model showing processing for exceptions to the normal process flow.

events (*296*) (UML) Classes that model the organization's transactions, usually affecting the organization's resources, such as sales and cash receipts; (BPMN) important occurrences that affect the flow of activities in a business process, including start, intermediate, and end events.

many-to-many relationship (*297*) Relationship that exists when instances of one class (e.g., sales) are related to many instances of another class (e.g., inventory) and vice versa. These relationships are implemented in Access and relational databases by adding a linking table to convert the many-to-many relationship into two one-to-many relationships.

one-to-many relationship (*297*) Relationship that exists when instances of one class are related to multiple instances of another class. For example, a customer can participate in many sales, but each sale involves only one customer.

orchestration (*287*) In BPMN, the sequence of activities within one pool.

product (*284*) Class representing the organization's goods held for sale—that is, the organization's inventory. This is considered a resource.

quote (*285*) Description of the products and/or services to be provided to a customer if ordered.

REA (*296*) Resource-event-agent framework for modeling business processes, originally developed by William McCarthy.

resources (*296*) Those things that have economic value to a firm, such as cash and products.

sales (*284*) Events documenting the transfer of goods or services to customers and the corresponding recognition of revenue for the organization.

sales order (*285*) Event documenting commitments by customers to purchase products. The sales order event precedes the economic event (sale).

subprocess (*287*) A series of process steps that are hidden from view in BPMN. The use of subprocesses in modeling helps reduce complexity.

type image (*298*) Class that represents management information (such as categorizations, policies, and guidelines) to help manage a business process. Type image often allows process information to be summarized by category.

Appendix A

Generic REA Model with Multiplicities for the Sales and Collection Process

GENERIC PATTERN WITH MULTIPLICITIES

Exhibit 7.A1 shows a generic sales and collection process UML diagram. There are two resources, *inventory* and *cash;* there are two events, *sales* and *cash receipts;* and there are two agents, *employees* (internal agent) and *customers* (external agent). In this example, let's assume that the inventory is something tracked by universal product code (UPC). UPC are those bar codes you see on literally millions of products, such as soap, breakfast cereal, and packages of cookies. The cash resource represents the various bank accounts that would make up this enterprise's cash balance on its balance sheet. The sales event records information about individual sales transactions (e.g., transaction number, date, total dollar amount). The cash receipt event records information about payments received

EXHIBIT 7.A1
Generic Sales and Collection UML Diagram

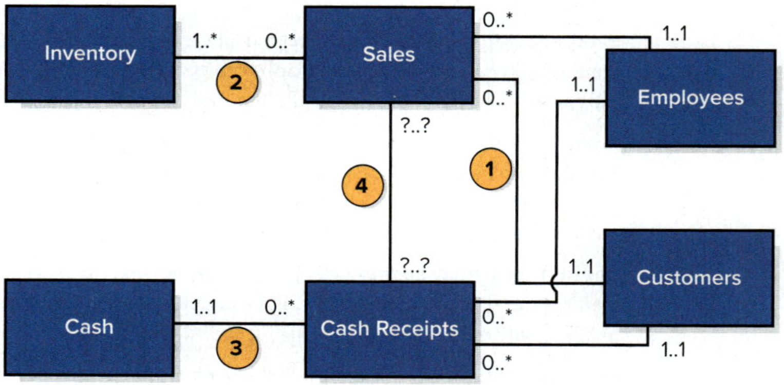

from customers and deposited into one of the bank accounts (e.g., receipt number, receipt date, receipt dollar amount, customer check number). The employees agent records information about the enterprise's employees, including those employees who handle sales transactions. The customers agent records information about actual and potential customers (let's assume that customer information is recorded in some cases when customers ask for product information and before they participate in their first sale, and let's also assume that the company only receives cash from customers).

Consider association 1 between *customers* and *sales.* The multiplicities indicate that each customer participates in a minimum of zero and a maximum of many sales. Does this seem reasonable? The minimum of zero means that we can record information about customers before they participate in any sale. On the other side of the association, the multiplicities indicate that each sale involves one and only one customer. Again, does this seem reasonable? Notice that the multiplicities for the other associations between agents and events are the same. In fact, these are the typical multiplicities for those associations. There are circumstances where they might be different, but those circumstances occur infrequently.

Next, consider association 2 between the *sales* event and *inventory* resource. The multiplicities indicate that each sale involves a minimum of one and a maximum of many inventory items. For example, you visit your local **Starbucks** and buy one coffee, a tea for your friend, plus two scones. The multiplicities also indicate that each inventory item can be sold zero times or many times. Starbucks has to put an item on its menu before it can be sold, so it could have inventory items that have not yet been sold. But the same inventory item can be sold many times—as long as the quantity on hand is greater than zero. The multiplicities on this association are typical when the inventory is carried at a type of product level, such as when the inventory is identified by UPC. If the company sells high-value items, the multiplicities would differ. (How?)

Now, consider association 3 between the *cash receipt* event and the *cash* resource. These multiplicities indicate that each cash receipt (e.g., one check from a customer) is deposited into one and only one account, and each account is associated with a minimum of zero cash receipts and a maximum of many cash receipts. These multiplicities reflect typical business practices. Cash receipts are deposited into one account (when you deposit money via an ATM, you are putting it in one account, right?).

Finally, consider the duality association 4 between the *sales* and *cash receipt* events. The question marks indicate that these multiplicities depend on the nature of the business. Some businesses require payment at the time of the sale. Some allow payment terms. Some provide revolving accounts for their customers. Some collect payments in advance of the sale (e.g., magazine subscriptions). So, there are no typical multiplicities for this association.

Although we discourage memorization of data modeling elements, students often find that multiplicities are easier to understand once they see the typical sets for particular associations. We therefore recommend that students recognize and use the standard patterns for multiplicities as shown in Exhibit 7.A1, remembering that those standard multiplicities could change depending on the particular circumstances of the business.

ANSWERS TO PROGRESS CHECKS

1. The collaboration model shown in Exhibit 7.4 highlights the interactions between Sunset Graphics and its customers. Exhibit 7.3 shows the sequence of activities for the sales process without identifying information coming into or out of each activity from an external party (i.e., customer).
2. The answer depends on the choice of firm. Take **Amazon.com,** for example. Amazon collects payments at the time of the order and does not invoice customers.
3. Companies that provide quotes typically build or tailor their products to the specific customer requirements compared to companies that simply sell available products.
4. The order event could be separated into orders and sales when one order could result in multiple sales or one sale could involve multiple orders.
5. The foreign key for the Customer to Cash Receipt association in Exhibit 7.21 would be posted in the Cash Receipt table.
6. The foreign key for the Orders to Cash Receipt association in Exhibit 7.21 would be posted in the Order table.

Multiple Choice Questions connect

1. **(LO 7-1)** Which of the following is not an activity within the sales and collection process?
   a. Selling products and services
   b. Billing customers
   c. Managing accounts receivable
   d. Recording payments from customers
   e. All of these options are sales and collection activities
2. **(LO 7-1)** The sales and collection process is the point of contact between the firm and which set of external business partners?
   a. Investors
   b. Customers
   c. Employees
   d. Vendors
   e. All of these options
3. **(LO 7-1)** Which of the following sales and collection process activities can result in the creation of an account receivable?
   a. Receiving a sales order from a customer
   b. Shipping ordered products to the customer
   c. Issuing a quote to the customer
   d. Recording payment from the customer
   e. None of these options
4. **(LO 7-2)** Which of the following describes message flows between pools?
   a. Orchestrations
   b. Sequence flows
   c. Choreography
   d. Intermediate events
   e. None of these options

5. **(LO 7-2, LO 7-3)** Which of the following statements is true?
   a. Each pool must have a start event.
   b. Sequence flows are shown by arrows with a dashed line.
   c. Message flows are shown by arrows with a solid line.
   d. Each pool must have more than one swimlane.
   e. Both a and b are true.
6. **(LO 7-3)** Which of the following is not a purpose of a subprocess in BPMN?
   a. Reducing complexity
   b. Presenting higher-level process descriptions
   c. Creating alternative process flows
   d. Developing a reusable model
   e. All of these options are purposes of subprocesses in BPMN
7. **(LO 7-3)** What is the purpose of an intermediate error event?
   a. Indicates a change in flow due to a process exception
   b. Indicates the end of a process
   c. Indicates the start of a collapsed subprocess
   d. Describes the activities that will occur when there is not an error
   e. None of these options
8. **(LO 7-4)** Which of the following is an example of a business rule implementing access controls?
   a. There shall be a physical count of inventory each quarter.
   b. User's recording collections cannot modify sales records.
   c. The computer system shall generate an audit trail.
   d. Internal auditors shall be used.
   e. None of these options are business rules implementing access controls.
9. **(LO 7-5)** Which of the following is not part of the REA framework?
   a. Agents
   b. Type images
   c. Resources
   d. Events
   e. Activities
10. **(LO 7-6)** How do you implement a one-to-many relationship in a relational database?
   a. Post a foreign key.
   b. Create a new table.
   c. Combine two fields to create a primary key.
   d. Create an association.
   e. None of these options.

Use this diagram to answer Questions 11 through 32.

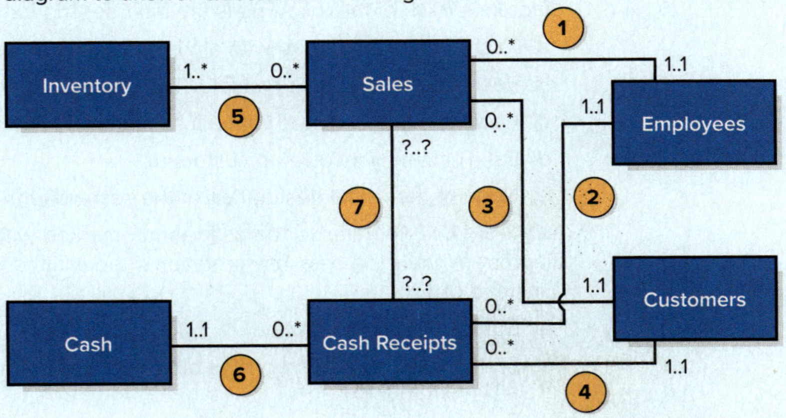

11. **(LO 7-5, LO 7-6)** Refer to the association marked with the number 1 in the preceding diagram. Which of the following is the best description of the association?
    a. Each employee participates in at least one sale.
    b. Each employee participates in a minimum of zero sales.
    c. Each employee participates in a maximum of one sale.
    d. Each employee participates in at least two sales.
    e. None of these is a description of the association.
12. **(LO 7-5, LO 7-6)** Refer to the association marked with the number 1 in the preceding diagram. Which of the following is the best description of the association?
    a. Each sale may involve multiple employees.
    b. Each sale may involve no employees.
    c. Each sale is associated with a minimum of one employee.
    d. Each sale is associated with a maximum of many employees.
    e. None of these is a description of the association.
13. **(LO 7-5, LO 7-6)** Refer to the association marked with the number 2 in the preceding diagram. Which of the following is the best description of the association?
    a. Only cashiers handle cash receipts.
    b. Each employee is associated with a maximum of one cash receipts.
    c. Each employee is associated with a maximum of many cash receipts.
    d. Each employee is associated with a minimum of one cash receipt.
    e. None of these is a description of the association.
14. **(LO 7-5, LO 7-6)** Refer to the association marked with the number 2 in the preceding diagram. Which of the following is the best description of the association?
    a. Each cash receipt may involve multiple employees.
    b. Each cash receipt may involve no employees.
    c. Each cash receipt is associated with only one employee.
    d. Each cash receipt is associated with a maximum of many employees.
    e. None of these is a description of the association.
15. **(LO 7-5, LO 7-6)** Refer to the association marked with the number 3 in the preceding diagram. Which of the following is the best description of the association?
    a. Each customer participates in a maximum of one sale.
    b. Each customer participates in at least one sale.
    c. Each customer participates in a minimum of zero sales.
    d. Each customer eventually participates in at least two sales.
    e. None of these is a description of the association.
16. **(LO 7-5, LO 7-6)** Refer to the association marked with the number 3 in the preceding diagram. Which of the following is the best description of the association?
    a. Each sale is associated with a minimum of one customer.
    b. Each sale may involve multiple customers.
    c. Each sale is associated with a maximum of many customers.
    d. Each sale may involve no customers.
    e. None of these is a description of the association.
17. **(LO 7-5, LO 7-6)** Refer to the association marked with the number 3 in the preceding diagram. What is the best interpretation if the minimum multiplicity next to Customers is 0 instead of 1?
    a. Some customers don't pay.
    b. Some customers place orders but don't pick up their items.

c. Some sales are made in cash and customer information is not recorded.

d. Some customers never buy anything.

e. None of these interprets this situation appropriately.

18. **(LO 7-5, LO 7-6)** Refer to the association marked with the number 4 in the preceding diagram. Which of the following is the best description of the association?

    a. Each customer pays in cash at the time of the sale.

    b. Each customer is associated with a maximum of many cash receipts.

    c. Each customer is associated with more than one cash receipt.

    d. Each customer is associated with a minimum of one cash receipt.

    e. None of these is a description of the association.

19. **(LO 7-5, LO 7-6)** Refer to the association marked with the number 4 in the preceding diagram. Which of the following is the best description of the association?

    a. Each cash receipt may involve no customers.

    b. Each cash receipt is associated with only one customer.

    c. Each cash receipt may involve multiple customers.

    d. Each cash receipt is associated with a maximum of many customers.

    e. None of these is a description of the association.

20. **(LO 7-5, LO 7-6)** Refer to the association marked with the number 5 in the preceding diagram. Which of the following is the best description of the association?

    a. Each sale may involve a maximum of many inventory items.

    b. Each sale may involve a minimum of zero inventory items.

    c. Each sale involves one inventory item.

    d. Each sale may involve two inventory items.

    e. None of these is a description of the association.

21. **(LO 7-4, LO 7-5)** Refer to the association marked with the number 5 in the preceding diagram. Which of the following is the best example of a business rule that constrains the association?

    a. Sales are allowed if they include at many inventory items.

    b. Sales are prohibited if they include more than one inventory item.

    c. Sales must include at least one inventory item.

    d. Sales are allowed with the manager's approval in advance.

    e. None of these is the best example of a business rule.

22. **(LO 7-5, LO 7-6)** Refer to the association marked with the number 5 in the preceding diagram. Which of the following is the best description of the association?

    a. Each inventory item must be sold at least once.

    b. Each inventory item could be sold many times.

    c. Each inventory item is associated with a minimum of one sale.

    d. Each inventory item is associated with a maximum of one sale.

    e. None of these is a description of the association.

23. **(LO 7-5, LO 7-6)** Refer to the association marked with the number 6 in the preceding diagram. Which of the following is the best description of the association?

    a. Each cash receipt is deposited into multiple cash accounts.

    b. Each cash receipt is associated with a minimum of zero cash accounts.

    c. Each cash receipt is associated with a maximum of many cash accounts.

    d. Each cash receipt is deposited into one cash account.

    e. None of these is a description of the association.

24. **(LO 7-5, LO 7-6)** Refer to the association marked with the number 6 in the preceding diagram. Which of the following is the best description of the association?
    a. Each cash account could be associated with many cash receipts.
    b. Each cash account is associated with one cash receipt.
    c. Each cash account is associated with a minimum of one cash receipt.
    d. Each cash account is associated with a maximum of one cash receipt.
    e. None of these is a description of the association.
25. **(LO 7-5, LO 7-6)** Refer to the association marked with the number 7 in the preceding diagram. Assume that customers pay for all sales in full at the end of the month. Which of the following is the multiplicity that should be found next to the cash receipts class?
    a. 0..*
    b. *..*
    c. 0..1
    d. 1..1
    e. 1..*
26. **(LO 7-5, LO 7-6)** Refer to the association marked with the number 7 in the preceding diagram. Assume that customers could be involved in many sales during the month and they pay for those sales in full at the end of the month. Which of the following is the multiplicity that should be found next to the sales class?
    a. 0..*
    b. *..*
    c. 0..1
    d. 1..1
    e. 1..*
27. **(LO 7-4, LO 7-5)** Refer to the association marked with the number 7 in the preceding diagram. Assume that customers could be involved in many sales during the month and they pay in full at the end of the month. Which of the following is the best example of a business rule that constrains the association?
    a. Customers are allowed to pay for sales on credit.
    b. Customers must pay for sales at the time of the sale.
    c. Customers are prohibited from paying for sales on credit.
    d. Customers may delay payment for a sale upon approval by the manager.
    e. None of these is an example of an appropriate business rule for the association.
28. **(LO 7-5, LO 7-6)** Refer to the association marked with the number 5 in the preceding diagram. What is the best description of the type of inventory that this company sells?
    a. High-value items such as automobiles
    b. Customized products
    c. Items identified by UPC (bar codes)
    d. Tickets to concerts
    e. None of these correctly describes the type of inventory
29. **(LO 7-5, LO 7-6, LO 7-7)** Assume you are implementing a database from the preceding diagram. How many tables would the database include?
    a. 6
    b. 7
    c. 5
    d. 4
    e. You can't tell from the information provided

30. **(LO 7-5, LO 7-6, LO 7-7)** Assume you are implementing a database from the preceding diagram. Which of these is the best way to implement the relationship identified by the number 3?
    a. Post the primary key of customers in sales as a foreign key.
    b. Post the primary key of sales in customers as a foreign key.
    c. Create a linking table between sales and customers.
    d. All of these are acceptable.
    e. None of these is acceptable.
31. **(LO 7-5, LO 7-6, LO 7-7)** Assume you are implementing a database from the preceding diagram. Which of these is the best way to implement the relationship identified by the number 6?
    a. Post the primary key of cash in cash receipts as a foreign key.
    b. Post the primary key of cash receipts in cash as a foreign key.
    c. Create a linking table between cash and cash receipts.
    d. All of these are acceptable.
    e. None of these is acceptable.
32. **(LO 7-5, LO 7-6, LO 7-7)** Assume you are implementing a database from the preceding diagram. Which of these is the best way to implement the relationship identified by the number 5?
    a. Post the primary key of sales in inventory as a foreign key.
    b. Post the primary key of inventory in sales as a foreign key.
    c. Create a linking table between sales and inventory.
    d. All of these are acceptable.
    e. None of these is acceptable.

Discussion Questions

1. **(LO 7-1)** The sales and collection process generates revenue, accounts receivable, and cash flow information for a firm's financial statements. What other information do you think managers would like to collect?
2. **(LO 7-1)** What kinds of businesses collect cash before recording the corresponding sales? How would that different sequence affect internal control requirements?
3. **(LO 7-2)** Draw a basic sales activity model using BPMN for a fast-food restaurant. Draw a second basic sales activity model using BPMN for a traditional restaurant. Discuss similarities and differences. How would you add taking reservations to the second model?
4. **(LO 7-2, LO 7-3)** Draw a collaboration diagram that shows two pools and the message flows between a fast-food restaurant and its customers. How would you change that diagram for a traditional restaurant?
5. **(LO 7-2, LO 7-3)** Draw UML class diagrams for fast-food and traditional restaurants. Discuss similarities and differences. How would you add taking reservations to the second model?
6. **(LO 7-3)** Using **Amazon.com** as an example, prepare a collaboration sales activity model. What is the difference between an online process and a traditional brick-and-mortar store process?
7. **(LO 7-4)** From your experience, think about the sales process for an online or brick-and-mortar store. Describe some business rules that help provide internal controls over that process.
8. **(LO 7-5)** What classes and associations would be included in a model that describes the information needed for a query that calculates the accounts receivable balance for each customer? Describe differences in the information for the *open-invoice method,* where customers pay according to specific invoices, versus the *balance-forward method,* where customers pay balances on monthly statements.

Problems connect

1. **(LO 7-5 , LO 7-6, LO 7-7)** The Beach Dude (BD) employs a legion of current and former surfers as salespeople who push its surfing-oriented products to various customers (usually retail outlets). This case describes BD's sales and collection process.

   Each BD salesperson works with a specific group of customers throughout the year. In fact, they often surf with their customers to try out the latest surf gear. The BD salespeople act laid-back, but they work hard for their sales. Each sale often involves hours of surfing with their customers while the customers sample all the latest surf wear. Because BD makes the best surfing products, the customers look forward to the visits from the BD salespeople, and they often buy lots of BD gear. Each sale is identified by a unique invoice number and usually involves many different products. Customers pay for each sale in full within 30 days, but they can combine payments for multiple sales.

   BD manages its clothing inventory by item (e.g., XL BD surfer logo T-shirts), identified by product number, but it also classifies the items by clothing line (the lines are differentiated by price points as well as the intended use of the clothing, e.g., surfing products, casual wear, etc.).

   Requirements:

   a. Draw a UML class diagram that describes the Beach Dude's sales and collection process.

   b. Using Microsoft Access, implement a relational database from your UML class diagram. Identify at least three fields per table.

   c. Describe how you would create queries in the relational database to determine the Beach Dude's accounts receivable.

2. **(LO 7-2, LO 7-3, LO 7-5, LO 7-6, LO 7-7)** The Bob White Karate Studio has been a local fixture for almost 40 years. The studio offers training in American Kenpo Karate to students from 3 years old to 80 years old. Students select one of several programs: (a) monthly payments, (b) semi-annual payments, or (c) the black belt program. Each of these programs allows them to take group classes as well as one or more private lessons with a qualified black belt instructor, depending on the program selected. For example, the monthly program includes one private lesson, the semi-annual program includes three private lessons, and the black belt program includes one lesson per week until the student attains black belt rank. Additionally, students may purchase additional private lessons, as well as uniforms, sparring gear, and various studio insignia and clothing items. The additional half-hour private lessons are priced as packages, which include 5, 10, 20, 40, or 60 lessons, and the price also varies depending on whether the lessons are provided by senior or junior instructors. When students purchase a package, they are assigned to a particular instructor for the duration of the package. Students pay for anything they buy at the time of their purchase by credit card. While all studio employees are also instructors, only a few employees handle sales transactions and accept payments.

   Requirements

   a. Draw a context diagram for Bob White Karate Studio's sales and collection process.

   b. Draw a basic BPMN activity diagram that describes the Bob White Karate Studio's sales and collection process.

   c. Prepare a UML class diagram with classes, associations, and multiplicities. Since all sales are paid at the time of the sale, there is no need for a separate cash receipt event. The sales event can be directly associated with the cash resource.

   d. Using the preceding narrative and the following attributes list, prepare a listing of the relational tables necessary to support Bob White Karate Studio's sales and collection process. List the tables in the following order: resources, events, agents, type images, and linking tables.

Attributes:

Cash account#
Cash account balance
Credit card number for this sale
Date sale paid
Employee/instructor#
Employee name
Employee rank
Instructor type
Inventory item#
Inventory item description
Inventory item price
Inventory item quantity on hand (QOH)
Private lesson package#
Private lesson package description
Private lesson package price
Program#
Program description
Program price
Quantity of instructors of this type
Quantity of this inventory item purchased on this sale
Sale#
Sale amount
Sale date
Sale paid (Y/N)
Student#
Student current rank
Student name
Student original enrollment date

3. **(LO 7-5, LO 7-6, LO 7-7)** Beach Rentals (BR) maintains an inventory of rental houses near universities and leases those houses primarily to student renters. This case describes their rental business process. BR agents—former marketing majors renowned for their fast-talking and flamboyant lifestyles—work with potential renters and sign the rental contracts for BR.

   BR tracks its houses by city, neighborhood, and distance from campus. BR assigns one specific BR agent to each neighborhood to manage rentals for all houses in that neighborhood, but each BR agent may be assigned to multiple neighborhoods. BR cashiers collect the rent and are bonded for security purposes. Because cashiers never become agents (or vice versa), BR tracks BR cashiers separately from BR agents, although both are identified by employee numbers.

   BR sets rental rates to its student customers by considering such matters as number of bedrooms and age of the house. Additionally, BR applies a monthly rental surcharge to each house that depends solely upon its neighborhood designation; for example, upscale neighborhoods have higher surcharges and less desirable neighborhoods have lower surcharges. The same surcharge applies for the life of the lease. Every house has a rental surcharge, and all houses in a particular neighborhood have the same surcharge.

   Prospective renters contact BR to inquire about renting a house. When a potential renter contacts BR, a BR agent is assigned to assist them. That BR agent remains the person's point of contact for as long as they continue to deal with Beach Rentals. BR records information on each potential renter as soon as they contact BR to inquire about a house.

BR agents negotiate the rental contracts with the students. Each rental contract must last at least 6 months, and 12-month contracts get a 5 percent discount. BR also charges a damage fee that is due along with the first month's rent when the rental contract is signed. The BR agent earns a 10 percent commission on each rental contract, and BR tracks the year-to-date (YTD) commission earned for each of the BR agents. Of course, the BR agents compete with one another to see who earns the highest commissions, and BR fosters the competition by giving an annual award to its "best" agent.

When multiple students want to rent one house, BR requires that they designate the primary renter—the one who will be responsible for paying the rent. However, BR also gathers information about all the other occupants of the house and designates them as secondary renters. All the renters sign the rental contract, and BR assigns a unique renter number to each occupant. The students may not change primary renter for the term of a contract. BR cashiers collect the rental payments monthly from the primary renters. BR records information concerning employees, house owners, bank accounts, cities, and neighborhoods in the database before the renters are involved in any events. Each neighborhood is located in only one city, and houses are in only one neighborhood.

Requirements:

a. Prepare a UML class diagram with classes, associations, and multiplicities.

b. Use the preceding narrative and the following attributes list to prepare a listing of the relational tables necessary to support this sales and collection process. List the tables in the following order: resources, events, agents, type images, and linking tables.

c. Using the list of relational tables prepared in (b), define the relational tables in Microsoft Access and establish the relationships among tables necessary to implement Beach Rentals' sales and collection process in Access.

Attributes:

Agent employee#
Agent name
Agent real estate license status
Bank account#
Bank account balance
Bank name and address
Cash receipt $ amount
Cash receipt#
Cashier employee#
Cashier name
City name
Damage fee
House street address
House zip code
Monthly rent
Neighborhood name
Number of bedrooms
Number of houses in this city
Rent discount for 12-month contract
Rental contract#
Rental contract begin date
Rental contract duration in months

Rental surcharge amount
Renter bank and routing numbers
Renter name
Renter number#
YTD rental commissions

Design Element: Duncan Smith/Getty Images

Chapter Eight

Purchases and Payments Business Process

A Look at This Chapter

This chapter examines the purchases and payments process. We continue the comprehensive example to develop activity and structure models of the process. We show how the activity model in conjunction with business rules can be used to develop, implement, and monitor control activities. We show how the structure model can be used to develop a relational database to support information processing requirements.

A Look Back

Chapter 7 examined the sales and collection processes. It began the comprehensive example that we use to examine typical process activities and data structures.

A Look Ahead

In Chapter 9, we examine the conversion process, whereby companies transform raw material into finished goods. We again use the basic modeling tools from Chapters 4 and 5 and database design methods presented in Chapter 6 to examine activity and structure models for the process.

Hero Images/Getty Images

In a 2002 interview,[1] David Norton, **Starbucks'** vice president of logistics, talked about its global supply chain: "Rapid global growth requires comprehensive, integrated strategies focused on the needs of our retail stores, license and joint venture partners. We have a formal process for developing both strategic and operating plans which ensures we link manufacturing, procurement, and logistics to the needs of the business."

Norton went on to describe the role of technology in a way that remains true today: "Technology has become increasingly a staple of the supply chain rather than a driver. There have been few significant advances on the physical distribution side of the supply chain in years. In the information arena, the pattern seems to be over-commit and under-deliver. Systems are generally harder, more costly, and take longer to implement than has been the promise. The evolution of systems over the past 15 years might be even characterized as a journey from homegrown proprietary systems through best-of-breed/homegrown combinations, and finally to monolithic ERP environments. And my experience is that the integrated, monolithic ERP environments simply lack the flexibility to meet unique business requirements. We believe the best place to be today is combining the best of different applications. And our IT professionals here at Starbucks are comfortable with this because of advances in business integration systems/tools that enable this approach."

Finally, describing what it takes to design and operate integrated supply chain management tools, Norton noted, "A lot of folks come into the business and don't understand that you need a solid item master, a solid price master, a solid customer master, a solid order management system, a solid inventory system—all tied in nicely with AP [accounts payable] and AR [accounts receivable]—and if you don't have any of that stuff right, you can just about forget everything else."*

Clearly, technology was—and is—important to Starbucks for the management of its supply chain. What kinds of information do you think Starbucks needs to manage and improve its supply chain?

1&*Source: Reported January 1, 2002, www.SupplyChainBrain.com.

CHAPTER OUTLINE

LEARNING OBJECTIVES

After reading this chapter, you should be able to:

8-1 Describe the business activities that constitute the purchase and payment process.

8-2 Develop an activity model of the purchase and payment process using BPMN.

8-3 Understand and apply different activity modeling options.

8-4 Develop business rules to implement controls for the purchase and payment process.

8-5 Develop structure models for the purchase and payment process using UML class diagrams.

8-6 Implement a relational database from the UML class diagram of the purchase and payment process.

LO 8-1

Describe the business activities that constitute the purchase and payment process.

PURCHASES AND PAYMENTS PROCESS

The purchases and payments process includes business activities related to buying inventory from **suppliers**, maintaining supplier records, and making payments to suppliers for trade accounts payable while taking appropriate **purchase discounts**. The purchases and payments process generates accounting transactions to record **purchases**, **accounts payable**, and **cash disbursements**. The process also affects inventory values as purchases are added to inventory. Exhibit 8.1 describes typical transactions resulting from the purchases and payments process.

EXHIBIT 8.1
Accounting Transactions for Purchases and Payments Process

Oct 1	**Purchases (or Inventory)***	**1,495.50**	
	Accounts Payable		**1,495.50**
	Purchased inventory on credit from Richardson & Sons, Inc.		
	Invoice 1125 dated Oct 1, terms 2/10, net 30.		
Oct 11	**Accounts Payable**	**1,495.50**	
	Purchase Discounts		**29.91**
	Cash		**1,465.59**
	Paid Richardson & Sons, Inc. for Invoice 1125 dated Oct 1		
	less 2% discount		

*Debit to Purchases or Inventory accounts depends on whether the company uses a periodic or perpetual inventory system.

We will apply the tools introduced in Chapters 4, 5, 6, and 7 to a comprehensive example of the purchases and payments process. We first describe the process activities using BPMN, and then we define the typical information structure using UML class diagrams. Finally, we use the UML class diagrams to build a database to collect and report relevant process information. We also describe business rules that establish potential process controls.

SUNSET GRAPHICS EXAMPLE

Company Overview

As described in Chapter 7, Virgil owns and operates Sunset Graphics. The company designs and sells signs and banners, lettering and vinyl graphics for vehicles and boats, corporate promotional items, and silk-screened t-shirts and embroidered gear, among other products. Recently, Virgil decided that it was time to review his business processes to develop better documentation, improve processes, and establish consistency in customer service. He also wanted to be sure that effective internal controls were in place. This comprehensive example assumes that we are business analysts who are helping Virgil accomplish these goals.

Sunset Graphics' Purchases and Payments Process Description

Virgil does most of the buying and also pays most of the bills for Sunset, so he explained the process. When Sunset needs to purchase items, it usually follows a straightforward process:

1. Research prices and product availability.
2. Select the best price and availability combination, and send a **purchase order** to the supplier.
3. Receive the items from the supplier (and record the purchase and accounts payable).
4. Pay the supplier according to the credit terms.

LO 8-2

Develop an activity model of the purchase and payment process using BPMN.

SUNSET GRAPHICS' ACTIVITY MODELS

Basic Purchases Activity Model

Virgil was more familiar with the process now, and he understood the value of business process models and a structure process to develop those models. First, we again identify the purpose of the business process model, and that is to document Sunset Graphics purchases and payments process. Second, we define the context for this process, identifying the external participants and the exchanges between Sunset Graphics and those participants. Exhibit 8.2 illustrates the context based on Virgil's description. The process is fairly typical. Sunset Graphics requests prices and availability of products from its vendors, but that part is informal, so we will leave that out of the model. The process starts when they issue purchase orders, then receive the items, and ends when they pay for the items.

EXHIBIT 8.2
Sunset Graphics Purchases Context

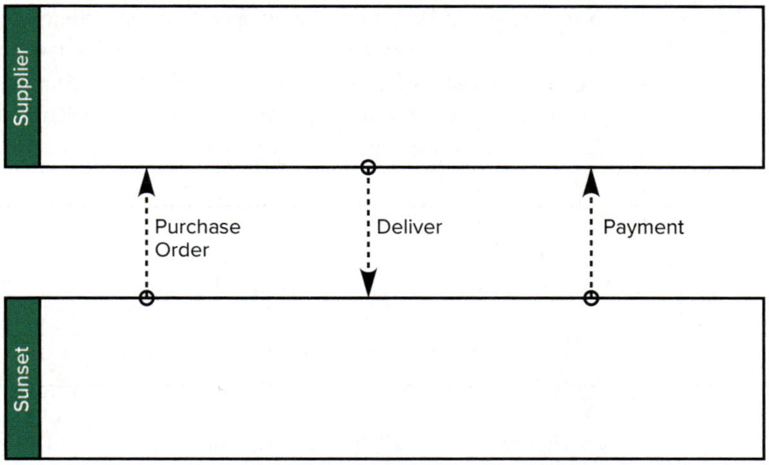

Third, we draw a basic business process model using BPMN. As shown in Exhibit 8.3, the start of the process occurs when Sunset needs to purchase items to fulfill a customer order or to replenish inventory. Then, a series of tasks takes place in sequence until Sunset pays for the items and the process ends. Sunset records purchases and updates inventory when it receives the items. It records cash disbursements when it sends the payment.

EXHIBIT 8.3
Basic Purchases Activity Model

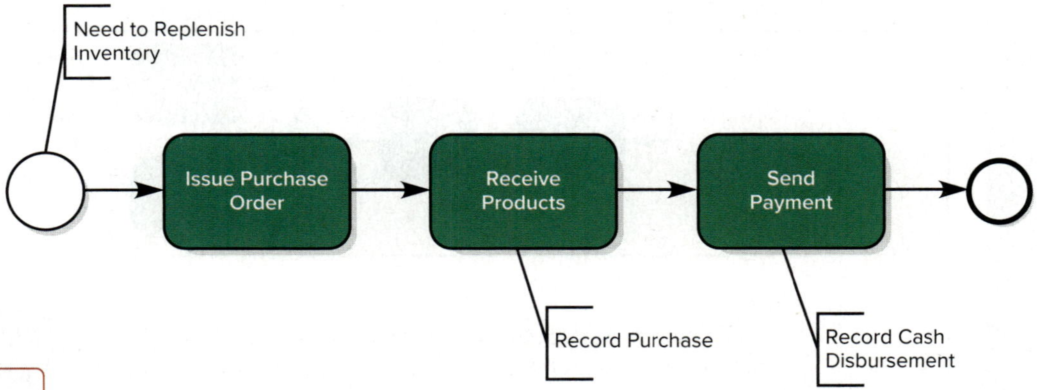

LO 8-3

Understand and apply different activity modeling options.

Refining the Model to Show Collaboration

The next steps in the process involve defining activities and refining the model. Virgil was starting to understand these models. He remarked that he liked the **collaboration** model because it shows the interactions with the external parties that Sunset relies on. So, he asked if we could prepare a collaboration model of the purchases and payments process. Of course, we said we could. In this case, the *pools* would show suppliers and Sunset, with *message flows* (shown by dashed arrows) between pools describing the interaction between participants, like the context diagram in Exhibit 8.2.

Virgil liked the choreography of interactions between the pools, but he reminded us that as Sunset grows, other employees would perform the buying and bill paying in the future. Because he was delegating those jobs, he thought that he should separate the buying duties from the payment duties for better internal control. He wondered if we could also differentiate jobs within Sunset. We reminded him about lanes in BPMN that allow us to model those different jobs. Virgil said that was exactly what was needed. Showing the different jobs would provide better process documentation and highlight the segregation of duties.

Virgil also noted that sometimes Sunset does not get acceptable items from the supplier. Sometimes, the entire shipment is unacceptable, but mostly, there are a few items in the shipment that do not meet specifications. So, Sunset can refuse the entire shipment or return the unacceptable items to the supplier. Also, Sunset waits 30 days before sending payment. He asked if we could include those changes to the process in the model. We prepared Exhibit 8.4 to show him a model with lanes that also allows for the return of deficient items and a delay in payment.

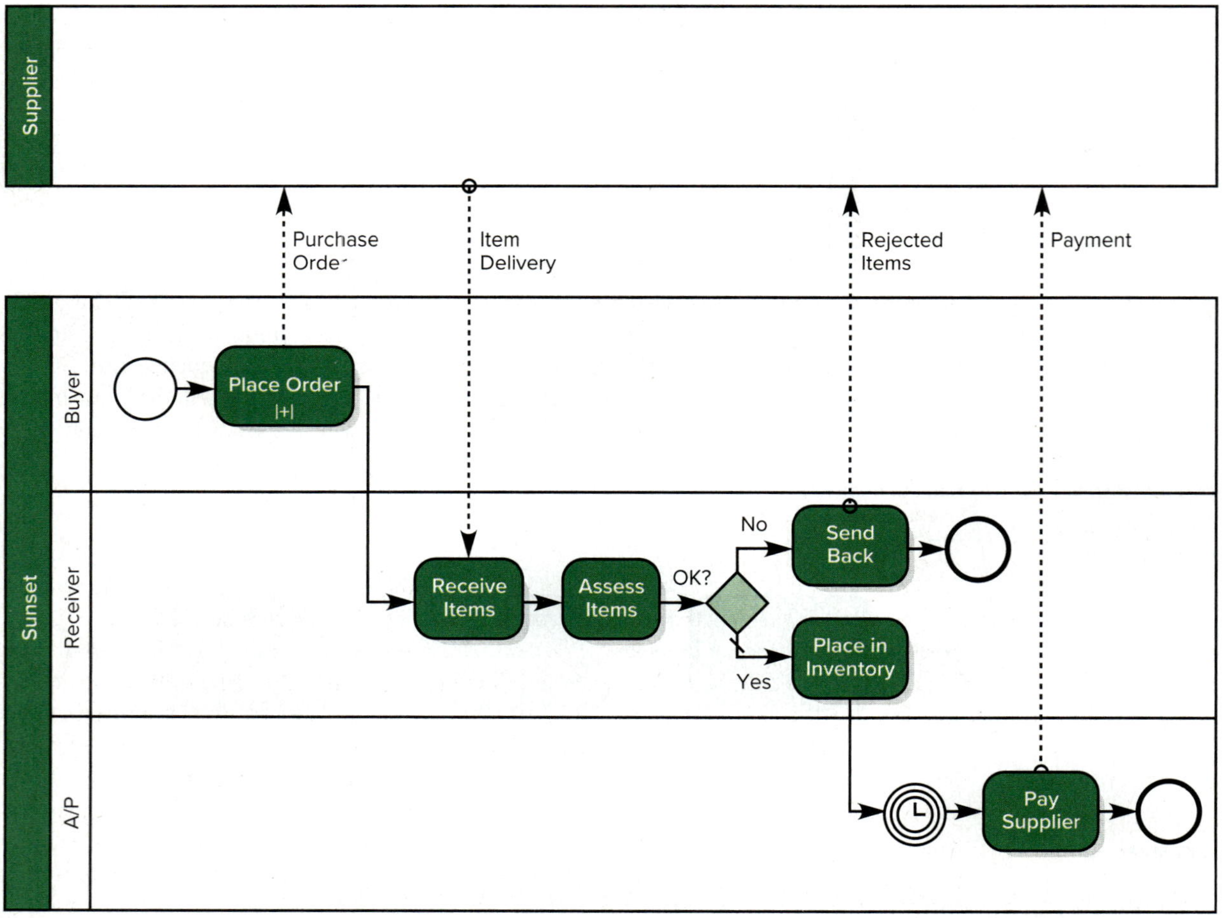

EXHIBIT 8.4
Expanded Collaboration Purchases Activity Model with Lanes

In Exhibit 8.4, we included lanes for the buyer, receiving, and accounts payable (A/P) jobs that will exist at Sunset after Virgil delegates those duties. We replaced the "Issue Purchase Order" activity in the original model shown in Exhibit 8.2 with a collapsed **subprocess** to reflect the interactions with suppliers to get prices and product availability before issuing the purchase order. We also added another step to assess the items after receiving them from the supplier. Then, we included a **gateway** to branch into two possible courses of action. If the items are not acceptable, Sunset returns them to the supplier and the process ends. If the items are acceptable, they are placed in inventory; 30 days later (depending on credit terms), Sunset sends a payment to the supplier. The slash across the sequence flow indicates the default path. Because there are two possible paths that do not reconnect, we include two end events.

We added some new notation to the diagram. The gateway, modeled with the diamond, indicates branching into two exclusive paths. We noted that with BPMN 2.0, gateways don't represent activity, so we include the activity, "Assess Items," before the gateway. We also included an **intermediate timer event** (the **intermediate event** symbol with clock hands) to represent the time delay before payment. **Timer events** represent a delay in the flow of a process. They can indicate a delay to (1) a specific date, such as December 31; (2) a relative time, such as 30 days; or (3) a relative repetitive date, such as next Friday at 5:00 p.m. As always, the *sequence flow* must be continuous from the *start event* to an *end event.* Remember that *sequence flows* do not extend outside a pool. *Message flows* connect pools. Because we elected to make the Supplier pool opaque, we connected the *message flows* to the edge of the pool. Otherwise, they would connect to an *activity* or *event* in the Supplier pool.

PROGRESS CHECK

1. In Exhibit 8.4, at what point would Sunset record the purchase?
2. From your own experience, describe how you would change Exhibit 8.4 to reflect another purchases and payments process. What if the customer purchased over the Internet and paid by credit card?

Refining the Model for Credit Card Payments

Virgil added that Sunset started using its business credit card for making routine purchases. So, the buyer makes the payment when the order is placed. The rest of the process is similar. Sunset receives and assesses items, sends back any unacceptable items for refund, and places the good items in inventory. We modified the purchases activity model as shown in Exhibit 8.5. Now Sunset makes both the order and payment at the same time at the beginning of the process, and there is no need for a separate payment activity at the end of the process. We also changed the "Send Back" activity to a *collapsed subprocess* since Sunset must follow up to ensure a refund to their credit card account. Virgil thought this looked correct, although he noted that this diagram clearly shows potential internal control issues, such as lack of segregation of duties. The same person is placing the order and making the payment. We replied that he was correct, but the receipt and storage of the items are assigned to another function. That should mitigate the risk. He may also want to consider an internal audit process that verifies all orders are received and all charges to the Sunset credit card are valid.

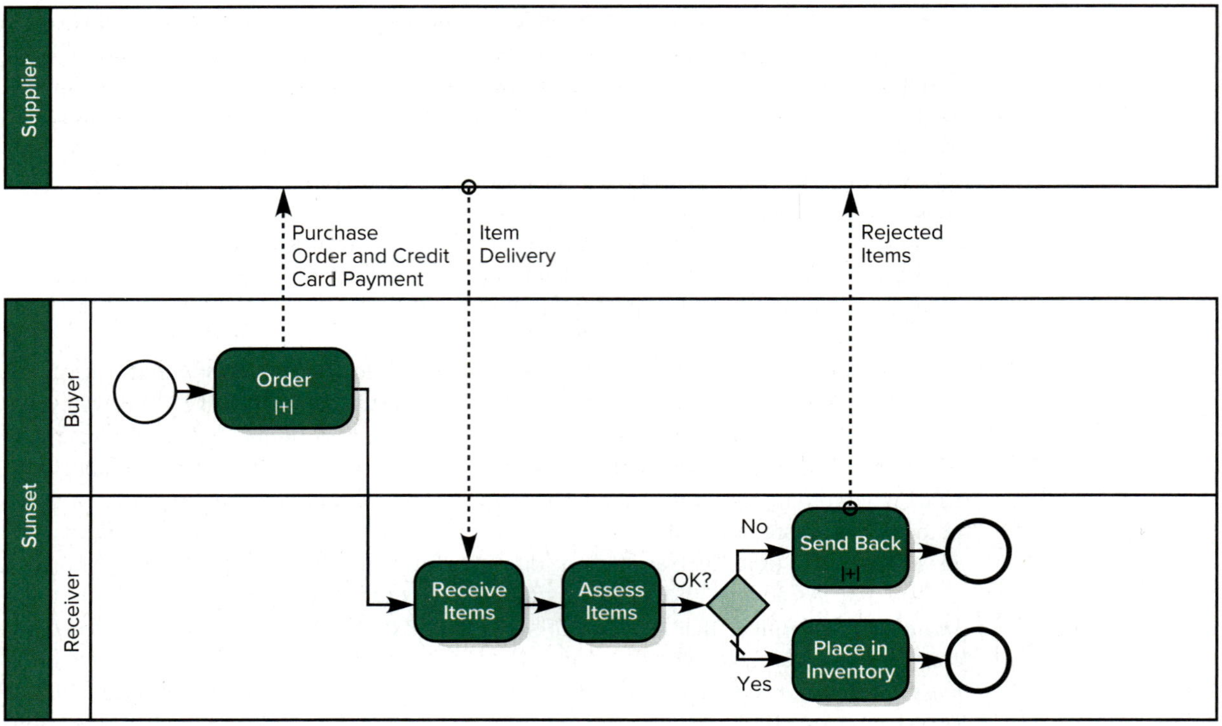

EXHIBIT 8.5
Purchases Model with Credit Card Payments

LO 8-4

Develop business rules to implement controls for the purchase and payment process.

PLANNING AND IMPLEMENTING PURCHASES AND PAYMENTS PROCESS CONTROLS

Next, we wanted to talk about planning controls over the purchases and payments process to give Virgil more confidence in the integrity of the process when they stepped back from the day-to-day operations. He remembered our discussion from the sales and collection process about using models and business rules to plan and implement internal controls. He was thinking about preventive, detective, and corrective controls. He suggested that the segregation of duties we documented in Exhibit 8.4 could be a preventive control. We agreed. He then wondered what control he could use when Sunset paid by credit card. We suggested that all the credit card payments should be properly authorized and tied to purchase orders as a preventive control. Then, there should be a process for reconciling credit card payments with purchase orders and receiving reports as a detective control. When any irregularities or errors are noted, then the employees should be disciplined or retrained as corrective controls.

Adding new purchases to inventory.
Alistair Berg/Getty Images

Since Virgil was delegating responsibility for purchase activities, it was important to establish and communicate relevant business rules, First, we need to identify important business events and define Sunset's intention or objective for each event. Then, we determine the appropriate actions to take based on the conditions. For example, let's examine Sunset's purchases and payments process in Exhibit 8.4 and develop some possible business rules to implement internal controls.

Virgil summarized objectives for each step in the process. Of course, the overall goal was to purchase needed items from reliable suppliers at the best possible prices to meet required delivery schedules. Sunset also wants these suppliers to be paid on time, taking prompt payment discounts where appropriate, so they could maintain positive, long-term relationships.

We outlined some standard controls over the purchases and payments process, suggesting segregation of ordering, receiving, and payment duties. Since Sunset's purchase process relied on its computer system, we discussed important access and application controls to ensure system integrity. We reiterated that *access controls* limit which of their partners can view and change records in the system and help implement appropriate segregation of duties. We also need *application controls* to ensure data integrity and an audit trail. For example, we need to control the assignment of purchase order and receiving report numbers to make sure all of them are accounted for. Plus, we need to establish appropriate ranges or limits for each value that Sunset's employees can add or change in the system.

With Virgil's direction, we developed an initial set of business rules for the purchases and payments process. He articulated intentions for every step in the process, and then we set business rules to segregate duties and limit partner authority appropriately. Exhibit 8.6 shows the initial set of business rules for Sunset's purchases and payments process. We noted that we would need to set application controls for almost every attribute updated during data entry.

Process Steps	Intention	Employee Authority/Action	Access Controls	Application Controls
Place Order	Order products from reliable suppliers at the best available prices to meet required delivery time.	Manager approval required for orders >$5,000; employee ordering products must not manage inventory.	Employee preparing purchase orders cannot modify product inventory records, receive items, or pay suppliers.	System must provide purchase order number control, default values, and range and limit checks and must create an audit trail.
Receive Items	Record receipt of items promptly and accurately.	Employee receiving items must not be same employee who ordered the items.	Employee receiving items cannot modify purchase orders or inventory records; they cannot view purchase order information regarding quantity ordered.	System must only allow employee to enter the number of items received, subject to range and limit checks on quantities received; date of receipt defaults to current date.
Assess Items	Reject defective items; record acceptance promptly and accurately.	Employee assessing items must not be same employee who ordered the items.	Employee assessing items cannot modify purchase orders or inventory records.	System must only allow employee to record the assessment; date of assessment defaults to current date.
Place in Inventory	Place accepted items in proper inventory locations promptly.	Employee placing the items in inventory must not be same employee who ordered the items.	Employee placing items in inventory cannot modify purchase orders.	System must specify where items are to be placed.
Send Items Back	Return defective items to suppliers promptly.	Manager approval required for defective items return.	Employee returning items cannot modify supplier information.	System must supply supplier return address.
Pay Supplier	Pay suppliers accurately, taking cost-effective discount terms.	Employee making payment must not be employee who ordered items or received/ accepted items.	Employee making payments cannot modify purchase orders and receipt/ acceptance records.	System must supply supplier payment information and amount of payment; payment date defaults to current date.

EXHIBIT 8.6
Using Business Rules to Implement Internal Controls

LO 8-5

Develop structure models for the purchase and payment process using UML class diagrams.

SUNSET GRAPHICS' STRUCTURE MODELS

Virgil seemed pleased with the business process models so far. However, he was also interested in planning Sunset's new database system. He'd already set up the sales and collection tables in Access, and he was waiting for the purchases and payments model so he could set up these tables, too. We proceeded to examine Sunset Graphics' purchases and payments information requirements. As described in Chapter 5, the primary purpose of our UML class diagram of the purchases and payments process is to create a blueprint for the development of a relational database to support the collection, aggregation, and communication of process information. As in Chapter 7, we follow the **REA** framework (**resources**, **events**, and **agents**) as a proven approach to describing business processes in a way that meets both accounting and broad management information requirements. See Appendix A to this chapter for a description of the generic REA framework for purchases and payments.

Basic UML Class Diagram for Purchases and Payments

Next, we prepared a UML class model for Sunset's purchases and payments process based on what Virgil described. A Sunset Employee (*agent*) selects the Supplier (*agent*) and issues a Purchase Order (*event*) as indicated by the number 1 on Exhibit 8.7. The Purchase Order specifies the prices and quantities of Products (*resource*) ordered. The Supplier (*agent*) sends and a Sunset Employee (*agent*) receives (Receipts *event*) the products (*resource*) as indicated by the number 2 on Exhibit 8.7. The **receipt** triggers the recognition of the purchase and the corresponding account payable in the accounting records. Then, when the payment is due, a Sunset Employee (agent) pays (cash disbursement event) the Supplier (agent) from a Cash account (resource) as indicated by the number 3 on Exhibit 8.7.[2] The payment reduces accounts payable.

EXHIBIT 8.7
Basic UML Class Diagram for Purchases and Payments

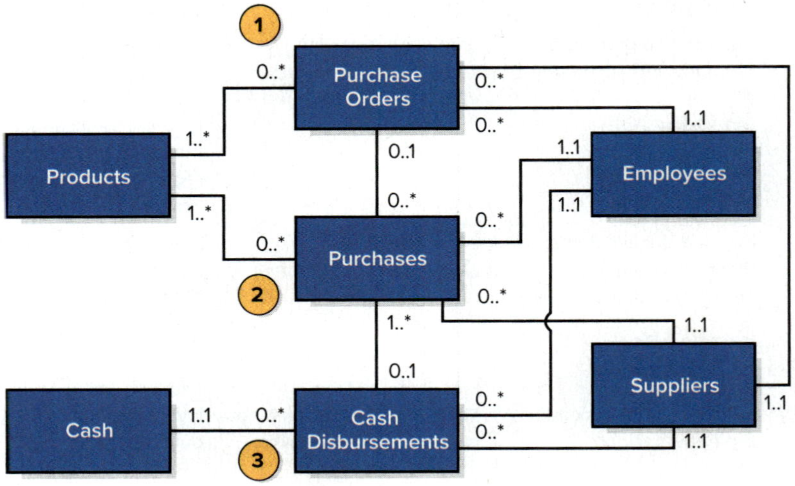

We showed Virgil the basic model, and he noticed that this model looked very similar to the sales and collection process model. Although the events were different, the resources and the Sunset Partner agent were the same. We said that this was a typical purchases and payments process. We always start with this basic diagram when we model the purchases and payments process, and then we modify it to reflect the unique information structure of a particular company. The Purchase Orders event represents Sunset's commitment to purchase **products** and pay the supplier, although commitments do not affect the financial statements.

[2]Note that UML class diagrams reflect data structure and do not necessarily reflect the sequence of events.

The Purchases event does affect the financial statements because it records the purchase for those items received and accepted and records the increases to accounts payable. The Cash Disbursement event also affects financial statements because it records decreases to **cash** and decreases to accounts payable.

Virgil said that he thought he understood multiplicities pretty well from our sales and collection process models, but he wanted to review a couple of them to make sure. For example, the multiplicities for the association between Purchase Orders and Products specify a **many-to-many relationship**. Each purchase order requests a minimum of one and a maximum of many products, and each product might not yet have been ordered and could be ordered many times.[3] We said that was correct but asked Virgil to explain the multiplicities for the Purchase Orders to Purchases association. He thought about it for a minute because he was not sure why a Purchase Order could be associated with multiple Receipts or why a Receipt could be related to a minimum of 0 Purchase Orders. We answered that we thought some Receipts were purchased over-the-counter from suppliers without first issuing a Purchase Order. Additionally, we thought that some Purchase Orders could result in partial shipments from the Supplier. Virgil responded that he could see how the model reflected those assumptions, but our assumptions were not correct. He said that Sunset always records a Purchase Order, even for over-the-counter purchases, and does not accept partial shipments.

Refining the UML Class Diagram for Purchases and Payments

Because Virgil said that Sunset always records Purchase Orders for a purchase and never accepts partial shipments, we revised the diagram. Because there is always a **one-to-one relationship** between Purchase Orders and Receipts, we can collapse the two classes into one and simplify the diagram (even though receipts happen after the orders). The new Purchases (event) class in Exhibit 8.8 would record purchase orders and include an attribute to indicate that the products were received. Because a different employee places the purchase order than receives the shipment, we need to include two associations between employees and purchase orders.

EXHIBIT 8.8
Revised UML Class Diagram for Purchases and Payments

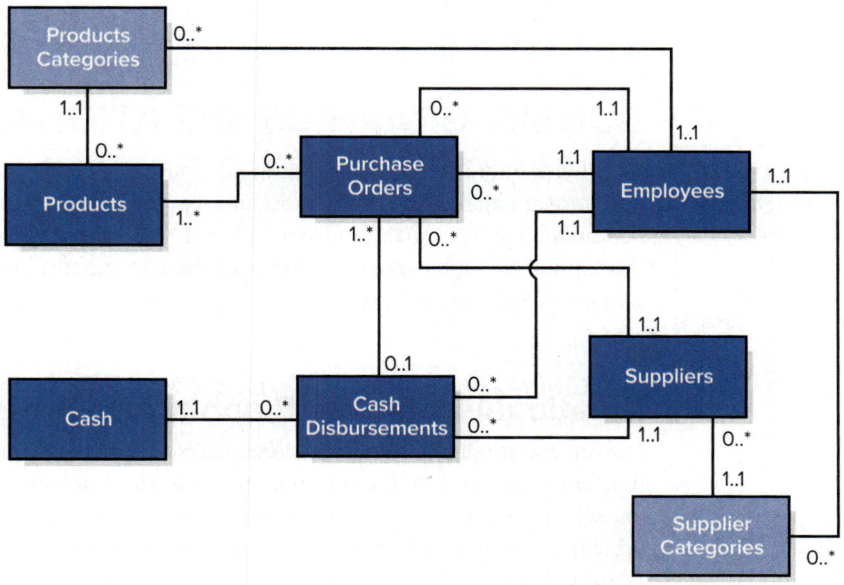

[3]We assume that products are identified before they are ordered.

The corresponding purchase orders table would have to include a field/attribute that reflects the date of receipt and acceptance.

Each Purchase is associated with a minimum of 0 and a maximum of 1 Cash Disbursement because Sunset usually pays for purchases 30 days after receipt and pays in full. Each Cash Disbursement is associated with a minimum of 0 and a maximum of many Purchases because Sunset writes checks for other purposes and combines payments for multiple purchases from the same supplier when possible.

We added the **type image** for Product Categories that we also identified in the sales and collection process. We also added the association between Sunset Employees and Product Categories to reflect the assignment association that we identified in the sales and collection process. Virgil then said that he was really starting to understand UML class diagrams. He said that Sunset also categorizes their suppliers, so he suggested that we add a type image for Supplier Categories. We also added an association between Employees and Supplier Categories, since purchasing employees work with specific categories of suppliers.

Virgil agreed that Exhibit 8.8 accurately reflected his purchases and payments process. He also correctly noted that this model would also accommodate the credit card purchases where Sunset made payments when the order was placed. He was anxious to get started on defining the database. He recognized the composition association between Purchases and Purchase Items reflected by the many-to-many relationship between Purchases and Products. He said he understood how to post the foreign keys (see Chapters 5 and 6).

PROGRESS CHECK

3. Describe when you would define two events—purchase orders and purchases—instead of combining them.
4. Review Exhibit 8.8, and explain when you might consider an association between Product Categories and Supplier Categories.

LO 8-6

Implement a relational database from the UML class diagram of the purchases and payments process.

SUNSET GRAPHICS' RELATIONAL DATABASE

Virgil was interested in implementing the purchases and payments UML class diagram in a relational database for Sunset. Again, we use Microsoft Access, but the process would be similar for any database-driven system. We encourage students to use the following description to implement a relational database to support information requirements for the purchases and payments process.

Relational Database Planning for Attributes

During the model development process, we reviewed Sunset's existing documents to determine specific data requirements for each class/table. We then followed the guidance in Chapter 5 to determine allocation of foreign keys. This resulted in a list of tables, attributes, data types, field sizes, and primary and foreign keys as shown in Exhibit 8.9.

PK/FK	Attribute Name	Type	Size
	Table: tblBankAccounts		
PK	Account_number	Text	10
	Bank_routing_number	Text	10
	Bank_balance	Currency	8
	Bank_name	Text	15
	Bank_branch	Text	15
	Bank_phone_number	Text	15
	Table: tblCashDisbursements		
PK	Check_Number	Text	10
	Check_Amount	Currency	8
	Check_Date	Date/Time	8
FK	Supplier_Number	Text	10
FK	Account_Number	Text	10
FK	Partner_Number	Text	10
	Table: tblEmployees		
PK	Employees_number	Text	10
	Employees_first_name	Text	15
	Employees_last_name	Text	15
	Employees_hire_date	Date/Time	8
	Employees_SocSecNo	Text	11
	Employees_Address	Text	50
	Employees_Address2	Text	50
	Employees_City	Text	20
	Employees_State	Text	2
	Employees_Zip	Text	10
	Employees_phone	Text	14
	Employees_cellphone	Text	14
	Table: tblProductCategory		
PK	Product_category_number	Text	10
	Product_category_description	Text	255
	Product_category_manager	Text	10
	Product_category_notes	Memo	—
	Table: tblProducts		
PK	Product_number	Text	10
	Product_description	Text	255
	Product_price	Currency	8
	Product_unit_of_sale	Text	10

PK/FK	Attribute Name	Type	Size
FK	Product_category	Text	10
	Product_quantity_on_hand	Integer	2
	Product_notes	Memo	—
	Table: tblPurchaseItems		
PK	Purchase_Order_number	Text	10
PK	Product_number	Text	10
	Purchase_Order_quantity	Integer	2
	Purchase_Order_price	Currency	8
	Received_quantity	Integer	2
	Accepted_quantity	Integer	2
	Table: tblPurchases		
PK	Purchase_Order_Number	Text	10
	Purchase_Order_Date	Date/Time	8
FK	Prepared_by	Text	10
FK	Supplier_Number	Text	10
	Received_Date	Date/Time	8
	Purchase_Order_Amount	Currency	8
	Required_by	Date/Time	8
FK	Check_Number	Text	10
	Memo	Memo	—
	Table: tblSupplierCategory		
PK	Supplier_category_number	Text	10
	Supplier_category_description	Text	255
	Supplier_category_purchases_YTD*	Currency	8
	Supplier_category_notes	Memo	—
	Table: tblSuppliers		
PK	Supplier_Number	Text	15
	Supplier_Name	Text	25
	Supplier_Contact_Name	Text	20
	Supplier_Address	Text	30
	Supplier_Address_2	Text	30
	Supplier_City	Text	20
	Supplier_State	Text	2
	Supplier_Zip	Text	5
	Supplier_phone	Text	15
	Supplier_website	Hyperlink	—
FK	Supplier_Category	Text	10

*Year to date

EXHIBIT 8.9
Sunset Database Table and Attribute Definitions

Creating the Database and Defining the Tables

The next step is to create a new, blank Microsoft Access database and create the tables described in Exhibit 8.8. Then, establish *relationships* between the tables as shown in Exhibit 8.10 and as described in Chapter 7 for the sales and collection process. At that point, Sunset's purchases and payments process database is set up.

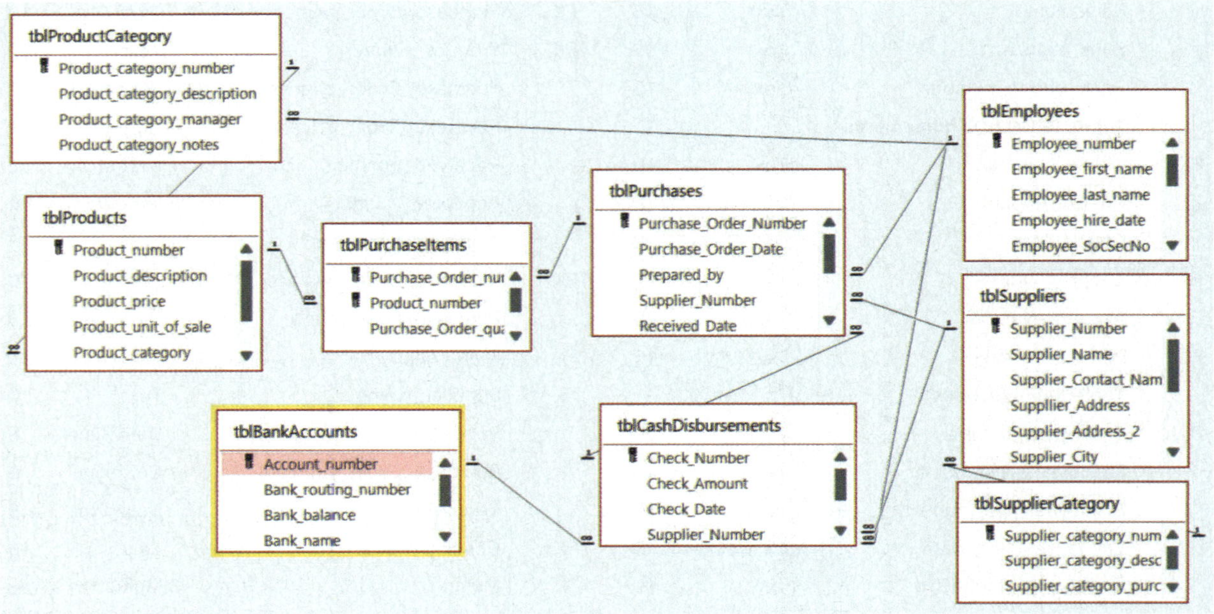

EXHIBIT 8.10
Linked Tables with Referential Integrity Enforced

Microsoft Access

Review Exercise: Baer Belly Bikinis' Purchases

This review exercise examines the purchases process for Baer Belly Bikinis Incorporated (BBB). As outlined in Chapter 7, BBB is a small business located in Santa Monica, California. It sells swimwear and related products to specialty stores throughout the United States. It also sells its products to individuals over a company website. Paige Baer founded BBB almost 10 years ago after she graduated from the Fashion Institute of Design and Merchandising. She recognized the need for swimsuits sold as separates. Her business has grown rapidly, and now BBB has a large following of customers who want to be able to mix and match to find their ideal swimsuit. Currently, BBB products are carried in more than 1,000 specialty swimwear boutiques and online retailers.

During an initial interview with Paige Baer, she outlined BBB's business processes. She acknowledged that she doesn't know much about accounting and information technology. As the business grew, her accounting suffered and information systems were added piecemeal, although she recently converted her swimsuit manufacturing to a completely automated process. So, she is looking forward to an assessment of her requirements and recommendations that would position BBB for substantial further growth.

This review exercise examines BBB purchases of fabric. BBB's production staff selects the fabric and materials for the swimsuits. BBB works closely with local fabric vendors to determine the color themes for each season's products. At the beginning of the summer swimsuit season, BBB estimates the quantity of swimsuits and products to manufacture. It then orders the required quantities of fabric and related materials from the fabric vendors. BBB pays each fabric vendor promptly (usually about 2 weeks). For each fabric order, there is one receipt. For each receipt of fabric, there is one order. Consequently, the order and purchases (receipts) events can be modeled as one event. This exercise also examines BBB purchases of miscellaneous supplies and services, such as the building lease, utilities, janitorial services, and shipping costs.

BBB Purchases of Fabric

Assessing fabric purchase requirements.

mavo/Shutterstock

Fabric Purchase Process

1. The Production supervisor places an order for fabric according to internal estimates of production quantities (the estimates are not part of the project).
2. Fabric vendors ship fabric in bulk to BBB usually within 2 weeks of the order.
3. A Shipping and Warehouse employee receives the bulk fabric and verifies quantities received.

BBB Miscellaneous Purchases

BBB also purchases miscellaneous services and supplies, such as utilities and janitorial services. It also makes monthly lease payments for its building, purchases office supplies, hires photo shoot models and photographers, and so on. BBB automatically pays its lessor on the 1st of each month. For routine expenses, such as utilities, janitorial services, and photo shoots, it assigns a purchase# to each invoice and then pays the vendor within about 2 weeks. BBB sometimes combines payments if it receives multiple invoices from one vendor during the month.

BBB Cash Disbursements

BBB assigns sequential numbers to each check issued. All checks for purchases (both fabric and miscellaneous) are written on its main bank account.

Exercise Requirements

1. Based on the preceding information, follow the steps outlined in Chapter 4 to create a business model that describes BBB's purchases process.
   a. The purpose of the model is to describe BBB's current purchase processes in preparation for business expansion.
   b. Develop a context diagram for BBB purchases that involves three participants: BBB, Fabric Vendors, and Miscellaneous Vendors, and the message flows between participants.
   c. Prepare a BPMN diagram showing the basic process flows.
   d. Next, define the activities, refine the model adding detail, and validate the model with stakeholders (your fellow students and instructor).
2. Based on the BBB process description and the attributes list at the end of the exercise, prepare a UML class diagram for BBB's purchases.
3. Use the UML class diagram to create an Access database. Your instructor will provide an Excel spreadsheet with the BBB information. Create a new Access database and import each worksheet in the spreadsheet into the database. Set appropriate primary keys and establish relationships among tables.

4. Use the Access database to create queries to determine the value of BBB's fabric purchases, miscellaneous purchases, total purchases, and cash disbursements during the 2nd quarter. Then, create queries to determine the change in BBB's accounts payable (total fabric plus miscellaneous purchases less total cash disbursements) during the 2nd calendar quarter.
5. Refer back to BBB's sales to retailers in Chapter 7. Create an integrated UML class diagram that shows both BBB's sales to retailers and BBB's fabric purchases. To reduce complexity, omit the miscellaneous purchases.

Attribute Listing for BBB

Bank Name
Cash Account#
Cash Account Balance Beginning (April 1)
Cash Account Description
Check#
Check Amount
Check Date
Employee#
Employee Address
Employee City
Employee Department
Employee First Name
Employee Hire Date
Employee Last Name
Employee Pay Amount
Employee Phone
Employee Salary/Wage
Employee Zip
Fabric Color Code
Fabric Color Name
Fabric Cost per Yard
Fabric Inventory Quantity on Hand
Fabric Purchase Date Received
Fabric Purchase Order#
Fabric Purchase Order Date
Fabric Purchase Quantity in Yards
Fabric Purchase Received By
Fabric Purchase Total Amount
Fabric Vendor#
Fabric Vendor Address1
Fabric Vendor Address2
Fabric Vendor Company
Fabric Vendor Item Number
Fabric Vendor State
Fabric Vendor Type
Fabric Vendor Zip
Miscellaneous Purchase#
Miscellaneous Purchase Amount
Miscellaneous Purchase Date
Miscellaneous Purchasing Employee#
Miscellaneous Vendor#
Miscellaneous Vendor Address1
Miscellaneous Vendor Address2
Miscellaneous Vendor Company
Miscellaneous Vendor Item Number
Miscellaneous Vendor State
Miscellaneous Vendor Zip
Order Employee# (hint: foreign key)
Pay Employee# (hint: foreign key)

Summary

- From an accounting standpoint, we must account for purchase orders, the receipt of goods and services (purchases), accounts payable, and cash disbursements (payments) in the purchases and payments process.
- Sunset Graphics Inc. provides a continuing example of how the purchases and payments process is modeled.

- BPMN activity diagrams can provide the basic sequence of tasks or can be extended to describe specific organizational responsibilities for tasks.
- Business rules implement controls over the purchases and payments process.
- UML class diagrams for the purchases and payments process are built on the standard REA pattern and look very similar to sales and collection process structure diagrams.
- Type images categorize information about agents and resources and show assignments.
- The structure models are the blueprint from which relational databases are designed and implemented.
- A comprehensive review exercise reinforces the concepts presented in the chapter.

Key Words

accounts payable (*324*) Amounts owed to suppliers for goods and services received. In a data modeling context, accounts payable are calculated based on receipts (purchases) from each supplier less the corresponding payments (cash disbursements) to those suppliers.

agents (*330*) The people or organizations, such as customers or salespeople, who participate in business events.

cash (*331*) The organization's monies in bank or related accounts. The instances of the class are individual accounts. This is considered a resource.

cash disbursements (*324*) Payments of cash to external agents (e.g., suppliers) and the corresponding reduction in cash accounts. This is considered an event.

collaboration (*325*) A BPMN model showing two participant pools and the interactions between them within a process.

events (*330*) (UML) classes that model the organization's transactions, usually affecting the organization's resources, such as sales and cash receipts; (BPMN) important occurrences that affect the flow of activities in a business process, including start, intermediate, and end events.

gateway (*327*) A BPMN symbol that shows process branching and merging as the result of decisions. Basic gateways are depicted as diamonds. Usually, gateways appear as pairs on the diagram. The first gateway shows the branching, and the second gateway shows merging of the process branches.

intermediate event (*327*) An event that occurs between start and end events and affects the flow of the process.

intermediate timer event (*327*) Intermediate events that indicate a delay in the normal process flow until a fixed amount of time has elapsed.

many-to-many relationship (*331*) Relationship that exists when instances of one class (e.g., sales) are related to many instances of another class (e.g., inventory) and vice versa. These relationships are implemented in Access and relational databases by adding a linking table to convert the many-to-many relationship into two one-to-many relationships.

one-to-one relationship (*331*) Exists when instances of one class (e.g., sales) are related to only one instance of another class (e.g., cash receipts) and each instance of the other class is related to only one instance of the original class.

product (*330*) Class representing the organization's goods held for sale—that is, the organization's inventory. This is considered a resource.

purchase discount (*324*) An offer from the supplier to reduce the cost of a purchase if payment is made according to specified terms, usually within a specified time.

purchase order (*324*) A commitment event that precedes the economic purchase event. It records formal offers to suppliers to pay them if the supplier complies with the terms of the purchase order.

purchases (*324*) Goods or services received from a supplier with a corresponding obligation to pay the supplier. These are considered events.

REA (*330*) Resource-event-agent framework for modeling business processes, originally developed by William McCarthy.

receipt (*330*) Same as the purchases event.

resources (*330*) Those things that have economic value to a firm, such as cash and products.

subprocess (*327*) A series of process steps that are hidden from view in BPMN. The use of subprocesses in modeling helps reduce complexity.

suppliers (*324*) In the UML diagram of the purchases and payments process, the external agents from whom goods and services are purchased and to whom payments are made.

timer events (*327*) Indication of a delay in the flow of a process to a specific date, an elapsed time (e.g., 30 days), or a relative repetitive date, such as every Friday.

type image (*332*) Class that represents management information (such as categorizations, policies, and guidelines) to help manage a business process. Type image often allows process information to be summarized by category.

Appendix A

Generic REA Model with Multiplicities for the Purchases and Payments Process

GENERIC PATTERN WITH MULTIPLICITIES

Exhibit 8.A1 shows a generic purchases and payments process UML diagram. There are two resources, *inventory* and *cash;* there are two events, *purchases* and *cash disbursements;* and there are two agents, *employees* (internal agent) and *suppliers* (external agent).

EXHIBIT 8.A1
Generic Purchases and Payments UML Diagram

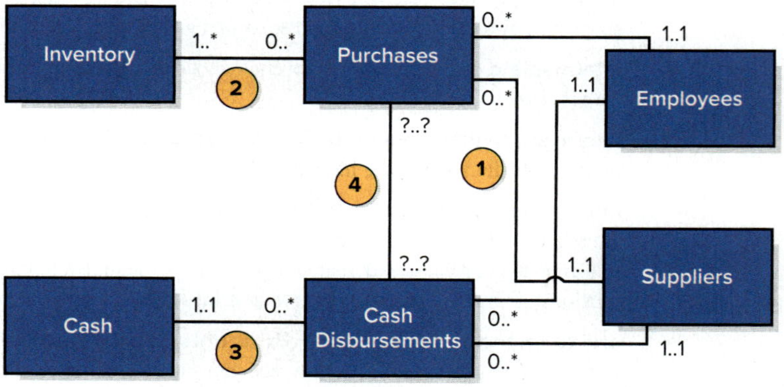

In this example, let's assume that the inventory is something tracked by universal product code (UPC). UPCs are those bar codes you see on literally millions of products, such as soap, breakfast cereal, and packages of cookies. The cash resource represents the various bank accounts that would make up this enterprise's cash balance on its balance sheet. The purchases event records information about individual purchase transactions (e.g., transaction number, date, total dollar amount). The cash disbursement event records information about payments made to suppliers from one of the bank accounts (e.g., check number, check date, check dollar amount). The employees' agent records information about the enterprise's employees, including those employees who handle purchases transactions.

The suppliers agent records information about actual and potential suppliers (let's assume that supplier information is recorded in some cases before the firm orders anything from them, and let's also assume that the company only writes checks to suppliers).

Exhibit 8.A1 shows the generic REA model. You should immediately notice the similarity with the sales and collection process diagram shown in Appendix A of Chapter 7. Consider association 1 between *suppliers* and *purchases*. The multiplicities indicate that each supplier participates in a minimum of zero and a maximum of many sales. Does this seem reasonable? The minimum of zero means that we can record information about suppliers before they participate in any sale. On the other side of the association, the multiplicities indicate that each purchase involves one and only one supplier. Again, does this seem reasonable? Notice that the multiplicities for the other associations between agents and events are the same. In fact, these are the typical multiplicities for those associations. There are circumstances where they might be different, but those circumstances occur infrequently.

Next, consider association 2 between the *purchases* event and *inventory* resource. The multiplicities indicate that each purchase involves a minimum of one and a maximum of many inventory items. The multiplicities also indicate that each inventory item can be purchased zero times or many times. The multiplicities on this association are typical when the inventory is carried at a type of product level, such as when the inventory is identified by UPC code.

Now, consider association 3 between the *cash disbursement* event and the *cash* resource. These multiplicities indicate that each cash disbursement (e.g., one check) is paid from one and only one account, and each account is associated with a minimum of zero cash disbursements and a maximum of many cash disbursements. These multiplicities reflect typical business practices. Think about paying bills using your bank's online banking feature. You log on, select the account, and then pay the bill. The amount of the payment is subtracted from that one account.

Finally, consider the duality association 4 between the *purchases* and *cash disbursement* events. The question marks indicate that these multiplicities depend on the nature of the business as well as the terms of the particular purchase. Payments could be made before, after, or at the same time as the purchase. One payment could be made for several purchases, or one purchase could involve several payments. So, there are no typical multiplicities for this association.

We recommend that students recognize and use the standard patterns for multiplicities as shown in Exhibit 8.A1, remembering that those standard multiplicities could change depending on the particular circumstances of the business.

ANSWERS TO PROGRESS CHECKS

1. Sunset would record the purchase when the items are received and accepted, so the purchase is recognized with the Place in Inventory activity.
2. If they purchased over the Internet, they would pay when they placed the order. The Pay Supplier activity would then occur during the Place Order process.
3. You would define two events when there is not a one-to-one relationship between purchase orders and purchases.
4. You would link Product Categories and Supplier Categories if summary information depended on both the product and supplier categories—for example, year-to-date sales for this product category and this supplier category.

Multiple Choice Questions connect

1. **(LO 8-1)** Which of the following is not an activity in the purchases and payments process?
   a. Request prices
   b. Receive items
   c. Pay for items
   d. Bill customers
   e. All are activities in the purchases and payments process
2. **(LO 8-1)** Which activity results in an increase to accounts payable?
   a. Request prices
   b. Place purchase order
   c. Receive items
   d. Return rejected items
   e. Send payment
3. **(LO 8-2, LO 8-3)** *Choreography* describes which of the following?
   a. Sequence of activities in a process
   b. Message flows between pools
   c. Process gateways
   d. Both (a) and (c)
   e. Both (b) and (c)
4. **(LO 8-4)** Which of the following is not an example of an application control?
   a. Range checks ensure that purchases are limited to valid amounts.
   b. Employee making disbursements cannot modify purchase orders.
   c. System requires passwords.
   d. System creates audit trail documenting all changes.
   e. All are examples of application controls.
5. **(LO 8-3)** Which of the following describes the purpose of an intermediate timer event?
   a. Indicates receipt of a message
   b. Indicates branching
   c. Indicates delay
   d. Both (a) and (c)
   e. Both (b) and (c)
6. **(LO 8-5)** Which of the following is a resource in a purchases and payments structure model?
   a. Employee labor
   b. Receipt of goods
   c. Paying by check
   d. Inventory
   e. Supplier
7. **(LO 8-5)** Which of the following is an agent in a purchases and payments structure model?
   a. Employee labor
   b. Receipt of goods
   c. Cash disbursement
   d. Inventory
   e. Supplier

8. **(LO 8-5)** Which of the following is an event in a purchases and payments structure model?
   a. Cash
   b. Inventory
   c. Employee
   d. Cash disbursement
   e. None of these options
9. **(LO 8-5)** Which of the following events would indicate recording of a purchase in the AIS?
   a. Issue Purchase Order
   b. Receive Goods
   c. Make Payment
   d. Transfer Inventory
   e. None of these options
10. **(LO 8-5)** In a typical relational database supporting the purchase and payment process, which of the following tables is likely to have the most foreign keys?
   a. Employee table
   b. Supplier table
   c. Inventory table
   d. Cash disbursement table
   e. Cash table

Use the following diagram to answer Questions 11 through 27.

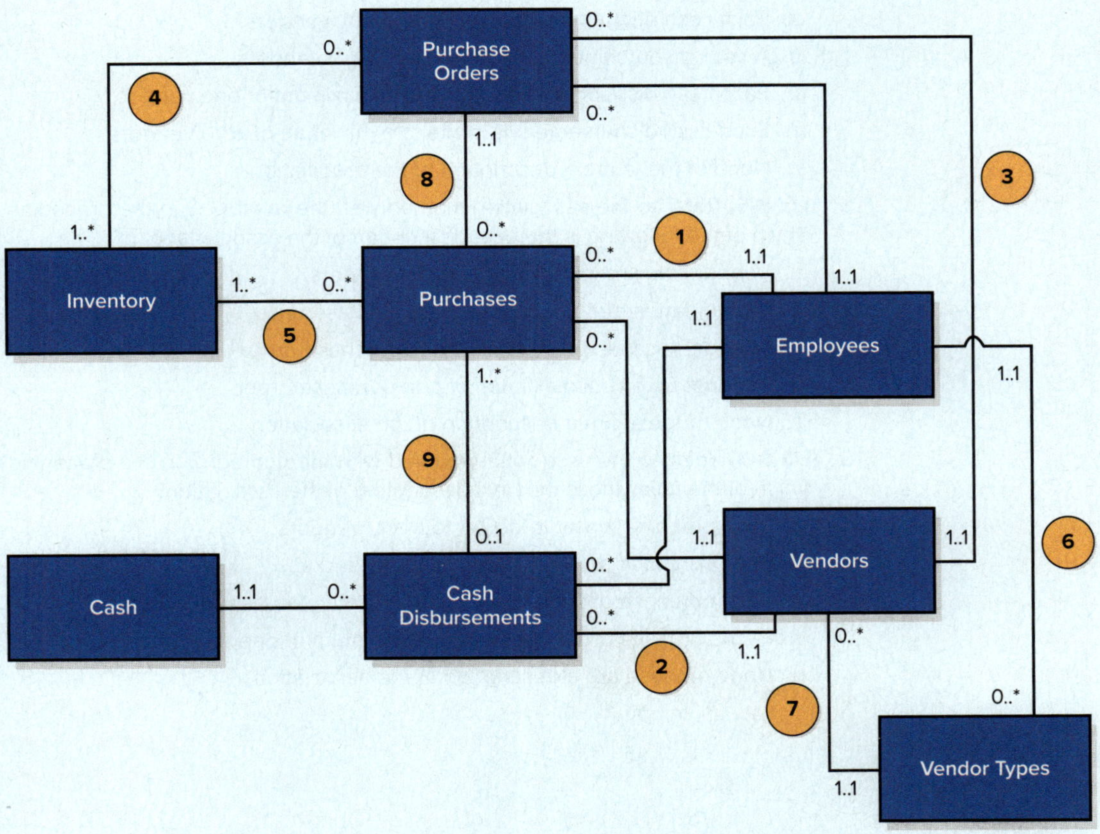

11. **(LO 8-5)** Refer to the association marked with the number 1 in the preceding diagram. Which of the following is the best description of the association?
    a. Each employee participates in a minimum of zero purchases.
    b. Each employee participates in at least one purchase.
    c. Each employee participates in a maximum of one purchase.
    d. Only employees in the shipping and receiving department receive purchases.
    e. None of these are a description of the association.
12. **(LO 8-5)** Refer to the association marked with the number 1 in the preceding diagram. Which of the following is the best description of the association?
    a. Each purchase is received by multiple employees.
    b. Each purchase is received by one employee.
    c. Each purchase can be received by a maximum of many employees.
    d. Each purchase can be received by a minimum of zero employees.
    e. None of these are a description of the association.
13. **(LO 8-5)** Refer to the association marked with the number 2 in the preceding diagram. Which of the following is the best description of the association?
    a. Each vendor always receives multiple cash disbursements.
    b. Each vendor receives a minimum of zero cash disbursements.
    c. Each vendor receives a maximum of one cash disbursement.
    d. Each vendor is paid by check.
    e. None of these are a description of the association.
14. **(LO 8-5)** Refer to the association marked with the number 2 in the preceding diagram. Which of the following is the best description of the association?
    a. Each cash disbursement is made to many vendors.
    b. A cash disbursement can be made to zero vendors
    c. Each cash disbursement is made to a maximum of one vendor.
    d. Each cash disbursement is made to a minimum of zero vendors.
    e. None of these are a description of the association.
15. **(LO 8-5)** Refer to the association marked with the number 3 in the preceding diagram. Which of the following is the best description of the association?
    a. Vendors may receive many purchase orders.
    b. Vendors must receive at least one purchase order.
    c. Vendors receive a minimum of one purchase order.
    d. Vendors receive a maximum of one purchase order.
    e. None of these are a description of the association.
16. **(LO 8-5)** Refer to the association marked with the number 3 in the preceding diagram. Which of the following is the best description of the association?
    a. Each purchase order is issued to many vendors.
    b. Each purchase order is issued to zero vendors.
    c. Each purchase order is issued to a maximum of many vendors.
    d. Each purchase order is issued to a minimum of one vendor.
    e. None of these are a description of the association.

17. **(LO 8-5)** Refer to the association marked with the number 4 in the preceding diagram. Which of the following is the best description of the association?
   a. Each purchase order specifies a type of inventory.
   b. Each purchase order is associated with a maximum of many inventory items.
   c. Each purchase order is associated with a minimum of zero inventory items.
   d. Some purchase orders do not list inventory items.
   e. None of these are a description of the association.
18. **(LO 8-5)** Refer to the association marked with the number 4 in the preceding diagram. Which of the following is the best description of the association?
   a. Each inventory item is ordered one time.
   b. Each inventory item is ordered zero times.
   c. Each inventory item is ordered on a minimum of zero purchase orders.
   d. Each inventory item is ordered on a minimum of one purchase order.
   e. None of these are a description of the association.
19. **(LO 8-5, LO 8-6)** Refer to the association marked with the number 4 in the preceding diagram. Which of the following is the best way to implement the association in a relational database?
   a. Post the primary key of purchase orders as a foreign key in inventory.
   b. Post the primary key of inventory in purchase orders as a foreign key.
   c. Create a linking table with a concatenated primary key.
   d. Record the date of the purchase order in the inventory table.
   e. None of these are a description of the correct implementation.
20. **(LO 8-5)** Refer to the association marked with the number 5 in the preceding diagram. Which of the following is the best description of the association?
   a. Each inventory item is associated with a minimum of one purchase.
   b. Each inventory item is purchased one time.
   c. Each inventory item is purchased zero times.
   d. Each inventory item is associated with a minimum of zero purchases.
   e. None of these are a description of the association.
21. **(LO 8-5, LO 8-6)** Refer to the association marked with the number 5 in the preceding diagram. Which of the following is the best description of the association?
   a. Purchases increase the quantity-on-hand of inventory items.
   b. Each purchase includes a minimum of zero inventory items.
   c. Each purchase includes a minimum of two inventory items.
   d. A purchase may be associated with a maximum of one inventory item.
   e. None of these are a description of the association.
22. **(LO 8-5)** Refer to the association marked with the number 5 in the preceding diagram. Which of the following is the best way to implement the association in a relational database?
   a. Create a linking table with a concatenated primary key.
   b. Post the primary key of purchases as a foreign key in inventory.
   c. Post the primary key of inventory in purchases as a foreign key.
   d. Post the purchases primary key in inventory and the inventory primary key in purchases.
   e. None of these are a description of the correct implementation.

23. **(LO 8-5)** Refer to the association marked with the number 6 in the preceding diagram. Which of the following is the best description of the association?
    a. Some employees are also vendor types.
    b. Employees only deal with authorized vendor types.
    c. Some employees are assigned to work with specific vendor types.
    d. Some vendor types are not issued purchase orders.
    e. None of these are a description of the association.
24. **(LO 8-5)** Refer to the association marked with the number 6 in the preceding diagram. Which of the following is the best way to implement the association in a relational database?
    a. Post the primary key of vendor types in employees as a foreign key.
    b. Post the primary key of employees as a foreign key in vendor types.
    c. Create a linking table with a concatenated primary key.
    d. The association does not require foreign keys.
    e. None of these are a description of the correct implementation.
25. **(LO 8-5)** Refer to the association marked with the number 7 in the preceding diagram. Which of the following is the best description of the association?
    a. Some vendors are not in a vendor type.
    b. Employees do not deal with vendors that are not in a vendor type.
    c. Vendors are classified by type.
    d. Each vendor type must contain at least one vendor.
    e. None of these are a description of the association.
26. **(LO 8-5)** Assume that you are drawing an activity (BPMN) diagram of the process. Which of the following is not true about your diagram?
    a. The issue purchase order task occurs before the receive purchases task.
    b. The purchases task could be modeled as a looping task to show multiple purchases following one purchase order.
    c. The process starts when a customer places a sales order.
    d. The process ends when the vendor is paid.
    e. All of these are true about the diagram.
27. **(LO 8-5)** Assume that you are drawing a collaboration activity (BPMN) diagram of the process. Which of the following would not be message flows on your diagram?
    a. Purchase order
    b. Delivery (of the purchase)
    c. Check/cash disbursement
    d. Inventory update
    e. All of these are message flows for the diagram.

Discussion Questions

1. **(LO 8-4)** Business rules implement internal controls. Review Exhibit 8.5 and describe which business rules implement segregation of duties. Classify each of those business rules as obligatory, prohibited, or allowed as described in Chapter 5.
2. **(LO 8-1)** **Walmart** uses a vendor-managed inventory system, where the inventory is owned and managed by the vendor until it is delivered from Walmart's distribution center to the stores. What implications does this system have for Walmart's purchases and payments process?

3. **(LO 8-2, LO 8-3)** Draw an activity model using BPMN for the process that you followed when you purchased your textbooks for the current semester.
4. **(LO 8-2)** Refer to Exhibit 8.5. Describe the types of businesses that would employ a similar diagram for their purchases and payments processes. What other alternative approaches are there? Describe some businesses that would use these alternatives for the purchases and payments process structure.
5. **(LO 8-5)** Recall that type images apply guidelines, constraints, and descriptive information, as well as categorizing the economic resources, events, and agents for a business process. Exhibit 8.7 shows two examples of type images for Sunset Graphics. Are there other possible type images that could be added to the diagram to help Sunset's managers manage the purchases and payments process?
6. **(LO 8-5)** Some larger companies and government entities issue contracts for major purchases and then issue specific purchase orders to their contractors according to the terms of the contract. The contract can specify prices and payment terms as well as other administrative procedures. How would the use of contracts affect the standard process flow as shown in Exhibit 8.4? How would it affect the UML class diagram for the purchases and payments process?
7. **(LO 8-5)** Sunset Graphics often buys inventory after receiving a sales order from the customer. Suppose you are asked to prepare one UML class diagram that combines both the sales and collection process and the purchases and payments process. What would be shared among those processes? What would be unique to each process? Why?
8. **(LO 8-5, LO 8-6)** What classes and associations would be included in a model that describes the information needed for a query that calculates the accounts payable balance for each supplier? Describe the logic of that query. (In other words, what steps would you follow to compute that balance?)

Problems connect

1. **(LO 8-5, LO 8-6)** The following narrative describes the purchase and payment process for The Tablet Store. Use the narrative to answer the questions below. The Tablet Store recently opened to sell iPads and other tablet computing devices. It purchases its tablets directly from the manufacturers (e.g., **Apple**, **Samsung**, and **Dell**). To order tablets, a Tablet Store employee submits a purchase order to the manufacturer electronically. Each purchase order could stipulate several different models of tablets from one manufacturer. The manufacturers typically deliver the tablets to the store within 2 weeks after they receive the purchase order. The Tablet Store pays for each shipment within 30 days after receipt. If there are multiple orders to the same manufacturer, the Tablet Store occasionally combines payments, issuing one check for multiple receipts. All of the Tablet Store checks are drawn on one bank account.
   a. Draw a UML class diagram that describes the Tablet Store's purchases and payments process.
   b. Using Microsoft Access, implement a relational database from your UML class diagram. Identify at least three fields per table.
   c. Describe how you would use the relational database to determine the Tablet Store's accounts payable.
2. **(LO 8-2, LO 8-3, LO 8-5)** The following narrative describes the purchase and payment process for Quick Jet Inc. Use the narrative to answer the questions below. Quick Jet Inc. provides air taxi service to the wealthy, including celebrities, sports stars, and business executives. Quick Jet employees negotiate long-term leases with airplane leasing companies. Each lease involves one plane. Quick Jet categorizes its planes according to passenger capacity and normal flying range. Quick Jet makes monthly lease payments for its planes. If it leases multiple planes from the same lease company, it combines payments.

Maintenance

The company has no maintenance staff of its own, so it also contracts with a number of airplane maintenance companies to perform the routine maintenance required to keep its fleet airworthy. It issues orders against the contracts for specific maintenance required for the planes. To comply with FAA regulations, it tracks the details of the specific maintenance performed on each plane. To facilitate the tracking, each maintenance order specifies the maintenance services for one plane. Quick Jet pays for all the maintenance performed by each maintenance contractor within 15 days, according to the terms of the contracts, and may combine payments.

Miscellaneous Purchases

Quick Jet also provides each of its pilots with credit cards so they can purchase fuel and miscellaneous supplies at the various airports they use. The pilots turn in detailed lists of their purchases that identify the supplier, the date, the amount purchased, and the prices, as well as the plane for which the items were purchased. Each list is assigned a miscellaneous purchase number. Quick Jet pays the credit card bills in full each month upon receipt from the credit card company.

Other Information

Quick Jet keeps information about the plane leasing companies, the plane maintenance contractors, miscellaneous suppliers, and the credit card companies in one vendor file. However, it tracks plane leases, maintenance contracts, maintenance orders, and miscellaneous purchases separately (separate events). Quick Jet categorizes its employees according to their job assignments (e.g., pilots, purchasing employees, A/P clerks). It also categorizes vendors according to the services/goods they provide. It puts information about its agents, resources, and type images in the database before linking to other classes.

a. Draw a context diagram showing Quick Jet's interactions with its suppliers.

b. Draw a BPMN activity diagram that describes Quick Jet's purchases and payments process.

c. Prepare a UML class diagram with classes, associations, and multiplicities.

d. Using the preceding information and the following attributes list, prepare a listing of the relational tables necessary to support this sales and collection process. List the tables in the following order: resources, events, agents, type images, and linking tables.

Attributes:

Cash account#
Cash account balance
Check#
Check amount
Check date
Date this misc. purchase billed by credit card company
Employee#
Employee hire date
Employee name
Employee type
Employee type description
Lease#
Lease date
Lease monthly payment amount
Misc. supply purchase#
Misc. supply purchase date
Number of vendors of this type

Plane#
Plane maintenance contract#
Plane maintenance contract date
Plane maintenance contract duration
Plane maintenance item performed on this order for this plane
Plane maintenance order#
Plane maintenance order date
Plane miles since last maintenance
Plane type
Plane type passenger capacity
Plane type range in miles
Vendor#
Vendor Name
Vendor type
Vendor type description
Year-to-date (YTD) purchases from this vendor type

3. **(LO 8-5)** The following narrative describes a purchase and payment process and a sales and collection process for BR Management Company. Use the narrative to answer the questions below. BR Management Company (BRMC) operates apartment complexes and earns revenues by renting out the apartments in those complexes. BRMC assigns an agent/manager to each complex (one manager can manage several complexes) to handle day-to-day operations, such as maintaining the property and signing rental contracts. This case describes the maintenance and rental processes.

Complexes and Apartments

BRMC has acquired 15 and built several more apartment complexes over the past 2 years. It identifies complexes by address and apartments by the combination of address and apartment number. BRMC categorizes each apartment according to a number of factors, including the quality of its furnishings, number of rooms, and size. There are 27 apartment categories at present, each identified by unique category number. Because each complex presents a unique set of luxury appointments and amenities, BRMC determines the standard monthly rental fee by considering both the apartment category and complex; for example, 2-bedroom, 1-bath apartments (category 21) rent for $850 per month in the Broadway complex, but the same category apartments rent for $1,450 per month in the Naples complex.

Maintenance

BRMC keeps its apartments and complexes in top condition. The BRMC agents monitor the condition of the facilities. Whenever the condition falls below BRMC standards, the agents hire contractors to bring the apartment back up to specifications. BRMC classifies each maintenance job by job type, and it matches the job type to the contractor type that can best perform the job. The BRMC agent then selects one specific contractor for the job from that contractor type. Each contractor may belong to several contractor types. Each maintenance job involves either one apartment or the common areas of the complex. BRMC tracks the maintenance performed on apartments and complex common areas.

Rentals

BRMC agents negotiate rental contracts with tenants. Each rental contract governs one year-long lease of an apartment. Although there is a standard monthly rental fee for each apartment in each building, agents may negotiate higher or lower rents if they see the need to do so. It is important to have a full record of the actual rent for all apartments. When there is more than one tenant per apartment, every tenant must sign the rental contract. BRMC assigns a unique tenant ID number to each tenant and issues them ID cards to control access.

Cash Receipts and Disbursements and Other Information

To simplify the case, the cash resource, the cashier agent, and the cash receipt and disbursement events (although they would certainly exist) are eliminated. You should *not* model those in your solution. All agents, resources, and types are put into the database before they are linked to other classes.

a. Prepare an integrated UML class diagram with classes, associations, and multiplicities.
b. Using the preceding information and the following attributes list, prepare a listing of the relational tables necessary to support BRMC's processes. List the tables in the following order: resources, events, agents, type images, and linking tables.

Attributes:

Actual completion date of job
Actual cost of this job
Actual monthly rent
Agent monthly salary
Agent name
Apartment category#
Apartment complex address
Apartment square footage
Apartment#
Category
Contractor name
Contractor phone number
Contractor quality rating
Contractor type
Contractor#
Count of rooms in apartment
Count of this type of contractor
Date complex was constructed
Employee#
Job type
Maintenance job#
Number of available apartments in this category
Projected completion date of job
Rental contract date
Rental contract#
Standard cost for this job type
Standard monthly rent
Tenant credit rating
Tenant ID#
Tenant name
Total complex square footage
Vendor#
Year to date (YTD) advertising $ for this
YTD $ spent on this job type
YTD $ spent on this job type in this complex

Design Element: Duncan Smith/Getty Images

Chapter Nine

Conversion Business Process

A Look at This Chapter

This chapter examines the conversion process whereby manufacturing companies convert raw material into finished goods. We continue our comprehensive example to develop activity and structure models of the process. We show how the activity model in conjunction with business rules can be used to develop, implement, and monitor control activities. We show how the structure model can be used to develop a relational database to support information processing requirements.

A Look Back

Chapter 8 examined the purchases and payments processes. It continued the comprehensive example that we are using to examine typical process activities and data structures.

A Look Ahead

Chapter 10 provides a hands-on project to review Chapters 7, 8, and 9.

Ingram Publishing/SuperStock

Starbucks roasts its coffee in roasting plants distributed around the United States. One plant is a nondescript, 320,000-square-foot warehouse building located in Kent, Washington. Other roasting plants are located in Carson Valley, Nevada; York, Pennsylvania; and Amsterdam, Netherlands. The coffee beans are stacked in 150-pound burlap bags, and each bag is marked to identify the country of origin.

The bags of green coffee beans are stacked over a large metal grate in the floor. A worker cuts open the bag and the beans pour through the grate. They are pulled into a washer that separates foreign material. After washing, the beans are weighed, sorted, and stored for roasting. They are transferred into large roasters that can hold up to 600 pounds of beans. The roasting process is carefully controlled by computer. As the beans roast, they slowly turn brown. When the beans pop, the flavor is released.

The beans are transferred to cooling vats that turn and toss them to stop further roasting. Workers test the roasted beans. Soon, they are bagged and boxed for shipment. On average, the roasted beans will be in stores within 3 days.

To keep a constant flow of quality product to their worldwide network of stores, Starbucks needs to monitor its conversion process closely. In addition to the cost information that affects its financial statements, what other information is necessary for Starbucks' management of this process?

CHAPTER OUTLINE

LEARNING OBJECTIVES

After reading this chapter, you should be able to:

9-1 Describe the business activities that constitute the conversion process.

9-2 Develop an activity model of the conversion process using BPMN.

9-3 Understand and apply different activity modeling options.

9-4 Develop business rules to implement controls for the conversion process.

9-5 Develop a structure model for the conversion process using UML class diagrams.

9-6 Implement a relational database from the UML class diagram of the conversion process.

LO 9-1

Describe the business activities that constitute the conversion process.

CONVERSION PROCESS

The conversion process is inherently more complicated than the sales and collections and purchases and payments processes described in the previous two chapters, primarily because of increased recordkeeping requirements and variations in the sophistication of the process itself among companies. Many types of businesses employ conversion processes, including bakeries, wineries, breweries, restaurants, car repair shops, construction companies, equipment manufacturers, automobile manufacturers, and so on.[1] The conversion process includes business activities related to maintaining inventories of raw material and finished goods, producing finished goods from raw material, tracking direct labor and direct equipment costs, and applying overhead.

The conversion process generates accounting transactions to record the transfer of raw material to work-in-process and work-in-process inventory to finished goods. In addition to the cost of raw materials, the conversion process must also account for direct labor and other direct costs incurred in determining the cost of goods manufactured. The allocation of overhead and indirect costs to work-in-process is typically based on direct labor, although overhead could be allocated based on a number of cost drivers in an activity-based costing system. More specifically, conversion costs are typically accounted for at standard, where the standard is based on management estimates, and then the costs are updated to reflect actual costs incurred. Exhibit 9.1 describes typical transactions resulting from the conversion process. In addition to the accounting transactions, the specific details of the conversion process are often tracked to the individual job.

EXHIBIT 9.1
Typical Conversion Process Accounting Transactions

Sep 1	**Work-in-Process Inventory**	**2,875.50**	
	Raw Materials Inventory		**2,875.50**
	Record transfer of raw materials to work-in-process		
Sep 2	**Manufacturing Wages**	**4,650.00**	
	Cash		**4,650.00**
	To record manufacturing payroll		
Sep 2	**Work-in-Process Inventory**	**3,250.00**	
	Manufacturing Wages		**3,250.00**
	To record direct labor		
	Manufacturing Overhead	**1,400.00**	
	Manufacturing Wages		**1,400.00**
	To record indirect labor		
Sep 2	**Manufacturing Overhead**	**1,945.25**	
	Utilities Payable		**1,945.25**
	To record manufacturing overhead costs		
Sep 2	**Work-in-Process Inventory**	**4,062.50**	
	Manufacturing Overhead		**4,062.50**
	To allocate manufacturing overhead to work-in-process inventory at 125% of direct labor		
Sep 3	**Finished Goods**	**10,188.00**	
	Work-in-Process Inventory		**10,188.00**
	Record transfer of work-in-process to finished goods		

[1]We focus on companies that use job cost accounting methods, although the models could apply generally to companies that also use process costing methods.

In this chapter, we continue to apply the tools introduced in Chapters 4 through 8 to a comprehensive example of the conversion process. We first describe the process activities using BPMN, and then we define the typical information structure using UML class diagrams. Finally, we use the UML class diagrams to build a database to collect and report relevant process information. We also describe business rules that establish potential process controls.

SUNSET GRAPHICS EXAMPLE

Company Overview

As described in Chapters 7 and 8, Virgil owns and operates Sunset Graphics. The company designs and sells signs and banners, lettering and vinyl graphics for vehicles and boats, corporate promotional items, and silk-screened t-shirts and embroidered gear, among other products. Recently, Virgil decided to expand the business. To plan the expansion carefully, he wanted to review Sunset's business processes to develop better documentation, improve processes, and establish consistency in customer service. He also wanted to be sure that effective internal controls were in place since he could not always directly supervise their employees after the expansion.

Sunset Graphics' Conversion Process Description

Until recently, Sunset didn't track its conversion costs. If labor was involved in preparing products for a customer's order, Sunset simply billed the customer a flat rate for the service. The company didn't assign any labor or overhead costs to its products. However, that changed when it signed a major contract to provide a variety of signs and banners to state agencies. The terms of the contract required that Sunset include direct labor, direct equipment costs, and overhead in the cost of its products. Virgil planned to open a dedicated location to service the state contract. He wondered if job costing could provide better information about the real costs of their products. If it did, he might change his accounting process at more locations.

Virgil explained the conversion process. Demand for products under the state contract fluctuated but often required short delivery times, so he decided to keep a safety stock of those products (**finished goods inventory**) on hand. When inventory levels dropped below certain levels, he then authorized production to replenish the inventory. To reduce delays, he also decided to maintain a **raw materials inventory**, although he wanted to keep those inventory levels as low as possible. It required some planning, but he created bills of material that identified the raw material required for each product and estimated the required inventory levels to keep production smooth and meet demand.

He summarized Sunset's conversion process as follows:

1. When the quantity on hand of a product drops below the minimum level, the item manager authorizes production to increase the quantity on hand.
2. Based on the bill of material for that item, they issue material into work-in-process.
3. Sunset employees then construct the items.
4. Upon completion, the products are placed in inventory.

LO 9-2

Develop an activity model of the conversion process using BPMN.

SUNSET GRAPHICS' ACTIVITY MODELS

Basic Conversion Activity Model

After gathering information about Sunset's conversion process, our first task was to draw a simple activity model using BPMN. Remembering our discussion about the sales and purchases process, Virgil asked why we didn't start with the context. We explained that the conversion process is internal, so there are no external participants for a context diagram. So, we start by laying out the basic process steps.

Sunset's conversion process is typical of most simple manufacturing companies. As shown in Exhibit 9.2, the process starts when Sunset needs to replenish finished goods inventory. Then, the production authorization starts production activities, including issue of materials (R/M) and use of direct labor. Work continues until the required quantity of the finished good item is prepared. At that point, production is complete and the finished goods inventory is updated.

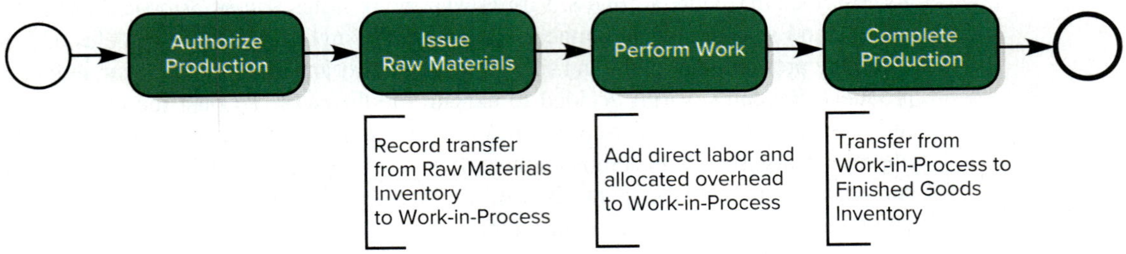

EXHIBIT 9.2
Basic Conversion Activity Model

> **LO 9-3**
> Understand and apply different activity modeling options.

Refining the Model

Virgil remarked that a collaboration model would also not make much sense here. All the work is within Sunset. We agreed, but we said that *lanes* with a *pool* could show the different functions within Sunset to help clarify responsibilities. Virgil then added that sometimes they performed the work in a series of batches to make the process more manageable. Often, it takes several batches to complete production. Each batch involves some setup activity, then raw materials are issued, work is performed, and when complete, we start the next batch. When all the batches are done, we transfer the products to finished goods inventory.

We said that it would be pretty easy to add those refinements to the model. Virgil then added that they always inspect the work before it is added to the finished goods inventory, and if it doesn't meet quality standards, they discard the bad items and produce new items to replace them. If the work passes the inspection, Sunset employees place the finished items in inventory, and the inventory manager updates the records.

Virgil was confident that he now understood BPMN and wanted to prepare this diagram himself. He suggested that the model could use multiple lanes and show the looping to reflect Sunset's conversion process. He then sketched the model shown in Exhibit 9.3. This model showed two lanes: (1) for the inventory manager and (2) for the Sunset employees who perform the work. This model shows the inventory manager authorizing production. Then, the conversion employees set up the batch, issue raw materials, and perform work making the finished good item. At that point, an employee inspects the work and if the work does not meet quality standards, the **intermediate error event** directs the process flow to the "Discard Errors" activity and the sequence loops back to issue more raw materials. If the batch is not finished, the **gateway** also directs the sequence flow back to issue more raw materials, and the steps are repeated until the batch is done. Then, a second gateway branches, depending on whether all batches are complete. If not, the sequence flow is directed back to the "Set up Batch" activity and the steps repeat until all batches are done. Conversion employees complete production by placing the finished items in inventory, and the inventory manager updates the inventory records.

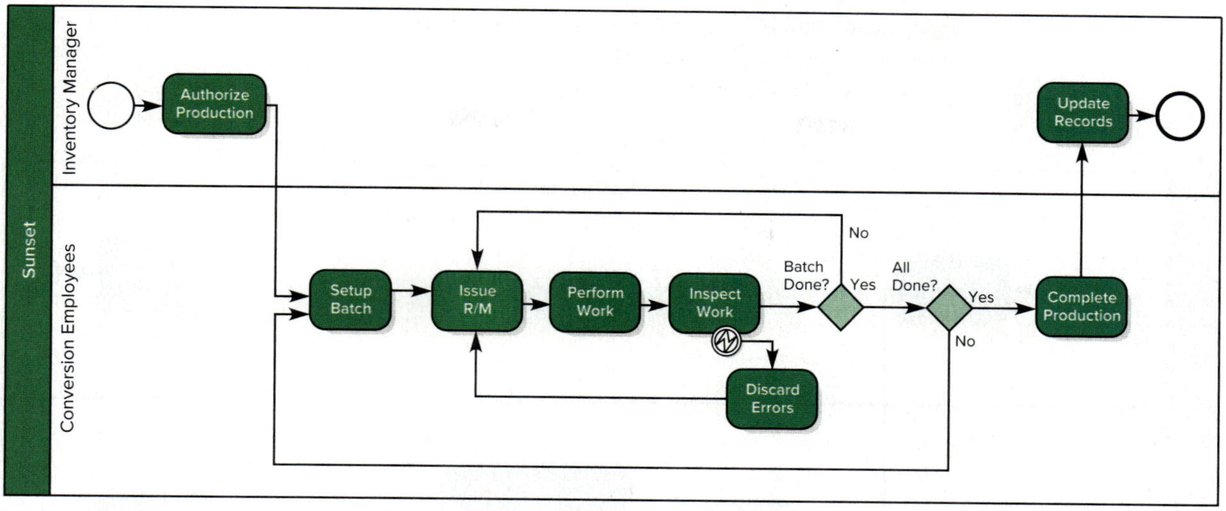

EXHIBIT 9.3
Conversion Process with Lanes and Loops

We congratulated Virgil on his understanding of activity modeling. We said that his model would work, but we added some minor refinements as shown in Exhibit 9.4. Each activity should only have one incoming and one outgoing sequence flow under normal circumstances. So, we added merging gateways for the batch and production looping flows. Then, only one activity has two incoming sequence flows, but the second flow is only in the case of rework for errors. It would be better though if we could also avoid that situation.

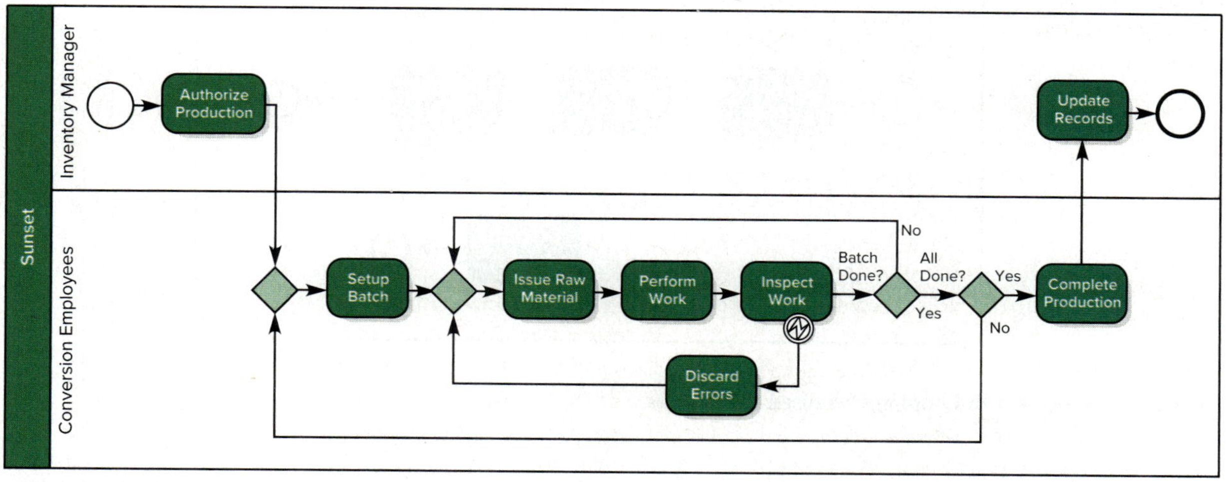

EXHIBIT 9.4
Conversion Process with Loops and Merging Gateways

After further discussion, we decided that we could simplify the presentation by using a looping collapsed subprocess (see Chapter 4) to represent the batch activities. We didn't need to link the "Discard Errors" activity back to "Issue R/M" because the batch needs to complete a designated number of good products. We just don't count the errors. The steps in the subprocess are then shown separately as in Exhibit 9.5. In this case, the original model was not that complicated, so either diagram is understandable. When certain parts of any process are complex, it can often improve understanding of the overall process if the complex parts are modeled separately. Then, one diagram shows the overall flow at a higher level, and the separate *expanded subprocess* shows additional detail. It is possible to include another collapsed subprocess in the expanded subprocess; thus, the models can have multiple levels of detail.

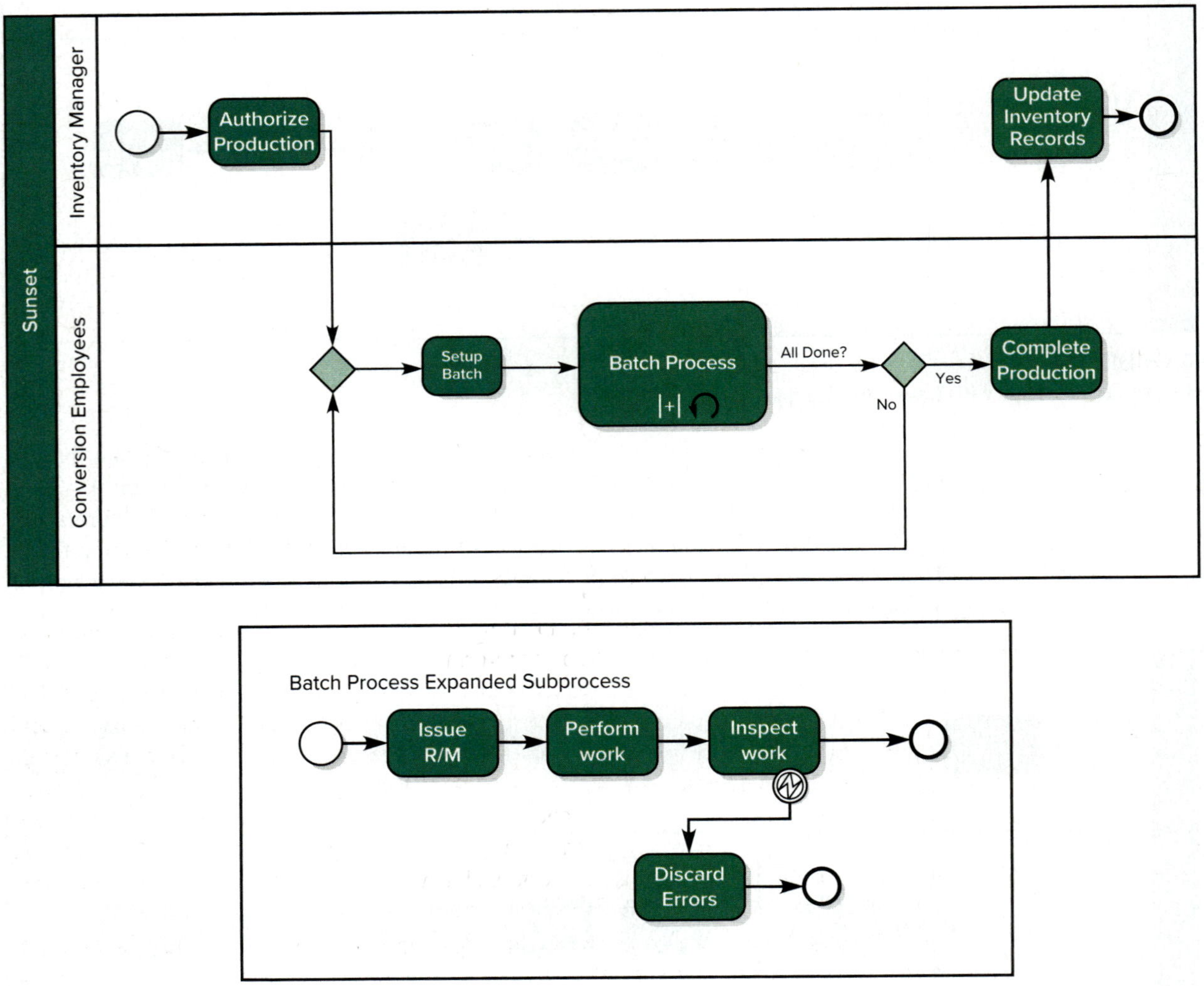

EXHIBIT 9.5
Conversion Process with Looping Collapsed Subprocess

Virgil agreed that both models accurately describe their process. He also understood the value of the looping subprocess to simplify the main diagram and allow separate modeling of the production batches. We noted that for internal control, we probably should have identified a third lane to show the separate "Inspect Work" function. The same employees that perform the work should not inspect the work. Virgil acknowledged that we were probably right, but we could leave that change for another day.

PROGRESS CHECK

1. How would you change Exhibit 9.4 to show a separate organization unit performing the inspect work function?
2. Could you model the intermediate error event with a gateway instead? What would that look like?

LO 9-4

Develop business rules to implement controls for the conversion process.

SUNSET GRAPHICS' CONVERSION PROCESS CONTROLS

Inspecting work and discarding defects.
guruXOX/Shutterstock

Again, we asked Virgil about controls over the conversion process. He thought that we had already incorporated some controls in the activity models. For example, preventive controls such as proper authorizations and segregation of duties are important features of Exhibits 9.4 and 9.5. He was concerned, though, about the effective operation of his information systems. We explained that a combination of information technology general controls (ITGC), access controls, and application controls helps ensure effective information systems. ITGC dictate how technology is used in an organization and protect against data breaches and system disruptions. *Access controls* limit which of their employees can view and change records in the system and help implement appropriate segregation of duties. *Application controls* ensure data integrity and an audit trail. For example, we need to control the assignment of production authorization and material issue numbers to make sure all of them are accounted for. In addition, we need to establish appropriate ranges or limits for each value that your partners can add or change in the system.

First, we need to identify important business events and define Sunset's intention or objective for each event. Then, we determine the appropriate actions to take based on the conditions. For example, we've already listed important business events in the activity models, so let's examine Sunset's conversion process in Exhibits 9.4 and 9.5 to develop some possible business rules to implement appropriate controls.

Virgil summarized his objectives for the steps in the process. Of course, the overall goal was to ensure finished products were available to meet expected demand. With Virgil's direction, we developed an initial set of business rules for the conversion process. He articulated intentions (goals) for every step in the process, and then we set business rules to segregate duties and limit employee authority appropriately. Exhibit 9.6 shows the initial set of business rules for Sunset's conversion process. We noted that we would need to set application controls for almost every attribute updated during data entry.

Process Steps	Intention	Employee Authority/Action	Access Controls	Application Controls
Authorize Production	Employee with proper authority authorizes production to ensure finished goods are available to meet expected demand.	Supervisor must authorize production >$5,000.	Employee authorizing production cannot modify inventory records.	System must provide authorization order number control, default values, and range and limit checks; must also create audit trail.
Issue Raw Material	Issues from raw material according to bill of material recorded accurately.	Employee issuing material must not be same emnployee who authorized production.	Employee recording issue of material cannot modify bill of material.	System must only allow employee to enter the number of items issued based on bill of material, subject to range and limit checks on quantities; date defaults to current date.
Perform Work	Direct labor costs recorded promptly and accurately.	Employee performing direct labor must not be same employee authorizing production.	Employee recording labor costs cannot modify production authorization.	System must provide control numbers, hours, costs range, and limit checks; date defaults to current date.
Inspect Work and Discard Defects	Inspection ensures that only products meeting quality standards are allowed.	Employee inspecting work must not be an employee performing work.	Employee recording inspection cannot modify inventory records.	System must provide limit checks; date defaults to current date.
Complete Production	Finished product inventory must be updated promptly and accurately.	Employee placing products in finished inventory must not be same employee authorizing production.	Employee recording update of inventory records cannot modify production authorization.	System must default date to current date; inventory update limit is based on authorization.

EXHIBIT 9.6
Using Business Rules to Implement Internal Controls

LO 9-5

Develop a structure model for the conversion process using UML class diagrams.

SUNSET GRAPHICS' STRUCTURE MODELS

Now, Virgil looked forward to adding the conversion process features to Sunset's new database. This would mean that his database could handle his entire supply chain encompassing purchasing, making, and selling his products. We proceeded to examine Sunset Graphics' conversion information requirements. As described in Chapter 5, the primary purpose of our UML class diagram of the conversion process is to create a blueprint for the development and operation of a relational database to support the collection, aggregation, and communication of process information. As in Chapters 7 and 8, we follow the **REA** framework (resources, events, and agents) as a proven approach to describing business processes in a way that meets both accounting and broad management information requirements.

Basic UML Class Diagram for Conversion

Based on what Virgil told us about their conversion process, we thought it was very close to a generic conversion process model shown in Exhibit 9.7. As indicated by numbers 1 and 2, an employee **(agent)** with supervisory responsibility authorizes production **(event)** of one or more finished goods items **(resources)**. Next, numbers 3 and 4 denote that an employee (agent) issues (event) the raw material (resource) into **work-in-process inventory** based on the bills of material for the finished goods items. Finally, number 5 shows that production employees perform work to make sure the finished goods items and their direct labor are recorded **(labor operations event)**.

EXHIBIT 9.7
Generic UML Class Diagram for the Conversion Process

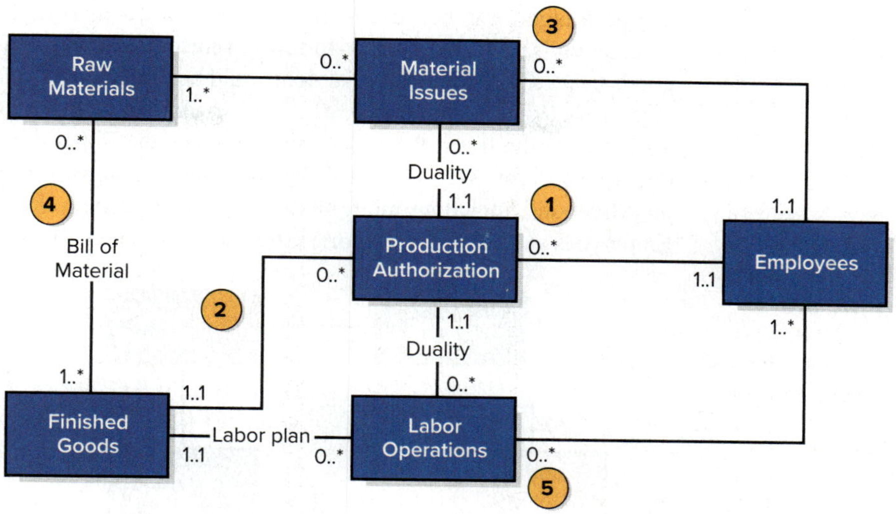

We explained that the association between finished goods and labor operations indicates the planned labor. The bill of materials association between finished goods and raw material indicates the planned material content of each finished goods item. The two duality associations link the raw material issue and labor operations events to the production authorization. Thus, the data structure captures information about both planned and actual conversion activity.

Virgil said that he understood most of the diagram, but where is the work-in-process inventory resource? We explained that we don't need to model a separate work-in-process inventory because we can calculate that value at any time. For example, the **raw material issue event** records the value of items issued into work-in-process. The labor operations event records the value of direct labor added to work-in-process. The labor plan association establishes standard overhead allocation rates. Until the job is complete, the accumulated material, labor, and overhead costs increase work-in-process inventory. When the job is complete, the initial **production authorization event** is updated and the cost of goods manufactured increases the finished goods inventory value.

Refining the UML Class Diagram for Sunset's Conversion Process

Virgil thought Sunset's bill of materials should be more than an association, although he agreed that the company's conversion process resembled the generic model. For Sunset, the bill of materials contains more than a simple link between Sunset's material (raw materials) and its final products (finished goods). He also said that they really had no defined labor plan. Sunset just recorded direct labor incurred and used a simple overhead allocation scheme.

Updating finished goods inventory.
Halfpoint Images/Moment/Getty Images

We replied that it was easy to modify the generic process diagram to reflect Sunset's information requirements for the conversion process. We could "promote" the bill of materials association to a **type image** class because there was more detail involved. Also, the bill of materials association is typically a **many-to-many relationship** between raw materials and finished goods because each raw material item could be used for multiple finished goods items, and vice versa. We would likely create a table to implement that association anyway. We could also remove the labor plan association between the finished goods resource and the labor operations event. We developed the class diagram shown in Exhibit 9.8 reflecting those modifications, including multiplicities, and also keeping the association between Sunset Employees and Product Categories from the sales and collection process.

EXHIBIT 9.8
Revised UML Class Diagram for Sunset's Conversion Process

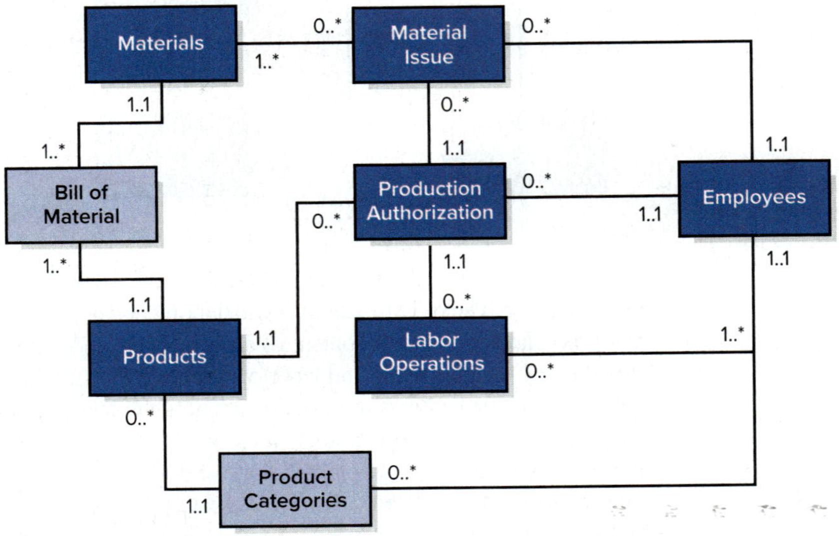

Virgil thought that the revised class diagram accurately reflected his information requirements. However, he had some hypothetical questions about modeling the conversion process to make sure he understood it perfectly. For example, he asked how we would modify the model if Sunset used equipment in the conversion process and wanted to record direct equipment costs. We replied that we would simply add an equipment resource to capture information about the equipment, and then we would add an equipment operations event to record the costs of the use of the equipment. An event records costs applied to work-in-process, and a resource captures permanent information about the things available for use in the process. We added that type images can specify the plan for resource use, and then the plan could be compared to the actual usage recorded in the events.

PROGRESS CHECK

3. Exhibit 9.8 dropped the labor plan association. Could Sunset instead have "promoted" the labor plan association to a type image? How would that affect the diagram?
4. Add the equipment resource and equipment operations event to the diagram, and define the multiplicities.

LO 9-6

Implement a relational database from the UML class diagram of the conversion process.

SUNSET GRAPHICS' RELATIONAL DATABASE

Virgil was now looking forward to implementing the conversion UML class diagram in a relational database for Sunset. Again, we use Microsoft Access, but the process would be similar for any database-driven system. We encourage students to use the following description to implement a relational database to support information requirements for the conversion process.

Relational Database Planning for Attributes

During the model development process, we again reviewed Sunset's existing documents to determine specific data requirements for each class/table. We then followed the guidance in Chapters 5 and 6 to determine allocation of foreign keys. This resulted in a list of tables, attributes, data types, field sizes, and primary and foreign keys as shown in Exhibit 9.9.

EXHIBIT 9.9
Sunset Database Tables and Attribute Definitions for the Conversion Process

PK/FK	Attribute Name	Type	Size
	Table: tblBill_of_Material		
PK	BOM_number	Text	10
	Issue_sequence	Integer	8
	Standard_quantity	Double	8
FK	Product_number	Text	10
FK	Material_number	Text	255
	Special_handling	Memo	—
	Table: tblLabor_Operations		
PK	Labor_ops_Number	Text	10
FK	Prod_auth_number	Text	10
	Labor_ops_description	Memo	—
	Table: tblLabor_Operations_Employees		
PK	Labor_ops_number	Text	10
PK	Employee_number	Text	10
	Actual_direct_labor_hours	Long Integer	4
	Actual_direct_labor_wage	Currency	8
	Table: tblMaterial_Issue		
PK	Material_Issue_number	Text	10
	Issue_date	Date/Time	8
FK	Issued_by	Text	10
FK	Prod_auth_number	Text	255
	Table: tblMaterial_Issue_Materials		
PK	Material_issue_number	Text	10
PK	Material_number	Text	10
	Qty_issued	Long Integer	4
	Table: tblMaterials		
PK	Material_number	Text	10
	Material_description	Text	255
	Material_price	Currency	8
	Material_quantity_on_hand	Integer	2
	Material_notes	Memo	—
	Table: tblEmployees		

(continued)

EXHIBIT 9.9
(Continued)

PK/FK	Attribute Name	Type	Size
PK	Employee_number	Text	10
	Employee_first_name	Text	15
	Employee_last_name	Text	15
	Employee_hire_date	Date/Time	8
	Employee_SocSecNo	Text	11
	Employee_Address	Text	50
	Employee_Address2	Text	50
	Employee_City	Text	20
	Employee_State	Text	2
	Employee_Zip	Text	10
	Employee_phone	Text	14
	Employee_cellphone	Text	14
	Table: tblProduct_Category		
PK	Product_category_number	Text	10
	Product_category_description	Text	255
FK	Product_category_manager	Text	10
	Product_category_notes	Memo	—
	Table: tblProduction_Authorizations		
PK	Prod_auth_number	Text	255
	Prod_auth_date	Date/Time	8
FK	Employee_number	Text	10
FK	Product_Number	Text	10
	Scheduled_qty_to_produce	Long Integer	4
	Actual_qty_produced	Long Integer	4
	Scheduled_completion_date	Date/Time	8
	Actual_completion_date	Date/Time	8
	Overhead_rate	Single	4
	Total_material_cost	Currency	8
	Total_direct_labor	Currency	8
	Total_overhead	Currency	8
	Total_COGM*	Currency	8
	Table: tblProducts		
PK	Product_number	Text	10
	Product_description	Text	255
	Product_price	Currency	8
	Product_unit_of_sale	Text	10
FK	Product_category_number	Text	10
	Product_quantity_on_hand	Integer	2
	Product_notes	Memo	—

Creating the Database and Defining the Tables

The next step is to create a new, blank Microsoft Access database and create the tables described in Exhibit 9.9. Then, establish relationships between the tables as shown in Exhibit 9.10 following the process outlined in Chapter 7. At that point, Sunset's conversion process database is set up.

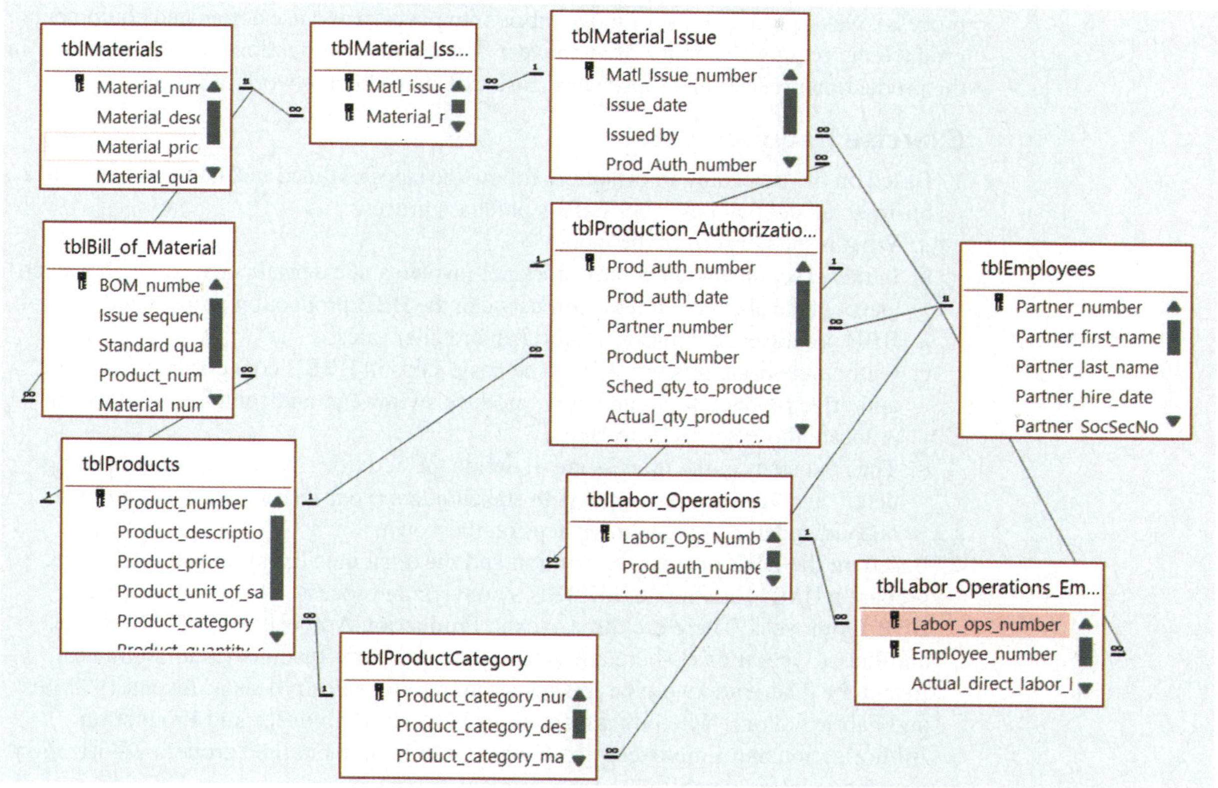

EXHIBIT 9.10
Linked Conversion Process Tables with Referential Integrity Enforced

Microsoft Access

Review Exercise: Baer Belly Bikinis' Swimwear Production

This review exercise examines the conversion process for Baer Belly Bikinis Incorporated (BBB). As outlined in Chapters 7 and 8, BBB is a small business located in Santa Monica, California. It sells swimwear and related products to specialty stores throughout the United States. It also sells its products to individuals over a company website. Paige Baer founded BBB almost 10 years ago after she graduated from the Fashion Institute of Design and Merchandising. She recognized the need for swimsuits sold as separates. Her business has grown rapidly, and now BBB has a large following of customers who want to be able to mix and match to find their ideal swimsuit. Currently, BBB products are carried in more than 1,000 specialty swimwear boutiques and online retailers.

During an interview with Paige Baer, she described BBB's conversion process. She recently converted her swimsuit manufacturing to an automated process, but it still requires the production staff to feed the machines, monitor the sewing, fold and package the swimwear, and add it to the swimwear inventory. So, she is looking forward to an assessment of her requirements and recommendations that would position BBB for substantial further growth.

This review exercise examines BBB conversion/production. BBB produces swimwear to order, so they respond to incoming sales orders. They schedule production to meet requested delivery dates. When the production supervisor is notified about a new sales order, the supervisor issues a production authorization to start the process. The supervisor then issues the necessary fabric into production (i.e., raw materials are issued into work in process). Next, production staff move fabric into position and use automated equipment to produce the required quantity of swimwear. BBB tracks production staff involvement in the production process, and those labor costs are also added to work in process.

Exercise Requirements

1. Based on the preceding information, follow the steps outlined in Chapter 4 to create a business model that describes BBB's purchase process.
   a. What is the purpose of the model?
   b. In this case, the model context does not involve and external participants; however, use pools to show the interaction between the BBB production process and other BBB processes: purchases of fabric and retailer sales.
   c. Outline the basic process flows. The basic steps in BBB's conversion process are authorize production, issue fabric, produce swimwear, and complete production. Allocate those activities to lanes.
   d. The next steps in the process are to define the activities, refine the model adding detail, and validate the model with stakeholders (your instructor). Students are encouraged to complete those steps on their own.
2. Based on the BBB process description and the attributes list at the end of the lab, prepare a UML class model for BBB's conversion process. There is one agent: BBB Employees. There are three events: Production Authorization, Fabric Issue, and Labor Operations. There are two resources: Fabric Inventory and Swimwear Inventory. There are two type images (from retailer sales process): Inventory Types and Fabric Colors. Note how associations between Employees and Production Authorization and Employees and Fabric Issue implement the "proper authorization" preventive internal control.
3. Use the UML class diagram to create an Access database. Your instructor will provide an Excel spreadsheet with the BBB information. Create a new Access database and import each worksheet in the spreadsheet into the database. Set appropriate primary keys and establish relationships among tables.
4. Refer back to BBB's sales to retailers in Chapter 7 and BBB's fabric purchases in Chapter 8. Create an integrated UML class diagram that shows BBB's sales to retailers, BBB's fabric purchases, and BBB's conversion process. Refer to the glossary of models for examples.

Attribute Listing for BBB

Authorized by (hint: foreign key)
Bill of Material Item Projected Cost
Catalog#
Color Code
Color Name
Employee Address
Employee City
Employee department
Employee First Name

Employee Hire Date
Employee Last Name
Employee Pay Amount
Employee Phone
Employee Salary/Wage
Employee Zip
Employee#
Fabric Cost for this Fabric Issue
Fabric Cost Per Yard
Fabric Inventory Quantity on Hand
Fabric Issue#
Fabric Quantity Yards Issued on this Fabric Issue
Inventory description
Labor Cost of this Employee for this Labor Operation
Labor Operations#
Production Authorization#
Production Date
Production Time Elapsed
Quantity Produced
Supervisor Employee#
Swimwear Inventory Type Code
Swimwear Inventory Wholesale Price
Swimwear Retail Price
Swimwear Size
Swimwear Standard Cost
Swimwear Type Use
Swimwear Type Yards Fabric Required
Total Labor Cost for this Labor Operation
Type Code Description
Yards Fabric Issued

Summary

- From an accounting standpoint, we must account for transfers of raw materials into work-in-process, direct labor, allocated overhead, and the cost of goods manufactured in the conversion process.
- Sunset Graphics provides an ongoing example of how to model the conversion process.
- Activity models can show the basic steps in the process and the collaborations between the company and its customers, as well as exceptions to the process.
- Business rules implement internal control activities.
- There is a standard structure model pattern that allows for collection of accounting information for the conversion process—including issues of raw material into work-in-process and recording direct labor and allocated overhead—such that cost of goods manufactured includes material, labor, and overhead costs.
- The standard pattern is tailored to a specific organization by adding type images to collect management information.
- The structure model provides a blueprint for a relational database that will collect, store, and report sales and collection information.

Key Words

agents (*358*) The people or organizations who participate in business events, such as customers and salespeople.

events (*358*) (UML) Classes that model the organization's transactions, usually affecting the organization's resources, such as sales and cash receipts; Important occurrences that affect the flow of activities in a business process, such as BPMN symbols to define start, intermediate, and end events.

finished goods inventory (*353*) For a manufacturing company, the inventory (REA resource) that has completed the manufacturing process and is held for sale to customers.

gateway (*354*) BPMN symbol that shows process branching and merging as the result of decisions. Basic gateways are depicted as diamonds. Usually, gateways appear as pairs on the diagram. The first gateway shows the branching, and the second gateway shows merging of the process branches.

intermediate error event (*354*) Occurs between start and end events and affects the flow of the process. Intermediate error events represent interruptions to the normal flow of the process and start the exception flow.

labor operations event (*358*) In the conversion process, an event that represents the recording of labor (and any associated overhead) costs applied to work-in-process.

many-to-many relationship (*360*) Exists when instances of one class (e.g., sales) are related to many instances of another class (e.g., inventory) and vice versa. These relationships are implemented in Access and relational databases by adding a linking table to convert the many-to-many relationship into two one-to-many relationships.

production authorization event (*359*) In a UML class model of the conversion process, an event that records the authorization to produce one or more finished good inventory items.

raw material issue event (*359*) In a UML class diagram of the conversion process, an event that records the transfer of raw materials into work-in-process.

raw materials inventory (*353*) For a manufacturing company, the inventory (REA resource) acquired for use (conversion) in the manufacturing process.

REA (*358*) Resource-event-agent framework for modeling business processes, originally developed by William McCarthy.

resources (*358*) Those things that have economic value to a firm, such as cash and products.

type image (*360*) Class that represents management information (such as categorizations, policies, and guidelines) to help manage a business process. Type image often allows process information to be summarized by category.

work-in-process inventory (*358*) For a manufacturing company, the value of raw materials, direct labor, and manufacturing overhead in production but not yet finished.

ANSWERS TO PROGRESS CHECKS

1. You could modify Exhibit 9.4 by creating an additional lane within the Sunset pool for the inspection organizational unit.
2. You could modify Exhibit 9.4 by adding an additional gateway following the Inspect Work activity with two branches: (a) linking to the Discard Items activity and (b) linking to the Batch Done gateway.
3. An association can be promoted to a type image if it needs to contain more information or link to other classes. Apparently, Sunset's labor operations do not vary according to the specific product. If they did, it could promote the labor plan association shown in Exhibit 9.8 to a labor plan class like the Bill of Material class in Exhibit 9.8. That type image class would link to the products class and the labor operations class.
4. An equipment class would be an additional resource. It would be linked to the products class if the equipment varied according to the specific product. The equipment operations class, like the labor operations class, would record the use of the equipment to add that cost to the costs of production.

Multiple Choice Questions connect

1. **(LO 9-1)** Which of the following is *not* an activity in the conversion process?
   a. Authorize production
   b. Issue raw material
   c. Perform work
   d. Transfer finished goods to customers
   e. All of these are activities in the conversion process.
2. **(LO 9-1)** Which of the following activities results in work-in-process moving to finished goods inventory?
   a. Authorize production
   b. Inspect work
   c. Complete production
   d. Issue raw material
   e. None of these options
3. **(LO 9-2, LO 9-3)** Which of the following describes the purpose of a lane within a pool in BPMN?
   a. Indicates the start of the process
   b. Indicates the end of the process
   c. Identifies different activity flow options
   d. Distinguishes specific responsibilities for performing different tasks
   e. None of these options
4. **(LO 9-2, LO 9-3)** Which of the following is *not* a purpose of using lanes to describe the conversion process?
   a. Document the sequence of activities in the process.
   b. Expose potential problems in the handoff between organizational units.
   c. Show important decision points, and identify responsibility for those decisions.
   d. Establish internal control activities, such as segregation of duties.
   e. All of these are purposes of lanes.
5. **(LO 9-4)** Which of the following is a business rule implementing access control for the conversion process?
   a. Employee authorizing production cannot modify inventory records.
   b. System must provide control numbers.
   c. System must default date to current date.
   d. System must create audit trail whenever records are changed.
   e. None of these options are access controls.
6. **(LO 9-5)** Consider a UML class diagram of the conversion process that uses the REA framework. Which of the following events begins a typical conversion process? Assign employees to departments
   a. Authorize production.
   b. Issue raw material into work-in-process.
   c. Sell finished goods.
   d. None of these options.
7. **(LO 9-5)** Review Exhibit 9.8. Which of the following describes the purpose of the Labor Operations event?
   a. Add the direct labor costs to work-in-process inventory.
   b. Control the specific labor activities.
   c. Ensure that labor is performed.
   d. Identify production employees.
   e. None of these options.

8. **(LO 9-5)** Review Exhibit 9.8. Which of the following is a correct posting of a foreign key to implement the model in a relational database?
   a. Labor Operations primary key becomes a foreign key in Production Authorization.
   b. Products primary key becomes a foreign key in Bill of Material.
   c. Product Categories primary key becomes a foreign key in Employees.
   d. Products primary key becomes a foreign key in Product Categories.
   e. All of these options are correct.
9. **(LO 9-1, LO 9-5)** Review Exhibit 9.8. Which of the following describes the purpose of the Bill of Material class?
   a. Record the invoices from suppliers for materials purchased.
   b. Record the planned raw material contents of each finished good.
   c. Record the authorization of production.
   d. Describe the labor required for each finished good.
   e. None of these options
10. **(LO 9-5)** Compare Exhibit 9.9 with Exhibit 9.10. Which of the following describes the differences between those two figures?
    a. Exhibit 9.10 includes *tblLabor_Operations_Employees* to implement the many-to-many relationship between *tblEmployees* and *tblLabor_Operations.*
    b. Exhibit 9.10 includes *tblMaterial_Issue_Material* to implement the many-to-many relationship between *tblMaterial_Issue* and *tblMaterials.*
    c. Exhibit 9.9 includes the minimum multiplicities to specify data integrity requirements.
    d. Exhibit 9.10 only shows maximum cardinalities between linked tables.
    e. All of these options are differences between the two figures.

Refer to the following integrated diagram, showing part of the purchases and sales processes linked to the conversion process, for Questions 11 through 25.

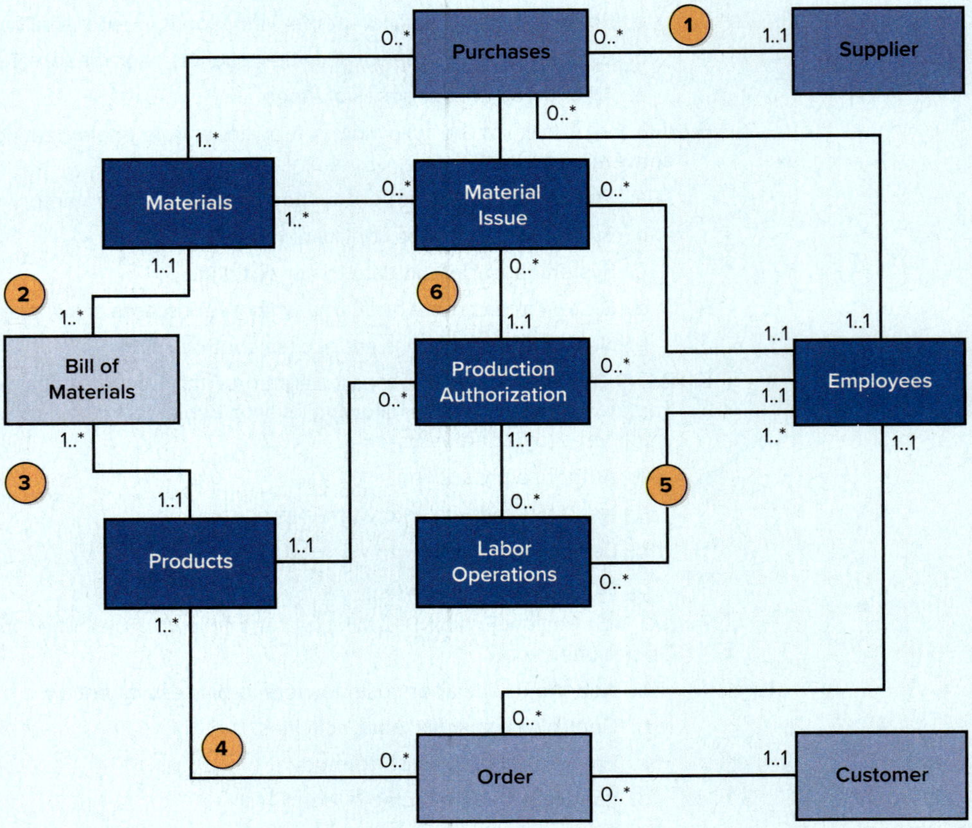

11. **(LO 9-5)** Refer to the association marked with the number 1 in the preceding diagram. Which of the following is the best description of the association?
   a. Each supplier participates in a minimum of zero purchases.
   b. Each supplier participates in at least one purchase.
   c. Each supplier participates in a maximum of one purchase.
   d. Supplier is the internal agent in the purchase process.
   e. None of these is a description of the association.
12. **(LO 9-5)** Refer to the association marked with the number 1 in the preceding diagram. Which of the following is the best description of the association?
   a. Each purchase involves one supplier.
   b. Each purchase involves multiple suppliers.
   c. Each purchase involves a minimum of zero suppliers.
   d. Some purchases are made after a production authorization.
   e. None of these is a description of the association.
13. **(LO 9-5)** Refer to the association marked with the number 2 in the preceding diagram. Which of the following is the best description of the purpose of the association?
   a. The association links products to the corresponding bill of materials.
   b. The association links purchases to raw materials.
   c. The association links raw materials to the bill of materials.
   d. All of these descriptions are purposes of the association.
   e. None of these is a description of the purpose of the association.
14. **(LO 9-5)** Refer to the association marked with the number 2 in the preceding diagram. Which of the following is the best description of the association?
   a. Each bill of materials entry specifies one raw material.
   b. Each bill of materials entry specifies multiple raw materials.
   c. Each bill of materials is related to a minimum of zero raw materials.
   d. Each bill of materials is related to a maximum of many raw materials.
   e. None of these is a description of the association.
15. **(LO 9-5)** Refer to the association marked with the number 2 in the preceding diagram. Which of the following is the best description of the association?
   a. Each raw material is related to a minimum of zero bills of materials.
   b. Each raw material is related to a maximum of one bill of materials.
   c. A raw material item could be related to multiple bill of materials entries.
   d. A raw material item could be related to no bill of materials.
   e. None of these is a description of the association.
16. **(LO 9-5)** Refer to the association marked with the number 2 in the preceding diagram. Which of the following is the best way to implement the association in a relational database?
   a. Post the primary key of bill of materials as a foreign key in raw materials.
   b. Post the primary key of raw materials as a foreign key in bill of materials.
   c. Create a linking table between raw materials and bill of materials.
   d. The location of the foreign key is optional.
   e. None of these is the best way to implement the relationship.

17. **(LO 9-5)** Refer to the association marked with the number 3 in the preceding diagram. Which of the following is the best description of the purpose of the association?
    a. Links actual material costs to each product produced.
    b. Links actual labor costs to each product produced.
    c. Specifies planned material costs for each product.
    d. Specifies planned labor costs for each product.
    e. None of these is a description of the purpose of the association.
18. **(LO 9-5)** Refer to the association marked with the number 3 in the preceding diagram. Which of the following is the best description of the association?
    a. Each bill of materials is related to a minimum of zero products.
    b. Each bill of materials is related to a minimum of one product.
    c. Each bill of materials is related to a maximum of many products.
    d. Each bill of materials is not necessarily related to a product.
    e. None of these is a description of the association.
19. **(LO 9-5)** Refer to the association marked with the number 3 in the preceding diagram. Which of the following is the best way to implement the association in a relational database?
    a. Post the primary key of bill of materials as a foreign key in products.
    b. Post the primary key of products as a foreign key in bill of materials.
    c. Create a linking table between products and bill of materials.
    d. The location of the foreign key is optional.
    e. None of these is the best way to implement the relationship.
20. **(LO 9-5)** Refer to the association marked with the number 4 in the preceding diagram. Which of the following is the best description of the purpose of the association?
    a. Shows that the conversion and purchases process are integrated via products.
    b. Shows that the conversion process is triggered by an order for a product.
    c. Links products produced by the conversion process to orders (by customers).
    d. Links products to subsequent cash receipts in the sales process.
    e. None of these is a description of the purpose of the association.
21. **(LO 9-5)** Refer to the association marked with the number 4 in the preceding diagram. Which of the following is the best description of the association?
    a. Each product is related to only one order.
    b. Each product can be related to many orders.
    c. Each product is related to a minimum of one order.
    d. Each product is related to a maximum of one order.
    e. None of these is a description of the association.
22. **(LO 9-5)** Refer to the association marked with the number 5 in the preceding diagram. Which of the following is the best way to implement the association in a relational database?
    a. Post the primary key of Employees as a foreign key in labor operations.
    b. Post the primary key of labor operations as a foreign key in Employees.
    c. Create a linking table between Employees and labor operations.
    d. The location of the foreign key is optional.
    e. None of these is the best way to implement the relationship.

23. **(LO 9-5)** Refer to the association marked with the number 5 in the preceding diagram. Which of the following is the best description of the association?
    a. Each labor operation is related to only one employee.
    b. Each labor operation is related to a maximum of many employees.
    c. Labor operations are related to a minimum of zero employee.
    d. Labor operations are related to a maximum of one employee.
    e. None of these is a description of the association.
24. **(LO 9-5)** Refer to the association marked with the number 6 in the preceding diagram. Which of the following is the best description of the purpose of the association?
    a. Authorizes the issue of raw materials.
    b. Controls the transfer of raw materials to work-in-process.
    c. Relates specific raw material issues to the controlling authorization.
    d. All of the above describe the purpose of the association.
    e. None of these describes the purpose of the association.
25. **(LO 9-5)** Refer to the association marked with the number 6 in the preceding diagram. Which of the following is the best description of the association?
    a. Each production authorization is related to a minimum of zero material issues.
    b. Each production authorization is related to a minimum of one material issue.
    c. Each production authorization is related to a maximum of one material issue.
    d. Each production authorization is related to a maximum of zero material issues.
    e. None of these is a description of the association.

Discussion Questions

1. **(LO 9-1)** Think about the roles of accountants presented in Exhibit 4.1 from Chapter 4. Why should accountants be involved in developing and reviewing the bills of materials?
2. **(LO 9-1)** Describe some businesses that use conversion processes. Do they all use the same sequence of activities? Do they all share the same information structure? Discuss some of the differences in those conversion processes.
3. **(LO 9-5)** Think about the UML class diagrams for the sales and collection process described in Chapter 7 and the purchases and payments process described in Chapter 8. If you were asked to prepare an integrated model that shows those two processes as well as the conversion process, where would the models intersect/integrate? Why? What elements are unique to each process?
4. **(LO 9-1, LO 9-5)** In Exhibit 9.8, the Labor Operations event tracks direct labor incurred in the conversion process. What event tracks indirect labor?
5. **(LO 9-1, LO 9-5)** Describe how you would change Exhibit 9.8 to implement an activity-based costing system with three different cost drivers.
6. **(LO 9-1, LO 9-5)** Put Exhibit 9.8 in the context of the overall supply chain that starts with the purchases and payments process (Chapter 8) and ends with the sales and cash receipts process (Chapter 7). How would you expand Exhibit 9.8 to describe Sunset's entire supply chain?
7. **(LO 9-4)** Business rules implement internal controls. Review Exhibit 9.6 and classify each of those business rules listed as access controls as obligatory, prohibited, or allowed, as described in Chapter 5. Select two of those business rules and rephrase them, so an obligatory rule is now a prohibited rule, a prohibited rule is now an allowed rule, and so on.
8. **(LO 9-5)** Compare the generic UML class diagram for the conversion process shown in Exhibit 9.7 with a generic sales and collection diagram, similar to Exhibit 7.20. Identify the similarities and differences, and then explain why they exist.

Problems connect

1. **(LO 9-5, LO 9-6)** The Rubber Duck Brewing Company is a new microbrewery. Rubber Duck's brewing process converts beer raw ingredients—malt extract, malted grain, adjuncts (rice or corn), hops, yeast, and water—into brewed beer. Rubber Duck assigns a unique ingredient number to each ingredient so it can track the quantity on hand. It tracks its brewed beer by the beer name: pale ale, amber ale, porter, stout, lager, pilsner, and so forth. Rubber Duck tracks its brewing equipment (e.g., mash tuns, whirlpools, fermenters, and conditioning tanks) by equipment item number, and it also tracks which equipment is used and how long it is used in each brewing step.

   Over time, Rubber Duck has developed a unique recipe for each of its brewed beers. The recipe describes the specific ingredients, the sequence of brewing steps, the specific equipment, and the type of employees required for each step in the brewing process for each beer. Each step in the recipe may involve multiple ingredients (e.g., barley, hops, malts, and yeast) and multiple pieces of equipment, but it only requires one type of employee.

   When Rubber Duck decides to brew one of its beers, a supervisor issues a "Brew Order" for that beer, specifying the quantity in gallons to be brewed. Then, the brewing process begins. In the first step, they thoroughly clean the equipment. Second, they mash the grains to activate enzymes. Third, they separate the wort from the grain, which is called *lautering*. Fourth, they boil the ingredients, adding hops per the recipe. Fifth, they prepare the wort for fermentation by quickly reducing the temperature, adding water and yeast.

   When the brewing process is complete, the brewed beer is stored in large copper tanks for aging. Ales require relatively little aging (less than 3 weeks), while lagers may require longer aging (up to 5 weeks). The copper tanks are tracked separately from other brewing equipment. Aging of the beer is not part of the brewing process; it takes place after the brewing process.

   a. Prepare a context diagram similar to the one shown in the Review Exercise showing the relationships with Rubber Duck conversion (brewing), purchasing, and sales processes.
   b. Prepare a BPMN diagram showing the basic steps in Rubber Duck's brewing process.
   c. Prepare a UML class diagram that captures Rubber Duck's brewing process.
   d. Using the preceding information and the following attributes list, prepare a listing of the relational tables, indicating the primary key (PK) and foreign keys (FK) for each table.
   e. Use the UML class diagram and the listing of relational tables to prepare a relational database in Access.

   Several Rubber Duck employees perform each brewing step. Rubber Duck tracks the amount of each raw ingredient actually used in each step as well as the time spent by each employee on each step. Each brewing step often requires more than one piece of equipment, and some pieces of equipment are used on multiple brewing steps, although many are used in only one step. For safety, Rubber Duck only allows employees to operate equipment that they are qualified to use.

   Attributes:

   Actual aging time to date for the brewed beer in this copper tank
   Actual quantity of this ingredient used in this brew step
   Actual time for this equipment used in this brew step
   Brew order date
   Brew order number (brew#)
   Brew quantity in gallons
   Brew step description

Brew step number (brew step#)
Brewed beer description
Brewed beer name
Brewed beer quantity on hand (QOH)
Brewing recipe step description
Brewing recipe step number (recipe step#)
Copper tank capacity in gallons
Copper tank number (tank#)
Date this employee qualified to operate this equipment
Employee name
Employee number (emp#)
Employee type
Employee type description
Equipment item description
Equipment item number (equip#)
Ingredient description
Ingredient number (ingred#)
Ingredient quantity-on-hand (QOH)
Number of employees of this type
Planned aging time for this brewed beer
Planned time for this equipment in this step
Quantity of beer in this tank (in gallons)
Standard quantity of this ingredient used in this recipe step
Time spent by this employee on this brew step

2. **(LO 9-2, LO 9-3, LO 9-5)** Penny loves pastries. She wanted everyone else to love pastries, too, so she started Penny's Pastries in Orange County about 3 years ago. After a shaky start, she scored a big contract with **Starbucks** to provide pastries to all stores in southern California. This case describes Penny's daily baking process. Penny's bakery starts preparing fresh pastries every morning about 1:00 a.m. for delivery to local stores by 5:30 a.m. The selection and quantity of pastries vary according to the day of the week as well as the time of the year.

Inventories

Although Penny has a number of her own specialties, she makes many of her baked products according to Starbucks' requirements. So, every day she makes some of her own pastries for sale in her bakeries as well as all the pastries for the various Starbucks locations. Currently, her finished goods inventory can include more than 50 different kinds of pastries and baked products. Because of the volume that Penny produces, she maintains an extensive inventory of the ingredients that she uses in her baked goods, such as flour, butter, milk, chocolate, and cinnamon.

Baking Plans

Penny carefully plans the contents and preparation of each finished product (pastry and baked good). There are two parts to her formal plans—an ingredient list and a recipe—for each baked product. The ingredient list specifies the quantity of each ingredient required for each finished product. The recipe defines the sequence of steps that her bakers follow to prepare each finished product. The recipe steps also set the standard number of labor-hours, as well as the specific equipment used, to prepare a standard batch of each finished product.

Daily Baking Process

Early each morning, the supervisor prepares a daily baking order that specifies the quantities of all the different finished products to be prepared that day. As soon as the various products and quantities are known, an inventory clerk uses the ingredient list to issue all the ingredients necessary for the day, moving them from the storeroom to the baking area. In some cases, the clerk may issue ingredients several different times for each daily baking order so that none of the refrigerated items are left out longer than necessary. Penny assigns sequential issue numbers to each issue during the day, and the clerk carefully records the quantity of each ingredient issued.

Penny's bakers prepare the finished products in batches. Each batch produces one finished baked good product. A supervisor (who could be different from the supervisor who issued the baking order) issues a batch order to start the baking process for that batch. The bakers then prepare the ingredients in a series of baking steps according to the recipe for that product using the equipment and ovens specified in the recipe. Penny's bakery has an array of ovens and baking equipment, tracked by equipment number, to keep up with the daily baking production volumes. Because each oven has different characteristics, the baking time for each product can depend on the particular oven used. The baking steps usually involve mixing ingredients, preparing the pastries, placing the prepared items in an oven for baking, and then removing the products and placing them on cooling racks, ready for packing. Each actual baking step may involve the use of multiple pieces of baking equipment and multiple bakers. Penny carefully tracks actual hours of labor and equipment use for each baking step.

General Information

Penny does not separately identify employees as supervisors, inventory clerks, or bakers. There is one employee entity. Information on ingredient lists, recipes, finished products, ingredients, and employees is put into the database before those entities are linked to events or type images.

a. Prepare a context diagram similar to the one shown in the Review Exercise showing the relationships between Penny's baking process and both ingredient purchases and pastry sales.
b. Draw a BPMN activity diagram that describes Penny's baking process.
c. Prepare a UML class diagram with classes, associations, and multiplicities.
d. Using the preceding case information and the following attributes list, prepare a listing of the relational tables necessary to support this conversion process. List the tables in the following order: resources, events, agents, type images, and linking tables.

Attributes:

Actual baking time for this baking step and this oven
Baking order#
Baking order date
Baking step#
Batch#
Batch finish time
Batch start time
Employee#
Employee hours worked on this baking step
Ingredient#
Ingredient cost
Ingredient description
Ingredient list#
Ingredient list description
Ingredient QOH
Ingredient unit of issue
Issue#
Issue date/time
Employee name

Employee pay rate
Equipment#
Equipment description
Equipment manufacturer
Finished product#
Finished product description
Finished product number of calories
Finished product price
Finished product QOH
Qty of this baked product ordered by this daily baking order
Qty of this baked product prepared in this batch
Qty of this ingredient issued on this issue#
Qty of this ingredient required for this finished product
Recipe step#
Recipe step description
Standard baking time for this recipe step with this oven
Standard labor hours for this recipe step
Total labor hours for this baking step

Chapter Ten

Integrated Project

A Look at This Chapter

This chapter builds on the business process modeling and database design material in earlier chapters. It describes how to approach a business analysis and integrated systems development project involving multiple business processes. The project itself, designed as a group assignment, is available separately. To complete the project successfully, each group must plan and execute a realistic systems design and development project. The finished product will include activity and structure models of a company's business processes, which can support enhanced internal controls, more effective use of an AIS and related information technology to improve the company's performance, and the development relational database system and appropriate queries necessary to prepare financial and managerial accounting reports.

A Look Back

Chapter 9 completed the comprehensive example describing Sunset Graphics' business processes. It presented basic activity and structure models for the company's conversion process, as well as a description of the database to support that process.

A Look Ahead

Chapter 11 discusses internal controls for accounting information systems.

Iain Masterton/Alamy Stock Photo

After **Starbucks** implemented the **Oracle** E-business Suite, it had the IT backbone necessary to leverage a variety of other applications to support its business processes. As part of the Oracle implementation, **Accenture** worked with Starbucks to standardize business processes around the world. The Oracle ERP system resides on top of Oracle's database system, and that allows reuse and redistribution of the information collected. Starbucks' enterprise data warehouse (EDW) leverages that data to support Starbucks' internal business users.

Since 2008, thousands of Starbucks' stores directly access the EDW through web-based dashboards. Using a business intelligence reporting tool from **MicroStrategy Inc.,** individual users could develop customized operational performance reports. MicroStrategy's reports can even be delivered by e-mail on preset schedules.

Since the economic downturn in 2009, Starbucks' revenues have increased steadily. Its revenue per store increased from $1 million to over $1.4 million annually in the United States. Its operating income has almost doubled, and its operating margin increased from 13.8 percent in 2010 to 14.3 percent in 2022. Clearly, Starbucks has been successful at reducing costs and increasing margins. Without standardized processes and integrated systems providing reliable and timely information for decisions, it is unlikely that it could have achieved this success.

CHAPTER OUTLINE

Integrated Project Options

Project Planning

Determine Business Requirements

Prepare Activity Models Using BPMN

Prepare Structure Diagram

Import Data into Access, Create Efficient Tables, and Set Relationships

Use Queries to Develop Financial Statement Information

LEARNING OBJECTIVES

After completing the project outlined in this chapter, you should be able to:

10-1 Plan and manage a business analysis project.

10-2 Develop activity models of multiple business processes, and use those models to assess potential risks and opportunities for process improvements.

10-3 Develop an integrated UML class diagram for a business.

10-4 Use the UML class diagram to design and implement a relational database system in Microsoft Access™.

10-5 Employ the relational database to answer a variety of business performance questions.

connect

INTEGRATED PROJECT OPTIONS

The integrated projects provide opportunities to apply the information presented in earlier chapters. There is no substitute for practice. Your instructor can select from three different projects. Two of the projects incorporate substantial use of UML class diagrams, BPMN, and Microsoft Access. The third project replicates a small business accounting software. The Y Not Flowers project can be offered as one integrated assignment or in three steps such that the assignment is started with step 1 following Chapter 7, extended with step 2 following Chapter 8, and then concluded with this chapter.

- **Y Not Flowers Project.** *Y Not Flowers* is a wholesale flower distributor with stores in several major metropolitan areas of the United States This project requires
  - Documenting business processes with BPMN.
  - Preparing UML class diagram(s) to plan data structures.
  - Moving Excel-based data into Access and preparing financial reports.
  - Reporting on findings.
- **Z Cheddr Project.** *Z Cheddr* is a successful chain of cheese and wine shops in Oregon that specialize in Oregon artisan cheeses and local wines. They also sell cheese and wine over the Internet. This project also requires
  - Documenting business processes with BPMN.
  - Preparing UML class diagram(s) to plan data structures.
  - Moving Excel-based data into Access and preparing financial reports.
  - Reporting on findings.
- **Y Not Flowers - Boston - Small Business Accounting.** This project emulates a small business accounting system for one of the Y Not Flowers stores. You would enter transactions in the same way that transactions are entered into a small business accounting system, such as Quickbooks, and review summary information to complete the accounting process for this store.

The remainder of this chapter describes how to approach the first two extensive integrated projects. These are challenging and realistic projects that require careful planning and well-managed execution to finish on time. The third project is standalone and your instructor will provide separate instructions.

LO 10-1

Plan and manage a business analysis project.

PROJECT PLANNING

Exhibit 10.1 describes a suggested sequence of activities to complete an integrated business analysis project. Such projects represent "ill-structured" problems that require careful planning and attention to detail. Thus, the first step is to prepare a project plan in as much detail as possible. Develop a problem statement and the timeline to accomplish the project on time. Identify the major steps you will undertake to complete the project, when they need to be completed, and who will perform them. There are additional project planning tools, such as Gantt charts, that can help define the elements of the plan. Refer to Chapter 16 of this text for a description of project planning/management elements. Regardless of the planning tool used, the plan should identify the specific tasks necessary to complete the project, when each task must be completed, and who will complete each task. The project plan then serves as the management tool to keep progress on track to successful and on-time completion.

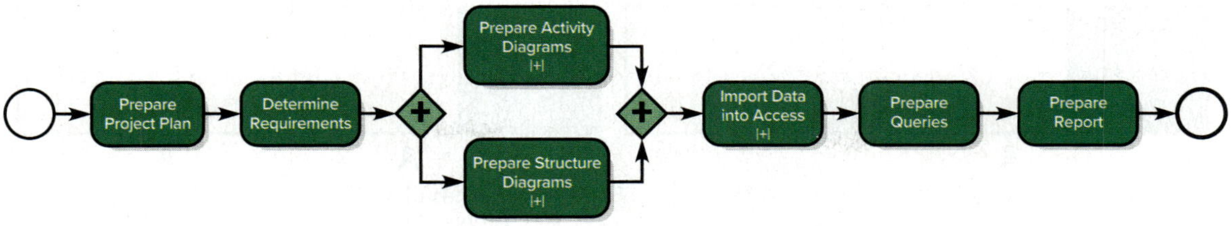

EXHIBIT 10.1
Suggested Project Steps

> **LO 10-2**
>
> Develop activity models of multiple business processes, and use those models to assess potential risks and opportunities for process improvements.

Determine Business Requirements

Step 2 is to determine the business requirements. The requirements discovery process involves fact-finding to determine who, what, when, where, why, and how business activities are performed. The process typically requires review of business documents as well as interviews with managers and employees.

Prepare Activity Models Using BPMN

Exhibit 10.1 shows Prepare Activity Diagrams as a collapsed subprocess. Exhibit 10.2 shows the expanded subprocess outlining the steps first described in Chapter 4.

EXHIBIT 10.2
Prepare Activity Diagrams Subprocess

The first task in the subprocess is to define the context. After determining the requirements, it is important to visualize them using a context diagram as shown in Exhibit 10.3. The focal organization is placed at the center of the diagram as an opaque pool. The external organizations that interact with "Your Company" are also shown as opaque pools. The goal is to identify all the message flows between the focal organization and the external organizations. The processes and systems within the focal organization must be able to respond to incoming message flows and efficiently deliver controlled outgoing message flows.

In this example, the focal organization (*Your Company*) interacts with four external organizations, Payroll Service, Suppliers, Customers, and the Bank. Exhibit 10.3 highlights the message flows (interactions) with each of the external organizations.

After gaining an understanding of the organization's business processes with the context diagram, the next step is to document each current process with a business process activity diagram using business process modeling notation (BPMN). This is often an iterative process. First, prepare simple diagrams that show the basic steps performed in each process identified from your context diagram. In this example, we will focus on the interactions with Customers for the sales process. Exhibit 10.4 shows a basic example of the sales process.

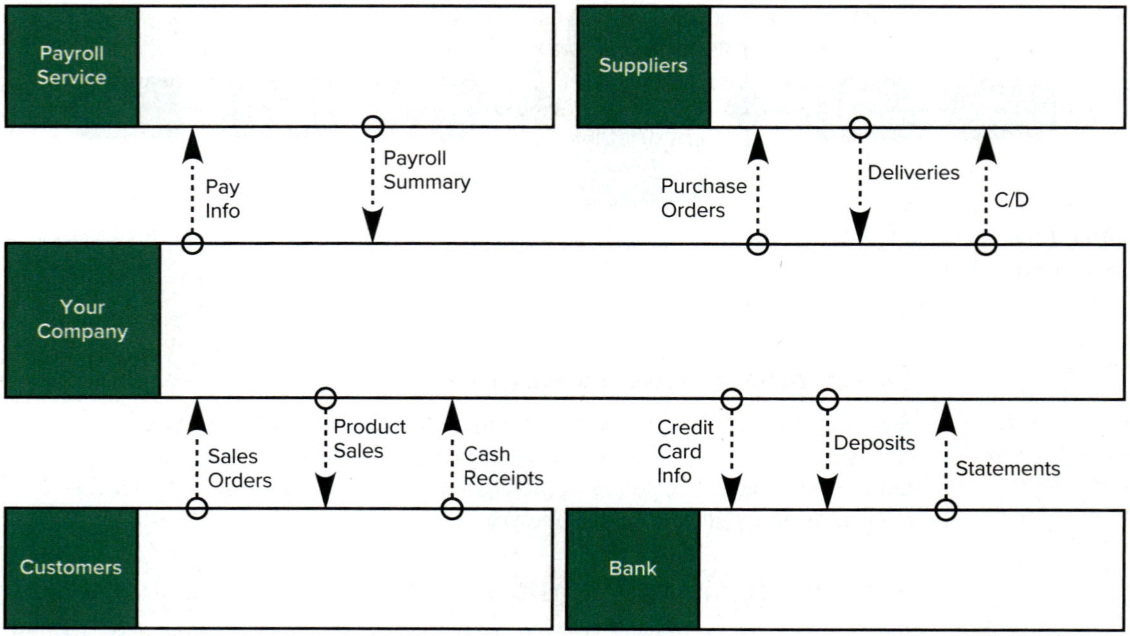

EXHIBIT 10.3
Project Context Diagram

C/D = cash disbursement.

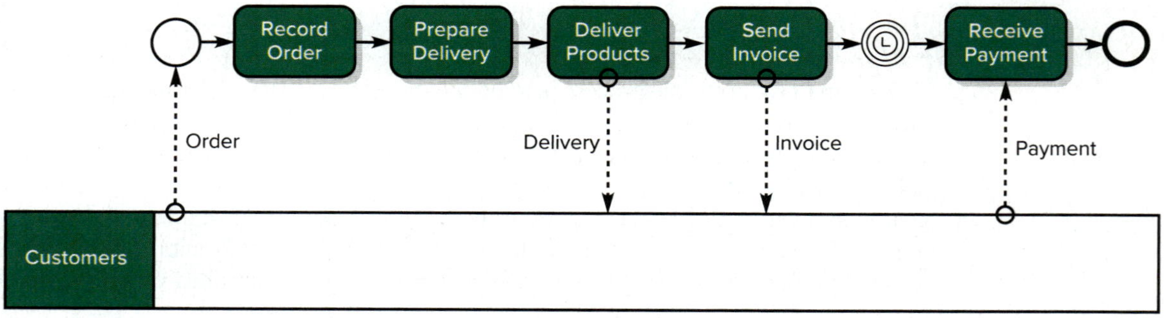

EXHIBIT 10.4
Basic Sales Process

After establishing that the basic diagram is correct, then, as described in Exhibit 10.2, define each activity including determining who performs the activity, which artifacts are created, updated, or used in the process, and whether there are exceptions to the planned sequence of activities. Then, the next step in Exhibit 10.2 is to refine and decompose activities in the model and add alternate process flows. For example, Exhibit 10.5 expands the sales process to show that the customer service department receives the order, and the shipping and receiving department prepares the delivery, and delivers the products to the customer. The accounting department then receives the payment at the end of the month.

Exhibit 10.5 also shows that the *Record Order* activity creates the Order form, which is used in the *Prepare Delivery* activity. The *Prepare Delivery* activity creates the Invoice (Inv), which is used in the *Receive Payment* process to confirm that the cash receipt matches the amount that the customer was billed.

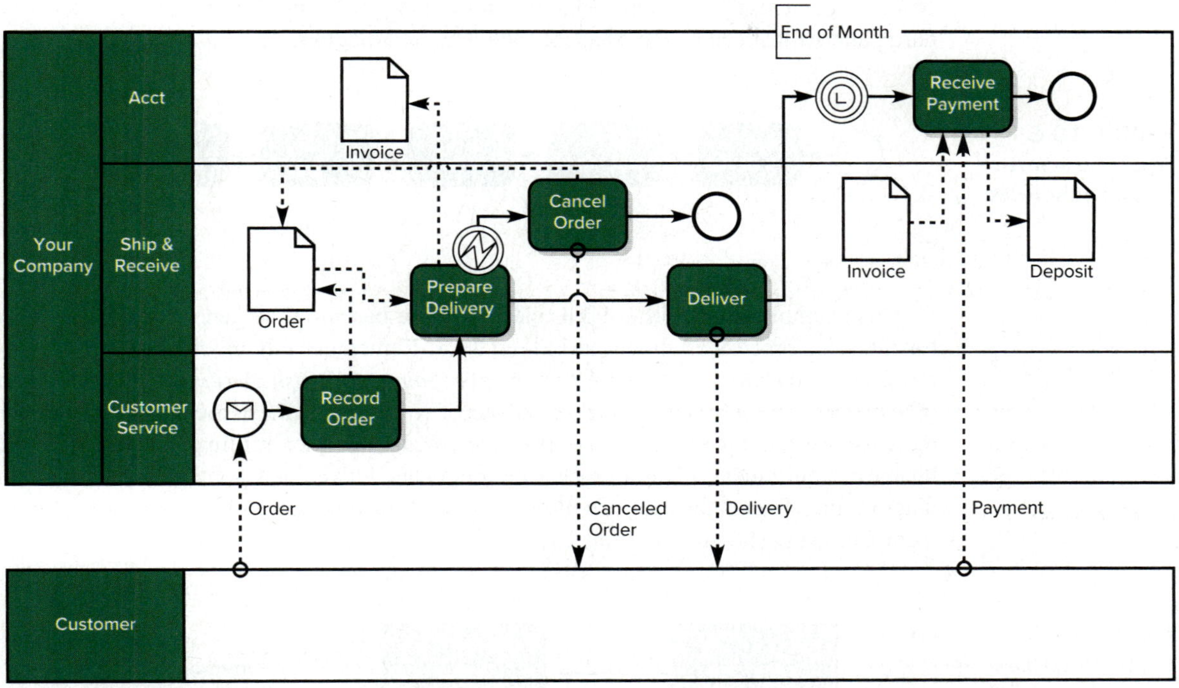

EXHIBIT 10.5
Expanded Sales Process

Exhibit 10.5 also adds an intermediate error event to the *Prepare Delivery* activity to model circumstances where products are not available. When the error event is triggered, the process flow diverts to the *Cancel Order* activity, which then updates the Order form to record the cancellation. The Cancel Order process also includes notifying the Customer of the cancellation. The project team should examine the models for potential changes to increase control or improve efficiency and document the business rules that guide decisions within each activity. At this point, the team should consider material in Chapters 11 and 12 of this text to ensure effective internal controls. To improve efficiency, each activity should be examined to determine whether it adds value to the process. Value-added activities are those that are essential for production regardless of the technology used. Activities that only add cost and not value should be eliminated where possible. Cost-added activities include those that involve nonessential movements, waiting, approvals, corrections, or revisions.

Finally, the last step in preparing activity models, Exhibit 10.2, is to validate the models with stakeholders. Once the project team confirms the accuracy of the models, the next step in Exhibit 10.1 is to prepare structure diagrams.

LO 10-3

Develop an integrated UML class diagram for a business.

Prepare Structure Diagram

Exhibit 10.6 outlines the tasks to prepare structure diagrams. Using the information gained from discovering the business requirements, the project team then prepares an integrated UML class diagram that shows the data requirements for the organization. The class diagram should articulate with the BPMN activity diagrams. In other words, the class diagram must include resources, events, and agents that capture information reflected by each data object in the activity diagrams. Material in Chapters 5, 6, and 7 of this text provides standard patterns that can be the basis for the integrated diagram.

EXHIBIT 10.6
Prepare Structure Diagram Subprocess

This example starts with a UML class diagram based on the generic REA framework for the sales process as shown in Exhibit 10.7. Remember this involves six classes, two resources (*Inventory* and *Cash*), two events (*Sales* and *Cash Receipts*), and two agents (*Customers* and *Employees*). The second step is to determine the associations, starting with the basic associations from the generic sales model and then refining to address specific business requirements. Third, process requirements define appropriate multiplicities. This diagram implements the data structures to support the interactions between Customers and Your Company shown in Exhibit 10.3.

EXHIBIT 10.7
Sample UML Class Diagram for Sales Process

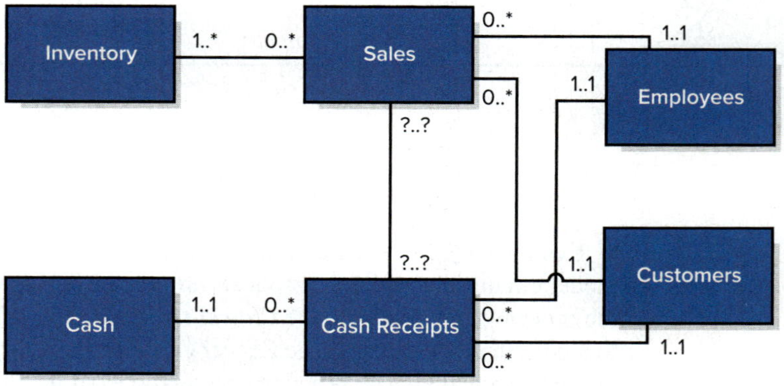

These steps—identify classes, identify associations, and define multiplicities—are repeated for each process indicated by the context diagram, see Exhibit 10.3. After UML class diagrams for each process are defined, they are combined in one integrated model as shown in Exhibit 10.8. This example includes three separate processes: Sales, Purchases of inventory, and Payroll. Chapters 7 and 8 provide examples of the sales and purchases process but not the payroll process. Essentially, the payroll process resembles a purchases process. The company acquires the employees' time (recorded in the *Timecard* event) and then pays employees (recorded in the *Payroll* event). Since there is no external agent in this simple example, there are multiple associations between the *Timecards* and *Payroll* events and the *Employees* agent, indicating that an employee supervises another employees work and an employee (payroll clerk) makes payments to other employees.

The integrated UML class diagram becomes the blueprint for implementing the database. The diagram also helps plan queries that will be used to develop the financial statements. For example, the *Sales, Timecards,* and *Purchases of Inventory* events support preparation of the income statement. The duality associations between events indicate potential payables and receivables for the balance sheet. Resources, such as *Inventory* and *Cash,* support asset balances on the balance sheet. *Cash Disbursement, Payroll,* and *Cash Receipt (C/R)* events affect the statement of cash flows.

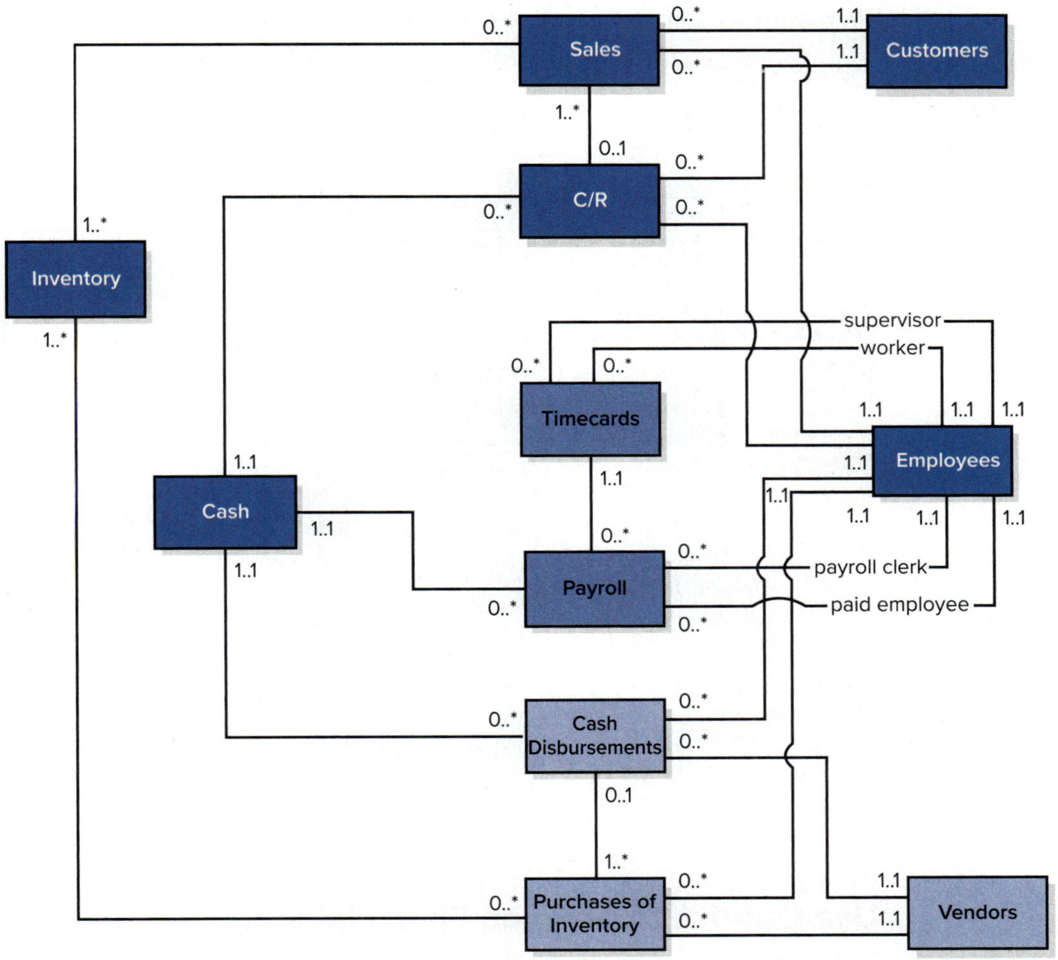

EXHIBIT 10.8
Integrated UML Class Diagram

> **LO 10-4**
>
> Use the UML class diagram to design and implement a relational database system in Microsoft Access™.

Import Data into Access, Create Efficient Tables, and Set Relationships

At this point, the project team is ready to create the Access database or more generally the AIS. For the purpose of the integrated project, your instructor will provide data in an Excel spreadsheet. In other projects, you might have to move data from existing systems into a new AIS. In either case, the UML class diagram will be the blueprint that you will follow. It is likely that the data will include redundancies and occasional typographical errors, which need to be corrected. After importing the data, set appropriate primary keys, check data types, and modify tables as necessary to be sure that they are structured efficiently. Then, create the relationships among tables, enforcing referential integrity. Failing to enforce referential integrity on relationships will affect the reliability of your queries.

Exhibit 10.9 shows the Access relationships implementing the integrated UML class diagram, see Exhibit 10.8. There are three notable differences between the integrated diagram and the resulting Access relationships. There are two new tables, sales items and purchase items, to implement the many-to-many relationships between sales and inventory and purchases and inventory. There is a new employees_1, a "ghost" image of employees created by Access, to allow two associations between employees and timecards and employees and payroll.

EXHIBIT 10.9
Access Relationships Implementing Integrated UML Class Diagram

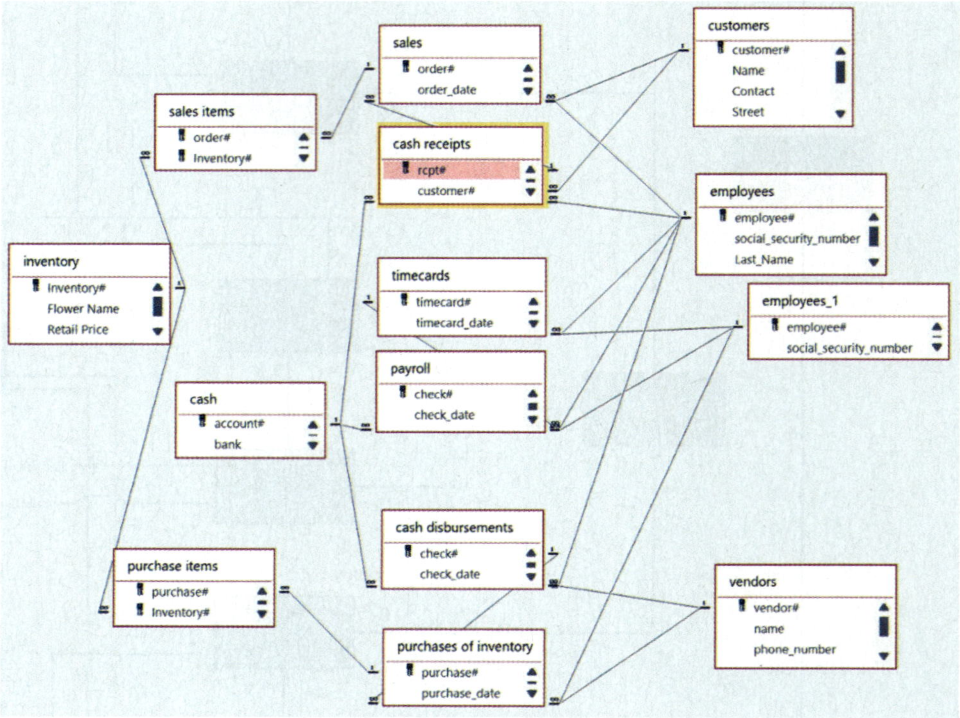

LO 10-5

Employ the relational database to answer a variety of business performance questions.

Use Queries to Develop Financial Statement Information

Developing financial statement information will require a series of queries. Refer to the integrated UML class diagram, Exhibit 10.8, as your guide. Some events affect the income statement; other events affect the balance sheet.

- Sales summarizes to revenue on the income statement.
- Purchases of Inventory summarizes to cost of goods sold.
- Timecards (and Payroll) summarizes to wages expense.
- Cash receipts and cash disbursements affect the cash balance on the balance sheet.
- Sales minus cash receipts is accounts receivable on the balance sheet.
- Purchases of Inventory and Sales affect the inventory balance on the balance sheet.
- Purchases minus corresponding cash disbursements determine accounts payable on the balance sheet.
- Any accumulated withholding and tax obligations in payroll determine taxes payable.

Summary

This chapter outlines the approach to an integrated business analysis project. The project involves

- Using project planning and management tools.
- Defining business requirements.
- Preparing an integrated UML class diagram.
- Preparing activity diagrams using BPMN.
- Importing data into Access from Excel.
- Cleaning and correcting data and data structures.
- Preparing queries to provide financial information.

Chapter Eleven

Accounting Information Systems and Internal Controls

A Look at This Chapter

This chapter provides a general discussion on control issues in accounting information systems. In particular, we examine issues in ethics and internal controls that are addressed by the Sarbanes–Oxley Act of 2002 and important factors in corporate governance. These related areas are critical to an organization's efficiency and effectiveness in operations, reliability in financial reporting, and compliance with applicable laws and regulations. In addition, important control and governance frameworks including COSO (Committee of Sponsoring Organizations), COSO ERM (COSO Enterprise Risk Management), COBIT (Control Objectives for Information and Related Technologies), and ITIL (Information Technology Infrastructure Library) are covered in this chapter.

A Look Back

Chapter 10 provided a comprehensive project in which we used BPMN to describe the business processes, integrated data models to create UML diagrams, and prepared a database that could be queried to develop important reports for decision making.

A Look Ahead

In Chapter 12, we discuss computer fraud and information security–related issues. The focus includes systems integrity and availability, as well as threats and risks in conducting business.

mauritius images GmbH/Alamy Stock Photo

You probably often visit **Starbucks** for coffee. Have you ever visited www.starbucks.com to learn more about the firm? You might be surprised to find more than just different types of coffee, a menu, store locations, and so on. You can find a lot of information under the tag called "Responsibility—Ethical, Local, Global." Starbucks believes businesses should be responsible to the communities they serve. The company is committed to "buying and serving the highest-quality, responsibly grown, ethically traded coffee to help create a better future for farmers." The philosophy and ethical values of a firm comprise one of the critical factors that form the firm's control environment. The Committee of Sponsoring Organizations (COSO) indicates that without a good control environment, even the best-designed control systems may fail. The control environment sets the tone of a firm and signifies how the firm values integrity and ethics of its employees.

CHAPTER OUTLINE

Introduction

Ethics, the Sarbanes–Oxley Act of 2002, and Corporate Governance

The Need for a Code of Ethics

Corporate Governance as Addressed by Sarbanes–Oxley

Control and Governance Frameworks

Overview of Control Concepts

Commonly Used Frameworks

COSO Internal Control Framework

COSO ERM Framework

COBIT Framework

Information Technology Infrastructure Library

ISO 27000 Series

Comparing Control/Governance Frameworks

Appendix: ERP Architecture and Control Issues

LEARNING OBJECTIVES

After reading this chapter, you should be able to:

11-1 Explain essential control concepts and why a code of ethics and internal controls are important.

11-2 Explain the control objectives and components of the COSO internal control framework and the COSO enterprise risk management framework.

11-3 Describe the overall COBIT framework and its implications for IT governance.

11-4 Describe other governance frameworks related to information systems management and security.

INTRODUCTION

Ethics, internal controls, and information security are three closely related areas critical to corporate governance. Safeguarding the assets of a firm has always been the responsibility of its management. Given the swift advancements in computing technology and the pervasive use of IT in all aspects of business operations, managers and accountants have to reexamine how to establish and monitor internal controls. For internal and external auditors, it is important to assess the effectiveness of internal controls to meet the mandate of the Sarbanes–Oxley Act.

LO 11-1

Explain essential control concepts and why a code of ethics and internal controls are important.

ETHICS, THE SARBANES–OXLEY ACT OF 2002, AND CORPORATE GOVERNANCE

The Need for a Code of Ethics

Ethical principles are derived from cultural values, societal traditions, and personal attitudes on issues of right and wrong. Integrity and individual ethics are formed through a person's life experience. Ethics plays a critical role when people make choices and decisions. Although individuals have their own values and may behave differently from one another, firms often choose to establish a formal expectation, through a **code of ethics**, on what is considered to be ethical within the group in order to promote ethical behavior. Ethical behavior prompted by a code of ethics can be considered a form of internal control. Given today's diversified and globalized business environment, a firm will have to rely on the ethics of its employees to operate efficiently and effectively. In addition, the importance of a code of ethics should be emphasized because employees with different culture backgrounds are likely to have different values.

In addition, many professional associations have developed codes of ethics to assist professionals in selecting among decisions that are not clearly right or wrong. Some examples include the American Institute of Certified Public Accountants (AICPA), the Information Systems Audit and Control Association (ISACA), the Institute of Internal Auditors (IIA), and the Institute of Management Accountants (IMA). The certification programs of these associations require the knowledge of the codes of ethics in developing professionalism.

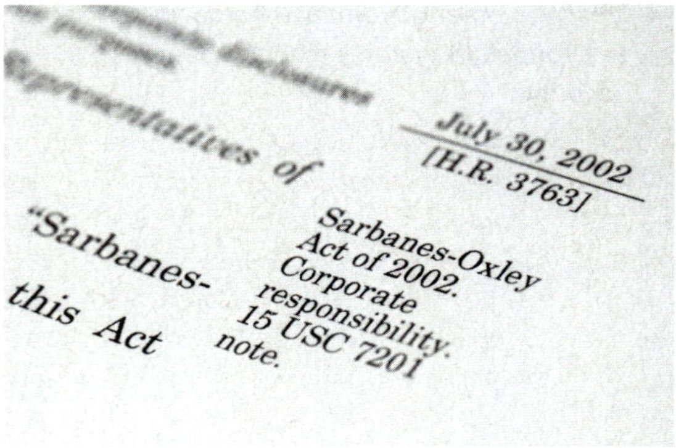

McKnight/Alamy Stock Photo

Corporate Governance as Addressed by Sarbanes–Oxley

The impact of public policy on the accounting profession through the enactment of laws and regulations has been well-documented and can be traced back to the 1930s.[1] Among those policies enforced, the **Sarbanes–Oxley Act of 2002 (SOX)** has probably had the most far-reaching effect on public companies and accounting firms. This bill was a response to business scandals such as Enron, WorldCom, and Tyco International. SOX requires public companies registered with the SEC and their auditors to annually assess and report on the design and effectiveness of internal control over financial reporting.

[1]See the Securities Act of 1933, Securities Exchange Act of 1934, and Foreign Corrupt Practices Act of 1977.

SOX also established the **Public Company Accounting Oversight Board (PCAOB)** to provide independent oversight of public accounting firms. The PCAOB issues auditing standards and oversees quality controls of public accounting firms. PCAOB Auditing Standard No. 5 (AS No. 5) encourages auditors to use a risk-based, top-down approach to identify the key controls. That is, auditors should start at the financial statement level when analyzing controls, focusing on entity-level controls[2] followed by reviewing significant accounts, disclosures, and management assertions.

SOX is arranged into 11 titles. As far as compliance for public companies, the most important sections within the other titles are considered to be 301, 302, 404, 406, 409, 802, 807, and 906 (see Exhibit 11.1).

EXHIBIT 11.1
Titles and Compliance Requirements of Sarbanes–Oxley Act

SOX Titles	Key Sections	Key Compliance Requirements
Title I: Public Company Accounting	101	Establishment
Oversight Board (PCAOB)	103	Auditing, quality control, and independence standards and rules
	104	Inspections of registered public accounting firms
Title II: Auditor Independence	201	Services outside the scope of practice of auditors
	203	Audit partner rotation
	204	Auditor reports to audit committees
	206	Conflicts of interest
Title III: Corporate Responsibility	301	Public company audit committees
	302	Corporate responsibility for financial reports
Title IV: Enhanced Financial Disclosures	404	Management assessment of internal controls
	406	Code of ethics for senior financial officers
	409	Real-time issuer disclosures
Title VIII: Corporate and Criminal Fraud Accountability	802	Criminal penalties for altering documents
	807	Criminal penalties for defrauding shareholders of publicly traded companies
Title IX: White-Collar Crime Penalty Enhancements	906	Corporate responsibility for financial reports

Do you consider SOX helpful to improve corporate governance? Is SOX relevant to a company's social responsibilities? You can find online that some public companies provide a sustainability report on their websites. What is the purpose of the sustainability report?

Corporate governance can be defined as a set of processes and policies in managing an organization with sound ethics, and internal and external control mechanisms to safeguard the interests of its stakeholders. Corporate governance also promotes accountability and transparency in the organization's relationship with its stakeholders. At the Global Corporate Governance Forum held by World Bank (2000), Adrian Cadbury[3] stated: "Corporate governance is concerned with holding the balance between economic and social goals and between individual and communal goals. The corporate governance framework is intended

[2]According to the PCAOB Release 2007-005, examples of entity-level controls include internal control environment, risk assessment and management, management override, centralized processing, and monitoring.

[3]Adrian Cadbury was the chairman of Cadbury and Cadbury Schweppes. He was a pioneer in raising the awareness and reforming corporate governance around the world. https://www.washingtonpost.com/business/adrian-cadbury-a-leader-in-corporate-governance-dies-at-86/2015/09/04/e87dd2fe-532e-11e5-8c19-0b6825aa4a3a_story.html, retrieved on May 4, 2016.

to encourage the efficient use of resources and to require accountability for the stewardship of those resources. The aim is to align as nearly as possible the interests of individuals, corporations and society." More specifically, OECD Secretary-General Angel Gurria indicated that "the purpose of corporate governance is to provide an environment of trust, transparency and accountability necessary for fostering long-term investment, financial stability and business integrity, thereby supporting stronger growth and more inclusive societies."[4]

PROGRESS CHECK

1. Why does a firm need a code of ethics? Is it important to corporate governance?
2. The Sarbanes–Oxley Act was enacted in 2002 and established PCAOB (see https://pcaobus.org/). What are the functions of PCAOB?

CONTROL AND GOVERNANCE FRAMEWORKS

Overview of Control Concepts

Internal control involves the processes that an organization implements to safeguard assets, provide accurate and reliable information, promote operational efficiency, enforce prescribed managerial policies, and comply with applicable laws and regulations. Appropriate internal controls support organizations' objectives through accountability and transparency for good corporate governance. According to SOX, the establishment and maintenance of internal controls is a management responsibility.

Firms use internal controls as a means of preventing errors and deterring fraud. The three main functions of internal control are prevention, detection, and correction. **Preventive controls** deter problems before they arise. Preventive controls require compliance with preferred procedures and thus stop undesirable events from happening. For example, a transaction should be authorized to ensure its validity. Hence, a signed source document should be required before recording a transaction. **Detective controls** find problems when they arise. These controls are procedures and techniques designed to identify undesirable events after they have already occurred. For example, bank reconciliations and monthly trial balances are prepared to catch mistakes. **Corrective controls** fix problems that have been identified, such as using backup files to recover corrupted data. Detective controls are often linked to accompanying corrective controls to remediate any issues that are discovered.

In a computerized environment, internal controls can also be categorized as general controls and application controls. **General controls** pertain to enterprisewide issues such as controls over accessing the network, developing and maintaining applications, and documenting changes of programs. **Application controls** are specific to a subsystem or an application to ensure the validity, completeness, and accuracy of the transactions. For example, when entering a sales transaction, use an input control to ensure the customer account number is entered accurately.

Given SOX, the SEC requires management to evaluate internal controls based on a recognized control framework such as the frameworks developed by the **Committee of Sponsoring Organizations (COSO)** of the Treadway Commission.

[4]OECD (2015), G20/OECD Principles of Corporate Governance, OECD Publishing, Paris, page 7, https://www.oecd-ilibrary.org/governance/g20-oecd-principles-of-corporate-governance-2015_9789264236882-en.

LO 11-2

Explain the control objectives and components of the COSO internal control framework and the COSO enterprise risk management framework.

Commonly Used Frameworks

COSO is composed of five nonprofit organizations: American Accounting Association (AAA), American Institute of Certified Public Accountants (AICPA), Financial Executives International (FEI), Institute of Internal Auditors (IIA), and Institute of Management Accountants (IMA). COSO is a voluntary initiative to improve corporate governance and performance through effective internal controls, enterprise risk management, and fraud deterrence. COSO examines the causal factors that lead to fraudulent financial reporting and develops recommendations for public companies, independent auditors, the SEC and other regulators, and educational institutions to improve the quality of financial reporting through internal controls and corporate governance.[5] COSO developed two frameworks to improve the quality of financial reporting through accountability, effective controls, risk management, and corporate governance. The Committee issued the "Internal Control—Integrated Framework" in 1992 and an updated version in 2013, and the "Enterprise Risk Management—Integrated Framework" in 2004 and an updated version in 2017. The COSO internal control framework is one of the most widely accepted authorities on internal control, providing a baseline for evaluating, reporting, and improving internal control. COSO 2013 internal control framework provides the principles for effective internal controls to address changes in the business and operating environments and to respond to expectations from stakeholders.

The COSO enterprise risk management (ERM) framework expanded the original COSO internal control framework to provide guidance in defining, assessing, managing, and transferring risk in order to maximize firm value. The COSO ERM focuses on the strategic alignment of the firm's mission with its risk appetite. Although most firms in the United States already use the COSO internal control framework in establishing and evaluating their internal control systems, many are still applying the concepts in COSO ERM as the basis for developing risk-based internal control systems. In 2017, an updated version of COSO ERM was published. It is now titled "Enterprise Risk Management—Integrating with Strategy and Performance" to stress the importance of considering risk in both the strategy-setting process and in driving performance. Therefore, the focus of both management and external auditors has become more in-line with the COSO ERM framework.

As a future business professional, do you think you need to know so much about control frameworks? Why is this knowledge critical to your success in your future career?

The **control objectives for information and related technology (COBIT)** framework is an internationally accepted set of best IT security and control practices for IT management released by the IT Governance Institute (ITGI). It is a control framework for the governance and management of enterprise IT. COBIT provides management with an understanding of risks associated with IT and bridges the gap among risks, control needs, and technical issues.

The **Information Technology Infrastructure Library (ITIL)** is a set of concepts and practices for IT service management. COBIT defines the overall IT control framework, and ITIL provides the details for IT service management. ITIL is released by the UK Office of Government Commerce (OGC) and is the most widely accepted model for IT service management. ITIL adopts a life-cycle approach to IT services, focusing on practices for service strategy, service design, service transition, service operation, and continual service improvement.

The **International Organization for Standardization (ISO) 27000 series** is designed to address information security issues. The ISO 27000 series—particularly, ISO 27001 and ISO 27002—have become the most recognized and generally accepted sets of information security framework and guidelines.

[5] See www.coso.org.

COSO Internal Control Framework

The updated COSO 2013 internal control framework defines internal control as a process—affected by an entity's board of directors, management, and other personnel—designed to provide reasonable assurance regarding the achievement of objectives in effectiveness and efficiency of operations, reliability of reporting, and compliance with applicable laws and regulations. Accordingly, the COSO framework indicates that[6]

1. Internal control is a process consisting of ongoing tasks and activities. It is a means to an end, not an end in itself.
2. Internal control is affected by people. It is not merely about policy manuals, systems, and forms. Rather, it is about people at every level of a firm who affect internal control.
3. Internal control can provide reasonable assurance, not absolute assurance, to an entity's management and board.
4. Internal control is geared toward the achievement of objectives in one or more separate but overlapping categories.
5. Internal control is adaptable to the entity structure.

According to the COSO 2013 framework, an effective internal control system should consist of three categories of objectives and five essential components. The three categories of objectives are

1. *Operations objectives:* effectiveness and efficiency of a firm's operations on financial performance goals and safeguarding assets.
2. *Reporting objectives:* reliability of reporting, including internal and external financial and nonfinancial reporting.
3. *Compliance objectives:* adherence to applicable laws and regulations.

To support a firm in its efforts to achieve internal control objectives, COSO 2013 suggests five components of internal control:

1. *Control environment*—sets the tone of a firm, influences the control consciousness of its employees, and establishes the foundation for the internal control system. Control environment factors include the management's philosophy and operating style, integrity and ethical values of employees, organizational structure, the role of the audit committee, proper board oversight for the development and performance of internal control, and personnel policies and practices.
2. *Risk assessment*—involves a dynamic process for identifying and analyzing a firm's risks from external and internal environments. Risk assessment allows a firm to understand the extent to which potential events might affect corporate objectives. Risks are analyzed after considering the likelihood of occurrence and the potential loss. The analysis serves as a basis for determining how the risks should be managed. This component will be discussed later in the chapter.
3. *Control activities*—occur throughout a firm at all levels and in all functions. A firm must establish control policies, procedures, and practices that ensure the firm's objectives are achieved and risk mitigation strategies are carried out. This component will be discussed later in the chapter.
4. *Information and communication*—supports all other control components by communicating effectively to ensure information flows down, across, and up the firm, as well as interacting with external parties such as customers, suppliers, regulators, and shareholders and informing them about related policy positions. Relevant information should be identified, captured, and communicated in a form and timeframe that enable employees to carry out their duties.

[6]See https://www.coso.org/.

5. *Monitoring*—the design and effectiveness of internal controls should be monitored by management and other parties outside the process on a continuous basis. Findings should be evaluated, and deficiencies must be communicated in a timely manner. Necessary modifications should be made to improve the business process and the internal control system.

The three objectives and five components of the COSO internal control framework are part of the COSO ERM framework. In addition, COSO 2013 codifies 17 relevant principles associated with the five components of internal control (see Exhibit 11.2). They are essential in assessing the five components. The 17 principles of effective internal controls are listed as follows:

EXHIBIT 11.2
COSO 2013 Control Components and Principles

Control Environment	1. Demonstrates commitment to integrity and ethical values
	2. Exercises oversight responsibility
	3. Establishes structure, authority, and responsibility
	4. Demonstrates commitment to competence
	5. Enforces accountability
Risk Assessment	6. Specifies suitable objectives
	7. Identifies and analyzes risk
	8. Assesses fraud risk
	9. Identifies and analyzes significant change
Control Activities	10. Selects and develops control activities
	11. Selects and develops general controls over technology
	12. Deploys thorough policies and procedures
Information and Communication	13. Uses relevant information
	14. Communicates internally
	15. Communicates externally
Monitoring Activities	16. Conducts ongoing and/or separate evaluations
	17. Evaluates and communicates deficiencies

Principles for Control Environment:

1. The organization demonstrates a commitment to integrity and ethical values.
2. The board of directors demonstrates independence from management and exercises oversight of the development and performance of internal control.
3. Management establishes—with board oversight—structures, reporting lines, and appropriate authorities and responsibilities in the pursuit of objectives.
4. The organization demonstrates a commitment to attract, develop, and retain competent individuals in alignment with objectives.
5. The organization holds individuals accountable for their internal control responsibilities in the pursuit of objectives.

Principles for Risk Assessment:

6. The organization specifies objectives with sufficient clarity to enable the identification and assessment of risks relating to objectives.
7. The organization identifies risks to the achievement of its objectives across the entity and analyzes risks as a basis for determining how the risks should be managed.
8. The organization considers the potential for fraud in assessing risks to the achievement of objectives.
9. The organization identifies and assesses changes that could significantly impact the system of internal control.

Principles for Control Activities:

10. The organization selects and develops control activities that contribute to the mitigation of risks to the achievement of objectives to acceptable levels.
11. The organization selects and develops general control activities over technology to support the achievement of objectives.
12. The organization deploys control activities through policies that establish what is expected and procedures that put policies into place.

Principles for Information and Communication:

13. The organization obtains or generates and uses relevant, quality information to support the functioning of internal control.
14. The organization internally communicates information, including objectives and responsibilities for internal control, necessary to support the functioning of internal control.
15. The organization communicates with external parties regarding matters affecting the functioning of internal control.

Principles for Monitoring Activities:

16. The organization selects, develops, and performs ongoing and/or separate evaluations to ascertain whether the components of internal control are present and functioning.
17. The organization evaluates and communicates internal control deficiencies in a timely manner to those parties responsible for taking corrective action, including senior management and the board of directors, as appropriate.

PROGRESS CHECK

3. What is the definition of internal control?
4. What are the three main categories of internal control?

COSO ERM Framework

All firms encounter uncertainty in daily operations. Uncertainty presents both risk and opportunity, with the potential to reduce or enhance the firm's value. For example, Paul Walsh, CEO of Diageo, indicated that

> Managing risk can be one of the most overlooked areas within a business' structure. It is critical, particularly for global companies such as Diageo, for risk management processes and strategies to be imbedded with its operations. At Diageo, we have an exclusive-level Audit and Risk Committee which is tasked with overseeing and implementing effective risk management and control in the business. Whether it's navigating the global financial crisis or contingency planning for global health epidemics such as avian flu, these are significant issues which can impact your business performance and sustainability.[7]

[7]Beasley, M. S., Bruce C. Branson, and Bonnie V. Hancock. "Enterprise Risk Oversight—A Global Analysis." CIMA and AICPA Research Series, September 2010, https://erm.ncsu.edu/az/erm/i/chan/library/erm-aicpa-cima-2010.pdf Accessed March 26, 2023.

COSO ERM—Integrated Framework (2004)

The COSO enterprise risk management framework (2004) defines **enterprise risk management (ERM)** as "a process, affected by the entity's board of directors, management, and other personnel, applied in strategy setting and across the enterprise, designed to identify potential events that may affect the entity, and manage risk to be within the risk appetite, to provide reasonable assurance regarding the achievement of objectives."[8]

Note that internal control is an integral part of enterprise risk management. In addition to internal controls, the COSO ERM—Integrated Framework expands the COSO internal control framework to provide a broader view on risk management to maximize firm value (see Exhibit 11.3). The relationship is depicted in a cube. The four objective categories—strategic, operations, reporting, and compliance—are represented by the vertical columns, the eight ERM components by horizontal rows, and the firm's units by the third dimension (such as entity, subsidiary, and division.)

EXHIBIT 11.3
COSO ERM 2004 Model

The Committee of Sponsoring Organizations of the Treadway Commission. Used with permission.

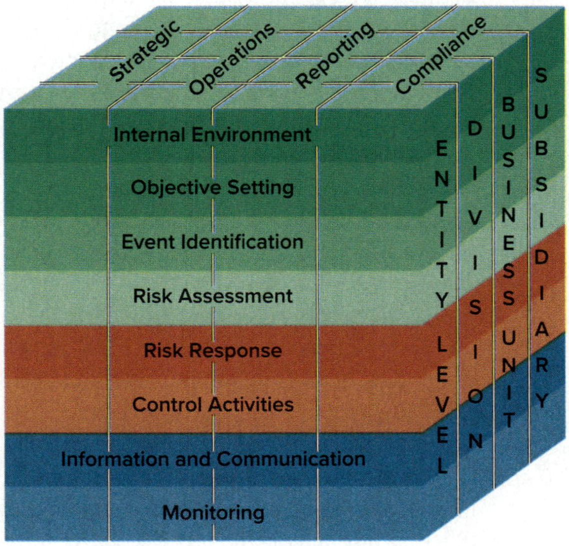

The ERM framework takes a risk-based, rather than a control-based, approach to achieve the firm's objectives in four categories:

1. *Strategic*—high-level goals, aligned with and supporting the firm's mission and vision.
2. *Operations*—effectiveness and efficiency of operations.
3. *Reporting*—reliability of internal and external reporting.
4. *Compliance*—compliance with applicable laws and regulations.

COSO ERM 2004 consists of eight interrelated components. ERM is not strictly a serial process; it is a multidirectional, iterative process in which each component can influence the others. These components are

1. *Internal environment*—provides the discipline and structure for all other components of enterprise risk management. It encompasses the tone of a firm, influences the risk consciousness of its people, and sets the basis for how risk is viewed and addressed by the firm. Internal environment factors include a firm's risk management philosophy

[8] Steinberg, Richard M., Miles E. A. Everson, Frank J. Martens, and Lucy E. Nottingham. "Enterprise Risk Management—Integrated Framework: Executive Summary," September 2004.

and risk appetite,[9] integrity and ethical values, organizational structure, board of directors and the audit committee, human resource policies and practices, assignment of authority and responsibility, commitment to competence, and development of personnel.

2. *Objective setting*—based on the firm's mission and vision, management sets specific objectives before identifying potential events[10] affecting their achievement. Management should have a process in place to set strategic, operations, reporting, and compliance objectives. Objectives are set at the strategic level, establishing a basis for operations, reporting, and compliance, and the chosen objectives shall support and align with the firm's mission and be consistent with its risk appetite.
3. *Event identification*—internal and external events affecting achievement of a firm's objectives must be identified. After identifying all possible events, management must distinguish between risks and opportunities. Opportunities are channeled back to management's strategy or objective-setting processes. Identified risks should be forwarded to the next stage for assessment and be managed according to the firm's risk appetite.
4. *Risk assessment*—the same as in the COSO internal control framework. This component will be discussed later in the chapter.
5. *Risk response*—management selects risk responses and develops a set of actions to align risks with the entity's risk tolerances and risk appetite. The four options to respond to risks are reducing, sharing, avoiding, and accepting risks. This component will be discussed later in the chapter.
6. *Control activities*—the same as in the COSO internal control framework. This component will be discussed later in the chapter.
7. *Information and communication*—the same as in the COSO internal control framework.
8. *Monitoring*—the process of evaluating the quality of internal control design and operation and the effectiveness of the ERM model. The ERM components and internal control process should be monitored continuously and modified as necessary. Determining whether a firm's enterprise risk management is effective is a judgment resulting from an analysis of whether the eight components are present and functioning properly. Thus, the components are also criteria for an effective enterprise risk management. Monitoring is accomplished through ongoing management activities and conducted by other parties outside the process. ERM deficiencies are reported to top management and the board.

Everyone in a firm is responsible for enterprise risk management. The chief executive officer (CEO) is ultimately responsible and should assume ownership. All others support the firm's risk management philosophy, comply with its risk appetite, and manage risks within their duties. The following comments from Jörg Pässler, group treasurer at Sappi Group Treasury, are about enterprise risk oversight:

> The financial crisis of 2008/09/10 has awakened the need to comprehensively review and manage risk, especially those that seem very remote. If Lehman Bros. can go under, if AIG can go to the brink due to material exposures to a specific market that was deemed "safe," and if government default is viewed as a possibility, then we need to re-assess our risks with a completely different mindset. The comment "that can never happen" will probably never be used in risk assessments again.[11]

[9]A company's risk appetite takes into consideration its risk-taking attitude and how this attitude relates to the expectations of its stakeholders.

[10]COSO defines an event as "an incident or occurrence emanating from internal or external sources that affects implementation of strategy or achievement of objectives. Events may have positive or negative impacts or both." Committee of Sponsoring Organizations of the Treadway Commission, *Enterprise Risk Management—Integrated Framework* (2004), p. 16.

[11]Beasley, Branson, and Hancock, *Enterprise Risk Oversight—A Global Analysis.*

Risk Assessment and Risk Response

Risk assessment is the process of identifying and analyzing risks systematically to determine the firm's risk response and control activities. It allows a firm to understand the extent to which potential events might affect corporate objectives. Given AS No. 5, risk assessment is also a first step in developing an audit plan to meet the mandate of SOX section 404. According to COSO ERM 2004, the risks of an identified event are analyzed on an inherent, control, and residual basis. **Inherent risk** is the risk related to the nature of the business activity itself. It exists already before management takes any actions to address it. For example, an inherent risk of a fast-food corporation is a high number of competitors in the industry. **Control risk** is the threat that errors or irregularities in the underlying transactions will not be prevented, detected, and corrected by the internal control system. For example, an accounts payable clerk is required to get approval if the total dollar amount on any specific purchase order (PO) is more than a predetermined limit (such as $1,000). The possibility that a clerk may create multiple purchase orders for one transaction to avoid the required authorization is a control risk. **Residual risk** is the product of inherent risk and control risk (i.e., Residual risk = Inherent risk × Control risk). In other words, it is the risk that remains after management's response to the risk or after the controls put in place to mitigate the risk. Firms should first assess inherent risk, develop a response or implement a control, and then assess residual risk.

According to COSO ERM 2004, management assesses risks from two perspectives—likelihood and impact—and uses a combination of both qualitative and quantitative risk assessment methodologies. When sufficient and/or credible data for quantitative assessment are not available, management often uses qualitative assessment techniques that depend largely on the knowledge, experience, and judgment of the decision maker. Regarding risk response, COSO ERM indicates four options:[12]

1. Reduce risks by designing effective business processes and implementing internal controls.
2. Share risks by outsourcing business processes, buying insurance, or entering into hedging transactions.
3. Avoid risks by not engaging in the activities that would produce the risk.
4. Accept risk by relying on natural offsets of the risk within a portfolio, or allowing the likelihood and impact of the risk.

In determining risk response, management should evaluate options in relation to the firm's risk appetite, cost versus benefit of potential risk responses, and degree to which a response will reduce impact and/or likelihood. Selections of responses should be based on evaluation of the portfolio of risks and responses.

The process to assess risks is as follows: (1) identify risks to the firm; (2) estimate the likelihood of each risk occurring; (3) estimate the impact (i.e., potential loss in dollars) from each risk; (4) identify controls to mitigate the risk; (5) estimate the costs and benefits of implementing the controls; (6) perform a cost/benefit analysis for each risk and corresponding controls; and (7) based on the results of the cost/benefit analysis, determine whether to reduce the risk by implementing a control, or to accept, share, or avoid the risk. Exhibit 11.4 illustrates this process.[13]

Cost/benefit analysis is important in determining whether to implement an internal control. The benefits of an internal control should exceed its costs. Costs are easier to measure than benefits. Costs incurred from implementing controls are often for personnel

[12]Ibid., p. 55.

[13]Adapted from M. B. Romney and P. J. Steinbart, *Accounting Information Systems*, 14th ed. (New York: Prentice Hall, 2018), p. 210.

EXHIBIT 11.4
Risk Assessment and Response Approach to Select Control Activities

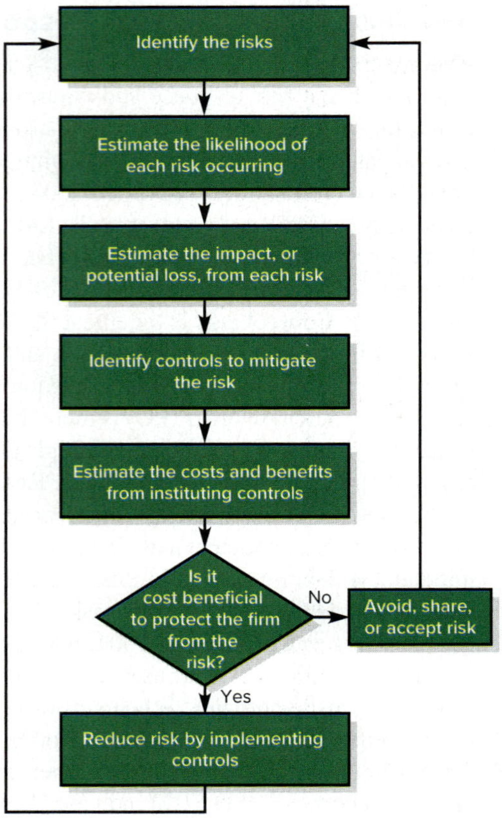

and technology, such as the price of a video camera and the value of additional hours of employee work incurred. They often can be quantified. Conversely, control benefits usually involve qualitative factors—such as increased productivity, improved customer satisfaction, better interaction with suppliers, or enhanced employee loyalty—and are difficult to measure. One way to measure the benefits of a control is using the estimated impact of a risk times the decreased likelihood if the control is implemented:

Expected benefit of an internal control = Impact × Decreased likelihood

For example, due to input errors in making sales orders, Carlsbad Bottle Company may ship goods to the wrong customers. The company estimates that if this happens, the impact of this type of event will cost about $15,000 due to lost revenue, rerouting expenses, and so forth. The likelihood of this risk is estimated as 10 percent. If Carlsbad Bottle Company implements a data validation step for input control, the likelihood of this risk could be only 0.5 percent. The cost to implement this control is $200. Given this information, the expected benefit = $15,000 × (10% – 0.5%) = $1,425. The expected benefit of implementing the control ($1,425) is larger than the cost ($200), contributing a net benefit of $1,225 (i.e., the difference between $1,425 and $200). Hence, Carlsbad Bottle Company should implement the control.

PROGRESS CHECK

5. What are the four options of risk response?
6. What is the calculation for the expected benefit of an internal control?

Control Activities

Control activities are the policies and procedures that help ensure that necessary actions are taken to address risks to achieve the firm's objectives. There are two categories of control activities: Manual controls and IT controls. IT controls are a subset of a firm's internal controls and are categorized as IT general and application controls.

Manual controls could involve the physical use of computing technology. These types of control activities include:

- Authorization to ensure transactions are valid.
- Segregation of duties to prevent fraud and mistakes.[14]
- Supervision to compensate imperfect segregation of duties.
- Accounting documents and records to maintain audit trails.
- Access control to ensure only authorized personnel have access to physical assets and information.
- Independent verification to double-check for errors and misrepresentations.

Business environments have continued to increase in complexity with ever-greater reliance on the information produced by IT systems and processes. **IT controls** involve processes that provide assurance for information and help to mitigate risks associated with the use of technology.[15] Firms need IT controls to protect information assets, remain competitive, and control costs in implementing IT projects.

IT general controls (ITGC) relate to enterprise-level controls over IT:

- *IT control environment*—sets the tone at the top and forms culture regarding IT service and management.
- *Access controls*—restrict access to IT facilities, programs, and data. Access controls in IT systems are related to proper authorization and segregation of duties.
- *Change management controls*—the processes of making sure changes to programs and applications are authorized and documented. Changes should be tested prior to implementation so they do not affect system availability and reliability.
- *Project development and acquisition controls*—related to the systems development life cycle (SDLC). The controls involve analysis, design, testing, implementation, and evaluation of IT projects. Through management review and approval and user involvement, a firm establishes a formal methodology for developing, acquiring, implementing, and maintaining information systems and related technologies.
- *Computer operations controls*—involve antivirus protection, backup and recovery procedures, minimizing system downtime, and patch management.

IT application controls are activities specific to a subsystem's or an application's input, processing, and output. Application controls include configured automated input controls, reports or data generated from the system and used in manual controls or accounting procedures, and automated calculations or data processing routines programmed into the application. The application controls are grouped into three categories to ensure information processing integrity: input, processing, and output controls. Most mistakes in an accounting information system occur while entering data. Control efforts are mainly focused on input rather than processing and output activities.

Input controls ensure the authorization, entry, and verification of data entering the system. Authorization of data entry is accomplished by using an access control matrix. This matrix specifies which portion of the system users are allowed to access and what

[14]The general guideline for segregation of duties (SOD) is that transaction authorization, recordkeeping, and asset custody should be separated from each other.

[15]www.theiia.org.

privilege(s) users have (e.g., view, create, update, and delete). Common data entry controls include the following:

- Field checks ensure the characters in a field are of the proper type.
- Size checks ensure the data fit into the size of a field.
- Range checks test a numerical amount to ensure that it is within a predetermined range.
- Validity checks compare data entering the system with existing data in a reference file to ensure only valid data are entered.
- Completeness checks ensure all required data are entered for each record.
- Reasonableness checks ensure the logical relationship between two data values is correct. For example, an hourly rate of $120 may pass the range check on pay rates (between $8.5 and $150). However, it is not a valid input because the data value of the record for position is "intern"—that is, the pay rate of $120 per hour is not reasonable for an intern.
- Check digit verifications prevent the transpositions of numbers such as entering 5168 for a valid number of 5186. A check digit generated by an algorithm is appended to the original number to create a combination. A number and check digit combination that does not satisfy the algorithm reveals an error.
- Closed-loop verifications retrieve and display related information to ensure accurate data entry. For example, when a receiving clerk enters a part number, the inventory system displays the description of the item so that the receiving clerk can verify that the correct part number had been entered.

Do you know that understanding internal controls is a critical success factor in being an auditor? SOX requires the external auditor of a public firm to express an opinion on the firm's effectiveness of internal controls.

Processing controls ensure that data and transactions are processed accurately. Important processing controls include the following:

- Prenumbered documents are generated internally to ensure that there is no duplicate or missing record. Prenumbered source documents are used in batch processing[16] to make sure authorized transactions are processed once and once only.
- Sequence checks ensure a batch of data is in sequence for batch processing.
- Batch totals ensure that a batch goes through the processing stages containing the same set of records, with no missing or duplicate record. Three commonly used batch totals are

    1. A record count indicates that the same total records are in the batch.
    2. A control total is the sum of a dollar amount field or a quantity field in the records. Sometimes, the sum of a field containing dollar values is called "financial total."
    3. A hash total is the sum of a numeric field, such as employee number, which normally would not be the subject of arithmetic operations.

- Cross-footing balance tests compare totals provided in multiple methods to ensure accurate processing.
- Concurrent update controls prevent two or more users updating the same record simultaneously.

Output controls provide output to authorized people and ensure the output is used properly. For example, only the required number of copies should be printed. Any additional copies should be disposed of following authorized procedures. Printed output should be delivered promptly to the designated party. Electronic, sensitive material should be encrypted for transmission and data storage.

[16]Batch processing, different from real-time processing, has a delay between the time a transaction occurs and the time it is processed. A batch consists of many records that have been accumulated for processing at the same time.

PROGRESS CHECK

7. Explain the purposes of physical controls.
8. What are application controls?
9. Give a few examples of input controls.

COSO ERM—Integrating with Strategy and Performance (2017)

The COSO Board published an updated ERM model in 2017, called *Enterprise Risk Management—Integrating with Strategy and Performance.* The purpose of this framework is for management and boards of all kinds of organizations to integrate ERM practices in accelerating growth and improving performance. According to this framework, ERM should be embedded into the activities of an organization including the mission, vision, and core values. This framework provides guidance on the critical role of risk management to long-term value creation and preservation.

The first part of COSO ERM 2017 presents the evolving concepts and applications of ERM. In this framework, ERM is defined as "the culture, capabilities, and practices that organizations integrate with strategy-setting and apply when they carry out that strategy, with a purpose of managing risk in creating, preserving, and realizing value."[17] ERM is critical to strategy-setting, corporate governance, internal control, communicating with stakeholders, and measuring performance.

The second part of COSO ERM 2017 offers five components with 20 principles that are applied in the process of strategic decision-making through performance measurement, at all levels and across all functions of the organization. Please refer to Exhibit 11.5 regarding the components and principles of COSO ERM 2017.

EXHIBIT 11.5
COSO ERM 2017 Components and Principles

5 Components	20 Principles
Governance & Culture	1. Exercise board risk oversight
	2. Establish operating structures
	3. Define desired culture
	4. Demonstrate commitment to core values
	5. Attract, develop, and retain capable individuals
Strategy & Objective Setting	6. Analyze business context
	7. Define risk appetite
	8. Evaluate alternative strategies
	9. Formulate business objectives
Performance	10. Identify risks
	11. Assess severity of risks
	12. Prioritize risks
	13. Implement risk responses
	14. Develop portfolio view
Review & Revision	15. Assess substantial change
	16. Review risk and performance
	17. Pursue improvement in ERM
Information Communication & Reporting	18. Leverage information and technology
	19. Communicate risk information
	20. Report on risk, culture, and performance

[17] *Enterprise Risk Management—Integrating with Strategy and Performance: Executive Summary,* June 2017, page 3, Accessed April 2, 2019, Retrieved at https://www.coso.org/Documents/2017-COSO-ERM-Integrating-with-Strategy-and- Performance-Executive-Summary.pdf.

Components of COSO ERM 2017

1. Governance and Culture—Risk governance sets the tone at the top and supports the importance of ERM oversight. Culture reflects ethical values and accountable decision-making. Both are required for effective ERM.
2. Strategy and Objective Setting—All aspects and implications of strategies need to be integrated with ERM in setting business objectives.
3. Performance—Risks that could affect realization of strategies and achievement of business objectives should be identified and assessed. These risks must be prioritized based on their severity and with consideration of the organization's risk appetite. Risk responses should be selected to form a portfolio view of risk.
4. Review and Revision—Reviewing organization performance is monitoring how risks or emerging risks affect performance. Revision is a process to improve risk management considering changes in the business environment.
5. Information, Communication, and Reporting—Information for decision making must be communicated across the organization and provide insight to key stakeholders. A continuous process to obtain and share relevant, timely information on risks is a critical part of ERM.

Principles of Governance and Culture:

1. Exercise Board Risk Oversight—Board members are responsible for risk oversight because risk governance and culture start at the top of an organization. Board members should have required experience and business knowledge on ERM.
2. Establish Operating Structures—The organization must execute high-level strategies and daily operations to achieve business objectives. The structure and governance of the organization's operating model are interrelated with business risks.
3. Defines Desired Culture—The organization should have a risk-aware culture regarding its risk attitude such as risk averse, risk neutral, or risk aggressive.
4. Demonstrate Commitment to Core Values—The operating style and personal conduct of executives and board of directors create the tone at the top and define the organizational culture. The top management and board need to demonstrate their commitment to core values of the organization, and ensure the desired culture is driven deep down into the organization.
5. Attracts, Develops, and Retains Capable Individuals—Management must determine the knowledge, skills, and experience necessary to execute the business strategy, and identify ways to attract, develop, and retain capable personnel and strategic partners.

Principles of Strategy and Objective-Setting:

6. Analyze Business Context—The organization must consider risks from changes in business context and internal/external stakeholders in executing strategy.
7. Define Risk Appetite—The organization should define risk appetite in the context of creating, preserving, and realizing firm value.
8. Evaluate Alternative Strategies—The organization evaluates alternative strategies based on risks and various assumptions, and then, selects the strategy to enhance firm value.
9. Formulate Business Objectives—Management establishes business objectives that align with and support the strategies considering the organization's risk appetite.

Principles of Performance:

10. Identify Risk—The organization identifies existing risks but not yet know and new/emerging risks to execution of its strategy with consideration of the changes in business context.

11. Assess Severity of Risk—Use qualitative and quantitative approaches in risk assessment processes based on the anticipated severity of the risk. Scenario analysis on severity may be necessary in assessing risks.
12. Prioritize Risk—Risks are prioritized for selecting risk responses using appropriate criteria. These criteria may include adaptability, complexity, velocity, persistence, and recovery, as well as tolerable variation in performance.
13. Implement Risk Responses—Risk responses include accept, avoid, exploit, reduce, and share risk. Management should select risk responses considering severity of the risk, the appetite for risk, cost and benefits, and the changes in the business context.
14. Develop Portfolio View—Portfolio view provides a comprehensive approach to evaluate the risks that the organization faces in achieving business objectives considering the nature, likelihood, relative size of risks, and how they may affect performance.

Principles of Review and Revision:

15. Assess Substantial Change—The organization should establish proper business processes to monitor substantial changes in daily operations. Substantial changes can cause significant performance gaps or require modifications of the underlying assumptions for strategies.
16. Review Risk and Performance—Management should work with those whom identify risks and are responsible for assurance to evaluate risk responses and ensure they are consistent with objectives of performance.
17. Pursue Improvement in ERM—Embedding continuous evaluations on ERM can systematically identify necessary improvements of the ERM processes.

Principles of Information, Communication, and Reporting:

18. Leverage Information and Technology—The organization uses information systems to obtain the data and information to support and implement ERM. In selecting technology, the management should consider marketplace needs, competitive requirements, and associated costs and benefits.
19. Communicate Risk Information—The management provides information on risk at various levels across the organization using different channels to communicate ERM concepts.
20. Report on Risk, Culture, and Performance—The management uses different types of reports on risk, culture, and performance to assist the board to fulfill their risk oversight responsibilities, as well as to inform various levels across the organization.

LO 11-3

Describe the overall COBIT framework and its implications for IT governance.

COBIT Framework

Information technology governance is a subset of corporate governance and includes issues regarding IT management and security. IT governance is the responsibility of management and consists of the leadership, organizational structures, and processes that ensure that the firm's IT sustains and extends its business objectives.[18] To achieve effective IT governance, controls should be implemented within a defined control framework for all IT processes to provide a clear link among IT governance requirements, IT processes, and IT controls. COSO is one of the generally accepted internal control frameworks for enterprises. COBIT (control objectives for information and related technology) was originated by the IT audit community, and has developed into a broad and comprehensive IT governance and management framework.

[18] IT Governance Institute, *COBIT 4.1 Executive Summary,* 2007, Retrieved May 5, 2016, https://www.isaca.org/Knowledge-Center/cobit/Documents/COBIT4.pdf.

COBIT provides a supporting toolset that bridges the gap among IT control requirements, technical issues, and business risks. The COBIT framework[19]

- Provides a business focus to align business and IT objectives.
- Defines the scope and ownership of IT process and control.
- Is consistent with accepted IT good practices and standards.
- Provides a common language with a set of terms and definitions that are generally understandable by all stakeholders.
- Meets regulatory requirements by being consistent with generally accepted corporate governance standards (e.g., COSO) and IT controls expected by regulators and auditors.

COBIT control objectives provide high-level requirements to be considered for effective control of IT processes. The overall control objectives are to increase business value or reduce risk; to establish and maintain policies, procedures, and organizational structures related to IT; and to provide reasonable assurance that business objectives will be achieved. According to COBIT, the key criteria of business requirements for information are as follows:

- *Effectiveness*—relevant and timely information.
- *Efficiency*—information produced economically.
- *Confidentiality*—protection of sensitive information.
- *Integrity*—valid, accurate, and complete information.
- *Availability*—information available when needed.
- *Compliance*—information produced in compliance with laws and regulations.
- *Reliability*—reliable information for daily decision making.

The most current version of the COBIT framework is COBIT 2019. As a generally accepted framework for IT governance and management, COBIT 2019 expands on COBIT 5 and integrates other major frameworks and standards, such as COSO ERM 2017, cloud standards, information security forum, ISACA's Val IT and Risk IT, the Information Technology Infrastructure Library (ITIL), NIST standards, and related standards from the International Organization for Standardization (ISO). COBIT 2019 assists firms in creating value from IT by maintaining a balance between realizing benefits and optimizing resource use. COBIT 2019 enables IT to be governed and managed in a holistic manner for the firm by taking in the end-to-end IT functional areas of responsibility and considering the IT-related interests of internal and external stakeholders. COBIT 2019 defines "governance" as ensuring that firm objectives are achieved by evaluating stakeholder needs; setting direction through decision making; and monitoring performance, compliance, and progress.[20] Per COBIT 2019, "management" includes planning (i.e., aligning, planning, and organizing), building (i.e., building, acquiring, and implementing), running (i.e., delivering, servicing, and supporting), and monitoring (i.e., monitoring, evaluating, and assessing) activities in alignment with the direction necessary to achieve the firm's objectives.[21]

COBIT 2019 has five domains: EDM (Evaluate, Direct, and Monitor), APO (Align, Plan, and Organize), BAI (Build, Acquire, and Implement), DSS (Deliver, Service, and Support), and MEA (Monitor, Evaluate, and Access). The first domain is about IT governance, and the other four domains are for IT management. Given these domains, COBIT provides comprehensive descriptions of 40 core governance and management objectives to guide firms to implement COBIT 2019 framework. In addition, this updated framework provides a design guide to assist firms in designing an effective IT governance system and an implementation guide to implement and optimize IT governance. In particular, a capability/maturity model is developed called COBIT Performance Management (CPM)

[19]*COBIT 4.1 Executive Summary*, p. 8.
[20]ISACA, *COBIT 2019 Framework: Introduction and Methodology*, p. 13.
[21]ISACA, *COBIT 2019 Framework: Governance and Management Objectives*, p. 11.

to guide firms to evaluate how well the IT governance and management system perform and how the system can be improved to achieve the required business objectives.

In summary, COBIT supports IT governance and management by providing a framework to ensure that IT is aligned with the business, IT enables the business and maximizes firm value, IT resources are used responsibly, and IT risks are managed appropriately.

PROGRESS CHECK

10. What are the IT resources and business requirements of information identified in the COBIT framework?

LO 11-4

Describe other governance frameworks related to information systems management and security.

Information Technology Infrastructure Library

The IT Infrastructure Library (ITIL) was developed by the UK government in the mid-1980s and has become a de facto standard in Europe for best practices in IT infrastructure management and service delivery. ITIL's value proposition centers on providing IT service with an understanding of the business objectives and priorities and the role that IT service has in achieving the objectives. The ITIL framework has evolved as a result of firms' increasing dependence on IT. In recent years, there has been growing global recognition and adoption of ITIL.[22]

ITIL 4 is the latest release of the ITIL framework (2019). ITIL 4 provides a digital operating model that builds on ITIL's decades of progress for the wider context of stakeholder experience, value streams, and digital transformation. Exhibit 11.6 illustrates the stages of the most current structure of the life cycle for ITIL 4 (2019). ITIL 4 is not a minor overhaul from ITIL 2011. It no longer defines the 26 processes in IT services and IT service management. ITIL 4 now describes 34 management practices in five high-level categories:

1. *Strategy for change*—the strategic planning of IT service management capabilities and the alignment of IT service and business strategies by identifying potential risks and opportunities for change.
2. *Service design and development*—the design of new services and improvement of existing IT services and service management processes based on the continuous assessments of stakeholders' requirements.
3. *Operational support and analysis*—the effective and efficient delivery and support of services, with a process for identifying, analyzing, reducing, or eliminating operational problems.
4. *Service transition*—realizing the requirements of strategy and design and maintaining capabilities for the ongoing delivery of a service.
5. *Service improvement*—ongoing improvement of the service and the measurement of process performance required for the service.

The ITIL life cycle starts with service strategy. In this phase, IT personnel should identify the customers or users of the IT services.[23] Then, IT personnel and business personnel (i.e., business strategists) should collaborate to develop IT service strategies that are aligned with and support the business strategy. The service design phase ensures that new and changed IT services are designed effectively to meet customer/user expectations in a cost-effective manner. Through the service transition phase of the life cycle, the IT service design is built, tested, and moved into production in order to ensure that the customer/

[22] C. Davis and M. Schiller, *IT Auditing Using Controls to Protect Information Assets,* 2nd ed. (New York: McGraw-Hill, 2011), p. 407.

[23] V. Arraj, *ITIL White Paper: The Basics,* May 2010, Accessed February 2013, Retrieved from http://www.best-management-practice.com/gempdf/itil_the_basics.pdf.

EXHIBIT 11.6
Overview of IT Infrastructure Library 4 Life Cycle (2019)

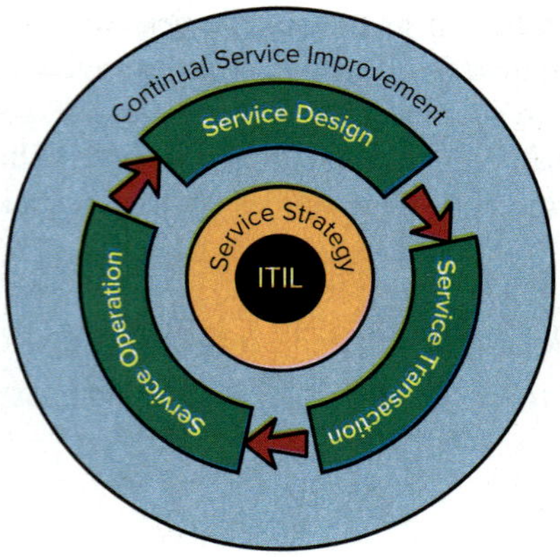

user can achieve the desired value. This phase involves managing changes; controlling the assets and configuration items (e.g., hardware, software, etc.); service validation; testing; and transition planning to ensure that users, support personnel, and the production environment have been prepared for the changed IT assets to function properly. Once transitioned, the service operation phase delivers and supports the service on an ongoing basis. This process includes managing disruptions to service through rapid restoration of incidents, determining the root cause of problems and detecting trends associated with recurring issues, handling daily routine end-user requests, and managing service access. The last phase of the IT service life cycle is continual service improvement. During this phase, a firm should offer a mechanism for IT to measure and improve the service levels, the technology, and the efficiency and effectiveness of IT processes.

ISO 27000 Series

The ISO 27000 series of standards are designed to address information security issues. Despite the evolving names and scope, the ISO 27000 series, particularly ISO 27001 and ISO 27002, have become the most recognized and generally accepted sets of information security framework and guidelines. ISO 27001/27002, ISO 17799, and BS 7799 are, essentially, the same core set of standards dealing with various aspects of information security practices and information security management. The ISO 27001 and 27002 standards were published in October 2005, replacing and enhancing BS 7799-1, BS 7799-2, and ISO 17799 standards with harmonization of other generally accepted international standards. Exhibit 11.7 presents a summary of the major operational standards in the ISO 27000 series.

The main objective of the ISO 27000 series is to provide a model for establishing, implementing, operating, monitoring, maintaining, and improving an information security management system (ISMS). The ISMS standard emphasizes using a "process approach,"

EXHIBIT 11.7
Summary of the Major Standards in the ISO 27000 Series

ISO 27001 This standard replaces BS 7799-2, providing specification for information security management systems (ISMSs).	**ISO 27002** This standard was called ISO 17799, providing guidance on the implementation of information security controls.
ISO 27003 A new standard offers guidance for implementing ISMSs.	**ISO 27004** This standard covers ISMS measurement and metrics; includes suggested ISO 27002-aligned controls.
ISO 27005 This standard provides the methodology for information security risk management.	**ISO 27006** This standard provides guidelines for accreditation of ISMS certification.

which is defined as "the application of a system of processes within an organization, together with the identification and interactions of these processes, and their management to produce the desired outcome."[24] It also employs the plan-do-check-act model (PDCA), which is used to structure the process approach. In the "plan" stage, an ISMS is established. Then, the IT personnel maintain and improve the ISMS in the "act" stage. The established ISMS is reviewed and monitored in the "check" stage, followed by the "do" stage to implement and operate the ISMS.

ISO 27001 and 27002 address 11 major areas with regard to information security and outline 133 security controls within those 11 areas:

1. Security policy.
2. Organization of information security.
3. Asset management.
4. Human resources security.
5. Physical and environmental security.
6. Communications and operations management.
7. Access control.
8. Information systems acquisition, development, and maintenance.
9. Information security incident management.
10. Business continuity management.
11. Compliance.

Exhibit 11.8 presents the basic steps required to set up an information security management system in accordance with ISO 27001/27002.

EXHIBIT 11.8
Steps to Establish an ISMS Following ISO 27001/27002

Source: http://iso-27000-series.blogspot.com/2008_06_01_archive.xhtml.

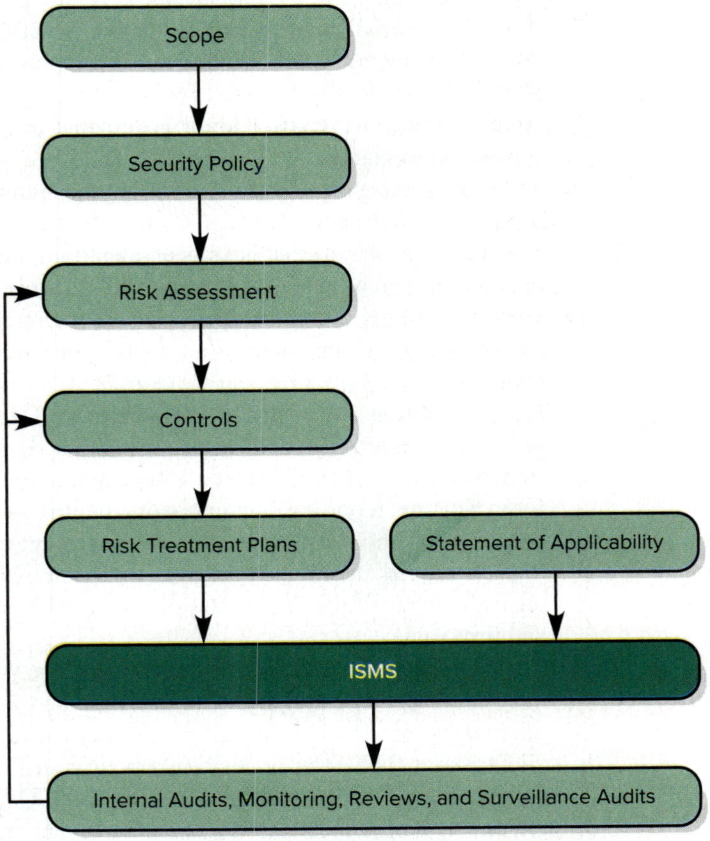

[24] The ISO 27000 Directory, www.27000.org/index.htm.

COMPARING CONTROL/GOVERNANCE FRAMEWORKS

As we know, COSO 2013 provides a general internal control framework that can be applied to all firms on various systems. COBIT 2019 is a comprehensive framework for IT governance and management and provides management and auditors with five domains, 40 objectives, risk and value drivers, best practices regarding information security, and a capability/maturity model for performance measurement to maximize the benefits from IT. ITIL 4 (2019) is a framework focusing on IT service management and digital service delivery. The ISO 27000 series is a framework for information security management. COBIT 2019 provides the biggest advantages because it includes other widely accepted standards, frameworks, and guidance for building effective IT governance and practices. A firm can implement a wide range of desirable IT processes and controls, as well as achieve its business objectives regarding IT security and service management.

Summary

- Given the mandate of the Sarbanes–Oxley Act of 2002, management is responsible for designing internal controls and evaluating the effectiveness of the controls based on a control framework. COSO is the most commonly accepted internal control framework. COBIT is a generally accepted framework for IT governance and management. Most American firms use COBIT for IT governance and to evaluate IT controls for SOX section 404 compliance.
- There are three general categories of internal controls. Preventive controls deter problems before they arise. Detective controls find out problems when they arise. Corrective controls fix problems that have been identified. In a computerized environment, internal controls can be categorized as general controls and application controls.
- General controls are those applicable to enterprisewide issues. Application controls are specific to a subsystem or an application including input, processing, and output controls.
- COSO publishes two control frameworks: COSO internal control integrated framework and COSO enterprise risk management (ERM) integrated framework. COSO 2013 framework is a widely accepted authority on internal control, providing a foundation for evaluating, reporting, and improving internal control. COSO ERM 2017 framework provides guidance on enterprise risk management in defining, assessing, managing, and transferring risk in order to maximize firm value. COSO ERM 2017 focuses on the strategic alignment of the firm's mission with its risk appetite to realize business objectives and firm value.
- The COBIT 2019 framework is a control framework for IT governance and management to ensure the integrity of information and information systems. Two additional governance frameworks related to information technology are the ITIL and the ISO 27000 series. ITIL 4 provides best practices in IT infrastructure management and IT service delivery. The main objective of the ISO 27000 series is to provide a model for establishing, implementing, operating, monitoring, maintaining, and improving an information security system.

Key Words

application controls (*390*) Controls specific to a subsystem or an application to ensure the validity, completeness, and accuracy of the transactions.

code of ethics (*388*) A formal expectation on what is considered to be ethical within an organization to promote ethical behavior.

Committee of Sponsoring Organizations (COSO) (*390*) Composed of several organizations (AAA, AICPA, FEI, IIA, and IMA); studies the causal factors that lead to fraudulent financial reporting and develops recommendations for public companies, independent auditors, the SEC and other regulators, and educational institutions to improve the quality of financial reporting through internal controls and corporate governance.

control objectives for information and related technology (COBIT) (*391*) An internationally accepted set of best IT security and control practices for IT management released by the IT Governance Institute (ITGI).

control risk (*397*) The threat that errors or irregularities in the underlying transactions will not be prevented, detected, and corrected by the internal control system.

corporate governance (*389*) A set of processes and policies in managing an organization with sound ethics to safeguard the interests of its stakeholders.

corrective controls (*390*) Fix problems that have been identified, such as using backup files to recover corrupted data.

cost/benefit analysis (*397*) Important in determining whether to implement an internal control.

detective controls (*390*) Find problems when they arise.

enterprise risk management (ERM) (*395*) A process, affected by the entity's board of directors, management, and other personnel, applied in strategy setting and across the enterprise, designed to identify potential events that may affect the entity, and manage risk to be within the risk appetite, to provide reasonable assurance regarding the achievement of objectives.

general controls (*390*) Pertain to enterprisewide issues such as controls over accessing the network, developing and maintaining applications, and documenting changes of programs.

Information Technology Infrastructure Library (ITIL) (*391*) A set of concepts and practices for IT service management.

inherent risk (397) The risk related to the nature of the business activity itself.

input controls (*399*) Ensure the authorization, entry, and verification of data entering the system.

International Organization for Standardization (ISO) 27000 series (*391*) This series contains a range of individual standards and documents specifically reserved by ISO for information security.

IT application controls (*399*) Activities specific to a subsystem's or an application's input, processing, and output.

IT controls (*399*) Involve processes that provide assurance for information and help to mitigate risks associated with the use of technology.

IT general controls (ITGC) (*399*) Enterprise-level controls over IT.

output controls (*400*) Provide output to authorized people and ensure the output is used properly.

manual controls (*399*) Mainly manual but could involve the physical use of computing technology.

preventive controls (*390*) Deter problems before they arise.

processing controls (*400*) Ensure that data and transactions are processed accurately.

Public Company Accounting Oversight Board (PCAOB) (*389*) Established by SOX to provide independent oversight of public accounting firms.

residual risk (*397*) The product of inherent risk and control risk (i.e., Residual risk = Inherent risk × Control risk).

risk assessment (*397*) The process of identifying and analyzing risks systematically to determine the firm's risk response and control activities.

Sarbanes–Oxley Act of 2002 (SOX) (*388*) A response to business scandals such as Enron, WorldCom, and Tyco International; requires public companies registered with the SEC and their auditors to annually assess and report on the design and effectiveness of internal control over financial reporting.

ANSWERS TO PROGRESS CHECKS

1. Ethics plays a critical role when people make choices and decisions. To promote ethical behavior, firms often choose to establish a formal expectation of what is considered to be ethical within the group. Ethical behavior prompted by a code of ethics can be considered a form of internal control, so a code of ethics is part of corporate governance.
2. The PCAOB was established by Congress to oversee the audits of public companies in order to protect investors and the public interest by promoting informative, accurate, and independent audit reports. In addition, auditors of U.S. public companies are subject to external and independent oversight by PCAOB. It also issues audit standards.
3. According to a COSO report, an internal control is "a process, affected by an entity's board of directors, management and other personnel. This process is designed to provide reasonable assurance regarding the achievement of objectives in effectiveness and efficiency of operations, reliability of financial reporting, and compliance with applicable laws and regulations."
4. Prevention, detection, and correction.
5. Reduce, share, avoid, and accept risks.
6. Expected benefit of an internal control = Impact (potential loss) × Decreased likelihood (due to control implementation).
7. a. Authorization to ensure transactions are valid.
   b. Segregation of duties to prevent fraud and mistakes.
   c. Supervision to compensate for imperfect segregation of duties.
   d. Accounting documents and records to maintain audit trails.
   e. Access control to ensure only authorized personnel have access to assets and information.
   f. Independent verification to double-check for errors and misrepresentations.
8. Application controls are input, processing, and output controls specific to a subsystem or application.
9. Field check, range check, closed-loop verification, reasonableness check, and so on.
10. IT resources are applications, information, infrastructures, and people. The business requirements for information are effectiveness, efficiency, confidentiality, integrity, availability, compliance, and reliability.

Appendix

ERP Architecture and Control Issues

Enterprise resource planning (ERP) systems have been steadily growing in popularity since the 1980s. Many firms have come to see integrated systems as essential to maintain a competitive edge; the ability to combine all of an enterprise's operations into an integrated system allows for greater visibility and control over its business concerns.

ERP architecture is generally designed around the needs of an organization from an operational standpoint. In general, a company will need to determine what business processes it needs to put into an ERP system and then determine the proper corresponding modules to purchase. Most ERP systems will utilize a financial accounting module to record accounting transactions and contain the enterprise's general ledger. Some companies will also need manufacturing/conversion modules to track all of the materials and processes required to produce finished goods. The current trend in ERP systems focuses more on business processes than modules (e.g., SAP S4 HANA) and with specialized or functional add-ons such as extended warehouse management system.

Modules within an ERP system generally tie together to promote easy integration. Concerning a sale transaction, costs associated with creating a product or delivering a service in the manufacturing module should easily flow into the cost of sales in the finance module. This easy integration and transferability of data is one of the major advantages granted by an ERP system. However, in some cases, companies still prefer to combine multiple systems to accomplish their business goals. One popular example of this is using a separate customer relationship management system in order to take customer orders and manage customer-facing interactions. In this case, data must flow from the CRM tool into the ERP system to create an order and then process that order to allow for invoicing and cash collections. This added systems layer produces heightened risk because it creates another repository—the middleware that manages the flow of data between the systems where controls must be put in place to protect the confidentiality and integrity of data.

The physical architecture of an ERP system must also be assessed to design a control structure that manages risks. Possible risk areas include

1. Where will the servers be hosted?
2. Will there be a client/server or a cloud, web-based architecture? If a third-party service provider (e.g., Amazon Web Services) is involved in cloud operations, what enterprise risk management issues should be considered?
3. How will data flow between the servers and the users, and are those lines of communication controlled by the company and secure?
4. Does the company need to utilize encryption or other controls to protect confidential data?
5. How will the company recover from a critical hardware failure or disaster?
6. How will the company maintain services during a primary systems outage?

Considering on-premise ERP systems, companies must ensure that their systems comply with relevant laws and regulations and contain safeguards to ensure the reliability of their financial reporting. One of the most important controls over an ERP system is the assurance of proper change management. Proper change management mandates the creation of at least three separate ERP system instances, referred to as "environments." The lowest environment, with the least number of controls, is the development environment. This is the only environment where code changes and configurations can be executed. From this environment, changes are migrated to the quality assurance environment for testing. Full testing should be executed in this environment before any changes can be moved to the final environment, production. Change management is designed to prevent disruptions to service or unauthorized code changes that could be used to commit fraud. All steps in the change management process should be monitored and well-documented to ensure proper authorization for changes.

ERP systems should be planned with consideration of the business' control structure. Control activities, like segregation of duties and access controls, should be utilized in the system security plan to limit the opportunities for fraud in a company's transactions. The company should use the control frameworks that it has adopted to govern its control structure to plan specific control activities. Controls should be considered for all steps of the systems management process:

1. Plan: Controls should first be considered in the planning stages of any ERP implementation. Business processes and risks should be assessed, and controls should be designed to mitigate the risks that are discovered.

2. Build: Controls need to be implemented properly in the build phase of the ERP's life cycle. This includes both initial implementation and any changes that are made through the change management process.
3. Run: Once implemented, controls will help to reduce risks to the business while the ERP system is operational. During this time, support needs to be provided to ensure continued operation of the control structure. An example of this activity is that new users must be properly trained and setup within the confines of the control structure.
4. Monitor: Once a company has set up an ERP system and integrated the enterprise's control structure, it should continue to monitor the implementation to ensure that the controls are effective. This includes activities such as monitoring for users with segregation of duties conflicts and providing internal audits of risk areas within the enterprise.

An ERP system's architecture and control structure are linked out of necessity. As the architecture of the ERP changes due to the addition of modules, middleware, or additional environments, control risk must be assessed and addressed to ensure the integrity of the system.

Multiple Choice Questions connect

1. **(LO 11-1)** Based on SOX, which of the following sections is about assessing internal controls?
   a. 302
   b. 401
   c. 404
   d. 906
2. **(LO 11-1)** SOX requires companies to use COSO or COSO ERM as the framework in evaluating internal controls.
   a. True
   b. False
3. **(LO 11-1)** Controls that are designed to prevent, detect, or correct errors in transactions as they are processed through a specific subsystem are referred to as
   a. general controls.
   b. application controls.
   c. processing controls.
   d. Both b and c are correct.
   e. None of these options are correct.
4. **(LO 11-2)** Which of the following is *not* a component in the COSO 2013 internal control framework?
   a. Effective operations
   b. Control activities
   c. Risk assessment
   d. Control environment
   e. Monitoring

5. **(LO 11-2)** Prenumbering of source documents helps to verify that
   a. multiple types of source documents have a unique identifier.
   b. all transactions have been recorded because the numerical sequence serves as a control.
   c. no inventory has been misplaced.
   d. documents have been used in order.
6. **(LO 11-2)** A field check is a(n)
   a. preventive control.
   b. detective control.
   c. corrective control.
   d. general control.
   e. output control.
7. **(LO 11-2)** Which is not an example of a batch total?
   a. Record count
   b. Financial total
   c. Hash total
   d. Exception total
8. **(LO 11-2)** Backup is a preventive control.
   a. True
   b. False
9. **(LO 11-2)** The computer sums the first four digits of a customer number to calculate the value of the fifth digit and then compares that calculation to the number typed during data entry. This is an example of a
   a. field check.
   b. parity check.
   c. check digit verification.
   d. batch total.
10. **(LO 11-3), (LO 11-4)** Which of the following statements is correct?
    a. SOX requires all public companies to use the COSO ERM framework to meet the requirements of section 404.
    b. Regarding IT control and governance, the COBIT framework is most commonly adopted by companies in the United States.
    c. ITIL is the best internal control framework for the high-tech industry.
    d. ISO 27000 series are best practices for IT service management.
11. **(LO 11-1)** Based on SOX, which of the following sections is not about corporate responsibility for financial reports?
    a. 101
    b. 302
    c. 404
    d. 906
12. **(LO 11-2)** Based on COSO 2013, which of the following statements is not correct?
    a. Employees at any level of an organization play a role in internal control.
    b. Internal controls can provide reasonable assurance only.
    c. Internal control is a process consisting of ongoing tasks and activities.
    d. The responsibility of monitoring the effectiveness of internal controls belongs to the internal audit group.

13. **(LO 11-2)** Which of the following is not one of the five essential components in the COSO 2013 framework?
    a. Control environment
    b. Control assessment
    c. Control activities
    d. Monitoring activities
14. **(LO 11-2)** Access control to ensure only authorized personnel have access to a firm's network is a
    a. general control.
    b. process control.
    c. output control.
    d. input control.
15. **(LO 11-4)** The ISO 27000 series are a framework for
    a. IT governance.
    b. IT general controls.
    c. data management.
    d. information security management.
16. **(LO 11-2)** Segregation of duty is a
    a. preventive control.
    b. detective control.
    c. corrective control.
    d. personnel general control.
17. **(LO 11-2)** The responsibility of enterprise risk management belongs to
    a. internal auditors.
    b. external auditors.
    c. controller.
    d. management.
18. **(LO 11-2)** Most input controls are designed to assess one field only. Which of the following input controls will need to examine a record to determine the control is effective or not?
    a. Range check
    b. Size check
    c. Completeness check
    d. Validity check
19. **(LO 11-2)** Which of the following is a correct statement about COBIT 2019 framework?
    a. It is a framework for enterprise risk management.
    b. It focuses on providing guidance for information security.
    c. It is designed for information and technology governance and management.
    d. It is a framework for IT audit conducted by public accounting firms.
20. **(LO 11-2)** Which of the following is a correct statement about COSO ERM 2017 framework?
    a. It is a framework developed by the IT audit profession.
    b. It stresses the importance of having one department responsible for risk management.
    c. It focuses on evaluating effectiveness of internal controls.
    d. It enhances alignment among strategy setting, decision making, and performance through enterprise risk management.

Discussion Questions connect

1. **(LO 11-1)** How has the Sarbanes–Oxley Act affected the audit profession and corporate governance of public firms?
2. **(LO 11-2)** What are the objectives and components of the COSO ERM 2004 framework?
3. **(LO 11-2)** Two commonly used frameworks developed by COSO are COSO 2013 internal control framework and the COSO ERM 2017 framework. What are the differences between the two frameworks?
4. **(LO 11-2)** Use a few sentences to describe IT general controls and application controls. Give a few examples of these two types of controls.
5. **(LO 11-3)** Why would a manager be inclined to use the COBIT framework as a guide for IT governance and management?
6. **(LO 11-4)** The ISO 27000 series serves different purposes than ITIL. Which one could be more important to accounting professionals and why?
7. **(LO 11-2)** Segregation of duties is an important internal control. What functions must be separated? If ideal segregation of duties is not economically feasible, what are some compensating controls that would help reduce the risk of fraud or error?
8. **(LO 11-2)** Use a flowchart to explain the risk assessment process.
9. **(LO 11-1)** There are three types of controls: preventive, detective, and corrective. List some examples of each type. Explain which type of control auditors would focus on while evaluating a company's effectiveness of controls and why?
10. **(LO 11-2)** Describe the control activities in the COSO framework. Why are these control activities important for most firms?

Problems connect

1. **(LO 11-2)** The global economic crisis of 2008–2010 has stimulated many boards of directors and executives to reevaluate how they assess and manage risks. Use a flowchart to describe the process of risk assessment.
2. **(LO 11-2)** A newly hired internal auditor discovered that immaterial thefts by employees are pervasive in the company; employees take books from the company's library, tools from the company's laboratories, supplies, products, and so forth. By interviewing some of the employees, the internal auditor discovered that most employees thought their behavior was not detrimental to the company because none of the items had significant value. What should the company do to prevent this type of employee behavior?
3. **(LO 11-2)** The sales department of a company received several claims from its customers that their payments were not credited to their accounts. Investigation uncovered that the accounts receivable clerk has been stealing some customer payments. What are some of the internal control procedures that could prevent and detect the problem?
4. **(LO 11-2)** The information system of Carlsbad Bottle Inc. is deemed to be 90 percent reliable. A major threat in the procurement process has been discovered, with an exposure of $300,000. Two control procedures are identified to mitigate the threat. Applying control A would cost $18,000 and reduce the risk to 4 percent. Implementing control B would cost $10,000 and reduce the risk to 6 percent. Using both controls would cost $26,000 and reduce the risk to 2.5 percent. Given the information presented, and considering an economic analysis of costs and benefits only, which control procedure(s) should Carlsbad Bottle choose to implement?

5. **(LO 11-2)** Which internal control(s) would you recommend to prevent the following situations from occurring?
   a. Authorization of a credit memo for a customer's account (on receivables) when the goods were never actually returned.
   b. Theft of funds by the cashier, who cashed several checks and did not record their receipt.
   c. Inventory stolen by receiving dock personnel. The receiving clerk claimed the inventory was sent to the warehouse, but the warehouse clerk did not record properly.
   d. Writing off a customer's accounts receivable balances as uncollectible in order to conceal the theft of subsequent cash collections.
   e. Billing customers for the quantity ordered when the quantity shipped was actually less due to back-ordering of some items.
6. **(LO 11-2)** Which types of input controls would best mitigate the following threats?
   a. Posting the amount of a sale to a customer account that does not exist.
   b. A customer entering too many characters into the five-digit zip code while making an online purchase, causing the server to crash.
   c. An intern's pay rate was entered as $150 per hour, not $15 per hour.
   d. Approving a customer order without the customer's address so the order was not shipped on time.
   e. Entering the contract number of a critical contract as 13688 instead of 16388, which is a serious mistake for the company.
7. **(LO 11-2)** The COSO 2013 internal control framework codifies 17 relevant principles associated with the five components of internal control. Match the following principles with the five components.

COSO Principles	COSO Components
a. Management establishes, with board oversight, structures, reporting lines, and appropriate authorities and responsibilities in the pursuit of objectives.	i. Control environment
b. The organization deploys control activities through policies that establish what is expected and procedures that put policies into place.	ii. Risk assessment
c. The organization considers the potential for fraud in assessing risks to the achievement of objectives.	iii. Control activities
d. The organization holds individuals accountable for their internal control responsibilities in the pursuit of objectives.	iv. Information and communication
e. The organization obtains or generates and uses relevant, quality information to support the functioning of internal control.	v. Monitoring activities
f. The organization evaluates and communicates internal control deficiencies in a timely manner to those parties responsible for taking corrective action, including senior management and the board of directors, as appropriate.	

8. **(LO 11-1)** Identify each of the following internal controls as a primarily preventive, detective, or corrective control.
   a. Limit access to petty cash funds.
   b. Reconcile the petty cash fund before replenishing it.

c. Require two signatures on checks above a specified limit.
d. Enable hidden flags or audit trails on accounting software.
e. Examine credit card statements and corresponding receipts each month, independently, to determine whether charges are appropriate.
f. Keep checks in a locked box or drawer and restrict the number of employees who have access to the key.
g. Back up accounting records daily.

9. **(LO 11-2)** Match the following internal controls with the categories of control activities.

Internal Controls	Control Activities
a. Separate handling cash (receipt and deposit) functions from recordkeeping functions (recording transactions in the accounts receivable subsidiary ledger).	i. Authorization
b. Require purchases, payroll, and cash disbursements to be authorized by a designated person.	ii. Segregation of duties
c. Require accounting department employees to take vacations.	iii. Supervision
d. Separate purchasing functions from payables functions.	iv. Accounting documents and records
e. Ensure that the same person isn't authorized to write and sign a check.	v. Access control
f. When opening mail, endorse or stamp checks "For Deposit Only."	vi. Independent verification
g. Periodically reconcile the incoming check log against deposits.	
h. Require supervisors to approve employees' time sheets before payroll is prepared.	
i. List customer checks on a log before turning them over to the person responsible for depositing receipts.	

10. **(LO 11-3), (LO 11-4)** Match the following control frameworks with their main purposes.

Purposes	Control Frameworks
a. Expand internal controls to provide a broader view on risk management to maximize firm value.	i. COSO 2013
b. Provide management an information technology (IT) governance model that helps in delivering value from IT and understanding and managing the risks associated with IT.	ii. COSO ERM 2017
c. Manage IT infrastructure and digital IT service delivery.	iii. COBIT 2019
d. Provide a framework and guidelines for information security.	iv. ITIL 4
e. Improve quality of financial reporting through internal controls and corporate governance.	v. ISO27000 series

11. **(LO 11-2)** The COSO ERM 2017 framework codifies 20 principles associated with the five components of enterprise risk management. Match the following principles with the five components.

COSO ERM Principles	COSO ERM Components
a. Report on risk, culture, and performance.	i. Governance and Culture
b. Review risk and performance.	ii. Strategy and Objective-setting
c. Pursue improvement in ERM.	iii. Performance
d. Exercise board risk oversight.	iv. Review and Revision
e. Attract, develop, and retain capable individuals.	v. Information, Communication, and Reporting
f. Prioritize risks.	
g. Define risk appetite.	
h. Assess substantial change.	

12. **(LO 11-3)** COBIT 2019 is a comprehensive framework for information and technology governance and management. This framework has five domains. Indicate if the purpose of each domain is for governance or management.

COBIT domains	Purpose
a. Align, plan, and organize	
b. Build, acquire, and implement	
c. Deliver, service, and support	
d. Evaluate, direct, and monitor	
e. Monitor, evaluate, and assess	

Design Element: Duncan Smith/Getty Images

Chapter Twelve

Cybersecurity and Computer Fraud

A Look at This Chapter

Given today's business environment, computers and networks are at the center of most firms' accounting information systems. Awareness of cybersecurity issues and computer fraud is critical to accountants and auditors. In this chapter, we introduce some frameworks relevant to cybersecurity and also provide examples of computer fraud and illustrate how AIS can be misused in order to achieve personal gains. We also discuss common vulnerabilities and how to manage and assess such vulnerabilities regarding cybersecurity.

A Look Back

In Chapter 11, we discussed internal controls and important factors in corporate governance that are critical to an organization's efficiency and effectiveness in operations, reliability in financial reporting, and compliance with applicable laws and regulations. We also provided detailed information on important control frameworks such as COSO 2013, COSO ERM 2017, and COBIT 2019.

A Look Ahead

Given the complicated information systems and the tremendous amount of data to be analyzed and reported, accountants must evaluate the design and monitor the integrity of an accounting information system. In Chapter 13, we examine the risks in accounting information systems and how auditors validate that systems are well designed with embedded internal controls and that the systems process data with integrity.

Tom Lasseter/MCT/Getty Images

Today, before going to work, you drop by **Starbucks** to grab a cup of coffee. Even early in the morning, Starbucks already has a line of customers waiting, looking at the menu, and deciding what they want to order. Perhaps they visit Starbucks regularly and have a specific drink they want to order. For example, you already have your drink in mind: iced caramel macchiato, nonfat milk, one extra shot of espresso, light ice, light caramel to start off the day.

While you are waiting, millions of Starbucks customers all over the world are also being served, many with drinks as unique as the one that you just ordered. Throughout the course of an entire day, all the individual Starbucks stores have made countless transactions, which all must be recorded accurately to provide reliable information for decision making to keep Starbucks competitive. The integrity of the systems and the quality of information are critical to companies such as Starbucks in supporting daily operations, as well as providing consolidated data for year-end financial reporting.

CHAPTER OUTLINE

Introduction

Information Security and Systems Integrity

Information Security Risks and Attacks

Encryption and Authentication

Cybersecurity Risk Management Framework by AICPA

Computer Fraud and Abuse

Computer Fraud Risk Assessment

Computer Fraud Schemes

Computer Fraud Prevention and Detection

General Data Protection Regulation

Vulnerability Assessments and Management

Types of Vulnerabilities

An Overall Framework for Vulnerability Assessment and Management

System Availability

System and Organization Controls (SOC) Examinations

Disaster Recovery Planning and Business Continuity Management

LEARNING OBJECTIVES

After reading this chapter, you should be able to:

12-1 Describe the risks related to information security and systems integrity.

12-2 Understand the concepts of encryption and authentication.

12-3 Describe computer fraud and misuse of AIS and corresponding risk-mitigation techniques.

12-4 Define *vulnerabilities,* and explain how to manage and assess them.

12-5 Explain issues in system availability.

12-6 Explain the concepts and issues in System and Organization Controls (SOC) reporting.

12-7 Describe the importance of disaster recovery and business continuity.

INTRODUCTION

Rapid development in digital technologies has been a driving factor of consumer demand, employee training, and efficient use of firms' resources. As a result of the maturing digital economy, firms across different industries will continue to be reshaped through the application of information technology. In this chapter, we present a discussion of one of the most critical impacts of technology on firms' operations—information security. We first introduce concepts and risks regarding information security and then provide examples of computer fraud and how AIS can be misused in achieving personal gains. We then explain common vulnerabilities and how to manage and assess those vulnerabilities, and the frameworks for vulnerability assessment and management. The AICPA has published guides for auditors to examine system and organization controls (SOC) for service organizations. Key concepts and differences of the three different SOC reports are described to enhance the selection of a SOC report that fits a specific set of circumstances. Last, disaster recovery planning and business continuity management are also presented in this chapter.

LO 12-1

Describe the risks related to information security and systems integrity.

INFORMATION SECURITY AND SYSTEMS INTEGRITY

The AICPA conducts a survey each year to identify the top 10 technology issues for certified public accountants (CPAs). The purpose of the survey is to indicate the CPAs' unique perspectives on how much each technology will affect financial management and the fulfillment of responsibilities such as safeguarding assets, overseeing business performance, and compliance with laws and regulations. For many years, information security management has been ranked as the top technology issue for CPAs. According to AICPA, "the primary focus of information security is the balanced protection of the confidentiality, integrity, and availability of data while maintaining efficient policy implementation and without disrupting organizational productivity."[1]

Information security is a critical factor in maintaining system integrity. If users can perform the intended functions of a system without being degraded or impaired by unauthorized manipulation, the system has maintained its integrity. Good information security ensures that systems and their contents remain constant for integrity. In general, the goal of information security management is to protect the confidentiality, integrity, and availability (CIA) of a firm's information.

- Confidentiality—information is not accessible to unauthorized individuals or processes.
- Integrity—information is accurate and complete.
- Availability—information and systems are accessible on demand.

Information Security Risks and Attacks

Given the popularity of the Internet and mobile devices and the complexity of computer technologies, important business information and IT assets are exposed to risks and attacks from internal (such as disgruntled employees) and external parties (such as

[1] https://www.aicpa.org/interestareas/informationtechnology/resources/information-security-cybersecurity.html.

hackers, competitors, etc.) Some of the more common information security risks and attacks include:[2]

- Virus—a self-replicating program that runs and spreads by modifying other programs or files.
- Worm—a self-replicating, self-propagating, self-contained program that uses networking mechanisms to spread itself.
- Trojan horse—a non-self-replicating program that seems to have a useful purpose in appearance, but in reality has a different, malicious purpose.
- Spam—sending unsolicited bulk information.
- Botnet (bot)—a collection of software robots that overruns computers to act automatically in response to the bot-herder's control inputs through the Internet.
- Denial-of-service (DoS)—the prevention of authorized access to resources (such as servers) or the delaying of time-critical operations.
- Spyware—software that is secretly installed into an information system to gather information on individuals or organizations without their knowledge; a type of malicious code.
- Spoofing—sending a network packet that appears to come from a source other than its actual source.
- Social engineering—manipulating someone to take certain action that may not be in that person's best interest, such as revealing confidential information or granting access to physical assets, networks, or information.

Do you know that mobile devices such as Android phones, tablets, and iPhones/iPads are often the targets for hackers to attack? In addition, mobile apps have emerged as a new attack vector for various security issues.

PROGRESS CHECK

1. What are the general goals of information security?
2. Give an example of social engineering.

LO 12-2

Understand the concepts of encryption and authentication.

Encryption and Authentication

Encryption is a preventive control providing confidentiality and privacy for data transmission and storage. It refers to algorithmic schemes that encode *plaintext* into nonreadable form or *cyphertext*. The receiver of the encrypted text uses a "key" to decrypt the message, returning it to its original plaintext form. The key is the trigger mechanism to the cryptographic algorithm. The main factors of encryption are key length, encryption algorithm, and key management. Longer key length provides for stronger encryption. In general, a key length of 56 bits or less is insufficient for sensitive data; 128-bit and longer key lengths are more than sufficient for secure data transmission. In addition, using a strong encryption algorithm and establishing a strong policy on key management are essential for information security.

In general, cryptographic algorithms are grouped into two categories: symmetric-key and asymmetric-key encryption methods. Exhibit 12.1 describes the process of using symmetric-key encryption to encrypt and decrypt data/documents in maintaining confidentiality. **Symmetric-key encryption** is fast and suitable for encrypting large data sets or messages. However, key distribution and key management are problematic because both the sender and the receiver use the same key to encrypt and decrypt

[2]Definitions of information security risks and attacks are quoted from National Institute of Standards and Technology (NIST), *Glossary of Key Information Security Terms* (Washington, DC: U.S. Department of Commerce, 2006).

EXHIBIT 12.1
Symmetric-Key Encryption Process

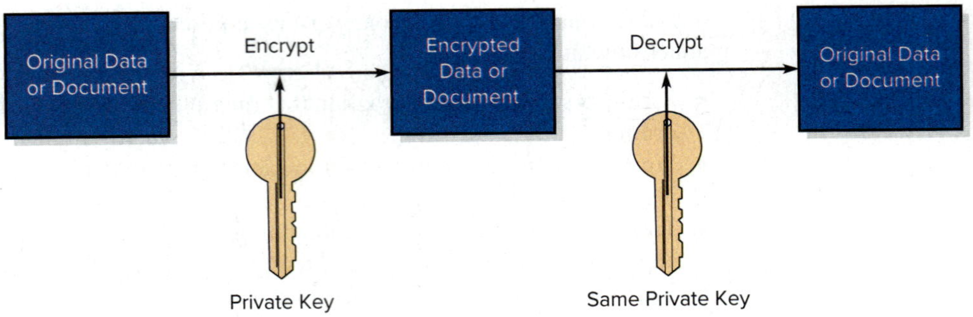

messages. If a firm has many employees and trading partners at different geographical locations, it is very difficult to always distribute keys in a secured way. In addition, managing one key for each pair of users, which results in exponential growth of the number of keys for each additional party, is not cost-effective given the large number of users among the firms.

Conversely, **asymmetric-key encryption** is slow and is not appropriate for encrypting large data sets. However, because each user has a pair of two keys—the **public key** and the **private key**—asymmetric-key encryption solves problems in key distribution and key management. The two keys are created as one pair and you use one to encrypt and the other to decrypt the data or document. The public keys are widely distributed and available to authorized users. The private key is kept secret and known only to the owner of the key. Hence, to transmit confidential information, the sender uses the receiver's public key to encrypt the message; the receiver uses his or her own private key for decryption upon receiving the message. Refer to Exhibit 12.2 regarding the process of how to use the asymmetric-key method to transmit data/documents in maintaining confidentiality. Two common names for asymmetric-key encryption are *public-key encryption* and *two-key encryption.*

EXHIBIT 12.2
Asymmetric-Key Encryption Process

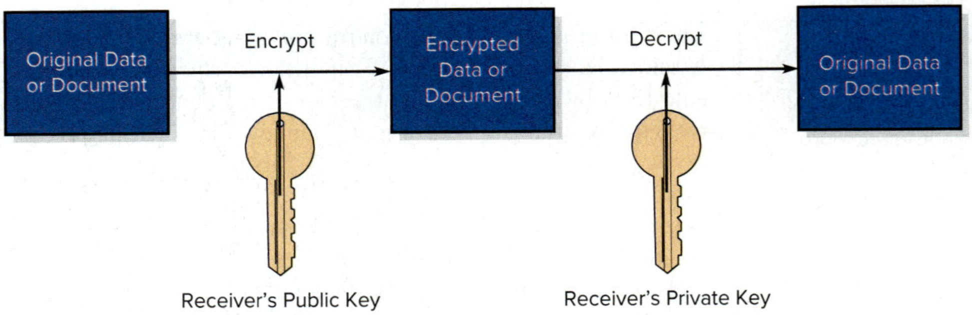

Authentication is a process that establishes the origin of information or determines the identity of a user, process, or device. It is critical in e-business because it can prevent repudiation while conducting transactions online. Using asymmetric-key encryption, authentication can be achieved for electronic transactions. For example, in Exhibit 12.3, to authenticate the receiver (B), the sender (A) emails a challenge message to B. B will use his or her private key to encrypt the challenge message and send it to A. If A is able to use B's public key to decrypt and get the plaintext of the challenge message, A has authenticated B successfully. Please notice that only the pair of one user's two keys is used for encryption and decryption. In this example, B used his or her private key to

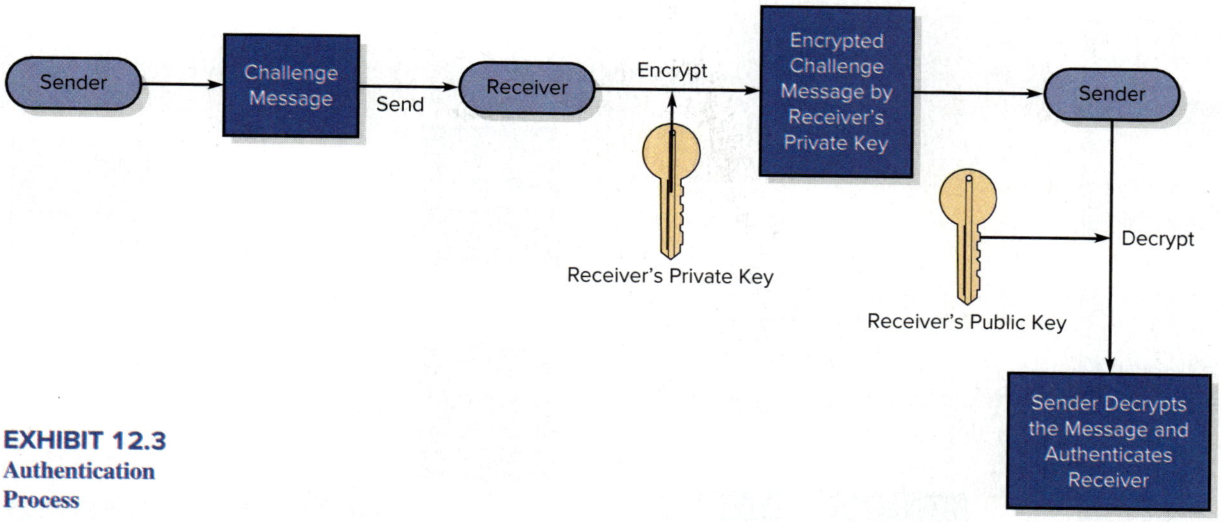

EXHIBIT 12.3
Authentication Process

encrypt the message, and A used B's public key to decrypt the message. Keys from different users cannot be mismatched for encryption and decryption purposes. Please note that this process would need to be repeated in reverse to authenticate both parties involved in the transaction.

To conduct e-business, most firms use a hybrid combination of both methods. We need to authenticate trading partners to avoid repudiation (using the asymmetric-key encryption method), as well as be able to transmit large data sets or documents fast (using symmetric-key encryption method). Specifically, we describe how to use both methods as follows:

1. Both the sender and receiver use the asymmetric-key encryption method to authenticate each other.
2. Either the sender (or the receiver) generates a symmetric key (called a **session key** because it is valid for a certain timeframe only) to be used by both parties.
3. Asymmetric-key encryption is used to maintain confidentiality in distributing the session key. (That is, the sender uses the receiver's public key to encrypt the session key and sends it to the receiver. The receiver uses his or her own private key to decrypt to get the session key.)
4. After both parties have the session key, the session key is used to transmit confidential data/information. The use of a symmetric key for encryption results in faster data transmission.

A **digital signature** is a **message digest (MD)** of a document (or data file) that is encrypted using the document creator's private key. An MD is a short code (256 bits or 32 characters) that is generated through a process called **hashing**, where the original document passes through an algorithm (a series of steps) to generate the MD. Because popular algorithms such as SHA-256 use every bit in the file to calculate the MD, the change of a single character would result in a completely different hash. Therefore, digital signatures can ensure **data integrity**. In addition, to create a digital signature, the document creator must use his or her own private key to encrypt the MD, so the digital signature also authenticates the document creator and serves the purpose of assuring nonrepudiation. Given the significant attributes of a digital signature (maintaining data integrity and authenticating the document/data creator), it serves a critical role in e-business: No one can record an electronic transaction and then later say that they had nothing to do with it. Exhibit 12.4 depicts

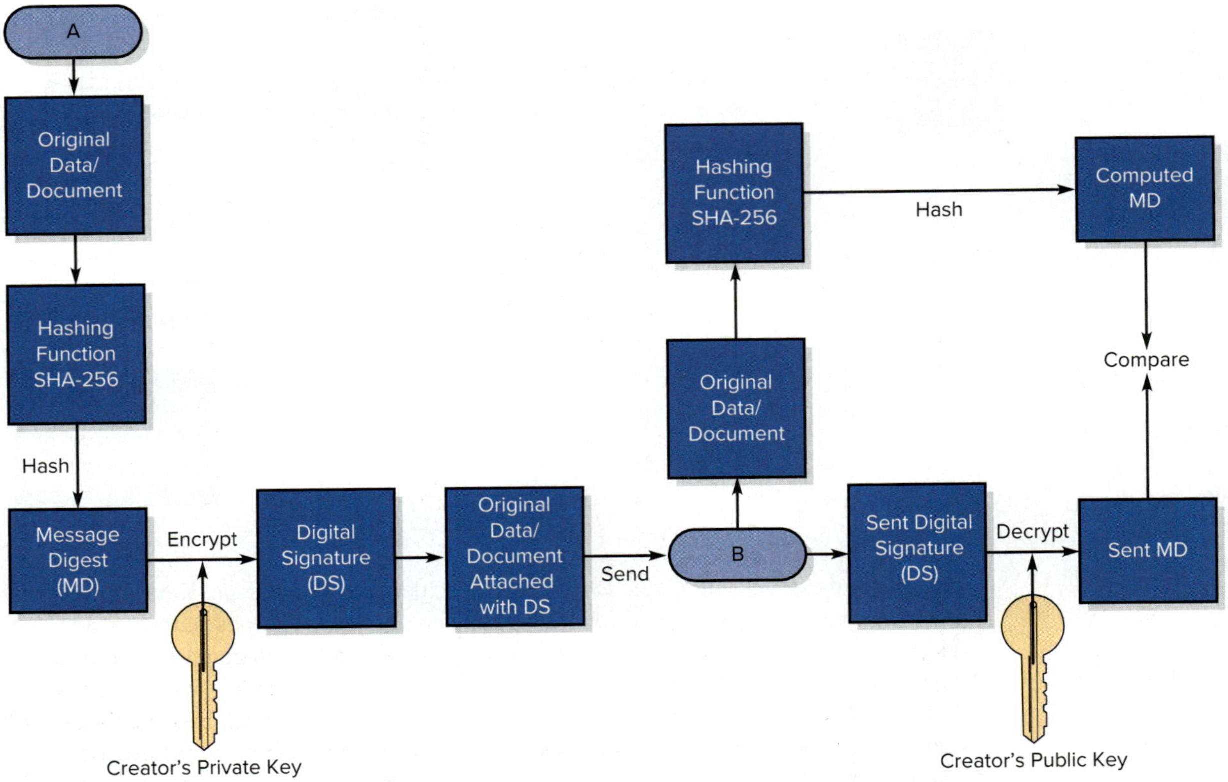

EXHIBIT 12.4
Digital Signature

the process of using a digital signature to ensure data integrity. The process is described as follows:

1. Both the sender (A) and receiver (B) use an asymmetric-key encryption method to authenticate each other.
2. A makes a copy of the document and uses SHA-256 to hash the copy and get an MD.
3. A encrypts the MD using A's private key to get A's digital signature.
4. A uses B's public key to encrypt the original document and A's digital signature (for confidentiality).
5. A sends the encrypted package to B.
6. B receives the package and decrypts it using B's private key. B now has the original document and A's digital signature.
7. B decrypts A's digital signature using A's public key to get A's original MD. B also authenticates that A is the document creator (to assure nonrepudiation).
8. B makes a copy of the received document and uses SHA-256 (must be the same algorithm used by the sender) to hash the copy and get a calculated MD.
9. If the original MD is the same as the calculated MD, B ensures data integrity (no changes made to the original document).

To ensure the asymmetric-key encryption method functions well, several key factors must be considered:[3]

1. A **Certificate Authority (CA)** is a trusted entity that issues and revokes digital certificates.
2. A **digital certificate** is a digital document issued and digitally signed by the private key of a Certificate Authority that binds the name of a subscriber to a public key.

[3]Definitions are quoted from NIST, *Glossary of Key Information Security Terms.*

The certificate indicates that the subscriber identified in the certificate has sole control and access to the private key.

3. A **public-key infrastructure (PKI)** refers to a set of policies, processes, server platforms, software, and workstations used for the purpose of administering certificates and public-/private-key pairs, including the ability to issue, maintain, and revoke public-key certificates.

PKI is an arrangement that issues digital certificates to users and servers, manages the key issuance, and verifies and revokes certificates by means of a CA. Because authentication and nonrepudiation are accomplished by using public keys in decryption, the CA plays the most significant role in assuring the effectiveness of asymmetric-key encryption.

PROGRESS CHECK

3. Can we use the symmetric-key encryption method to authenticate users? Why?
4. What is a digital signature? Why do we need it?

Cybersecurity Risk Management Framework by AICPA

The AICPA believes cybersecurity is an important part of risk management. A company's cybersecurity is an essential consideration for investors when deciding whether or not to invest in a company. Public accounting firms may provide attestation and advisory services to clients to enhance the reliability of a company's cybersecurity representations.

Public accounting firms and their clients' management have similar obligations regarding cybersecurity as they do for financial audits. Management is responsible for describing and asserting the effectiveness of its cybersecurity. The accounting firm is responsible for providing an opinion regarding its client's cybersecurity. The AICPA created *Reporting on an Entity's Cybersecurity Risk Management Program and Controls: Attestation Guide* in 2017. This framework provides CPAs guidance on performing cybersecurity examinations for clients.

Companies should consider using cybersecurity risk management reporting framework developed by the AICPA when assessing a company's cybersecurity. The reporting framework consists of two criteria. The first set of criteria is a description of the company's cybersecurity risk management system. It provides description criteria in the following areas: nature of business and operations, nature of information at risk, cybersecurity objectives, factors significantly affecting inherent cybersecurity risks, cybersecurity risk governance structure, cybersecurity risk assessment process, cybersecurity communications and quality of cybersecurity information, monitoring of the cybersecurity risk management program, and cybersecurity control processes. The second set of criteria is an evaluation of the company's cybersecurity controls. It provides the trust services criteria and principles for security, availability, processing integrity, confidentiality, and privacy.

LO 12-3

Describe computer fraud and misuse of AIS and corresponding risk-mitigation techniques.

COMPUTER FRAUD AND ABUSE

The International Professional Practices Framework[4] (IPPF) of the Institute of Internal Auditors (IIA) defines fraud as any intended illegal act characterized by deceit, concealment, or violation of trust. "Frauds are perpetrated by parties and organizations to obtain money, property, or services; to avoid payment or loss of services; or to secure personal or

[4]The IPPF is the conceptual framework that provides authoritative guidance promulgated by IIA.

business advantage."[5] It is important to understand that intent is a key component defining and differentiating fraud from other acts and behaviors. In addition, the *Statement of Auditing Standards (SAS) No. 99,* "Consideration of Fraud in a Financial Statement Audit" states that an entity's management has primary responsibility for establishing and monitoring all aspects of the entity's fraud risk-assessment and prevention activities and has both the responsibility and the means to implement measures to reduce the incidence of fraud.

Some of the most valuable items desired by individuals committing computer fraud are the digital assets maintained by the firm. Most firms gather, create, utilize, store, and discard data that have value to others outside the firm. Such data can be in the form of employee or customer personal information such as government-issued identification numbers, bank account numbers, credit card numbers, other personal information, confidential company information, and/or trade secrets. Whether the perpetrator is an individual with authorized access to the data or a hacker, this data can be sold to others or used for personal gain for crimes such as identity theft, unauthorized purchases on stolen credit cards, or stealing or diverting money from a bank account.[6]

Insiders, having legitimate access to their firms' data, systems, and networks, pose a significant risk to their firms. Employees experiencing financial problems may tend to use the systems they access at work to commit fraud such as stealing confidential data, proprietary information, or intellectual property from their employers. According to the **fraud triangle** (see Exhibit 12.5), three conditions exist for a fraud to be perpetrated. First, there is an *incentive* or pressure that provides a reason to commit fraud. Second, there is an *opportunity* for fraud to be perpetrated (e.g., absence of controls, ineffective controls, or the ability of management to override controls.) Third, the individuals committing the fraud possess an attitude that enables them to *rationalize* the fraud. Because research indicates that more than half of the malicious incidents in IT security are caused by insider abuse and misuse, firms should implement a sound system of internal controls to prevent and detect computer frauds perpetrated by insiders. However, the reality seems to be that threats from inside have been overlooked by many firms.[7] We address this gap by introducing computer fraud risks, typical fraud schemes, and strategies/techniques to prevent and detect computer frauds.

Fraud cases bring negative publicity to many companies.

Getty Images, Inc.

EXHIBIT 12.5
The Fraud Triangle

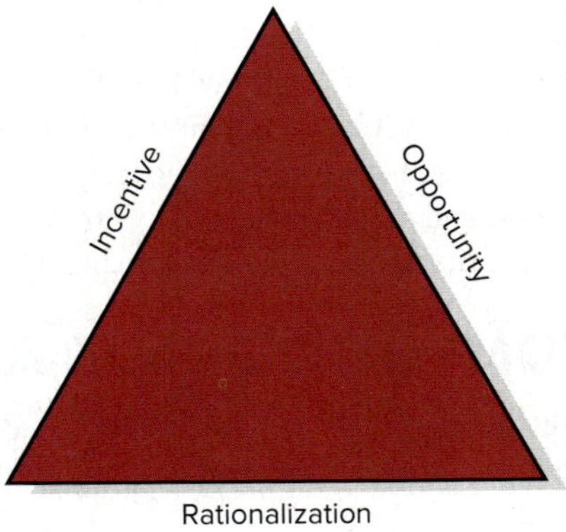

[5]Global Technology Audit Guides (GTAG), *Fraud Prevention and Detection in an Automated World* (2009).
[6]Ibid.
[7]K. C. Brancik, *Insider Computer Fraud: An In-depth Framework for Detecting and Defending against Insider IT Attacks* (Danvers, MA: Auerbach Publications, 2008).

Computer Fraud Risk Assessment

The Computer Fraud and Abuse Act (CFAA) of 1986 is U.S. legislation that made it a federal crime to access a protected computer without proper authorization. CFAA was originally designed to protect computer systems operated by the U.S. government and some financial institutions, but expanded in scope after several amendments. According to Global Technology Audit Guides (GTAG) provided by IIA, common computer frauds include the following:

1. The theft, misuse, or misappropriation of assets by altering computer-readable records and files.
2. The theft, misuse, or misappropriation of assets by altering the logic of computer software.
3. The theft or illegal use of computer-readable information.
4. The theft, corruption, illegal copying, or intentional destruction of computer software.
5. The theft, misuse, or misappropriation of computer hardware.

Concerning computer fraud risks, management should first review potential risk exposures. Given an identified possible fraud, exposures are management's estimates of the potential loss from the fraud. Computer fraud risk assessment is a systematic process that assists management and internal auditors in discovering where and how fraud may occur and identifying who may commit the specific fraud. A computer fraud risk assessment is often a component of a firm's enterprise risk management (ERM) program.

Similar to an enterprise risk assessment, a computer fraud risk assessment focuses on fraud schemes and scenarios to determine whether the controls exist and how the controls might be circumvented. According to GTAG, computer fraud risk assessments usually include the following key steps:[8]

1. Identifying relevant IT fraud risk factors.
2. Identifying potential IT fraud schemes and prioritizing them based on likelihood and impact.
3. Mapping existing controls to potential fraud schemes and identifying gaps.
4. Testing operating effectiveness of fraud prevention and detection controls.
5. Assessing the likelihood and business impact of a control failure and/or a fraud incident.

Computer Fraud Schemes

It is important to identify potential fraud schemes related to computer systems and include them in the enterprisewide risk assessment plan. The following scenarios are provided to help you understand general computer fraud schemes regarding unauthorized access to systems/data and unauthorized changes to systems programs/data for personal gains.

1. In November 2013, computer hackers breached Target's IT security and stole customer information, including credit card data and debit card PIN numbers. The hackers used stolen credentials from third-party vendors to gain access and install software to collect customer information from the stores' point-of-sale systems. It was the largest retail hack in U.S. history, encompassing 1,797 stores and resulting in 40 million credit card numbers and 70 million addresses, phone numbers, and other pieces of personal information being stolen. Target's IT security software would have stopped the data breach, but the company's security team manually turned off the automated detection function.[9]

[8]GTAG, *Fraud Prevention and Detection in an Automated World,* p. 2.

[9]http://www.bloomberg.com/news/articles/2014-03-13/target-missed-warnings-in-epic-hack-of-credit-card-data.

2. In September 2014, the same point-of-sale data collecting technology that hacked Target stores also breached Home Depot. The costs associated with these types of cyber attacks were quite expensive and resulted in loss of customer confidence and lost business, lawsuits, regulatory fines, and expenses to cover identity theft and credit monitoring services for customers victimized by the attack. Home Depot estimates that approximately 56 million credit and debit card numbers were exposed. Estimated costs to the company could be as high as $10 billion or $176 billion per compromised record.[10]
3. In January 2015, the health insurance company Anthem discovered that around 80 million medical and personal data records had been accessed by cyber thieves. The data included names, birthdays, medical IDs, Social Security numbers, street addresses, email addresses, employment information, and income data. Anthem's public communication about the attack indicated that the attack was so sophisticated that they could not possibly defend against it. However, it turned out that a general laxity exists in regard to cyber security with Anthem.[11]
4. In March 2017, the IRS indicated that in a scheme involving the IRS Data Retrieval Tool, used to complete the Free Application for Federal Student Aid (FAFSA), around 100,000 taxpayers' personal information was stolen. The IRS shut down the Data Retrieval Tool because identity thieves who had obtained some personal information outside of the tax system were using the tool to access additional data. The IRS estimated that around 8,000 fraudulent returns were filed and refunds were issued, costing $30 million. About 52,000 returns were stopped by IRS filters, and 14,000 illegal refund claims were halted as well.[12]
5. In early 2019, IT security and cloud data management provider, Rubrik, exposed a database containing customer information including names, contact information, and other details related to corporate accounts. The data leak was discovered on an unprotected Amazon Elasticsearch server that didn't require a password. The data leak could be traced back to October 2018. Data breach can happen in any type of organization, even professional IT security and data management service providers.[13]
6. In March 2019, Facebook admitted that since 2012, it has not properly secured the passwords of as many as 600 million users. These passwords were stored in plaintext and able to be accessed by more than 20,000 of the company's employees.[14] In addition, later in April, two third-party-developed Facebook Apps exposed their datasets to the public Internet, including information such as detailed comments, likes, reactions, account names, and Facebook IDs. While Facebook did not directly cause the data breach, it created the avenue by which the third party had the opportunity to gather this information and expose it to the public Internet.[15]

In addition, the U.S. Secret Service and Computer Emergency Response Team (CERT) have also identified computer fraud in the systems development life cycle (SDLC). Exhibit 12.6 is a summary of such frauds and the corresponding oversights.[16]

One of the main reasons computer fraud is possible is weak access control. The best control over unauthorized access to sensitive information is to require passwords for accessing individual files or subsystems. Logon user IDs should be automatically locked out if the wrong password is entered a predefined number of times. Once locked, a logon

[10]http://krebsonsecurity.com/tag/target-data-breach/.
[11]https://www.bankinfosecurity.com/new-in-depth-analysis-anthem-breach-a-9627.
[12]https://www.identityforce.com/blog/2017-data-breaches.
[13]https://techcrunch.com/2019/01/29/rubrik-data-leak/.
[14]https://www.identityforce.com/blog/facebook-user-password-privacy.
[15]https://www.upguard.com/breaches/facebook-user-data-leak.
[16]U.S. Secret Service and CERT Coordination Center/SEI, *Insider Threat Study.*

Phase	Scenario	Oversights
Requirements definition phase	195 illegitimate drivers' licenses are created and sold by a police communications officer who accidentally discovers they can create them.	Lack of authentication and role-based access control requirements Lack of segregation of duties
System design phase	A special function to expedite handling of cases allows two caseworkers to pocket $32,000 in kickbacks.	Insufficient attention to security details in automated workflow processes
	An employee realizes there is no computerized control in the firm's system, so they entered and profited from $20 million in fake health insurance claims.	Lack of consideration for security vulnerabilities posed by authorized system access
System implementation phase	An 18-year-old former web developer uses backdoors they inserted into their code to access their former firm's network, spam its customers, alter its applications, and ultimately put the firm out of business.	Lack of code reviews
System deployment phase	A computer technician uses their unrestricted access to customers' systems to plant a virus on their networks that brings the customers' systems to a halt.	Unrestricted access to all customers' systems
	A software engineer intentionally did not document or back up their source code and then deleted the only copy of the source code once the system was in production.	Lack of enforcement of documentation practices and backup procedures
System maintenance phase	A foreign currency trader covers up losses of $691 million over a 5-year period by making unauthorized changes to the source code.	Lack of code reviews End-user access to source code
	A logic bomb sits undetected for six months before finally performing a mass deletion of data of a telecommunications firm.	Ineffective backup processes

EXHIBIT 12.6
Fraud Schemes in Systems Development Life Cycle

user ID should be activated only by appropriate personnel, such as a system administrator. A system itself should enforce password changes on a regular basis (i.e., every 30, 60, or 90 days) and should not permit previous password(s) to be used again for a certain period of time. In addition, the use of two or more types of authentication credentials can achieve a greater level of security. This approach is called a multi-factor authentication. For example, requiring a user entering a password and also inserting a smart card in a device is more secure than using either method alone.

Computer Fraud Prevention and Detection

A fraud prevention program starts with a fraud risk assessment across the entire firm, taking into consideration the firm's critical business divisions, processes, and accounts and is performed by management. Management is responsible for fraud risk assessments, while the audit committee typically has an oversight role in this process.[17] The audit committee often works with the internal audit group to ensure that the fraud prevention and detection program remains an ongoing effort. The audit committee also interacts with the firm's external auditor to ensure that fraud assessment results are properly communicated.

Inappropriate use of IT resources by users exposes an enterprise to fraud risks as well as other information security risks. Making employees aware of their obligations concerning fraud and misconduct begins with practical communication and training. Communicating the firm's policy to employees is one of the most important responsibilities of management. Before new employees receive access to information systems, they should be required to sign an acknowledgment called an acceptable use policy (AUP) or an end-user

[17]KPMG, *Fraud Risk Management: Developing a Strategy for Prevention, Detection, and Response* (2006).

computing policy. The AUP should explain what the firm considers to be acceptable computer use, with the goal of protecting both the employee and the firm from any illegal act.

A fraud detection program should include an evaluation by internal auditors on the effectiveness of business processes, along with an analysis of transaction-level data to obtain evidence of the effectiveness of internal controls and to identify indicators of fraud risk or actual fraudulent activities.[18] An effective approach is to have a continuous monitoring system with embedded modules to create detailed logs for transaction-level testing.

General Data Protection Regulation

General Data Protection Regulation (GDPR), effective on May 25, 2018, is to protect European Union (EU) citizens from privacy and data breaches. GDPR aims to provide customers greater control of their personal data.

GDPR applies to all companies processing the personal data of EU citizens, regardless of the company's location. Hence, it is also relevant to companies in the United States. According to GDPR, personal data including name, identification number, location data, or online identifier reflect changes in technology and the way organizations collect information about people. Proposed regulations surrounding data breaches primarily relate to the notification policies of companies that have been breached. Data breaches that may pose a risk to individuals must be notified to the authority or government agencies within 72 hours and to the affected individuals without undue delay. Organizations in breach of GDPR can be fined up to 4 percent of annual global turnover or €20 million (whichever is greater).

PROGRESS CHECK

5. Given your understanding of computer fraud, do you think it happens often? Why or why not?
6. Use the fraud triangle to explain a hypothetical fraudulent scenario.
7. Search over the Internet to find a recent computer fraud scheme. Given the scenario, identify the oversights of the firm.

LO 12-4

Define *vulnerabilities,* and explain how to manage and assess them.

VULNERABILITY ASSESSMENT AND MANAGEMENT

The Information Systems Audit and Control Association (ISACA) defines vulnerability as "the characteristics of IT resources that can be exploited by a threat to cause harm."[19] The GTAG considers vulnerabilities as weaknesses or exposures in IT assets or processes that may lead to a business risk, compliance risk, or security risk.[20] Vulnerability management and risk management have the same objective: Reduce the probability of the occurrence of detrimental events. The subtle difference between risk management and vulnerability management is that risk management is often a more complex and strategic process that may take many months or years and is mostly conducted using a top-down, risk-based approach, whereas vulnerability management is often a tactical and short-term effort that may take weeks or a few months and is frequently conducted using an IT asset-based approach. The purpose of an asset-based approach is to categorize and prioritize further investigation efforts on each asset and to identify appropriate control measures based on meaningful criteria, such as a monetary value of assets and significance of the corresponding risks. To use this approach, it is important to properly maintain asset inventory on an ongoing basis.

[18]GTAG, *Fraud Prevention and Detection in an Automated World.*

[19]ISACA, *Certified Information Systems Auditors Examination Review Manual* (2009).

[20]GTAG, *Managing and Auditing IT Vulnerabilities* (2006).

Types of Vulnerabilities

Because vulnerabilities are the weaknesses or exposures in IT assets or processes, gaining an understanding of existing controls is important to identify vulnerabilities. In general, vulnerabilities are categorized based on where they commonly exist: within a physical IT environment, within an information system, or within the processes of IT operations. Exhibits 12.7, 12.8, and 12.9 provide examples of different types of vulnerabilities.

EXHIBIT 12.7
Examples of Vulnerabilities within a Physical IT Environment

Threats	Vulnerabilities
Physical intrusion	• External parties entering facilities without permission and/or providing access information • Unauthorized hardware changes
Natural disasters	• No regular review of a policy that identifies how IT equipment is protected against environmental threats • Inadequate or outdated measures for environmental threats • Lack of a disaster recovery plan
Excessive heat or humidity	• Humidity alarm not in place • Outdated devices not providing information on temperature and humidity levels
Water seepage in a data center	• Server room located in the basement • Clogged water drain
Electrical disruptions or blackouts	• Insufficient backup power supply • No voltage stabilizer

EXHIBIT 12.8
Examples of Vulnerabilities within an Information System

Threats	Vulnerabilities
System intrusion (e.g., spyware, malware, etc.)	• Software not patched immediately • Open ports on a main server without router access • Outdated intrusion detection/prevention system
Logical access control failure	• Work performed not aligned with business requirements • Poor choice of password or sharing of passwords • Failure to audit and terminate unused accounts in a timely manner
Interruption of a system	• Improper system configuration and customization • Poor service level agreement (SLA) monitoring of service providers

EXHIBIT 12.9
Examples of Vulnerabilities within the Processes of IT Operations

Threats	Vulnerabilities
Social engineering	• Employee training not providing information about social engineering attempts
Unintentional disclosure of sensitive information by employee	• Inappropriate data classification rule • Poor user access management allows some users to retrieve sensitive information not pertaining to their roles and responsibilities
Intentional destruction of information	• Approval not required prior to deleting sensitive data • Poor employee morale • Writable disk drive containing data that shall not be deleted, such as transaction logs
Inappropriate end-user computing	• Ineffective training as to the proper use of computer • End-user computing policy not reviewed • Poor firewall rules, allowing users to access illegitimate websites

PROGRESS CHECK

8. Search the Internet to find additional definitions of vulnerability.
9. Search the Internet to find examples of recent cases for each type of vulnerability presented in Exhibits 12.7, 12.8, and 12.9.

An Overall Framework for Vulnerability Assessment and Management

There are two prerequisites for vulnerability management. First, a firm should determine the main objectives of its vulnerability management because the firm's resource for managing vulnerabilities is limited. In some cases, a primary purpose of vulnerability management could be to comply with applicable laws, regulations, and standards—in that case, the firm should determine which laws, regulations, and standards it should comply with.

Second, a firm should assign roles and responsibilities for vulnerability management. Management may designate a team (i.e., internal audit group, risk management committee, etc.) to be responsible for developing and implementing the vulnerability management program. When assigning roles and responsibilities (i.e., assigning an owner of each IT asset and/or process, implementing a control self-assessment program, etc.), it is important to note that management's commitment and support, as well as the integration of vulnerability management efforts within all levels of the firm, are critical success factors.

Exhibits 12.10 and 12.11 provide the overall view and main components of vulnerability management and assessment, as well as brief descriptions of each component.[21]

EXHIBIT 12.10
Main Components of Vulnerability Management and Assessment

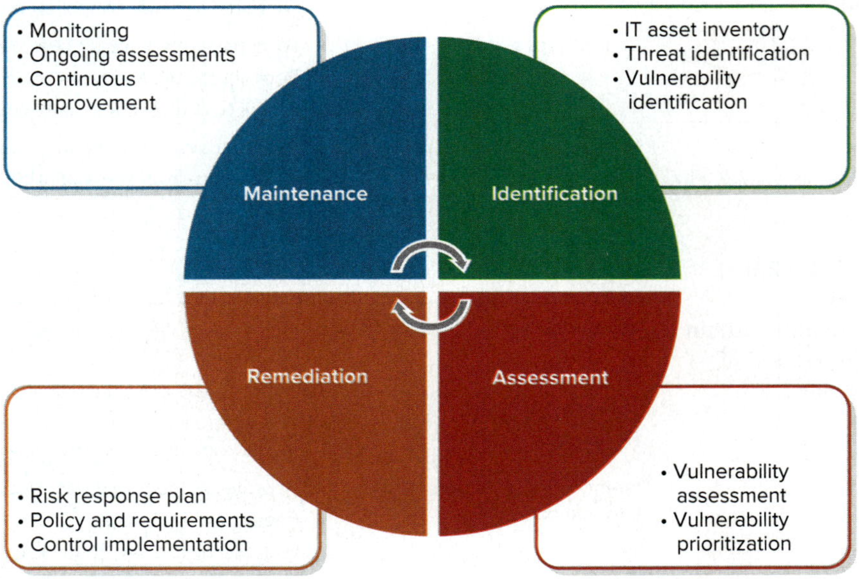

[21]GTAG, *Managing and Auditing IT Vulnerabilities.*

VULNERABILITY ASSESSMENT		VULNERABILITY MANAGEMENT	
I. Identification	**II. Risk Assessment**	**III. Remediation**	**IV. Maintenance**
IT Asset Inventory Ensure that all critical IT assets are identified. Ensure IT assets identified are grouped and prioritized. Ensure IT assets are identified and updated periodically.	**Vulnerability Assessment** Identify the approach and criteria to be consistently used for assessing the identified vulnerabilities throughout the organization. Quantify and/or qualify the identified vulnerabilities.	**Risk Response Plan** Understand the firm's risk appetite. Conduct a cost/benefit analysis. Select controls and policies to implement.	**Monitoring** Ensure IT assets are maintained in a standardized format to help track logical and physical elements of the IT asset such as model, applications installed, and patches. Ensure change and incident management are integrated with configuration management.
Threat Identification Identify the threats related to each IT asset. If a network scanning or a monitoring tool is used, ensure that the tool reflects updated threats and is used periodically.	**Vulnerability Prioritization** Ensure business impact is included as a measurable priority identifier. Prioritize vulnerabilities based on the significance of risks in an area of focus.	**Policy and Requirements** Policy and procedures for remediation should be consistent across the organization. The following five policies are generally of high importance to vulnerability management: • Change management • Configuration management • Incident management • Patch testing • Contingency plans	**Ongoing Assessment** Conduct monitoring on an ongoing basis to verify whether controls are operating effectively as initially implemented. Automatically scan the systems and devices to detect new vulnerabilities and to meet changes in regulatory requirements.
Vulnerability Identification Identify vulnerabilities associated with each identified threat and IT asset.		**Control Implementation** Analyze whether controls are effective to combat identified vulnerabilities. Any changes of control should be authorized and tested prior to implementation. Changes of control should cause minimal disruptions to business.	**Continuous Improvement** Continuously improve processes to reach best practice, based on prior findings, ongoing assessment, and the benchmark in the industry.

EXHIBIT 12.11
Brief Descriptions of the Main Components of Vulnerability Management and Assessment

LO 12-5

Explain issues in system availability.

SYSTEM AVAILABILITY

A key component of IT service delivery and support is making sure the data are available at all times or, at a minimum, in the moment the data are needed. Even a short period of system downtime on an e-commerce application can result in a loss of e-commerce sales and, potentially, a loss of trust in the provider.

Firms continue to monitor system availability. Backups are used to alleviate problems of file or database corruptions. An **uninterruptible power supply** is a device using battery power to enable a system to operate long enough to back up critical data and shut down properly during the loss of power. **Fault tolerance** uses redundant units to provide a system with the ability to continue functioning when part of the system fails. Many firms implement a redundant array of independent drives (RAID) so that if one disk drive fails, important data can still be accessed from another disk.

Virtualization and **cloud computing** are often considered good alternatives to back up data and applications. Cloud computing uses redundant servers in multiple locations to host virtual machines. A virtual machine contains system applications and data backups. If the server hosting a virtual machine fails, the virtual machine can be installed to any other redundant server immediately. Using virtualization and cloud computing for system availability could be cost-effective.

Recently, cloud computing has become a popular model for business operations. In general, cloud computing refers to a service model in which a third-party service provider offers computing resources, including hardware and software applications, to cloud users over the internet, and the service provider charges on a per-user basis. A cloud user company often shares the computing resources with other user companies, and a cloud provider bears the responsibility for managing and maintaining the resources. A survey result showed that 43 percent of 2,014 IT leaders in 50 countries indicated that their companies were projected to have most of their IT efforts running in the cloud by 2015.[22] A user company must evaluate a cloud provider's credibility, controls, and security of the systems and networks and its financial viability carefully before using the cloud provider. It is important that a cloud user company obtains and reviews a service organization control (SOC) report from the cloud provider prior to signing an agreement for the service.

LO 12-6

Explain the concepts and issues in System and Organization Controls (SOC) reporting.

SYSTEM AND ORGANIZATION CONTROLS (SOC) EXAMINATIONS

It is important that companies obtain and review **system and organization controls (SOC) reports** from their service providers prior to signing agreements for specific services. Common examples of service organizations include cloud service providers, payroll processing, accounts receivable processing, health insurance claims, and application service providers. If the specific business operations are critical to the service user company (such as storing its confidential data and hosting critical applications), the user company should consider requiring an SOC 2 or SOC 3 report. The SOC 1 report focuses on the impact of the service provider's controls on the user company's financial statements. On the other hand, SOC 2 and SOC 3 reports provide the evaluations on a broader set of controls relevant to security, availability, processing integrity, confidentiality, or privacy implemented by the service provider.

The AICPA has published guides for each SOC report with detailed procedural steps. SOC 1 report provides auditor opinions on the service organizations' controls relevant to the user company's internal control over financial reporting. SOC 2 report provides auditor opinions on the service organizations' internal control based on trust services criteria developed by AICPA. SOC 3 is a summarized SOC 2 report and it is for general use. SOC reporting process is consistent with most auditing process: (1) management designs and implements the internal control system; (2) management reports on the effectiveness of the internal controls; (3) the auditor reviews the internal controls and the report prepared by the management; (4) the auditor gives an opinion on the fairness of management's report; (5) the auditor gives an opinion on appropriateness of controls; and (6) in some instances, the auditor tests and provides an opinion about control effectiveness over a time period.

Two Types of SOC 1 reports[23]

Per AICPA, SOC 1 examines "controls at a service organization relevant to user entities' internal control over financial reporting (ICFR)." The use of SOC 1 report is restricted

[22] Gartner Inc., *Reimagining IT: The 2011 CIO Agenda,* January 2011, Retrieved at: http://www.gartner.com/id=1524714.

[23] https://us.aicpa.org/interestareas/frc/assuranceadvisoryservices/aicpasoc1report.

to the management of the service organization, user companies, and user auditors. It is an auditor-to-auditor report.

SOC 1 Type 1 reports on (1) the fairness of the presentation of management's description of the service organization's system and (2) the suitability of the design of the controls to achieve the related control objectives as of a specified date.

SOC 1 Type 2 same as above, but the examination should be throughout a specified period.

Two Types of SOC 2 reports[24]

Per AICPA, SOC 2 examines "controls at a service organization relevant to security, availability, processing integrity, confidentiality or privacy." "These reports are intended to meet the needs of a broad range of users that need detailed information and assurance about the controls at a service organization . . ." AICPA indicates that SOC 2 reports can play an important role in corporate governance and risk management, vendor management programs, regulatory oversight, etc.

Please note that the broad range of users does not mean the general public. The use of SOC 2 report is for current and prospective customers and/or government regulators. Sometimes, the depth of these reports may reveal competitive secrets. Many service organizations closely control dissemination of their SOC 2 reports.

SOC 2 Type 1 reports on (1) the fairness of the presentation of management's description of the service organization's system and (2) the suitability of the design of the controls to achieve the related control objectives as of a specified ***date***.

SOC 2 Type 2 reports on (1) the fairness of the presentation of management's description of the service organization's system and (2) the suitability of the design and operating effectiveness of the controls throughout a specified ***period***.

SOC 3 reports[25]

Per AICPA, SOC 3 examines service organizations based on the Trust Services criteria and is a report for general use. These reports are designed to meet the needs of users who need assurance about the controls at a service organization but do not need or do not have the knowledge necessary to make effective use of a SOC 2 report. SOC 3 report is not detailed and can be freely distributed.

	Users	Purposes	Contents
SOC 1 Type 1 or Type 2*	The auditors and the management of the user company	To audit the user company's financial reports	Service provider's internal controls relevant to the user company's financial reporting
SOC 2 Type 1 or Type 2*	Management of a service organization, Regulators, Others	To assess governance, risk management, and compliance programs. To provide due diligence and oversight.	Examination on security, availability, processing integrity, confidentiality or privacy
SOC 3	Any users with need for confidence in the service organization's controls	To provide a general understanding and for marketing purposes	A report easy to read by the general public in a summary format on security, availability, processing integrity, and confidentiality or privacy

EXHIBIT 12.12
SOC Report Comparison
* Type 1 reports are for a specific date; Type 2 reports are for a period of time.

[24] https://us.aicpa.org/interestareas/frc/assuranceadvisoryservices/aicpasoc2report.
[25] https://us.aicpa.org/interestareas/frc/assuranceadvisoryservices/aicpasoc3report.

Recently, AICPA offered enhanced SOC 2 reports: (1) SOC for Cybersecurity examination and report[26] and (2) SOC for Supply Chain reporting framework (https://us.aicpa.org/interestareas/frc/assuranceadvisoryservices/soc-for-supply-chain). In addition, AICPA provides whitepapers on the Implications of the Use of Blockchain in SOC for Service Organization examinations[27]. These SOC 2 reports go beyond the Trust Service Principles to include more regulatory and industry sets of standards. For example, SOC for Cybersecurity is often based on the standards or practices of

- National Institute of Standards and Technology (NIST)
- International Standardization Organization (IS): ISO 27001
- Health Information Trust Alliance (HITRUST): HIPAA
- Cloud Security Alliance (CSA): Cloud Controls Matrix
- PCI-DSS: privacy standards on credit cardholder data

In addition, frameworks such as COBIT and GDPR are often included as relevant cybersecurity frameworks. As described in Chapter 11, COBIT is a framework for managing and governing enterprise IT controls and security; GDPR is for data protection procedures and practices on privacy issues. The GDPR impacts all organizations that collect and store the private data of EU citizens—including U.S. businesses.

There are potential issues of SOC reports for the user auditor. If the user auditor received a SOC 1 Type 1 report prepared by an inexperienced accounting firm, there could be an audit quality issue. Sometimes, a SOC 1 Type 2 report might have a period during which controls effectiveness was evaluated which does not match the user company's fiscal period. If the service provider has a SOC 2 or SOC 3 report only, it may not be easy for the user auditor to evaluate the impact of the service provider's internal controls on the client's financial report.

LO 12-7

Describe the importance of disaster recovery and business continuity.

DISASTER RECOVERY PLANNING AND BUSINESS CONTINUITY MANAGEMENT

Adverse events happen in every daily business environment. For any firm, it is essential to establish and maintain a proper plan to recover from a disaster or any disruptive event and to continue its business operations. In recent years, the severe experience of natural disasters (such as the tsunami in Japan and the tornados in the United States) reinforced the importance of disaster recovery planning and business continuity management.

Disaster recovery planning (DRP) is a process that identifies significant events that may threaten a firm's operations and outlines the procedures to ensure that the firm will resume operations if such events occur. DRP must include a clearly defined and documented plan that covers key personnel; resources, including IT infrastructure and applications; and actions required to be carried out in order to continue or resume the systems for critical business functions within planned levels of disruption. A disaster recovery plan should be reviewed and tested periodically to analyze weaknesses and explore possible ways to improve the plan.

Both DRP and BCM are important to firms because they are about whether the firms can continue their business or not.

While DRP is the process of rebuilding the operations and/or infrastructure after a disaster has occurred, **business continuity management (BCM)** refers to the activities required to keep a firm running during a period of displacement or interruption of normal operations. DRP and BCM are the most critical corrective controls, and DRP is a key component of BCM.[28] BCM is broader than DRP and is concerned with the entire business process, rather than particular assets such as IT infrastructure and applications. To achieve

[26]https://drive.google.com/file/d/1NmCgikN8k9d2GxmeYITp637DBdbl-2P_/view.

[27]https://drive.google.com/file/d/15qA0gaArjgnGBWmZ-Mm8735zi2XY8Q79/view.

[28]R. Muthukrishnan, "The Auditor's Role in Reviewing Business Continuity Planning," *Information Systems Control Journal*, 2005.

business objectives, a firm must continue to perform its critical business processes, as well as IT functions that support the business processes.

International Organization for Standardization (ISO) 22301 is the commonly accepted standard for BCM. It establishes the process, principles, and terminology of continuity management for business and its IT functions. ISO 22301 provides a framework to plan, establish, implement, operate, monitor, review, maintain, and continually improve a business continuity management system (BCMS). It is expected to help organizations protect against, prepare for, respond to, and recover when disruptive incidents arise.[29] As shown in Exhibit 12.13, BCM often includes the following components: (1) understanding the firm and identifying risks; (2) analyzing business impact of the risks; (3) determining BCM strategy and developing plans for the BCM; and (4) testing, maintaining, and improving the firm's BCM practices.

EXHIBIT 12.13
Components in Business Continuity Management Life Cycle

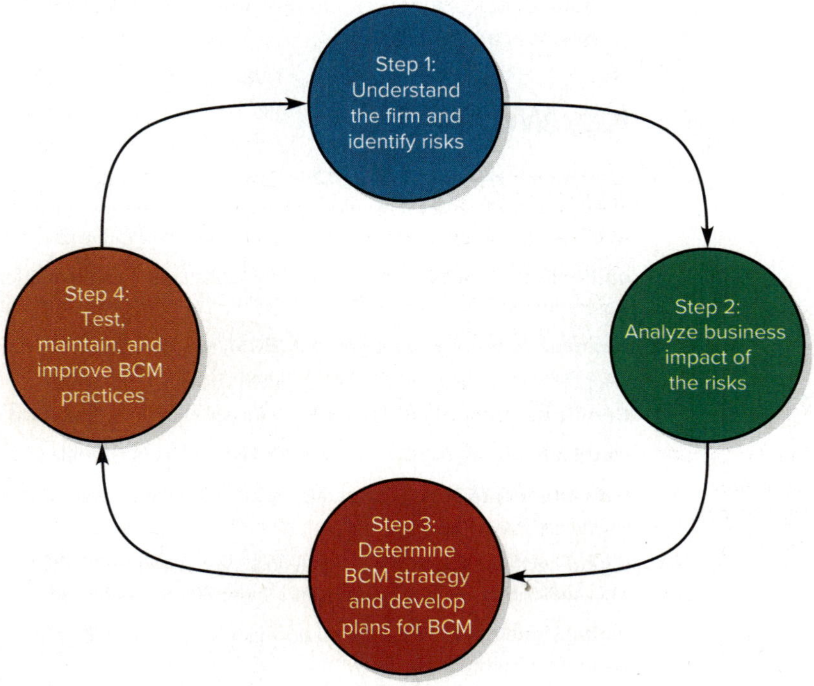

[29]International Organization for Standardization, https://www.iso.org/news/2012/06/Ref1587.html.

Summary

- Proper use of encryption, authentication, and digital signature technology are important to maintaining information security. Most firms use both symmetric-key and asymmetric-key encryption methods for e-business. Authentication ensures transactions are valid. Encryption maintains confidentiality during data transmission. Digital signatures achieve data integrity and confirm nonrepudiation while conducting e-business.
- System and Organization Controls (SOC) reports are important to companies that use service providers. Companies should review SOC reports prior to signing agreements for specific services. In addition, SOC reports are often used by these companies' external auditors regarding the impact of internal controls of the service providers on the audited financial reports.

- In today's data-driven world, cybersecurity is a crucial part of an organization's daily operations. The AICPA suggests that cybersecurity is important to an organization's risk management and created the *Reporting on an Entity's Cybersecurity Risk Management Program and Controls: Attestation Guide* in 2017. This framework provides CPAs guidance on performing cybersecurity examinations for clients.
- Disaster recovery planning (DRP) identifies significant events that may threaten a firm's operations, outlining the procedures that ensure the firm's smooth resumption of operations in the case such an event occurs. DRP must include a clearly defined and documented plan that covers key personnel, resources, and actions required to be carried out to resume the systems necessary for critical business functions within a defined, acceptable timeframe. DRP is an essential component of business continuity management (BCM), which refers to the activities required to keep a firm running during a period of interruption of normal operations. BCM is broader than DRP and is concerned with all key business processes, rather than particular assets such as IT infrastructure and applications. To achieve business objectives, a firm must continue to perform its critical business processes, as well as IT functions that support the business processes.

Key Words

asymmetric-key encryption (*424*) To transmit confidential information, the sender uses the receiver's public key to encrypt the message; the receiver uses his or her own private key for decryption upon receiving the message. Also known as public-key encryption or two-key encryption.

authentication (*424*) A process that establishes the origin of information or determines the identity of a user, process, or device.

business continuity management (BCM) (*438*) The activities required to keep a firm running during a period of displacement or interruption of normal operations.

Certificate Authority (CA) (*426*) A trusted entity that issues and revokes digital certificates.

cloud computing (*436*) Using redundant servers in multiple locations to host virtual machines.

data integrity (*425*) Maintaining and assuring the accuracy and consistency of data during transmission and at storage.

digital certificate (*426*) A digital document issued and digitally signed by the private key of a Certificate Authority that binds the name of a subscriber to a public key.

digital signature (*425*) A message digest of a document (or data file) that is encrypted using the document creator's private key.

disaster recovery planning (DRP) (*438*) A process that identifies significant events that may threaten a firm's operations and outlines the procedures to ensure that the firm will resume operations when the events occur.

encryption (*423*) Using algorithmic schemes to encode plaintext into nonreadable form.

fault tolerance (*435*) Redundant units providing a system with the ability to continue functioning when part of the system fails.

fraud triangle (*428*) Three conditions exist for a fraud to be perpetrated: incentive, opportunity, and rationalization.

hashing (*425*) A process to run an original document or data through an algorithm to generate a message digest.

message digest (MD) (*425*) A short code, such as one 256 bits long, resulting from hashing a plaintext message using an algorithm.

private key (*424*) A string of bits kept secret and known only to the owner of the key.

public key (*424*) A string of bits created with the private key and widely distributed and available to other users.

public-key infrastructure (PKI) (*427*) A set of policies, processes, server platforms, software, and workstations used for the purpose of administering certificates and public-/private-key pairs, including the ability to issue, maintain, and revoke public-key certificates.

session key (*425*) A symmetric key that is valid for a certain timeframe only.

symmetric-key encryption (*423*) Both the sender and the receiver use the same key to encrypt and decrypt messages.

system and organization controls (SOC) reports (*436*) SOC 1 report focuses on the impact of the service provider's controls on the user company's financial statements. SOC 2 and SOC 3 reports provide the evaluations on a broader set of controls relevant to security, availability, processing integrity, confidentiality, or privacy implemented by the service provider.

uninterruptible power supply (*435*) A device using battery power to enable a system to operate long enough to back up critical data and shut down properly during the loss of power.

virtualization (*436*) Using various techniques and methods to create a virtual (rather than actual) version of a hardware platform, storage device, or network resources.

ANSWERS TO PROGRESS CHECKS

1. The general goals of information security are to safeguard critical systems and to maintain confidentiality, integrity, and availability of information from internal and external security threats.

2. Social engineering could be an attempt to trick someone into revealing information, such as a password, that can be used to attack systems or networks. For example, a hacker may find a phone number of a salesperson from the company's website. The hacker then pretends that they are one of the IT staff working at the helpdesk and calls the salesperson to ask for the salesperson's password in "fixing" a problem on accessing certain files. If the salesperson gives their password to the hacker, the hacker can obtain access to the company's network.

3. We cannot use the symmetric-key encryption method to authenticate users because both the sender and the receiver are using the same key. This method does not provide a unique key for each user when transmitting information among different parties.

4. A digital signature is a message digest encrypted using the sender's private key. We use a digital signature to achieve two purposes. The main purpose is to maintain data integrity. The second purpose is to authenticate the sender. If the receiver can use the sender's public key to decrypt the digital signature, the receiver authenticates the sender. The receiver compares the calculated message digest with the sent-over message digest to confirm data integrity.

5. Computer fraud includes a variety of illegal acts that involve a computer or network. If the internal control of a company is not adequate, the wide use of technologies, computers, and other electronic devices in the business world provide an environment for frequent occurrences of computer fraud.

6. Scenario: The loose access control of a company's information system may provide the employee an opportunity to obtain confidential information after leaving the position. The associate lured the employee to disclose the confidential information for their business by providing financial benefits to the employee (i.e., an incentive). The employee committed the identity theft. They rationalized their behavior—because their position had changed, they were no longer responsible for keeping employees' account information confidential.

7. A phishing attack happened to Prisma Health in November 2018. The company gave hackers unauthorized access to several employee email accounts. An investigation into the data breach determined that 23,811 patients' personal health information was exposed, including names, health insurance information, Social Security numbers, and financial information.[30]
8. The Internet Engineering Task Force (IETF) defines vulnerability as a flaw or weakness in a system's design, implementation, or operation and management that could be exploited to violate the system's security policy. The European Network and Information Security Agency (ENISA) defines vulnerability as the existence of a weakness, design, or implementation error that can lead to an unexpected, undesirable event compromising the security of the computer system, network, application, or protocol involved. The Committee on National Security Systems of United States of America defines vulnerability as weakness in an IS, system security procedures, internal controls, or implementation that could be exploited.
9. Examples for each type of vulnerability:
   a. Vulnerabilities in physical IT system

      Threats: Fire

      Vulnerabilities:
      - Nonsensitive automatic fire detection response systems
      - Improper storage of combustible materials
      - Use of malfunctioning heating devices
      - Insufficient training of people about fire prevention and reaction
   b. Vulnerabilities in an information system

      Threats: System intrusion

      Vulnerabilities: No virus scanner on each computer
   c. Vulnerabilities within the process of IT operations

      Threats: Unintentional deletion of information

      Vulnerabilities:
      - Employee mistakes caused by inadequate training about operation
      - Lack of a backup of data and information

[30] Source: https://www.hipaajournal.com/phi-of-23811-palmetto-health-patients-exposed-in-phishing-attack/.

Multiple Choice Questions connect

1. **(LO 12-2)** (CISA exam, adapted) Authentication is the process by which the
   a. system verifies that the user is entitled to enter the transaction requested.
   b. system verifies the identity of the user.
   c. user identifies him- or herself to the system.
   d. user indicates to the system that the transaction was processed correctly.
2. **(LO 12-2)** (CMA exam, adapted) Data processing activities may be classified in terms of three stages or processes: input, processing, and output. An activity that is not normally associated with the input stage is
   a. batching.
   b. recording.
   c. verifying.
   d. reporting.

3. **(LO 12-2)** (CISA exam, adapted) To ensure confidentiality in an asymmetric-key encryption system, knowledge of which of the following keys is required to decrypt the received message?
    a. Private key
    b. Public key
    c. Both keys are required.
    d. Neither the private key nor the public key is required.
4. **(LO 12-2)** To authenticate the message sender in an asymmetric-key encryption system, which of the following keys is required to decrypt the received message?
    a. Sender's private key
    b. Sender's public key
    c. Receiver's private key
    d. Receiver's public key
5. **(LO 12-2)** To ensure the data sent over the Internet are protected, which of the following keys is required to encrypt the data (before transmission) using an asymmetric-key encryption method?
    a. Sender's private key
    b. Sender's public key
    c. Receiver's private key
    d. Receiver's public key
6. **(LO 12-3)** Which of the following groups/laws was the earliest to encourage auditors to incorporate fraud examination into audit programs?
    a. COSO
    b. COBIT
    c. PCAOB
    d. SAS No. 99
    e. Sarbanes–Oxley Act
7. **(LO 12-3)** Incentive to commit fraud usually will include all of the following, *except*
    a. inadequate segregation of duties.
    b. financial pressure.
    c. personal habits and lifestyle.
    d. feelings of resentment.
    e. alcohol, drug, or gambling addiction.
8. **(LO 12-7)** (CPA exam, adapted) An information technology director collected the names and locations of key vendors, current hardware configuration, names of team members, and an alternative processing location. What is the director most likely preparing?
    a. Internal control policy
    b. System hardware policy
    c. System security policy
    d. Disaster recovery plan
    e. Supply chain management policy

9. **(LO 12-2)** A message digest is the result of hashing. Which of the following statements about the hashing process is true?
   a. It is reversible.
   b. Comparing the hashing results can ensure confidentiality.
   c. Hashing is the best approach to make sure that two files are identical.
   d. None of the options are true.
10. **(LO 12-4)** Which one of the following vulnerabilities would create the most serious risk to a firm?
   a. Using open source software (downloaded for free) on the firm's network.
   b. Employees recording passwords in Excel files.
   c. Employees writing instant messages with friends during office hours.
   d. Unauthorized access to the firm's network.
11. **(LO 12-1, LO 12-2, LO 12-6, LO 12-7)** Which of the following statements is correct?
   a. A spam will send a network packet that appears to come from a source other than its actual source.
   b. Multi-factor authentication is less secure than requiring a user to always enter a password to access a network.
   c. Fault tolerance uses redundant units to provide a system with the ability to continue functioning when part of the system fails.
   d. SOC 1 reports provide the evaluations on a broader set of controls implemented by the service provider.
12. **(LO 12-7)** Which of the following can be considered as a good alternative to back up data and applications?
   a. Continuous monitoring
   b. Disaster recovery planning
   c. Business continuity management
   d. Cloud computing
13. **(LO 12-2)** A digital certificate
   a. is used to certify public-key and private-key pairs.
   b. is a trusted entity to certify and revoke Certificate Authorities (CA).
   c. indicates that the subscriber identified has sole control and access to the private key.
   d. ensures that the symmetric-key encryption method functions well.
14. **(LO 12-2)** The symmetric-key encryption method
   a. is slow.
   b. is not appropriate for encrypting large data sets.
   c. solves problems in key distribution and key management.
   d. uses the same key for both senders and receivers for encryption and decryption.
15. **(LO 12-3)** The fraud triangle indicates which of the following condition(s) exist for a fraud to be perpetrated?
   a. Rationalization
   b. Pressure
   c. Legal environment
   d. Only (a) and (b) are correct
   e. (a), (b), and (c) are correct

16. **(LO 12-2)** To prevent repudiation in conducting e-business, companies must be able to authenticate their trading partners. Which of the following encryption methods can be used for authentication purpose?
   a. Symmetric-key encryption method
   b. Asymmetric-key encryption method
   c. Both symmetric-key and asymmetric-key encryption methods are good for authentication.
17. **(LO 12-3)** Regarding GDPR, which of the following statements is/are correct?
   a. It is a regulation enforced by EU.
   b. It is to protect EU citizens' personal data.
   c. It is not relevant to the companies in the United States.
   d. (a) and (b) are correct.
   e. (a), (b), and (c) are all correct.
18. **(LO 12-2)** Which organization created the *Reporting on an Entity's Cybersecurity Risk Management Program and Controls: Attestation Guide* in 2017?
   a. SEC
   b. AICPA
   c. U.S. Congress
   d. Department of Homeland Security
19. **(LO 12-7)** Business continuity management is a
   a. preventive control.
   b. detective control.
   c. corrective control.
   d. Two of these options are correct.
20. **(LO 12-2)** Encryption is a
   a. preventive control.
   b. detective control.
   c. corrective control.
   d. Two of these options are correct.
21. **(LO 12-5)** What is fault tolerance?
   a. A policy allowing employees to make mistakes.
   b. Using redundant units to continue functioning when a system is failing.
   c. An application that can detect mistakes and correct mistakes automatically.
   d. Two of these options are correct.
22. **(LO 12-2)** Comparing encryption with hashing,
   a. hashing process is reversible.
   b. encryption is used to ensure data integrity.
   c. hashing results are large data.
   d. encryption results are called cyphertext.
23. **(LO 12-7)** Disaster recovery plan is a
   a. preventive control.
   b. detective control.
   c. corrective control.
   d. Two of these options are correct.

24. **(LO 12-2)** Select a correct statement describing encryption or hashing process.
    a. Encryption process is reversible.
    b. Hashing results are called message digests.
    c. Hashing process could be used to obtain a digital signature.
    d. Symmetric-key encryption process is to maintain confidentiality.
    e. All of these statements are correct.
25. **(LO 12-2)** Select a correct statement regarding encryption methods.
    a. Most companies prefer using asymmetric-key encryption method for data transmission.
    b. Symmetric-key encryption method is used to authenticate trading partners.
    c. Only asymmetric-key encryption method can ensure confidentiality.
    d. Asymmetric-key encryption method is used to create digital signatures.
26. **(LO 12-6)** Why would a company need a SOC report?
    a. The external auditor needs to know the effectiveness of internal controls of the company's service provider(s).
    b. The company wants to use it for marketing purposes.
    c. It could be require by a government agency to provide a SOC report.
    d. All of these options are correct.
27. **(LO 12-6)** Which of the following statements regarding SOC is correct?
    a. SOC 1 report is prepared for the general public to use.
    b. SOC 2 report is focused on the impact of the service provider's controls on the user company's financial statements.
    c. Type 1 reports are for a specific date.
    d. SOC 3 report is prepared for auditors and management to use.
    e. All of these options are correct.
28. **(LO 12-6)** Which of the following frameworks could be used for SOC cybersecurity?
    a. NIST
    b. HIPPA
    c. PCI-DSS
    d. All of these options are correct.
    e. Two of these options are correct.
29. **(LO 12-5)** Using an uninterruptible power supply is a
    a. preventive control.
    b. detective control.
    c. corrective control.
30. **(LO 12-5)** Implementing a redundant array of independent devices (RAID) is a preventive control.
    a. True
    b. False

Discussion Questions

1. **(LO 12-1)** Phishing is an example of social engineering where the attacker attempts to trick people into giving them personal information. Give two examples of phishing.
2. **(LO 12-1)** If social engineering is a common reason that confidential information was revealed, what needs to be done to prevent this from occurring?

3. **(LO 12-1)** What is the goal of each of the general security objectives (e.g., confidentiality, integrity, availability, access control)? Why should a company care about these?
4. **(LO 12-6)** There are restrictions on how U.S. companies store and share customer data. For health care providers, HIPAA is designed to protect patient data. A handful of states require companies processing customer payments to comply with PCI-DSS. Search the Internet for information about these regulations, and discuss the major requirements of each.
5. **(LO 12-3)** Consider the following scenarios and identify the incentive, opportunity, and rationalization that exist that would enable a person to commit fraud:
   a. A manager increases the value of inventory in the computer system so she can show higher cost of goods sold. As a result, she embezzles the additional income.
   b. A college student pirates a newly released movie over the Internet.
   c. An employee creates a new vendor account for his spouse and submits invoices for services that were never performed.
6. **(LO 12-2)** What are the differences between authentication and authorization?
7. **(LO 12-2)** Explain how to use the asymmetric-key encryption method to maintain confidentiality in transmitting a business document electronically.
8. **(LO 12-2)** What is hashing? Does it serve the same purpose as encryption? Why?
9. **(LO 12-2)** How can data integrity be ensured when conducting e-business? Why is it critical to e-business?
10. **(LO 12-4)** Chapter 11 identifies COBIT and ISO 27000 as information security frameworks. How do they relate to GTAG's Vulnerability Assessment? What similarities and differences are there among these three?
11. **(LO 12-7)** Disaster recover planning (DRP) and business continuity management (BCM) help businesses manage security risks. What similarities and differences exist between these two approaches?

Problems connect

1. **(LO 12-2)** Compare and contrast symmetric-key and asymmetric-key encryption methods in conducting e-business. Why do companies prefer one method over the other? If a company chooses to use both methods, what might be the reasons? How can the company truly use both methods for e-business?
2. **(LO 12-1)** Many internal auditors and IT professionals believe wireless networks and mobile devices pose high risks in a firm's network system. Collect information to examine whether this concern is valid. If so, identify the risks and the general controls to help reduce these risks.
3. **(LO 12-2)** Under PKI, Certification Authority (CA) plays a critical role in the success of maintaining information security. Search the Internet to find a few public firms that are CAs. Compare these firms, and provide suggestions on how to choose a CA as part of information security management.
4. **(LO 12-2)** Match the descriptions with each encryption method.

Descriptions	Encryption Method
a. Good for large datasets	i. Symmetric-key encryption
b. Slow in processing	ii. Asymmetric-key encryption
c. Convenient for key distribution and key management	
d. Each user has a public key and a private key	
e. Good for authentication	

5. **(LO 12-5)** and **(LO 12-7)** Match correct statement(s) with each term regarding system availability.

Internal Controls	System Availability Terms
a. Activities required to keep a firm running during a period of displacement or interruption of normal operations	i. Uninterruptible power supply
b. A process that identifies significant events that may threaten a firm's operations and outline the procedures to ensure that the firm will resume operations if such events occur	ii. Fault tolerance
c. A service model in which a third-party service provider offers computing resources, including hardware and software applications, to cloud users over the Internet, and the service provider charges on a per-user basis	iii. Cloud computing
d. A clearly defined and documented plan that covers key personnel, resources including IT infrastructure and applications, and actions required to be carried out in order to continue or resume the systems for critical business functions	iv. Disaster recovery planning
e. Using redundant units to provide a system with the ability to continue functioning when part of the system fails	v. Business continuity management
f. A device using battery power to enable a system to operate long enough to back up critical data and shut down properly during the loss of power	

6. **(LO 12-4)** Identify the main components of vulnerability management and assessment.

Component	Category
a. Prioritize vulnerabilities	i. Vulnerability management
b. Design a risk response plan	ii. Vulnerability assessment
c. Monitor vulnerabilities	
d. Establish policy and requirements	
e. Identify vulnerabilities	

7. **(LO 12-3)** There are five types of fraud schemes in systems development cycles (refer to Exhibit 12.6). Identify an example of each type.
8. **(LO 12-4)** Internal auditors are often tasked with testing vulnerabilities. How would you suggest testing for system intrusion, logical access control, natural disasters, and intentional destruction of information?
9. **(LO 12-5)** Browse the Internet to identify some recent cases related to system availability. What are the risks and issues in system availability of these cases? Indicate possible controls to mitigate the risks.
10. **(LO 12-3)** Consider each of the following fraud cases. Identify the incentive, opportunity, and rationalization present in each case.
    a. An employee of a telecommunications firm's payroll department moved to a new position within the department in which she no longer has privileged access to payroll accounts. However, when changing positions, her access rights to the payroll accounts were left unchanged. An associate told her that he was starting a financial service business and needed some contact information. Using the privileged access rights that she had retained, the employee provided her associate with confidential information of many employees, including 401(k) account numbers, credit card account numbers, and social security numbers, which he then used to commit more than 100 cases of identity theft. The insider's actions caused more than $1 million worth of damages to the firm and its employees.[31]

[31] U.S. Secret Service and CERT Coordination Center/SEI. Insider Threat Study: Illicit Cyber Activity in the Information Technology and Telecommunications Sector (2008), https://resources.sei.cmu.edu/library/asset-view.cfm?assetid=52257 Accessed March 26, 2023.

b. A database analyst of a major check authorization and credit card processing company went beyond his authorized computer access rights. The employee obtained his firm's consumer information of 8.4 million individuals. The stolen information included names and addresses, bank account information, and credit and debit card information. He sold the data to telemarketers over a 5-year period.[32]

c. An IT consultant working under contract for an offshore oil platform company was denied an offer for a permanent job with the same company. He then accessed the firm's computer systems without approval and caused damage by impairing the integrity and availability of data.[33]

d. A manager responsible for payment authorization hired an offshore programmer to insert a couple of independent contractors to the vendor table of his company's database. He then authorized payments to the independent contractors on fictitious services for personal gain. He spent the stolen money on luxury items and extravagant purchases for himself, his family, and friends.

11. **(LO 12-6)** Match correct purposes, contents, and users regarding SOC reports.

Purposes/Contents/Users	SOC Reports
a. Easy to read by the general public in a summary format on security, availability, processing integrity, and confidentiality or privacy	i. SOC 1
b. To assess governance, risk management, and compliance programs	ii. SOC 2
c. Reports for a period of time	iii. SOC 3
d. To provide a general understanding and for marketing purposes	iv. Type 1 SOC reports
e. To be used by the auditors and the management of the user company	v. Type 2 SOC reports
f. Reports for a specific date	
g. To be used by the management of a service organization, regulators, and others	
h. To examine security, availability, processing integrity, confidentiality or privacy policy, and practice of the service organization	

Design Element: Duncan Smith/Getty Images

[32]U.S. Department of Justice Website, Computer Crime and Intellectual Property Section, http://usdoj.gov/criminal/cybercrime.

[33]Ibid.

Chapter Thirteen

Monitoring and Auditing AIS

A Look at This Chapter

In today's business environment, almost all firms rely on computerized systems in daily operations—in particular, to perform accounting functions. The swift advances in technologies have changed business models and the approaches to collecting data and communicating business information. Given the complicated information systems and the tremendous amount of data to be analyzed and reported, it is challenging for managers, accountants, and auditors to validate that the systems are well designed with embedded internal controls and that they process data with integrity. Accountants' role in the business world is to provide quality information for decision making. Hence, they must understand and be involved in monitoring and auditing accounting information systems.

A Look Back

In Chapter 12, we provided examples of computer fraud and illustrated how AIS can be misused in order to achieve personal gains. The concepts of cybersecurity and understanding on the audit reports such as SOC 1 and 2 are important to professionals in accounting, tax, and auditing. We also discussed common vulnerabilities in information security and how to manage and assess such vulnerabilities.

A Look Ahead

Chapter 14 provides a description of how AIS facilitates management reporting, including using data warehouses, business intelligence, and dashboards. In addition, it also explains the development and emerging use of eXtensible Business Reporting Language (XBRL).

Tim Boyle/Getty Images

If you visit the website of **Starbucks Corporation** (starbucks.com), at the bottom of the page, under "Investor Relations," you can access its annual reports in the Financial Data section. In each year's annual report, you can find the audit report as part of Financial Statements and Supplementary Data, titled "Report of Independent Registered Public Accounting Firm." In addition, Starbucks also has a separate report on Global Environmental and Social Impact. For 2022, the auditor's opinion by **Deloitte & Touche LLP** is on pages 80–81 of Starbucks' 2022 annual report. This audit report is the auditor's opinion on whether the financial statements of Starbucks Corporation fairly represent the company's financial conditions. Item 9A of the annual report is on Controls and Procedures (see page 82). On page 83, you can find the second audit report that examines the internal control over financial reporting of Starbucks Corporation. The external auditors from Deloitte & Touche LLP conducted audits on the information systems, internal controls, and financial information of Starbucks before they rendered these audit opinions. External auditors need to understand a firm's information systems and examine the reliability of the systems before they audit the financial information that is produced by those systems.

CHAPTER OUTLINE

Introduction

Computer Hardware and Software

The Operating System

Database Systems

LANs and WANs

Wireless Networks

Computer-Assisted Audit Techniques

Continuous Monitoring and Continuous Auditing

LEARNING OBJECTIVES

After reading this chapter, you should be able to:

13-1 Understand the risks involved with computer hardware and software.

13-2 Understand and apply computer-assisted audit techniques.

13-3 Explain continuous monitoring and continuous auditing in AIS.

INTRODUCTION

In Chapters 11 and 12, we provided a general discussion of control, cybersecurity, and fraud issues in accounting information systems with regard to managing threats and risks in conducting business. In Chapters 7, 8, and 9, we indicated specific internal controls for each major business process—such as sales, cash collections, purchases, cash disbursement, and conversion/manufacturing. This chapter discusses important concepts of monitoring and auditing controls and verifying the accuracy and completeness of the information produced by the systems. We introduce fundamental concepts of critical computer hardware and software, including the operating system, the database, local area networks and wide area networks, and wireless networks. More importantly, we discuss computer-assisted audit techniques (CAATs) and continuous auditing in AIS.

LO 13-1

Understand the risks involved with computer hardware and software.

COMPUTER HARDWARE AND SOFTWARE

Chapter 12 discussed information technology-related frauds, cybersecurity, and vulnerabilities of information security. To enhance the understanding of those concepts, in this section we discuss important computer hardware and software: the operating system (OS), database systems, local area networks (LANs) and wide area networks (WANs), wireless networks, and remote access.

The Operating System

The **operating system (OS)** is the most important system software because it performs the tasks that enable a computer to operate. The operating system is comprised of system utilities and programs that[1]

- Ensure the integrity of the system.
- Control the flow of multiprogramming and tasks of scheduling in the computer.
- Allocate computer resources to users and applications.
- Manage the interfaces with the computer.

To consistently and reliably perform these tasks listed, the operating system must achieve five fundamental control objectives:[2]

- *The operating system must protect itself from users.* User applications/software must not be able to gain control of or damage the operating system.
- *The operating system must protect users from each other.* One user must not be able to access, destroy, or corrupt the data or programs of another user.
- *The operating system must protect users from themselves.* A user's applications/software may consist of several modules stored in separate memory locations, each with its own data. One module must not be allowed to destroy or corrupt another module.
- *The operating system must be protected from itself.* The operating system is also made up of individual modules. No module should be allowed to destroy or corrupt another module.
- *The operating system must be protected from its environment.* In the event of a power failure or other disaster, the operating system should be able to achieve a controlled termination of activities from which it can later recover.

Operating system security should be included as part of IT governance in establishing proper policies and procedures for IT controls that determine who can access the operating system, which resources (e.g., files, programs, printers, or servers) they can use, and what

[1]Information Systems Audit and Control Association (ISACA), *CISA Exam Review Manual* (2011), p. 260.
[2]F. M. Stepczyk, "Requirements for Secure Operating Systems," *Data Security and Data Processing* 5 (1974).

actions they can take.[3] With an ever-expanding user community sharing greater levels of computer resources, operating-system security becomes one of the most important IT control issues.

It should be noted that many firms are now turning toward virtualization of their computer resources and using cloud computing. In this architecture, hardware resources are split among multiple separate operating systems that exist only as separate environments on the server. In this situation, additional care must be taken to govern and secure the IT environments used.

Database Systems

In today's competitive business environment, data are often the core assets of many companies. In our electronic world, all or most accounting records are stored in a database. A **database** is a shared collection of logically related data that meet the information needs of a firm. Understanding a **database system** is crucial to accounting professionals. Because they have superior knowledge of risks, controls, and business processes, accountants increasingly participate in designing internal control systems and improving the business and IT processes in a database environment.

A **data warehouse** is a centralized collection of firmwide data that are stored for a relatively long period of time. The data in a data warehouse are pulled periodically from each of the operational databases (ranging from a couple of times a day to once a year), and the data are maintained in the data warehouse for 5–10 years. Firms use **operational databases** for daily operations. An operational database often includes data for the current fiscal year only. The data in an operational database are updated when transactions are processed. Such updates do not happen in a data warehouse, so the data in a data warehouse are nonvolatile. Periodically, new data are uploaded to the data warehouse from the operational databases for analysis. The purpose of a data warehouse is to provide a rich dataset for management to identify patterns and to examine trends of business events.

Data mining is the process of searching for patterns in the data within a data warehouse and analyzing these patterns for decision making. Data mining is often used to identify patterns in predicting customers' buying behavior for making better selling and production decisions. The tools used in data mining are called online analytical processing (OLAP). Typical approaches in OLAP include drill-down, consolidation, time series analysis, exception reports, and what-if simulations.

Data governance, a discipline that has emerged in recent years, has an evolving definition. It is the convergence of data quality, data management, data policies, business process management, regulation compliance, and risk management surrounding the handling of data in a firm.

Connection with Practice

Downtime Despair: The Impact of Online Banking Outages

With the popularity of online banking, many of us have been on the receiving end of messages alerting us that bank's online system is down or experiencing an outage.

According to Bank of America's (BOA) 2021 Annual Report, over 2 million active banking customers were added during 2021, totaling 54 million verified

(continued)

[3] J. A. Hall, *Information Technology Auditing,* 4th ed. (Boston, MA: Cengage Learning, 2016), p. 71.

Online banking.
Hill Street Studios/Getty Images

users. BOA estimated that in the fourth quarter of 2021, 86 percent of all deposit transactions were digital. So on the morning of October 1, 2021, when customers were greeted with an error message and unable to access the bank's website, Down Detector noted they were hit with over 12,000 customer complaints even though the site was back up by midday.

Outages are not new to online banking. In February 2018, a rollout of new technology caused a 3-day outage at BB&T Bank, and the bank later spent $300 million on a new data center. The bank sued technology firm Hitachi Vantara, who supplied disk storage and related services to the bank's mainframe computer systems. A settlement was agreed to in February 2022, where they agreed to dismiss the claims. In February 2019, Wells Fargo's online and mobile banking systems and ATM machines were down due to some issues in a data center. Many companies were affected and could not send out payments to meet deadlines. This is a typical example of how critical companies must control system downtime.

Sources: Taylor Rains, "Bank of America's online banking went down Friday, locking thousands of customers out of their accounts," *Business Insider,* October 1, 2021, https://www.businessinsider.com/bank-of-america-online-service-app-went-down-friday-2021-10;

Dan Swinhoe, "US bank Truist reaches settlement with Hitachi over 2018 outage," *Data Center Dynamics,* March 7, 2022, https://www.datacenterdynamics.com/en/news/us-bank-truist-reaches-settlement-with-hitachi-over-2018-outage/.

LANs and WANs

A **local area network (LAN)** is a group of computers, printers, and other devices connected to the same network that covers a limited geographic range such as a home, small office, or a campus building. LAN devices include **hubs** and **switches**. A packet, which is a formatted, small unit of data, is part of the message or dataset that is transmitted over the networks.

A hub contains multiple ports. When a data packet from a computer arrives at one port of a hub, it is copied to *all* other ports so that all other equipment connected to the LAN can receive the arrived packet (like a broadcast). A switch is an intelligent device that provides a path for each pair of connections on the switch by storing address information in its switching tables. From a security perspective, switches provide a significant improvement over hubs because each device connected via the network only sees traffic that has been directed to it via its designated **MAC (media access control) address** and cannot eavesdrop on network traffic intended for other recipients. Exhibit 13.1 illustrates a sample local area network.

Wide area networks (WANs) are networks that cover broad geographic areas including cities, regions, or nations. A WAN links different sites together, transmits information across geographically dispersed LANs. The three main purposes of WANs are (1) to provide remote access to employees or customers, (2) to link two or more sites within the

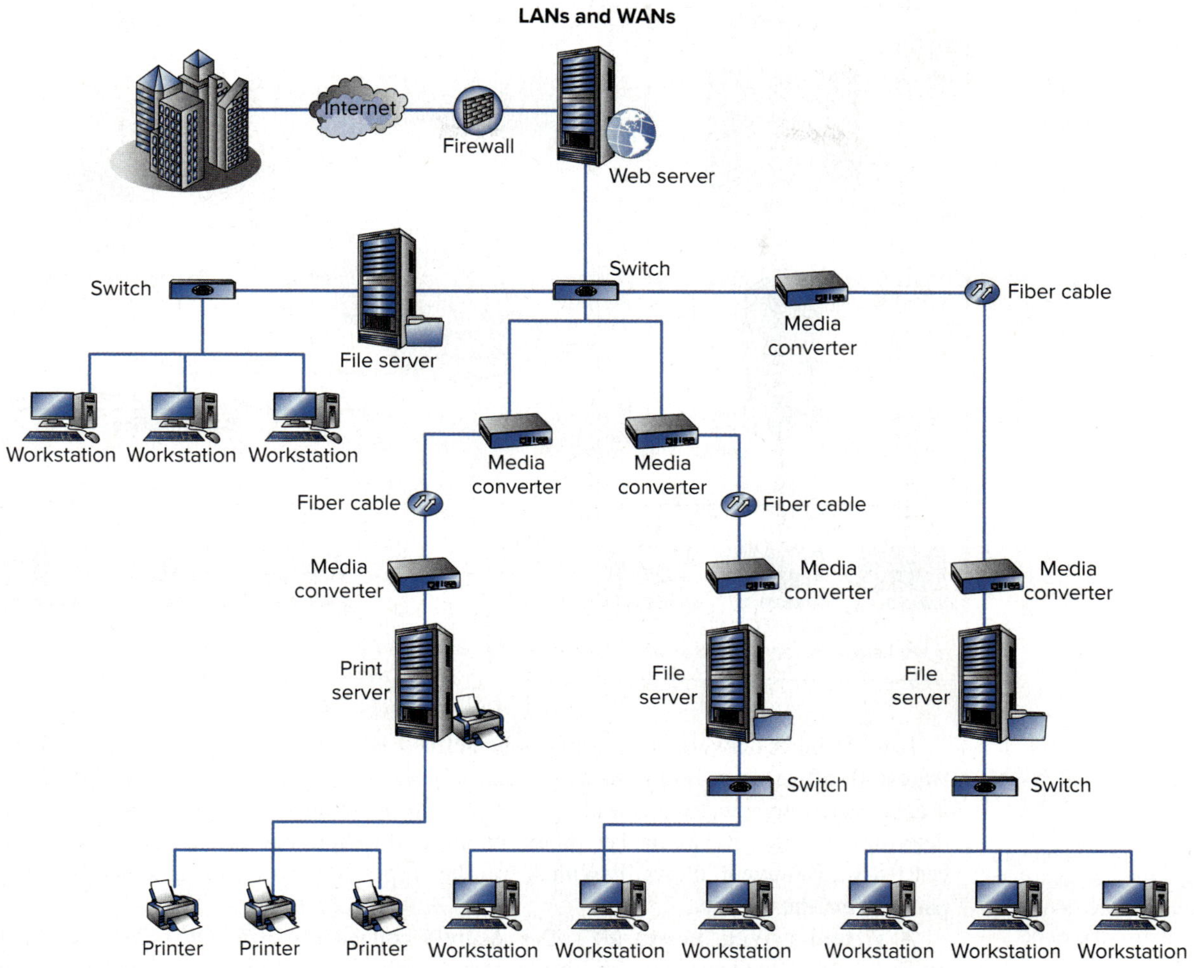

EXHIBIT 13.1
A Local Area Network Sample

Source: SanketShukla Blog, http://sanketshukla.blogspot.com/2009/11/local-area-network-lan.html.

firm, and (3) to provide corporate access to the Internet.[4] In general, WANs are slower than LAN communication in transmitting data but are often implemented over connectivity that offers guaranteed data rates. Enterprises are often willing to pay for these connections because of the guaranteed quality of service (QoS) and security offered by the point-to-point dedicated connection. WAN devices include **routers** and **firewalls**. Exhibit 13.2 illustrates a sample wide area network.

A router connects different LANs. Routers are software-based intelligent devices that choose the most efficient communication path through a network to the required destination. A router examines the Internet Protocol (IP) address of senders and recipients and makes decisions to direct the packet to its recipient's IP address through the most efficient communication path. Routers can also divide and interconnect network segments or link two more physically separate network segments, similar to a switch.

[4]R. Panko and J. Panko, *Business Data Networks and Telecommunications,* 8th ed. (Upper Saddle River, NJ: Prentice Hall, 2011).

EXHIBIT 13.2
A Wide Area Network Sample

Source: OTC company, http://www.otc.pl/en/tm_med.html.

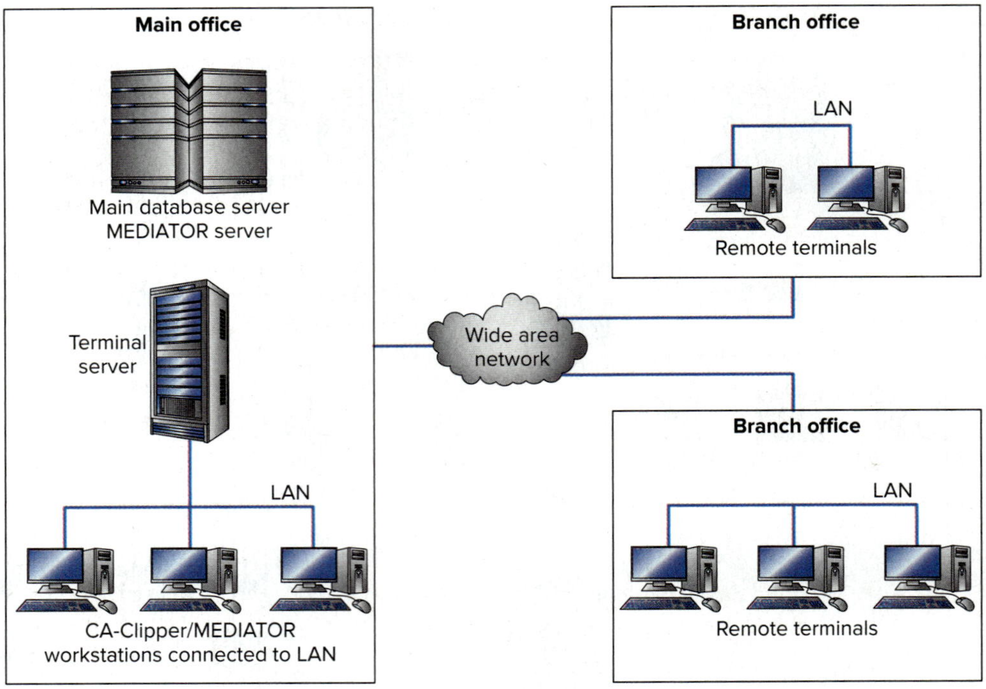

In today's business environment, VPN is an important technology. Many firms need to provide secure remote access for employees who are traveling and for those who work from home.

In a computer network, a firewall can be defined as a security system comprising hardware and software that is built using routers, servers, and a variety of software.[5] Whenever a data packet arrives, the firewall examines each incoming and outgoing data packet to determine whether a data packet should be allowed to continue in the transmission process. Also, a firewall allows individuals on the corporate network to send/receive a data packet from the Internet.

A **virtual private network (VPN)** securely connects a firm's WANs by sending/receiving encrypted packets via virtual connections over the public Internet to distant offices, salespeople, and business partners. Rather than using expensive dedicated leased lines, VPNs take advantage of the public Internet infrastructure with encryption and authentication technology to create a virtual private network that provides users with secure, **remote access** to their firm's network using the Internet. VPNs are a cheaper alternative to leased lines, yet they carry the disadvantage of not having guaranteed QoS. VPNs allow for companies to utilize a widely dispersed workforce without losing the productivity provided by a LAN.

PROGRESS CHECK

1. Identify one LAN and one WAN that you have been using.

Wireless Networks

Wireless technologies, which use radio-frequency transmissions and electromagnetic signals as the means for transmitting data, enable devices to communicate without physical connections. According to the Institute of Electrical and Electronics Engineers (IEEE) 802.11 standard, a **wireless network** is a network connecting hosts without using physical

[5]Ibid.

wires. A wireless network comprises two fundamental architectural components: access points and stations. An **access point** is a device to offer logical connections to a firm's network (LAN). Access points can also logically connect wireless stations with each other in an ad hoc wireless network.[6] A **station** is a wireless endpoint device equipped with a wireless network interface card (NIC). Common benefits of using wireless technology include[7]

- *Mobility*—convenient online access without a physical network using cables for connections.
- *Rapid deployment*—time saved on implementing networks because of reduction in using physical cables/media.
- *Flexibility and scalability*—freely setting up or removing wireless networks at different locations.

General security objectives for both wired LANs and wireless LANs include

- *Confidentiality*—ensure that communication cannot be read by unauthorized parties.
- *Integrity*—detect any intentional or unintentional changes to the data during transmission.
- *Availability*—ensure that devices and individuals can access a network and its resources whenever needed.
- *Access control*—restrict the rights of devices or individuals to access a network or resources within a network.

Most threats with regard to wireless LANs involve an attacker with access to the radio link between a station and an access point or between two stations. The most common security threats for wireless LANs include[8]

- *Eavesdropping*—the attacker passively monitors wireless networks for data, including authentication credentials.
- *Man-in-the-middle*—the attacker actively intercepts communications between wireless clients and access points to obtain authentication credentials and data.
- *Masquerading*—the attacker impersonates an authorized user and gains certain unauthorized privileges to the wireless network.
- *Message modification*—the attacker alters a legitimate message sent via wireless networks by deleting, adding to, changing, or reordering it.
- *Message replay*—the attacker passively monitors transmissions via wireless networks and retransmits messages, acting as if the attacker was a legitimate user.
- *Misappropriation*—the attacker steals or makes unauthorized use of a service.
- *Traffic analysis*—the attacker passively monitors transmissions via wireless networks to identify communication patterns and participants.
- *Rogue access points*—the attacker sets up an unsecured wireless network near the enterprise with an identical name and intercepts any messages sent by unsuspecting users who log onto it.

Security controls for wireless networks can be categorized into three groups: management, operational, and technical controls.[9] Management controls are security controls that focus on management of risk and information system security. Management controls include, but are not limited to, assigning roles and responsibilities, creating policies and

[6]National Institute of Standards and Technology (NIST), "Establishing Wireless Robust Security Networks: A Guide to IEEE 802.11i," SP 800-97 (2007), p. 22.

[7]Cyber Security Malaysia, *Wireless Local Area Network (WLAN) Security Guideline* (2010), p. 12.

[8]NIST, "Establishing Wireless Robust Security Networks: A Guide to IEEE 802.11i," pp. 27–28.

[9]Federal Information Processing Standards (FIPS), "Minimum Security Requirements for Federal Information and Information Systems," Publication 200 (2006).

procedures, and conducting risk assessment on a regular basis. Examples include determining which parties are authorized and responsible for installing and configuring access points and other wireless network equipment; types of information that may or may not be sent over wireless networks; and how transmissions over wireless networks should be protected, including requirements for the use of encryption and for cryptographic key management.[10]

Operational controls in wireless networks typically include protecting a firm's premises and facilities; preventing and detecting physical security breaches; and providing security training to employees, contractors, or third-party users. For example, a firm should define and document the security roles and responsibilities of employees, contractors, and third-party users for the firm's policies, procedures, and security requirements. It is also important to produce terms and conditions of employment that state the responsibilities of the employees, contractors, and third-party users for the firm's wireless network. They should agree to and sign the terms and conditions of their employment contract prior to beginning work. In addition, conducting appropriate awareness training on wireless networks and providing regular updates on organizational policies and procedures to employees, contractors, and third-party users can strengthen a firm's security control.

Technical controls are security controls that are primarily implemented and executed through mechanisms contained in computing-related equipment, including access-point management and encryption setup. A firm should immediately change the default configuration of all access points that have been deployed, including the service set identifier (SSID), administrator credentials, radio signal strength, remote web-based configuration (e.g., administrator's username and password), and Internet protocol service configuration.[11] Regarding data transmission security, all access points should be configured with encryption to maintain confidentiality and data integrity. Using the wired equivalent privacy (WEP) algorithm is not recommended because it is not secure enough. It is better to use the wi-fi protected access (WPA) or the WPA2 algorithm as the cryptography technique to provide more effective authentication and for encryption.

PROGRESS CHECK

2. Do you own a few mobile devices in addition to a laptop? Can you identify a few security issues while using these devices over a wireless network?

LO 13-2

Understand and apply computer-assisted audit techniques.

COMPUTER-ASSISTED AUDIT TECHNIQUES

For most large and medium-sized enterprises, there are few business processes that are not driven by computers.[12] Almost all the data needed while conducting an audit are digital. Given today's business environment, it is very difficult to audit effectively and efficiently without using technology, such as **computer-assisted audit techniques (CAATs)**.

CAATs are essential tools for auditors to conduct an audit in accordance with heightened auditing standards. Generally accepted auditing standards (GAAS) are broad guidelines regarding an auditor's professional responsibilities in three areas: general standards, standards of fieldwork, and standards of reporting. GAAS require auditors to gather sufficient and appropriate evidence in the course of audit fieldworks. The Information Systems Audit and Control Association (ISACA) issues Information Systems Auditing Standards (ISASs) that provide guidelines for conducting an IS/IT audit. Recently, ISASs

[10] NIST, "Guide to Securing Legacy IEEE 802.11 Wireless Networks," SP 800-48 Rev 1 (2008), p. 29.
[11] Cyber Security Malaysia, *Wireless Local Area Network (WLAN) Security Guideline*, p. 12.
[12] S. A. Sayana, "Using CAATs to Support IS Audit," *Information Systems Control Journal*, 1 (2003).

were renamed as IT Standards, Guidelines, Tools, and Techniques for Audit and Assurance and Control Professionals. In "Performance of Audit Work" (S6), ISACA indicates that "during the course of the audit, the IS auditor should obtain sufficient, reliable, and relevant evidence to achieve the audit objectives. The audit findings and conclusions are to be supported by appropriate analysis and interpretation of this evidence."[13] In addition, according to the Institute of Internal Auditors' (IIA) professional practice standard section 1220.A2, internal auditors *must* consider the use of computer-assisted, technology-based audit tools, and other data analysis techniques when conducting internal audits.[14]

The *term computer-assisted audit techniques* refers to any automated audit techniques that can be used by an auditor to perform audits in achieving audit objectives. In particular, CAATs enable auditors to gather and analyze audit evidence to test the adequacy and reliability of financial information and internal controls in a computerized environment. Some common areas in which auditors can use CAATs include

- Test of details of transactions and balances.
- Analytical review procedures.
- Compliance tests of IT general and application controls.
- Operating system (OS) and network vulnerability assessments.
- Application security testing and source code security scans.
- Penetration testing.

Auditors may use two CAAT approaches in auditing systems: **auditing around the computer (or black-box approach)** and **auditing through the computer (or white box approach)**. Using the black-box approach, auditors test the reliability of computer-generated information by first calculating expected results from the transactions entered into the system. Then, the auditors compare these calculations to the processing or output results. If they prove to be accurate and valid, it is assumed that the system of controls is effective and that the system is operating properly. That is, auditors do not need to gain detailed knowledge of the systems' internal logic. The advantage of this approach is that the systems will not be interrupted for auditing purposes. The black-box approach could be adequate when automated systems applications are relatively simple.

The white-box approach requires auditors to understand the internal logic of the system/application being tested. Using this approach, auditors need to create test cases to verify specific logic and controls in a system. The auditing through the computer approach embraces a variety of approaches: the test data technique, parallel simulation, integrated test facility (ITF), and embedded audit module.[15]

The **test data technique** uses a set of input data to validate system integrity. When creating the test data, auditors need to prepare both valid and invalid data to examine critical logics and controls of the system. **Parallel simulation** attempts to simulate the firm's key features or processes. Under this approach, the auditors write a computer program to reprocess the firm's actual data for a past period to generate simulated results. The simulated results are compared with the actual results to determine the validity of the system. The **integrated test facility (ITF)** approach is an automated technique that enables test data to be continually evaluated during the normal operation of a system. The auditor creates fictitious situations and performs a wide variety of tests over the system. This approach requires more computer expertise and is time-consuming and expensive. The **embedded audit module (EAM)** is a programmed audit module that is added to the system under review. Hence, the auditors can

[13]ISACA, *IT Standards, Guidelines, Tools, and Techniques for Audit and Assurance and Control Professionals* (2010), www.isaca.org.

[14]Institute of Internal Auditors (IIA), *International Standards for the Professional Practice of Internal Auditing (Standards)* (2010), www.theiia.org.

[15]Hall, *Information Technology Auditing and Assurance.*

monitor and collect data over online transactions. The collected data are analyzed by auditors in evaluating control risks and effectiveness. The application of this approach requires auditors to have good knowledge and skills in computer programming.

In addition to the aforementioned techniques in auditing controls in a system, one widely used tool in auditing a system is **generalized audit software (GAS)**. GAS is frequently used to perform substantive tests and to test controls through transactional data analysis.[16] GAS refers to standard software that has the capability to directly read and access data from various database platforms. GAS provides auditors with an independent means to gain access to data for analysis and the ability to use high-level, problem-solving software to invoke functions to be performed on data files.[17] Features include mathematical computations, stratification, statistical analysis, sequence checking, duplicate checking, and re-computation. Two of the most popular software packages are Audit Command Language (ACL) and Interactive Data Extraction and Analysis (IDEA). GAS is ideal for investigating large data files to identify records needing further audit scrutiny.

LO 13-3

Explain continuous monitoring and continuous auditing in AIS.

CONTINUOUS MONITORING AND CONTINUOUS AUDITING

The acceleration of variety and velocity of business transactions and data and disruptive technology advancements—including blockchain, machine learning, and artificial intelligence—require a shift in monitoring and auditing methodology. For management, related continuous monitoring activities are control, security and performance monitoring, use of the Balanced Scorecard for total quality management, and enterprise risk management. Continuous monitoring provides holistic information about the effectiveness of business processes and internal controls that enhances the accuracy of transactions processed and improves information security. With continuous monitoring, companies are potentially alerted to issues on a timely basis and thus can identify and resolve the problems before they spread. While it is beneficial for companies to be more aware of the effectiveness of their controls, it also increases a company's accountability in case something does go wrong and not fixed.

A **continuous audit** occurs when audit-related activities are performed on a continuous basis. With continuous auditing, theoretically, an audit report/opinion can be issued *simultaneously* with, or shortly after, the occurrence of the events under review.[18] Testing in continuous audits often consists of continuous controls monitoring and continuous data assurance.[19] Using automated audit procedures, the audit activities related to continuous auditing range from continuous control assessment to continuous risk assessment and include internal control assurance, financial attestation, fraud examination, audit scope and objective identification, audit records follow-ups, and annual audit plans preparation. Continuous auditing enables internal and external auditors to continually collect audit evidence from the IT systems, including information and data from transactions and processes. Because continuous auditing is highly dependent on automated audit procedures, technology plays a key role in analyzing trends and patterns of transactions, identifying exceptions and anomalies, and testing controls.[20] Exhibit 13.3 illustrates the concepts and hierarchy of continuous auditing.

[16] M. V. Cerullo, "Impact of SAS No. 94 on Computer Audit Techniques," *Information Systems Control Journal* 1 (2003).

[17] ACL and IDEA are the most widely used GAS applications for data analysis.

[18] Global Technology Audit Guides (GTAG), *Continuous Auditing: Implications for Assurance, Monitoring, and Risk Assessment* (2005), p. 7.

[19] M. G. Alles, A. Kogan, and M. A. Vasarhelyi, "Putting Continuous Auditing Theory into Practice: Lessons from Two Pilot Implementations," *Journal of Information Systems* 22, no. 2 (2008), pp. 195–214.

[20] GTAG, *Continuous Auditing.*

<table>
<tr><th>Approach</th><th>Focus</th><th>Analysis Techniques</th><th>Related Audit Activities</th><th>Related Management Activities</th></tr>
<tr><td>Continuous controls assessment</td><td>Control-based (ensure financial controls are working)</td><td>Real-time/detailed transaction testing on financial data</td><td rowspan="2">Control assurance
Financial data attest
Fraud/waste/abuse examination
Audit scope and objectives
Follow-up on audit recommendations
Annual audit plan</td><td rowspan="2">Control monitoring
Performance monitoring
Balanced Scorecard
Total quality management (TQM)
Enterprise risk management (ERM)</td></tr>
<tr><td>Continuous risk assessment</td><td>Risk-based (identify and assess risks on financial and operational controls)</td><td>Trend/comparison analysis on financial and operational data</td></tr>
</table>

Exhibit 13.3
Concepts in Continuous Auditing

Source: D. Coderre, "Concepts in Continuous Auditing," Continuous Auditing, Pub/2005, https://www.iia.nl/.

There are many benefits of conducting continuous audits. Most firms can reduce errors and frauds, increase operational effectiveness, better comply with laws and regulations, and increase management confidence in control effectiveness and financial information. In addition, continuous auditing allows internal and external auditors to monitor transaction data in a timely manner; better understand critical control points, rules, and exceptions; perform control and risk assessments in real time or near real time; notify management of control deficiencies in a timely manner; and reduce efforts of routine testing while focusing on more valuable investigation activities. However, if costs outweigh benefits, continuous auditing should not be implemented.

A 2006 study by Kuhn and Sutton analyzes the particular fraudulent activities that WorldCom's management used to deceive investors and assesses whether the "continuous auditing alarms" would have caught the fraudulent activities. This study provides guidance to auditors who are establishing continuous auditing initiatives to leverage the lessons learned from the WorldCom debacle and ensure that their continuous auditing routines are able to identify the type of financial fraud that occurred at WorldCom.[21]

Exhibit 13.4 summarizes the Kuhn and Sutton study and indicates the fraud schemes and the corresponding proposed alarms under continuous audits that would have flagged the activity for further review.

Although the concept of continuous auditing was introduced decades ago, it was not widely implemented by firms before the proliferation of information technologies in recent years. Today's advanced data analytics, ERP systems, and web-based programming languages such as Extensible Markup Language (XML) and eXtensible Business Reporting Language (XBRL) make the implementation of continuous auditing more feasible and less costly than before.

Common IT techniques needed to implement continuous auditing include database management systems, transaction logging and query tools, data warehouses, and data mining or CAATs. Using these techniques, some key functions of continuous audits can be performed, such as accessing and normalizing data from across the enterprise, extracting large transactional volumes without having a negative impact on operational system performance, and testing data and reporting results in a timely manner.

[21] J. R. Kuhn and S. G. Sutton, "Learning from WorldCom: Implications for Fraud Detection through Continuous Assurance," *Journal of Emerging Technologies in Accounting* 3, no. 1 (2006), pp. 61–80.

EXHIBIT 13.4
Continuous Auditing Alarms and the WorldCom Fraud Schemes

WorldCom Fraud Scheme	Proposed Continuous Auditing Alarm
Operating expenses were illegitimately reclassified as capital expenditures, which improved the "expenditure-to-revenue" (E/R) ratio by reducing the amount of expenses recorded in current fiscal year.	Create an alarm that simultaneously identifies (1) reductions in operating expenses that exceed the industry average and (2) increases in capital expenditures that exceed the industry average.
Book values of acquired entities were illegitimately reclassified as goodwill on the books, which improved the E/R ratio by increasing the effective amortization period of the amounts in question.	Create an alarm that identifies increases in plant, property, equipment, and goodwill that differ significantly from historical averages.
"Taking a bath" by excessively writing down the assets included in the corporate acquisitions gave "the false impression that expenses were declining over time in relation to revenue (i.e., reducing the E/R ratio and increasing net income from operations)."	Benchmark key ratios (e.g., E/R) against industry averages, and generate an alarm when there is a significant discrepancy between the two.
Allowance for doubtful accounts was underestimated (along with the corresponding expense entry bad debts expense) to falsely improve the E/R ratio.	Generate an alarm if the allowance for doubtful accounts differs significantly from the last month's ratio (i.e., to Accounts Receivable).

The most significant nontechnical barriers[22] and technical challenges[23] encountered in implementing continuous auditing include

- Perceived negative impact of continuous auditing on the firm, such as the cost of initial investments, changes in internal audit group's head count, and the quality of audits.
- Priority of implementation in determined key areas, such as which controls should be monitored on a continual basis and which audit activities could be automated.
- Readiness of the internal audit group to develop and adopt continuous auditing.
- Unrealistic expectations of the benefits of continuous auditing.
- Access to all relevant data in a timely manner.
- Accumulating and quantifying the risks and the exposures that have been identified.
- Defining the appropriate analytic that will effectively identify exceptions to controls.
- Developing a suitable scoring/weighting mechanism to prioritize exceptions.
- Balancing the costs and efforts of reviewing large volumes of exceptions against the exposures of the exceptions themselves.

Although there is no universal, well-accepted approach to implement continuous auditing, there is a general template that a steering team or the internal audit function can use.[24] When a firm considers whether or not to implement continuous auditing, it should first evaluate the overall benefit and cost of having continuous auditing as part of the firm's overall governance, risk, and compliance (GRC) effort. After careful evaluations to rationalize the decision, the firm should develop a strategy in identifying and prioritizing potential areas for continuous audits. Once the strategy is developed, the firm should plan and design how to implement continuous auditing, such as determining the scope of the audit objectives, designing the continuous auditing processes, allocating resources, and creating a reasonable timeline for implementation. Once the resources are approved and in place, the firm can implement continuous auditing followed by periodic performance monitoring on the implementation.

[22] Deloitte & Touche, *Continuous Monitoring and Continuous Auditing: From Idea to Implementation* (2010), p. 10.
[23] ACL, *Building and Implementing a Continuous Controls Monitoring and Auditing Framework* (2005), p. 3.
[24] Deloitte & Touche, *Continuous Monitoring and Continuous Auditing,* p. 10.

Summary

- Essential concepts of critical computer hardware and software are introduced in this chapter, including the operating system, the database, local area networks, wide area networks, and wireless networks.
- There are two approaches to auditing an information system: auditing around the computer (the black-box approach) and auditing through the computer (the white-box approach).
- Most auditors would like to use computer-assisted audit techniques (CAATs) in auditing a system, such as the test data technique, parallel simulation, and the embedded audit module. CAATs are often used in continuous auditing. Performing audit-related activities on a continuous basis may narrow the gap between daily operations and the required improvements resulting from an audit.

Key Words

access point (*457*) Logically connects stations to a firm's network.

audit around the computer (or black-box approach) (*459*) An audit that tests the reliability of computer-generated information by first calculating expected results from the transactions entered into the system and then comparing these calculations to the processing or output results.

audit through the computer (or white-box approach) (*459*) An audit that requires auditors to understand the internal logic of the system/application being tested.

computer-assisted audit techniques (CAATs) (*458*) Essential tools for auditors to conduct an audit in accordance with heightened auditing standards.

continuous audit (*460*) Performance of audit-related activities on a continuous basis.

data governance (*453*) The convergence of data quality, data management, data policies, business process management, and risk management surrounding the handling of data in a firm.

data mining (*453*) A process of using sophisticated statistical techniques to extract and analyze data from large databases to discern patterns and trends that were not previously known.

data warehouse (*453*) A centralized collection of firm-wide data that are stored for a relatively long period of time.

database (*453*) A shared collection of logically related data for various uses.

database system (*453*) A term typically used to encapsulate the constructs of a data model, database management system (DBMS), and database.

embedded audit module (EAM) (*459*) A programmed audit module that is added to the system under review.

firewall (*455*) A security system comprising hardware and software that is built using routers, servers, and a variety of software.

generalized audit software (GAS) (*460*) Software that is frequently used to perform substantive tests and to test controls through transactional data analysis.

hub (*454*) Contains multiple ports.

integrated test facility (ITF) (*459*) An automated technique that enables test data to be continually evaluated during the normal operation of a system.

local area network (LAN) (*454*) A group of computers, printers, and other devices connected to the same network that covers a limited geographic range such as a home, small office, or a campus building.

MAC (media access control) address (*454*) A designated address that is connected to each device via the network and only sees traffic.

operating system (OS) (*452*) Performs the tasks that enable a computer to operate; comprises system utilities and programs.

operational database (*453*) Database that often includes data for the current fiscal year only.

parallel simulation (*459*) A technique that attempts to simulate the firm's key features or processes.

remote access (*456*) Connection to a data-processing system from a remote location—for example, through a virtual private network.

router (*455*) Software-based intelligent device that chooses the most efficient communication path through a network to the required destination.

station (*457*) A wireless endpoint device equipped with a wireless network interface card.

switch (*454*) An intelligent device that provides a path for each pair of connections on the switch by storing address information in its switching tables.

test data technique (*459*) A testing technique that uses a set of input data to validate system integrity.

virtual private network (VPN) (*456*) Securely connects a firm's WANs by sending/receiving encrypted packets via virtual connections over the public Internet to distant offices, salespeople, and business partners.

wide area network (WAN) (*454*) Links different sites together; transmits information across geographically dispersed LANs; and covers a broad geographic area such as a city, region, nation, or an international link.

wireless network (*456*) Comprises two fundamental architectural components: access points and stations.

ANSWERS TO PROGRESS CHECKS

1. Two or more computers in a small office connected to the same printer form a local area network. The Internet is the most popular and largest wide area network.
2. Mobile devices are subject to man-in-the-middle attacks when using unsecured wi-fi networks. Also, an iPad user who gets applications from any apps store is at risk of getting malicious applications from the store.

Multiple Choice Questions connect

1. **(LO 13-1)** A local area network (LAN) is best described as a(n)
   a. computer system that connects computers of all sizes, workstations, terminals, and other devices within a limited proximity.
   b. system that allows computer users to meet and share ideas and information.
   c. electronic library containing millions of items of data that can be reviewed, retrieved, and analyzed.
   d. method to offer specialized software, hardware, and data-handling techniques that improve effectiveness and reduce costs.
2. **(LO 13-1)** Which of the following network components is set up to serve as a security measure that prevents unauthorized traffic between different segments of the network?
   a. Switch
   b. Router
   c. Firewall
   d. Virtual local area networks (VLANs)
3. **(LO 13-1)** Unauthorized alteration of records in a database system would impair which of the following components of the CIA (related to security)?
   a. Confidentiality
   b. Integrity
   c. Availability
   d. Authorization

4. **(LO 13-1)** Which of the following is not a task performed by an operating system?
   a. Translate high-level languages to machine-level language.
   b. Manage job scheduling and multiprogramming.
   c. Support applications and facilitate their access to specified resources.
   d. Provide controlled access to data and process data.
5. **(LO 13-1)** Managers at a consumer products company purchased personal computer software from only recognized vendors and prohibited employees from installing nonauthorized software on their personal computers by enforcing a new end-user computing policy. To minimize the likelihood of computer viruses infecting any of its systems, the company should also
   a. restore infected systems with authorized versions.
   b. recompile infected programs from source code backups.
   c. institute program change control procedures.
   d. test all new software on a stand-alone personal computer.
6. **(LO 13-1)** Unauthorized alteration of records in a database system can be prevented by employing
   a. key verification.
   b. computer matching.
   c. regular review of audit trails.
   d. database access controls.
7. **(LO 13-1)** An organization is planning to replace its wired networks with wireless networks. Which of the following approaches provides the most secure wireless network?
   a. Implement wired equivalent privacy (WEP) protocol.
   b. Allow access to only authorized media access control (MAC) addresses.
   c. Disable the network interface card (NIC).
   d. Implement wi-fi protected access (WPA2).
8. **(LO 13-3)** The vice president of human resources has requested an audit to identify payroll overpayments for the previous year. Which would be the best audit technique to use in this situation?
   a. Test data
   b. Generalized audit software
   c. Integrated test facility
   d. Embedded audit module
9. **(LO 13-2)** Which of the following statements about CAATs is not correct?
   a. Parallel simulation attempts to simulate or reproduce the firm's actual processing results.
   b. The test data technique uses a set of hypothetical transactions to examine the programmed checks and program logic in programs.
   c. The integrated test facility is a programmed module or segment that is inserted into an application program to monitor and collect data based on daily transactions.
   d. The embedded audit module may require the auditor to have a good working knowledge of computer programming and a solid understanding of IT risks that may exist in a system.
10. **(LO 13-3)** Which of the following audit techniques should an IS auditor use to detect duplicate invoice records within an invoice master file?
   a. Test data
   b. Generalized audit software
   c. Integrated test facility
   d. Embedded audit module

11. **(LO 13-1)** A group of computers, printers, and other devices connected to the same network and covering a limited geographic range is called a
    a. LAN.
    b. VAN.
    c. VPN.
    d. WAN.
12. **(LO 13-1)** The most common security threats for wireless LANs include
    a. man-in-the-middle.
    b. system malfunction.
    c. social engineering.
    d. virus.
13. **(LO 13-3)** The test data technique uses
    a. a programmed audit module that is added to the system under review.
    b. a computer program to reprocess the firm's actual data for a past period to generate simulated results.
    c. a set of input data to validate system integrity.
    d. an automated technique that enables test data to be continually evaluated during the normal operation of a system.
14. **(LO 13-1)** Which of the following is not one of the main purposes for a WAN?
    a. Provide remote access to employees and/or customers.
    b. Link two or more geographically dispersed sites within a company.
    c. Provide corporate access to the Internet.
    d. Securely connect a network to distant offices in a building by sending encrypted packets.
15. **(LO 13-1)** An operational database
    a. contains data that are volatile.
    b. covers the data of current and previous fiscal years.
    c. is updated before transactions are processed.
    d. contains data that are uploaded from a data warehouse.
16. **(LO 13-1)** What is the main purpose of using VPN today?
    a. Secure the data transmission between e-business trading partners.
    b. Examine the Internet traffic and to prevent DoS attacks.
    c. Maintain a secured data transmission or communication for remote access.
    d. None of these options are correct.
17. **(LO 13-1)** Select the correct statement(s) regarding network devices.
    a. Firewalls are used to screen and secure data transmitted among internal networks.
    b. Routers use IP addresses for data transmission over the Internet.
    c. Hubs are used for transmitting packets over internal networks.
    d. (a) and (b) are correct.
    e. (b) and (c) are correct.
18. **(LO 13-1)** Select a correct statement regarding routers.
    a. Routers are used for data transmission over internal networks.
    b. Routers use MAC addresses to pass the packets over the Internet.
    c. Routers and hubs using the same approach in transmitting packets.
    d. None of these options are correct.
19. **(LO 13-1)** Select a correct statement regarding database systems.
    a. Data mining is often used to analyze data in the data warehouse.
    b. A data warehouse is the operational database.
    c. A company's ERP system is often the same as the data warehouse.
    d. Two of these statements are correct.

20. **(LO 13-2)** Which of the following is not a generalized audit software (GAS)?
  a. ACL
  b. SAP
  c. IDEA

Discussion Questions connect

1. **(LO 13-1)** What are the main reasons for using a VPN?
2. **(LO 13-1)** Consider the computer attacks in the previous chapters. How would a VPN protect a user from one or more of them?
3. **(LO 13-1)** We often use regression analyses in data mining. Are accountants required to understand data mining? Why?
4. **(LO 13-1)** What is the main purpose of using firewalls? Search the Internet to find its importance for cybersecurity.
5. **(LO 13-1)** Firewalls rely on a list of allowed and blocked services and locations. What would happen if a company's firewall rules were too weak? If the firewall rules were too strict?
6. **(LO 13-1)** Are there differences among hubs, switches, and routers?
7. **(LO 13-1)** Identify a few critical security issues in using a wireless network.
8. **(LO 13-1)** Using a brute-force attack, hackers can crack the password to a WEP access point in about 5 minutes and WPA2 in about 2 days. What does this tell you about the security of wireless networks?
9. **(LO 13-2)** Auditors are constantly developing new CAAT analyses to help them in the assurance process. Use a search engine to identify three of the techniques that are being used currently.
10. **(LO 13-2)** When would an auditor prefer to conduct a black-box audit? A white-box audit?
11. **(LO 13-3)** Continuous auditing allows auditors to validate data and monitor transactions in near real-time. What advantages does this provide to auditors? What are some potential problems with continuous auditing?
12. **(LO 13-2)**, **(LO 13-3)** Auditing an accounting information system requires knowledge and skills in both accounting and computers. However, most auditors may not have sufficient expertise in the technical side of computing and information systems. Given today's business environment, how much computer- and information systems-related knowledge and skills must an auditor have to be effective in performing auditing?

Problems connect

1. **(LO 13-1)** Match the descriptions with each type of network.

Descriptions	Network
a. This computer network covers a broad area (e.g., includes any network whose communications link cross metropolitan, regional, or national boundaries over a long distance).	i. LAN
b. The Internet is a good example of this type of network.	ii. WAN
c. This type of network often uses Layer 2 devices like switches and Layer 1 devices like hubs.	iii. VPN
d. The purpose of this type of network is mainly for remote access.	iv. Wireless LAN
e. This type of network comprises of two fundamental architectural components: stations and access points.	
f. This type of network has a large geographical range generally spreading across boundaries and often needs leased telecommunication lines.	

2. **(LO 13-1)** Match correct descriptions with each network device.

COSO ERM Principles	Network Devices
a. Using IP address to transport packets	i. Hubs
b. Using MAC address to transport packets	ii. Switches
c. Using rules to screen incoming and outgoing packets	iii. Firewalls
d. Do not use source or destination addresses to transport packets	iv. Routers
e. Always used for Internet transportation of packets	
f. Broadcast to all devices when transport packets for internal networks	

3. **(LO 13-3)** Match the continuous auditing alarms to flag the fraud schemes.

Fraud Scheme	Continuous Auditing Alarms
a. Operating expenses were illegitimately reclassified as capital expenditures, which improved the "expenditure-to-revenue" (E/R) ratio by reducing the amount of expenses recorded in the current fiscal year.	i. Generate an alarm if the allowance for doubtful accounts differs significantly from the last month's ratio (i.e., to Accounts Receivable).
b. Book values of acquired entities were illegitimately reclassified as goodwill on the books, which improved the E/R ratio by increasing the effective amortization period of the amounts in question.	ii. Benchmark key ratios (e.g., E/R) against industry averages and generate an alarm when there is a significant discrepancy between the two.
c. Excessively wrote down the assets included in the corporate acquisitions, which gave "the false impression that expenses were declining over time in relation to revenue (i.e., reducing the E/R ratio and increasing net income from operations)."	iii. Create an alarm that identifies increases in plant, property, equipment, and goodwill that differ significantly from historical averages.
d. Allowance for doubtful accounts was underestimated (along with the corresponding expense entry bad debts expense) to falsely improve the E/R ratio.	iv. Create an alarm that simultaneously identifies (1) reductions in operating expenses that exceed the industry average and (2) increases in capital expenditures that exceed the industry average.

4. **(LO 13-3)** (CIA adapted) As an internal auditor, you have been assigned to evaluate the controls and operation of a computer payroll system. To test the computer systems and programs, you submit independently created test transactions with regular data in a normal production run. Identify advantages and disadvantages of this technique.
5. **(LO 13-2)** Describe how an auditor would use each of the following audit techniques: ITF, parallel simulation, EAM, and GAS.
6. **(LO 13-3)** Identify the key features of a continuous audit and the common techniques to implement the audit.
7. **(LO 13-2), (LO 13-3)** (CMA adapted) As chief executive auditor, Mallory Williams heads the internal audit group of a manufacturing company in southern Texas. She would like to purchase a CAAT tool to assist her group in conducting internal audit functions. She has asked you to prepare a report on the following tools: ACL, IDEA, Microsoft Visio, Oversight, and Tableau. In your report, identify key features and how an auditor would incorporate the tool into the audit, and recommend one or two of the tools for purchase.

Chapter Fourteen

Reporting Processes and eXtensible Business Reporting Language (XBRL)

A Look at This Chapter

In this chapter, we explain how accounting information systems facilitate management reporting, including using data warehouses, business intelligence, and dashboards. We then explain the development and emerging use of eXtensible Business Reporting Language (XBRL). We also discuss the potential for XBRL and other emerging technologies to address reporting needs.

A Look Back

In Chapter 13, since an accountant's role in the business world is to provide quality information for decision making, they must understand and be involved in monitoring and auditing accounting information systems.

A Look Ahead

Blockchain and artificial intelligence are important emerging topics in information systems and accounting. In Chapter 10, we provide an overview of those topics. While we recognize that each topic could be an entire accounting course, instead we focus on the general concepts important for critical for accountants to understand.

ridvan_celik/Getty Images

Throughout this textbook, we've been trying to make the case that **Starbucks** is a technology company that happens to sell coffee. Look no further than Starbucks' relationship with its fellow *Fortune* 500 company from the Seattle area, **Microsoft**!

The history of both Seattle companies has long been intertwined. How? Both began as a company in the 1970s. What's more? Twenty-five years ago, Bill Gates used Microsoft technology that combined words, images, charts, and sounds in a single document to demonstrate how Starbucks could formulate its quarterly financial statements. In fact, this chapter discusses how XBRL is used to report financial performance to all sorts of users of Starbucks' financial statements. Satya Nadella, Microsoft's CEO, even sits on Starbucks' board of directors.

Even today, Starbucks stores many of its data warehouses on Microsoft's Azure cloud services and works closely with Microsoft as it rolls out new initiatives.

So, is Starbucks a technology company or a coffee company?

Source: David McCracken, "Starbucks Brews a Tech-Infused Future, with Help from Microsoft", 2018, https://www.fastcompany.com/40568165/starbucks-brews-a-tech-infused-future-with-help-from-microsoft (Accessed October 2022).

CHAPTER OUTLINE

LEARNING OBJECTIVES

After reading this chapter, you should be able to:

14-1 Explain how data warehouses are created and used.

14-2 Describe the basic components of business intelligence and how they are utilized in a firm.

14-3 Describe how digital dashboards allow for continuous tracking of key metrics.

14-4 Explain how XBRL works and how it makes business reporting more efficient.

INTRODUCTION

Earlier chapters in this textbook demonstrated how information is gathered and accumulated in a database. We are now interested in the reporting of that information to both internal and external users. We introduce the overall concept of a data warehouse and then specifically explain how data warehouses may be used in business intelligence settings. We also discuss how dashboards are used to manage a company's operations. Finally, we explore the use of XBRL to share financial and nonfinancial information with external users like the Securities and Exchange Commission, the Internal Revenue Service, financial analysts, lenders, and current or potential investors.

LO 14-1

Explain how data warehouses are created and used.

DATA WAREHOUSES AND DATA MARTS

Our discussion thus far in this book has been about operational systems primarily designed and optimized to capture business transactions, such as sales and purchases. In contrast, a data warehouse is essentially a new (often independent) repository designed to be optimized for speed and efficiency in data analysis. More specifically, a **data warehouse** is a collection of information gathered from an assortment of external and operational (i.e., internal) databases to facilitate reporting for decision making and business analysis. Data warehouses often serve as the main repository of the firm's historical data (or, in other words, its corporate memory) and will often serve as an archive of past firm performance.

Like a data warehouse, a **data lake** integrates data from different sources, but it can maintain much larger amounts of data, including both structured and unstructured data. It may seem that a data lake is always preferable to a data warehouse because of the added flexibility that comes with maintaining more data, including unstructured data. However, data lakes do have an important limitation: The more data that are stored, the greater is the risk of delayed reporting and information overload. A data lake can make it more difficult for business analysts to focus on precisely the data they need to perform their analysis.

While both data warehouses and data lakes store and integrate data, remember that analysts must work with data, not just collect data. A variety of programming languages can be used to retrieve the data, such as SQL, R, and Python, and a processing application called an OLAP cube can also be built on top of a data warehouse. **OLAP (online analytical processing)** aids in processing transactional and structured data in a data warehouse, even when the data originate from disparate databases or external sources.

However, if a company is using a data lake to store unstructured data in addition to structured data and an analyst wishes to perform analysis on the unstructured data, then OLAP may not be useful. In this instance, an upgrade to distributed computing is recommended. In **distributed computing**, data are stored across multiple databases, which allows greater storage of data and increased speed of analysis.

An example of a framework that supports distributed data lakes is **Hadoop,** an open-source framework for storing and processing Big Data. Hadoop was a trailblazing framework for Big Data, and many organizations continue to use it to work with Big Data. For a company to acquire the computation power necessary to run Hadoop (or any other big data framework) with massive data sets, it must shift to cloud storage. Cloud storage vendors such as **Amazon Web Services (AWS), Cloudera,** and **Microsoft Azure** provide cloud solutions to support the storage of massive amounts of data. All are compatible with Hadoop.

The best way to illustrate a data warehouse is by using a exhibit. Exhibit 14.1 shows operational and external databases that are used as inputs into the data warehouse. The operational databases may all come from within the company's enterprise system or various systems throughout the firm. The external databases may come from a variety of places, including purchased data from the Gartner Group, the Federal Reserve, and industry organizations.

EXHIBIT 14.1
Model of Data Warehouse Design

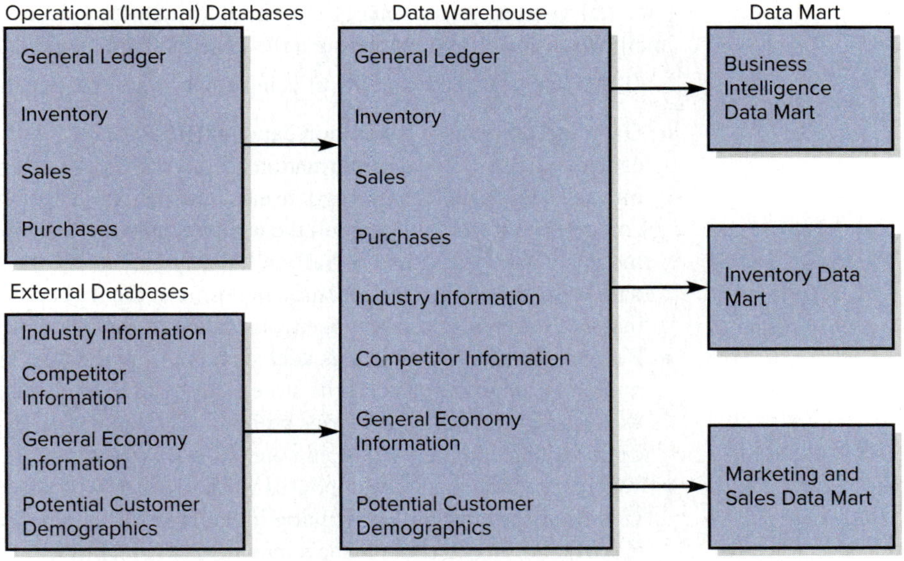

The actual data warehouse may become too big and overwhelming for specific groups within the firm to use. A **data mart** takes a subset of the information from the data warehouse to serve a specific purpose, such as a marketing data mart, an inventory data mart, or a business intelligence data mart. Whereas a data warehouse is a repository for the overall firm, the data mart is a subset of the data warehouse for a specific purpose or function. In essence, a data warehouse is made up of many data marts.

The opening vignette suggests **Starbucks** continues to use a data warehouse and data marts within its organization. Exhibit 14.2 provides an example of a potential data warehouse design for Starbucks. The exhibit highlights four types of data marts (although the

EXHIBIT 14.2
Potential Data Warehouse Design for Starbucks

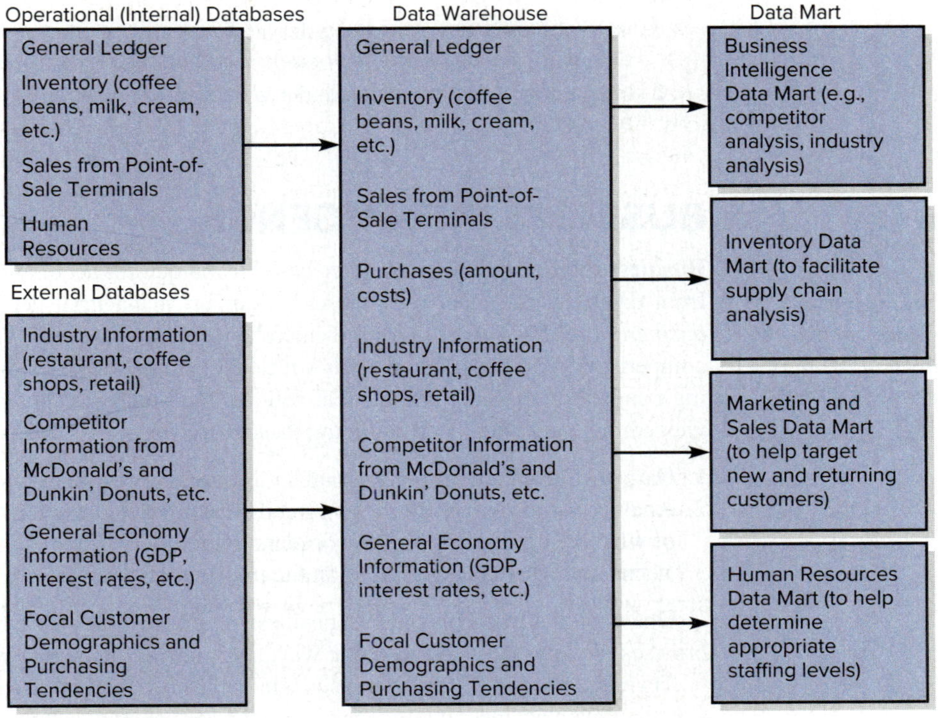

potential number of data marts is unlimited) that may be useful to Starbucks: business intelligence, inventory, marketing and sales, and human resources.

The advantages and benefits of using a data warehouse include the following:

- Data warehouses use a common data model for all data in the warehouse, making it easy to quickly compare information all the way from customer invoices, bills of lading, sales journals, purchasing journals, and general ledgers to industry information, competitor information, potential customers, and the like. We discussed some data models in Chapters 5 and 6. Suffice it to say that before the data are loaded into the data warehouse, any data inconsistencies from the input databases are removed so that the data warehouse has homogeneous data that can be readily accessed and analyzed.
- Because the data warehouse is kept separate from the operational database, the information in the warehouse can be stored safely for extended periods of time, and data warehouses can run data queries without affecting the performance (i.e., slowing down) of the company's ongoing operational systems.
- When appropriate, data warehouses work together with operational systems to provide necessary insight, particularly in the case of customer relationship management (CRM) and supply chain management (SCM) systems.
- Data warehouses are often designed to facilitate decision making (such as those often addressed in managerial accounting) and management by exception (such as variance reports, trend reports, variance analysis reports, and reports that show actual performance compared with budgeted information). Often, the type of system used to support managerial decision making is called a **decision support system (DSS)**.

It should also be noted that a key disadvantage of a data warehouse is that it can quickly become obsolete with outdated data unless there is a mechanism to continuously update the internal and external databases as time passes.

PROGRESS CHECK

1. Why would **Apple**'s marketing department only use a subset of the data (using a data mart) instead of the entire data warehouse?
2. Imagine what might be included in a data warehouse for **Best Buy**. How might it be useful?

LO 14-2

Describe the basic components of business intelligence and how they are utilized in a firm.

BUSINESS INTELLIGENCE

Business intelligence is a computer-based technique for accumulating and analyzing data from databases and data warehouses to support managerial decision making. The term *business intelligence* is often used interchangeably with *competitive intelligence.* While competitive intelligence often deals with the examination of external information regarding competitor strategic and tactical actions, the process of business intelligence can be viewed more generically as including these three steps:

1. Gather information (either internal data sources, external data sources, or both).
2. Analyze (or discern) patterns and trends from that information to gain understanding of what the competitor is doing or planning to do.
3. Make strategic decisions based on the information gained.

One way that firms may gather business intelligence is by use of a web crawler, which browses the Internet in a systematic way, automatically indexing website content.

There are many different settings in which business intelligence is used. Perhaps the best way to explain business intelligence is to consider potential settings where it might be used.

Airlines rely on business intelligence to price their flights.
Matej Kastelic/Shutterstock

- Imagine **Tesla** using business intelligence to determine the cost of a battery at **Rivian** and **Canoo**, two key competitors in the electric vehicle space.
- Imagine **American Airlines** trying to decide how to price its flights from New York La Guardia to Dallas-Fort Worth. It can use business intelligence to track its competitor's prices over different times, days of the week, and so on. It can also use business intelligence to decide the right mix of first-class, business, and economy passengers to maximize revenue. It can also use business intelligence to decide the costs of canceling a flight based on its mix of first-class and economy-class customers.
- Imagine **Morgan Stanley** trying to price an initial public offering of stock for a firm like **AirBNB** or **Doordash**. It can use business intelligence to assess market conditions, assess how other similar firms are performing in the stock market, and assess how initial public offerings have recently performed.
- Imagine **Dunkin' Donuts** using business intelligence to track information about its competitors and where they choose to place the next coffee/donut shop.
- Imagine **Progressive** or other insurance carriers using business intelligence to determine forecast claim amounts and medical coverage costs, and important elements that affect medical coverage for each of its competitors.
- Imagine **GoPro** using business intelligence to track pricing information for various, assorted cameras and video products of its offline and online competitors so that the management can price products appropriately to stay competitive in the market.

Data mining is one technique used to analyze data for business intelligence purposes. Data mining is the process of using sophisticated statistical techniques to extract and analyze data from large databases to discern patterns and trends that were not previously known. Data mining is often used to find patterns in stock prices to assist technical financial stock market analysts, or in commodities or currency trading. Another example of data mining might be analyzing the point-of-sale terminal at **Walmart** to find the following trends:

- Items frequently bought in combination (e.g., cereal and milk; wieners, hot dog buns, ketchup, mustard, and relish; ice cream and cones; cayenne pepper and antacid; turkey and stuffing; chips and pop; diapers and baby food).
- Items frequently included in a large $200-plus grocery bill.
- Items frequently purchased by people making relatively small purchases, with "small" perhaps being defined by a dollar amount (i.e., less than $20) or defined by the fact that the customer used the express check-out counter.[1]

The main caveat about data mining is making sure the results are reasonable (or even plausible). While data mining may find a statistical correlation or relationship between two data items, it may or may not have a plausible relationship in the real world. There is a classic example that ice cream sales are correlated with drownings, suggesting that as ice cream sales increase, the number of drownings also increases. That does not mean that ice cream sales cause drownings or that drownings cause more ice cream sales, but rather that

[1]www.cs.ubc.ca/nest/dbsl/mining.html, accessed July 2010.

warm weather caused both. So it is clear that professional judgment must be used when using data mining techniques.

We must also be careful to communicate clearly (i.e., give or receive information to use appropriate language to describe the relationship) the results of a data mining exercise. For example, if we are describing a correlation, we should use words like *is associated with, is linked to,* or *is related to* to describe the relationship. In contrast, if causation is implied, we could use words like *causes, impacts, affects, enhances,* or *improves.*

PROGRESS CHECK

3. How would **Starbucks** use business intelligence to monitor **Dunkin' Donuts** or other competitors (like **McDonald's**)? What sources would it monitor?
4. How would the concepts behind business intelligence and data mining be used by the Golden State Warriors of the **National Basketball Association** to best compete on the court with the Boston Celtics?

LO 14-3

Describe how digital dashboards allow for continuous tracking of key metrics.

DIGITAL DASHBOARDS

Your car has a dashboard that is easy to read and contains information that is critical to the driver (engine status, engine heat, rpms, speedometer, odometer, fuel levels, etc.). The original automobile dashboard designers carefully considered the most important metrics of the automobile's performance and conveniently put them in the best place for the driver to see. Exhibit 14.3 illustrates an automobile dashboard.

EXHIBIT 14.3
Automobile Dashboard

Just like automobile dashboards, digital dashboards offer timely, critical information to the decision maker.
Sjoerd van der Wal/Getty Images

In accounting information systems (AISs), a **digital dashboard** is designed to track a firm's process or its performance indicators or metrics to monitor critical performance. Examples of the metrics that might be continuously tracked include month-to-date orders, days that receivables are outstanding, budget variances, and days without an accident on the assembly line. While the data on the main dashboard may monitor high-level processes, lower-level data can be quickly accessed by clicking through the links. This high-level summary with the lower-level detail allows executives not only to see the summary, but also to drill down deeper as questions arise.

Specialized dashboards may track overall corporate processes and performance or be specialized by function or department. These dashboards may track building projects, customer relationships, sales and marketing, security, operations, and the like. Exhibit 14.4 presents an example of a digital marketing dashboard that provides an example of how marketers are tracking the performance of their online marketing activities. While digital marketing activities may span multiple marketing channels (including social media and more traditional marketing activities like calls, emails, and subscriptions), this dashboard is designed to be representative of what a digital marketing manager might use to monitor performance on a continuous basis. The metrics displayed are selected to inform a wide audience, which may span from digital marketing specialists to marketing executives, where the marketing efforts stand.

EXHIBIT 14.4
Example of Digital Marketing Dashboard

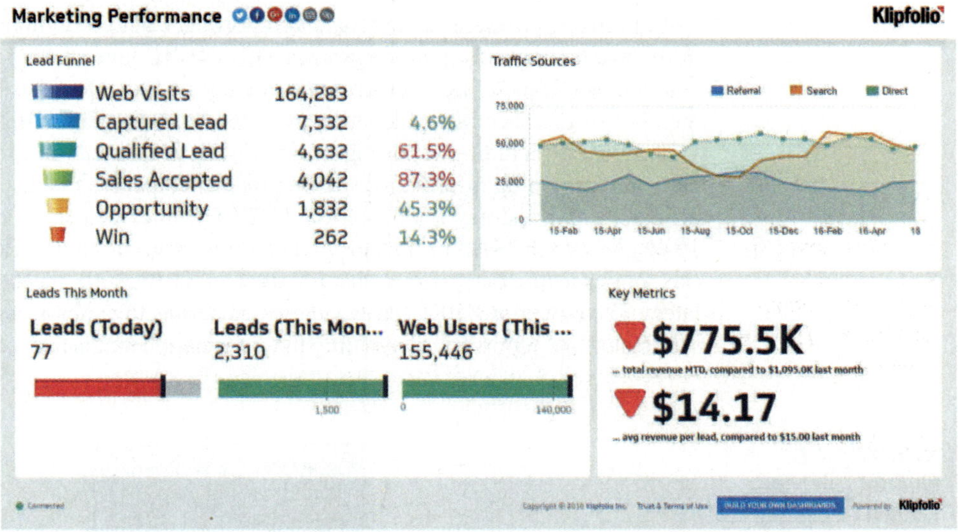

https://www.klipfolio.com/resources/dashboard-examples/marketing/current-performance.

PROGRESS CHECK

5. What business processes could be on a digital dashboard for your business school? As retention of students becomes increasingly important for universities and business schools, what metrics could be displayed to monitor and support retention?
6. Why is a dashboard more useful than a standard report shared periodically?

FINANCIAL REPORTING AND XBRL

LO 14-4

Explain how XBRL works and how it makes business reporting more efficient.

XBRL stands for e**X**tensible **B**usiness **R**eporting **L**anguage and is based on the **XML** language (**Extensible Markup Language**), a standard for Internet communication among businesses. XBRL is specifically designed to electronically communicate business information and is used to facilitate business reporting of financial and nonfinancial data.

One of the advantages of XBRL is that it greatly enhances the speed and accuracy of business reporting. **XBRL International** has developed a taxonomy to describe and tag thousands of financial statement items.

XBRL provides major benefits in the preparation, analysis, and communication of business information. Instead of treating financial information as just a block of text that has to be manually reentered into a computer (or digitized) to give it meaning, XBRL gives each financial statement item (both text and numbers) its own unique tag that is computer readable and searchable. Total assets, for example, has its own unique tag telling the database exactly what it is. Accounts receivable has its own tag, and inventory has yet a third tag.

In February 2009, the U.S. Securities and Exchange Commission (SEC) passed a new rule titled "Interactive Data to Improve Financial Reporting," which required all large domestic and foreign accelerated filers to begin formatting their financial statements using XBRL. The new rule also requires these same public companies to format their financial statements using XBRL on their corporate websites. XBRL US, a division of XBRL International, was chosen to develop a single taxonomy for SEC financial reporting. Details regarding XBRL and the SEC are available at the SEC's XBRL website: http://xbrl.sec.gov/.

Exhibit 14.5 presents how financial reporting would look under XBRL. The data start in the accounting information system (AIS). XBRL tags are then assigned to each financial and nonfinancial item either automatically by the enterprise system or manually by a member of the accounting department or its designee. The XBRL tags are available for various uses, including reporting on the firm's website, filing to regulators (SEC, IRS, etc.), and providing information to other interested parties (such as financial analysts, loan officers, and investors). Each interested XBRL user can either access standard reports (i.e., 10-K going to the SEC or the corporate tax return going to the IRS) or specialized reports (i.e., only specific data) using what is called an XBRL style sheet (discussed in more detail later). The power of XBRL allows interested parties to either access standardized financial statements and reports or access only the information that is needed most for their own use.

EXHIBIT 14.5
Financial and Nonfinancial Reporting Using XBRL: From the Accounting Information System to the End User

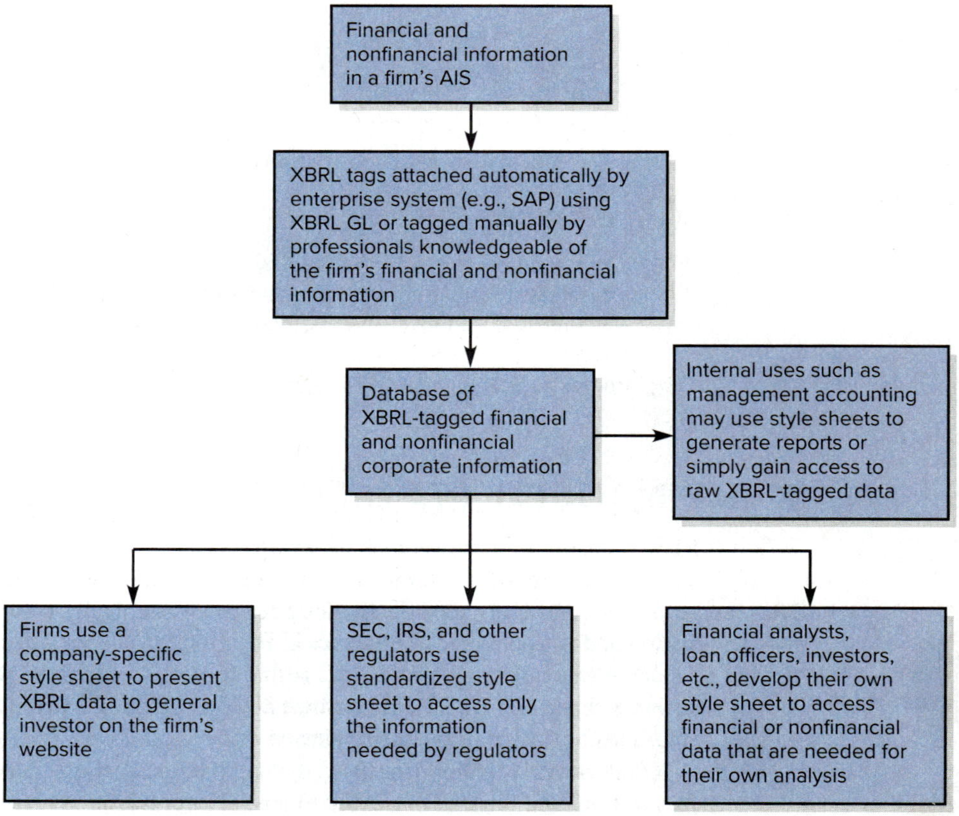

How XBRL Works

In this section, we present a description of how the data go from the AIS to ultimately an XBRL report. Exhibit 14.6 provides a model of how XBRL works.

EXHIBIT 14.6
How XBRL Works

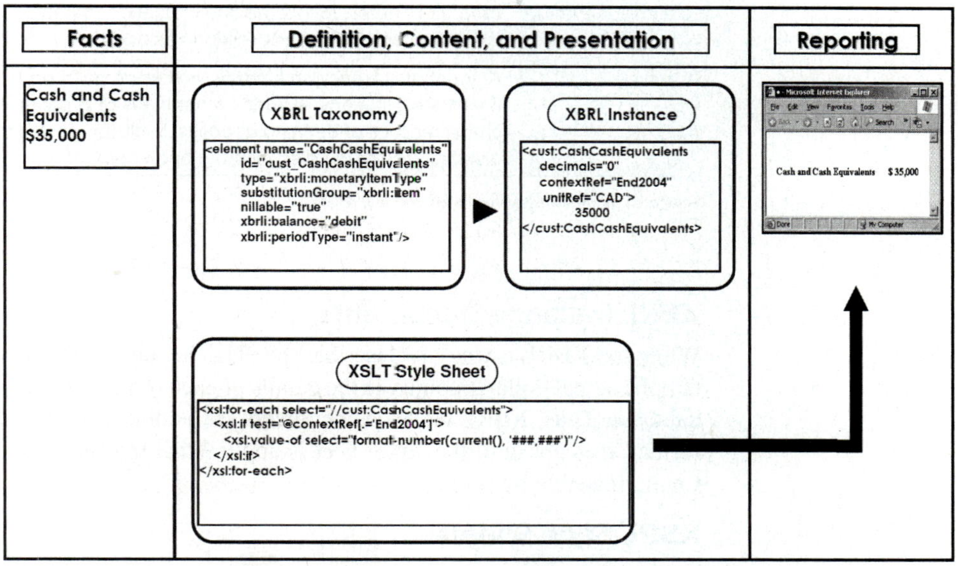

Source: David Nichtman, "Interactive Data: The Impact on Assurance," Assurance Working Group of XBRL International, XBRL, published November 2006. https://www.xbrl.org/, accessed May 23, 2016.

The **XBRL specification** (currently version 2.1) outlines the technical framework for XBRL. It provides the underlying technical details of what XBRL is and how it works.

XBRL Taxonomy and Tags

The **XBRL taxonomy** defines and describes each key data element (total assets, accounts, payable, net income, etc.). Because each national jurisdiction may have different accounting rules and regulations, each country may have its own taxonomy for financial reporting. That is why there are different taxonomies for each country: XBRL–Australia, XBRL–Canada, XBRL–Germany, XBRL–IASB, XBRL–Japan, XBRL–Netherlands, and XBRL–UK.

Taxonomies continue to be developed to enable filings to regulators (such as banks), tax authorities (such as the IRS), and other governmental entities. For example, U.S. banks are required to submit their quarterly report "Report of Condition and Income" or their Call Report to the Federal Deposit Insurance Corporation (FDIC) using XBRL. The Federal Financial Institutions Examination Council (FFIEC) is responsible for creating XBRL Call Report taxonomy to facilitate filing call reports.

You can think of the XBRL tags for U.S. GAAP as just a big chart of accounts that companies use to tag all of their accounts (or line items or major categories of accounts). The number of potential tags is huge, with the 2022 XBRL taxonomy containing around 17,000 tags! A listing of the tags can be viewed at https://fasb.org/Page/PageContent?PageId=/xbrl/2022financial.html.

Exhibit 14.7 provides an example of some sample tags.

EXHIBIT 14.7
A Description of XBRL Elements (Tag Names)

XBRL Element (Tag Names)	Description of Element (Tag Names)
PrepaidRent	Amount of asset related to consideration paid in advance for rent that provides economic benefits within a future period of one year or the normal operating cycle, if longer.
NetIncomeLoss	The portion of profit or loss for the period, net of income taxes, which is attributable to the parent.
DeferredRevenue	Amount of deferred income and obligation to transfer product and service to customer for which consideration has been received or is receivable.
Cash	Amount of currency on hand as well as demand deposits with banks or financial institutions. Includes other kinds of accounts that have the general characteristics of demand deposits. Excludes cash and cash equivalents within disposal group and discontinued operation.

Source: xbrlview.fasb.org, accessed February 2019.

XBRL Instance Documents

While the XBRL taxonomy describes the data elements, **XBRL instance documents** contain the actual dollar amounts or the details of each of the elements within the firm's XBRL database. Thus, XBRL instance documents are a collection of data in a computer-readable format. It is not until the style sheet is applied that the financial statement information is finally readable by people.

XBRL Style Sheets

XBRL style sheets take the instance documents and add presentation elements to make them readable by people. The data may be presented in a number of formats, including HTML, PDF, Microsoft Word, and Microsoft Excel (among others). The style sheet is made in conformance with a standardized language called Extensible Stylesheet Language (XSL). The official XSL specification for the XSL language is XSLT. This language is not governed by XBRL but is a standard means for taking data from XBRL or XML and presenting computer readable data in a way that is readable to humans. As discussed in Exhibit 14.6, different users will have different style sheets to access the exact data they are interested in. While the SEC may be interested in a standardized style sheet to retrieve a standardized report, a bank loan officer or financial analyst may be interested in developing his or her own to facilitate analysis.

Using XBRL Tags to Display Financial Statements

Calcbench is an example of an aggregator that uses XBRL tags to report its financial statements. Exhibit 14.8 shows an example of the specific XBRL tags (see red highlight box for XBRL tags) used in reporting the income statement for Alphabet (Google). As shown in this income statement, specific line items of Alphabet's financial statement are called out, including European Commission fines and basic net income and diluted net income per share. Each of these line items can be effortlessly retrieved for whatever time period using XBRL's functionality within Calcbench.

XBRL Assurance

Before the SEC mandated XBRL submissions, **assurance** on any voluntary XBRL filings generally followed guidance from the Public Company Accounting Oversight Board (PCAOB), which relied on the auditor comparing a paper output of the XBRL-related

EXHIBIT 14.8
Google Financial Statements Using XBRL Tags

Exported from Calcbench: 10/19/2022 4:41:11 PM - Numbers in 1000000's				
Alphabet Inc. (GOOG)				
CONSOLIDATED STATEMENTS OF INCOME				
Fiscal Period		Y 2021	Y 2020	Y 2019
Period Start		1/1/2021	1/1/2020	1/1/2019
Period End		12/31/2021	12/31/2020	12/31/2019
		10-K	10-K	10-K
Revenues	Revenues	$257,637	$182,527	$161,857
Costs and expenses:	CostsAndExpensesAbstract			
Cost of revenues	CostOfRevenue	$110,939	$84,732	$71,896
Research and development	ResearchAndDevelopmentExpense	$31,562	$27,573	$26,018
Sales and marketing	SellingAndMarketingExpense	$22,912	$17,946	$18,464
General and administrative	GeneralAndAdministrativeExpense	$13,510	$11,052	$9,551
European Commission fines	LossContingencyLossInPeriod	$0	$0	$1,697
Total costs and expenses	CostsAndExpenses	$178,923	$141,303	$127,626
Income from operations	OperatingIncomeLoss	$78,714	$41,224	$34,231
Other income (expense), net	NonoperatingIncomeExpense	$12,020	$6,858	$5,394
Total	IncomeLossFromContinuingOperationsBeforeIncomeTaxesExtraordinaryItemsNoncontrollingInterest	$90,734	$48,082	$39,625
Provision for income taxes	IncomeTaxExpenseBenefit	$14,701	$7,813	$5,282
Net income	NetIncomeLoss	$76,033	$40,269	$34,343
Basic net income per share (in dollars per share)	EarningsPerShareBasic	$113.88	$59.15	$49.59
Diluted net income per share (in dollars per share)	EarningsPerShareDiluted	$112.20	$58.61	$49.16

Calcbench

documents to the information in the official EDGAR (Electronic Data Gathering, Analysis and Retrieval) filing to note any possible differences. Now that the use of XBRL is mandated by the SEC, assuring those XBRL documents is not required. It is expected that investors and other financial statement users will ultimately demand some assurance from an auditor or external party on a firm's use of XBRL.

There is no clear way to predict the future, but we can predict that the assurance afforded to XBRL will be quite different from the common external auditor's report on the auditee's financial statements and more than just matching a paper copy of the financial statements to the output of XBRL reports. However, we do believe that XBRL assurance will include assurance that

1. The most current, standardized XBRL taxonomy is used.
2. The underlying financial and nonfinancial data that are used in XBRL tagging are reliable.
3. The XBRL tagging is accurate and complete.
4. The reports generated using XBRL are complete and received on a timely basis.

XBRL allows highly disaggregated data, so not only is it possible to know the level of sales, but it is possible to know sales revenue in much more detail. For example, it is possible for firms to apply XBRL tagging to sales by state or by country, by product line, by store or by office, and so on. While the extent of disaggregated data that a company will provide is still in question, the possibility allows opportunities for firms to provide this potentially helpful data to external parties. As firms begin to use XBRL to disclose disaggregated data, assurance will be needed on items that have never before been disclosed to investors. It will be especially critical for these items to receive assurance as mentioned under item 2 to ensure that the underlying financial and nonfinancial data used in XBRL tagging are reliable.

XBRL GL

Thus far, we have focused on XBRL for external financial reporting. That type of XBRL is meant to facilitate efficient communication between firms and external parties (e.g., shareholders, regulatory bodies like the SEC and IRS, and the like). In contrast, **XBRL GL** (also known as **XBRL Global Ledger Taxonomy**) serves as a means to facilitate efficient communication *within a firm.* XBRL GL allows the representation of anything that is found in a chart of accounts, journal entries, or historical transactions—financial and nonfinancial. The ability to tag using XBRL is generally supported by enterprise systems (ERPs) such as **SAP**, **Oracle**, and **Workday**.

According to XBRL International, the advantages of XBRL GL include the following:

- XBRL Global Ledger is *reporting independent.* It collects general ledger and after-the-fact receivables, payables, inventory, and other nonfinancial facts and then permits the representation of that information using traditional summaries and through flexible links to XBRL for reporting.
- XBRL Global Ledger is *system independent.* Any developer can create import and export routines to convert information to XBRL GL format. This means that accounting software developers need only consider one design for their XML import/export file formats. Application service providers can offer to supply XBRL import and output so end users can more easily use their own data. Companies developing operational products, such as point-of-sale systems or job costing, or reporting tools can link with many accounting products without needing specialized links to each one.
- XBRL Global Ledger permits *consolidation.* Popular low-end products and mid-market solutions are not designed to facilitate consolidating data from multiple organizations. XBRL GL can help transfer the general ledger from one system to another, be used to combine the operations of multiple organizations, or bring data into tools that will do the consolidation.
- XBRL Global Ledger provides *flexibility,* overcoming the limitations of other approaches such as electronic data interchange (EDI). It offers an *extensible, flexible, multinational solution* that can exchange the data required by internal finance, accountants, and creditors.[2]

PROGRESS CHECK

7. Using Exhibit 14.6 as a guide, how will XBRL GL facilitate the process of tagging the data that are generated by the firm's AIS?
8. What is the XBRL tag for Research and Development Expense (see Exhibit 14.8)? And the XBRL tag for Diluted Earnings per Share?

Summary

- Data warehouses serve as a repository of information that is separate from the operating databases of the firm. Data warehouses include data from a number of operational (internal) and external sources that will be helpful in providing information supportive for decision making across a number of functions in the firm. Data marts represent a slice of data from the data warehouse to meet a specific need.
- Business intelligence uses computer-based techniques to accumulate and analyze data that might be helpful to the firm's strategic initiatives.
- Digital dashboards track critical firm performance in a way that is easily accessible to executives.
- XBRL serves as a means to electronically communicate business information to facilitate business reporting of financial and nonfinancial data to users. XBRL greatly enhances the speed and accuracy of business reporting.

[2]Source: www.xbrl.org/GLTaxonomy/, accessed July 20, 2010, used with permission.

Key Words

assurance (*480*) Independent, professional opinions that reduce the risk of having incorrect information.

business intelligence (*474*) A computer-based technique for accumulating and analyzing data from databases and data warehouses to support managerial decision making.

data lake (*472*) A repository for a large amount of both structured and unstructured data (internal and external) to be integrated for reporting and data analysis.

data mart (*473*) A subset of the information from the data warehouse to serve a specific purpose.

data mining (*475*) A process of using sophisticated statistical techniques to extract and analyze data from large databases to discern patterns and trends that were not previously known.

data warehouse (*472*) A collection of information gathered from an assortment of external and operational (i.e., internal) databases to facilitate reporting for decision making and business analysis.

decision support system (DSS) (*474*) A computer-based information system that facilitates business decision-making activities.

digital dashboard (*476*) A display to track the firm's process or performance indicators or metrics to monitor critical performance.

distributed computing (*472*) The storage of data across multiple databases, allowing greater storage of data and increased speed of analysis.

Online Analytical Processing (OLAP) (*472*) A means of processing transactional and structured data, even when the data originate from disparate databases or external databases. OLAP tools are often used to access data stored in a data warehouse.

XBRL (eXtensible Business Reporting Language) (*477*) An open, global standard for exchanging financial reporting information.

XBRL Global Ledger Taxonomy (XBRL GL) (*481*) Serves as a ledger using the XBRL standard for internal purposes.

XBRL instance document (*480*) A document containing XBRL elements.

XBRL specification (*479*) Provides the underlying technical details of what XBRL is and how it works.

XBRL style sheet (*480*) Adds presentation elements to XBRL instance documents to make them readable by people.

XBRL taxonomy (*479*) Defines and describes each key data element (e.g., total assets, accounts payable, net income, etc.).

XML (Extensible Markup Language) (*477*) Open, global standard for exchanging information in a format that is both human- and machine-readable.

ANSWERS TO PROGRESS CHECKS

1. Specific functions in a firm, such as marketing, often do not need the whole data warehouse but would prefer a data mart that most closely addresses their needs. **Apple** may be interested in the demographics of the customer segment that purchases iPhones and iPads to best identify those most likely to buy an Apple Watch or other Apple innovation.
2. To answer this question, we'll use Exhibit 14.2 as a guide. Among other things, **Best Buy** would be interested in general ledger, inventory, sales, and cost information from its internal databases. The company would also be interested in data from the retail industry, specifically from the retail segment that includes consumer electronics, personal computers and entertainment software, gaming, and appliances. General economic information and focal customer demographics would all be useful.

3. **Starbucks** could use business intelligence to monitor websites, news articles, court filings, and the like for **Dunkin' Donuts'** prices, the locations for potential stores, and proposed new products.
4. Business (perhaps better termed as "competitive") intelligence and data mining could be used in the **NBA** to see which defenses work best, who to foul at the end of the game, who would usually take the end-of-the-game shot, who to cover and when to play tight defense at the three-point line, and so on. This would be particularly helpful in a playoff series of five to seven games, where the team plays its competitor in successive games.
5. A business school might use a digital dashboard to track its performance. Many items might be tracked, but if the business school is particularly interested in retention, it might be interested in
   a. Number of students enrolled each semester and number of students returning from previous semesters.
   b. Grades of students dropping out (are they dropping out due to poor performance or for other reasons?).
   c. Student loans of students dropping out (are they experiencing financial trouble, etc.?).
   d. Job placement rates in each major (are students getting jobs when they graduate?).
6. A dashboard is used to monitor, and display, in a user-friendly way, the critical business processes that most affect firm performance. Standard reports may always be used but may not be as accessible as a digital dashboard.
7. XBRL GL will automatically tag the various financial and nonfinancial elements in the enterprise system software. This makes this step of tagging trivial for the firm to perform.
8. The appropriate XBRL tag for Research and Development Expenditures is ResearchAndDevelopmentExpense (no spaces) and EarningsperShareDiluted as shown in Exhibit 14.8.

Multiple Choice Questions connect

1. **(LO 14-1)** A subset of a data warehouse is called a
   a. small data warehouse.
   b. data mart.
   c. data martian.
   d. business intelligence.
2. **(LO 14-1)** A data lake may include
   a. an XBRL style sheet.
   b. process diagrams.
   c. a digital dashboard.
   d. both structured and unstructured data.
3. **(LO 14-2)** **American Airlines** may use business intelligence to
   a. track the cost of snacks on its airplanes.
   b. monitor the cost of its pilots and flight attendants.
   c. track the cost of its airplane fuel.
   d. monitor prices on competitive routes.
   e. All of these options.
4. **(LO 14-2)** The computer-based technique to accumulate and analyze data to learn about a competitor is called
   a. business intelligence.
   b. data warehouse.
   c. digital dashboard.
   d. XBRL.

5. **(LO 14-2)** The steps in business intelligence include
    a. analyze data for patterns, gather information, make decision.
    b. create data warehouse, query data warehouse, make decision.
    c. query data warehouse, create data warehouse, make decision.
    d. gather information, analyze data for patterns, make decision.
6. **(LO 14-3)** A digital dashboard tracks, in a user-friendly way:
    a. automobile speed.
    b. critical business failures.
    c. critical business processes.
    d. critical business markets.
7. **(LO 14-4)** XBRL facilitates business reporting of
    a. business processes.
    b. the XML language.
    c. financial and nonfinancial information.
    d. only financial information.
8. **(LO 14-4)** The first person to propose using XML as a means to electronically deliver financial information was
    a. Albert Gore.
    b. Charles Hoffman.
    c. Robert Byrd.
    d. Herb Hackett.
9. **(LO 14-4)** XBRL GL, or XBRL Global Ledger Taxonomy, is different from XBRL U.S. GAAP because it facilitates
    a. efficient communication between the firm and external parties.
    b. efficient communication within a firm.
    c. efficient communication with the supply chain.
    d. efficient communication with customers.
10. **(LO 14-4)** The stated advantages of XBRL GL do not include
    a. reporting independence.
    b. system independence.
    c. scalability.
    d. flexibility.
11. **(LO 14-3)** What is the mechanism called that firms may use to track their marketing efforts?
    a. XBRL
    b. Business intelligence
    c. Data analytics
    d. Digital dashboard
12. **(LO 14-4)** XBRL assurance might include all but which of the following?
    a. The most current, standardized XBRL taxonomy is used.
    b. The XBRL tagging is accurate and complete.
    c. The reports generated using XBRL are complete and received on a timely basis.
    d. The XBRL tagging is useful to investors.
13. **(LO 14-4)** The XBRL style sheet is made in conformance with which standardized language?
    a. XML
    b. XSL
    c. XBRL GL
    d. XL

14. **(LO 14-4)** Which body mandated that operating firms in its jurisdiction submit their financial reports using XBRL?
    a. FASB
    b. GASB
    c. SEC
    d. NYSE
15. **(LO 14-2)** Which technique or tool is used to analyze data for business intelligence purposes?
    a. Data mining
    b. Decision support systems
    c. Data marts
    d. Big Data

Discussion Questions connect

1. **(LO 14-1)** Using Exhibit 14.2 as a guide, name three internal and three external databases that you think should be included in a data warehouse for **Bank of America, Wells Fargo,** or your local bank. Support your answer.
2. **(LO 14-1)** Using Exhibit 14.2 as a guide, name three internal and three external databases that you think should be included in a data warehouse for your university. Support your answer.
3. **(LO 14-3)** Name five items that you think would be included in a digital dashboard for **ESPN** or for **Disney.** Why are these critical business processes for that company?
4. **(LO 14-4)** Who will rely on XBRL data for decision making? Why is assurance needed on XBRL data? Support your answer.
5. **(LO 14-4)** Why is there a different XBRL taxonomy for each country, including XBRL-Australia, XBRL-Canada, XBRL-Germany, XBRL-Japan, XBRL-Netherlands, XBRL-US, and XBRL-UK? What would happen if there was only one XBRL taxonomy for all countries?
6. **(LO 14-4)** How would the XBRL style sheets be different for financial analysts as compared to the Securities and Exchange Commission? How would XBRL style sheets be different for a firm's website as compared to bank loan officers?
7. **(LO 14-4)** Why is XBRL needed in the financial community? In your opinion, why did the Securities and Exchange Commission mandate its usage? What does it provide that was not available before XBRL?
8. **(LO 14-4)** Why would XBRL be used for internal uses such as management accounting? (*Hint*: See Exhibit 14.5.)
9. **(LO 14-1)** Why do companies need both internal and external databases in a data warehouse?
10. **(LO 14-3)** How is a digital dashboard different from a financial report?

Problems connect

1. **(LO 14-1)** Using Exhibits 14.1 and 14.2 as guides, name four internal and four external databases that you think should be included in a data warehouse for the marketing function of **Procter & Gamble** (or the consumer packaged goods company with which you are most familiar). Procter & Gamble has products like Gillette razors, Charmin tissue, and Head and Shoulders shampoo. Why are these eight databases you recommend critical to the effective functioning of the marketing department to sell more products? Support your answer.

2. **(LO 14-4)** Which of the four predicted assurance needs do you believe is most critical to ensuring XBRL accuracy? Support your answer.
3. **(LO 14-4)** XBRL allows disaggregated data to be presented to interested external parties. Financial analysts often forecast earnings many years ahead and then suggest whether an investor should buy, sell, or hold a stock. Which type of disaggregated data do you think financial analysts would be most interested in receiving when predicting 1-year-ahead earnings: detailed sales data, detailed expense data, detailed asset data, and/or detailed liability data? Support your answer. In your opinion, which disaggregated XBRL data would be most useful information in predicting whether an investor should buy, sell, or hold a stock?
4. **(LO 14-2)** The effectiveness of data mining has been criticized by the *Wall Street Journal*. In one article, the author notes that academic studies have shown that by using data mining, analysts could accurately predict changes in the stock market based on either the population of sheep in Bangladesh, the number of 9-year-olds at a given time, or whether it is smoggy on a given day.[3] While the statistical correlation may be valid, there must be a logical reason that a particular factor will predict stock returns.

   Required:

   a. Do you think these findings represent valid relationships or spurious correlations?

   b. What measures do you think might be valid predictors of stock market returns?
5. **(LO 14-4)** XBRL touts as its primary advantage that it will increase efficiency for the firm and those interested in its business reports.

   Required:

   a. How is XBRL more efficient for the firm that reports its business performance? Does the use of XBRL GL in a firm's accounting software make XBRL more or less efficient than when XBRL GL is not used?

   b. How is XBRL more efficient for those using its business reports for regulator, investing, or other purposes?

   c. Are there any cases when it is less efficient to use XBRL?
6. **(LO 14-2)** How would **Coca-Cola** use business intelligence to monitor **Pepsi Cola**'s operations in Argentina? What sources of data need to be gathered? How would they be analyzed?
7. There are four stated advantages of XBRL GL: reporting independence, system independence, consolidation, and flexibility. Match the advantage with the characteristic of XBRL GL.

1. XBRL GL offers an extensible, multinational solution that can exchange the data required by internal finance, accountants, and creditors.	A. Reporting independence
2. Any developer can create import and export routines to convert information from any system to XBRL GL format.	B. System independence
3. Permits the representation of information using traditional summaries and through flexible links.	C. Consolidation
4. XBRL GL can be used to combine the operations of multiple organizations.	D. Flexibility

8. **(LO 14-4)** Match the description of these XBRL terms with their descriptions.

1. A document containing XBRL elements.	A. XBRL instance document
2. Adds presentation elements to XBRL instance documents to make them more readable to people.	B. XBRL specification
3. Defines and describes each key data element (e.g., total assets, accounts payable, and net income).	C. XBRL style sheet
4. Provides the underlying technical details of what XBRL is and how it works.	D. XBRL taxonomy

[3]http://online.wsj.com/article/SB124967937642715417.html, accessed May 2016.

9. **(LO 14-1, LO 14-2)** Match the description with these business process terms.

1. A subset of the information from the data warehouse to serve a specific purpose.
2. A computer-based information system that facilitates business decision-making activities.
3. A collection of information gathered from an assortment of external and operational (i.e, internal) databases to facilitate reporting for decision making and business analysis.
4. A computer-based technique for accumulating and analyzing data from databases and data warehouses to support managerial decision making.

A. Business intelligence
B. Data mart
C. Data warehouse
D. Decision support system (DSS)

10. **(LO 14-3)** The following exhibit represents a digital cockpit (or dashboard) for Advanced Environmental Recycling Technologies.

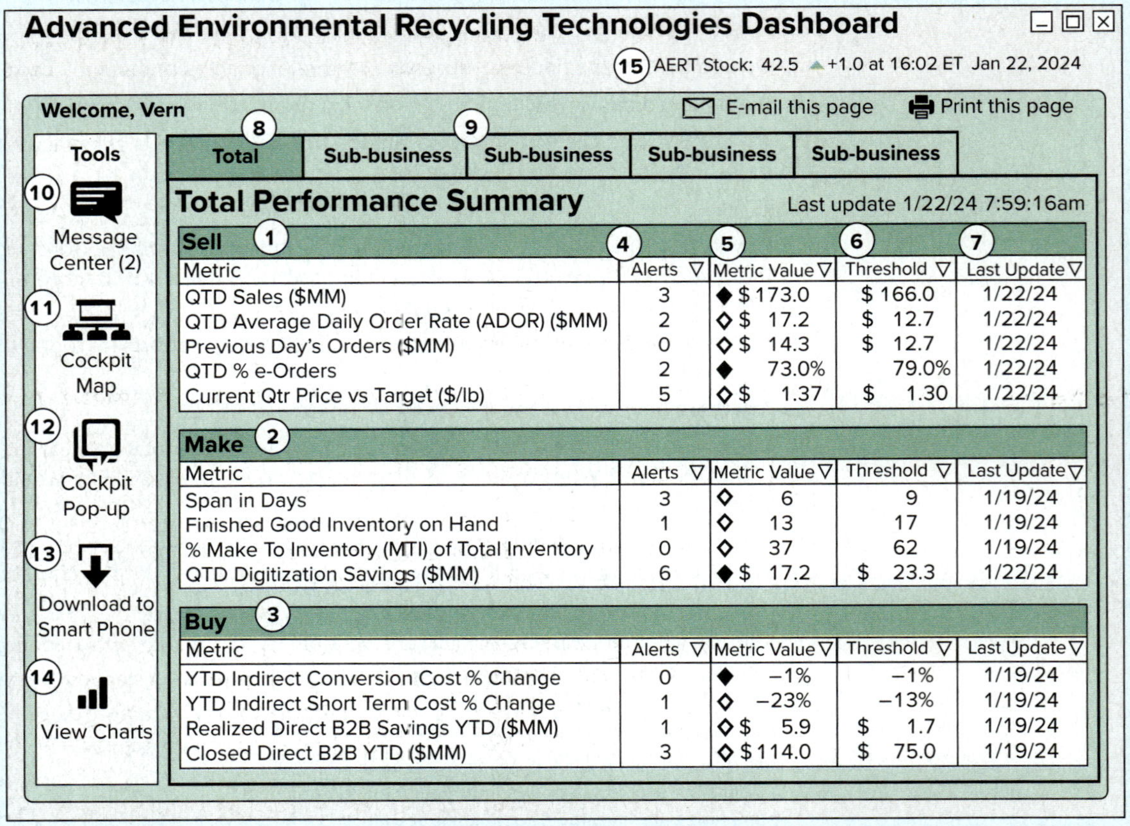

Source: Based on http://www.ge.com/annual01/letter/cockpit/.

The cockpit has 15 items highlighted. Identify which numbered item tracks or shows the following data:

a. The sales of Advanced Environmental Recycling Technologies
b. The detail of the sub-business
c. The previous day's orders
d. The current AERT stock price
e. The column reporting the most recent update
f. The "alerts" that need to be investigated further

g. The column reporting the current performance

h. The conversion cost percentage

11. **(LO 14-2)** Data mining is the process of using sophisticated statistical techniques to extract and analyze data from large databases to discern patterns and trends that were not previously known. The patterns we find are correlations, but not necessarily causation.

Every time we see a link between the occurrence of one event or action with another, we generally assume that one event or action caused the other. But simply linking one occurrence with another does not always prove that the result has been caused by the other.

For example, such data mining might suggest the following relationship between arcade revenue and computer science doctorates awarded in the United States, with a correlation of 0.985.

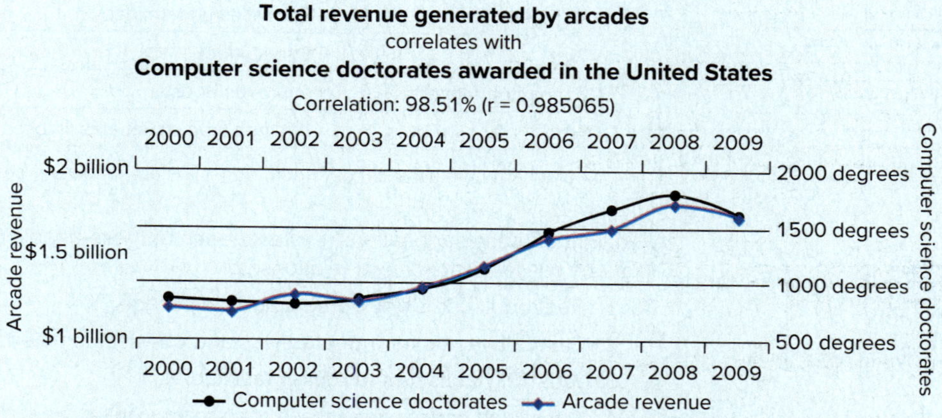

Data sources: U.S. Census Bureau and National Science Foundation (accessed at https://tylervigen.com/spurious-correlations February 2023).

a. Is this simply a correlation? Or is there a possibility that computer science doctorates affect total revenue generated by arcades or vice versa? Explain your answer.

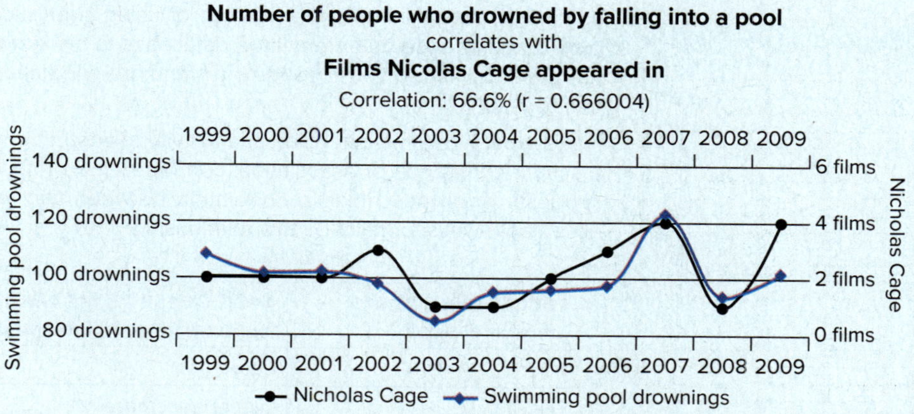

Data sources: U.S. Census Bureau and National Science Foundation (accessed at https://tylervigen.com/spurious-correlations February 2023).

b. Is this simply a correlation? Or is there a possibility that the number of people who drowned was affected by the films Nicolas Cage appeared in? Explain your answer.

12. **(LO 14-2)** Data mining is the process of using sophisticated statistical techniques to extract and analyze data from large databases to discern patterns and trends that were

not previously known. The patterns we find are correlations, but we do not necessarily find causation.

Newspaper headlines often link one activity to another and imply causation, rather than a simple correlation or association. Jon Mueller, a professor at North Central College, suggests that when describing a correlation between two variables, there are some acceptable ways to describe this relationship.

ACCEPTABLE TERMS for Correlations	AVOID THESE TERMS When Discussing Correlations (but they are acceptable when asserting causation)
Get	Cause
Have	Increase/decrease
Linked	Benefits
More	Impacts
More/less, less	Enhances/undermines
Tied	Effect/affect
Connected/related	Improves/boosts
Tend	If → then type statements (implies one-direction)

Source: http://jfmueller.faculty.noctrl.edu/100/correlation_or_causation.htm.

In light of these suggestions, evaluate each of these headlines as to whether they suggest a causal or noncausal relationship:

1. Facebook users get worse grades in college
2. Link between over-indebtedness and obesity identified
3. Kids' TV habits tied to poorer test scores
4. Recession causes increase in teen dating violence
5. Snooze or lose: Memory retention enhanced by sleep
6. Soda causes obesity, researchers assert
7. Disciplinarian parents have fat kids
8. Social isolation may have a negative effect on intellectual abilities

13. **(LO 14-2)** Data mining is the process of using sophisticated statistical techniques to extract and analyze data from large databases to discern patterns and trends that were not previously known. The patterns we find are correlations, but we do not necessarily find causation.

Newspaper headlines often link one activity to another and imply causation, rather than a simple correlation or association. Jon Mueller, a professor at North Central College, suggests when describing a correlation between two variables that there are some acceptable ways to describe this relationship.

ACCEPTABLE TERMS for Correlations	AVOID THESE TERMS When Discussing Correlation (but they are acceptable when asserting causation)
Get	Cause
Have	Increase/decrease
Linked	Benefits
More	Impacts
More/less, less	Enhances/undermines
Tied	Effect/affect
Connected/related	Improves/boosts
Tend	If → then type statements (implies one-direction)

In light of these suggestions, evaluate each of these headlines as to whether they suggest a causal or noncausal relationship:

1. Obese girls less likely to attend college, research shows
2. Migraine often associated with psychiatric disorders
3. Your parents are correct, scholars report: Studying pays off
4. Tooth loss in elderly linked to mental impairment
5. Eating fatty fish lowers risk of dementia
6. Political bias affects brain activity, study finds
7. Child anxiety linked to ecstasy use

14. **(LO 14-4)** Consider each of the following statements and state whether they are true or false:

    1. XBRL allows tagging of highly disaggregated data.
    2. XBRL GL allows the representation of anything that is found in a chart of accounts, journal entries, or historical transactions—financial and nonfinancial.
    3. XBRL style sheets take the instance documents and add presentation elements to make them readable.
    4. XBRL stands for **eXtensible Base Reporting Language**.
    5. XBRL instance documents contain the actual dollar amounts or the details of each account.
    6. XBRL for U.S. GAAP has approximately 2,000 element labels or tags.
    7. Assurance of XBRL is required by the Securities and Exchange Commission.
    8. XBRL GL serves as a ledger using the XBRL standard for internal purposes.
    9. XBRL GL does not allow consolidation of the financials of multiple organizations.
    10. There is a specific XBRL style sheet required by financial analysts.

15. **(LO 14-4)** Find the XBRL element (tag) name and description for Cost of Goods and Services Sold and Dividends in the 2022 XBRL taxonomy using the Search Command.

    Steps:

    1. Open a web browser, and go to xbrlview.fasb.org.
    2. Click the+ next to US GAAP (2022), highlight "All (Main/Entire)" and click "Open".
    3. Find the **Search** window at the bottom of the screen to search for "Cost of Goods and Services Sold" and "Dividends," and select the appropriate XBRL element/account name.
    4. Copy the documentation, or definition of the selected XBRL account.

16. **(LO 14-4)** Find the XBRL element (tag) name and description for Current Liabilities and Cash in the 2022 XBRL taxonomy using the Search Command.

    Steps:

    1. Open a web browser, and go to xbrlview.fasb.org.
    2. Click the + next to US GAAP (2022), highlight "All (Main/Entire)" and click "Open".
    3. Find the **Search** window at the bottom of the screen to search for "Current Liabilities" and "Cash," and select the appropriate XBRL element/account name.
    4. Copy the documentation or definition of the selected XBRL account.

Chapter Fifteen

Emerging Technologies: Blockchain and AI Automation

A Look at This Chapter

Blockchain and artificial intelligence are important emerging topics in information systems and accounting. This chapter provides an overview of those topics, recognizing that each topic could be an entire course. Because this is an overview, we focus on the general concepts important for understanding the topics.

A Look Back

Chapter 14 provided a description of how AIS facilitates management reporting, including using data warehouses, business intelligence, and dashboards. In addition, we also explained the development of eXtensible Business Reporting Language (XBRL) in electronic financial reporting.

A Look Ahead

As managers of information systems and business partners, accountants are often involved in formulating and implementing company strategies. Chapter 16 explains how the Balanced Scorecard might be used to formulate, implement, and monitor strategic performances on information technology and information systems.

Westend61/Getty Images

Do you know that **HSBC**, one of the largest bank institutions, settled $250 billion of transactions in 2018 using blockchain technology? In that calendar year, this amounted to more than 3 million blockchain-based foreign exchange transactions. The company used "FX everywhere" to process 150,000 payments since the platform's launch in February 2018. To most people, this comes as astonishing news. Blockchain is not just a buzzword or hype that surrounds the business world; it has already happened and is heavily used by HSBC and many other institutions.

HSBC is just one of many organizations that has adopted blockchain technology in their business operations. A consortium led by R3, a company applying the blockchain technology to the financial industry, has assembled more than 300 institutions across different industries to develop a **distributed ledger** technology suitable for all areas of business. This will enable institutions to transact using smart contract and ensure privacy and security. R3's Corda platform is being used in such wide-ranging industries as financial services, insurance, health care, and shipping.

Hyperledger project is an open source project to develop cross-industry distributed ledger blockchain technology. **IBM** has successfully deployed the Hyperledger technology to many clients across many industries such as public health, supply chain, asset registration, fraud prevention and compliance, payment solutions, insurance, and food.

CHAPTER OUTLINE

Blockchain
- *A Brief History of Blockchain*
- *What Is Blockchain?*
- *When Is Blockchain Useful?*
- *How Does Blockchain Work?*
- *Popular Cryptocurrency Applications*
- *Types of Blockchain*
- *Platforms Using Blockchain Technology*

Blockchain Applications
- *Blockchain Use Cases*
- *Current Challenges with Adopting Blockchain Technology*
- *The Impact of Blockchain on Audit and Assurance*
- *Getting Started with Blockchain*

Artificial Intelligence
- *Introduction to Artificial Intelligence*
- *Assessing Performance*

AI Applications Important to Accounting
- *Natural Language Processing*
- *Robotic Process Automation*

LEARNING OBJECTIVES

After reading this chapter, you should be able to:

- **15-1** Describe the history of blockchain technology.
- **15-2** Understand the emergent blockchain technology and its benefits.
- **15-3** Differentiate between the blockchain applications Bitcoin and Ethereum.
- **15-4** Describe public blockchain, private blockchain, and consortium blockchain.
- **15-5** Discuss blockchain use cases.
- **15-6** Explain the potential impact of blockchain on audit and assurance.
- **15-7** Define artificial intelligence.
- **15-8** Understand the differences among artificial intelligence, machine learning, and deep learning.
- **15-9** Appreciate the structure of neural networks.
- **15-10** Describe the types of learning.
- **15-11** Assess model performance.
- **15-12** Recognize applications of AI in accounting.

LO 15-1

Describe the history of blockchain technology.

BLOCKCHAIN

A Brief History of Blockchain

In traditional business, we rely on intermediaries as the trusted parties to ensure that transactions can occur as described in the business processes. The intermediaries take some time to validate the accuracies of the transactions, but they also charge a proportional fee for each business transaction. These validation processes usually take time depending on the type of business transactions.

For example, an international wire transfer in the financial industry usually takes a few days before the receiver can actually use the wired money. The relevant banks need to make sure that the bank accounts provided are valid, ensure there are sufficient funds in the sender's account, determine the currency exchange rate on the date of the transfer, and so on. For real estate transactions, escrow companies take even longer to verify these processes. They must put together the deed, lien, tax, and mortgage documents, while ensuring compliance with all the related regulations in order to close the transaction. In these types of business transactions, banks and escrow companies are the intermediaries. They take time to verify that business transactions can occur without any errors. For these services, a fee is usually charged for every transaction, which could total a significant sum. These fees are justified by the fact that the information required to complete the deal is often scattered throughout several different organizations. This necessitates additional time and effort to pull together the related information.

Intermediaries and middlemen were needed to perform these types of business transactions. This was until Satoshi Nakamoto published a white paper in 2008 titled "Bitcoin: A Peer-to-Peer Electronic Cash System,"[1] which introduced a concept for a new type of technology. In 2009, Nakamoto used a distributed ledger system through resource intensive mining to eliminate the need for intermediaries in trustless, online, peer-to-peer digital currency transactions. This paper proved that peer-to-peer transactions can be accomplished anonymously and safely together with the public history transactions in the bitcoin network. The internal data structure of transactions in this system is packaged in blocks and chained together, thus, this technology eventually became popularized as **blockchain**. With this underlying blockchain technology, **Bitcoin** completely eliminated middlemen to achieve the peer-to-peer transactions. Because there are no middleman involved, the time it takes for the whole transaction to complete is 10 minutes. The first known bitcoin transaction was made in 2010 to use 10,000 bitcoins to purchase a $25 pizza.

Initially, due to the nature of the Bitcoin platform—with no regulation, open participation in the network, and anonymous transactions—Bitcoin was not attractive to corporations. In 2014, blockchain 2.0 emerged as a more robust and sophisticated technology to pull together logic and business rules into contracts represented in code called "smart contracts" through **Ethereum**. Rather than hard coding a fixed business rule in Bitcoin to transfer only digital currency or tokens as specified in Nakamoto's paper, "smart contracts" are programmable in Ethereum. This flexibility drew the attention of corporations and government agencies. Since then, blockchain technology has become a hot topic in many industries. Many startups have emerged to develop different applications across a myriad of industries, such as finance, supply chain management, health care, and government. Some examples include tracking food deliveries, medical records verification, mortgage/loan record history, crowd funding, voting, vehicle registries, land titles, birth/death certificates, and wills.

[1] Nakamoto S., "Bitcoin: A Peer-to-Peer Electronic Cash System," 2008, https://bitcoin.org/bitcoin.pdf.

LO 15-2

Understand the emergent blockchain technology and its benefits.

What Is Blockchain?

Due to the rise of cryptocurrencies like Bitcoin and Ethereum, blockchain is the nascent technology with the most hype. However, cryptocurrencies are just one application that can be built on top of the blockchain technology.

In a traditional system, we do a lot of business through independent, trustworthy, third-party intermediaries. These third-party intermediaries help verify the validity of the business transactions and also keep ledgers of the transactions. Assume that Bob, living in Chicago, wants to wire transfer $1,000 to Alice, who lives in Tokyo. He must go to his bank and fill out the wire transfer paper work to initiate the $1,000 wire transfer. The bank employee needs to complete the following: (1) Verify that Bob's account has an adequate balance, (2) verify both the SWIFT code of Alice's bank and her account information, (3) exchange U.S. dollars to foreign currency, and (4) enter Bob's request through a SWIFT network for the wire transfer. Once the information is in the SWIFT network, there are many other banks involved in this transaction before the money becomes available in Alice's account. Bob's bank first collects a $40 service fee for the wire transfer from him, so the net amount Alice receives is the remaining $960. Normally, Alice must wait 2 or 3 days before the remaining $960 becomes available in her account.

Exhibit 15.1 shows the difference of a wire transfer between the traditional banking system and a blockchain wire transfer application. In this simple wire transfer transaction, the trusted third-party banks are called middlemen or intermediaries. There are three important concepts involved in this transaction: the middleman, the delay, and the service fee. In a blockchain wire transfer application, Bob can use his wallet to accomplish the same goal without any middleman involved and yet with much faster transaction time (minutes versus days of delay) and a lower service fee. These three factors make blockchain very attractive as the desired wire transfer mechanism.

EXHIBIT 15.1
Differences between a Traditional Banking System and a Blockchain Network

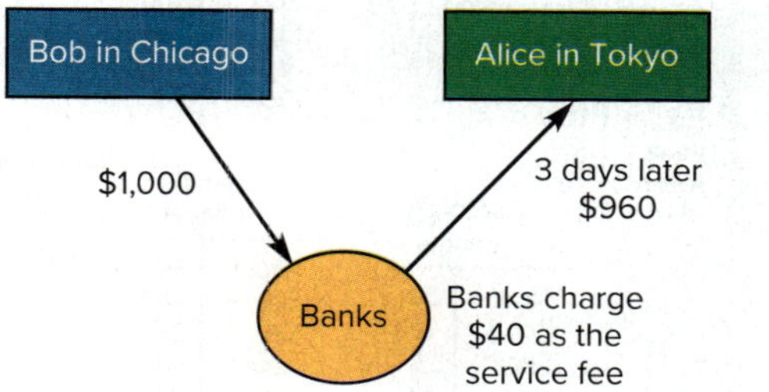

Bob wire transfers $1,000 to Alice through banks

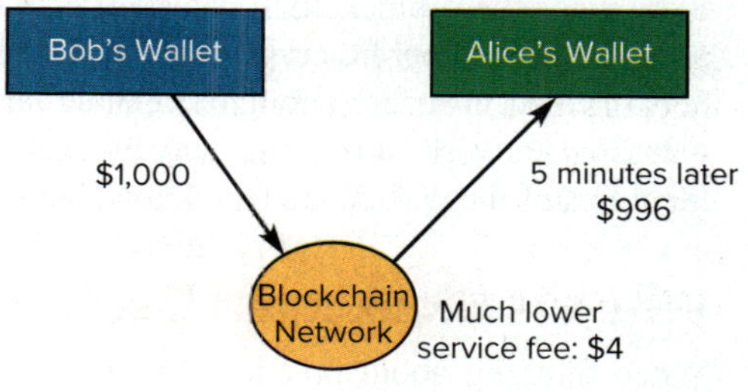

Bob transfers $1,000 to Alice through a blockchain network

There are a few major differences between a blockchain system and a traditional system. First, a traditional system is centralized and generally requires a middleman to approve and record transactions. At a high level, with blockchain, all data are distributed safely, and everyone participating in the network has a copy of the data. As shown in Exhibit 15.2, there is only one copy of the ledger in a centralized ledger system, but multiple copies exist in a distributed ledger system. These distributed copies contain the same transaction records. When a new transaction occurs, the information is guaranteed to be propagated to all the participants to keep all nodes in sync. Exhibit 15.2 shows that all ledgers in a distributed system credit Alice's account $20 and debit Bob's account $20 after Bob transfers $20 to Alice. There is no central authority that can alter the existing transactions in the network. No middleman is needed. The technology utilizes cryptography to ensure there are no fraudulent transactions, and consensus must be reached between the participants before transactions are committed to the blockchain. Information cannot be added or deleted without the knowledge of the entire network. Blockchain also has characteristics of a traditional ledger in which you cannot edit or alter past information once it has been committed to the network; it is a write-once, read-many type of system.

EXHIBIT 15.2
Centralized Ledger versus Distributed Ledger System

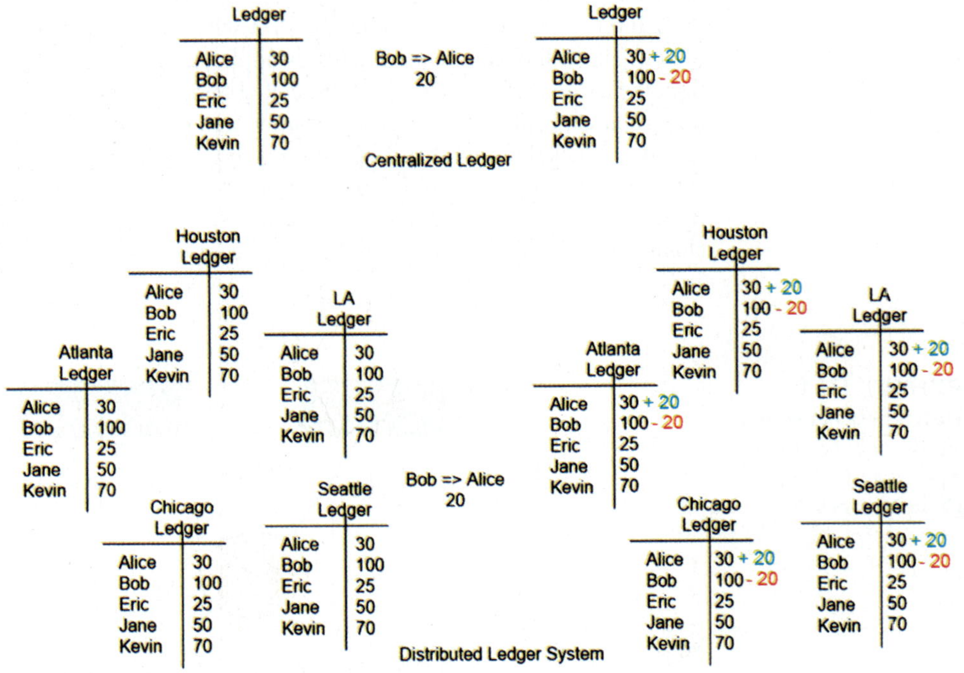

With this type of secure, distributed data store, there are various applications across industries where blockchain can be transformative. The most widely known blockchain applications are public cryptocurrencies. These are possible through a public blockchain network that is secure enough to enable large-scale, trustless transactions. In addition to untrusted networks, there are many blockchain applications in permissioned settings where identities of the participants are known and participation in the network is gated.

When Is Blockchain Useful?

When thinking about potential blockchain projects and applications to build, you must consider a few factors to evaluate whether or not leveraging blockchain makes sense for your business scenario. Think about where blockchain would add the most value.

One major benefit of blockchain is enabling multiple parties that do not fully trust each other to collaborate with a shared source of truth. For example, a shared source of truth is the distributed ledger system deployed in a peer-to-peer cryptocurrency transaction network such as Bitcoin. In this use case, where multiple parties need to share and potentially manipulate the same data, blockchain allows these parties to see the latest updates in real time.

Another perspective helpful in evaluating blockchain's usefulness is through thinking about whether or not there are intermediaries involved in a particular business process. If there are third-party middlemen involved that control the data source, blockchain can help with eliminating these intermediaries, thus accelerating transaction settlement and verification. For example, a voting system with blockchain technology can eliminate the middleman, reflect the voting result for all candidates in real time, and eliminate fraud or potential human errors in the vote counting process.

Another aspect where blockchain can be useful is in scenarios where there is a need for manual verification. Blockchain automatically keeps an immutable audit history of all transactions that have happened, which can help cut costs and resources that would normally be spent on manual efforts required to accomplish this. Hence, some may question whether blockchain technology might eliminate the need for a financial statement audit by a CPA. Although the blockchain technology verifies the occurrence of a transaction in each block, an audit involves an assessment that each recorded transaction is supported by evidence that is relevant, reliable, objective, accurate, and verifiable. Auditors can benefit from this technology to focus on collecting and evaluating evidence to support the transactions.

Because blockchain is currently considered one of the newest technologies, there are many companies that wish to leverage it. In evaluating use cases for blockchain, it is critical to evaluate whether there truly are benefits. For example, for completely internal scenarios, you may want to consider whether blockchain can really add value or if it will simply increase complexity for the organization. If there is complete trust between the parties involved in the use case, it is more efficient to leverage a centralized solution instead.

PROGRESS CHECK

1. Blockchain is a new technology that many companies want to use. Find two examples that you consider most innovative in using blockchain.

How Does Blockchain Work?

Suppose you have a smart ledger you can rely on for doing your business that allows you to add journal entries to the ledger. Once an entry is entered, it cannot be altered or deleted from the ledger; thus, finality of the entry is guaranteed. The entry is cryptographically saved in the ledger, so it is highly secure such that only the related parties can view it and nobody can tamper with the entry. This smart ledger is also shared among multiple parties to achieve a consistent view of the ledger. This is often called distributed ledger due to its distributed nature.

A blockchain entry may consist of **smart contracts**. Smart contracts define the terms, business rules, and transfer of assets in a piece of software code. Smart contracts can be examined among the trading partners and regulators. Once agreed and executed, smart contracts ensure that the business rules and processes are followed through in every step of the transactions as specified in the contract. It helps resolve disputes and provides end-to-end transparency for each transaction.

As with all types of technology, there are different implementations of blockchain. To be characterized as blockchain, there must be a few components that are met. In public networks where there can be malicious actors, the technology must be designed carefully to ensure that participants are incentivized to act properly:

1. *Distributed and decentralized.* The data are distributed and synchronized among all the participants in the network. Data are decentralized in the aspect that participation in the network is fair.
2. *Consensus.* Every transaction that is submitted to the network is validated by participants in the network and packaged into blocks. Before the blocks are confirmed to be added to the network, agreement in the network must be reached among the parties. All parties will be aware of transactions that take place on the network and agree to the transactions being written to the blockchain.
3. *Immutability.* Once transactions are confirmed on the blockchain, they are tamper-proof and cannot be altered.

To get a bit more into the details, there are a few different ways that this can work. We will conceptually cover a few of the currently popular consensus algorithms. These consensus algorithms determine whether to add a new block to the chain or to drop a fraudulent block. A new block is always added to the longest chain as seen by the majority of the computers.

Proof of Work

To fully understand this consensus algorithm, we need to first explain the concept of **miners**. Miners are the nodes in the blockchain network creating and validating blocks. This consensus algorithm is designed for all miners in the network to compete to create the next block to be committed to the blockchain. This is done by solving a complex mathematical problem.

As the miner is generating a valid block, there are a few pieces of work that need to be done. The miner needs to give a hash of the transactions in the block, as well as another hash which proves that the computer work was done to generate this block and solve the mathematical problem. A hash function is a one-way function that converts an input into an output of fixed length. You can think of it as a unique signature for that particular input. The first miner to provide this hash broadcasts the valid block and receives a reward for mining the block.

For example, the mathematical problem in Bitcoin is finding a random number N such that SHA256 (transaction data, previous hash value, N) is less than a target value where SHA256 is an industry standard hash function that generates a 32-byte digital signature of its input data. Bitcoin protocol adjusts the target value in a manner that only one new block is committed to the chain at a rate of 10 minutes. That is, this protocol is not regulated nor practical for most transactions.

Proof of work requires that the miners use computer power to solve this problem. This prevents attacks as it requires either one bad actor to own tons of computer power to overcome all the other good actors in the network or requires a large number of participants in the network to be maliciously working together.

Proof of Authority

Proof of authority is another consensus algorithm that requires a few members in the network with known identities. This algorithm is designed for a subset of the participants in the network, called administrators, to be the ones creating blocks for the rest of the network. The administrator identities are known and reputable.

There are several methods to implement this, but for simplicity, let us say that for each round of getting consensus, one of the administrators is selected at random to create the next block. This administrator has nodes in the network that then create the block and add the block to the blockchain. Because administrator identities are known, this prevents malicious behavior, and the rest of the network can vote for admin removal in case of malicious behavior found in the network.

Proof of Stake

Proof of stake is another type of consensus algorithm that can be used in blockchain networks. It has a number of variations based on how the reward is distributed. Essentially, there is a set of validators in the network who work on proposing the next block to be added to the blockchain. These validators lock up an amount of their cryptocurrency as a deposit to ensure honest behavior. If others find that the block was not created honestly, then the block validators lose their staked cryptocurrency. The main incentive for the miner to act honestly in this scenario is so they do not lose their staked amount. Some of the benefits of the proof of stake consensus algorithm are reduced computer costs and reduced centralization risks.

As the technology gets more advanced, there are more people investigating different consensus algorithms to continually improve blockchain.

LO 15-3

Differentiate between the blockchain applications Bitcoin and Ethereum.

Popular Cryptocurrency Applications

The following two sections describe the two most popular cryptocurrency applications using blockchain technology.

Bitcoin

Utilizing blockchain technology to keep track of all the transactions, Bitcoin was the first cryptocurrency. The key concepts behind Bitcoin are as follows:

1. A cryptocurrency that eliminates the ability to double spend.
2. Anonymous peer-to-peer transactions, no middleman involved.
3. Public blockchain—anyone can join or leave the blockchain network at any time.
4. Validation through proof of work and rewards as an economic incentive via a resource intensive computation called mining.
5. Immutable history of transactions.
6. Distributed ledger.
7. Addition of one block to the blockchain approximately every 10 minutes.
8. The First-Mover—the first blockchain application in production.

The size of a block in the Bitcoin network varies but usually contains thousands of transactions in one block. Each block contains transaction data such as the sender, receiver, and the quantity of Bitcoin to be transferred. A block also contains a 32-byte hash value from SHA256, the digital digest of the block, the hash value from the previous block, and a timestamp of the block transaction in a chronological order. A small change of the data will completely change the digest, making it almost impossible to tamper with once a block is added to the chain. Bitcoin also introduces the "proof of work" algorithm through mining and rewards to ensure the finality of a block and to prevent the existing blocks from being tampered with. Any party can join the Bitcoin network at any time and keep a copy of the existing transactions. Before adding a new block, each party must validate the work of the new block and achieve a network consensus. All transaction blocks are chained together in such a way that it is extremely secure and difficult to break. Exhibit 15.3 shows the approach to add a new Bitcoin block to the chain. First, we need to feed the hash value of the previous block and the transaction data of the new block, and continuously guess a random number as the input data to SHA256 until we find a number N (called nonce) such that SHA256 (previous block's hash, transaction data, N) < target. There is also difficulty involved in this calculation. The easiest target is when difficulty is 1, where you need about 2^{32} hashes (the leading 32 bits of SHA256 are zeros) to find a nonce N. Normally, "difficulty" is a very large number and will be changed to an even larger number over time. Crypto analysts estimate that 99% of Bitcoin will have been mined by 2032 and 100% of the total Bitcoin will be mined by 2040. Assume that difficulty is 7,182,852,319,938 and consider all the mining machines in the whole Bitcoin network. Only one block is added every 10 minutes and the total number of hashes required for adding a new block is around 50 million tera hashes, an incredibly large number. As you can imagine, this type of computation consumes lots of energy and computational resources and is not economically efficient.

EXHIBIT 15.3
Add a Bitcoin Block

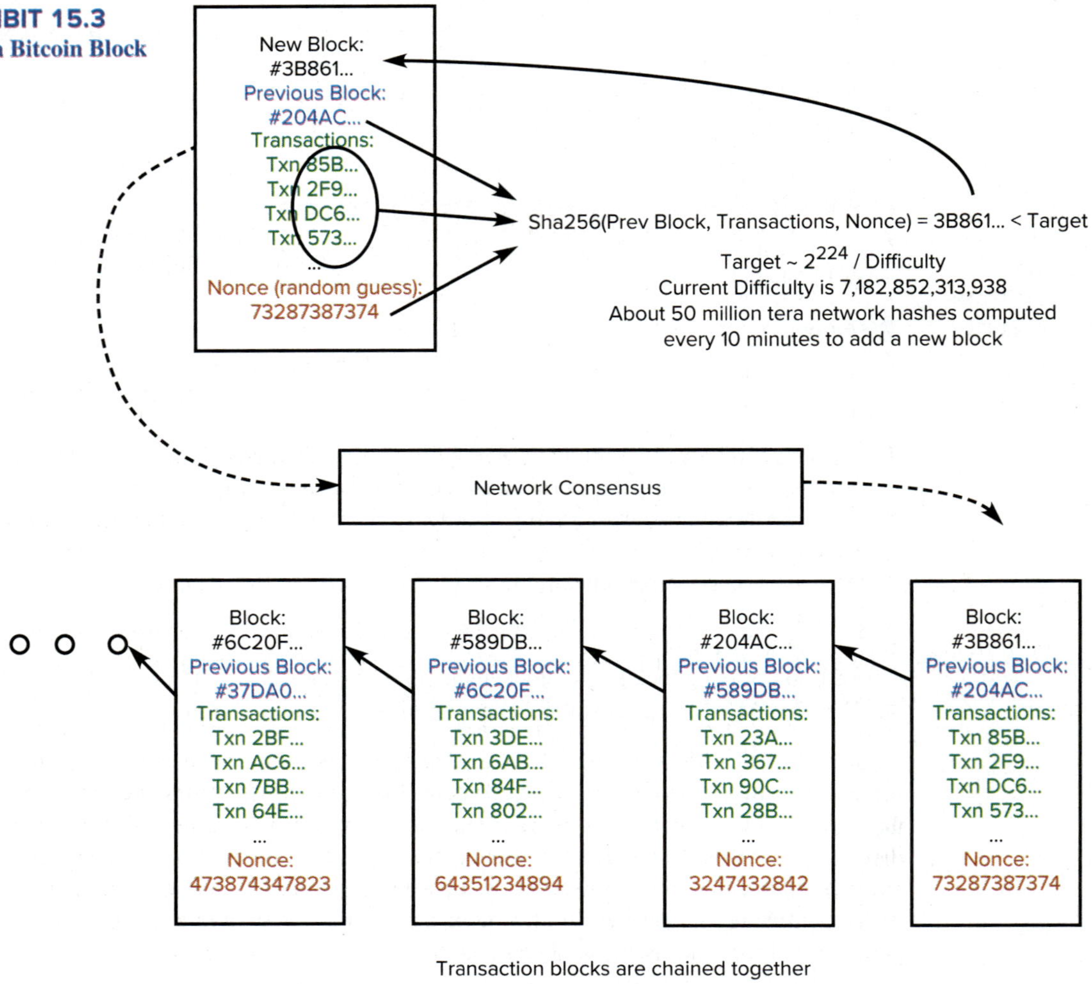

Ethereum

Due to the anonymous nature of the Bitcoin network, the cryptocurrency is classified as an unregulated shadow currency and is often rejected in many business organizations and government agencies. However, its underlying blockchain technology has been revised and modified to become more flexible and suitable for business transactions. Smart contracts—computer programs that facilitate the exchange of digital assets—have been introduced and implemented in a blockchain platform called Ethereum. The terms and conditions of a mutually agreed-upon contract between peers can be specified in a smart contract. In an enterprise context, a smart contract is business logic that is converted to a piece of software code. When executed, it guarantees the business rules are followed among the anonymous parties in the Ethereum network without the need of a central authority. In other words, every node in the Ethereum network keeps a history of all transactions, a history of all smart contracts, and the current state of the smart contracts. Once a contract is executed, it cannot be altered or tampered with.

Ethereum was proposed in 2013 by Vitalik Buterin. Ethereum employs similar concepts as Bitcoin but differs in the following ways:

1. Ether is the cryptocurrency that runs on the Ethereum network, which is used to pay for the computational resources and transaction fees.
2. One block is added every 12 to 15 seconds, compared to 10 minutes in the Bitcoin platform.
3. Transaction fees differ by computational complexity, while Bitcoin transaction fees differ by block size.
4. Mining of Ether occurs at a constant rate, while Bitcoin mining reduces by 50 percent every 4 years.
5. Smart contracts (programmable business rules) are used rather than fixed business rules.
6. Ethereum uses Ethash algorithm to reduce the advantage of ASICs in mining machine versus SHA-256.
7. Mining reward is 2 Ether versus 6.25 Bitcoins as of today.
8. Transaction fees are considerably lower for Ether than Bitcoin.
9. Account is debited/credited in Ethereum versus Bitcoin's unspent transaction output system (spending cash and receiving change).
10. Ethereum deprecated Bitcoin's Proof of Work (PoW) approach and moved to Proof of Stake (PoS) in 2022. PoS relies on validators who also own Ethers in the Ethereum network. By adapting to PoS, 99.95 percent of the energy is saved in Ethereum's mining process.
11. The Ethereum virtual machine is used to run the Ethereum smart contracts.

It is important to know that many applications can be built on the Ethereum network. For example, in a digital voting case, all the polls are publicly visible. The Ethereum network ensures transparency and a fair democracy by eliminating any errors or malpractices in the voting process. In a banking and payment application, it is very difficult for hackers to have access to personal information, perform illegal transactions, or tamper with the existing transactions in the distributed ledger system. In the shipping industry, it helps track cargo, monitor the entire shipping process, and prevent the cargo from being misplaced. You can track how the cargo is handled from the source to its final destination in real time. With Ethereum's smart contracts, agreements can be maintained and executed without any disputes or alternations. The Ethereum network can also be utilized to build other applications, such as market predictions, super computing platforms, electronic sports, and social networks.

LO 15-4

Describe public blockchain, private blockchain, and consortium blockchain.

Types of Blockchain

There are three types of blockchain: public blockchain, private blockchain, and consortium blockchain.

Public Blockchain

Public blockchain has no access restrictions in relation to the viewing or participation in the blockchain network. Anyone interested in the public blockchain can join or leave the network at any time without disrupting the overall network. This type of network usually offers economic reward for the computational proof of work in mining. It is often called permissionless blockchain.

Private Blockchain

Private blockchain usually is controlled by one organization and it requires permission to join the network. Hence, it is permissioned blockchain. One cannot join a private blockchain unless he or she is invited to join the network. Instead of going through the proof of work in mining, transaction data and validation are restricted. Corporations that want to deploy the blockchain technology to replace their traditional bookkeeping, but do not want to expose the internal information to the public, may take this approach. This type of blockchain is also referred to as enterprise blockchain.

Consortium Blockchain

Consortium blockchain is another type of permissioned blockchain. It allows several organizations to participate in its management. A selected set of organizations may run a blockchain node separately for keeping the transaction records. Administrators from the organizations establish the access rights and permissions for each participant, which allows private channels to exist in the consortium blockchain. In addition, the consensus protocol is executed only on a limited set of trusted nodes. That is, the consortium blockchain can be considered a kind of private blockchain, but its different permission structure can permit more complicated enterprise behaviors.

PROGRESS CHECK

2. Among the three different types of blockchain, which one would involve many organizations/companies to deploy the blockchain?
3. Search on the Internet to find one example for each type of blockchain.

Platforms Using Blockchain Technology

As previously mentioned, there are different ways of implementing blockchain technology. Think of different flavors of a technology, similar to how there are different flavors of mobile phones (iOS and Android) and computers (MacBook and PC). With the increasing popularity in this technology, there are over a hundred different blockchain implementations. There are a handful of blockchain platforms that are popular with enterprises, a couple of which we will go into more detail as follows.

Corda

R3, formed in 2014, is a software company utilizing distributed ledgers and database systems to apply blockchain technology focused on financial services scenarios to achieve more transparency, security, speed, and traceability with reduced cost. It is made up of a consortium of more than 200 firms.

Corda, an open source blockchain platform, was developed by R3 in 2016. It uses smart contracts for its business rules while ensuring privacy and security in the business transactions. In contrast to the permissionless or public blockchain approaches in Bitcoin or Ethereum, Corda is a consortium blockchain network where only relevant parties can join the network and only the related parties will be informed for each transaction. It is a permissioned blockchain, and access to each Corda network is restricted to the participating companies or organizations. The administrators of a Corda blockchain platform can be formed from many organizations that may run a node on the blockchain network. The administrators define and restrict each user's access rights to the transaction records. In a Corda network, only a restricted set of trusted nodes execute the consensus protocol. Therefore, this type of blockchain is normally classified as a business blockchain.

Corda differs from public blockchain protocols in the following areas:

1. *Known identity versus anonymity.* When we do business, we need to know the identity of our business partners.
2. *Selective endorsement versus proof of work.* Corda has authorities that play the notary role. For the network to trust a transaction, the endorsement work should be done by these authorities instead of relying on the public to provide the proof of work. Mining is not required in Corda because the validation is done by the notary. Corda is usually run in a secure and trusted network.
3. *Asset versus cryptocurrency.* Business transactions generally involve some sort of asset transfer or an alteration to asset records. Different assets require different representations on the blockchain; it is impossible to represent all assets in the same form as cryptocurrency.
4. *Smart contracts.* Again, we need flexibility for different business transactions. Each type of transaction needs a list of requirements to be satisfied before the actual transaction can occur. Smart contracts are a perfect fit for representing these types of transactions. It allows users to specify a list of business rules into a single contract before the contract is submitted. The consensus can be achieved only when the specified business rules in a contract are met.
5. *Access control rules.* These rules can be deployed to define the roles of the participants, such as the access rights of everyone in the network.
6. *Privacy.* Business blockchain ensures appropriate visibility and that transactions are secure, authenticated, and verifiable. For example, if only two parties are involved in a private transaction, other participants will not be able to see the details of that transaction.

Hyperledger

Hyperledger is an open source blockchain platform created by the **Linux Foundation** in 2016. Its main objective is to achieve cross-industry collaboration with blockchain technology and distributed ledgers in a more efficient, reliable, and traceable environment so that it can be used in global business transactions prevalent in financial institutions or supply chain companies. It is a permissioned blockchain, and only members have access rights to interact with the information stored in the blockchain. For its smart contracts and consensus protocol, Hyperledger's original source code was contributed by a few companies such as **IBM**, **Digit Asset**, and **Intel**. Later, this evolved into various Hyperledger projects. Among them, Hyperledger Fabric is a permissioned blockchain with capabilities of handling smart contracts, configurable consensus, and member management services.

The membership-identity-service manages and authenticates participants' identities. The access control list (ACL) provides an additional layer of permission around role-based access control. For example, the ACL provides read-only permissions on transaction records for persons with auditor roles, read/write permissions to bank tellers, and consensus rights to the business management teams. Hyperledger Fabric uses chaincode, a piece of code that is written in one of the supported languages such as Go or Java, to represent the business logic that defines transaction instructions about an asset or assets.

There are three types of nodes—client nodes, peer nodes, and ordering nodes. Client nodes submit the transactions to the endorsers and broadcast the transactions to the ordering nodes. Peer nodes are responsible for executing and verifying transactions, while ordering nodes are responsible for communication service with a delivery guarantee.

A blockchain log file is created to store the sequenced transaction records in blocks. It helps keep track of the provenance of transactions. Hyperledger Fabric also stores the current state of the blockchain in the blockchain database to facilitate the speed of verification. This can be seen by comparing this to how it is accomplished in a traditional blockchain. For example, in the Bitcoin network, to make sure a user has enough funds for a transaction, it needs to fetch a list from the most recent block to earlier blocks until funds are verified. In Hyperledger Fabric, you can query the current state of a user with a simple command, like an SQL command. This implementation speeds up the verification and saves computing power and resources while still maintaining efficiency and privacy.

One special feature in Hyperledger Fabric is private channels. Private channels provide restricted message paths to ensure privacy for participating parties only. The transactions through the private channels are invisible to ungranted business parties or individuals. This allows competing business corporations to coexist in the same permissioned Hyperledger Fabric network.

In summary, Hyperledger Fabric contains the following features:

1. It can define the asset types and consensus protocol.
2. A membership identify service provides permissioned networks. It manages user IDs and authenticates all participants in the Hyperledger network. ACL can be used to provide additional layers of role-based access control.
3. There are three types of nodes: client node, peer node, and ordering node.
4. Ledger consists of a transaction log and a database for current state.
5. Assets are added, updated, and transferred with chaincode.

BLOCKCHAIN APPLICATIONS

Goldman Sachs & Co. describes blockchain as a new technology redefining the way we transact.[2] It will change the way we buy or sell. Some government agencies have started deploying blockchain as the core technology for bookkeeping. It will affect the way we interact with the government and many other organizations. Many things—from property deeds, to food delivery, to music—can be disrupted by blockchain technology. It combines the openness of the internet with cryptography to give everyone a faster and trustful way to verify key information and conduct business. Blockchain has already started to take off, and we can expect the impacts of the technology in the coming years. Organizations and individuals will need to be prepared to adopt this technology as it matures along the way.

The blockchain technology gives users and corporations the ability to create value, authenticate identities, and transfer digital assets in a secure and transparent way. Many areas of blockchain applications are under development. Here, we list a few of them:

- Health care
- Sharing economy
- Voting
- Crowdfunding
- Cryptocurrency
- Banking and payment systems
- Governance
- Supply chain management and auditing
- File storage

[2]https://www.goldmansachs.com/insights/pages/blockchain/.

- Prediction markets
- Protection of intellectual property
- Internet of Things (IoT)
- Insurance
- Identity management
- Private transport and ride sharing
- Energy management
- Music
- Data management
- Property records
- Stock trading

LO 15-5

Discuss blockchain use cases.

Blockchain Use Cases

Now that we have a high-level understanding of what blockchain is and where it can be useful, we can look at various industries and some common scenarios where we can evaluate potential use of blockchain technologies. We see these possibilities in industry cases for asset transfer and cross organizational workflows, such as in various supply chain scenarios. Let us walk through some examples.

Supply Chain

In a refrigerated transportation supply chain scenario (such as transporting ice cream or seafood), there may be certain temperature ranges that goods must be transported with; otherwise, it may not be safe for the retail store to sell the goods to the consumers.

In a traditional case without blockchain, it is very difficult for the retailer to have transparency concerning the conditions of the goods during the transportation process because data among the different counterparties responsible for handling and transporting the goods may be siloed as each organization has its own data stores. Because the goods are being handled by multiple different parties, to understand the status of the shipment and whether or not each party is in compliance with the temperature regulations, the retailer will have to contact each party individually to get the entire picture.

With blockchain and Internet of Things (IoT) sensors installed in the transportation vehicles, each counterparty—the suppliers and the retail stores—has direct access and real-time visibility into the conditions of the shipment. In this case, once the temperature falls out of the allowable range, an alert is triggered, and the retail store knows exactly who bears responsibility for the shipment at that point in real time and thus can react quickly and claim the loss with the correct party.

In use cases with cross-organizational workflows, such as supply chain, you can automate the shared workflows among the different organizations to simplify the number of parties involved in the reconciliation process. In the refrigerated transportation example, the retailer knows exactly which counterparty to work with in the case there was a breach in the temperature compliance conditions.

Loyalty Program

In a loyalty program scenario, there are multiple partners that need to access the same data, such as a customer's frequent flier miles. We are seeing increasing flexibility in how people can redeem their frequent flier miles, whether it be buying a plane ticket, buying meals with the airline's restaurant partners, or even using the points at retail stores to buy material goods.

This type of program with multiple partners is difficult to manage because each partner needs to be able to recognize a customer using loyalty points to redeem for services or goods. They later need to claim revenue from the airline based on the agreement that is in place. In a traditional system, it requires both the airline, as well as the partner, to keep track of the points that are redeemed and ensure that this is reflected across both systems each time to avoid inaccuracies across the board.

With a blockchain-enabled solution, the partners and the airline can have a record of all customers and their points. When a customer finishes a flight, the added points are reflected in the customer point account, so both the airline and all partners know the updated amount. When a customer redeems points at a partner location, the partner can update the point account in real time, which is reflected across the board. All other partners and the airline always have visibility into the customer's account. Redeeming revenue with the airline becomes easier, as well as determining whether or not the customer has enough points to buy certain items or services at the partner location.

Auto Industry

In a blockchain-enabled auto industry, a buyer can enter an order to purchase a car from a car seller. They specify the model, exterior color, options, and their driver's license in an order that is then delivered to the car seller. The car seller puts together a smart contract, indicating the purchase rules such as financial terms and eligible license information, and makes it available to the blockchain network. The bank is informed in order to validate that the buyer has sufficient funds in their bank, while the DMV ensures the driver's license information is valid. The seller then creates a vehicle identification number and posts the information for the car company to produce this car. The car company adds auto parts information into the blockchain network, and the regulators constantly monitor the source of auto parts coming from reputable sources. Once the car is finished, the regulators are instructed to check and digitally authenticate the car's compliance. At this stage, the car is ready for delivery. The buyer is informed, and the bank will get authorization from the buyer to transfer the money to the seller. Once the seller receives the payment, the car is delivered to the buyer. All the transaction steps, including the payment information, vehicle information, auto parts, buyer, seller, and car delivery time are recorded in the shared distributed ledger.

Current Challenges with Adopting Blockchain Technology

There are a myriad of benefits with incorporating blockchain technology into an organization's existing business processes. Blockchain also unlocks a number of transformative cross-organizational scenarios. You may be wondering why there is still doubt in various industries concerning the integration of blockchain with the day-to-day business scenarios. One of the main reasons is because blockchain was originally built to support public, trustless, cryptocurrency scenarios. It was not originally designed to support enterprise use cases.

In enterprise blockchain scenarios, there are a few challenges that need to be addressed. First, blockchain protocols designed for public network cryptocurrencies are lacking in areas such as speed, confidentiality, and governance requirements that are critical to enterprise use cases. For certain enterprise use cases, there may be a need for having certain transactions only visible to a part of the blockchain network. Furthermore, most enterprises are opting to start with permissioned or private blockchain networks, which require a method to govern who is eligible to participate in the network (whether it be through a majority vote, a delegate in the existing network who has the privileges to add or remove members, etc.). With public networks, these two requirements are irrelevant because all participants are free to join and leave as they like, and all transactions, by nature, are visible to the entire network.

These challenges led to organizations building their own blockchain protocols with these enterprise requirements in mind, such as the **Linux Foundation**'s Hyperledger family of blockchain frameworks and tools, and **R3**'s Corda. There are also variations of Ethereum such as **JPMorgan**'s Quorum. These are a few examples of blockchain protocols with differing levels of support for confidentiality and governance.

Furthermore, while there are many tools now to help you get started in setting up a private blockchain network, there are still challenges to integrating with existing enterprise solutions. There are nuances to sending input to the blockchain as well as getting data from the blockchain.

The Impact of Blockchain on Audit and Assurance

LO 15-6

Explain the potential impact of blockchain on audit and assurance.

Blockchain technology has the potential to affect the bookkeeping industry and how a transaction is initiated, authorized, executed, and reported. Changes in the business models with blockchain also affect CPAs in the financial reporting and tax preparation industries. The source document in a blockchain network resides in the chained blocks. The means by which CPAs or auditors parse and extract the desired information from the blockchain network plays a critical role in collecting audit evidence and assurance of the business conduct.

Furthermore, the records residing in the blockchain network may not provide sufficient information for auditors. Illegal, fraudulent, or unauthorized transactions can reside in the blockchain. Information stored in the blockchain network and relational databases further complicate the tasks for auditors. How auditors access the business information and provide a reasonable assurance of financial statements for business entities will be challenging.

With the emergence of blockchain technology, audit and assurance tasks become more difficult due to the complicated protocols involved in the distributed ledger system. To audit a business with blockchain technology, an auditor needs to understand how the business logic is implemented and how the business uses blockchain technology in its end-to-end business applications. Does a company run its business with only blockchain technology or a combination of traditional systems alongside blockchain? Auditors need to understand not only how the business is conducted in traditional systems, but also how the same business is conducted under blockchain technology. Unfortunately, there is no easy way to convert the traditional audit approaches and apply them directly to blockchain technology. To begin with, many different blockchain platforms exist. This is further muddied by the fact that a greater number of blockchain applications, such as Bitcoin and Ethereum, exist. In blockchain platforms such as Corda and Hyperledger, the protocols and terms are quite different. The business terms, rules, and compliance information are often defined and enforced by the software code in smart contracts. A complete understanding of smart contracts requires the knowledge of programming skills and may not be straightforward to most auditors. Acquiring the skill sets necessary to understanding smart contracts is crucial for auditors to successfully audit the upcoming blockchain use cases. As blockchain technology has begun to appear in many applications, auditors are encouraged to learn the related skills to prepare themselves for the advancement of this new technology.

Continuous Audit Becomes Possible

With blockchain technology, traditional audit activities such as reconciling ledgers and providing proof of ownership can be eliminated or reduced to the minimum. Due to the distributed nature and real-time information retrieval of blockchain technology, it is possible for auditors to conduct a continuous audit over time. From the business rules, auditors can create scenarios to enter violation cases and see how the business logic responds with the violations in addition to the normal business operations. To create the normal business transactions and the violation cases, auditors also need to understand the business rules and terms defined in smart contracts.

Opportunities for Future Roles in CPA

There are new challenges for auditors and CPAs due to the emergence of blockchain technology. There are also immense new opportunities that come with blockchain technology. Auditors and CPAs familiar with blockchain and its applications will capitalize most on these new opportunities. Among these opportunities, smart contracts will be one of the key areas for auditors and CPAs to focus on. All business rules, terms, regulations, asset transfers, participants, liabilities, violations, triggers, and the like are specified clearly in smart contracts. Due to the complexities of smart contracts, software companies may develop smart contract libraries and sell them for asset transfers, recordkeeping, asset allocation among participants, asset management, identity verification, and credit verification. Once the libraries become available, smart contracts built on top of the libraries will appear. To understand business activities, auditors are forced to understand the business rules embedded in the smart contracts and the related libraries. Furthermore, auditors also need to verify the tax code and regulations are considered and handled properly in the smart contracts.

New Approaches for Future Audit Tasks

Future audit tasks that come with blockchain technology require a broad understanding of technology. Accounting firms will give their opportunities to auditors who understand blockchain technology and smart contracts well. Because technology is not the major focus for auditors, it will be difficult for accounting firms to recruit their ideal auditors. A more realistic approach for them is to recruit auditors with enough understanding of blockchain technology and IT background. They then offer them enough training in smart contracts and other areas in IT before doing the real auditing tasks. Another alternative approach for them is to recruit the people with either software or IT background and then do the onsite audit training. The last approach for them is to form an audit team of two to three people, combining the expertise of information technology, taxation, law, accounting, and auditing. In this team, the auditor may have to rely on the work of other professionals such as an IT expert to understand the business rules in smart contracts, how the business activities occur, and how the transactions are recorded or rejected in blockchain network.

Getting Started with Blockchain

With a basic understanding of blockchain technology, examples of how it can be used in industry, as well as challenges to be aware of, you can start brainstorming what scenarios in your current organization and industry could benefit from the help of blockchain.

Coming up with a good use case can be difficult. A method that is helpful is to model the use case as a workflow with multiple states and transitions between the states. You can then define various roles, which roles are able to take actions at which states, and what actions move the workflow from one state to another. This will be helpful in translating the business logic to code, which will run on the blockchain network.

ARTIFICIAL INTELLIGENCE

Introduction to Artificial Intelligence

When we consider **artificial intelligence**, the first thing that often comes to mind is a robot like Sophia, shown in Exhibit 15.4. Sophia was developed by **Hanson Robotics** and activated in 2016. She was reintroduced with legs for mobility at the Consumer Electronics Show in 2018. Sophia is humanlike in appearance and action. She imitates human gestures, recognizes people and things, and carries on basic conversations. However, most current artificial intelligence applications are very different from Sophia. In this part of the

EXHIBIT 15.4
Sophia the Robot

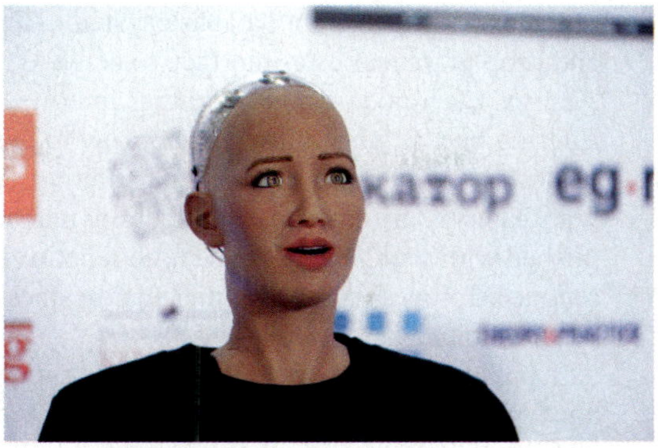

Anton Gvozdikov/Shutterstock

chapter, we will describe artificial intelligence, define some of the buzzwords associated with artificial intelligence, review various types of artificial intelligence applications, and examine the potential benefits of artificial intelligence to accounting and accountants.

LO 15-7

Define artificial intelligence.

What Is Artificial Intelligence?

According to **McKinsey Global Institute**, artificial intelligence can create up to $5.8 trillion annual value across all business sectors. Artificial intelligence, or AI, is intelligence exhibited by machines rather than humans. It is the ability of computers to perform tasks that require features normally associated with human intelligence, such as thinking logically and acting rationally. Thus, artificial intelligence applications are also called cognitive technologies. AI also includes technologies related to other human characteristics, such as visual perception, speech recognition, and language translation. So, robots and self-driving cars are examples of AI. However, there are aspects of human thought and perception that machines struggle with—emotions, intuition, ethics, etc. AI can only approximate some of the features associated with human intelligence.

Artificial intelligence is also a broad field in computer science with foundations in philosophy, mathematics, economics, neuroscience, psychology, cybernetics, and linguistics. The AI field began in the 1950s, but advances were limited by primitive computers and programming tools. Nevertheless, computer scientists made advances in the use of neural networks, expert systems, and probabilistic reasoning. Since 1995, the advent of the Internet and very large data sets led to further advances in AI.

Intelligent agents or bots are now widely used Internet tools. Large data sets spurred the development of **machine learning** so computers could learn new patterns without human intervention. With more sophisticated computing capability and larger data volumes, cognitive technologies—such as machine learning, neural networks, robotic process automation (RPA), bots, and natural language processing—employ self-learning algorithms that allow computers to examine connections and notice patterns. New approaches to data management increasingly provide new and dynamic approaches to gathering, classifying, and correlating data. Consequently, the development and implementation of new AI applications is exploding.

Examples of RPA Applications

In recent years, a few new technologies have been developed to automate business operations. For example, Alteryx is designed for analytic process automation; UiPath is a commonly used tool for robotic process automation (RPA).

Alteryx is a software designed to automate processes of data extraction, filtering, blending, and analytics that enables computer and business professionals to manage and manipulate scientific/business data from various data sources. These data sources can be as simple as plain text files, Excel files, comma separated values (CSV) data files, or as complex as files from a database system. Alteryx implements its application with a drag and drop graphical user interface to achieve a low code or no code process as desired. In Alteryx, each node generates either intermediate or final results. Data manipulation and filtering occurs when drawing an arrow to feed the intermediate results as an input to the next stage of computation or data filtering. When a user is building business processes with Alteryx, the entire data extraction, manipulation, and further analyses can be accomplished with a single click to be used repetitively. This type of automation solves the recurrent tasks/processes for analytics that business professionals face every day and increases work efficiency.

Applications such as UiPath, Blue Prism, Automate Anywhere, and Power Automate are typical applications for robotic process automation. One of the leading applications in RPA is UiPath. In UiPath's definition, RPA is a software technology automating any repetitive tasks for digital transformation. To automate repetitive or mundane tasks, users can select their desired drag and drop activities to build bots with minimum coding. UiPath also integrates very well with web browsers such as Google Chrome or Microsoft Edge which allows users to feed data or to extract data from the web. Regarding file management, UiPath provides Microsoft office integrations such as Excel, Word, PowerPoint, and Outlook into drag and drop activities. Other integrations include PDF file information extractions and processing, and handwritten document transcription. UiPath also has an orchestrator that allows companies to deploy and manage their robot workforce on the web at the enterprise level. The bots can be scheduled to run at any desired time with access control. The one goal of automation to increase overall productivity could be achieved by using a tool for analytics automation (i.e., data as the input source for Alteryx) or, using self-designed bots to complete repetitive tasks for all kinds of purposes (i.e., RPA with UiPath, etc.).

LAB CONNECTION

Hands-on Lab 15-1 using Alteryx and Lab 15-2 UiPath are available in Connect to provide examples of using the software to complete tasks.

LO 15-8

Understand the differences among artificial intelligence, machine learning, and deep learning.

Types of AI

One way to differentiate artificial intelligence applications is based on the ability to perform task without using explicit instructions. Initially, the development of AI applications used rules-based approaches where the logic was programmed into the application. Machine learning, however, involves the computer's ability to learn from experience rather than specific instructions. Exhibit 15.5 describes machine learning as a subset of the AI applications, and **deep learning** is then a subset of machine learning.

Machine Learning

Machine learning is a technique by which a software model is trained using data. In this case, a model is a mathematical representation of some process. The model learns from training cases or data. The model then makes predictions for new products or data. Those new products then generate new data, which improves its ability to make predictions. This is sometimes named the virtuous cycle of machine learning as shown in Exhibit 15.6. When designed properly, a machine learning application improves its ability to analyze patterns as it processes more data. The essence of machine learning is to explain with examples and not instructions.

EXHIBIT 15.5
AI, Machine Learning, and Deep Learning

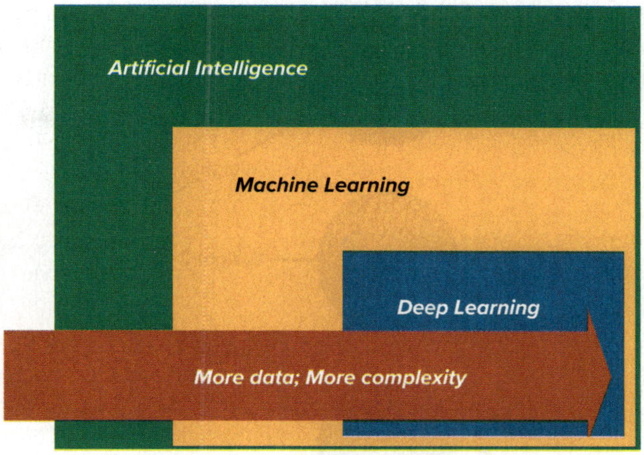

EXHIBIT 15.6
Virtuous Cycle of Machine Learning

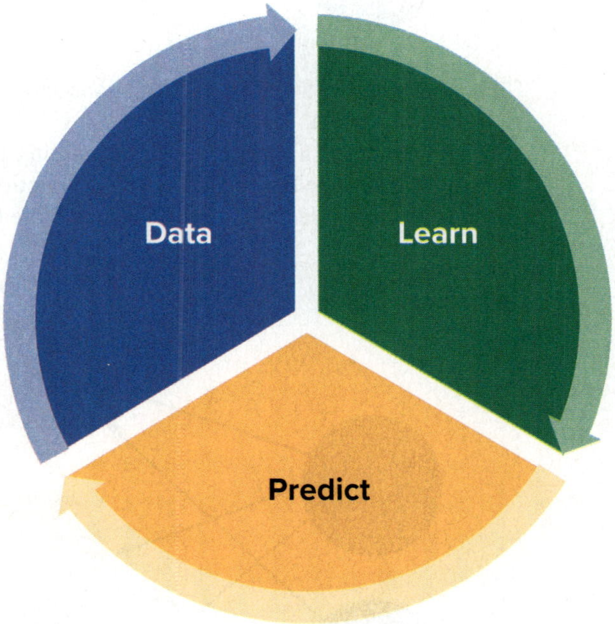

PROGRESS CHECK

4. Can you describe how the virtuous cycle of machine learning would work in a real-world example?

LO 15-9

Appreciate the structure of neural networks.

Neural Networks

Artificial neural networks are the engines of machine learning. See Exhibit 15.7 for an example of a simple neural network that consists of inputs, a neuron or node, and outputs. Neural networks are mathematical models that convert inputs to outputs/predictions. For machine learning, these models can be nested so the overall neural network consists of multiple layers. In feed-forward neural networks, information moves in one direction from the input layer, through hidden layers, to the output layer. In recurrent neural networks, the connections between neurons include loops that allow a sequence of inputs. Training a neural network involves using a training set of data that is cleaned and well-defined.

EXHIBIT 15.7
Simple Neural Network Example

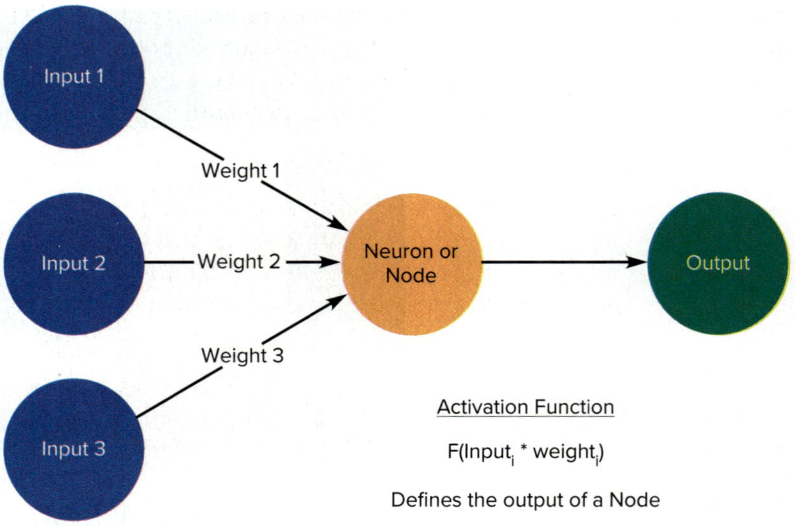

These data are used to optimize predictions and then the model is applied to more test data or to real-world data.

Deep learning is a form of machine learning that involves complex, multilayer (deep) neural networks. See Exhibit 15.8 for a description of a neural network with hidden, non-output layers. Deep learning networks have more than two nonoutput layers. This structure

EXHIBIT 15.8
Neural Network with Layers

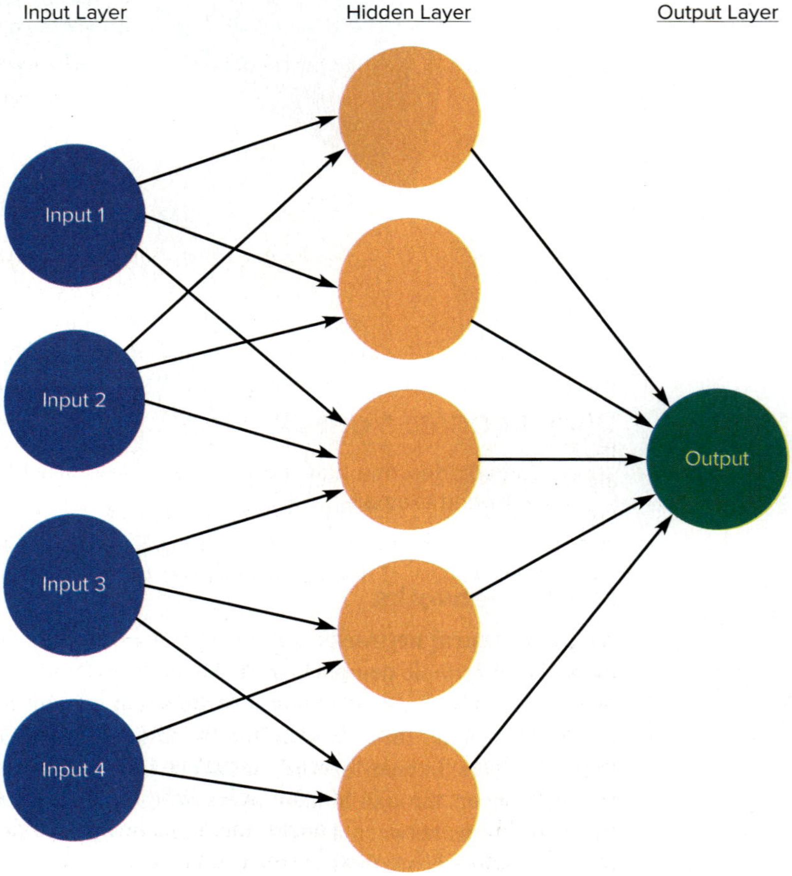

provides more power to solve sophisticated problems, such as computer vision, but also creates model complexity. Modern neural network learning algorithms allow effective training of very deep neural networks. In some cases, these networks include hundreds of layers. In practice, however, many business problems can be solved with two or three hidden layers.

LO 15-10

Describe the types of learning.

Classification and Regression

Most machine learning applications are designed to perform either some form of classification or regression. This makes them well-suited to business problems involving clustering, anomaly detection, ranking, recommendations, and continuous estimation. Different algorithms help machine learning applications answer five basic questions shown in the table below:

EXHIBIT 15.9
Questions That AI Can Answer

Questions AI Answers	Family of Algorithms	Business Questions
1. Is it A or B?	Two-class classification	Will this toy break in less than 30 days? Does a 20 percent discount code attract more customers?
2. Is it different?	Anomaly detection	Is this website safe? Is this transaction fraudulent?
3. How much?	Regression algorithms	What is this house price? What will revenue be in the 3rd quarter?
4. How are these alike?	Clustering algorithms	Which customers like these types of products? Do these cell phone models all fail in the same way?
5. What should I do next?	Reinforcement learning algorithms	Self-driving: Should I stop or go left? Game playing: What action should I take?

PROGRESS CHECK

5. Can you think of other business questions the five AI questions answer?

Classification problems seek to assign labels, dividing the input into output groups. For example, a problem determining whether an incoming email is spam or not. So, the algorithm takes a variety of input and maps it to the interval from 0 (not spam) to 1 (spam). Regression problems seek to predict real numbers, such as the price of a house. So, the algorithm seeks to minimize the difference between the prediction and actual house values. There are several neural network techniques to train the system and optimize the link between input and correct output: supervised learning, unsupervised learning, semi-supervised learning, and reinforcement learning.

Supervised Learning

Supervised learning is the type of machine learning most commonly used in practice. In supervised learning, the output is a known set of values that the neural network seeks to predict using the input dataset. The data includes pairs of input and output. Input could be anything, but output is typically a real number or a label. For example, the input could be characteristics of houses for sale such as location, size, number of bedrooms, and number of bathrooms. The output might be the labels indicating whether the house sold or the real number price at which the house sold.

Assume that you are building a model to detect email spam; the inputs could be features of email messages, and the outputs would be two classes, spam or not spam. Each example is labeled—for example, each email is designated as *spam* or *not spam*—to facilitate network training. The data analyst must first decide how to convert email messages into a set of features, such as encoded words. The learning algorithm uses the encoded input to find the optimal input weights (see Exhibit 15.7) to predict the output.

Unsupervised Learning

In **unsupervised learning**, the computer gets unstructured data rather than labeled data. There are no input–output pairs, so the computer discovers patterns in the data. In this case, the goal usually involves clustering or dimension reduction. The model discerns how elements of the dataset are alike or not. The output set would have fewer features than the input dataset. Alternatively, the output could identify outliers in the input dataset. The groups or clusters are not known in advance and different parameters can result in different results.

Semi-Supervised Learning

In **semi-supervised learning**, some of the data are labeled (the input–output pairs are defined), but some labels can be incorrect or missing. The computer discerns values for the incorrect and missing outputs. One form of semi-supervised learning is called active learning. Active learning involves querying the user to discover the right label/output. **Netflix** recommendations or **Amazon** suggestions are examples of active learning.

Reinforcement Learning

In **reinforcement learning**, the machine/model learns by trial-and-error. The program acts and learns by feedback from those actions as it works toward a desired goal. The goal, however, may be dynamic so it can change over time based on circumstance. Reinforcement learning examples include games, robotic control, and other applications where the problems are well-defined. Reinforcement learning is less successful in more complex situations where rewards are not as clearly defined.

LO 15-11

Assess model performance.

Assessing Performance

After training the network, a data analyst would assess how well the model worked. For regression models, the data analyst can use standard regression metrics such as mean squared error or similar average loss functions. For classification models, there are several options.

Confusion Matrix

A **confusion matrix** is a table summarizing the prediction results. A confusion matrix would have as many rows and columns as there are classifications to predict. Continuing the example of spam prediction, there are two classifications and four possible situations. A true positive (TP) is a correct prediction of spam email. A true negative (TN) is a correct prediction of email that is not spam. Those categories both represent correct predictions. For incorrect predictions, there is the option that the model predicted spam but the email was not spam. That is a false positive (FP) prediction. Then, there is the option that the model predicted not spam but the email is spam. That is a false negative (FN). The confusion matrix can be used to calculate other performance metrics, such as precision, recall, and accuracy.

	Prediction	
True Situation	**Spam**	**Not Spam**
Spam	20 (TP)	2 (FN)
Not spam	5 (FP)	650 (TN)

Precision. Precision ratio is the ratio of correct positive predictions to the number of positive predictions. In the spam prediction example, precision equals 20 (TP) divided by 25 (TP plus FP) or 0.80.

Recall. Recall ratio is the ratio of correct positive predictions to the true positive values in the dataset. In the spam prediction example, recall equals 20 (TP) divided by 22 (TP plus FN) or 0.91.

Accuracy. Accuracy ratio is the ratio of correct classifications to total values in the dataset. In the spam example, accuracy equals 670 (TP plus TN) divided by 677 (TP plus FP plus FN plus TN) or 0.99.

In practice, data analysts trade-off precision and recall depending on the cost of false predictions. In the spam example, failure to properly identify some spam emails is not critical, but we don't want to classify legitimate email messages as spam. Thus, we would favor precision over recall in assessing the model's performance to limit false positive predictions.

PROGRESS CHECK

6. If your machine learning application was classifying things into four categories, how many rows and columns would be in the confusion matrix?

LO 15-12

Recognize applications of AI in accounting.

AI APPLICATIONS IMPORTANT TO ACCOUNTING

Natural Language Processing

Humans communicate through language, both written and spoken. For machines to assume human activities, machines also need to understand and communicate using written and spoken language using **natural language processing (NLP)** and **natural language understanding (NLU)** techniques. Also, machines need to translate text or spoken word in one language into another language. So, AI applications have been developed to understand text, extract semantic meaning, and discern sentiment from natural language. We see examples of this in products such as Alexa from **Amazon** and Siri from **Apple**. In late November 2022, OpenAI launched ChatGPT (Chat Generative Pre-trained Transformer). It is a chatbot with supervised learning techniques. ChatGPT interacts with users in a conversational way. This approach guides ChatGPT by using reinforcement learning from human feedback. ChatGPT can debug codes and answer questions in various domains. In an accounting context, **KPMG International**, in partnership with **IBM**, recently announced products that automate the extraction of lease contract data to facilitate compliance with new lease accounting standards.

Robotic Process Automation

Robotic process automation (RPA) in accounting is defined as the use of automation applications to reduce the amount of human labor required to process accounting and finance department transactions. RPA is a tool that can perform high-volume repetitive accounting tasks, such as preparing tax returns, managing accounts payable, determining cost allocations and account classification, and preparing financial statements. Accounting RPA can reduce costs and improve accuracy in a variety of accounting processes. RPA is not necessarily an AI tool, but recent advances increase the possibility of creating an artificially intelligent accounting workforce.

Machine Learning in Audit and Assurance

All major accounting firms have machine learning applications in use or under development to assist with the audit process. Some applications use structured and unstructured information to assess risk. Other applications are aimed at detecting anomalies in large volumes of data. Still other applications extract salient information from financial documents. For example, **PwC** developed GL.ai, an AI application trained to replicate the thinking and decision making of expert auditors. It examines every transaction, user, amount, and account to find unusual transactions that could indicate potential error or fraud in the general ledger.[3] **Deloitte** employs machine learning technology to review contracts to identify and extract key terms. This reduces time necessary to review contracts and allows auditors to review and assess larger samples in less time.[4] **EY** developed a machine learning tool called Helix GLAD to detect anomalies in large databases.[5] **KPMG** recently launched CLARA, its smart audit platform, which incorporates machine learning capabilities to identify potential risk. **BDO** uses neural network technology to manage information in multiple languages during global audits.

[3] See https://www.pwc.com/gx/en/about/stories-from-across-the-world/harnessing-the-power-of-ai-to-transform-the-detection-of-fraud-and-error.html.

[4] See http://www.cfo.com/auditing/2015/06/artificial-intelligence-can-boost-audit-quality/.

[5] See https://www.ey.com/en_gl/better-begins-with-you/how-an-ai-application-can-help-auditors-detect-fraud.

Summary

- Blockchain is a distributed ledger system that eliminates the need for intermediaries in a variety of transactions.
- No central authority can modify existing transactions in a blockchain network.
- Blockchain allows multiple parties that do not fully trust each other to collaborate with a single, shared source of truth.
- Blockchain reduces the need for middlemen.
- Blockchain technology must be designed carefully to ensure participants act properly. So, Blockchain is distributed, new transactions require consensus of the participants before they can be added to the network, and transactions cannot be modified after they are confirmed on the blockchain.
- Miners are nodes in the blockchain network that creates blocks. Miners create proof of work when adding transactions to the chain. Network administrators create proof of authority to add new blocks. Miners must offer proof of stake so they are at risk when creating blocks.
- Bitcoin cryptocurrency is a prominent example of the use of blockchain networks.
- Ethereum is a blockchain platform to facilitate exchange of a variety of digital assets.
- There are three types of blockchain: public, private, and consortium. Public blockchains have no access restrictions. Private blockchains usually require permissions to join the network. Consortium blockchains are administered by one or more organizations that establish access rights and permissions.
- There are many existing and potential applications of blockchain technology, and it has the potential to affect the accounting industry through changes in the ways transactions are initiated, authorized, executed, and reported. This will further impact how auditors collect evidence and assure business conduct.

- Artificial intelligence (AI) can create up to $5.8 trillion in annual value across business sectors.
- AI or cognitive technologies have been aided by advances in computer systems and the availability of data. Machine learning is a subset of AI applications, and deep learning is a subset of machine learning.
- Artificial neural networks are the engine of machine learning applications. Neural networks consist of one or more layers with neurons or nodes. Neurons process input data to deliver output predictions.
- Deep learning applications involve complex, multilayer neural networks.
- Most machine learning applications perform either classification or regression. Classification involves two or more labeled outputs or classes. Regression involves predictions of real numbers. There are five basic questions that AI/machine learning can answer, but those questions can address many business problems.
- There are several types of learning for machine learning applications: supervised, unsupervised, semi-supervised, and reinforcement. These differ in how the training data are constituted.
- The performance of machine learning models that produce classification predictions can be assessed with confusion matrices and precision, recall, and accuracy ratios.

Key Words

accuracy ratio (*515*) Machine learning performance ratio formed by dividing the correct classifications by the number of values in the dataset.

artificial intelligence (*508*) Intelligence exhibited by machines rather than humans.

artificial neural network (*511*) The mathematical model underlying machine learning; consists of inputs, nodes or neurons, and outputs in one or more layers.

Bitcoin (*494*) One cryptocurrency.

blockchain (*494*) Distributed ledger system originally designed for Bitcoin exchange but now used to exchange a variety of digital assets.

confusion matrix (*514*) Matrix showing the correct and incorrect classifications after training a machine learning model.

consortium blockchain (*502*) Blockchain network governed by one or more organizations.

deep learning (*510*) Machine learning models that include neural networks with more than two non-output layers.

distributed ledger (*493*) A ledger where individual entries are separate in time and location.

Ethereum (*494*) A blockchain platform allowing exchange of more than cryptocurrencies.

machine learning (*509*) Artificial intelligence applications where the computer learns from example and experience rather than specific instructions.

miners (*498*) Miners are the nodes in the blockchain network creating and validating blocks.

natural language processing (NLP) (*515*) Natural Language Processing (NLP) is a branch of AI that allows computers to understand, analyze, and respond to written and spoken human language.

natural language understanding (NLU) (*515*) Natural Language Understanding (NLU) is a subset of NLP that focuses on interpreting the meaning and establishing the proper intent of written and spoken human language.

precision ratio (*515*) The ratio of correct positive predictions to the total number of positive predictions after training a machine learning model.

private blockchain (*502*) A blockchain network where participants need permission to join the network.

proof of authority (*498*) Assurance that new blocks are added only by known administrators.

proof of stake (*499*) Miners must stake a portion of their own cryptocurrency to ensure blocks are created honestly.

proof of work (*498*) The blockchain miner completes proof of work that a block was added to the network by sending a hash of the transactions in the block as well as a hash to prove that the computer work was done.

public blockchain (*501*) A blockchain network where participants do not need permission to join the network.

recall ratio (*515*) The ratio of correct predictions to true positive values in the training dataset.

reinforcement learning (*514*) Where the machine learns by trial-and-error learning from feedback as it works toward a desired goal.

robotic process automation (RPA) (*515*) Robotic Process Automation (RPA) is the use of technology, such as AI, to automate structured business processes.

semi-supervised learning (*514*) Supervised training but with missing and incorrect output labels in the training dataset.

smart contracts (*497*) Smart contracts define the terms, business rules, and transfer of assets in a piece of software code. Smart contracts should be examined among the trading partners and/or regulators.

supervised learning (*513*) Where the dataset includes matched input–output data for training.

unsupervised learning (*514*) Where the dataset only includes input data for training.

ANSWERS TO PROGRESS CHECKS

1. Two examples follow:

   A. Tracking fruit from vine to table

   Naturipe Farms is a partnership among four highly esteemed fresh berry growers. The company is going to implement blockchain technology to help export fresh fruits faster. With blockchain technology, the company can trace types of fruits back to where they were harvested, have proof of the grower's sustainability practices, and export fresh fruits faster.

   Example video: https://www.youtube.com/watch?v=1FhbNl_9a2Y

   B. Identifying counterfeit pharmaceuticals

   Boehringer Ingelheim is a family-owned, global pharmaceutical company. The company is using a blockchain-based system to verify the authenticity of pharmaceutical products and combat counterfeits. The company works with **SAP** to establish a blockchain-based system that ensures the unique identification and verification of individual medicine packages. The blockchain technology supports the company's battle with counterfeit pharmaceuticals in their supply chain.

   Example: https://news.sap.com/2021/11/boehringer-ingelheim-smart-app-prototype-counterfeit-pharmaceuticals/

2. Consortium blockchain

3. Examples of different types of blockchain:

   A. Public blockchain—Bitcoin

   Newegg.com is one of the biggest computer parts stores online, and they sell virtually everything related to computers and electronics, such as PlayStation 4, laptops, or a television. Newegg will let you use Bitcoin at checkout. Bitcoin is on a public blockchain.

B. Private blockchain—JPM Coin

The example of a private blockchain is **JPMorgan's** digital currency. It was first launched in February 2019. The JPM Coin runs on a private blockchain, which is permissioned by JPMorgan only.

https://www.marketwatch.com/story/jpmorgans-digital-currency-runs-on-a-private-blockchain-heres-what-makes-it-different-from-public-blockchains-2019-02-19

C. Consortium blockchain—we.trade

In early 2017, several global financial institutions got together and formed the Digital Trade Chain. Members included **Deutsche Bank, UniCredit** and **Rabobank**. Their platform is called we.trade (https://we-trade.com), a financial service blockchain.

4. The virtuous cycle of machine learning involves using data to learn and make optimal predictions, then when applied to more data, the results can be assessed and the model can be improved. Take **Netflix**, for example; they might test their recommendation engine on a set of training data to establish a prediction model. Then, they would expand the data and see if the recommendations were still correct. Finally, they would go live and see whether the Netflix subscribers liked the predictions.
5. There are many business questions that can be answered by the five types of AI questions. Some examples include (1) Will this firm report a material weakness in internal control? (2) Does this amount of overtime seem reasonable? (3) What is the value of this potential acquisition? (4) Is this patient likely to get cancer? (5) What action should this drone take to avoid this power line?
6. If your machine learning application classified things into four categories, the confusion matrix would have four rows and four columns.

Multiple Choice Questions connect

1. **(LO 15-2)** Ben goes to his bank to wire transfer $1,000 to his sister Jennifer. The role of the bank in this transaction is best described as
   a. miner.
   b. blockchain.
   c. middleman.
   d. consensus.
2. **(LO 15-1)** Which of the following statements is true?
   a. Because blockchain transactions are stored in chronological order, you may trace a block from an earlier transaction block to the most recent block in the blockchain.
   b. Both permissioned and public blockchains need miners to determine which transaction block should be added next.
   c. Ethereum is a private blockchain.
   d. Smart contract was introduced in Ethereum.
3. **(LO 15-3)** Which feature cannot be found in Bitcoin?
   a. Double spend
   b. Anyone can join and leave the Bitcoin network at any time
   c. Immutable history of transactions
   d. A new block is added every 10 minutes

4. **(LO 15-3)** In the Ethereum network
   a. transaction fees are higher than Bitcoin.
   b. mining of Ether occurs at a constant rate.
   c. because a smart contract describes business rules and is also flexible for different industries, it can be modified to fit the business after a block is inserted to the Ethereum network.
   d. miner uses SHA256 to determine if a block is a valid block.
5. **(LO 15-4)** A selected set of organizations may run a blockchain node separately for keeping the transaction records. Administrators from the organizations establish the access rights and permissions for each participant. This type of blockchain is often called
   a. public blockchain.
   b. permissionless blockchain.
   c. private blockchain.
   d. consortium blockchain.
6. **(LO 15-4)** Which of the following statements is false?
   a. A distributed ledger contains many copies of the same ledger.
   b. A distributed ledger stores the same set of transaction records.
   c. Because a distributed ledger exists in a blockchain network, a computer consisting of all transaction records may crash and cause the syncing issue in the blockchain network.
   d. A transaction record cannot be added to the blockchain unless there is network consensus.
7. **(LO 15-4)** Which of the following statements is false?
   a. Hyperledger is an open source blockchain platform created by the Linux foundation.
   b. Hyperledger is a permissioned blockchain with capabilities of handling smart contracts.
   c. The main objective of Hyperledger is to achieve cross-industry collaboration with blockchain technology.
   d. Hyperledger is a public blockchain.
8. **(LO 15-4)** Which of the following statements is false?
   a. Private blockchain requires permission to join the network.
   b. Bitcoin uses smart contract to specify the business rules.
   c. In Ethereum, a new block is added every 12 to 15 seconds.
   d. Blockchain transactions are immutable.
9. **(LO 15-5)** When we refer to smart contract in blockchain, we mean
   a. a contract that can be edited at any time for business rules.
   b. a digital copy of paper contract such as a Word file.
   c. a digital contract that can be distributed to the participants with all terms defined.
   d. a piece of software code that can be executed or triggered by business activities.
10. **(LO 15-3)** Which of the following is created mainly for cryptocurrency application?
    a. Ethereum
    b. Hyperledger
    c. Corda
    d. Bitcoin
11. **(LO 15-1)** What information does a block in the Bitcoin network not contain?
    a. The sender
    b. The receiver

c. The quantity of Bitcoins to transfer

d. a and b

e. None, a block contains all of this information.

12. **(LO 15-4)** What is a requirement of the proof of authority algorithm?

a. A few members have known identities.

b. A portion of the miner's blocks will be locked until it is validated.

c. Large quantities of computer power are required to solve a complex mathematical problem.

d. None of these are a requirement of the proof of authority algorithm.

13. **(LO 15-7)** Which of the following is not true with respect to artificial intelligence?

a. AI is a broad field in computer science.

b. AI is intelligence exhibited by machines rather than humans.

c. AI began in the 1990s.

d. AI is also called cognitive technologies.

e. None of these is true.

14. **(LO 15-8)** Which of the following best describes the difference between artificial intelligence and machine learning?

a. Machine learning is a subset of AI.

b. Machine learning only applies to deep learning algorithms.

c. AI and machine learning are the same thing.

d. Machine learning requires less data than AI.

e. None of these.

15. **(LO 15-8)** Which of the following best describes machine learning?

a. Machine learning is driven by programming instructions.

b. Machine learning is a different branch of computer science from AI.

c. Machine learning is a technique where a software model is trained using data.

d. Machine learning is the ability of a machine to think on its own.

e. None of these.

16. **(LO 15-8)** Which of the following is not part of the virtuous cycle of machine learning?

a. Model

b. Learn

c. Predict

d. Data

e. None of these.

17. **(LO 15-9)** Which of the following best describes artificial neural networks?

a. Training a neural network involves the use of real-world data.

b. Deep learning is required for a neural network.

c. Neural networks consist of inputs, neurons or nodes, and outputs.

d. Neural networks only have two layers.

e. None of these.

18. **(LO 15-8)** Which of the following best describes deep learning?

a. Deep learning is used to solve philosophical problems.

b. Deep learning involves complex, multilayer neural networks.

c. Deep learning is different from machine learning in fundamental ways.

d. Deep learning provides more output values than machine learning.

e. None of these.

19. **(LO 15-9)** Which of the following is not directly related to one of the five questions that machine learning/AI is best suited to answer?
    a. Which business strategy will be most successful?
    b. Is this firm a good merger candidate?
    c. What type of customer will like this new product?
    d. How much can we sell this product for?
    e. None of these.
20. **(LO 15-10)** Which of the following best describes supervised learning?
    a. The training data contain missing labels or incomplete data.
    b. The training data match inputs to nodes in the network.
    c. The training data contain input–output pairs.
    d. The training data only include input values.
    e. None of these.
21. **(LO 15-10)** Which of the following best describes unsupervised learning?
    a. The training data contain missing labels or incomplete data.
    b. The training data match inputs to nodes in the network.
    c. The training data contain input–output pairs.
    d. The training data only include input values.
    e. None of these.
22. **(LO 15-10)** Which of the following best describes semi-supervised learning?
    a. The training data contain some missing labels or incomplete data.
    b. The training data match inputs to nodes in the network.
    c. The training data contain input–output pairs.
    d. The training data only include input values.
    e. None of these.
23. **(LO 15-10)** Which of the following best describes reinforcement learning?
    a. The model determines how elements of the dataset are alike.
    b. The training data match inputs to nodes in the network.
    c. The training data contain input–output pairs.
    d. The model learns by trial-and-error.
    e. None of these.
24. **(LO 15-11)** Which of the following best describes a confusion matrix?
    a. It is a table summarizing the prediction results.
    b. It has as many rows and columns as classifications to predict.
    c. It can be used to calculate other performance metrics.
    d. All of these.
    e. None of these.
25. **(LO 15-11)** If a confusion matrix shows 46 TP, 6 FN, 500 TN, and 4 FP, what is the precision ratio?
    a. 0.90
    b. 0.92
    c. 0.98
    d. 0.88
    e. None of these.

26. **(LO 15-11)** If a confusion matrix shows 46 TP, 6 FN, 500 TN, and 4 FP, what is the recall ratio?
    a. 0.90
    b. 0.92
    c. 0.98
    d. 0.88
    e. None of these.
27. **(LO 15-11)** If a confusion matrix shows 46 TP, 6 FN, 500 TN, and 4 FP, what is the accuracy ratio?
    a. 0.90
    b. 0.92
    c. 0.98
    d. 0.88
    e. None of these.
28. **(LO 15-11)** If a confusion matrix shows 25 TP, 5 FN, 1000 TN, and 5 FP, what is the precision ratio?
    a. 0.90
    b. 0.92
    c. 0.99
    d. 0.83
    e. None of these.
29. **(LO 15-11)** If a confusion matrix shows 25 TP, 5 FN, 1000 TN, and 5 FP, what is the recall ratio?
    a. 0.90
    b. 0.92
    c. 0.99
    d. 0.83
    e. None of these.
30. **(LO 15-11)** If a confusion matrix shows 25 TP, 5 FN, 1000 TN, and 5 FP, what is the accuracy ratio?
    a. 0.90
    b. 0.92
    c. 0.99
    d. 0.83
    e. None of these.

Discussion Questions connect

1. **(LO 15-3)** Bitcoin was introduced in 2009. The total Bitcoin amount that exists today is much more than the total Bitcoin amount in 2009 or 2010. How can this happen?
2. **(LO 15-3)** Since Bitcoin uses blockchain technology and is cheaper than the traditional way of doing business, why is Bitcoin not accepted by many government agencies?
3. **(LO 15-3)** Why is Ethereum a better choice over Bitcoin for business-related applications?
4. **(LO 15-4)** What are the three types of blockchain? What are major differences among these blockchains?

5. **(LO 15-6)** You have been tasked with forming an audit and assurance team to work with companies that have adopted blockchain technology. What skill sets will you emphasize when choosing your team members and why?
6. **(LO 15-7)** Recently, more than 20 percent of companies surveyed indicated they were testing or considering artificial intelligence applications in their business, but only 4 percent were actively using AI. Why do you think companies (a) are interested in AI and (b) are having trouble implementing AI?
7. **(LO 15-8), (LO 15-9)** Review the five basic questions that AI/machine learning can answer. Develop additional business questions for each question.
8. **(LO 15-12)** Visit the websites of major accounting firms. Search for what they are doing with AI/machine learning. How do you think this will affect the accounting profession over the next 10 years?
9. **(LO 15-7)** Give examples of process automation applications.

Design Element: Duncan Smith/Getty Images

Lab 15-1 Using Alteryx to Audit Accounting Data

Keywords

Alteryx, auditing

Lab Insight

In this lab you will use Alteryx to aggregate and analyze accounting data, which you can then write to an Excel spreadsheet. Before working on this assignment, you should review the concepts on accounting treatment of cash and accounts receivable.

Refer to the step-by-step instructions in Connect or those provided by your instructor for creating an aging analysis of accounts.

Follow the instructions and answer questions provided in Connect or your LMS. Additional information and links to helpful videos on installing Alteryx are also available in Connect.

Lab 15-2 Introduction to Robotic Process Automation (RPA) and UiPath

Keywords

UiPath, robotic process automation

Lab Insight

Before working on this RPA lab, you need to Sign in UiPath, download UiPath, and install UiPath to your computer. Please make sure that you have UiPath installed and can login before working on this Lab. **Refer to the installation instructions including links to helpful videos on downloading and installing UiPath available in the Connect Library.**

Follow the step-by-step instructions in Connect or provided by your instructor to complete this Lab.

Chapter Sixteen

The Balanced Scorecard, Business Model Canvas, and Business Value of Information Technology

A Look at This Chapter

As managers and designers of IT systems as well as business partners, accountants are often involved in helping formulate and implement company strategy. The Balanced Scorecard is a well-known strategic performance management system that many companies use to formulate, implement, and monitor strategic performance. In this chapter, we explain concepts embodied in the Balanced Scorecard and describe how information technology supports a company's strategic objectives from a Balanced Scorecard viewpoint. We also examine other strategic tools such as the Val IT framework and the Business Model Canvas.

A Look Back

Chapter 15 explained the accountants' role in the business when monitoring and auditing accounting information systems.

A Look Ahead

Chapter 17 presents a process for assessing the business value of IT initiatives. As users, managers, designers, and evaluators of the firm's IT systems, accountants are important members of the team that will develop the business case for AIS initiatives. Additionally, as users, managers, and evaluators, they can also be asked to review business cases for IT initiatives in general.

Atstock Productions/Shutterstock

With 31,000 stores worldwide and 400,000 partners serving 100 million customers a week, **Starbucks** leadership suggests scale and complexity are two of the company's biggest challenges. Starbucks leadership also knows technology will figure heavily into the 49-year-old company's success for the next 50 years. So, how will Starbucks balance the power of technology with the commitment to the company's mission to nurture the human spirit? And how can technology actually enhance the ability to enhance that mission?

This chapter focuses on how technology can be used to support the Balanced Scorecard. The Scorecard is a well-known strategic performance management system that many companies use to formulate, implement, and monitor strategic performance.

Source: https://stories.starbucks.com/stories/2020/how-starbucks-plans-to-use-technology-to-nurture-the-human-spirit/ (Accessed October 2022).

CHAPTER OUTLINE

Balanced Scorecard Framework

Learning and Growth Perspective

Process Perspective

Customer Perspective

Financial Perspective

Framework Integrating Strategy, Operations, and IT Investment

Role of AIS/IT in a Balanced Scorecard Framework

Using a Balanced Scorecard Management Process

Role of AIS/IT in the Balanced Scorecard Management Process

IT Governance Institute Val IT Framework

Implementing Val IT Governance

Business Model Canvas

Elements of the Business Model Canvas

Impact of Information Technology

Similarities with Strategy Maps

LEARNING OBJECTIVES

After reading this chapter, you should be able to:

16-1 Describe the Balanced Scorecard framework.

16-2 Explain the purpose of strategy maps.

16-3 Describe different types of IT and why IT initiatives can be difficult to evaluate.

16-4 Define the Balanced Scorecard management process.

16-5 Describe how an AIS system contributes to a Balanced Scorecard management process.

16-6 Describe the IT Governance Val IT framework.

16-7 Explain how organizations implement the Val IT framework.

16-8 Describe the purpose of a business model canvas.

16-9 Articulate and define the nine building blocks of a business model canvas.

16-10 Describe the potential impact of IT on an organization using the business model canvas.

LO 16-1

Describe the Balanced Scorecard framework.

BALANCED SCORECARD FRAMEWORK

Investments in information technology, such as AIS, best take on value only in the context of the company's strategy. Indeed, a recent survey by KPMG[1] suggests that 66 percent of organizations have been extremely effective at using digital technology to advance their business strategy. Executives should analyze each proposed digital investment as part of a portfolio of potential investments that help to implement a strategy.[2]

The Balanced Scorecard provides a tool that can describe the contribution of IT to the company's strategy. The Balanced Scorecard is a performance measurement framework that allows managers to measure the firm's performance from multiple perspectives that follow from the firm's mission, strategy, and objectives. According to the Balanced Scorecard Institute (www.balancedscorecard.org),

> The balanced scorecard is a strategic planning and management system that is used extensively in business and industry, government, and nonprofit organizations worldwide to align business activities to the vision and strategy of the organization, improve internal and external communications, and monitor organization performance against strategic goals.

The **Balanced Scorecard framework** describes performance from four different perspectives based on the firm's strategy to achieve shareholder value. Objectives for each perspective describe the strategy in a series of cause-and-effect relationships (see Exhibit 16.1).

EXHIBIT 16.1
Relationships between Balanced Scorecard Perspectives

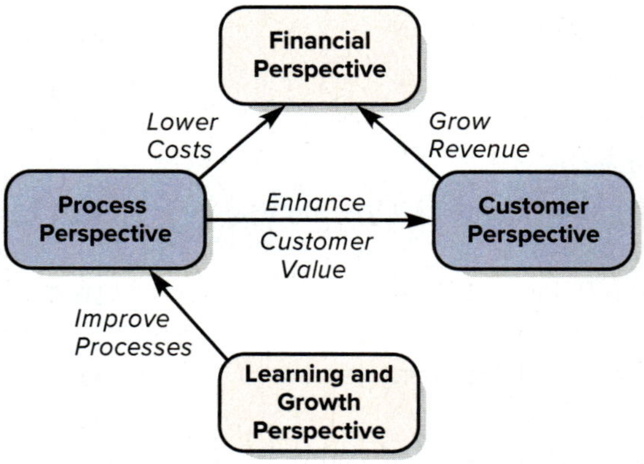

Connection with Practice

Bain and Company, a prominent consulting company, conducts an annual survey of almost 1,500 international executives. The survey asks about the use of the 25 most popular management tools and techniques. For 2017, 29 percent of respondents were using some form of the Balanced Scorecard for strategic management.

[1]Digital to the Core: KPMG 2022 U.S. Technology Survey Report, page 11, https://advisory.kpmg.us/content/dam/advisory/en/pdfs/digital-to-the-core.pdf (accessed October 2022).

[2]See, for example, Deloitte, *Value Matters: Getting Back to What's Really Important in Planning, Budgeting, and Forecasting,* Deloitte Consulting, LLP (2010).

Learning and Growth Perspective

Tim Pannell /Fuse/Getty Images

The **learning and growth perspective** describes the firm's objectives for improvements in tangible and intangible infrastructure. The firm addresses its goals for investments in human capital, information capital, and organizational capital to make sure that the firm is strategically ready to continuously improve its process performance. Managers use metrics to focus investments, such as employee training or new systems development, to achieve the firm's learning and growth objectives and also link those changes to process objectives. Those metrics are considered leading indicators of performance because investments in learning and growth in this period will affect customer and financial metrics in the future.

Process Perspective

The **process perspective** describes the firm's objectives for its business processes so that the firm operates efficiently while delivering products and services that meet its customers' requirements. In their book, *Strategy Maps,*[3] Kaplan and Norton describe four types of business processes:

1. Operations management processes, such as supply, production, distribution, and risk management.
2. Customer management processes, such as those involved with the selection, acquisition, and retention of customers and growth of the firm's market.
3. Innovation processes, such as identifying opportunities, research and development, product design and development, and product launch.
4. Regulatory and social processes, such as financial reporting, accounting, and those that manage environmental, safety and health, employment, and community issues.

Firms invest in learning and growth to improve business process performance, which in turn affects customer and financial performance objectives. Process performance is measured generally in terms of cost, time, quality, and throughput. Process cost directly affects financial productivity measures, as shown in Exhibit 16.2. Time measures, such as cycle time and on-time delivery, directly affect customer service. Process quality affects product quality and customer service and thus drives customer satisfaction and retention. Throughput describes the quantity of products and services that the process can deliver. Financial perspective productivity measures, such as return on assets or return on sales, relate costs to throughput. In general, companies seek to lower process costs, lower cycle times, improve process quality, and increase process throughput to deliver their value proposition to their customers and achieve financial objectives. Process perspective metrics are considered leading indicators of firm performance because they affect future customer and financial metrics.

[3] R. S. Kaplan and D. Norton, *Strategy Maps: Converting Intangible Assets into Tangible Outcomes.* (Boston: Harvard Business School Press, 2004).

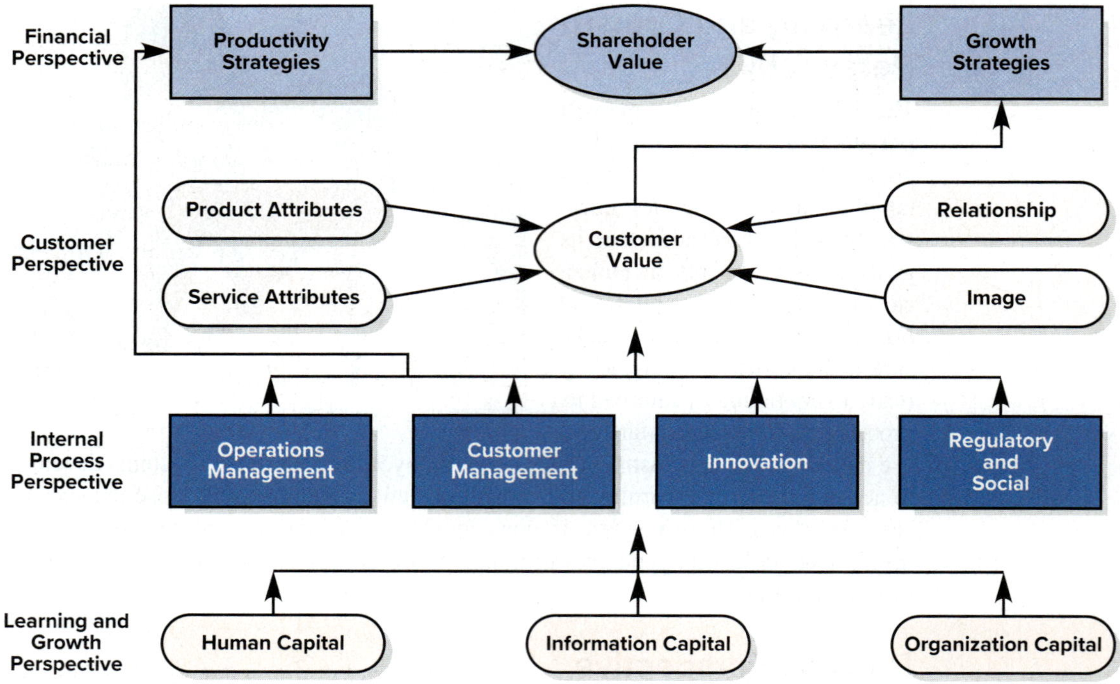

EXHIBIT 16.2
Generic Strategy Map

Customer Perspective

Within the **customer perspective**, customer satisfaction is considered a lagging indicator of firm performance, since it describes customers' satisfaction with products purchased in the past. By operating its business processes, the firm creates a **value proposition** that differentiates it from its competition. The value proposition includes attributes of the firm's products, such as price, quality, and selection, as well as attributes of its relationship with its customers, such as the level of service and efforts to build long-term relationships, and its brand image (see Exhibit 16.2). When the firm's value proposition meets or exceeds customers' requirements, customer satisfaction results in customer retention and new customer acquisition, which drives sales growth.

Financial Perspective

The final measure is the **financial perspective**. Accounting-based performance measures are considered lagging indicators of firm performance. They confirm the success of the firm's investments in learning and growth, process performance, and ability to deliver value to customers. Balanced Scorecard financial objectives usually relate to firm productivity and long-term growth, both of which drive shareholder value.

LO 16-2

Explain the purpose of strategy maps.

FRAMEWORK INTEGRATING STRATEGY, OPERATIONS, AND IT INVESTMENT

The Balanced Scorecard provides a useful integrating framework to examine a company's strategy/operations management system as well as the potential contributions of IT to company success. A Balanced Scorecard strategy map illustrates the various components of a company's strategy across the four perspectives described in the preceding section.

Perspective	Performance Objectives	Critical Success Factors	Key Performance Indicators
Financial	How does the firm's performance drive shareholder value?	Demonstrate productivity and growth necessary to create shareholder value.	Return on assets/equity/sales, earnings per share growth rate, sales growth rate, and market value added
Customer	How does the firm deliver value to its customers to create long-term growth?	Create customer value necessary to drive revenue growth.	Market share, new customer acquisition rate, repeat purchase rate, and customer satisfaction
Process	How do the firm's processes deliver value to customers while operating efficiently?	Conduct business processes to create customer value and achieve profitable growth.	Process cost, quality, timeliness, and outputs
Learning and growth	How do investments in employee, organizational, and information-system capabilities support continuous improvement of the firm's business processes and customer relationships?	Invest in human capital, organizational capital, and information capital to improve processes and deliver strategic objectives.	Assessments of employee knowledge, skills, and values; employee change readiness and strategic awareness surveys; readiness ratings of software applications; levels of spending

EXHIBIT 16.3
Balanced Scorecard Perspectives, Objectives, Sample Critical Success Factors, and Key Performance Indicators

One important feature of strategy maps is the identification of expected cause-and-effect links among perspectives.

A **strategy map** is a one-page representation of the firm's strategic priorities and the cause-and-effect linkages among those strategic priorities.[4] It illustrates the firm's strategic objectives (also called critical success factors, as shown in Exhibit 16.3) for each perspective as well as the cause-and-effect links among perspectives. A strategy map allows firms to assess and prioritize gaps between their current and desired performance levels.

LO 16-3

Describe different types of IT and why IT initiatives can be difficult to evaluate.

ROLE OF AIS/IT IN A BALANCED SCORECARD FRAMEWORK

A Balanced Scorecard framework allows companies to assess the value of IT investments in terms of contribution to strategic objectives, regardless of whether they employ a Balanced Scorecard performance management system. A Balanced Scorecard framework recognizes the difference between investments in tangible information technology and the capabilities provided by that technology. **Information capital** is an intangible asset that reflects the readiness of the company's technology to support strategic internal processes. In other words, information capital includes

- Computing hardware, such as individual computers.
- Infrastructure, such as communications networks.
- Applications, such as accounting and decision support software.
- Employees' abilities to use the technology effectively.

To understand the value of IT in a Balanced Scorecard framework and the importance of portfolios of IT investments rather than individual investments, it is helpful to consider different ways to characterize the nature of IT. The following classifications (see Exhibit 16.4) characterize the nature of information technologies and can indicate which initiatives could be harder to implement and evaluate:[5]

[4]Ibid.
[5]A. McAfee, "Mastering the Three Worlds of Information Technology," *Harvard Business Review*, November 2006, pp. 141–149.

EXHIBIT 16.4
Three Categories of Information Technologies

IT Category	Description	Characteristics
Function IT	Assists execution with discrete tasks.	Does not require complements, but impact can increase with users' skill.
Network IT	Facilitates interactions.	Does not require complements, but impact increases with users' skill and extent of teamwork.
Enterprise IT	Specifies the nature of business processes and requires interactions.	Requires complements and impact often depends on users' skills, teamwork, changes to the way work is performed, and changes in the way decisions are made.

1. **Function IT (FIT)**—a type of information technology that performs a single function, such as enhancing worker productivity for stand-alone tasks. Examples of FIT include word-processing and spreadsheet applications and computer-aided design applications. Function information technologies can improve the productivity of skilled workers, but they can be used without affecting the remainder of the organization.
2. **Network IT (NIT)**—a type of information technology that allows people to communicate with one another. Examples of NIT include email, instant messaging, network technologies, and blog applications. Network information technologies allow collaboration, foster teamwork, and improve information exchange within the organization, but they do little to change the way that work is performed or decisions are made.
3. **Enterprise IT (EIT)**—a type of information technology that restructures interactions within the organization as well as with external partners. Examples of EIT include customer relationship management (CRM) and supply chain management (SCM) applications. Enterprise information technologies often change the way business processes are performed as well as the way decisions are made.

Compared to function and network IT, enterprise IT provides more capabilities but requires more complementary resources to achieve its potential benefits. Enterprise IT can provide the following organizational capabilities:

- *Transaction automation*—EIT can automate transaction processing, replacing personnel while ensuring that each transaction is performed in a uniform and controlled manner. This allows—and forces—standardized work flow and applications of business rules.
- *Process management automation*—EIT can automate administrative processes, incorporating business rules and decision heuristics and reducing the need for administrative specialists.
- *Process integration*—EIT can integrate processes previously managed separately, reducing the need for separate systems and separate administration.
- *Customer service*—EIT can provide general and customized service to both internal and external clients, thereby reducing the need for customer service agents.
- *Performance monitoring and decision support*—EIT can record various process performance indicators and more timely summarize information on **key performance indicators** for management use.

After enterprise IT is implemented, its performance becomes embedded in one or more organizational processes, making it difficult for firms to evaluate the benefit of the IT investment separately from the performance of the process. However, the performance of business processes usually depends on a variety of factors. For example, when an EIT improves decision support, the impact on business value depends on the decisions, and it can take 3 to 5 years for managers to learn how to use better and timelier information.

IT systems provide relative few business benefits on their own. The value of IT can depend on the existence of complementary organizational capabilities, such as skilled workers, teamwork, the way that work is performed, and the authority to make decisions. Furthermore, the level of these complementary resources can change over time after an IT system is implemented.

PROGRESS CHECK

1. Describe how you think IT creates value for **Starbucks,** whose CIO is now also general manager of digital ventures. Based on what you know about the company, what category of IT best describes Starbucks' digital ventures?
2. From your own experience, describe examples of function IT and network IT.

LO 16-4

Define the Balanced Scorecard management process.

USING A BALANCED SCORECARD MANAGEMENT PROCESS

While the relationships among Balanced Scorecard perspectives shown in the generic strategy map (Exhibit 16.2) show how information capital contributes to critical business processes, which in turn contribute to customer acquisition and retention and result in financial performance, the strategy map does not describe how companies go about implementing their strategy. According to the creators of the Balanced Scorecard, companies can plan, implement, and monitor performance using the following **Balanced Scorecard management process.**[6] The steps in the process can be thought of as continuous, with the last step feeding back to the first step, as shown in Exhibit 16.5.

1. *Formulate*—the company examines its competitive environment and identifies ways in which it can best compete consistent with its mission, vision, and values.
2. *Translate*—the company establishes specific objectives, measures, targets, and initiatives and develops capital, initiative, and other long-term budgets to guide resource allocation and action according to its strategy.

EXHIBIT 16.5
Balanced Scorecard Management Process

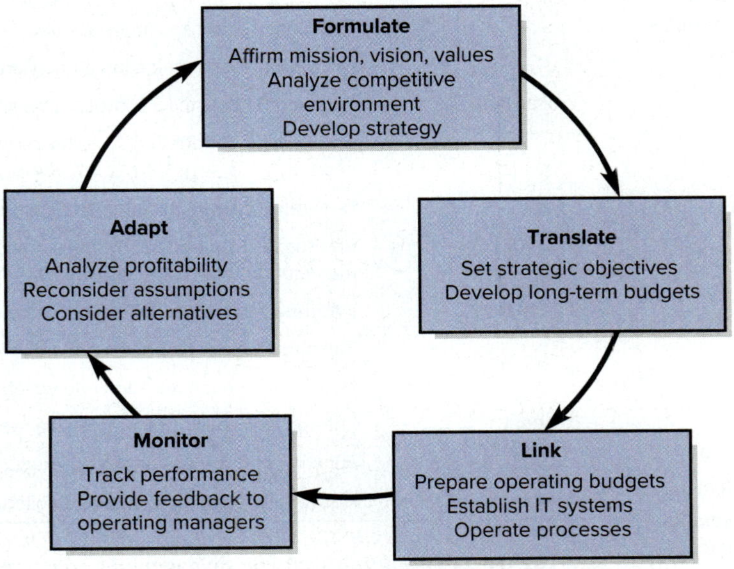

[6] R. S. Kaplan and D. Norton, *The Execution Premium* (Boston: Harvard Business Press, 2008).

3. *Link to operations*—the company prepares operating budgets, prioritizes business process improvements, and develops key performance indicators. At this point, it establishes necessary IT systems to support strategic business processes as well as management reporting and review capabilities.
4. *Monitor*—the company monitors performance to ensure processes are meeting objectives and provides feedback to operating managers for continuous improvement.
5. *Adapt*—the company evaluates the effectiveness of its strategy, conducts profitability analytics, tests the cause-and-effect assumptions of the strategy, and identifies potential alternatives.

LO 16-5

Describe how an AIS system contributes to a Balanced Scorecard management process.

ROLE OF AIS/IT IN THE BALANCED SCORECARD MANAGEMENT PROCESS

IT also has an important role in implementing and managing a Balanced Scorecard management process or similar planning, forecasting, and budgeting processes. Beginning with strategy formulation, companies rely on a variety of information technology systems and capabilities to support their strategy execution and management process. Exhibit 16.6 provides some examples. Business intelligence and financial reporting systems provide data to support strategy development, and business analytics systems provide forecasts and analysis to support senior executives' decisions. Those broad strategic decisions are translated into objectives that guide the capital budgeting process, supported by a variety of systems. Strategic objectives then link to operations. Specific budgets are set, and the company conducts operations, supported by appropriate enterprise IT, such as ERP systems. The enterprise IT performance monitoring and decision support capabilities then assess operational performance against the strategic objectives. Operational managers adjust operations based on feedback. Finally, senior executives use information from business intelligence and financial reporting systems to reevaluate the strategy and consider alternatives.

EXHIBIT 16.6
AIS/IT Contributions to the Balanced Scorecard Management Process

Process Step	Information Technology Capabilities
1. Formulate	Enterprise IT (business intelligence systems, financial reporting systems)
	Function IT (business analytics, executive dashboards)
	Network IT (communication and collaboration)
2. Translate	Function IT (Balanced Scorecard systems, business analytics)
	Enterprise IT (budgeting systems, performance monitoring, and decision support)
	Network IT (communication and collaboration)
3. Link to operations	Enterprise IT (budgeting systems, transaction processing, process management, customer service, process integration)
4. Monitor	Integrated Enterprise IT (performance monitoring and decision support)
	Function IT (operational dashboards with key performance indicators)
	Network IT (communication and collaboration)
5. Adapt	Enterprise IT (business intelligence systems)
	Function IT (business analytics, executive dashboards)
	Network IT (communication and collaboration)

Think about how the models that you prepared in Chapters 6, 7, and 8 would support the information requirements outlined here.

The use of structured strategic management processes, such as the Balanced Scorecard, ties the effective use of supporting technologies, as described in Exhibit 16.6, to successful performance. Standardized, integrated, and networked technology enhances decision making and performance management. While the capabilities of function IT systems, such as business analytics and executive dashboard applications, are important, companies need to gather data from multiple sources, linking dashboards to an integrated view of operating processes. A complete picture of the company's value chain enhances data analysis and accelerates decision making and planning.

LO 16-6

Describe the IT Governance Val IT framework.

IT GOVERNANCE INSTITUTE VAL IT FRAMEWORK

Recently, the IT Governance Institute also developed a structured framework for IT investment and management. The **Val IT** framework is intended to help managers create business value from IT investments. It aligns with and complements the COBIT control framework described in Chapter 13. Val IT is aimed at the management of IT benefits over an investment's life cycle net of any costs and adjusted for risk. It is similar to the Balanced Scorecard since it requires organizations to define value in terms of the organization's strategic objectives.

Val IT requires managers and executives to focus on the following four major questions,[7] illustrated in Exhibit 16.7:

1. Are we doing the right things? To answer this question, managers must examine whether investments are consistent with their business principles and contributing to the achievement of strategic objectives.
2. Are we doing them the right way? This requires managers to consider whether the investment is consistent with their current IT architecture and other IT initiatives.
3. Are we doing them well? This question focuses on processes. Managers must evaluate whether the organization has the right technical and business resources to support the investment.
4. Are we getting the benefits? Managers must understand what the investment will deliver and establish clear metrics to help assess whether the investment delivers those benefits.

EXHIBIT 16.7
Fundamental Val IT Questions

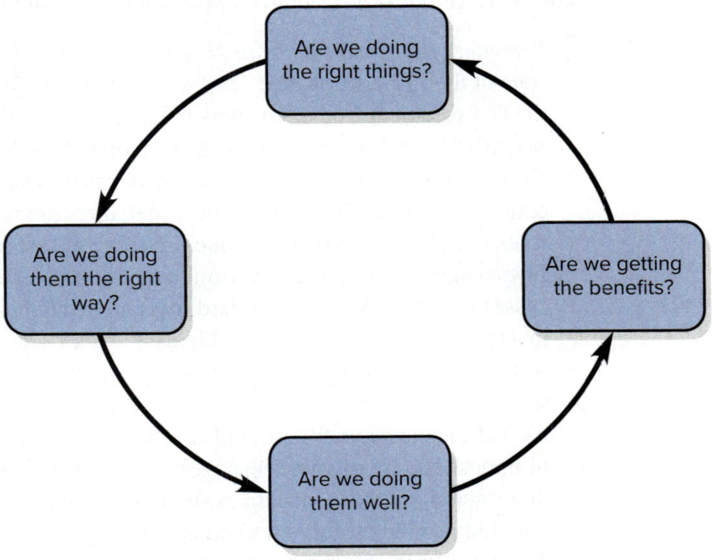

[7]For further information on Val IT, see *Enterprise Value: Governance of IT Investments - The Val IT Framework 2.0,* published by the IT Governance Institute.

Val IT distinguishes among (1) projects, activities to deliver a defined capability; (2) programs, structured groups of interdependent projects; and (3) portfolios, groups of programs, projects, services, and other IT resources. The Val IT framework establishes three domains with corresponding governance, portfolio management, and investment management processes:

1. Value governance establishes the governance part of the framework, which includes defining the various portfolios as well as mechanisms for monitoring the effectiveness of all Val IT processes.
2. Portfolio management establishes strategic priorities, determines required characteristics of the investment portfolios, and monitors the performance of the overall portfolio. It also sets program priorities within funding constraints, based on strategic alignment, net benefits, and risks.
3. Investment management proposes potential programs and the projects that make up those programs, executes authorized programs, reports investment and program performance, and retires programs when the desired business value is delivered or it is clear that the business value cannot be delivered.

Thus, the three domains interact to provide oversight and management of individual projects, combinations of projects within programs, and programs within the overall portfolio.

When properly implemented, Val IT focuses on delivering business value while COBIT focuses on managing risk. Both are essential elements of IT governance.

LO 16-7

Explain how organizations implement the Val IT framework.

IMPLEMENTING VAL IT GOVERNANCE

The steps to implement and use Val IT are similar to the steps of the Balanced Scorecard management process outlined earlier in this chapter. Organizations often fail to realize value from their IT investments. Experts agree that the most common problem is the lack of a structured approach; however, the second most common problem is lack of knowledge of how to begin. Four Val IT implementation steps are designed to assist organizations in developing a structured approach to managing IT investments:

1. *Recognize problems with prior IT investments.* In this step, organizations should assess the state of their IT governance. They should consider whether the roles and responsibilities of the IT function and other business functions are clearly defined. They should also assess whether IT and business functions collaborate fully to deliver value from IT investments.
2. *Define characteristics of the ideal future state.* These include awareness and communication of roles and responsibilities. Managers are responsible and accountable for their roles in delivering business value. Investments are aligned with business strategies. Investment performance is continuously monitored against goals. Management processes are effective, and standard tools are available across the enterprise to evaluate investments and respond to problems.
3. *Assess the organizations' readiness to undertake IT business value management.* This self-assessment examines whether the organization is aware of and recognizes the need for Val IT management principles. This assessment provides insight into current levels of understanding of value management principles and the commitment to practices that implement those principles. It also provides information about gaps between current and desired attitudes and practices.
4. *Take action.* Build awareness of value management principles. Redefine processes, roles, and responsibilities. Identify and create an inventory of IT investments both planned and ongoing. Review the business cases for individual investments. Evaluate and prioritize investments to form new programs and an overall portfolio.

LO 16-8

Describe the purpose of a business model canvas.

BUSINESS MODEL CANVAS

A business model describes how a business operates or plans to operate. Strategy maps are a form of business model and strategy implementation tool. A business model integrates business strategy, business organization, and the application of technology as shown in Exhibit 16.8. A business model is influenced by external forces, such as the social and legal environment in which the business operates, competitive forces in the industry, customer demand, and technological change. The business model implements business strategy and determines how technology will be used within the organization.

The **business model canvas** is a relatively new, but widely used, tool that organizations can use to describe the essential elements of their business model in one page.[8] Like strategy maps, the business model canvas is easy to understand, helps focus business model discussion, and shows the connections between investments in the business and desired outcomes. It is also useful in describing how information technology can support, or change, a business model.

EXHIBIT 16.8
Business Model Integrates Strategy, Organization, and Technology[9]

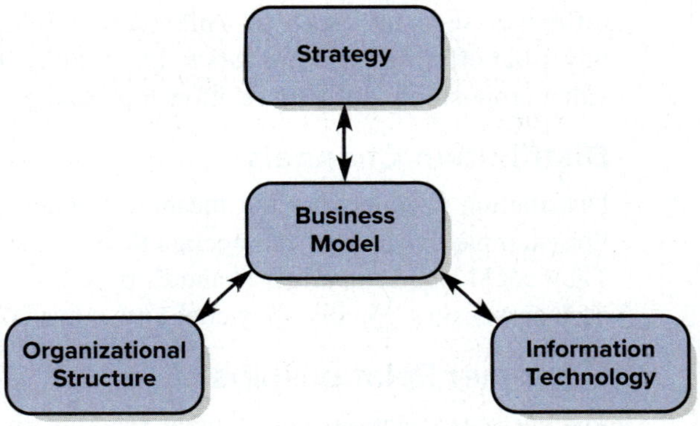

LO 16-9

Articulate and define the nine building blocks of a business model canvas.

Elements of the Business Model Canvas

The business model canvas has nine building blocks as shown in Exhibit 16.9. Importantly, it is not only the blocks but the relationships among those blocks that defines a business model, like the cause-and-effect relationships in a strategy map described earlier in this chapter.

EXHIBIT 16.9
Canvas Example

Source: Osterwalder, Alexander, and Yves Pigneur, *Business Model Generation* (John Wiley & Sons, Inc., 2010).

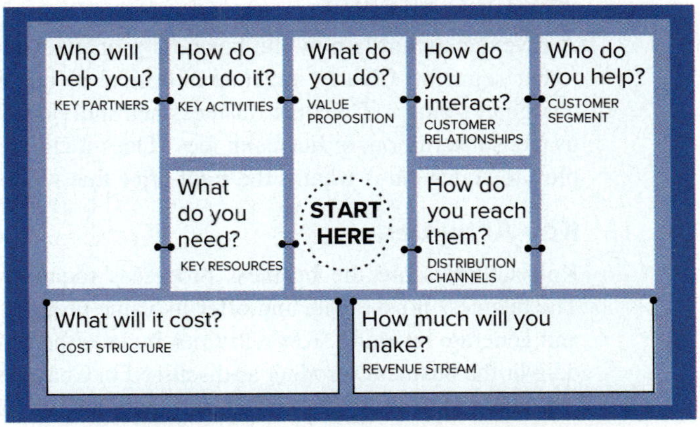

[8]Based on Alexander Osterwalder, *The Business Model Ontology: A Proposition in a Design Science Approach,* figure 8, (Hoboken NJ: John Wiley & Sons, Inc., 2004).
[9]Business model canvas templates are available at https://www.strategyzer.com/.

Value Proposition

Again, like a strategy map, the value proposition is the heart of the business model canvas. Thus, Exhibit 16.9 labels the value proposition element of the canvas with "start here." This is where a business defines what it does to attract and retain customers. A value proposition includes the characteristics of a bundle of products or services that are expected to be valued by a specific customer segment. Product characteristics like quality, design, price, convenience, and functionality affect the customers' willingness to buy. Brand image also influences many customers.

Customer Segments

Customer segments represent the group or groups of customers that the business intends to serve. Examples include mass market, niche market, or segmented market. Business models focusing on the mass market don't distinguish among segments. These businesses assume all their customers have similar needs. Niche market models focus on a specialized subset of customers with distinct characteristics, such as **Ferrari** focusing on wealthy car enthusiasts. Businesses with segmented customers offer variations of their products to difference segments, such as **Volkswagen** selling less-expensive cars to the typical car buyer but offering **Porsche** cars to the wealthy buyers. Each segment involves a different value proposition, different relationships, and potentially different profitability.

Distribution Channels

Distribution channels are the means by which products and services get to customers. For example, businesses can operate their own channels, such as retail stores or websites. They could also use partner channels by selling through wholesalers, partner retailers, or partner websites. Finally, they could use a mix of their own and partner channels.

Customer Relationships

The customer relationships element specifies the relationship that the business wants to establish with each customer segment. For example, a customer segment may require personal assistance. These customers must be able to communicate with a real person to solve problems or assist. Other customers may prefer self-service, so the business needs to create all necessary means for those customers to help themselves. Some customers need automated services that could be supported by artificial intelligence. Still other customers are deeply involved with the business' products and seek to co-create business value.

Revenue Streams

A revenue stream is how the business monetizes its products and services for each customer segment. Clearly, revenue is critical to business success. The question is how to charge customers. Does the business sell individual products for a price? Does it charge usage, subscription, or licensing fees? Does it charge a brokerage fee? For all these examples, the question is what is the right price that will optimize the revenue stream.

Key Activities

Key activities are the business processes required to make the business model work. The business must create and offer its value proposition, maintain customer relationships, and generate revenues. Key activities include the business processes to source, make, and deliver the business' product as discussed in Chapters 6, 7, and 8. Additionally, key activities can include innovation processes that allow the business to develop new products and solve customer problems.

Key Resources

The tangible or intangible assets that make the business model work are the company's key resources. The resources can be physical—such as **Starbucks**' local shops, **Amazon**'s vast computing power, or **Walmart**'s supercenters—or intellectual—such as **Nike**'s ability to design new and desired consumer products. They can include human resources, such as pharmaceutical companies engaged in creating new drugs. They can also include financial resources, such as those that give businesses the flexibility to operate key activities and acquire other key resources as necessary.

Key Partners

Key partners provide the array of inputs that allows the business to function. Partnerships include strategic alliances and partnerships, joint ventures, and buyer–supplier relationships. Key partners allow businesses the benefit of economies of scale, risk reduction, and access to resources that would otherwise be unavailable. These also include firms to which the business has outsourced key activities.

Cost Structure

Cost structure means the major costs incurred by the business. It indicates whether the business focuses on lean operations or provides premium services. Companies like Walmart and **Southwest Airlines** focus on lean operations and cost reduction. Luxury hotels instead focus on value creation for their unique customer segment. Cost structure recognizes the categories of cost, such as fixed and variable. It is affected by economies of scale and scope.

Example

Exhibit 16.10 is a hypothetical simplified business model canvas for Starbucks. Starbucks offers a value proposition based on brand image, quality, and availability. Starbucks customers include coffee (and tea) drinkers at home and coffee shop patrons

EXHIBIT 16.10
Canvas Example

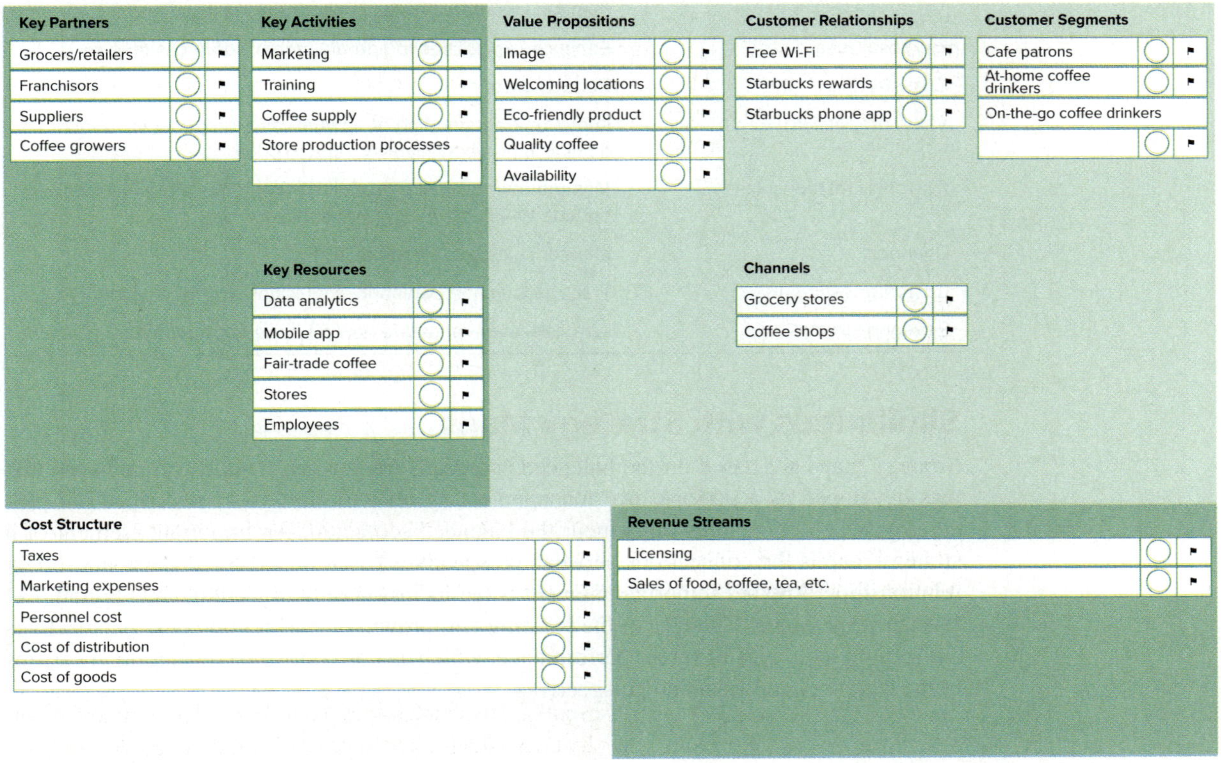

away from home. They reach those customers through their coffee shop and retail grocery store channels. They build customer relationships through their rewards programs, a phone app that allows customers to order ahead, and in-store amenities such as free Wi-Fi. Revenue streams include sales of coffee, tea, and food products as well as licensing fees.

To deliver the value proposition, operate their stores, and maintain relationships, they perform key activities such as in-store production, coffee acquisition, roasting and distribution, marketing, and employee/franchisee training. Key resources include their stores, employees, fair-trade coffee, and their technology supporting their mobile app and data analytics. Key partners include growers, suppliers, franchisees, and grocery stores/retailers that sell packages of Starbucks products. Important elements of their cost structure include cost of goods, personnel cost, distribution cost, marketing, and taxes.

LO 16-10

Describe the potential impact of IT on an organization using the business model canvas.

Impact of Information Technology

Information technology can reduce costs, increase revenue, or completely change business models. The business model canvas allows the assessment of potential impacts. Continuing with the Starbucks example presented earlier, Exhibit 16.11 shows potential impacts of information technology on all nine elements of Starbucks' business model canvas. The business model canvas shows the kinds of data that might be created and exploited by Starbucks. For example, the rewards program and mobile app allow Starbucks to capture customer preferences and assist with marketing particular products to individual customers. Store sales data (channels) allow Starbucks to plan inventory replenishment and distribution (key activities). Store staffing (key activities) can be matched to customer satisfaction (customer segment) to refine staffing levels and update training requirements.

EXHIBIT 16.11
Impacts of IT on the Business Model Canvas

Business Model Canvas Element	Potential Impact of Information Technology
Key partners	Share information among partners
Key activities	Automate processes, improve security, manage staffing, manage inventory levels, monitor performance
Key resources	Enhance capabilities to operate stores, serve customers
Cost streams	Reduce costs
Value proposition	Improve understanding of optimal value proposition, monitor quality, improve availability, reduce price
Customer relationships	Manage rewards, tailor products to customer's preferences, provide Wi-Fi and in-store network services
Channels	Monitor sales and inventory levels
Customer segments	Track satisfaction, retention, acquisition; expand market
Revenue streams	Increase revenue; create new revenue opportunities

Similarities with Strategy Maps

Strategy maps are based on the balanced scorecard framework. This is a framework that was developed as a performance management system. Exhibit 16.11 described the process by which companies implement the balanced scorecard. An important element of a strategy map is the connections between perspectives based on expected cause-and-effect relationships. Another important element is the inclusion of both leading and lagging performance measures. Changes to the learning and growth or business process perspectives are leading indicators of future performance, which can be confirmed by lagging measures in the customer and financial perspectives.

The business model canvas had its origins in research that integrated multiple established business models. It was not specifically based on a performance management system with established objectives and measures. Thus, financial performance is not as prominent in the canvas compared to strategy maps. Also, there is no clear starting point (such as the learning and growth perspective) for making investments to improve performance. Nevertheless, the business model canvas is customer-focused and easy to understand. It provides a flexible tool to communicate and examine changes to a business model. Like a strategy map, the connections among the nine building blocks are essential to understand performance drivers. To make effective use of the business model canvas to implement changes, companies should establish performance objectives and corresponding measures (i.e., key performance indicators) for each of the nine building blocks.

Summary

- The Balanced Scorecard provides a framework that allows managers to measure firm performance from multiple perspectives using both financial and nonfinancial measures.
- The four Balanced Scorecard perspectives are as follows:
  - Learning and growth
  - Business processes
  - Customer
  - Financial
- Strategy maps illustrate the components of a company's strategy across the four Balanced Scorecard perspectives.
- Investments in AIS/IT create information capital.
- Three classes that describe the nature of information technologies are as follows:
  - Function IT supports individual employees.
  - Network IT allows collaboration among employees.
  - Enterprise IT structures interactions within the organization and with external partners.
- The Balanced Scorecard management process involves
  - Formulating ways to improve competitiveness.
  - Translating objectives into specific targets and initiatives to attain those targets.
  - Linking objectives and initiatives to operations.
  - Monitoring performance.
  - Adapting to continuously improve performance.
- The Val IT framework helps managers create business value from IT investments.
  - It examines IT investments in terms of contribution to strategic objectives.
  - Investments should be consistent with current IT architecture and other IT initiatives.
  - Organizations should develop resources necessary to support the investments.
  - Investments should deliver benefits according to established metrics.
- Val IT creates an investment management hierarchy.
  - Projects are structured into programs, and overall portfolios include programs and projects as well as supporting resources.
  - Value governance involves implementing and maintaining the Val IT framework.
  - Portfolio management sets priorities for investments and monitors performance.
  - Investment management executes authorized IT investment programs.
- Organizations implement Val IT in four major steps:
  - Recognize issues with prior performance.
  - Define characteristics of desired future state.

- Assess readiness to undertake change.
- Institute the necessary change.

- The business model canvas is a framework that allows companies to describe important elements of their business model in one page.
- The business model canvas integrates strategy, organizational structure, and the use of information technology.
- The business model canvas provides nine building blocks designed to answer essential questions about what the business does.

Key Words

Balanced Scorecard framework (*528*) An integrating framework that describes organizational performance relative to its strategic objectives across four perspectives: learning and growth, process, customer, and financial. Objectives for each perspective describe the strategy in a series of cause-and-effect relationships.

Balanced Scorecard management process (*533*) The process by which companies plan, implement, and monitor performance. It consists of five steps: formulate the strategy, translate the strategy, link the strategy to operations, monitor performance, and adapt.

business model canvas (*537*) A one-page representation of the nine building blocks of a company's business model.

customer perspective (*530*) The Balanced Scorecard perspective that describes the organization's customer-related objectives and corresponding customer measures; it views organization performance from the customers' perspective.

enterprise IT (EIT) (*532*) A type of information technology that restructures interactions within an organization and with external partners, such as customer relationship management systems.

financial perspective (*530*) The Balanced Scorecard perspective that describes the organization's financial objectives and corresponding financial measures of performance; it views organizational performance from the shareholders' perspective.

function IT (FIT) (*532*) A type of information technology that performs/supports a single function, such as spreadsheet applications.

information capital (*531*) An intangible asset that reflects the readiness of the company's technology to support strategic internal processes. It includes computing hardware, infrastructure, applications, and employees' abilities to use technology effectively.

key performance indicator (*532*) Those measures that the organization feels best indicate the performance of a particular activity.

learning and growth perspective (*529*) The Balanced Scorecard perspective that describes the organization's objectives and corresponding measures related to improvements in tangible and intangible infrastructure, such as human, information, and organizational capital.

network IT (NIT) (*532*) A type of information technology that allows people to communicate with one another, such as email and instant messaging.

process perspective (*529*) The Balanced Scorecard perspective that describes the organization's internal, process-related, objectives and corresponding measures; it views organizational performance from an internal perspective.

strategy map (*531*) A one-page representation of the firm's strategic priorities and the cause-and-effect linkages among those strategic priorities.

Val IT (*535*) An IT investment framework developed by the IT Governance Institute.

value proposition (*530*) Communicates the expected financial benefits of choosing each possible alternative IT investment to help firm's senior executives decide whether to allocate resources to it.

ANSWERS TO PROGRESS CHECKS

1. At the least, IT creates value by supporting operations management processes, including supply chain management. It also creates value in the regulatory and social process by supporting internal and external financial reporting and compliance with myriad local laws, regulations, and tax requirements. **Starbucks**' digital ventures are most likely an example of network IT because they will support content delivery.
2. The answers can vary, but function IT includes individual tax preparation software and other personal applications. Network IT includes email, local wireless networks, and perhaps social media.

Multiple Choice Questions connect

1. **(LO 16-1)** Which of the following is not a Balanced Scorecard perspective?
    a. Learning and growth
    b. Customer
    c. Business process
    d. Financial
    e. All of these are Balanced Scorecard perspectives.
2. **(LO 16-1)** Which of the following is not a type of business process in the Balanced Scorecard framework?
    a. Operations management
    b. Customer management
    c. Innovation
    d. Regulatory and social
    e. All of these are types of business processes.
3. **(LO 16-2)** Which of the following describes the purpose of a strategy map?
    a. A graphical description of expected cause-and-effect linkages among Balanced Scorecard perspectives
    b. A list of the company's mission, vision, and values
    c. A representation of the company's strategic priorities
    d. Both (a) and (b)
    e. Both (a) and (c)
4. **(LO 16-4)** Which of the following does not describe a step in the Balanced Scorecard management process?
    a. Formulate the strategy
    b. Translate the strategy into strategic objectives
    c. Link objectives to operations
    d. Monitor performance and provide feedback
    e. All of these describe steps in the Balanced Scorecard management process.
5. **(LO 16-3)** Which of the following do not describe characteristics of enterprise IT?
    a. Enhance individual worker productivity
    b. Automate transaction processing
    c. Integrate processes
    d. Provide general customer service
    e. Monitor performance and support decision making

6. **(LO 16-3)** Which of the following would be an example of network IT?
   a. Spreadsheets
   b. Email
   c. ERP systems
   d. CRM systems
   e. None of these options
7. **(LO 16-3)** Which of the following is an example of function IT?
   a. Spreadsheets
   b. Email
   c. ERP systems
   d. CRM systems
   e. None of these options
8. **(LO 16-5)** Which of the following is not a role of IT in the Balanced Scorecard management process?
   a. Strategy development support
   b. Long-term budget forecasting
   c. Transaction processing
   d. Reporting
   e. All are roles of IT in the Balanced Scorecard management process.
9. **(LO 16-1)** What is one reason a Balanced Scorecard might be considered "balanced"?
   a. It includes four perspectives.
   b. It includes both leading and lagging performance indicators.
   c. It includes a large base.
   d. It is widely used by organizations around the world.
   e. All of these are reasons that it is balanced.
10. **(LO 16-1, LO 16-2)** Which of the following is the ultimate objective for the financial perspective in for-profit organizations?
    a. Brand image
    b. Productivity
    c. Growth
    d. Shareholder value
    e. None of these is the ultimate objective.
11. **(LO 16-1)** Which of the following is part of an organization's value proposition?
    a. Product price
    b. Product quality
    c. Product availability
    d. Brand image
    e. All of these are part of the value proposition.
12. **(LO 16-1)** Which of the following is a typical key performance indicator for the financial perspective?
    a. Process cost
    b. Satisfaction
    c. New customer acquisition rate
    d. Return on equity
    e. Change readiness

13. **(LO 16-1)** Which of the following is a typical key performance indicator for the customer perspective?
    a. Process cost
    b. Satisfaction
    c. Process quality
    d. Return on equity
    e. Change readiness
14. **(LO 16-1)** Which of the following is a typical key performance indicator for the process perspective?
    a. Return on equity
    b. Employee skills
    c. Market share
    d. Process cycle time
    e. Sales growth
15. **(LO 16-1)** Which of the following is a typical key performance indicator for the learning and growth perspective?
    a. Return on equity
    b. Market share
    c. Process cost
    d. Sales growth
    e. Employee skills
16. **(LO 16-1)** Information capital can include which of the following?
    a. Employee ability to use technology
    b. Communications networks
    c. Accounting systems
    d. Computing hardware
    e. All of these are information capital.
17. **(LO 16-6)** Which of the following is the best description of Val IT?
    a. A Balanced Scorecard system
    b. A customer relationship management system
    c. An enterprise resource planning system
    d. A structured IT investment management system
    e. None of these describe Val IT.
18. **(LO 16-6)** Which one of the following is not one of the four major questions that Val IT focuses on?
    a. Doing the right thing
    b. Doing things differently
    c. Doing things well
    d. Doing things the right way
    e. Getting the benefits
19. **(LO 16-6)** In the Val IT framework, a program is which of the following?
    a. An IT governance practice
    b. An individual IT investment
    c. The description of a portfolio
    d. A collection of interdependent projects
    e. All of these are programs.

20. **(LO 16-6)** In the Val IT framework, portfolio management includes which of the following?
   a. Establishing strategic priorities
   b. Determining required characteristics of the portfolio
   c. Monitoring performance of the portfolio
   d. Setting program priorities under funding constraints
   e. All of these are portfolio management.
21. **(LO 16-6)** In the Val IT framework, investment management includes which of the following?
   a. Governs the Val IT framework
   b. Establishes strategic priorities
   c. Monitors portfolio performance
   d. Executes projects within authorized programs
   e. None of these are investment management.
22. **(LO 16-6)** Val IT is designed to work in concert with COBIT. Which of the following is true with respect to the roles of these two frameworks?
   a. Val IT focuses on delivering business value; COBIT focuses on managing risk.
   b. Val IT focuses on IT; COBIT does not.
   c. Val IT focuses on portfolio management; COBIT focuses on project management.
   d. Val IT focuses on financial performance; COBIT focuses on process performance.
   e. None of these is true about the two frameworks.
23. **(LO 16-7)** Which of the following is the first step in implementing Val IT?
   a. Forming programs of IT investments
   b. Making specific IT investments
   c. Recognizing problems with prior IT investments
   d. Assessing the readiness to change
   e. None of these is the first step.
24. **(LO 16-7)** Which of the following is the second step in implementing Val IT?
   a. Defining the ideal future state for IT investments
   b. Making specific IT investments
   c. Recognizing problems with prior IT investments
   d. Assessing the readiness to change
   e. None of these is the second step.
25. **(LO 16-7)** Which of the following is the third step in implementing Val IT?
   a. Defining the ideal future state for IT investments
   b. Making specific IT investments
   c. Recognizing problems with prior IT investments
   d. Assessing the readiness to change
   e. None of these is the third step.
26. **(LO 16-7)** Which of the following is the fourth step in implementing Val IT?
   a. Defining the ideal future state for IT investments
   b. Taking action to redefine processes, roles, and responsibilities
   c. Recognizing problems with prior IT investments
   d. Assessing the readiness to change
   e. None of these is the fourth step.
27. **(LO 16-8)** Which of the following is not integrated in a business model?
   a. Internal controls
   b. Business strategy

c. Information technology
d. Organizational structure
e. None of these

28. **(LO 16-9)** In the business model canvas, a description of the value proposition should answer which of the following questions?
    a. What do we do for our customers?
    b. How do we produce our products?
    c. How much does it cost to produce our products?
    d. How do we reach our customers?
    e. How do we interact with our customers?
29. **(LO 16-9)** In the business model canvas, a description of the revenue streams should answer which of the following questions?
    a. What do we do for our customers?
    b. How much do we make by serving our customers?
    c. How much does it cost to produce our products?
    d. How do we reach our customers?
    e. How do we interact with our customers?
30. **(LO 16-9)** In the business model canvas, a description of the cost structure should answer which of the following questions?
    a. What do we do for our customers?
    b. How do we produce our products?
    c. How much does it cost to produce our products?
    d. How do we reach our customers?
    e. How do we interact with our customers?
31. **(LO 16-9)** In the business model canvas, a description of the key resources should answer which of the following questions?
    a. What do we need to produce our products?
    b. How do we produce our products?
    c. How much does it cost to produce our products?
    d. How do we reach our customers?
    e. How do we interact with our customers?
32. **(LO 16-9)** In the business model canvas, a description of the key partners should answer which of the following questions?
    a. How do we produce our products?
    b. How much does it cost to produce our products?
    c. How do we reach our customers?
    d. Who helps us produce our products?
    e. How do we interact with our customers?
33. **(LO 16-9)** In the business model canvas, a description of the channels should answer which of the following questions?
    a. How do we produce our products?
    b. How much does it cost to produce our products?
    c. How do we reach our customers?
    d. How do we interact with our customers?
    e. How do we get our products to a particular customer segment?

Discussion Questions connect

1. **(LO 16-2)** Consider a company that competes on price, such as **Walmart**, in comparison to a company that competes on other factors, such as **Starbucks**. Describe how their Balanced Scorecard objectives and the corresponding measures would differ across the four perspectives.
2. **(LO 16-1, LO 16-2)** One criticism of the Balanced Scorecard is that it can lead to information overload by measuring too many performance indicators. Do you agree with this criticism? Why or why not?
3. **(LO 16-1, LO 16-2)** If a company does not want to implement a formal Balanced Scorecard performance management system, is it still beneficial for the company to develop a strategy map? Why or why not?
4. **(LO 16-1, LO 16-2)** Some companies create a Balanced Scorecard by taking some current objectives and key performance indicators (KPIs) and assigning them to the four Balanced Scorecard perspectives. Describe the advantages and disadvantages of that approach.
5. **(LO 16-1, LO 16-2)** Does the Balanced Scorecard framework provide a performance measurement system or a performance management system? Why?
6. **(LO 16-1, LO 16-2)** A biotech company is considering developing an IT system that will track the progress of its drug compounds through the **Food and Drug Administration (FDA)** approval process. Describe, as specifically as possible, how that IT initiative might affect performance across all four Balanced Scorecard perspectives.
7. **(LO 16-1, LO 16-2)** A company is developing key process indicators (KPIs) for the information capital aspect of its learning and growth. It is considering measuring the amount spent on information technology hardware and software as its measure. What advice would you give it about that choice?
8. **(LO 16-1, LO 16-2)** Outline a Balanced Scorecard for your business school. How would using your Balanced Scorecard system affect the management of the school?
9. **(LO 16-1, LO 16-2)** Describe likely differences in a Balanced Scorecard between a for-profit company and a not-for-profit (or governmental) organization. Which perspectives are each organization more likely to focus on?
10. **(LO 16-1, LO 16-2, LO 16-3)** The CEO of a midsized company is considering purchasing an ERP system but may not have fully considered the other changes that the company needs to make to maximize the value of the system. Using a Balanced Scorecard framework, create a strategy map that describes how the ERP system could benefit company performance with the right set of complementary changes.
11. **(LO 16-8)** Consider a large, Fortune 500 company. They are probably too complicated for one business model canvas. What advice would you give them about how to divide up their business into multiple business model canvases?
12. **(LO 16-9)** Name a company that sells to a mass market customer segment. What are some characteristics of that company's products?
13. **(LO 16-9)** Name a company that sells to a niche market customer segment. What are some characteristics of that company's products?
14. **(LO 16-9)** Name a company that segments their customer segment. What are some characteristics of that company's products?

Problems connect

1. **(LO 16-1, LO 16-2)** Select a prominent public company, such as **Apple, Google,** or **Microsoft**. Obtain recent annual reports and news articles about the company. Using that information, develop a strategy map that describes the company's performance. Start by defining its value proposition and then identifying key business processes that deliver that value proposition.
2. **(LO 16-1, LO 16-2)** Use the company that you selected for Problem 1. Identify examples of its learning and growth efforts and explain how those might affect its business process performance.

3. **(LO 16-1, LO 16-2)** Select a prominent company that experienced problems during the 2008–2010 economic downturn, such as **Bank of America, Goldman Sachs,** or **AIG.** Use annual reports and news articles from that time to develop a strategy map that describes the elements that caused the company's financial problems.
4. **(LO 16-1, LO 16-2)** Using the following objectives, create a strategy map that places them at the proper perspective and links them together. For each objective, develop two possible measures.
   a. Manage the product portfolio for superior innovation.
   b. Acquire new customers.
   c. Improve fixed asset utilization.
   d. Lower cost of serving customers.
   e. Grow revenue.
   f. Create a climate of knowledge sharing.
   g. Implement an IT infrastructure necessary to support growth.
   h. Improve return on assets.
   i. Increase market share.
   j. Achieve just-in-time supplier capability.
5. **(LO 16-1, LO 16-2)** A company has elected to pursue the initiatives listed in part a. For each initiative, describe which Balanced Scorecard perspectives the initiative will address and, specifically, which of the performance measures in part b it will affect.
   a. Initiatives
      Purchase new, more efficient, production equipment.
      Train employees.
      Renovate older retail stores.
      Implement a business intelligence/business analytics system.
      Create a new advertising campaign.
   b. Performance measures
      Sales growth percentage.
      Percent of repeat customers.
      Employee turnover.
      Percent of defective products.
      Number of new customers.
      Number of product warranty claims.
      Employee satisfaction.

For Problems 6–10 you may consider using sites such as www.vizologi.com, which offers an online tool to help create business model canvases.

6. **(LO 16-8)** Select a prominent public company, such as **Apple**, **Google**, or **Microsoft**. Obtain recent annual reports and news articles about the company. Using that information, develop a business model canvas that describes their business. Start by defining their value proposition.
7. **(LO 16-8, LO 16-9)** Use the company that you selected for problem 6. Identify examples of their key resources and explain how those might affect their business model performance.
8. **(LO 16-8, LO 16-9)** Use the company that you selected for problem 6. Identify examples of their key activities and explain how those might affect their business model performance.
9. **(LO 16-8, LO 16-9, LO 16-10)** Use the company that you selected for problem 6. Identify ways that they use information technology in each building block of the canvas. Structure your answer like table 16.4 and be as specific as possible.
10. **(LO 16-8, LO 16-9)** Use the company that you selected for problem 6. Find a direct competitor of that company. Develop a business model canvas that describes the competitor's business. Start by defining their value proposition. Examine differences in the two business model canvases. Which company is better? Why?

Chapter Seventeen

Justifying and Planning IT Initiatives Using Project Management Techniques

A Look at This Chapter

In this chapter, we describe the process by which firms plan and justify IT initiatives. Accounting information systems and information technology initiatives in general often involve substantial costs. As users, managers, designers, and evaluators of the firm's IT systems, accountants are important members of the team that will develop the business case for IT initiatives. Additionally, as users, managers, and evaluators, they can also be asked to review business cases for IT initiatives in general.

Once the IT initiative is approved, project management techniques are used to implement them. This chapter also describes constraints to successful IT implementations and tools that are used to overcome them. Additionally, it discusses a model that indicates whether a new system will actually be useful to the intended IT users.

A Look Back

Chapter 16 described the Balanced Scorecard framework and explained how information technology delivers value by supporting a company's strategic objectives. It also outlined a Balanced Scorecard management process whereby companies plan, implement, monitor, and adjust strategic objectives and showed AIS/IT roles in that context.

SamaraHeisz5/Shutterstock

Starbucks Chief Technology Officer Gerri Martin-Flickinger leads the global IT function and plays a key role in shaping the technology agenda across the Starbucks business.

In the press release announcing her hire, Starbucks noted, "Gerri is a technologist at heart and has a 30-year track record of leveraging technology-based solutions to *drive business value*. As we continue to shape our global technology agenda at Starbucks, we needed leadership talent with deep experience in cloud, big data analytics, mobile and security to take us to the next level. As we searched for that leader, Gerri stood out as someone who has years of experience in Silicon Valley and brings deep management and technical expertise to help us navigate the future."

One example of new technology Starbucks hopes will pay off is to make a more seamless experience for those who choose convenient mobile ordering. When you go into our busiest (mobile-connected) stores, you see something called a Digital Order Manager that baristas use to indicate that your drink is ready. Customers also get a notification that their drink is ready, facilitating the handover from barista to customer.

You can be sure that Gerri will carefully evaluate all AIS investments to ensure that they drive business value as well as enhance the customer experience. There may well be some great new technologies for Starbucks to try, but if they do not create value, you can guess that Gerri and the rest of the C-suite executives will not approve the investment.

Starbucks Corporation

CHAPTER OUTLINE

LEARNING OBJECTIVES

After reading this chapter, you should be able to:

17-1 Articulate similarities and differences between major IT initiatives and other capital investments.

17-2 Explain the major steps in the economic justification of an IT initiative.

17-3 Explain potential benefits of IT initiatives and how to evaluate them.

17-4 Assess potential costs of IT initiatives and how to evaluate them.

17-5 Describe potential risks of IT initiatives and corresponding risk-mitigation techniques.

17-6 Apply capital budgeting techniques to assess the value proposition for an IT initiative.

17-7 Describe each phase in the systems development life cycle.

17-8 Explain the core principles of information systems planning.

17-9 Define *project management,* and describe the positions of those who lead the project.

17-10 Explain why IT projects are challenged and the tools that are used to overcome these challenges.

LO 17-1

Articulate similarities and differences between major IT initiatives and other capital investments.

LARGE IT PROJECTS REQUIRE ECONOMIC JUSTIFICATION

Information technology (IT) projects involve substantial costs and offer important benefits to organizations. **Gartner Inc.**, a prominent consulting firm, suggests that global IT spending will reach $4.5 trillion in 2022.[1] It is estimated that approximately 70 percent of that spending will be in the form of capital expenditures. When managed well, these investments offer organizations significant opportunities to create value. However, Gartner estimates that 30 percent of all IT spending is often wasted.[2]

Most organizations have developed specific techniques for evaluating IT projects based on these reasons:

1. IT projects often require large amounts of capital, and for most firms, capital resources are limited.
2. Selecting one investment often means forgoing other potentially value-increasing investments.
3. IT projects often involve changes in business processes that will affect substantial portions of the organization.

Capital budgeting techniques provide a systematic approach to evaluating investments in capital assets. Yet, many organizations find it difficult to evaluate IT projects using traditional capital budgeting techniques. To understand why IT projects can be difficult to evaluate, managers need to consider the unique characteristics of IT.

LO 17-2

Explain the major steps in the economic justification of an IT initiative.

THE BUSINESS CASE FOR IT INITIATIVES

"A goal without a plan is just a wish."
—Antoine de Saint-Exupéry, French writer and aviator

Good governance requires that all significant investments be justified. Therefore, information technology planning requires thorough consideration of alternative approaches and justification of the value of the selected alternative. According to the International Federation of Accountants, a global organization committed to the development of the

[1]Gartner, "Gartner Forecasts Worldwide IT Spending to Grow 3% in 2022," https://www.gartner.com/en/newsroom/press-releases/2022-06-14-gartner-forecasts-worldwide-it-spending-to-grow-3-percent-in-2022 (accessed November 2022).

[2]Smarter MSP, *Survey Suggests Large Portions of IT Budgets Are Being Wasted* (2019), https://smartermsp.com/survey-suggests-large-portions-of-it-budgets-are-being-wasted/ (accessed November 2022).

[3]International Federation of Accountants, *Managing Information Technology; Planning for Business Impact,* Information Technology Committee Guideline 2 (December 1999).

accounting profession, organizations should create a **business case** for an IT investment. That business case should answer the following questions:[3]

1. Why are we doing this project?
2. How does it address key business issues?
3. How much will it cost, and how long will it take?
4. What are the return on investment and the payback period?
5. What are the risks of doing the project?
6. What are the risks of not doing the project?
7. What are the alternatives?
8. How will success be measured?

ESB Professional/Shutterstock

As users, managers, designers, and evaluators of the firm's IT systems, accountants are important members of the team that will develop business cases for AIS initiatives. Additionally, as users, managers, and evaluators, they can also be asked to review business cases for IT initiatives in general.

So, how do firms create a business case to justify their IT initiatives? Exhibit17.1 describes this **economic justification process**.[4]

1. The project team assesses the business requirements for the IT initiative.
2. The team identifies potential solutions that will address those business problems.
3. For each alternative solution, the team evaluates potential benefits, costs, and risks.
4. All of the information gathered is combined to form the estimated value propositions for the alternatives and the team formalizes their business case recommendations.

The following sections describe each step in this process.

EXHIBIT 17.1
Economic Justification Process

Note: The gateway symbol with the plus sign indicates that the process takes all three paths.

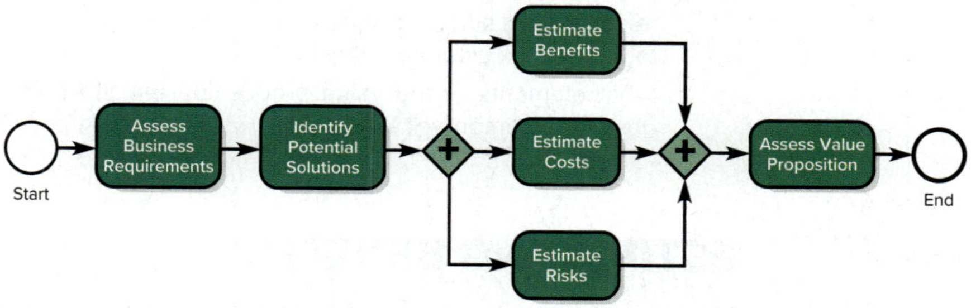

Assessing Business Requirements for IT Initiatives

In a company, IT exists to support the business goals and business strategies. To support those goals and strategies, IT must carefully align with the business requirements. IT initiatives should reduce one or more gaps between the firm's current and desired performance levels as indicated by the firm's strategy map. Therefore, the project team must

[4]See Microsoft Corporation's *Rapid Economic Justification, Enterprise Edition* (2007), for additional information.

explicitly link the proposed technology with the overall business performance improvements for one or more selected critical success factors. IT alone is usually not sufficient to achieve important changes, so the project team must also consider other enabling changes that, in conjunction with the technology, will accomplish substantial business change, as shown in Exhibit 17.2.

EXHIBIT 17.2
Benefit Dependency

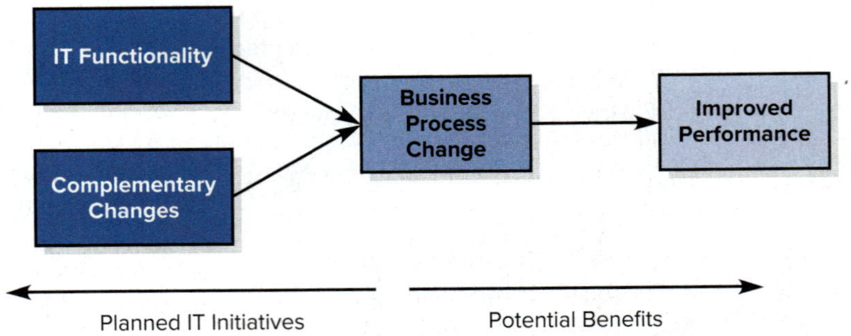

Examples of complementary changes include providing training, redefining job descriptions, reconfiguring tasks, or offering incentives. For each critical success factor to be addressed by the IT initiative, the project team identifies (1) the specific business processes that affect that critical success factor, (2) problems with those business processes, (3) opportunities to address those problems, and (4) the specific technology that would enable changes.

PROGRESS CHECK

1. Think back to the discussion of the Balanced Scorecard framework in Chapter 16. Like other firms, **Starbucks**' value proposition includes attributes of its products, such as price, quality, and selection; attributes of its relationship with its customers, such as the level of service and efforts to build long-term relationships; and its brand image. Which of those attributes are most important to Starbucks customers' satisfaction?
2. What elements of the value proposition are **Starbucks**' digital ventures likely designed to improve? Why?

LO 17-3

Explain potential benefits of IT initiatives and how to evaluate them.

ESTIMATING BENEFITS

Once the opportunities for improvement are identified and alternative solutions are proposed, the project team next assesses the potential benefits of each alternative. A **benefit** is a positive consequence—such as a reduction in the performance gaps for a critical success factor—of an IT investment. Benefits should be measurable in financial terms:

1. *Revenue enhancement*—creating all-new sales opportunities, such as using e-commerce capabilities to expand the firm's market.
2. *Revenue protection*—protecting existing revenue streams. For example, a data encryption system protects the loss of customer data and encourages customers to share data.

Ultimately, benefits must be measured in terms of the financial impact of the project.

3. *Cost savings*—opportunities to modify business processes to reduce low value-added or manually intensive activities, to improve capabilities to manage assets to increase efficiencies, or to reduce errors. For example, improving inventory management information allows reduced inventory investments.
4. *Cost avoidance*—opportunities to modify business processes to avoid cost increases in the future, such as installing current software that will accommodate changes to international financial reporting standards when required.

Note that the benefits should be measured in comparison to the revenues and costs that will occur if the IT initiative is not implemented. These revenues and costs can be different than current levels of revenues and costs. Often, the project team must estimate the amount and timing of future benefits for a number of reasonable alternative situations without complete information. There are several possible approaches that can be used to quantify expected benefits:

- *Simulation*—using simulation software to test the impact of a change in a key performance indicator on the firm's financial statements under a variety of assumptions to establish the likely benefit.
- *Expert opinion*—consulting with experts to establish the likely benefit or the probability of achieving a particular level of benefit.
- *Real option theory*—using sophisticated financial techniques that compare the probability of achieving benefits with an investment against the benefits of not making that investment.
- *External benchmarks*—using the actual experience of other firms that made similar investments in similar contexts to estimate the likely benefit.

These approaches start with an assessment of the effectiveness of current performance based on the current outputs and inputs for the process or processes under consideration, as shown in Exhibit 17.3. Then, they consider the potential impact of the change and forecast the long-term benefit.

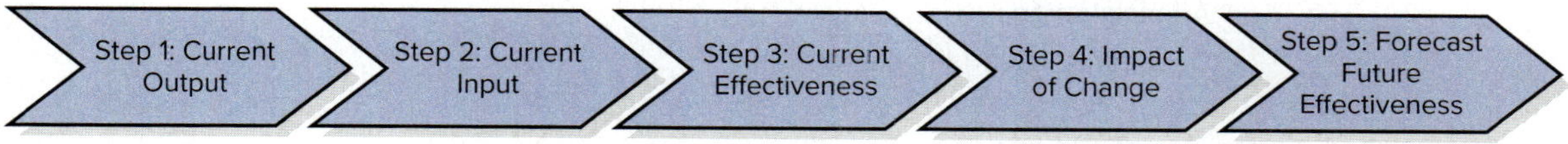

EXHIBIT 17.3
Forecasting Effects of Change

LO 17-4

Assess potential costs of IT initiatives and how to evaluate them.

ESTIMATING COSTS

Relevant costs include the incremental expense of developing, implementing, and operating the proposed IT initiative over its life cycle. The total **acquisition cost** includes all direct and indirect costs required to acquire and deploy the technology. The total **operation cost** includes all direct and indirect costs of operating, maintaining, and administering the technology over its expected life. Technology consulting firms, such as **Gartner Inc.** and **International Data Corporation**, publish widely used total cost of ownership figures for various technologies, and Gartner has developed an extensive chart of accounts to classify IT initiative costs.[5]

[5]https://books.google.com/books?id=YHR4UGwF6BIC, accessed March 2019.

Acquisition Costs

Direct Costs

The direct acquisition costs include all costs necessary to acquire and implement the IT initiative:

Hardware
Software
Networking and communications
Development
Project management
Consulting
Training

Indirect Costs

The indirect acquisition costs include costs not directly related to the acquisition and implementation, such as business disruption and employee downtime.

Operating Costs

Direct Costs

The direct operating costs include all costs necessary to operate, maintain, and administer the technology:

Hardware replacements
Software upgrades
Maintenance contracts
Help desk support
Ongoing training
Administration
Decommissioning the old system

Indirect Costs

The indirect operating costs include costs of user downtime and lost productivity, such as time spent on self-training, peer support, and end-user data management.

The project team must also estimate the amount and timing of the direct and indirect costs of acquisition and operation of IT initiatives without complete information. The various approaches to quantifying benefits, outlined earlier, also apply to estimating costs. Additionally, there are several commercial software products designed to help firms estimate total cost of ownership.

PROGRESS CHECK

3. Do you own a laptop, a cell phone, or an iPad? What is your total cost of ownership for each of those? Is it more expensive than just the initial purchase? Do you have any indirect costs of owning those products?

LO 17-5

Describe potential risks of IT initiatives and corresponding risk-mitigation techniques.

ASSESSING RISKS

Each alternative IT initiative carries risks of failing to achieve the prospective benefits and exceeding the estimated costs. To help identify risks, it is usually helpful to consider the following categories of risks. One classification scheme is as follows:[6]

- **Alignment risk**—the solution is not aligned with the strategy of the firm.
- **Solution risk**—the solution will not generate projected benefits.
- **Financial risk**—the solution will not deliver expected financial performance.
- **Project risk**—the project will not be completed on time or within budget.
- **Change risk**—the firm or part of the firm will not be able to change.
- **Technological risk**—the technology will not deliver expected benefits.

After identifying relevant risks, the project team should assess the financial impact on the firm if the risk scenario occurs, the probability that the risk scenario will occur, and costs of mitigating the risk. Some of the risk assessment can be done during the quantification of costs and benefits, and the estimated costs and benefits can be adjusted for risk. Risk-mitigation techniques include considering portfolios of IT initiatives, rather than single initiatives, and considering outsourcing where contracts can protect against certain risks. Exhibit 17.4 describes examples of risk-mitigation techniques for each risk category.

EXHIBIT 17.4
Examples of Risk-Mitigation Techniques

IT Initiative Risks	Risk-Mitigation Examples
Alignment risk	Use the Balanced Scorecard framework (Chapter 16) to assess the link to strategy.
Solution risk	Use sensitivity analysis to consider likely alternative benefit levels.
Financial risk	Interview other users of similar IT; follow a structured Balanced Scorecard management process (Chapter 16).
Project risk	Ensure active top management support for the project.
Change risk	Conduct training, and create employee incentives for successful use of the new IT.
Technological risk	Require hardware and software vendors to demonstrate that their systems can meet requirements.

Systems implementation problems kept Hershey's from accepting Halloween orders.

Scott Olson/Getty Images

PROGRESS CHECK

4. A few years ago, **Hershey's Corp.**, a leading manufacturer of chocolates, confectionaries, and beverages, implemented SAP's R/3 enterprise resource planning software using a big bang approach, where all the software was implemented at the same time. Because of problems with the implementation during a busy period, Hershey's could not take orders or deliver products for Halloween. By the time the problems were corrected, they had cost Hershey's more than $100 million. What risks were involved? Was this the fault of the software? Do you think Hershey's planning allowed for this contingency when it justified the IT initiative?

[6]Risk categories taken from Microsoft Corporation, *Rapid Economic Justification, Enterprise Edition* (2007).

LO 17-6

Apply capital budgeting techniques to assess the value proposition for an IT initiative.

DEVELOPING THE VALUE PROPOSITION

The last step in the IT economic justification process is to combine the information developed in the previous steps to describe the **value proposition** for the preferred alternative. The value proposition communicates the expected financial benefits of choosing each possible alternative IT investment which helps a firm's senior executives decide whether to allocate resources to it. The project team will employ capital budgeting techniques using the expected cash flows for each alternative:

The business case establishes the value proposition for the preferred alternative or alternatives.

1. Determine the relevant time frame for costs and benefits.
2. Select appropriate discount rates to apply.
3. Prepare capital budgeting financial metrics.
4. Assess the sensitivity of results to the assumptions.

The relevant time frame for most IT initiatives is 3 years or less because technology changes rapidly. The appropriate discount rates usually run from 5 to 15 percent, depending on the firm's cost of capital and the riskiness of the particular project. Financial metrics commonly used include the following and are summarized in Exhibit 17.5.

EXHIBIT 17.5
Financial Metric Strengths and Weaknesses

Financial Metric	Strength	Weakness
Payback period	Easy to calculate and understand. Widely used.	Ignores the time value of money as well as both costs and benefits occurring after the payback period.
Accounting rate of return	Relates estimates to standard accounting ratios using accrual accounting. Shows impact on operating income.	Ignores the time value of money. Assumes cash flows in all periods are similar.
Net present value	Considers the time value of money. Incorporates cash flows over the life of the IT initiative. Compares the dollar value of the benefits from an IT initiative to the initial investment.	Larger projects tend to have larger net present values. Does not show rate of return on investment. Sensitive to discount rate applied.
Internal rate of return	Considers the time value of money. Incorporates cash flows over the life of the IT initiative. Computes the unique rate of return for the initiative. Not sensitive to a selected discount rate.	Fails to consider the size of the project. Sensitive to timing of the cash flows.

- **Payback period** and **breakeven analysis**—both compare the costs with benefits of an IT project. The breakeven point is where the total value of benefits equals that of total costs. The payback is the number of periods needed to recover the project's initial investment.

$$\text{Payback period} = \text{Initial investment/Increased cash flow per period}$$

Assume an IT project is expected to cost \$20,000 up front, and it will provide net benefits that average \$16,000 per year for the next 3 years.

$$\text{Payback period} = \$20{,}000/\$16{,}000 = 1.25 \text{ years}$$

- **Net present value (NPV)**—sum of the present value of all cash inflows minus the sum of the present value of all cash outflows. Each cash outflow/inflow is discounted to its present value.

$$\text{Present value} = CF_t/(1 + r)^t$$

where
CF_t = cash flow for period t
r = discount rate (typically the firm's weighted average cost of capital).

Again, assume an IT project that is expected to cost $20,000 up front and return $16,000 per year for 3 years. Assume a discount rate of 10 percent. Then, the NPV is calculated as follows:

Year 0	Present value = −$20,000/(1.10^0)	−$20,000
Year 1	Present value = $16,000/(1.10^1)	14,545
Year 2	Present value = $16,000/(1.10^2)	13,223
Year 3	Present value = $16,000/(1.10^3)	12,021
NPV	Sum of present values	$19,790

- **Internal rate of return (IRR)**—the discount rate that makes the project's net present value equal to zero. There is no solvable formula for internal rate of return. Instead, financial calculators and spreadsheet software, such as Microsoft Excel, use an iterative technique for calculating IRR. Starting with a guess, they cycle through the calculations until the result is accurate. The IRR and NPV functions are related in that if you use the IRR as the discount rate (r) in calculating NPV, your NPV is zero.[7]
- **Accounting rate of return (ARR)**—the average annual income from the IT initiative divided by the initial investment cost.

ARR = (Average annual income from IT initiative)/(Total IT initiative investment cost)

Again, using the same assumed initial outlay and subsequent net cash flows described earlier, the accounting rate of return would be calculated as follows.

$$\text{ARR} = \$16{,}000/\$20{,}000 = 80\%$$

Exhibit 17.6 shows an example of the financial metrics applied to an IT initiative with an implementation cost of $20,000 in year zero and positive net cash flow for the subsequent 3 years. The two projects have equal payback periods, but project 1 has a higher net present value (NPV), and project 2 has a higher internal rate of return (IRR). This illustrates how risks resulting in increased costs and reduced benefits can affect the value of the IT initiative, especially when considering the time value of money.

[7]Note that Excel assumes that the cash flows occur at the end of the year, so the initial outlay would be assumed to be for year 1. Try this by entering the data and using the Excel NPV and IRR functions.

EXHIBIT 17.6
Example Comparing Payback, NPV, and IRR

Discount Rate	10%					
Project 1	**Year 0**	**Year 1**	**Year 2**	**Year 3**	**Total**	**Average**
Benefits		$20,000	$20,000	$30,000	$70,000	$23,333
Costs	$20,000	$7,500	$7,500	$7,500	$42,500	$10,625
Cash flow	–$20,000	$12,500	$12,500	$22,500	$27,500	$15,833
Payback	1.26					
NPV	$18,598.80					
IRR	52%					
Project 2	**Year 0**	**Year 1**	**Year 2**	**Year 3**	**Total**	**Average**
Benefits		$30,000	$20,000	$20,000	$70,000	$23,333
Costs	$20,000	$7,500	$7,500	$7,500	$42,500	$10,625
Cash flow	–$20,000	$22,500	$12,500	$12,500	$27,500	$15,833
Payback	1.26					
NPV	$20,176					
IRR	71%					

Note that total cash flow is equal, but NPV and IRR are not, due to time value of money.

Test the Sensitivity of Estimates to Changes in Assumptions

Before prioritizing the alternative IT initiatives based on the financial metrics, the project team should test the impact of changes in assumptions on the various financial metrics. These tests can be performed using spreadsheet or simulation software. The assumptions can also be reviewed by subject matter experts. Because each financial metric has both strengths and weaknesses, IT initiatives should be evaluated using several metrics (see Exhibit 17.7).

EXHIBIT 17.7
Project Value

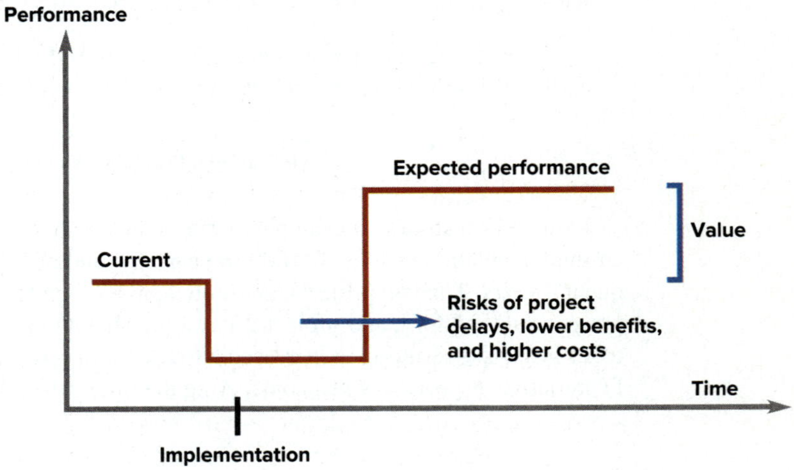

Prepare the Value Proposition

The final step is to assemble the analysis for each alternative IT initiative and recommend the preferred alternatives. The value proposition must address the business case questions listed earlier in the section "The Business Case for IT Initiatives" especially focusing on these five areas:

1. The change and technology proposed.
2. The anticipated benefits (related to the firm's critical success factors).
3. The group(s) within the firm that will benefit.
4. The timing of the benefits.
5. The likelihood of achieving those benefits as planned.

LO 17-7

Describe each phase in the systems development life cycle.

THE SYSTEMS DEVELOPMENT LIFE CYCLE

We have learned about many of the processes and components of an accounting information system (AIS) thus far in this book. Another key component in understanding the accounting information system is to know how these AIS systems are envisioned, designed, and ultimately brought into operation. In an organization, accountants play a key user role in telling systems developers what information is needed in an accounting information system and often play an important role in implementing projects. Managing and carrying out the systems development life cycle to achieve an intended outcome is called **project management** and is a topic of this chapter.

To best understand the design, use, management, and evaluation of an accounting information system, it is important to understand the systems development life cycle. The **systems development life cycle (SDLC)** is the process of creating or modifying information systems to meet the needs of its users. The SDLC is generally viewed as the foundation for all systems development that people use to develop such systems. The SDLC has five phases: planning, analysis, design, implementation, and maintenance.

1. The **planning phase** of the SDLC begins with a business need for a new or better information system. This phase involves summarizing the business needs with a high-level view of the intended project. A feasibility study is often used to evaluate economic, operational, and technical practicability. This includes making a business case for the system. It is also used as a basis to get buy-in and funding from upper management.
    - *Example:* Let's suppose that the **Starbucks** marketing department wants to analyze what type of pastries sell best with its various hot and cold drinks. In order to do so, it will need to change the software on its POS (point-of-sale) terminals and develop an easy system for the marketing department to run what-if analyses with its data. A feasibility analysis suggests that it is operationally and technically practical to make this change, and if this information is captured, the chief marketing officer of Starbucks will be much more successful when she presents her case for potential marketing promotions featuring the sale of both drinks and pastries. The marketing officer expects the payoff in profits for such systems to be greater than the approximately $63,000 needed to plan, design, and implement this system.
2. The **analysis phase** of the SDLC involves a complete, detailed analysis of the systems needs of the end user. The analysis phase further refines the goals of the project into carefully specified functions and operations of the intended system. This step may involve looking at the entire system in different pieces and drawing various flowcharts and diagrams to better analyze the situation and project goals.
    - *Example:* The **Starbucks** systems analysis team meets with all of the desired users of the enhanced system (including the chief marketing officer). The users want to make sure that considerable flexibility is built into the system in order to address both current and potential data analysis needs it may have in the future.

3. The **design phase** of the SDLC involves describing in detail the desired features of the system that it uncovered in the analysis phase. These features may be described using screen layouts, process and event diagrams (such as we learned earlier in this book), and other documentation. A **systems analyst** is responsible for both determining the information needs of the business and designing a system to meet those needs.
   - *Example:* The **Starbucks** systems designers take the requested business requirements from the analysis stage and begin to design how the new, what-if Starbucks analysis system would look on a screen and the business rules and process diagrams needed to make such a change in the system.

4. The **implementation phase** of the SDLC involves development, testing, and implementation of the new proposed system. Development is the process of transforming the plan from the design phase into an actual, functioning system. The testing of the system involves testing for errors, bugs, and interoperability with other parts of the system. It also serves to verify that all of the business requirements from the analysis phase are met. Implementation involves placing the system into production such that users can actually use the system that has been designed for them.
   - *Example:* The **Starbucks** systems developers write the computer code and test it. Once testing is complete and the business requirements are met, the users are trained and given incentives to use the new system, and the new software is put into actual use. At this point, the users can begin to perform what-if analyses using the new software.

5. The **maintenance phase** of the SDLC is the final phase and includes making changes, corrections, additions, and upgrades (generally smaller in scope) to ensure the system continues to meet the business requirements that have been set out for it. The maintenance phase continues indefinitely because the system must continue to evolve as the underlying business evolves.
   - *Example:* The **Starbucks** system undergoes continuous and regular maintenance to ensure that it meets the underlying business requirements. Specifically, as new products are introduced and new information is needed, the system continues to be modified and upgraded. The bigger the needed changes, the more likely that the SDLC will start all over again to address the expected changes.

During the maintenance phase, new, substantive changes are often needed to meet the changing, evolving needs of the firm. The systems development life cycle starts again and the planning phase begins anew in a recursive manner to assess whether a new or upgraded system needs to be developed. This recursive nature is a reason why it is called a life cycle. The recursive nature of the systems development life cycle is illustrated in Exhibit 17.8.

EXHIBIT 17.8
The Recursive Nature of the Systems Development Life Cycle

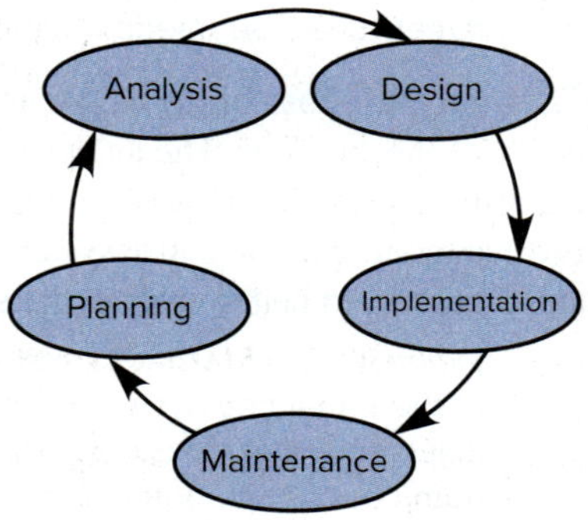

The Waterfall Model and the Agile Model of Systems Development

There are two different methodologies for systems development: the waterfall model and the agile model.

The **waterfall model** is a traditional, sequential method that requires the team to complete each project phase before the next phase begins. So, the planning phase would need to be completed first, and then the analysis phase would begin and so forth until the systems development is complete.

The **agile model** allows the team to work on different phases of the project simultaneously in a cyclic and collaborative way. For example, the planning phase and the analysis might be able to be done at the same time as can other phases as development continues.

If the project timeline is fixed and sufficient, the waterfall model will likely offer a more predictable, more certain outcome. However, if the project needs to be delivered in a short amount of time to deal with rapidly changing market conditions or opportunities, the agile model would be the more appropriate choice.

Connection with Practice

The Information Systems Audit and Control Association (ISACA) and the IT Governance Institute (ITGI) developed Control Objectives for Information and Related Technology (COBIT) to serve as a set of best practices for information technology (IT) management. COBIT provides managers, auditors, and IT users with a set of generally accepted measurements, processes, indicators, and best practices to assist them in maximizing the benefits derived through the use of information technology. COBIT's guidance corresponds to the SDLC—namely, plan and organize, acquire and implement, deliver and support, and monitor and evaluate.

LO 17-8

Explain the core principles of information systems planning.

EFFECTIVE INFORMATION TECHNOLOGY PLANNING

As the title of this chapter suggests, we want to emphasize the importance of effective IT planning. During the first phase of the SDLC, the planning phase, an information technology plan should be developed to support the overall firm strategy. The plan should provide a roadmap of the information technology required to support the business direction of a firm. This should include an outline of the required resources and the expected benefits that will be realized when the IT plan is implemented. While each information technology plan is unique to the needs and circumstances of a firm, the International Federation of Accountants suggests that these 10 core principles be followed to ensure effective information technology planning:[8]

- *Alignment*—the planning phase should support and complement the business strategy of a firm.
- *Relevant scope*—the overall scope of the planning phase should be established to facilitate formulation of effective ways to address the business needs.

[8]International Federation of Accountants, *Managing Information Technology Planning for Business Impact* (January 1999).

- *Relevant timeframe*—the appropriate planning horizon should be formulated that provides both short- and medium-term deliverables as well as long-term alignment with the business strategy.
- *Benefits realization*—costs of implementation should be commensurate with the tangible and intangible benefits that are expected to be realized. The expected benefits should be bigger than the costs.
- *Achievability*—the planning phase should recognize the capability and capacity of the firm to deliver solutions within the stated planning timeframe.
- *Measurable performance*—the planning phase should provide a means to measure and monitor project performance and serve as a means of communicating success to both stakeholders inside and outside the firm.
- *Reassessment*—the plan should be periodically reassessed to ensure it is relevant to the evolving business strategy of the firm.
- *Awareness*—the resulting plan that comes out of the planning phase should be communicated widely.
- *Accountability*—identification of those responsible for implementing the plan should be explicitly clear.
- *Commitment*—management commitment to the plan's implementation should be clear and evident.

Each of these core principles is important for effective information technology planning.

PROGRESS CHECK

5. Why is the systems development life cycle recursive? Will systems development ever be completed?
6. Why is measurable performance important to consider in the planning phase of the systems development life cycle?

The Sarbanes–Oxley Act of 2002 (SOX) highlights the importance of accounting information system controls by requiring management and auditors to report on the effectiveness of internal controls over the company's accounting information system.

Consider these two excerpts taken from two companies announcing that their financial statements had errors and had to be restated. In both cases, the firms revealed a material weakness in their accounting information system that allowed a material misstatement in the financial reports.

Consider this 10-K filing from **Landauer Inc.** (2014):

> We did not design and maintain processes and procedures that restrict access to key financial systems and records to appropriate users and evaluate whether appropriate segregation of duties is maintained. Specifically, certain personnel had access to financial application, programs and data beyond that needed to perform their individual job responsibilities without independent monitoring.
>
> U.S. Securities and Exchange Commission

Landauer provides technical and analytical services, outsourced medical physics services, and radiology-related medical products worldwide. This misstatement in the accounting information system suggests that the software was not designed to restrict access to the accounting systems or to provide adequate segregation of duties. Had the software been designed correctly, it would not have caused a misstatement.

This one is from **WaferGen Bio-Systems Inc.**'s 8-K filing:

> In addition, due to a spreadsheet error, the Company's previously filed financial statements recorded basic and diluted net loss per share in the nine months ended September 30, 2013, based on a weighted average of 709,639 shares outstanding during the period, when the correct number of shares was 1,226,570.
>
> U.S. Securities and Exchange Commission

WaferGen Bio-Systems presents a case of ineffective controls around the use of spreadsheets. As accountants understand the design of accounting information systems, they are better equipped to address potential weaknesses in the accounting information system.

A more recent example (2019) is from auditors expressing concern regarding Stitch Fix needing to work with third-party IT service providers to properly provide reports that aligned with its fiscal year, suggesting that if that problem isn't fixed, errors in the financial statements would certainly arise.

Connection with Practice

Segregation of Duties

In nearly all accounting textbooks, the importance of segregation of duties (SOD) is discussed. The general rule is that accounting controls, whether they be manual or computerized, should be set up to separate (1) custody of assets, (2) authorization of transactions, and (3) recordkeeping responsibilities.

As in the case of **Landauer** disclosed earlier, it notes that the company "did not design and maintain processes and procedures that restrict access to key financial systems and records to appropriate users and evaluate whether appropriate segregation of duties is maintained."

Segregation of duties is not just a concept you read in a textbook. It continues to be a real issue at companies today.

U.S. Securities and Exchange Commission

In these examples, the design of the information system was ineffective and was the source of a potential material weakness in the accounting information system. This highlights the real need for accountants to understand the design and development of accounting information systems, which is the topic of this chapter.

LO 17-9

Define *project management,* and describe the positions of those who lead the project.

PROJECTS, PROJECT MANAGEMENT, AND PROJECT SPONSORS

Projects are a series of tasks that are generally performed in a defined sequence to produce a predefined output. The history of project management has its roots in engineering and construction projects. In an information technology setting, a project might include the creation of a new, unique IT product or service such as replacing old computers, moving data to a different cloud computing environment, installing a new financial reporting database, or merging financial reporting databases. For example, can you imagine merging an accounting information system from two different systems into one? We'll highlight this IT project management setting throughout the rest of this chapter.

Can you imagine merging the databases of customers, flights, accounting information, and frequent flyer miles for the merger of **American Airlines** and **US Airways**? Now that's a big project!

As defined earlier in the chapter, project management is the planning, organizing, supervising, and directing of an IT project. A **project manager** is the lead member of the project team and is responsible for the project. The project manager's mission is to coordinate the entire project development process to successfully complete the project. A project manager must also be able to analyze the project charter, a document that details the objectives and requirements of the project.

The third important concept surrounding a project is the presence of a project (or executive) sponsor. The **project sponsor** will often be a senior executive in the company who takes responsibility for the success of the project. The project sponsor is generally a different person than the project manager but often serves as the project champion. In addition, this person takes on critical roles in the project, including the following:

- Supporting the project manager in managing the project.
- Advocating for the project to the company management and also to those outside the company (e.g., vendors, suppliers, and shareholders).
- Obtaining necessary resources for successful completion.
- Monitoring overall scope for the project to ensure successful completion and work to prevent scope creep (as discussed later).
- Accepting responsibility for issues and problems that arise that the project manager cannot handle alone.

All IT projects move through these five phases of the project management life cycle: initiating, planning, executing, monitoring and controlling, and closing. These phases contain the needed processes to move the project from the initial idea to project implementation and subsequent maintenance.

The modern project management concept began with the Manhattan Project, which the U.S. military led to develop the atomic bomb.

Bettmann/Getty Images

PROGRESS CHECK

7. Why is the project sponsor so important?
8. Why should accountants be interested in project management?

LO 17-10

Explain why IT projects are challenged and the tools that are used to overcome these challenges.

CHALLENGES OF IT PROJECT MANAGEMENT

Before we get too far into discussing the details of the challenges of IT project management, it should be noted that IT projects are frequently canceled, late, or over budget or don't deliver the intended consequences. To illustrate the problem, here are some statistics on the outcomes of recent IT projects. Every few years, the Standish Group performs a survey to evaluate the outcomes of IT projects. Exhibit 17.9 provides a summary of its 2021 report.

The report shows that software projects in 2021 have a 16 percent success rate, compared with 23 percent from the previous study in 2018 and 16 percent in 1994. On the other hand, 53 percent of projects were challenged (i.e., late, over budget, and/or with less

EXHIBIT 17.9
Information Technology Project Outcomes

	2021	2018	2015	2012	2009	2006	2004	2002	2000	1998	1996	1994
Successful	16%	23%	29%	39%	32%	35%	29%	34%	28%	26%	27%	16%
Challenged	53	58	52	43	44	19	53	15	23	28	40	31
Failed	31	19	19	18	24	46	18	51	49	46	33	53

than the required features and functions) while 31 percent failed (i.e., canceled prior to completion or delivered and never used). This low success rate can be attributed to poor project management and helps illustrate why project management is so critical in firms today. In the next section, we consider the specific obstacles, or constraining factors, that project managers face and the tools to overcome those challenges.

CONSTRAINING FACTORS OF IT PROJECTS

There are many reasons information technology projects fail to meet expectations. First, there are project management concerns that exist for all projects—such as deadlines, budget constraints, and limited resources (i.e., people) to focus efforts on completing the project successfully. Second, information technology projects face unique challenges because technology continues to change and oftentimes has glitches. These changes and glitches may come from hardware, operating systems, or databases. Third, there might also be security risks or interoperability issues between computer systems.

A project manager is generally told that a project must be completed by a certain date or for a certain cost or both. All information technology and other projects are constrained by three factors: cost, scope, and time constraints. This is often called the Dempster's triangle or the **triple constraints**. For a project to be successful, these three constraints must be held in balance. Once any of the constraints becomes out of balance, the project is likely headed for an unsuccessful outcome. Exhibit 17.10 provides an illustration of the triple constraints. Notice that in the center of these three constraints is quality. While the triple constraints do need to be carefully addressed, some level of quality must be met to be useful to the firm. As a project manager, you are often told that a project must be completed by a certain date or for a certain amount of money (cost) or both. At the same time, the deliverable (or result) of your project must also meet some minimum specifications (quality) to meet the firm's intended purposes.

EXHIBIT 17.10
The Triple Constraints of Project Management (Dempster's Triangle)

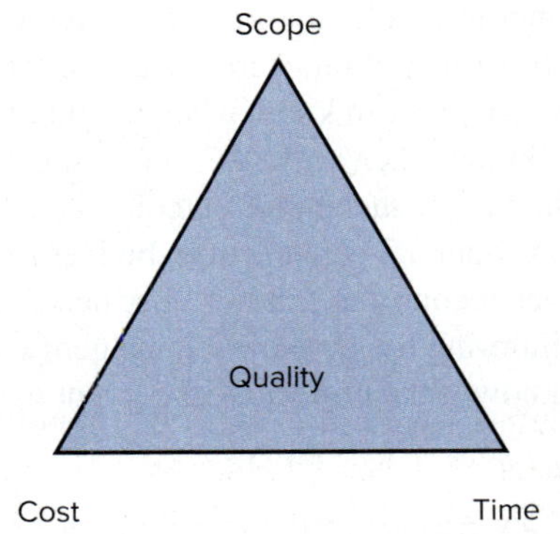

Scope

The size or scope of the project is often defined in the initial stages of the project. However, in most projects, the scope begins to expand when additional features are added to the original specifications to add desired functionality. **Scope creep** is the broadening of a project's scope that occurs after the project has started. The change in scope often comes about from small, relatively insignificant change requests that the project team accepts to keep the project sponsor satisfied (e.g., information system available in Spanish or an e-commerce program able to transact with euros as well as U.S. dollars). Eventually, the number of change requests may become numerous enough to become significant, or some of the individual requests may be big enough to require much more work than originally expected.

The larger the scope expands beyond its initial specifications, the more the project will drift away from its original purpose, timeline, and budget. To help control scope creep, the project sponsor must be involved in the process to ensure that scope changes are absolutely needed and to assess if the benefits of the enhanced scope outweigh the costs. If the project scope is expanded, there must be additional time and funding to complete it.

Cost

A major challenge for IT projects is keeping the project within the planned budget. Often, the initial budget may not reflect all of the costs to bring the project to completion. As the IT project manager becomes aware of the costs to date and the expected costs to complete the project, they must share this information with the project sponsor and other company leadership. They then suggest a reconfiguration of resources or tasks that do not significantly change the scope of the project. This can be a challenge if additional costs are needed to successfully complete the project but additional needed funds are not available.

Time

Due to the rapid evolution of business and technology, most information technology projects are constrained by time. The results of these information systems often serve as a basis for a competitive advantage within the firm. Sometimes, systems implemented quickly can have a first-mover advantage. For this reason, the project manager is often given a deadline by which the project needs to be completed and delivered. Likewise, if software or hardware vendors don't deliver their solutions on time, the project will not be completed on time. To help address these time constraints, there are several project management tools available, including the PERT and Gantt charts, which are discussed later.

The 15-15 Rule

Sometimes, it is important to know when an IT project will not reach a successful conclusion. At that point, it may make sense to stop investing in the IT project. As some would say, you need to know when to "quit throwing good money after bad" or in a poker game, "to know when to fold." One indicator that the project might have serious difficulty in achieving a successful outcome is called the **15-15 rule**, which states that if a project is more than 15 percent over budget or 15 percent off the desired schedule, it will likely never recoup the time or cost necessary to be considered successful. Of course, careful monitoring by the project manager (and possibly the project sponsor) is necessary in order to know if the project is 15 percent over budget or 15 percent off the desired schedule.

PROGRESS CHECK

9. What are the triple constraints of project management? How can scope creep cause distortions in cost and time?
10. When should the project manager and project sponsor approve scope changes? When should they deny scope changes?

PROJECT MANAGEMENT TOOLS

The previous section mentioned that one of the triple constraints of projects is time. There are two project management tools to help with this time constraint by scheduling, organizing, and coordinating the tasks within a project. The most popular tools in use today are the PERT and Gantt charts.

PERT is actually an acronym for **Program Evaluation Review Technique**. PERT was originally developed in the 1950s by the U.S. Navy to manage the building of the Polaris submarine missile.

The first step in a PERT chart is to identify all tasks needed to complete a project. This breakdown of all of the project tasks is often called the **work breakdown structure (WBS)**. These tasks generally define all events and deliverables. After the tasks have been identified, the next step is to establish the sequencing of those events. The sequencing suggests which tasks need to precede the other tasks and which are dependent on the other tasks. A key part of making sure the PERT and the Gantt chart work is being able to define all of the tasks—including all internal, external, and interim tasks. This identification of all tasks is sometimes called the **100% rule**. The 100% rule, therefore, requires thorough and complete project planning.

The best way to explain a PERT chart is to see one and explain how it works. Consider the PERT chart in Exhibit 17.11. A PERT chart is a graphical representation of a project that consists of numbered *nodes* (either circles or rectangles) representing milestones in the project linked together by labeled directional lines representing tasks that need to be completed in the project. The numbers on the various directional lines indicate how much time has been allotted to the task. The sequencing of the tasks is denoted by the direction of the arrows on the lines. Some of the tasks must be completed in a certain sequence, like the set of tasks between numbered nodes 1, 6, 7, and 9 in Exhibit 17.11. These are called *dependent tasks* because they require that the previous task be completed before they can begin the next task. The tasks between nodes 10 and 11 cannot begin until all the preceding tasks (incoming directional lines) for node 10 are completed, including tasks 5, 8, and 9.

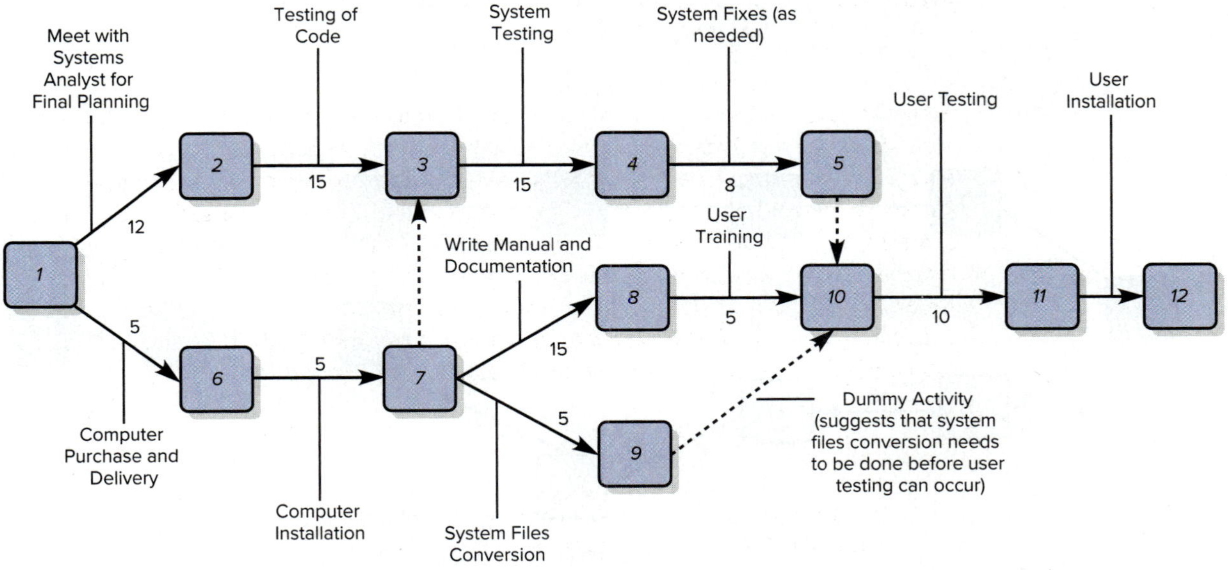

EXHIBIT 17.11
Example of a PERT Chart

Because these all must be done in order, the longest string of time allotted to dependent tasks must be determined. We call this the critical path. The **critical path** is the longest path for a project and represents the minimum amount of time needed for the completion of the project when sufficient resources are allocated. The critical path helps the project manager figure out how resources should be allocated in order to complete the project within the shortest amount of time. In Exhibit 17.11, that path is 1, 2, 3, 4, 5, 10, 11, 12.

Some tasks are not dependent on the completion of one to start the other, such as the tasks between nodes 7 and 8, and nodes 7 and 9. Tasks 5 and 8 are called *parallel,* or *concurrent tasks* because they can be done at the same time. Tasks that must be completed in a specific sequence but don't require additional resources or a specific completion time are considered to have *task dependency.* These are called *dummy tasks* and are represented by dashed lines with arrows. For example, the dashed lines between nodes 9 and 10 suggest that the software testing and related fixes must be completed before user testing can take place.

Another similar, but complementary project management tool is the use of the Gantt chart. A **Gantt chart** is a graphical representation of the project schedule by mapping the tasks to a project calendar. Gantt charts are especially useful when monitoring a project's progress.

Henry Gantt, an American mechanical engineer, is generally credited with inventing the Gantt chart.

A Gantt chart illustrates the start and finish dates of the various tasks of the project. Some Gantt charts also show the dependency between the tasks. Exhibit 17.12 shows an illustration of both a PERT chart and a related Gantt chart and how they might work together. Each letter represents a task to be performed. The PERT chart shows the critical path; the Gantt chart also shows the term "margin" and ". . ." to signify the slack time

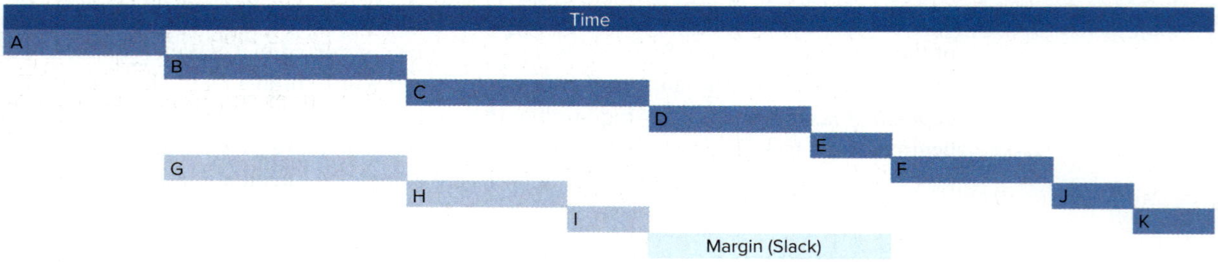

Gantt Chart

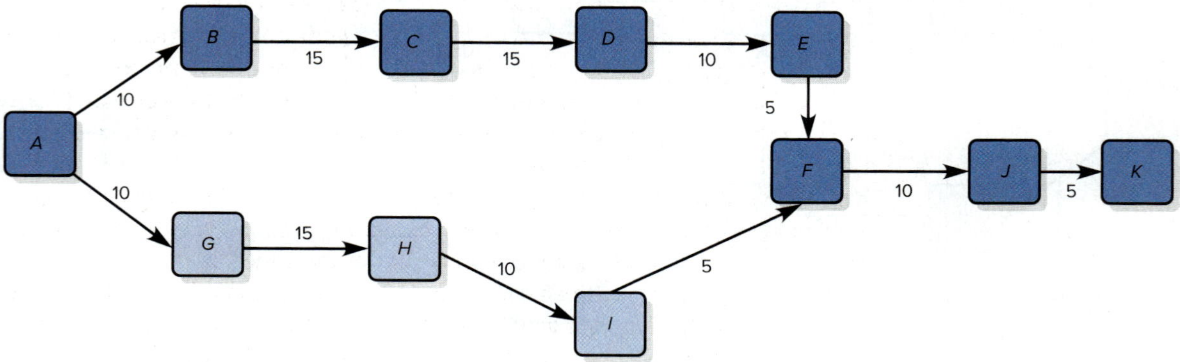

PERT Chart

EXHIBIT 17.12
Example of Gantt Chart and Its Relationship to the PERT Chart

before the next critical path task needs to be completed. As the project progresses through time, the Gantt chart is used to show the current status.

One noted advantage of the PERT chart over the Gantt chart is that it clearly illustrates the dependence of one task on another. At the same time, one disadvantage of the PERT chart is that it can be much more difficult to interpret, especially on complex projects.

PROGRESS CHECK

11. Why is the 100% rule critical for identifying the work to be done? How is it different from the 15-15 rule?
12. What is a parallel or concurrent task? Are these tasks required to be done at the same time? If you have to choose, which parallel or concurrent task should be done first?

Summary

- Large projects require economic justification comparing the costs against the benefits.
- One step in the economic justification process is the preparation of the business case that identifies the purpose of the project, costs, expected return on investment, risks of doing the project, risks of not doing the project, alternatives considered, and how success will be measured.
- The economic justification process occurs in a series of steps:
  - Assess business requirements.
  - Identify potential solutions.
  - Estimate costs, benefits, and risks.
  - Assess the overall value proposition for each potential solution.
- IT initiatives must also include complementary changes in business processes to improve performance. Estimated benefits involve revenue enhancement, revenue protection, cost savings, and cost avoidance. Estimated costs involve direct and indirect acquisition and operating costs over the life cycle of the project.
- The value proposition depends on capital budgeting financial metrics that consider the time value of money and the anticipated timing of the costs and benefits.
- Users and auditors of an accounting information system need to understand the basics of AIS project management to understand how accounting information systems are developed.
- The systems development life cycle is the foundation for all development, models, and methodologies that people use to develop such systems. The SDLC has five phases: planning, analysis, design, implementation, and maintenance.
- Effective information systems planning is of critical importance to the firm because it is the stage that the firm uses to evaluate needed changes to the system. Ten core principles of effective information systems planning were highlighted.
- Scope, time, and cost represent the triple constraints of project management. If any of these constraints get out of control, the project will likely face overwhelming challenges. The project manager and project sponsor use various project management tools to monitor and control the scope, time, and costs.

Key Words

100% rule (*569*) A rule requiring 100 percent planning of all tasks, including all of the internal, external, and interim tasks.

15-15 rule (*568*) A rule suggesting that if a project is more than 15 percent over budget or 15 percent off the planned schedule, it will likely never recoup the time or cost necessary to be considered successful. At this point, a decision needs to be made on if or how to proceed.

accounting rate of return (ARR) (*559*) The average annual income from the IT initiative divided by the initial investment cost.

acquisition costs (*555*) All direct and indirect costs necessary to acquire and implement the IT initiative.

agile model (*563*) An agile model allows the team to work on different phases of the project simultaneously in a cyclic and collaborative way.

alignment risk (*557*) The risk that an IT initiative is not aligned with the strategy of the organization.

analysis phase (*561*) The phase of the SDLC that involves a complete, detailed analysis of the systems needs of the end user as well as a proposed solution.

benefits (*554*) The positive consequences to the organization of an IT investment.

breakeven analysis (*558*) Analysis to determine the breakeven point, where the total value of benefits equals total costs.

business case (*552*) Economic justification for an IT investment or other major project.

change risk (*557*) The risk that the organization will be unable to make the changes necessary to implement the IT initiative successfully.

critical path (*570*) The longest path for a project and represents the minimum amount of time needed for the completion of the project when sufficient resources are allocated.

design phase (*562*) The phase of the SDLC that involves describing in detail the desired features of the system that were uncovered in the analysis phase.

economic justification process (*553*) The process by which an organization creates a business case for an IT investment or other major project.

financial risk (*557*) The risk that the IT investment will not deliver expected financial benefits.

Gantt chart (*570*) A graphical representation of the project schedule that maps the tasks to a project calendar.

implementation phase (*562*) The phase of the SDLC that involves development, testing, and implementation of the new proposed system.

internal rate of return (IRR) (*559*) The discount rate (return) that makes a project's net present value equal to zero.

maintenance phase (*562*) The final phase of the SDLC that includes making changes, corrections, additions, and upgrades (generally smaller in scope) to ensure the system continues to meet the business requirements that have been set out for it.

net present value (NPV) (*559*) The sum of the present value of all cash inflows minus the sum of the present value of all cash outflows related to an IT investment or other capital investment.

operation cost (*555*) The recurring cost necessary to operate, maintain, and administer an IT initiative.

payback period (*558*) The amount of time necessary to recoup a project's initial investment.

planning phase (*561*) The phase of the SDLC that summarizes the business needs with a high-level view of the intended project.

Program Evaluation Review Technique (PERT) (*569*) A project management tool used to help identify all tasks needed to complete a project. It is also helpful in determining task dependencies.

project (*565*) A series of tasks that are generally performed in a defined sequence to produce a predefined output.

project management (*561*) The process of carrying out the systems development life cycle to achieve an intended outcome.

project manager (*566*) The lead member of the project team who is responsible for the project.

project risk (*557*) The risk that the project will not be completed on time or within budget.

project sponsor (*566*) Generally a senior executive in the company who takes responsibility for the success of the project.

relevant costs (*555*) Those costs that will change as a result of an IT initiative or other major project.

scope creep (*567*) The change in a project's scope after the project work has started.

solution risk (*557*) The risk that the proposed solution will not generate expected benefits.

systems analyst (*562*) Person responsible for both determining the information needs of the business and designing a system to meet those needs.

systems development life cycle (SDLC) (*561*) The process of creating or modifying information systems to meet the needs of its users. It serves as the foundation for all processes people use to develop such systems.

technological risk (*557*) The risk that the technology will not perform as expected to deliver the planned benefits.

triple constraints (*567*) Three factors that constrain information technology and other projects: cost, scope, and time. Also known as Dempster's triangle.

value proposition (*558*) Communicates the expected financial benefits of choosing each possible alternative IT investment to help firm's senior executives decide whether to allocate resources to it.

waterfall model (*563*) A traditional, sequential method of systems development that requires the team to complete each project phase before the next phase begins.

work breakdown structure (WBS) (*569*) The process of identifying all tasks needed to complete a project.

ANSWERS TO PROGRESS CHECKS

1. **Starbucks** competes on quality, image, and relationship. All three are important to the company's customer satisfaction, but one could argue that image gets the customer into the store and quality and relationship keep the customer coming back.
2. Digital ventures seem to be aimed at (a) improving the customer relationship and (b) expanding their selection so new and returning customers buy more per visit.
3. Each of these personal devices costs far more than the original investment in hardware. You have to buy applications (software), Internet access, and perhaps insurance. Each time you purchase one of these, you incur indirect costs of self-training, potential loss of personal information, and any loss of productivity connected with using the new device.
4. The **Hershey** ERP project likely carried all the risks listed in Exhibit 17.4. The fault was not likely related to the software alone. It was more likely related to the way the software was implemented and the way Hershey employees were trained to use it. It is highly unlikely that Hershey considered this possibility in its planning, or the company would have had contingency plans to mitigate the problems.
5. The recursive nature of the SDLC reflects that the firm continues to evolve, always needing new and different information. While a particular system may be completed and put into use, a firm's systems development should never be considered complete because the business is always changing.
6. It is important to set expectations clearly and measure whether a system has met those expectations (or not). This is particularly important to consider in the earliest planning phases.
7. For a project to be successfully implemented, there must be executive support. A project sponsor ensures that the project has initial and continuing executive support to ensure

that the necessary and appropriate resources are available. One of the most important responsibilities of the project sponsor is to monitor the overall scope of the project and make sure there is enough support for any scope changes that might occur.

8. Accountants use and audit the information that comes out of an accounting information system. But how was the system designed? Can they trust the numbers that come out of the system? Accountants must understand the design and development of an accounting information system to be able to trust the information coming out of that system.
9. Scope, cost, and time are the triple constraints of project management. If the scope becomes different and/or larger, the cost and time to complete can quickly become overwhelming and become a source of failure.
10. Generally, scope changes are made to satisfy potential users and executives. They may make the system more usable and have desired features. The project manager and project sponsor must assess and balance the costs and benefits of scope changes. If a change has too little impact, costs too much, or can easily be done in a future upgrade to the system, the project manager and project sponsor should deny the scope change.
11. In order to plan the project, the work breakdown structure must be complete, or 100 percent planned. This will help in sequencing the tasks, figuring out which tasks are dependent on other tasks, and allowing for planning of the complete project. In contrast, the 15-15 rule states that if a project is more than 15 percent over budget or 15 percent off the desired schedule, it will likely never recoup the time or cost necessary to be considered successful.
12. A parallel, or concurrent, task is a task that can be done or completed at the same time as another task. All other things equal, the parallel task that is on the critical path should be completed first because subsequent tasks depend on that task being completed.

Multiple Choice Questions connect

1. **(LO 17-2)** Which of the following is a question that companies should answer when preparing the business case for an IT investment?
   a. How much will it cost?
   b. What are the risks?
   c. What are the alternatives?
   d. How will success be measured?
   e. All of these.
2. **(LO 17-2)** What is the first step in the economic justification process?
   a. Identify potential solutions.
   b. Assess the value proposition.
   c. Assess business requirements.
   d. Estimate costs.
   e. All of these.
3. **(LO 17-2)** Which of the following is a not an example of a complementary change necessary to allow an IT initiative to achieve its goals?
   a. Outsource the IT initiative.
   b. Retrain employees.
   c. Redefine job descriptions.
   d. Provide incentives for employees to make the change successfully.
   e. None of these.

4. **(LO 17-3)** Which of the following is not an example of benefits of an IT investment?
   a. Increased revenues from access to new markets
   b. Decreased costs from automating manual tasks
   c. Facilitating employee work-from-home arrangements
   d. Allowing compliance with new federal regulations
   e. Reducing the number of inventory count errors
   f. All of these.
5. **(LO 17-3)** Which of the following can be used to quantify benefits on an IT investment?
   a. Gathering expert opinions
   b. Benchmarking against competitor performance
   c. Comparing against the probability of future benefits if investment is forgone
   d. Conducting simulations
   e. All of these.
6. **(LO 17-4)** Which of the following are examples of direct costs of acquiring and implementing an IT investment?
   a. Cost of hiring consultants to assess system requirements
   b. Personnel costs of the project team
   c. Training costs of employees who will use the system
   d. Cost of new computer hardware necessary to run the system
   e. All of these are direct costs of acquiring and implementing an IT investment.
7. **(LO 17-4)** Which of the following are not examples of operating costs for an IT investment?
   a. Costs of routine hardware replacements over time
   b. Cost of contract for help desk support
   c. Costs of disposal of electronics at end of life
   d. Costs of software license renewals
   e. All of these are examples of operating costs.
8. **(LO 17-5)** Which of the following is not a category of IT initiative risk?
   a. Alignment
   b. Technological
   c. Financial misstatement
   d. Solution
   e. All of these are examples of IT initiative risk.
9. **(LO 17-6)** If an IT project costs $150,000 and returns net cash flows of $100,000 per year, what is the payback period?
   a. 1 year
   b. 1.5 years
   c. 2 years
   d. 2.5 years
   e. None of these.
10. **(LO 17-6)** If an IT project costs $150,000 and returns net cash flows of $100,000 per year, what is the accounting rate of return?
   a. 33 percent
   b. 50 percent
   c. 67 percent
   d. 75 percent
   e. None of these.

11. **(LO 17-2)** What is the order of events for the economic justification process?
   a. Identify potential solutions ⟶ Assess business requirements ⟶ Estimate costs ⟶ Assess value.
   b. Assess business requirements ⟶ Estimate costs ⟶ Identify potential solutions ⟶ Assess value.
   c. Identify potential solutions ⟶ Estimate benefits ⟶ Assess business requirements ⟶ Assess value.
   d. Assess business requirements ⟶ Identify potential solutions ⟶ Estimate costs ⟶ Assess value.
   e. None of these.
12. **(LO 17-7)** Which methodology of systems development requires one phase be completed before the next phase begins?
   a. Agile model
   b. Waterfall model
   c. Scrum model
   d. Sequential model
13. **(LO 17-7)** The IFAC suggested 10 core principles of effective information technology planning. Which of the following is *not* one of those 10 core principles?
   a. Achievability
   b. Justifiable cost
   c. Reassessment
   d. Accountability
14. **(LO 17-10)** Projects are considered challenged if they:
   a. are late, are over budget, or do not have the required features and functions.
   b. are canceled prior to completion.
   c. are delivered but never used.
   d. are completed early.
15. **(LO 17-10)** The triple constraints of project management do not include the constraint of:
   a. technical issues.
   b. time.
   c. cost.
   d. scope.
16. **(LO 17-10)** The 100% rule suggests that before a PERT chart is done, a project manager must:
   a. make sure 100 percent of the project is funded.
   b. make sure the project team is devoted solely, or 100 percent, to the project.
   c. make sure that each person on the project team got 100 percent on his or her project management final exam.
   d. make sure 100 percent of the project tasks are defined.
17. **(LO 17-10)** The critical path in a PERT chart represents:
   a. the sequencing of tasks.
   b. the most important tasks of the whole project.
   c. the longest path of tasks needed for project completion.
   d. the tasks that must be completed without errors.

18. **(LO 17-8)** The Sarbanes–Oxley Act's section 404 reports require management and auditors to report on:
    a. the financial condition of the firm.
    b. the quality of the project management planning.
    c. the academic background and experience of the company's accounting leadership.
    d. the effectiveness of the internal controls of the company's accounting information system.
19. **(LO 17-9)** In this chapter, *projects* are defined as:
    a. a series of tasks performed in a defined sequence.
    b. turning raw talent into an NFL-quality quarterback.
    c. turning blueprints from an architect into a completed building.
    d. merging two databases into one.
    e. address technical difficulties.
    f. none of these.
20. **(LO 17-7)** Which phase of the systems development life cycle would include describing in detail the desired features of the system?
    a. Analysis phase
    b. Design phase
    c. Planning phase
    d. Maintenance phase
    e. Implementation phase

Discussion Questions

1. **(LO 17-2)** An important first step in the economic justification process is to assess business requirements. How would the Balanced Scorecard framework presented in Chapter 16 help companies assess their business requirements for IT?
2. **(LO 17-2)** Chapter 16 described three types of IT: function, network, and enterprise IT. Consider the diagram shown in Exhibit 17.2. Which type of IT is likely to have the greatest impact on business performance? Which type of IT would require the most complementary changes? Why?
3. **(LO 17-3)** The benefits of an IT initiative should be measured in comparison to the revenues and costs that will occur if the IT initiative is not implemented. What issues would a project team face when making this comparison? How does it affect the team's assessment of risks?
4. **(LO 17-6)** Use Microsoft Excel to assess the NPV of an IT initiative. The initiative will require an initial investment of $250,000 in year zero and is expected to return $150,000 per year for the next 3 years. Assume a discount rate of 10 percent. What is the NPV? How does the NPV change if the discount rate is 15 percent? Describe how changes in the discount rate assumption can affect the NPV.
5. **(LO 17-6)** Use Microsoft Excel to assess the internal rate of return for an IT initiative. Suppose the initial investment is $60,000 in year zero. The returns on investment in dollars for the following 5 years are (a) $10,000, (b) $12,000, (c) $15,000, (d) $21,000, and (e) $26,000. Use the IRR function to compute the internal rate of return after 2, 4, and 5 years. Next, assume that the loan for the initial $70,000 is at 8 percent and you are earning 16 percent on the annual returns. Use the MIRR function to calculate the internal rate of return. Is the annual rate of return higher when using the MIRR function than the IRR function? Under what circumstances would it be lower?

6. **(LO 17-6)** Consider two projects. Project 1 costs $262,000 and returns $60,000 per year for 8 years. Project 2 costs $390,000 and returns $70,000 per year. Project 2 is determined to be less risky, so your company only requires an 8 percent minimum annual return compared to 10 percent for project 1. What is the NPV of each project? What is the absolute maximum that the company should consider investing in each project?
7. **(LO 17-6)** Your company has just completed a major IT initiative and is reviewing the outcome. It notes that the project took 3 months longer than expected. As part of the project, the company wanted to use some automatic bar code readers, but the rate of correct bar code reads was below the expected rate. Although managers were worried about employee acceptance of the new system, it appears that the employees have embraced it and, as a result, are making it work better than expected. Refer to Exhibit 17.4 and identify how these results address the risk categories listed in the table.
8. **(LO 17-6)** Moore's law suggests that computing power for the same cost doubles every two-and-a-half years. A combination of Moore's law and the commoditization of computer components has made it possible to buy a $500 computer today that is more powerful and portable than a similar offering that cost $2,000 just a few years ago. How does this affect planning for major IT projects?
9. **(LO 17-8)** Rank the 10 core principles of effective information technology planning in order of importance in your opinion. Provide support for your top five important principles.
10. **(LO 17-9)** Imagine the role of the project sponsor when a leader of the accounting bookkeepers comes to complain that the new information system could possibly result in the loss of five bookkeeper jobs. The bookkeepers argue that they will get the union involved if needed to protect their jobs. What should the project sponsor do?
11. **(LO 17-10)** Explain the 100% rule. Assume you are telling your roommate about this rule, and use an example that is relevant to him or her.
12. **(LO 17-10)** Compare and contrast a PERT chart and a Gantt chart. How do they complement each other?
13. **(LO 17-10)** Using the 15-15 rule as a guide, when would a project manager and/or project sponsor proceed with completion of a project even if it is both 15 percent over budget and 15 percent off the initial schedule?

Problems connect

1. **(LO 17-6)** SlowRider Inc. had a rudimentary business intelligence (BI) system. Analysts at SlowRider Inc. pulled data from three different ERP systems, loaded the data into Excel spreadsheets, and emailed those spreadsheets to the senior managers each month. However, some managers complained that they didn't understand how to get the information they needed, others complained that the data were not accurate, and still others ignored the spreadsheets. SlowRider established a project team to look at acquiring a state-of-the-art business intelligence system. After several interviews with all the managers, the project team was ready to develop the business case.

   The project team estimated benefits of the new BI system as follows:

   - 5 percent increase in sales through better-focused sales campaigns, which should increase gross margins by $200,000 in year 1 and $300,000 in years 2 and 3.
   - 10 percent increase in inventory turnover through better purchasing, which should reduce inventory carrying costs by $100,000 in year 1 and $150,000 in years 2 and 3.

   The project team estimated costs over an expected 3-year life as follows:

Cost Element	Year 0	Year 1	Year 2	Year 3
Acquisition cost (new software and implementation)	$400,000			
Operating cost (annual licenses, upgrades, support)		$50,000	$50,000	$50,000
Training	$ 10,000	$ 5,000	$ 5,000	$ 5,000
Lost productivity during implementation	$ 20,000			
Total	$430,000	$55,000	$55,000	$55,000

After interviewing managers at other firms that have already implemented similar BI systems, the project team then estimated that the initiative would have the following risks.

Risk Description	Probability	Mitigation Steps
Managers will not use the system, resulting in:		Top management support; incentives to use the system
Revenue growth of 3%	25%	
Inventory turnover increase of 5%	25%	

a. Disregarding the risk, calculate the following for the BI investment:
   1. Payback period
   2. NPV (assume 10 percent discount rate)
   3. IRR
   4. Accounting rate of return (annual)

b. Recalculate the payback period, NPV, IRR, and ARR considering the risk.

c. Prepare a value proposition for the BI investment. Should SlowRider pursue the investment? What other issues should they consider?

2. **(LO 17-6)** The Beach Dude Inc. (BD) sells surf gear and clothing to retail stores around the country. It outsources the production of most of its items, so its warehouse is very busy receiving incoming shipments and preparing deliveries to customers. After a thorough review of its warehouse processes, the company determined that it could save substantial employee time and improve its on-time delivery rates if it adopted a warehouse management system using RFID chips and readers. RFID (radio-frequency identification) is a technology that uses radio waves to automatically identify people or objects. RFID tags are applied to packages, and then RFID readers can be used to track the location and movement of the inventory.

   BD estimates that the RFID system—including fixed and mobile scanners, software, servers, installation, and integration with its existing AIS—will cost $400,000. The system has an expected useful life of 5 years and is expected to have a negligible value at that time. Training for the warehouse, IT, and accounting employees is expected to cost an additional $25,000. Additionally, the company's estimate for the cost of RFID tags is $30,000 per year based on the current $0.15 cost per tag. However, it believes there is a 50 percent probability that the cost per tag will decrease to $0.10 per tag in 2 years. BD estimates that it will save $150,000 per year in reduced employee overtime, fewer priority shipments, reduced inventory losses, and improved inventory turnover. Assume that BD has a cost of capital of 6 percent.

   a. Calculate the following for BD's investment, assuming there is no reduction in the cost of RFID tags:
      1. Payback period
      2. NPV
      3. IRR
      4. Accounting rate of return (average income/initial cost)

   b. Recalculate those values, assuming that the cost of RFID tags does decrease in 2 years as expected.

   c. Identify some potential risks and possible omissions in BD's planning. Provide examples of situations that would lead to the risks that you identify.

3. **(LO 17-3; LO 17-6)** Refer to the Starbucks vignette at the beginning of this chapter. Starbucks has aggressively pursued digital ventures to improve the customer experience and increase the amount of customer transactions per visit. Among other things, Starbucks mines the data from customer loyalty cards to examine buying patterns to predict what customers will buy in the future. It is looking for an increased "wallet-share."

   a. Describe why it is difficult to evaluate Starbucks' digital ventures' investments using traditional capital budgeting techniques.

   b. What are some other ways that Starbucks could evaluate the benefit of its digital ventures?

4. **(LO 17-6)** Sunset Graphics is considering two mutually exclusive projects. Both require an initial investment of $100,000. Assume a marginal interest rate of 10 percent and no residual value for either investment. The cash flows for the two projects are expected to be the following:

Year	Project 1	Project 2
1	$30,000	$ 0
2	$30,000	$20,000
3	$30,000	$20,000
4	$30,000	$50,000
5	$30,000	$75,000

   a. Compute the NPV, payback, and IRR for both projects. Which is more desirable?
   b. Assume straight-line depreciation is used for both projects; compute the accounting rate of return. What do you think of the ARR criterion?
   c. Assume a change in interest rate to 15 percent. Does that change your views on which project the company should adopt?
   d. Assume a change in interest rate to 6 percent. Does that change your views on which project the company should adopt?
   e. For investments in technology, which cash inflow projection is most likely?

5. **(LO 17-6)** Sunset Graphics is considering moving to a cloud-based accounting system because its current system only runs on outdated computers. The cloud-based system is very similar to the current system, so there would be no additional training required. The cloud-based system will cost $1,500 per month for the next 36 months. The company will write off its old equipment and record a corresponding loss of $2,000. It will buy five new computers to access the cloud at a total cost of $2,200.

   Its alternative is to purchase a new local accounting system. If it pursues this alternative, the company will also spend $2,200 on five new computers and write off the old hardware and software. The new software will cost $40,000. Sunset Graphics uses a discount rate of 10 percent.

   a. Which alternative is the better solution? Why? What factors would influence your decision?
   b. Assume the local accounting system is expected to last 5 years but will require a major upgrade costing $15,000 at the end of year 3. Also, assume that the cost of the cloud-based system will fall to $1,200 per month for months 37–60. Neither alternative will have any residual value. Compare the two alternatives again.

6. **(LO 17-5)** Each alternative IT initiative carries risk of failing to achieve the respective benefits and exceeding the estimated costs. Match the description of risk with each risk term.

1. The solution will not generate projected benefits.	A. Project risk
2. The solution is not aligned with the strategy of the firm.	B. Solution risk
3. The project will not be completed on time or within budget.	C. Alignment risk
4. The solution will not deliver expected financial performance.	D. Financial risk

7. **(LO 17-5)** After identifying relevant risks, the project team often employs risk-minimization techniques to lessen the probability or impact of the risk. Match the description/example of the risk mitigation technique with the type of risk being mitigated.

1. Ensure active top management support for the project.	A. Change risk
2. Use sensitivity analyst to consider likely alternative benefit levels.	B. Project risk
	C. Technological risk
3. Ask **Microsoft** to demonstrate that its software can meet the system requirements.	D. Solution risk
4. Give employees adequate incentive to use the new IT.	

8. **(LO 17-6)** Match the description of these financial metrics to their terms.

1. The average annual income from the IT initiative divided by the initial investment cost
2. The sum of the present value of all cash inflows less the sum of the present value of all cash outflows
3. The discount rate (return) that makes a project's net present value equal to zero
4. The amount of time necessary to recoup a project's initial investment

A. Accounting rate of return
B. Internal rate of return
C. Net present value
D. Payback period

9. **(LO 17-3)** Project benefits may come from a variety of sources. Match the examples of these project benefits to their terms.

1. The new system will be able to identify additional products that customers might be interested in.
2. Installing an accounting system that supports international financial standards will lower the cost when international financial standards are required.
3. A supply chain system will help us source cheaper sources of raw materials to build our projects.
4. Adding tracking information to shipments was important to not lose sales to competitors.

A. Revenue enhancement
B. Revenue protection
C. Cost savings
D. Cost avoidance

10. **(LO 17-4)** Which of these project costs would be considered to be acquisition costs and which would be considered to be operating costs?

1. Hardware replacement
2. Help desk support
3. Software upgrade
4. Development
5. Initial training
6. Ongoing training
7. Maintenance contracts
8. Project management

11. **(LO 17-3)** There are several approaches to quantifying expected project benefits. Which of the following uses simulation, external benchmarks, real option theory, or expert opinion to help with the quantification?

1. Software that allows you to consider the impact under a variety of assumptions
2. Compare and contrast the results with projects of competitors or similar firms
3. Sophisticated financial analysis comparing the probability of achieving expected benefits
4. Consulting with a seasoned consultant to establish a likely benefit

12. **(LO 17-6)** A firm is considering two projects. Both have an initial investment of $1,000,000 and pay off over the next 5 years in this fashion. The cost of capital is 6 percent.

Year	Option 1	Option 2
Year 0	−1,000,000	−1,000,000
Year 1	1,000,000	250,000
Year 2	0	250,000
Year 3	0	250,000
Year 4	0	250,000
Year 5	100,000	250,000

a. Which of these has a faster payback period?

b. Which of these options has a higher net present value?

c. Which of these options has a higher internal rate of return (IRR)?

13. **(LO 17-6)** A firm is considering two projects. Both have an initial investment of $1,000,000 and pay off over the next 5 years in this fashion. The cost of capital is 8 percent.

Year	Option 1	Option 2
Year 0	−1,000,000	−1,000,000
Year 1	1,000,000	500,000
Year 2	100,000	500,000
Year 3	200,000	400,000
Year 4	300,000	300,000
Year 5	400,000	200,000

a. Which of these has a faster payback period?

b. Which of these options has a higher net present value?

c. Which of these options has a higher internal rate of return (IRR)?

14. **(LO 17-8)** As part of effective IT planning in the systems development life cycle, a return on investment (ROI) calculation may be performed as part of the economic feasibility analysis. Often, many of the benefits from a new information system may be intangible benefits (e.g., system is easier to use or system enhances customer service) that are hard to quantify in an income statement. How would you suggest this be included in the economic feasibility analysis?

15. **(LO 17-7)** In the chapter, we discussed an example of **Starbucks** using the systems development life cycle to develop the capability to analyze what type of pastries sell best with its various hot and cold drinks. Now, let's suppose that **NASDAQ** requires all of the firms trading on the exchange to report their financial statements not only using GAAP but also International Financial Reporting Standards (IFRS). Because Starbucks' current system cannot handle the IFRS requirements, the financial reporting system must be modified. Using Starbucks as an example, explain what types of activities would occur in each of the five phases of the systems development life cycle in preparation for reporting financial results according to IFRS.

16. **(LO 17-9)** Accountants generally do not have all of the necessary systems analyst and systems development skills needed to develop accounting information systems. Why should you be interested in project management of an accounting information system?

17. **(LO 17-7, LO 17-8)** For your personal consulting business, you decide to set up an accounting information system to help with taxes as well as to help monitor your revenues and expenses. You've heard that **QuickBooks** is easy to set up, so you buy it, install it on your computer, enter in recent transactions, and begin to use it.

Required:

1. Explain one or two ways you could be a user of this accounting information system. (*Hint:* Use the discussion in the text considering the role of accountants in accounting information systems.)
2. Explain one or two ways you could be a manager of this accounting information system. (*One possibility:* What practices do you employ to make sure your system is safe?)
3. After a few months, you decide to expand your QuickBooks with additional modules (payroll, inventory, etc.). Access the QuickBooks website (http://quickbooks.intuit.com) and consider one or two ways in which you could be a designer of your accounting information system.

18. **(LO 17-10)** Brainstorm a list of reasons why 84 percent (including 53 percent challenged plus 31 percent failed) of the information technology projects either failed or were

challenged in 2021. Consider specifics of each of the elements of the triple constraints model and any other common delays, including the challenges of working with programmers, software and hardware suppliers and vendors, and the like. What is the best way to overcome these issues and decrease the number of projects failed or challenged?

19. **(LO 17-10)** The following PERT chart (Exhibit 17.13) represents the tasks to be done to implement a system. Can you think of other steps that should be included? Is there adequate time for training given the technology acceptance model's recommendation to focus on perceived usefulness and perceived ease of use? What is the critical path for this project?

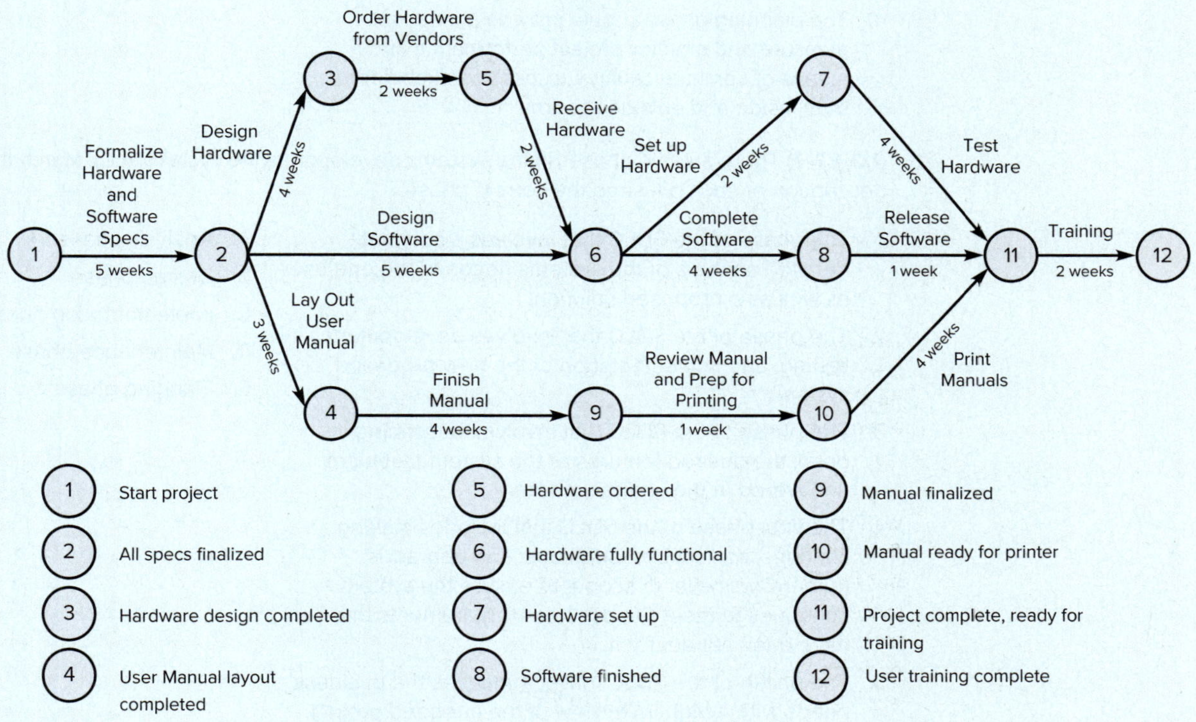

EXHIBIT 17.13
PERT Chart for Problem 7

20. **(LO 17-10)** Consider the triple constraints diagram in Exhibit 17.10. Why is quality included in that figure even if it is not one of the triple constraints? Why is quality a concern (or not a concern, based on your point of view) for the project manager and project sponsor?

21. **(LO 17-8)** We discussed 10 core effective information technology planning principles. Match the description of each with its respective principle.

1. The planning phase should support and complement the business strategy of the firm.	A. Alignment
2. Costs of implementation should be commensurate with the tangible and intangible benefits expected to be realized.	B. Relevant scope
3. An appropriate planning horizon should be developed.	C. Relevant timeframe
4. The overall scope of the planning phase should be established to facilitate formulation of effective ways to address the business needs.	D. Benefits realization

22. **(LO 17-8)** We discussed 10 core effective information technology planning principles. Match the description of each with its respective principle.

1. The resulting plan that comes out of the planning phase should be communicated widely.
2. The planning phase should recognize the capability and capacity of the firm to deliver solutions within the stated planning timeframe.
3. The plan should be periodically reassessed to ensure it is relevant to the evolving business strategy of the firm.
4. The planning phase should provide a means to measure and monitor project performance and a means of communicating success to stakeholders both inside and outside the firm.

A. Achievability
B. Awareness
C. Reassessment
D. Measurable performance

23. **(LO 17-7)** There are five phases in the systems development life cycle (SDLC). Match the description of each phase to the correct phase.

1. The phase of the SDLC that involves a complete, detailed analysis of the systems needs of the end user as well as a proposed solution.
2. The phase of the SDLC that involves development, testing, and implementation of the new proposed system.
3. The phase of the SDLC that involves describing in detail the desired features of the system that were uncovered in the analysis phase.
4. The final phase of the SDLC that includes making changes, corrections, additions, and upgrades (generally smaller in scope) to ensure the system continues to meet the business requirements that have been set out for it.
5. The phase of the SDLC that summarizes the business needs with a high-level view of the intended project.

A. Analysis phase
B. Design phase
C. Implementation phase
D. Maintenance phase
E. Planning phase

24. **(LO 17-10)** For each of the following, please define these as either work breakdown structure, triple constraint, 100% rule, or 15-15 rule.
   1. The process of identifying all tasks needed to complete a project.
   2. Three factors that constrain information technology and other projects: cost, scope, and time.
   3. A rule requiring 100 percent planning of all tasks, including all of the internal, external, and interim tasks.
   4. A rule suggesting that if a project is more than 15 percent over budget or 15 percent off the planned schedule, it will likely never recoup the time or cost necessary to be considered successful. At this point, a decision needs to be made on if or how to proceed.

Glossary of Models

This glossary presents various structure and activity models to show modeling options. It is not intended to be all inclusive, but rather to provide examples of how to model common situations. For the structure models, the basic assumption is that resources, agents, and type images are added to the database before they are linked to other classes, so the minimum multiplicity is zero. Otherwise, the models show the most common multiplicities.

The glossary presents examples of structure models in the following section and then presents some generic activity models in the last section. The models are presented in the following order: sales and cash receipts process, purchases and cash disbursements process, and the conversion process, and for the structure models, it includes miscellaneous and integrated models.

STRUCTURE MODELS USING THE REA FRAMEWORK

1. Sales—Generic Model

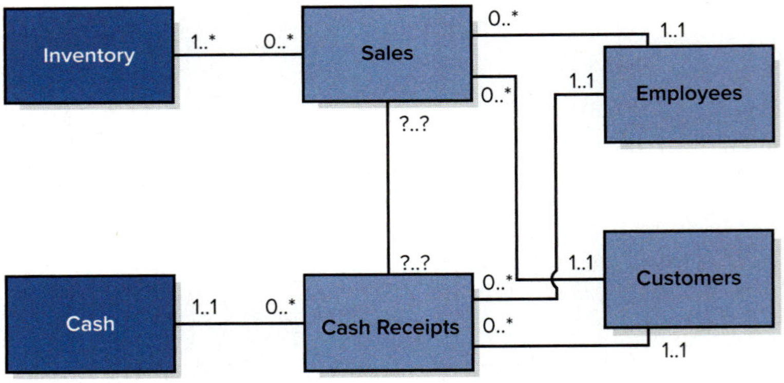

The generic model represents typical economic resources, events, and agents involved in the sales process. This model assumes that inventory items are not tracked individually (like high-value items such as automobiles and houses) but rather by UPC code such that all products with the same UPC code are considered to be the same item.

2. Sales—With Invoice Tracking

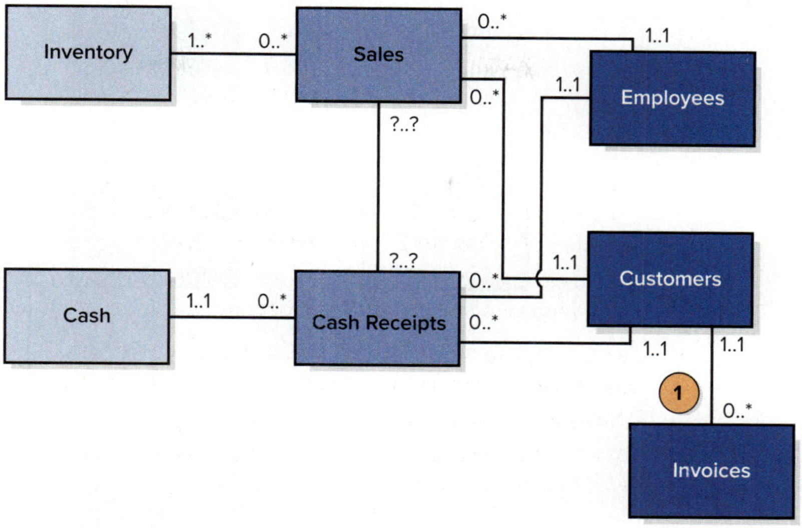

This model extends the generic model to track the invoices issued to each customer as shown in the association (1) between Customers (Agent) and Invoices (Type Image).

3. Sales—Where Employees Are Assigned to Service Particular Customers

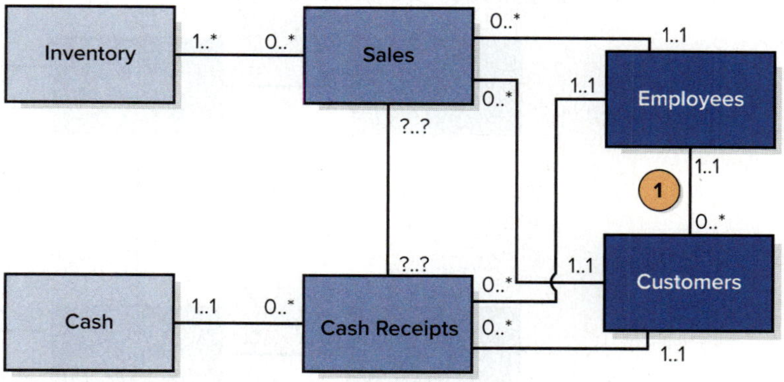

This model extends the generic model to represent assignment of employees to customers. The association (1) links customers to the assigned employee, such as when sales take place on commission. Similarly, employees can be assigned to inventory when specific employees manage specific inventory items.

4. Sales with Summary

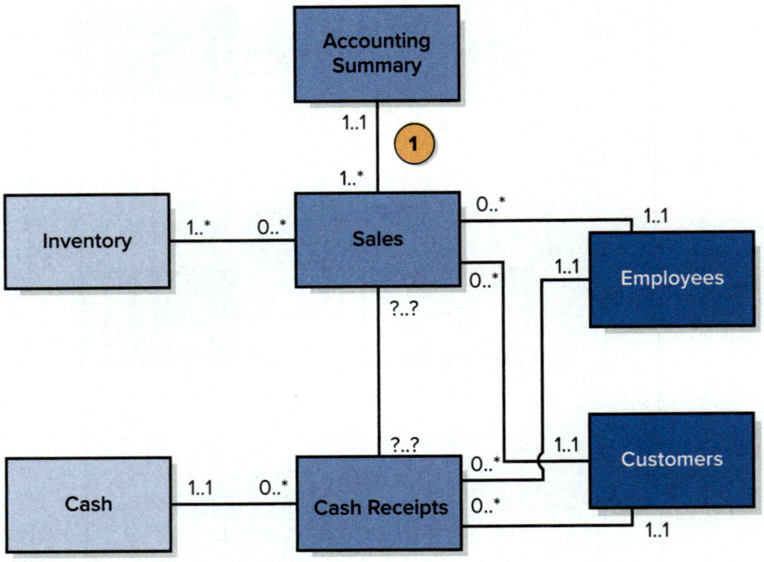

This model presents a simplified example of the summarization of economic activity by fiscal period in order to prepare financial reports. In this case, sales are summarized by fiscal period as shown in the association (1) between Accounting Summary and Sales.

5. Purchases—Generic Model

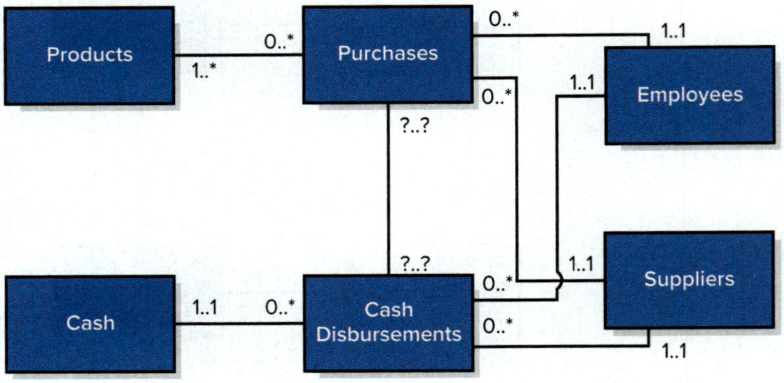

The generic model represents typical economic resources, events, and agents involved in the purchases process. Like the generic sales model, this model assumes that inventory items are not tracked individually but rather by UPC code or similar identifier.

6. Purchases—With Commitment Event

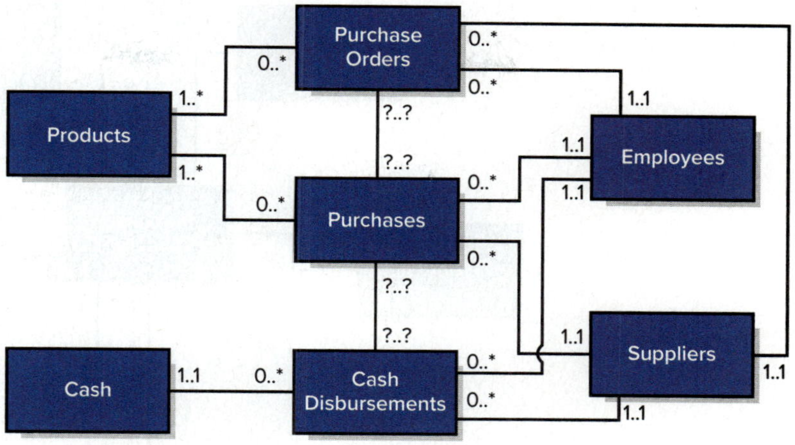

This model adds the commitment event, Purchase Orders, to the generic model. A commitment precedes the economic event. It records anticipated purchases but does not directly affect the financial statements. Note that this model requires tracking both the items ordered and the items received, which is a level of complication that many organizations avoid. Thus, they use a structure that combines the Purchase Orders and Purchases event as shown in the next model.

7. Purchases—With Combined Purchase Orders and Purchases

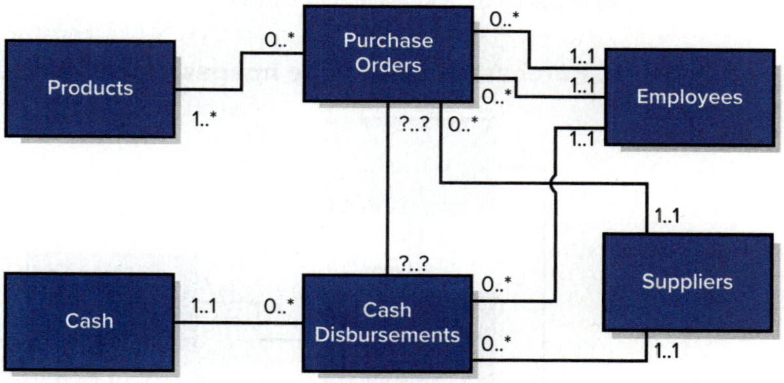

This model shows the combined Purchase Orders and Purchases event (still titled Purchase Orders). The Purchase Order class would track both the date of the order and the date of the receipt of products (the purchase date). The organization is now concerned with only one association between Purchase Orders/Purchases and the Products classes. However, there are now two associations between the Employees and Purchase Orders class, representing the requirement to track the two roles (purchasing agent and receiving agent) separately for internal control.

8. Purchases—With Type Images to Manage the Purchases Process

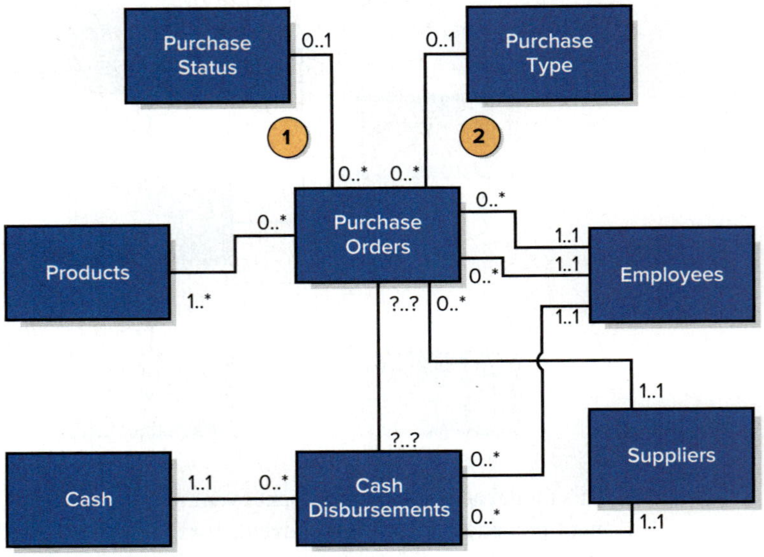

This model shows potential use of two type images to manage the purchase process. The Purchase Status type (1) would summarize information based on the point in the purchase process at the end of a fiscal period—for example, amounts on order, amounts received, and amounts paid. The Purchase Type (2) would summarize information according to the type of purchase—for example, routine organizational supplies and services, inventory replenishment, and asset acquisition.

9. Purchases—With Type Images Linked for Summary Information

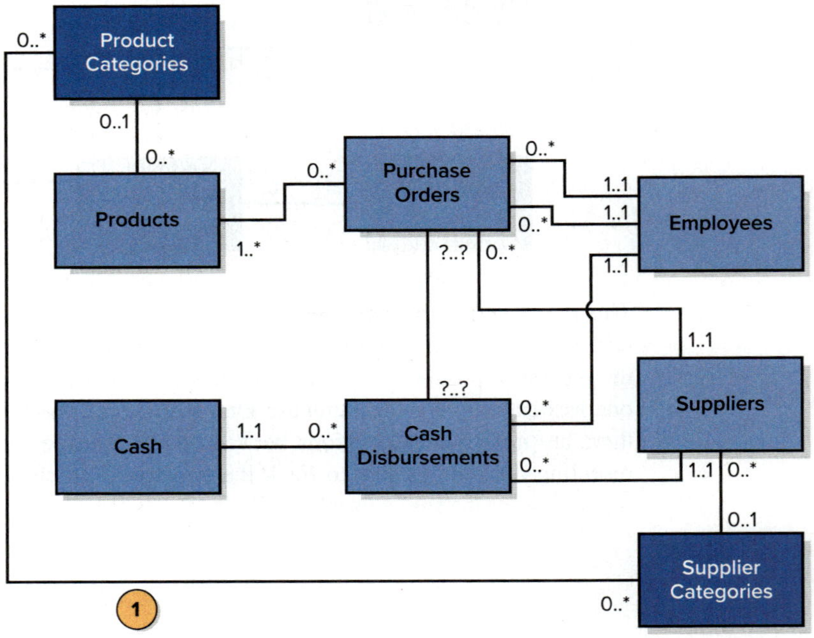

This model provides an example of the use of type images to summarize information. In this case, the organization could use the category classes to obtain summary information about supplier characteristics and activity, about product characteristics and activity, and about the common activity for each product and supplier category combination (1). For example, annual sales for each supplier category and product category combination would be recorded in the linking table between those two type images.

10. Conversion—Basic Model

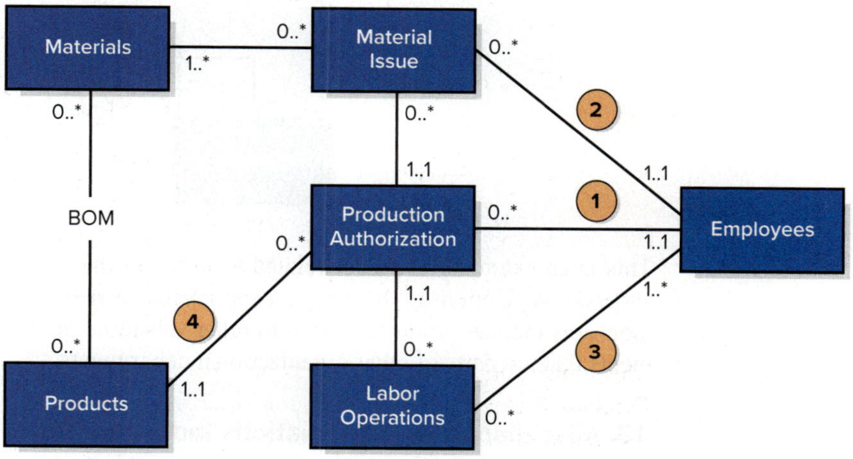

This basic conversion process model shows the structure related to (1) a supervisor authorizing production, (2) raw material issued into work-in-process, (3) labor applied to work-in-process, and (4) finished goods (products) increased when production completes.

11. Conversion—Production in a Series of Steps

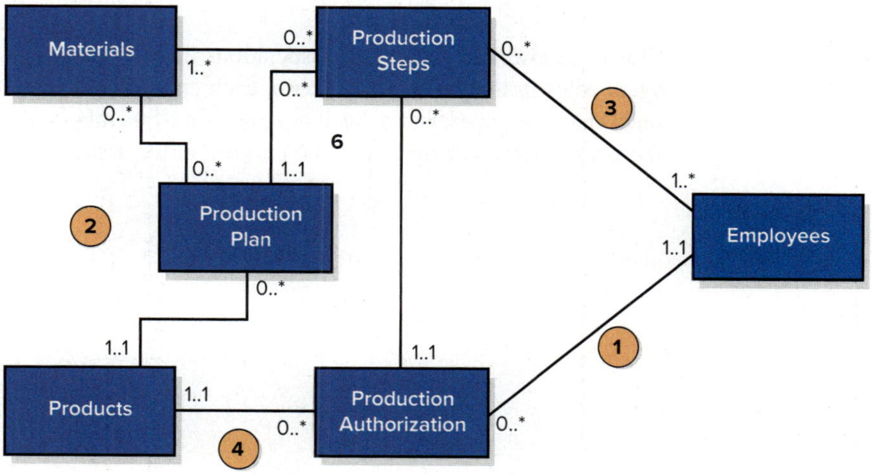

This revised conversion model shows production in a series of steps according to a production plan (a type image). The model shows (1) the supervisor authorizing production, (2) the production plan determining the raw material and labor needed to produce a specific product, (3) how employees work and materials are issued into work-in-process, and (4) how finished goods (products) increase when production completes. This model can be expanded to include accounting for equipment (a resource) use in the production steps.

12. Miscellaneous—Recursive Relationships

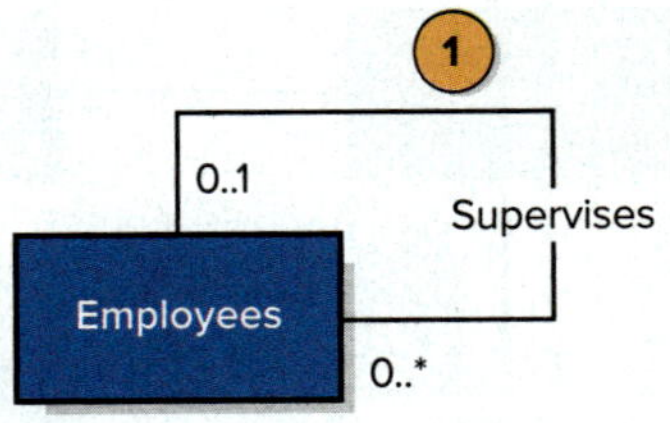

This is an example of a class related to itself. In this case, the association describes the supervisory relationship between an employee and several other employees. Similar common uses include products related to other substitute products and organizational departments that are parts of other organizational departments.

13. Miscellaneous—Associations Indicating Roles

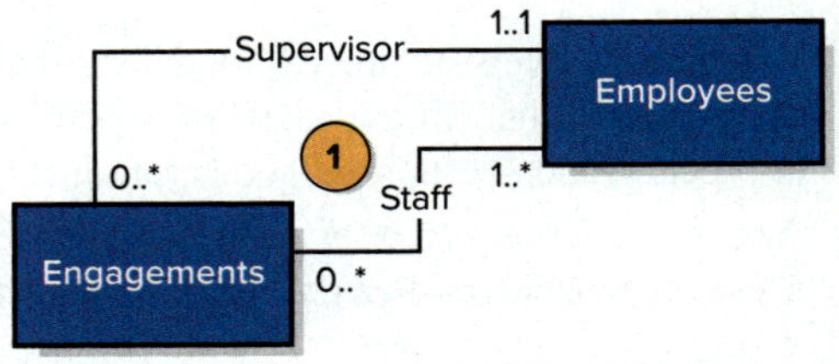

This is an example where two associations link the same two classes to indicate different agent roles in the event. In this case, each engagement (e.g., audit or consulting engagement) has one supervisor as well as several staff members. Placing the name of the role on the association can help clarify the purpose of the associations.

14. Integrated Models—Sales and Purchases

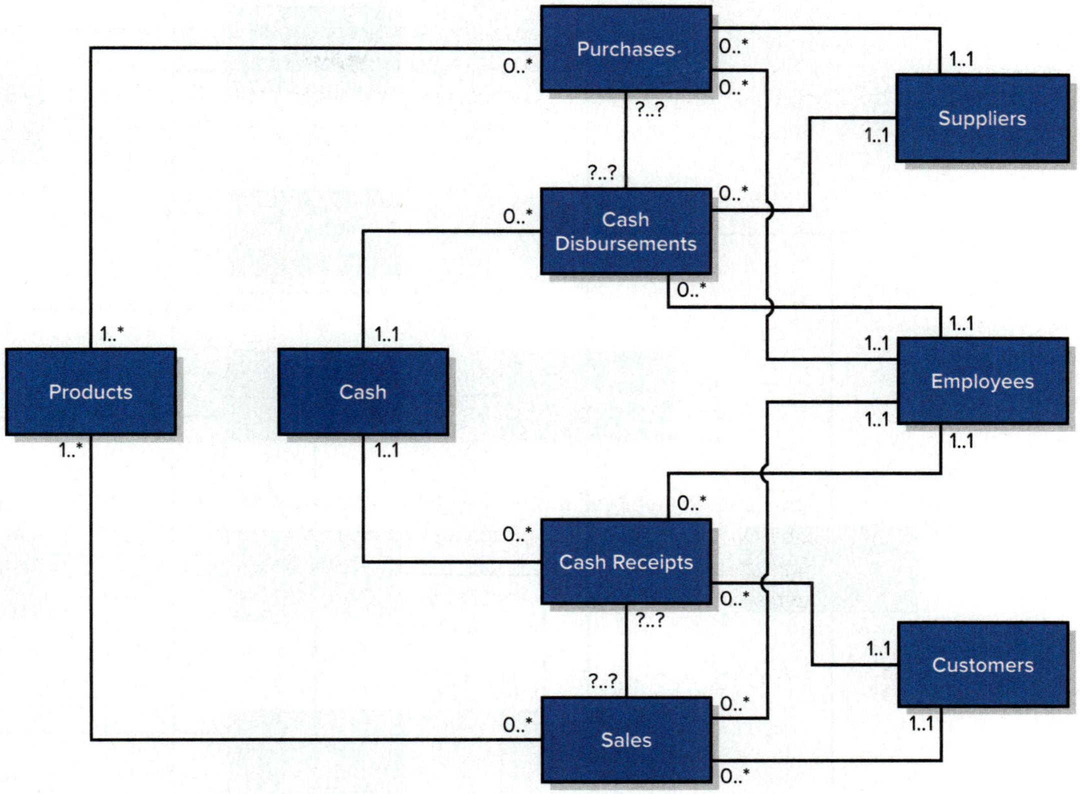

This is a basic example of a model integrating the sales (and cash receipts) and purchases (and cash disbursements) processes. Note that the two duality events (Purchases and Cash Disbursements or Sales and Cash Receipts) as well as the external agents (Customers and Suppliers) are unique to one process. However, the internal agent (Employees) and resources (Products and Cash) are shared across processes.

15. Integrated Models—Sales, Conversion, and Purchases

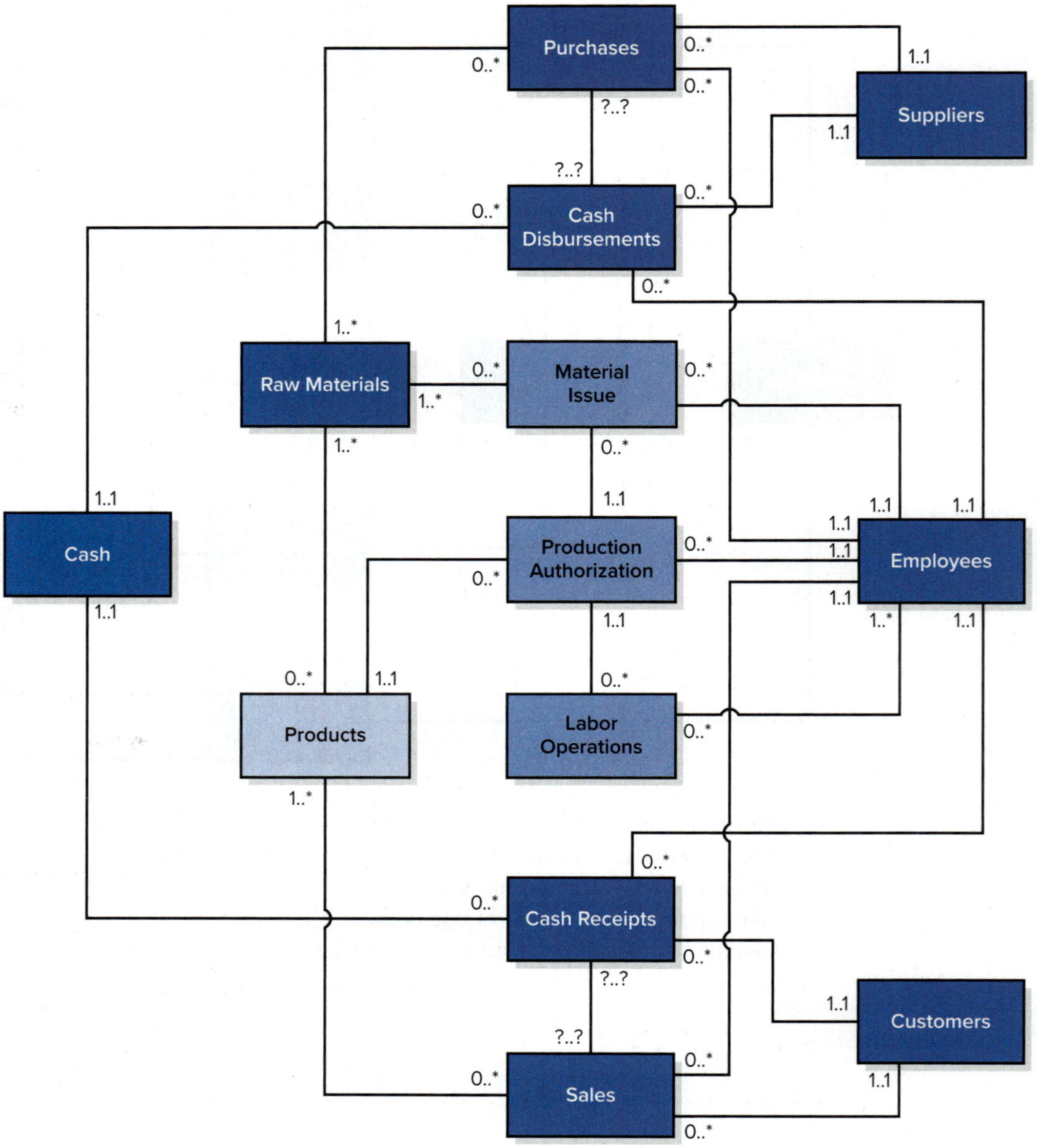

This is an example of a model integrating the sales (and cash receipts), conversion, and purchases (and cash disbursements) processes. In this case, the organization purchases raw materials that are converted into products (finished goods) that are then sold to customers. Again, the duality events (Purchases and Cash Disbursements, Sales and Cash Receipts, Production Authorization and Material Issue and Labor Operations) as well as the external agents (Customers and Suppliers) are unique to one process. However, the internal agent (Employees) and resources (Raw Materials, Products, and Cash) are shared across processes.

ACTIVITY MODELS USING BPMN

16. Sales—Basic Model

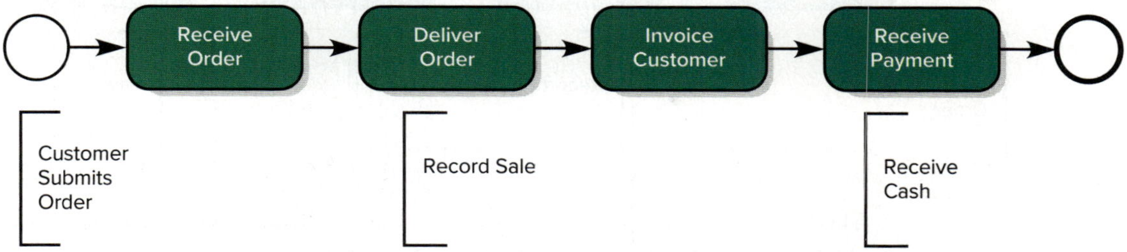

This model shows typical activity flow for a business that takes orders. Note that the steps in the model generally correspond to events in an REA diagram: commitment (receive order), sale (deliver order), and cash receipt (receive payment).

17. Sales—Basic Model with Pools and Swimlanes

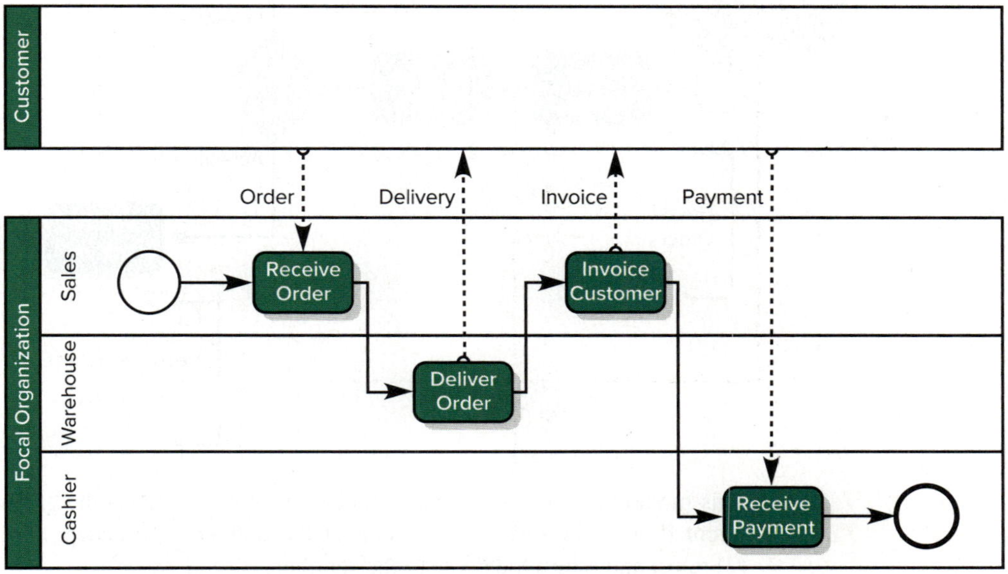

This is the basic model with pools and swimlanes to show responsibility for the various tasks. Note that there are no visible activities in the Customer pool because we are normally not interested in the specific steps they take. Instead, the focus moves to the interactions between pools, shown as message flows (dashed lines). It is good practice to put labels on the message flows to clarify the nature of the interactions. Within the pool of interest, the sequence flows connect the start and end events without any break.

18. Purchases—Basic Model

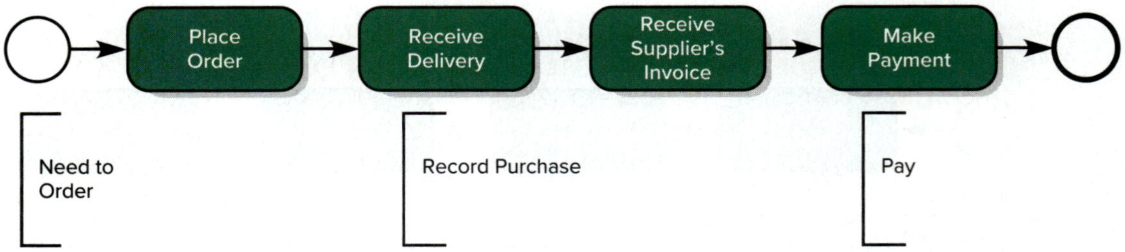

This model shows typical activity flow related to issuing purchase orders. Note that the steps in the model generally correspond to events in an REA diagram: commitment (place order), purchase (receive order), and cash disbursement (make payment).

19. Purchases—Basic Model with Gateway

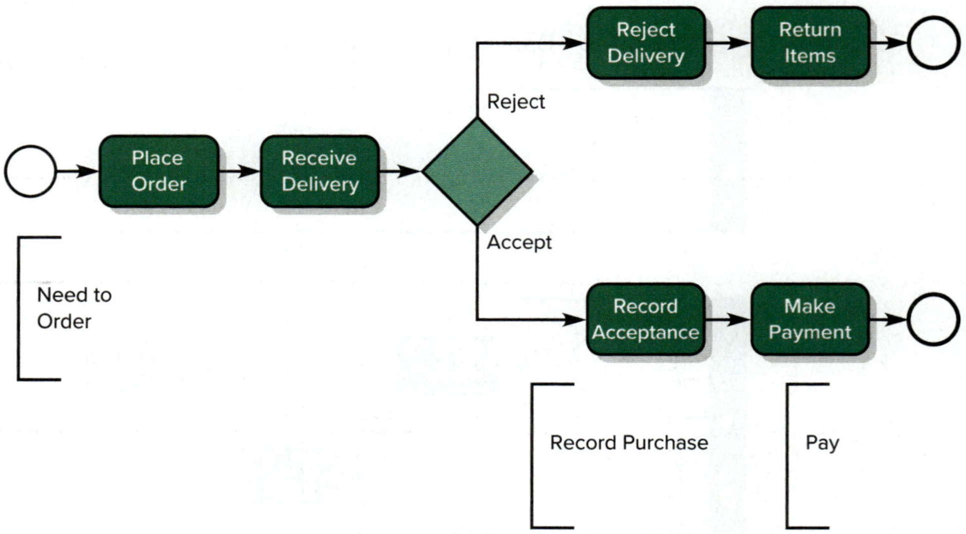

This model is similar to the basic model, except it includes the gateway to show the different flow options after the receipt of the delivery: (1) accept and make payment and (2) reject and return the items to the supplier.

20. Purchases—Basic Model with Error Event

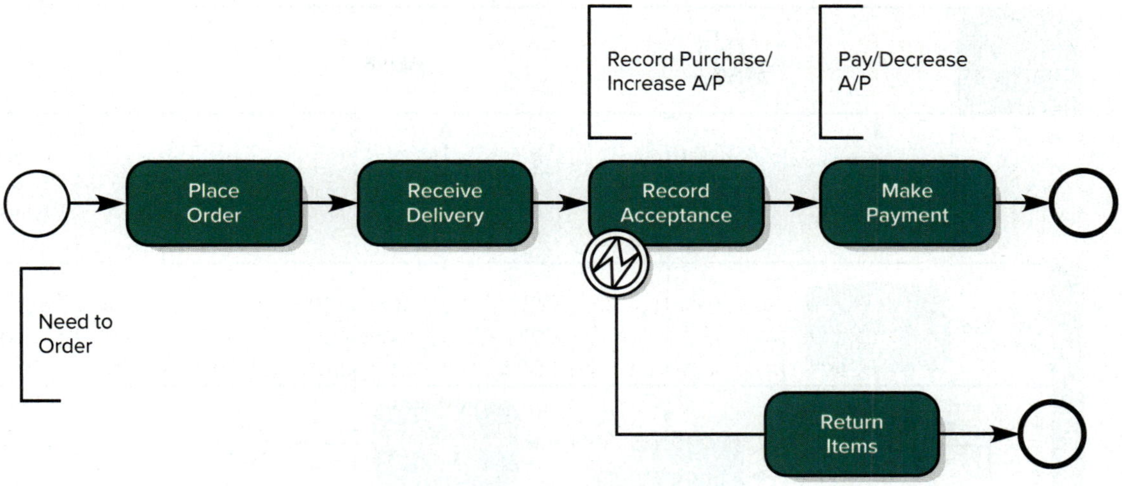

In this model, the intermediate error event shows flow when the items are rejected.

21. Purchases—With Pools and Lanes

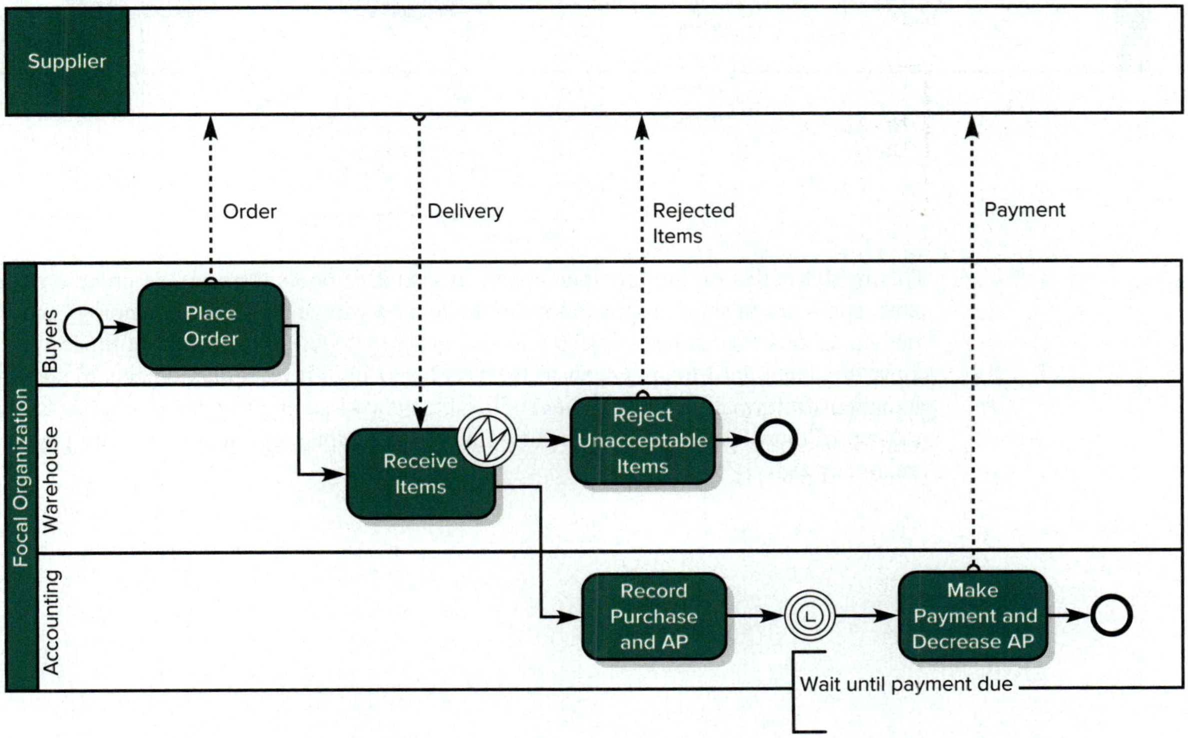

This model uses pools to show the process participants and lanes to show responsibility in the focal organization. It again employs an intermediate error event to show rejected items. It includes an intermediate timer event to show the delay until the payment to the supplier is due.

22. Purchases—With Pools and Lanes and Data Objects

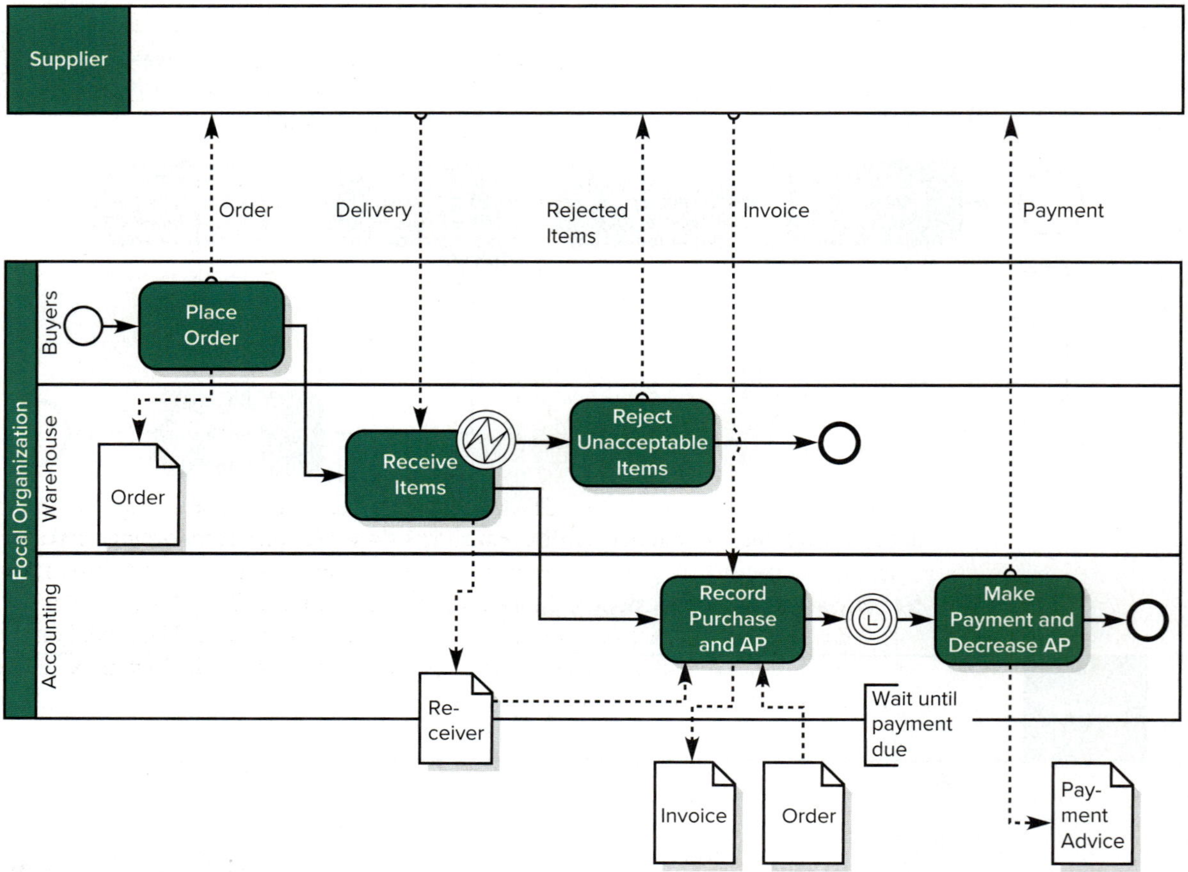

This model builds on the previous model. It also uses pools to show the process participants and lanes to show responsibility in the focal organization. It again employs an intermediate error event to show rejected items, and it includes an intermediate timer event to show the delay until the payment to the supplier is due. It adds data objects to show the documents/information being created or used at the various steps in the process. It assumes a standard three-way match—matching invoices, receipts, and orders—before payments are authorized.

23. Conversion—Basic Model with Repeated Activities or a Looping, Collapsed Subprocess

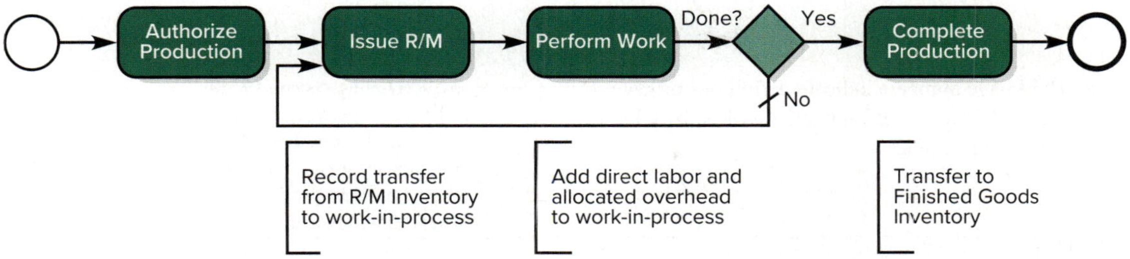

These models provide alternate descriptions of the basic conversion process. The model on top is closely related to the REA model that shows (1) the authorization, (2) raw material issue into work-in-process, (3) labor (and equipment) applied to work-in-process, and (4) completion of production and transfer to finished goods. The gateway routes the flow back until all production to carry out the authorization is complete. The model on the bottom places work-in-process activities in a collapsed subprocess. The looping arrow shows that the process loops until complete.

24. Conversion—Basic Model with Repeated Activities and Batches

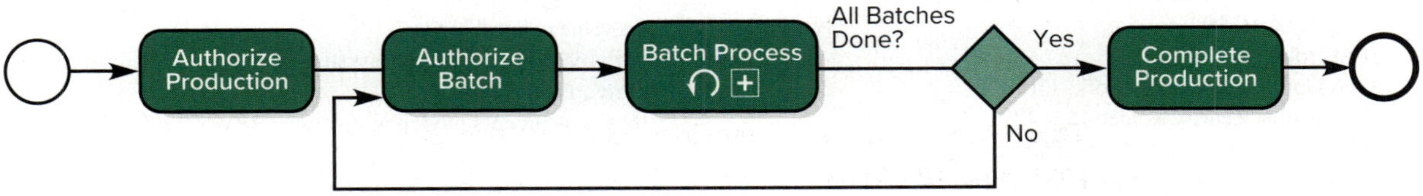

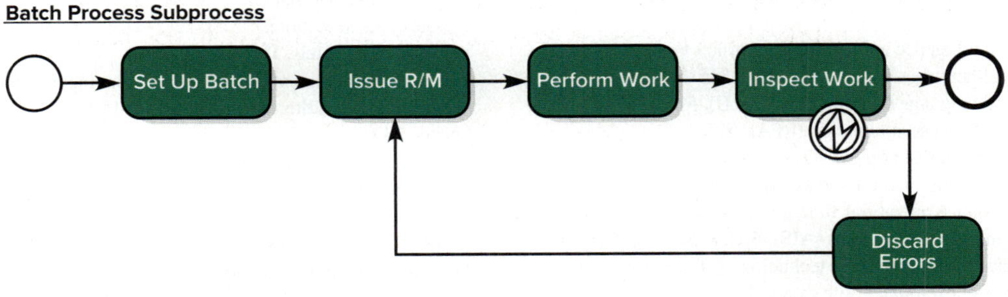

This model expands on the previous model to include batches. In this case, the flow starts with production authorization, to batch authorization, to the batch process, which then repeats until all batches are done. The contents of the collapsed Batch Process subprocess are shown separately. The subprocess also includes an intermediate error event that halts the normal process flow when items fail inspection.

Index

Note: **Bold** page numbers indicate definitions or key discussions of terms; page numbers followed by *n* indicate footnotes or source notes.

B